A History of Women

IN THE WEST

Georges Duby and Michelle Perrot, General Editors

V. Toward a Cultural Identity
in the Twentieth Century

D1057199

A HISTORY OF WOMEN

IN THE WEST

V. Toward a Cultural Identity in the Twentieth Century

Françoise Thébaud, Editor

The Belknap Press of
Harvard University Press
Cambridge, Massachusetts
London, England

Copyright © 1994 by the President and Fellows
of Harvard College
ALL RIGHTS RESERVED
Printed in the United States of America
Fourth printing, 2000

Originally published as *Storia delle donne in Occidente*, vol. V,
Il Novecento. © Gius. Laterza & Figli Spa, Rome and Bari, 1992.

First Harvard University Press paperback edition, 1996

Text design by Lisa Diercks

Library of Congress Cataloging-in-Publication Data

(Revised for vol. 5)

A history of women in the West.

    Translation of: Storia delle donne in Occidente.
    Spine title: A history of women.
    Includes bibliographical references and indexes.
    Contents: 1. From ancient goddesses to Christian
    saints / Pauline Schmitt Pantel, editor — [etc.] —
    3. Renaissance and Enlightenment paradoxes / Natalie
    Zemon Davis and Arlette Farge, editors — [etc.] —
    5. Toward a cultural identity in the twentieth century /
    Françoise Thébaud, editor.
        1. Women—History. 2. Women—Europe—History.
    I. Duby, Georges. II. Perrot, Michelle. III. Pantel,
    Pauline Schmitt. IV. Title: History of Women.
    HQ1121.S79513   1992   305.4'094   91-34134
    ISBN 0-674-40374-6 (cloth)
    ISBN 0-674-40365-7

Contents

Writing the History of Women

Georges Duby and Michelle Perrot

WOMEN WERE LONG RELEGATED to the shadows of history. The development of anthropology and the new emphasis on the family, on a history of *mentalités* centered on everyday life, on what was private and individual, have helped to dispel those shadows. The women's movement and the questions it has raised have done even more. "Where have we come from? Where are we going?" These are questions that women have begun asking themselves. Both inside and outside the university they have set out in search of their forebears and attempted to understand the roots of their domination and the changes in male-female relations across space and time.

"The History of Women" is a convenient and attractive title, but the idea that women in themselves are an object of history must be rejected firmly. What we want to understand is the place of women, the "condition" of women, women's roles and powers. We want to investigate how women acted. We want to examine their words and their silences. We want to look at their many images: goddess, madonna, whore, witch. Our history is fundamentally relational; because we look at society as a whole, and our history of women is necessarily also a history of men.

It is a history of the *longue durée*: five volumes cover the history of the West from antiquity to the present. And our history covers only the West, from the Mediterranean to the Atlantic. Histories of the women of the Orient, Latin America, and Africa are sorely needed, and we hope that one day the women and men of those regions will write them.

Our history is "feminist" in that its outlook is egalitarian. Our intention is to be open to the spectrum of interpretations. We want to raise questions, but we have no formulaic answers. Ours is a plural history: a history of *women* as seen from many different points of view.

It is also the work of a team. Georges Duby and Michelle Perrot are responsible for the overall coordination. Each volume has one or two editors: Pauline Schmitt Pantel (antiquity), Christiane Klapisch-Zuber (Middle Ages), Natalie Zemon Davis and Arlette Farge (early modern period), Geneviève Fraisse and Michelle Perrot (nineteenth century), and Françoise Thébaud (twentieth century) have chosen their own collaborators—some sixty-eight scholars in all, and we hope a representative sample of those working in this field in Europe and the United States.

We see this series as a provisional summary of the results achieved to date and as a guide to further research. We also hope that it will bring the pleasures of history to new readers and act as a stimulus to memory.

A History of Women

IN THE WEST

Toward a Cultural Identity
in the Twentieth Century

Explorations of Gender

Françoise Thébaud

OBSERVING WOMEN WHOSE lives have spanned this century, one is struck by their tragedy and greatness. Buffeted by war, revolution, and dictatorship, they also witnessed a major upheaval in relations between the sexes. Have we now reached an "end" of women's history, the culmination of years of steady, ineluctable progress toward emancipation? Not at all. If the geopolitical twentieth century that was born in the maelstrom of the First World War and the Russian Revolution is now definitively over, the notion of an "end of history" following the triumph of liberalism after the collapse of the Eastern bloc did not survive the assault of events in Europe and elsewhere. What might an end of history mean for women, anyway? A twilight of male domination and the dawn of a new society? A new era in which sexual division would all but disappear?[1] Or a world in which men and women could maintain their distinctive identities yet enjoy equal rights and opportunities? Contemporary feminists are still arguing over these issues. Although their goal is to establish women as subjects of history, constant tension arises between the need to construct a feminine identity and the further need to demolish the category "woman" altogether. Separatism no longer seems a viable option; some form of coexistence with men on terms yet to be defined appears to be increasingly desirable. What does a woman want? What do women want? Readers of this book—gendered actors in a history that is still unfolding—will find not answers to these questions (for it is not the place of scholars to give such answers) but rather food for thought.

Readers may be surprised that the volume contains no chronological narrative of women's liberation. That women's lives no longer resemble the lives of their mothers is a fact so obvious that it hardly needs to be stated. There is no denying all that women have achieved: the right to vote, a dramatic reduction of risk in childbearing, contraception, new opportunities in the workplace. But just what is an "achievement"? A social construct—just the kind of icon that stands in urgent need of deconstruction. What did the women's movement achieve? Who opposed and who supported specific changes? And what were the issues and consequences—symbolic as well as real? These are questions that need to be asked. And remember, too, that no achievement is definitive: the strength of the present-day anti-abortion movement and the spread of AIDS stand as reminders of this important truth. Women's history grew out of the women's movement, but those militant beginnings must not mislead us into thinking that the story we have to tell is essentially one of progress. It is actually a good deal more complex.

The image of the twentieth century as a time of progress for women, in stark contrast to the Victorian era, is based on a series of clichés. One forgets the massacres and world wars and remembers only the flapper of the Roaring Twenties, the liberated woman set free by "the pill," or the superwoman of the 1980s, that creature of feminism and consumer society, capable of juggling career, children, and lovers without missing a beat. In fact, the stereotypes of the flapper and the liberated female were more often invoked to denounce the collapse of the sex barrier and the double standard than to applaud the victories of the women's movement. And the superwoman image, which Betty Friedan criticized in *The Second Stage* (1981), is at the very least ambiguous: few women can live up to such an ideal, and the tensions arising out of the contradictory demands it imposes are swept under the rug. Indeed, Rose-Marie Lagrave has argued that the social function of the superwoman ideal is to conceal growing inequality between the sexes.

Like the critique of the movement's achievements, these stereotypes are nevertheless interesting for the questions they raise about what events are significant for the history of women, and how they fit or jar the masculine chronology of standard history. It must also be emphasized that the history of women is unthinkable without a history of representations, that is, a decoding of images and discourses shaped by the male imagination and masculine social norms. The twentieth century—the century of psychology and images—has demonstrated, among other things, that Western culture has developed few positive ways of representing women. Although Freud complicated the whole business of sex and sexual identity, philosophy and social science went right on reflecting the sexism of society at large: women were seen as filling a special role in service of men and the family. Decked out in the trappings of modernity, approved by science, publicized in film, newspapers, magazines, and advertising, the model of the housewife and mother was triumphantly democratized. Governments—and not just dictatorial ones—made population growth a matter of official concern. Child-rearing became a medical specialty. Psychologists issued normative pronouncements about mother-child relations. All these factors created new pressures for women to stay at home. Sexuality was now regarded as a legitimate source of pleasure and the sexuality of women was recognized, but marriage was held to be the proper place for its expression, and women worried about failing to live up to new ideals of beauty symbolized by impossibly slender film stars, models, and beauty queens. Meanwhile, a new image of the modern woman took hold: she was a professional homemaker, at once queen of the household and shrewd consumer. Advertisements sold images along with merchandise. The new woman might seem flashier than the old, but at bottom not much had changed, as advertising simultaneously turned women themselves into sexual objects, desirable commodities. Pervasive, intrusive pornographic images were promulgated in magazines and video tapes. Meanwhile, however, growing numbers of women began to speak out and seize control of their own visual identities. Emphasizing the political importance of representation, they tried to break down old stereotypes and to suggest a variety of ways in which women might fulfill themselves. At no time in history has the image of women changed as rapidly as it has in recent years. We will attempt to measure, date, and comprehend that change.

This volume is not simply a narrative of women's liberation or a history of representations. Like the authors of the four previous volumes in this series, we conceive our task in more ambitious terms, informed by twenty years of work in women's history. This is not the place to explore the far-reaching debates on what the subject of that history ought to be.[2] Let me simply give a quick overview of the common approach to our subject that transcends differences among individual contributors and leads, we hope, to a new interpretation of the twentieth century.

History was for a long time the history of men, presented as typical of the human race. More recently, numerous works (thousands have been written about the twentieth century alone) have shown that women, too, have a history; indeed, that they have been full participants in the history of humankind. But to study women in isolation from men, as if in a vacuum, is a theoretical dead-end and a possible source of historical misunderstandings. What we propose, rather, is a gendered approach. Relations between men and women are an important dimension of history. These relations are not a natural fact but a social construct, and they are constantly being redefined. This redefinition is at once an effect and a cause of the social dynamic. Hence relations between the sexes are a useful category of analysis, on a par with other categories more familiar to historians, such as relations between classes, races, nations, and generations. Like any new way of looking at the past, this change of perspective yields new knowledge. It may even lead to rewriting history in such a way as to take account of a wider range of human experience than earlier approaches allowed for. For example, a gendered approach to Nazi racism leads to the conclusion that Hitler's policy toward women was not pronatalist and based on a cult of motherhood but rather antinatalist and based on a cult of virility and mass extermination of inferior people, in which women were the preferred and easiest targets. Wherever relevant, contributors have tried to relate gender and class, gender and nationality, gender and age, gender and religion: gender turns out to be a differentiating factor within groups too often treated as homogeneous.

Readers should therefore ask themselves not about women's achievements but about the evolution of the "gender system," by which I mean the set of gendered social roles together with the system of ideas and representations that culturally define masculine and feminine and thus shape sexual identity. Changes in the condition of women must be seen in relation to changes in the condition of men. If, for example, on one end of the scale the feminization of certain trades perpetuates a disparity between men and women, on the other end modern methods of birth control do not merely allow women to avoid unwanted pregnancies but to take control by themselves of the reproductive cycle. The development of new contraceptives must therefore be seen in relation to simultaneous changes in the law, changes that ended women's subservience to men in the domestic sphere. Readers should also ask themselves what it was that gave meaning and value to the respective activities of men and women. What are the functions and consequences of the gender symbolism promoted in one way or another by governments, individuals, and groups? Such symbolism is most commonly used to establish hierarchies and represent relations of power and tends to impede change rather than accelerate it. Although war in general and World War I in particular have often been described as liberating for women, armed conflict (whose psychological and social aftereffects generally persist long after the cessation of hostilities) is in fact profoundly conservative because it encourages, even within the feminist frame, thinking of gender issues in terms of dichotomy. Or consider politics: when all men received the right to vote, the term "universal suffrage" was misleadingly applied to a situation that still excluded women. More than that, politics is still a male preserve: only a handful of elected officials are women even where women voters are in the majority. Women tend to be relegated to certain designated areas of government, preserving the age-old division between the male world of politics and the female world of social concerns. Female officials are often seen as intruders by their male colleagues and as marginal even by one another. Yet women in government deserve credit for what they have accomplished. For instance, the Russian revolutionary Alexandra Kollontai, the Spanish anarchist Federica Montseny, and the French politician Simone Veil, all three ministers of health, worked to legalize abortion in their respective countries.

This history of women therefore has a subtext: that men, too, are gendered individuals. Readers should be aware of how the story told here modifies and contributes to our picture of history in general. Obviously it has something to add to social history. But it also leads to revision of the conventional periodization of cultural history and, more surprisingly perhaps, of political history, which remains one of the most influential ways of looking at the past. Our approach leads, for example, to a new interpretation of paternalistic wartime policies for the protection of women. It leads to reflection on the nature of fascism and Nazism, which, among other things, intended to quell gender conflict in the interest of more efficient exploitation. It reveals distinctive features of the

Vichy and the "Catholic nationalist" Franco regimes. It leads to a reconsideration of the origins and workings of the welfare state, which took early feminist demands for public recognition of the social utility of motherhood and reinterpreted them in a paternalistic sense. It also helps us to understand the uniqueness of Quebec, whose history is interpreted here in feminist-nationalist terms. And it sheds new light on the reasons for the failure of Soviet-style communism, which imposed a voluntaristic, economistic model even in the sphere of gender relations. Alexandra Kollontai, who did not believe in the self-generated "withering away" of the bourgeois family and dreamed of a new working-class morality, was criticized for "George-Sandism." But since she preached her doctrine in a poor agricultural nation under siege, where civil society in general and women in particular were subject to constant interference from the central authorities, she was most likely ahead of her time.

The history of feminism and women's movements is of course an integral part of Western political history. Much work remains to be done in this area. The period 1920–1960, long regarded as a fallow patch between two "waves" of feminism, is just now being explored for the first time, yet understanding it is essential to understanding the century as a whole. How did the movement for women's rights, steeped as it was in nineteenth-century rationalism and liberalism, cope with the challenges of mass politics, communism, nationalism, and Freudianism? What was the relation between this earlier movement and the women's liberation movement that grew out of the New Left, the anticolonial movement, and the sexual liberation of the 1960s? In attempting to understand all this, it is best to be wary of pejorative labels such as "bourgeois feminism" and to question whether there really was a hard-and-fast distinction between egalitarian feminism and the "feminism of difference."[3] The question of gender can lead to a renewal of political thought, because it forces one to recognize that equality requires the acceptance and inclusion of difference. Women's history can also enrich general history by examining itself and history in general as a cognitive process. By analyzing the gendered categories that structure our culturally determined notions of sexual difference, we learn to look at sources in new ways and to revise our methodologies appropriately. Although women's history is sometimes criticized for being a "discourse on discourse," such an approach is a necessity, not a fad or a device for avoiding hard work.

Other fields of knowledge have also been influenced, along with history, by contemporary feminist thought: philosophy, law, sociology, political science, and literary criticism have also played a role in the preparation of this book.[4] A one-sided approach can no longer be mistaken for universal. Feminist critique questions the ideological assumptions that may lie hidden in even the most learned studies or the most comprehensive statistics. This is particularly true of labor studies and statistics. It is invariably assumed that women are responsible for child care and housework, as if work outside the home were a natural right for men and an anomaly for women. Contemporary political economists, like their nineteenth-century predecessors, try to justify the sexual division of labor by arguing that it is grounded in nature.[5]

But what about the twentieth century? It has been, of course, the bloodiest century in the history of humankind, a century of total war, whose victims, civilian as well as military, number in the tens of million, and a century of genocide, which has shown women no special mercy and indeed exterminated Jewish and Gypsy women purposefully to prevent the birth of a new generation. Women have had to suffer, too, for their political choices. Repression, harsh for all its victims, was sometimes aimed particularly at women, whose heads were shaved, whose bodies were violated. And totalitarian regimes frequently resorted to the terrifying idea of family guilt. In memory of all the victims of totalitarian regimes, let me mention here the names of two extraordinary women who became friends while interned at Ravensbrück: the Czech journalist Milena Jesenká, Kafka's friend and translator and an ardent enemy of oppression in all its forms, and the German communist Margarete Buber-Neumann, who not only told the world about the camps of Stalin and Hitler but also kept alive the memory of her friend, who died in 1944.[6]

Yet this century has also been one in which women at last— and long after men—entered the modern world. Modern technology brought women as well as men the boon of better health and longer lifespans. Infant mortality has been dramatically reduced. Women have obtained the finest educations available. The growth of cities and the proliferation of consumer goods have changed the way we live. Less of life is given over to toil and pain, and on balance this must be counted as progress, even granting the failures and inequalities of consumer society. For women this has meant changes in the nature of housework and child-rearing. Since less time needs to be devoted to these activities, more is left over for participation in social life. But for women modern life means something else as well. Long trapped in the web of that natural community, the family, women failed to reap the benefits of the dynamic expansion of individual rights initiated by the French Revolution. Hence for them modernity has meant the achievement of individuality and full citizenship status and the conquest of economic, legal, and symbolic independence vis-à-vis fathers and husbands. A once powerful vise-like grip has thus been loosened, as any number of monographic studies have shown.[7]

When did this revolution in gender relations begin, and how are we to explain it? It appears to have been the cause of a crisis of masculine identity, signs of which are numerous though difficult to grasp. The end of the Second World War, which ushered in a lasting period of democracy and economic growth in the West, is not the crucial date in this history (although it did bring women in France the right to vote). For the second time in this century, the end of a world war signaled a return of women to the private sphere. Since the children of the next generation were declared to be the key to national reconstruction, women were told that it was their civic duty to return home, just as it had been their duty a few years earlier to join the workforce. Indeed, in several countries the wartime generation turned out to be the least active professionally and the most prolific in terms of childbearing. This generation of women had little taste for politics in the usual sense: the 1950s saw the apotheosis of the housewife, whose ideological conditioning by the media—to say nothing of psychoanalysis—Betty Friedan denounced in *The Feminine Mystique* (1963), history's best-selling book about women, a fundamental text on feminism along with Virginia Woolf's *A Room of One's Own* (1929) and Simone de Beauvoir's *The Second Sex* (1949). In the case of France, the Vichy regime broke politically with the republican past but continued the family policies of previous governments: from the 1920s to the 1960s French women were expected to serve as mothers while their husbands worked for a living. Few democrats questioned the totalitarian potential in such policies, just as few advocates of the separation of church and state questioned the influence of religion on this government's meddling in the nation's bedrooms.

More space might have been devoted to advocates of birth

control such as Margaret Sanger in the United States or Madeleine Pelletier and Jeanne and Eugène Humbert in France.[8] And we might have said more about the proponents of family planning and single-woman motherhood, many of whom were also active in the international movement for sexual reform of the 1920s and 1930s. We might have tried to gauge the place of religion in the lives of women: the issue is important but vast. Gender difference is one of the cornerstones of the Catholic Church, which seems to have been more conservative than most on the issue: witness its refusal to countenance contraception in any form, to permit priests to marry, and to ordain women. This intransigence gave rise to generations of Catholic militants, reformers who helped to bring about change in the Church and in the condition of women. Even so, there has been an unmistakable decline in religious practice in France.[9]

But it was not until the middle of the 1960s, more than fifty years after the first hopes of the Belle Epoque, that gender relations began to change in most Western countries. It is not easy to say what factors were most responsible. Peace, prosperity, and scientific discoveries certainly helped, and I must at least mention the name of Gregory Pinkus, the inventor of the contraceptive pill.[10] But the student unrest of 1968 was also important: the student movement is a field that remains open for future scholars to explore from a gender-conscious point of view. And, above all, there is the women's movement, which fervently denounced "patriarchy" and all its icons. Change has been greatest, it seems, in the private sphere: the idea that husband and wife are equal partners in marriage, and that the man is not "head of the household," is one that influenced first American and British law and, later, continental legal systems as well. The law now admits a variety of family types and female roles. More liberal attitudes toward contraception and abortion have enabled women to reclaim possession of their bodies and sexuality. Women can now determine when they wish to have children, and governments have been forced to abandon the most coercive family policies. When feminists insisted on a woman's right to determine when and if she would have children, they were in fact giving voice to a wish to privatize a reproductive function that, for better or for worse, had throughout the century been seen as a public duty. In a more fundamental sense, they were seeking to redefine the relation of women to childbearing. Few contemporary feminists have followed their predecessors on this controversial issue. Liberation, it seems, is more easily attained through self-fulfillment in the workplace and private pressure on husbands to share in parental responsibilities, than through seeking to gain state recognition and assistance for motherhood as a social function.

Change is best measured, however, not by opposing public and private but by noting how the two spheres interact. There is no single cause, no primary factor, in producing social change. Rather, we must look at the interaction of causes and effects. As more and more women entered the labor market and participated in cultural and political activities, private law also evolved. The diminished burden of housework itself encouraged women to participate more fully in the public sphere. Although social legislation and tax codes continued to embody the marital inequalities of the past, discouraging many women from working, the advent of the welfare state afforded women greater independence. It not only offered protection but also created new jobs and lightened the burden of family care. Women sought schooling and work in record numbers, and although the educational system favored boys and many jobs were reserved for men, the effects of these changes were nevertheless considerable. Autocracy in marriage disappeared, along with the traditional housewife. And women increasingly tended to vote for the left, contradicting their reputation for political conservatism. In France, in fact, younger women of the present generation are more likely than their male counterparts to vote for left-wing candidates. Perhaps, too, there has been a democratization of family life, although that is more difficult to measure. The culture of love may have evolved, and men and women may have come to see each other in a new light. In all these changes, especially the conquest of political and symbolic autonomy (the ability to say "we women"), the feminism—or, rather, feminisms—of the 1960s and 1970s played a key role by establishing womanhood as a fundamental political category and by organizing themselves as a group capable of deconstructing and reconstructing its meaning. In using the past tense here, I mean to imply only that the pace of change has been rapid, not that the process is complete. I do not claim that women have won a victory, nor am I suggesting that there has been a return to more "normal" gender relations following the alleged "excesses" of the feminist era. The apparent decline of feminism (which has led some commentators to speak of a "postfeminist era") is as much a transformation as a loss:

history continues, constantly shaking things up in ways that are unpredictable yet wholly implicit in the past.

Furthermore, in using the plural "women," I do not mean to prejudge the question of whether they constitute a unified group. Feminism discovered the multiplicity of individual female subjects as a result of conflicts between different groups of women: disagreements between black and white women activists in the United States, for example, or, even more dramatically, accusations of imperalism leveled at Europeans and Americans by Third World women at international conferences. Even in Western Europe and the United States not all women have an equal opportunity to live as they choose: social background, professional status, nationality, and ethnicity are important factors. The difficulties faced by single mothers today are reminiscent of those faced by unmarried women in the past. Women face other problems as well, and we will go into greater detail about some of them, but it may be that we have paid too little attention to women in marginal situations.

This book, I must emphasize, has no pretensions to universality or even to exhaustive coverage of its chosen field. It is a history by Western historians of Western women. Indeed, narrowing it down still further, it is a history of white women born in the West. It does not touch on the West's relation to the rest of the world, about which little research has been done from this particular angle. Nor do we consider the domination of the South by the North, which in the postcolonial era involves not only economic and/or cultural imperialism but also the problem of immigration. I am particularly sorry that there is no essay on mass consumption. The wide array of consumer goods available today has transformed the household, but on a global scale inequalities remain. The issue of gender and race is another unexplored area. How are we to interpret contacts between women colonists and women among the colonized peoples?[11] When two civilizations clash, how do women relate to women, and how do men relate to women and vice versa, on either side of the divide? What is the place of imagery and sexual fantasies in this confrontation? What role have immigrant women (and their daughters) played in preserving ethnic identities or in fostering a desire for integration?

Our decision to focus on the West may seem, as in the case of the previous volumes in the series, at once justifiable and presumptuous. What I am calling the West—essentially Europe and North America—possesses not only a geographic and cultural unity but also, in the twentieth century, an economic and political unity: the countries we study are by and large wealthy, developed societies with a shared history. But we cannot overlook the Soviet experiment, which from the first proposed to establish new relations between the sexes, as well as between the classes. For decades Soviet society served as an ideal for communists the world over; it was also a source of puzzlement as to the persistent disparities between the utopian ideal and the reality.

Our approach is chronological as well as thematic. In looking at the first half of the century we call attention to national differences: in Europe there were efforts to "nationalize" women, by which I mean efforts by various nations to propose their own models of womanhood in opposition to those associated with communism on the one hand and the United States on the other. Subsequently, however, the trend has been toward internationalization, not to say standardization, often under the aegis of the United States: that is where things stand today. It may be, therefore, that we do not devote as much space to the American case as it deserves. Our comparative work leads to a set of models, when what is needed, perhaps, is an analysis of the complex relations among these various models, which would require explorations of mass culture, immigration, and international interactions.[12]

The reader, we hope, will therefore begin to have a sense of the variegated geography and history of gender relations. Some countries were veritable experimental laboratories: the United States, which, despite periodic bouts of puritanism, was the birthplace of both the "modern woman" and "women's lib," and social-democratic Sweden are perhaps the best examples. There are important historical and cultural differences between northern Europe and the Latin countries of the Continent: France developed under the weight of the Napoleonic Code, while the countries of the Mediterranean struggled with the remnants of legal systems based on the confessional, as well as with dictatorial regimes. Given the decline of birth and marriage rates, the increase in the number of working women, and the democratization of marriage as well as politics—phenomena common to all the West—southern Europe's recent advances seem all the more remarkable. This progress has fostered new centers of women's history: in Spain there is pride in rediscovering forgotten filiations with the bold experiments of the republican era and in exploding Francoist myths. And perhaps we should extend to the countries of Eastern Europe an invitation to join us in this realm as they have begun to do in others.

One other point needs to be made in order to avoid any possible misunderstanding. The fact that there are no male contributors to this volume is not the result of deliberate exclusion but the reflection of a historiographical reality. The history of women in the twentieth century, because it is our history and the history of our mothers and grandmothers, has—to an even greater degree than the history of women in earlier periods—been written by women. An author's sex, however, is not enough to effect a change in intellectual outlook. The unity, not to say the originality, of this volume and this series lies in its approach, its way of interrogating the past and the present. It is up to readers—common readers as well as professional historians—to say whether that approach seems fruitful.

Women's history does not claim to offer the ultimate vantage point from which it is possible at last to see history whole.[13] But at a time when history, buffeted by current events, is reexamining both its identity as a discipline and the principles in terms of which it understands reality, women's history may be one way of adding new depth to our models of the past.[14] Nothing less ambitious can hope to reveal the true complexity of social processes.

TRANSLATED FROM THE FRENCH BY ARTHUR GOLDHAMMER

FOR EVERY FIGHTER
A WOMAN WORKER

Y·W·C·A·

BACK OUR SECOND LINE OF DEFENSE
UNITED WAR WORK CAMPAIGN

one

The Nationalization
of Women

In the Service of the Fatherland

The first half of the twentieth century witnessed not only two world wars but years of slaughter, worldwide depression, and totalitarian dictatorship. The first eight essays in this volume will reexamine this history from the standpoint of relations between the sexes. In so doing the authors also find occasion to reconsider the notions of equality and difference, resistance and consent, emancipation and oppression.

Owing to America's technological lead as well as to early feminist struggles there, a new female type emerged in the United States in the 1920s. This image of the "modern woman" has shaped our view of changing sexual roles, but it was as much an image of conformity as of liberation. In the East, the young Soviet Union produced an industrious workforce in which male and female workers seemed all but indistinguishable. In fact, however, Soviet women were the first victims of new laws regarding the family, laws promulgated without debate and modified at the whim of the central authorities. Caught between the two, the nations of Europe, shaken by World War I and invaded by American culture, reacted by defending their distinctive national characters. Faced with the dual challenge of democratization and the "population question" (which was seen as a matter not only of demographic decline but also of changing relations between men and women), most European countries swept aside old distinctions between private and public, family and government, individuals and the state. Governments of every stripe—from social-democratic Sweden to the fascist and Nazi dictatorships, and including first republican and later Vichy France—attempted to "nationalize" their female citizens. Their methods were more authoritarian in some countries, less so in others. Maternity became a matter of public policy. The first steps were taken toward the institution of the welfare state. Women were mobilized in service of the embattled fatherland or enlisted in organizations dedicated to promoting the grandeur of the nation.

Nazi Germany is of course a case apart. The genocide of the Jews and Gypsies precludes comparison with other totalitarian regimes, despite revisionist contentions to the contrary.[1] Under the Nazis the nationalization of Germany's women destroyed traditional family values and placed women, whether mothers, party activists, or workers, at the service of the German *Volk*. Marxist and feminist believers in emancipation through work have long argued that authoritarian regimes assigned women to the functional role of motherhood. This cannot withstand scrutiny. The fascists, Nazis, and Vichyites tempered their natalist ideology to fit the economic realities. In the case of the Nazis, moreover, pronatalist policies frequently conflicted with racist antinatalism. And in any case, efforts to expand the population were by no means the most distinctive feature of these regimes.

How does this nationalization of women relate to what Rita Thalmann has called "the nationalist temptation?"[2] And what light does this history shed on the contradictory roles played by women under Nazism? These are important and difficult questions. Debate over these issues has influenced feminist discussion, which has tended, in seeking continuity in patriarchal oppression, to look upon German "women as victims—often just victims and sometimes the only victims."[3] Wherever possible, national questions have been assigned to a historian from the country in question. The Nazi case posed a particular challenge. Gisela Bock tries to relate the sexism and the racism of the Nazis. Her essay makes a useful confirmation and counterpoint to the work of Rita Thalmann (from France) and Claudia Koonz (from the United States).[4] Together the work of these historians gives us a better idea of the various German movements of the 1920s—lay and religious, masculine and feminine, modernist and traditionalist—that attacked Weimar and called for the regeneration of the German people. They allow us to see beyond the crimes of a racist male order and to understand the attractions that the Third Reich may have held for many women interested in the restoration of morality and the family and avid for female *Lebensraum.*

But what are the merits of the current debate over the degree of responsibility of German women and their representative groups for the crimes of the Nazis? Do women bear a primary share of the blame on the grounds that, as wives and mothers, they not only subscribed to Nazism but paved the way for male violence by comforting the executioners and humanizing the regime's image? Can the Nazi state be seen as a consequence and ultimate form of the division of male and female spheres? I do not think so. Nevertheless, the question of consent (resistance, still in need of further study, seems not to have been widespread) by both men and women leads to further questions about the dangers of such division, as well as about the risks of subtle adaptation to totalitarianism and racism.

This long historical section also raises questions about the place of war in this century and, on a more modest level, about the gendered character of wartime policy. It is difficult, however, to draw any general conclusions about World War II, whose effects varied so widely from country to country.

War traditionally was man's business, the very essence of virility. But modern war requires mobilization in the rear as well as at the front and makes victims as well as participants of both sexes. In the long run, however, it is more a conservative, even reactionary, force than a force for change. Not even the Spanish Civil War, in which many women fought, and the French Resistance, participation in which earned so many women deportation and death, established the right of women to shoulder the responsibility of battle or to share the credit. When resistance turned to armed combat, when regular military units were organized, women were excluded from command. And whenever a war ended, women were reminded of the uniqueness of the female role. Wars of national liberation proved to be no exception to the rule. Although some have led to changes in the individual behavior of women who were combatants (former rebels in Algeria have fewer children than their sisters, for example),[5] wholesale changes in gender relations are rare. As for armed struggle in the Third World and urban guerilla movements in the West, only the Red Army Faction (also known as the Baader-Meinhof Gang after its leaders Andreas Baader and Ulrike Meinhof)—which reformulated the terrorist tradition—appears to have allowed women anything other than a subordinate role.[6] It is interesting, regardless of whether or not one approves of the change, to consider in this light the current feminization of Western armies, a feminization that Germany, incidentally, has so far refused to accept.[7]

F.T.

1

The Great War and the Triumph of Sexual Division

Françoise Thébaud

"IT IS THE FIRST hour in history for the women of the world. This is the woman's age," proclaimed Mrs. Raymond Robins, a delegate to the American Women's Trade Union League Congress in 1917.[1] As if in echo from across the sea, the French essayist Gaston Rageot and the feminist historian Léon Abensour hailed, respectively, "the dawn of a new civilization" and "the advent of women in the life of the nation."[2]

The idea that the Great War had done more to redefine relations between the sexes and emancipate women than years or even centuries of previous struggle had accomplished was widespread during and immediately after the conflict. It was a commonplace in the literature and political speeches of the time, whether hailed or reviled, strictly scrutinized or magnified out of all proportion to reality. Yet later memory of the war was shaped by living veterans and commemoration of their fallen comrades. Only the names of heroes and battlefields survived. Across Europe, monuments to the dead (some 30,000 of them in France alone) put each sex in its proper place. Women were evoked only in allegory: as Victory, as the weeping widow, occasionally as the mother cursing the war.[3] Meanwhile, a new and scandalous scent floated in the air, that of a new woman, the **"garçonne,"** masculine in manners and appearance: one of this new breed became the eponymous heroine of Victor Margueritte's 1922 best-seller *La Garçonne* (translated into English as *The Bachelor Girl*), a work allegedly conceived as "a virtuous fable." Despite the return of peacetime conformism, the book sold over a million copies, a *succès de scandale* that earned its author expulsion from the Legion of Honor. Translated into a dozen languages, it attracted a following throughout the Continent.[4]

After the arms fell silent, tens of thousands of books were written in the hope of understanding the extraordinary events just past. Untold suffering and millions of dead: that was the price that Europe had paid to be catapulted into the twentieth century. In all this postwar writing, however, there was little discussion of women. There were, to be sure, occasional anecdotes about life behind the lines, but serious attention was focused elsewhere, on the war's causes, aims, and costs, as well as on military strategy and tactics. Economic and political approaches predominated in works ranging from the Carnegie series[5] to Georges-Henri Soutou's magisterial work *L'Or et le Sang* (Gold and Blood).[6] More recently, of course, social history, which has blazed many new trails and is in any case, by the nature of its inquiry, more keenly attuned to the home front, could hardly fail to note the presence of women, particularly those who contributed to the war effort.[7] But the real pressure for a fresh look at this period came from the feminist movement of the 1960s and 1970s. What did women in the belligerent countries do? What happened to them? Did the war affect them in the same way it affected men? If men were subjected to the extended trauma of battle, did women know nothing but mourning, melancholy, and mothering? Given the breakdown of the family and the social order and the availability of new kinds of work, wasn't this also a time of possibility for women? These questions gave rise to a new area of historical inquiry: what was the place of war in the long march toward women's emancipation? In their study of British women, David Mitchell and Arthur Marwick suggested a rather enthusiastic response.[8]

Indeed, it is difficult to imagine a subversion of the established order comparable to that brought about by the war. Showing that warfare had not been an exclusively male activity meant identifying women who had filled new roles and positions of responsibility: as heads of family, munitions workers, streetcar conductors, and even auxiliaries in the military. Their experience gave them new mobility and self-confidence. Sources demonstrate that the activities of women were commented on, judged, caricatured, and photographed. In Great Britain their contribution to the war effort earned official recognition by the Women's War Work Subcommittee of the Imperial War Museum (IWM). In France and Germany women had to content themselves with the unofficial honors bestowed by organizations such as L'Effort Féminin, which promoted an often rather uncritical view of their wartime role. In the 1970s, when historians interviewed women who had participated in the war effort, nearly all expressed a sense of liberation and retrospective pride. "Out of the cage" was a sentiment often voiced in interviews with researchers from the IWM and the Museum of Southampton.[9] Elderly women in France reported that, yes, they had done all sorts of things during the war and that afterward nothing was the same.[10]

Nevertheless, James F. MacMillan, writing in 1977, noted the tenacity of French conservatism in regard to sex roles. In his view, the war had only reinforced the image of women as housewives and mothers.[11] In the 1980s younger historians also challenged the notion that the war had had a liberating effect. A critical rereading of the sources showed that the changes had been temporary or superficial.[12] Wartime innovation had been followed by a return to normalcy. The whole idea of emancipation had been illusory. More than that, the war was thought to have halted an emancipation movement that had been on the march throughout Europe earlier in the century. Imaginative as well as egalitarian, that movement had created the model of a "new woman," economically and sexually independent.[13] Thus, we are told, the war bolstered a male identity that had been in crisis on the eve of the conflict and restored women to their place as prolific mothers and efficient homemakers. If it liberated them at all, it was for the purpose of making them even more efficient household managers and more dutiful and admiring wives.

Viewing women's history in terms of emancipation has proved valuable and productive, and many historians continue to find it so. The problem, however, is that it isolates women and their history from the rest of humanity, and in recent years the approach has come under increasing criticism. Ute Daniel, one of the first

German historians to write on the subject, suggests that emancipation should not be measured against present-day conceptions. Our goal, rather, should be to recover the perceptions and experience of historical individuals, whose views often differed from the official positions of governments and organizational leaders.[14] Meanwhile, American historians have opened up new prospects with their concept of the gender system. For them, the question is no longer how the war affected men and women but, rather, how it redefined the reality and symbolism of male-female relations. Proponents of this approach, exemplified by the participants in the "Women and War" conference held in January 1984, attach great importance to official discourse and representations.[15] What historians must study, in their view, is the rhetoric of gender and other cultural reactions to the sexual upheaval stemming from the war, along with the power of such cultural manifestations to impede change. The end result of this approach is to rewrite the history of the war in gendered terms, moving women from the edges of the picture toward the center. Joan Scott, I think, goes even further in this direction in her attempts to move the history of women toward the center of political history.[16] Gender in effect emerges as an organizing principle of wartime policy, indeed a veritable weapon of war: its construction and deconstruction became an additional front in a war involving governments, groups, and individuals.

The Mobilization of Men and Women

Much has already been written about women in the First World War. The following summarizes work in this field and discusses it in the light of current gender history. In addition, I hope to bring out not only the similarities in the experience of women in different countries but also some of the differences.

1914: A Year of Women and War

July 1914. It had been a beautiful summer, and no one anticipated the imminence of disaster. In France the press barely mentioned the assassination of Austrian Archduke Franz Ferdinand in Sarajevo on June 28. Readers were less interested in the far-off Balkans than in the last great political scandal of the Belle Epoque: the trial of Henriette Caillaux [for killing the publisher of *Le Figaro,* who had attempted to blackmail her politician husband Joseph Caillaux with details of her extramarital affairs—Trans.]. Feminists departed on vacation after honoring Condorcet in a major suffragist demonstration on July 5. That rally marked the high point of the feminist campaign for political equality, which had gained wide support. The Union Française pour le Suffrage des Femmes (UFSF), more than 9,000 strong, favored a moderate, step-by-step approach. That summer it had circulated a nationwide petition in support of the Dussaussoy-Buisson Bill granting French women the right to vote in the municipal elections of 1916. The Confédération Générale du Travail (CGT), the country's largest labor union, had placed women's labor on the agenda of its fall congress; it had taken this action in the wake of the Emma Couriau affair, which had resulted in the virtual exclusion of women from the printing trades.[17]

In Great Britain, a more radical feminist movement had attacked the Victorian ideology of "two spheres" (a public male sphere and a private female one) and the sexual double standard. In the turbulent period just before the war, the "woman question" was the number one political issue, taking precedence over both the Irish question and social unrest. Borrowing socialist strategy and propaganda techniques, the Women's Social and Political Union (WSPU), first organized in Lancashire in 1903, focused on the right to vote; ultimately, however, the organization was destroyed by the combined effects of a cycle of violence and repression and the authoritarianism of the Pankhursts. In the summer of 1914 Christabel fled to France to avoid prison, but Mrs. Fawcett's National Union of Women's Suffrage Societies (NUWSS), which enjoyed strong support among Liberals and Laborites, staged a huge parade in London to demonstrate the strength of its 480 affiliated groups and 53,000 members. Thus 1914 could have been the year of women; but the war came instead, putting both sexes back in their places.

Between July 28 and August 4 Europe erupted. Although stupor was the immediate popular reaction, it soon gave way to resignation in some quarters, enthusiasm in others (enthusiasm was more prevalent in urban than in rural areas and more common among men than among women). People did not reject the idea of war, because they were mentally prepared for it. French schools had kept alive the memory of the provinces lost to Germany in the Franco-Prussian War of 1870–71 and taught that the Republic, a government of laws and of peace, could not possibly wage an unjust military action. Germans, proud of their economic success and convinced of the superiority of their civilization, set out to conquer a "barbaric" Russia and an "effeminate" France.[18] Nearly everyone in uniform imagined a brief, chivalrous war in which soldiers would be able to demonstrate the highest moral values and enjoy the comradeship of the ranks. Such anachronistic images were sustained by uniforms and rituals: the red trousers worn by French troops, the drums that accompanied the maneuvers of the Germans.[19] Everywhere the departure of troops for the front took place amid collective demonstrations of patriotism, in which social distances vanished and women's cheers were more welcome than their tears.

It was a strange summer, one that radically segregated the sexes while restoring, after the turbulence of the prewar period, a modicum of sexual harmony. The mobilization of the men strengthened family feelings and revived the myth of the man as protector of the motherland and loved ones. Soldiers' early letters home were full of filial piety, protestations of love, and in some cases longing for the children.[20] Although most history books note that, in all the belligerent countries, political parties and social classes closed ranks to form a "national front" or "Union sacrée" to save the nation, the "solidarity of the sexes" is seldom evoked. In France, however, contemporaries hailed the emergence of a real Woman, pure, conscious of her deeper nature and eternal duties, and fountain of universal love and class solidarity. This true woman was the embodiment of the nineteenth-century bourgeois ideal.[21]

Service became the watchword of the French women who comforted soldiers in railway canteens, cared for the wounded in Red Cross hospitals, and fed the homeless of every description: the refugees who fled to the rear of the retreating allied armies, those deprived of employment in the chaos of war zones, and families of mobilized soldiers left without means of support. In Germany, and Britain, too, women did charity work. In England, for example, the trade unionist Mary Macarthur joined with Queen Mary to establish the Queen's Work for Women Fund. Needy women were offered jobs sewing or in some other typically female line of work in exchange for a meal or a modest wage.

Feminists shared the general enthusiasm for service. They temporarily dropped their demands and sought to prove themselves by zealous performance of their womanly duties. Marguerite Durand resumed publication of *La Fronde* in the last two weeks of August 1914. Her position was essentially the same as that expressed by Mrs. Fawcett in *Common Cause* on August 14: "Ladies, your country needs you. Let us show ourselves worthy of citizenship, whether our claim [the right to vote] is recognized or not." And Jane Misme, the editor of *La Française,* the leading journal of moderate feminism, said this in her first wartime issue: "So long as our country's suffering endures, no one is permitted to speak of rights. We have only duties now."[22] Granted amnesty, the Pankhursts transformed themselves into veritable recruiting sergeants. Their rhetoric was sexist and militaristic: men, do your duty and take up a noble cause if you want to look women in the eye. This was not very different fare from that served up by official government recruiting posters, which depicted stoic, unbending women standing in the windows of their homes and exhorting their men to join up; the caption read, "Women of Britain say 'Go!'"[23]

Counting on the war being short, governments expected that women would resign themselves to it and were glad to have feminists rally to the national cause. Yet while they welcomed women volunteers for charity work, they spurned offers to serve in other ways, including a few applications to enlist in the military. The Bund Deutscher Frauenvereine (BDF) had proposed a year of social service for young women at its 1912 congress. On August 3, 1914, the Bund created the Nationaler Frauendienst (NFD), which assisted the government by providing social services and doing supply work.[24] In Britain some female volunteers were accepted for farm work or service as city police auxiliaries. When Dr. Elsie Inglis submitted a plan for a series of overseas hospitals (later to be known as the Scottish Women's Hospitals of France and Serbia), the War office told her to "go home and keep quiet."[25] France's sexist policies were typical: on August 5 the wives of mobilized soldiers were authorized to collect an allowance from the government, out of concern not for the welfare of the family but for the morale of the troops. On August 7 French Prime Minister Viviani issued an appeal to French women. Actually, it was addressed to peasant women, whose services the government believed were urgently needed in farm fields abandoned by their husbands. Viviani adopted the virile language of military glory for the occasion: "Rise up, women and children of France, daughters and sons of the nation. Take the place in the field of labor of those who are now on the field of battle. Be ready to show them, very soon now, the cultivated land, the completed harvest, the seeded fields! In these grave hours no toil is insignificant. Whatever serves the country is great. Arise! To action! To work! Tomorrow there will be glory enough for everyone."[26] But when Marguerite Durand proposed that women serve as auxiliaries in the military, she was dismissed, as was the writer Mme Jack de Bussy when she sought to organize a Ligue des Enrôlées (League of Women Volunteers) as early as July 30.

All the belligerent governments except the United States established what the British called separation allowances, which were paid to common-law as well as legitimate wives and varied in amount according to the number of children. The British allowance, paid from the early days of the war right through to the end, was fairly generous, slightly higher, in fact, than the average wage of a single woman. France and Germany, however, persisted in viewing these payments as a form of welfare, hence kept the amounts low. Furthermore, it was illegal to combine separation allowances with unemployment benefits, which in theory were reserved for the needy and were paid only until the recipient found work that provided a living wage. Even so, the French, German, and British governments were slow to move on these measures. Thus the emotional trauma of the war on the lower classes was compounded by economic disaster. No degree of patriotic fervor was enough to make people forget circumstances so dire that many were forced to seek charity or scour the want ads. Unemployment in highly feminized sectors such as the textile, clothing, and luxury goods industries was extensive and long-lived. In August 1914 the number of women employed in French commerce and industry fell to around 40 percent of prewar levels and had recovered to only 80 percent by July 1915. Paris, owing to the nature of its industry and its proximity to the front, was particularly hard-hit. Except for nurses, who found employment with agencies that helped the wounded, and peasants and shopkeepers, who filled in for absent husbands, the female workforce was slow to be enlisted in the war effort. Full mobilization did not come until people began to recognize that the war would not end quickly. Doubts about female workers had to be laid to rest as well. But what really tipped the scales was the realization that existing labor pools simply could not get the job done.

The Mobilization of Women

The war did not go as expected. With no clear victor apparent by the end of fall, a more or less stagnant front stretched for more than five hundred miles from Flanders to the Swiss border. With illusory hopes of rapid victory dispelled, the belligerents could no longer count on their industrial reserves to get them through and had to gear up production once again. A long and costly war in terms of both men and materiel, the First World War could not have been sustained without support from the rear—and without the cooperation of women. In the course of four and a half years of fighting, 8 million men, or more than 60 percent of the workforce, were mobilized in France, 13 million in Germany, and 5.7 million in Great Britain, which for two years relied on volunteers before instituting a draft in May 1916. Lethal battles devoured men and munitions, and new weapons were rushed into service. Governments set up agencies to oversee the conversion of national arsenals and private factories into a modern weapons industry, which absorbed greater numbers of workers as output rose to unprecedented levels.[27] Modern warfare mobilized minds as well as bodies: that war was fought on two fronts, the battle front and the home front. Combat was exclusively a man's world, whereas women were in the majority behind the lines. These general remarks apply to all the belligerent countries. To delve further into the policy and practice of mobilizing women, however, we must examine each one individually.

In France, where there were already 7.7 million women (including 3.5 million *paysannes*) working prior to 1914, the mobilization of women was largely *ad hoc,* notwithstanding the best efforts of men like Etienne Clémentel, the minister of commerce, and Albert Thomas, the socialist minister of armament. Women were more likely to respond to a newspaper advertisement, act on a tip from a neighbor, or knock at factory gates than they were to sign up for work with one of the regional employment offices established by the ministry of labor in 1915. Often a soldier would be replaced by a family member: a wife, daughter, or sister might be offered a job by the man's employer to tide the family over. That way, there would be no contention over the post when the war was over, and the men at the front could rest assured that someone was watching over the virtue of the women left behind. Although this practice was rare in industry, it was common in business, banks, the transportation sector, and certain government agencies. France had its *financières* (bank ladies) and *cheminottes* (railway ladies); women punched tickets in the Metro, worked in sales, collected bills, and even drove trolleys. In the munitions factories, though, women were always the last resort, after all available civilians had been hired, 500,000 already mobilized workers had been recalled by the Dalbiez Law, and additional workers had been brought in from the colonies and elsewhere abroad.

In the fall of 1915 government ministries began urging industrialists to employ women wherever possible. Posters went up on walls, and hiring offices proliferated throughout France. Although women's charitable organizations tried, with the backing of leading feminists, to rationalize recruitment procedures, female workers streamed into wartime factories from every quarter, attracted by high wages and by the need to find work. Women were assigned to an ever wider variety of tasks. By 1918 some 400,000 women were employed in war industries, or one-quarter of the total workforce (one-third in the Paris region). They symbolized not only the contribution of women to the war effort but also the influx of women into traditionally male sectors of industry.

Nevertheless, there were limits to the mobilization of women, and the labor market was by no means inundated with a flood of female workers. According to statistics of the labor ministry, the number of women employed in industry and commerce did not return to prewar levels until 1916, and by the end of 1917, when female employment reached its highest level, it stood just 20 percent above the prewar mark. Women then accounted for 40 percent of the total workforce, compared with 32 percent before the war. But in France, at least, no sector of industry was paralyzed by a shortage of labor, whereas in Germany the mobilization of women apparently proved insufficient to compensate for the loss of male workers.

That, at any rate, is the view of Ute Daniel, who rejects the conventional argument that the war saw a dramatic increase in female labor.[28] In particular, Daniel challenges the validity of the source most widely cited in support of the conventional view: health insurance statistics. To be sure, German women were mobilized for work in war industries. At first their contribution was minor and sporadic, despite the efforts of the NFD, but recruitment was intensified and centralized in the latter part of the war, as the economy was organized in military fashion and government leaders realized that there could be no victory unless women were brought into the workforce. The Hindenburg Program of November 1916, which tightened the military's grip on domestic policy, assigned the task of industrial mobilization to General Groener's Kriegsamt, or War Office. The armaments industry was naturally assigned top priority: a supply of labor was guaranteed by compulsory auxiliary service *(Hilfdienst)* instituted on December 5, 1916, for all men between the ages of seventeen and sixty. The inclusion of women was considered and rejected by civilian authorities; the feminists of the BDF advised against it, moreover, proposing instead that women be placed in charge of the recruitment of women and that new social policies be instituted for the protection of female workers. To that end the Kriegsamt established a Frauenreferat, or Department of Women in charge of recruitment, and a Frauenarbeitszentrale (FAZ), or Central Office for Women's Labor, which was responsible for the well-being of female workers. By early 1918 these departments employed around a thousand women under the leadership of Marie-Elisabeth Lüders of the BDF.

To be sure, this mobilization led to an increase in the absolute and relative numbers of women working in the heavy metals, electrical, and chemical industries, especially in the largest firms. Some German historians claim an increase of more than 50 percent in companies employing more than ten workers. Krupp represents an extreme case, with more than 30,000 women in a total workforce of 110,000 by the war's end.[29] But this growth came at the expense of sectors of industry that traditionally employed women, sectors that were sacrificed in a Germany whose sources of raw materials and markets were closed off by the allied blockade. Furthermore, the growth in industrial employment seems to have been less important than the expanded use of home-based workers to supply the war machine, a finding confirmed by any number of local estimates. Seamstresses in the Black Forest were put to work manufacturing munitions; corset-makers were assigned to make tents and mess kits; and women who had never worked before were given jobs making rucksacks, gas masks, socks, and even complete uniforms.

What other incentives were offered to induce women to respond to the guilt-inducing appeals of the authorities or the patriotic speeches of Gertrud Bäumer, the president of the BDF? Ringing words alone could not conceal internal conflicts within the German bureaucracy. And some trade unions and employers had doubts about taking women into the workforce: prospective female employees were sometimes forced to sign undated letters of resignation as a condition of employment. In any case, accepting a job in a wartime factory often meant moving to a new location, and many women were tied down by family responsibilities. By 1915 there were shortages of everything, and coping with these shortages proved to be the nub of wartime experience for German women. It took backbreaking effort at home just to get by, and the potential appeal of higher wages for factory work was offset by the need to do work around the house. The government, moreover, provided many families with just enough cash (in the form of unemployment benefits and bonuses paid to *Kriegerfamilien,* or war families) to buy what little remained in the shops. Thus social policies designed to assure soldiers at the front that the government was taking care of the family back home tended to disrupt the labor market and thwart efforts to enlist female workers.

In England Mrs. Pankhurst, backed by the newly created Ministry of Munitions, organized a "Right to Serve" march on July 17, 1915: "The situation is serious," read signs carried by some of the marchers. "Women must help to save it." This demonstration marked the suffragettes' total commitment to the national cause as well as the response of the Asquith government to the political crisis stemming from the shortage of war materiel. It was also a turning point in the mobilization of British women. The recruitment of women was accelerated first by conscription and later by the actions of the Lloyd George government that came to power in December 1916. The government, trade unions, and employers together worked out policies for dealing with the sharp increase in the number of working women.

The second decade of the twentieth century, and especially the wartime years, marked a high point of British trade unionism. Union membership grew, and labor leaders found governments ready and willing to cooperate in social and industrial reform.[30] For the first few months of 1917 the unions were even granted the authority to issue labor cards entitling the bearer to exemption from military service. In return, the unions agreed to accept the principle of "dilution," according to which skilled workers called into the military could be replaced by semiskilled or unskilled employees, and the principle of "substitution," both of which permitted women to take positions previously regarded as "men's jobs." In many branches of industries so-called dilution agreements were negotiated, sometimes after arduous discussion, specifying what jobs could be temporarily assigned to women. At the end of the war these women were to be dismissed, and male workers and returning mobilized workers were guaranteed a return to the status quo or better.

Women first replaced men in commercial establishments and offices, where labor unions were weak and the work was considered respectable. Later they moved into other branches of industry as well, as documented in monthly statistics issued by the Board of Trade for Labour Supply. Although Britain was on the whole more hostile to women's work than France, the figures, which do not include domestic servants, home workers, or women employed by small shops, nevertheless show an increase of 50 percent in the number of women working between July 1914 (admittedly a moment of high unemployment) and November 1918, from 3.3 to 4.9 million. A workforce that had included 24 percent women was now 38 percent female.[31] The change was facilitated by a sharp increase in the number of younger female employees, a shift from home work in traditional trades to industrial employment, and a rise in employment among married women and mothers. The increase was particularly marked in certain sectors, generally the same as in France: the munitions industry (which employed one million women in 1918, many of them in vast arsenals such as those at Gretna and Woolwich), and on a lesser scale in transportation, banking, and the civil service. A desire to serve one's country seems to have been a factor along with the attraction of good pay: 9 percent of the workforce in the war industries consisted of women of the middle and upper classes.

Britain also stands out in another respect: it was the first country to establish a Women's Army Auxiliary Corps (WAAC) in the spring of 1917. By November 1918 the WAACs had enlisted some 40,000 women, 8,500 of whom were sent abroad. The Corps's very murky history is an index of just how difficult it was for contemporaries, both military and civilian, to imagine women as soldiers. Serbia had female soldiers who wore men's uniforms, and Russia had its famous women's death battalion, but France was slow to employ women in either the military or the war ministry. It was late in 1916 when it finally allowed women into military-related posts, but they were required to enter and leave at different times from the men, and there was a special corps of *inspectrices*. Postcards, a prosperous French industry as well as a national passion, gave ribald illustration to the theme by depicting *poilues* (the feminine of *poilu,* slang for infantryman) in extreme décolleté, panties, and ankle boots. Newspapers distributed to the troops in the trenches reflected soldiers' dreams of recreation behind the lines.

The WAAC grew out of the determination of leaders such as Katherine Furse to coordinate the work of a large number of voluntary service organizations. Her plans for a military-style organization were eventually chosen, not without conflict and bitterness, over those of Violet Markham, who thought there should be nothing like a military structure or organization of women's activities, and of the Marchioness of Londonderry, who founded the Women's Legion in 1915. After much hesitation, the War Office opted for an official women's corps led by Mrs. Chalmers Watson. It was to be endowed with the usual panoply of ranks, regulations, and uniforms, in the hope that its status would help to control and perhaps even absorb other women's groups. Men were freed up to fight at the front as the first women recruits were sent to France to work as cooks, clerks, and mechanics. Recruiting efforts were meanwhile expanded at home, and the air force and navy also established women's auxiliaries. Yet critics went right on accusing the new auxiliaries of dishonoring the king's uniform, soaked in the blood of generations of soldiers, as well as denying their sex by "aping" men in a tasteless parody of the real army. Recruits were also widely suspected of immoral if not homosexual proclivities. This bad reputation persisted despite the favorable report of a humiliating investigative commission appointed in 1918 to look into the charges. The very existence of the WAAC somehow disturbed the psychosexual economy of the war—men fighting to protect women and children—and confused male and female identities.[32] More than any other female worker, the WAAC crystallized the fear, so characteristic of the period, that women would be "masculinized."

The Masculinization of Women

Esther Newton and Carroll Smith-Rosenberg have shown how nineteenth-century men shifted the debate over the social and political role of the "new woman" to the sexual realm, where they could express their fears and intimidate their companions. Emancipated women were first branded "uterine deviants" and later, especially under the influence of the German psychiatrist Richard von Krafft-Ebing (1840–1902), "virile lesbians," dangerous, shameless "wo-men."[33] In 1912 the celebrated German physician A. von Moll blamed the emancipation of women for "masculinizing" them, leading to a decline in fertility and a perversion of sexuality.[34] The war, which thrust women into previously male roles and challenged existing concepts of femininity, did more to encourage than to discredit this line of thinking.

Occasionally the literature reveals surprised admiration at what women had proved capable of. More often, however, it reflects outright hostility, ostensibly justified by the alleged physical and mental weaknesses of the female sex: it is astonishing to discover how much was written about the dangers of allowing women to drive trolleys. Fear was the dominant emotion in the male reaction to the mobilization of women. In testimony given in March 1917 to the Reichstag's committee on commerce and industry, which was already planning for demobilization, a representative of the ministry of the interior worried about changes in women's minds and bodies: "Today, when we look at women performing the most difficult tasks, we must look closely to be sure that we are looking at a woman and not a man."[35] One French physician, Dr. Huot, employed the then new term "masculinization" in an ambitious article published in the *Mercure de France:* he acknowledged that he had been wrong about women's "sensitivo-emotive" constitution yet alleged that confusion of the sexes posed a danger of "moral anarchy."[36]

Commentators of all nationalities searched obsessively for feminine metaphors to characterize the work of women doing "masculine" jobs: they "strung" artillery shells like "pearls" or "knitted" steel beams with "grace," "steadfastness," and "finesse." The commentators, it seems, needed to reassure themselves that the world had not changed, that the boundary line between the sexes remained fixed, that the present situation was only temporary. The June 16, 1917, issue of the magazine *J'ai vu* contains a fine example of the genre. An article extolling the "Ouvrière de la victoire" contains a picture of a smiling female worker cradling a huge artillery shell under her left arm while holding a rifle with her right, above the following caption: "Answering the call of the endangered motherland, the women of the Great War have given their all. One finds them wearing men's coveralls in factories, machining shells, making steel for cannons, and manufacturing explosives. Yet in this atmosphere of death, while performing hard labor fit only for men and so taxing to their fragile limbs, they have managed to remain women, sacrificing none of their grace." The very word *munitionnette,* with its charming diminutive, has an inescapably feminine ring.

The patriotic bombast of government propaganda has often been described, but few historians have tried to gauge propaganda's ambiguous effects on the public's perception of male and female roles. In its public pronouncements the French ministry of armament struck the note of family solidarity, urging women to take jobs in the factories in order to save the lives of their *poilus* at the front, but the ministry's official journal, *Le Bulletin des usines de guerre,* was all business, discussing technology, machinery, and the technical capabilities of women. The British government called on women to work as "temporary replacements": "Do your bit. Replace a man for the front." But photographs of women at work made at the behest of the War Office and circulated around the country to persuade employers to hire women emphasized the new and unusual, and portrayed proud, smiling women with agile bodies deft at working with machines.[37] On both sides of the Channel the rhetoric of sacrifice could scarcely conceal the advertisement of competence. In general, however, the press and literature devoted more space to the traditional wartime role of women—as nurses, aid workers, correspondents of soldiers at the front—than to the work of women in the factories. In cartoons in the five leading French dailies, women are all but absent except as Marianne, symbol of the Republic, or "the wife" holding down the fort at home while her man fights at the front.

The war did more to revive the symbolism of woman as the agent of salvation or consolation than to prove female competence. Feminists, however, emphasized the efficiency of female workers and tried to draw a parallel between male and female service by adopting a military vocabulary. In 1916 Friedrich Naumann and Gertrud Bäumer published their journal under the double symbol of the sword and the kernel of wheat; as the *Kriegschronik* (war chronicle) appeared in *Die Hilfe,* the *Heimatchronik* (home-front chronicle) appeared in the monthly magazine *Die Frau,* which emotionally paid tribute to "the service of women to the fatherland." In *La Française* of March 6, 1915, Jane Misme wrote that the "soldiers of the rear" had answered "the nation's call" and held "the second front" in order to "help break" one "more bar of the cage in which women have been confined for centuries." The cover of *La Vie féminine* for April 15, 1917, featured a diminutive *midinette,* or dressmaker, the very type of the working woman of the prewar period, facing a tall, powerful *munitionnette* against a background of factory smokestacks. Whereas the German feminists of the BDF saw women as achieving integration by developing specific types of competence, French feminists hoped to use their wartime experience as a springboard to equality in the workplace, or at any rate toward greater opportunities and a higher level of skills for female workers. They called for occupational training, opened new schools, promoted existing ones, and laid the groundwork for further progress by undertaking a vast survey of educational and career opportunities available to women.

Still, the mobilization of women was different from the mobilization of men. For every woman who worked, one more man could be sent to the front. According to Teresa Noce, politically conscious working-class families in Turin gave female workers at Fiat a hard time: by working, it was alleged, they were sending men to their death.[38] The age-old hostility of working-class men to female labor, fed by fears of competition, long-standing guild loyalties, and attachment to the traditional role of woman as mother and homemaker, was now compounded by fears of death. Women who took factory jobs were sometimes accused of being profiteers and gravediggers (*Totengräber* in German). French anarchists and pacifists, who formed a minority within the CGT and SFIO (French Section of the Workers' International), reacted against female employment, perhaps out of frustration but with ferocity nonetheless. Raymond Péricat of the Building Trades Union and Alphonse Merrheim of the Metalworkers Union accused women of being lower than animals: even wolf bitches protect their young, they charged, but French women had done nothing to keep their men from going to the front in 1914 and in fact had sold them out for twenty-five sous (the amount of the separation allowance). While men died in combat, women had a ball at home.

The Women's Age?

Was the experience of women during the war a positive one? To put it even more provocatively, was the war a happy time for women? To one degree or another a variety of sources suggest that it was, including oral histories of French and British women and photographs compiled by the Imperial War Museum. The Museum of Southampton has a collection of photographs from a studio to which women in various trades, especially transportation, went to have portraits made of themselves in their working garb: we see women proud of their work (and perhaps of their uniforms as well).[39] In France contemporary observers did not fail to note the "fantastic" wages and "insane" expenditures of women in the munitions industry: some purchased boots and silk stockings with their earnings, while others preferred oranges and chickens. While all feminist writing of the period emphasized the desire to serve, to prove one's mettle, and to hasten the emancipation of women, some British and American writers also mentioned the pleasure of being with other women. Harriot Stanton Blatch described England in 1918 as "a world of women." Gone was the self-effacing spinster, replaced by the "capable woman, bright-eyed, happy." Others looked back on those years as a "good time," a "fine time."[40] Women's literature—from wartime poems and novels to later memoirs and essays, from the English propagandist Jessie Pope to the American novelist Willa Cather—frequently rejoiced in the reversal of sex roles: "All the world is topsy-turvy." Women were glad to be able at last to express their desires openly.[41] Lesbians like Amy Lowell and Gertrude Stein produced their most erotic work during the war (*Lifting Belly,* for example), and it was in 1915 that Charlotte Perkins Gilman published *Herland,* a utopian novel about a world without men.

A female apotheosis? Poets and novelists such as D. H. Lawrence, T. S. Eliot, Wilfred Owen, Siegfried Sassoon, and Ernest Hemingway suggested as much by describing the war as an apocalyptic turning point in the battle of the sexes, a sacrifice of young men to fathers and women and, in Sandra Gilbert's phrase, "a festival of female misrule." Emasculation, real or imaginary, is an obsessive theme in this literature of modern antiheroes, paralyzed, sterile, or maimed. Paul Fussell and Eric Leed have called attention to literary evidence for the traumatic psychological effects of the war on those who fought it.[42]

There is no denying that the Great War was indeed one long trauma for the troops: mass slaughter made nonsense of manly images of war and victory, indeed of the values of Western civilization itself. Bogged down in the mud and blood of the trenches with nothing to do but wait for a murderous assault or artillery barrage, some soldiers succumbed to that old female disorder, hysteria, now renamed "shell shock" by English doctors.[43] The troops felt that they had been returned to a primitive state of total helplessness, public as well as private. In the past, when men had gone off to fight the enemy, their women had waited piously at home. Now, however, the men left and the women took over, shouldering public responsibilities and keeping the war machine running, and the troops at the front were afraid of returning home only to find themselves penniless cuckolds.

French wartime literature was, I think, on the whole less aggressive and less misogynist, although it does express the *poilu*'s resentment of the home front and need to emphasize manly values. "There're two countries, I tell you, we're divided into two foreign countries. Out there, at the front, there're too many unhappy people. And back here in the rear, there're too many happy ones," says one of the heroes of Henri Barbusse's popular novel, *Feu* (1916). Stéphane Audoin-Rouzeau's work on soldiers' newspapers also shows the ambivalence of the troops' feelings about women and the home front.[44] On the one hand, woman symbolized "the opposite of war." She was the soldier's helpmate, the mother of his children, the archangel who made it possible to conceive of a future away from the horror and chaos of the present. She was the beloved of whom the trooper spoke constantly to his comrades, the woman of his dreams. She, along with other close relatives, was treated as an exception to the rule that civilians failed to understand the suffering of the troops and believed the propaganda served up by the "brain-stuffing" press. Yet she was also the subject of the soldier's nightmares, constantly suspected of infidelity. Men were afraid that when they returned home on leave they would no longer recognize their wives, for they knew full well that behind the lines life continued as before. Misunderstandings sometimes led to painful ruptures. While the writer Roland Dorgelès was crawling among corpses, his mistress sprained her ankle dancing.

An Experience of Freedom

The war offered women unprecedented freedom and responsibility. Serving their country in previously inaccessible occupations, many found pleasure in working with new tools and technologies. The war broke down age-old barriers and opened many prestigious professions to women. In 1914 there were only a few hundred female doctors in all of France and only a few dozen female lawyers. But Maria Vérone and Jeanne Chauvin were allowed to plead cases before military courts, and young women were admitted to business and engineering schools, including the prestigious Ecole Centrale, which accepted its first female student in 1918. Female teachers were welcomed with open arms as teachers in boys' schools and generously praised. The teaching profession became increasingly female, to the dismay of male teachers, who feared that they would be driven out. In many rural villages the female teacher became the community spokesperson, taking the place of the absent mayor. Girls found their way into all the bastions of higher education from Oxford to the Sorbonne. Women working in cafés, hotels, commercial establishments, banks, and government offices gave women a public presence. If a few were unpleasant, many were appreciated for their honesty and discretion.

Most working women recognized their skills and valued their new financial independence. Wartime work was well paid, particularly in munitions factories, where women could often earn twice what they made in the traditional female occupations. In France and Britain domestics seized a once-in-a-lifetime opportunity to turn their backs on meager wages and tyrannical masters, and this, along with the departure of the *Fraüleins,* deepened a "servant crisis" that had begun even before the war. In some areas competition forced employers in the textile trade to increase the pay schedule, and the unpopular "leaving certificate" was intended to prevent women from quitting one armaments factory in search of higher-paid employment in another. Women no longer worked for "pin money" (*salaire d'appoint* or *Zuverdienst*): a skilled arsenal worker at Woolwich could earn several pounds a week (as many as six for a welder), and a driver working for the army up to five pounds, a good middle-class wage.

For women and girls of the middle and upper classes, accustomed to charity work, the war was a period of feverish service, which helped to break down social barriers and stiff bourgeois forms. In France the venerable custom of receiving guests on set days fell by the wayside as former hostesses now gave hours of their time to charity work and balls. The demise of the corset, along with shorter skirts and simplified outfits (most notably Gabrielle Chanel's creation of the jersey blouse) liberated the body and facilitated movement. The loss of their chaperones left young women frightened and dazzled by their newfound freedom, among them young Clara Goldschmidt (later the wife of writer André Malraux), who stalwartly rose to the challenge of defending her family against xenophobic prejudice.[45]

Older girls, like their mothers, joined the Red Cross and other charitable organizations. As nurses and nurses' aides, they were quickly introduced to life's realities: they discovered men, sex, the working class, and even people of color. Although a certain "uniformed snobbery" was denounced early in the war, it could not survive long days of hard labor and daily contact with suffering. Overwhelmed by the numbers of the wounded, military hospitals took on thousands of volunteer workers (more than 70,000 in France, compared with 30,000 paid staff). Some were assigned to auxiliary hospitals, while others drove ambulances and a few were even sent to the front (the French were more reluctant to do this than the British). There, in Flanders, Salonika, and Serbia, their devotion was rivaled only by their courage. Many died, while many others returned with medals and fabulous stories to tell. While Marie Curie and her daughter organized a squadron of radiological ambulances to provide X-ray services to wartime surgeons, the British press dubbed two Scottish women, Mairi Chisholm (born 1896) and Mrs. Knocker (the future Baroness of T'Serclaes), the "heroines of Pervyse." As members of an ambulance squad in Belgium, the pair had set up a field dispensary in a ruined village close to the trenches, and despite constant bombardment by enemy artillery they remained at their posts until 1918, when they were seriously injured in a gas attack. The press also reported the prefect of Constanza's comment on the death of Elsie Inglis in Serbia in November 1917: "No wonder England is a great country if the women are like that."[46]

The nurse was the very embodiment of devotion, at once angel of mercy and mother. No other group of women drew more praise for its wartime service than did nurses, who became a favorite subject of contemporary artists. One Red Cross poster featured "The Greatest Mother in the World." The image—a gigantic nurse cradling a miniature man lying on a stretcher—hinted at a new relation between the sexes. While soldiers, many of them of lower-class background, appreciated the quiet of the hospital, they felt humiliated and infantilized by the rather aloof women who cared for them like children, saw all their weaknesses, and in the end sent them back to the front. Obsessed by this maternal stereotype, contemporaries seemed to have imagined the nurse as a figure of power, a fantasy that also comes out in persistent references to her supposedly prodigious sexual appetite.

Although postwar discourse emphasized the ascetic existence of men at the front and the fidelity of their wives back home, we actually know very little about the more intimate aspects of the war beyond what can be gleaned from memoirs, letters, and indirect evidence such as the rise in illegitimacy during the conflict and the sharp increase in divorce when the troops returned home. Some relationships succumbed to the pervasive obsession with death, which could not only sharpen the pangs of love but make the whole idea of love seem foolish. Lengthy engagements became a thing of the past. The war may even have contributed, as Michelle Perrot has suggested, "to the emergence of the modern couple, whose core is self-fulfillment rather than inherited wealth."[47] Enforced separation and a widespread "changing of partners" (the soldier-writer Jean Norton Cru called it a *chassé-croisé des ménages*) kindled new desires, reflected in erotic postcards, magazines, and theatrical productions as well as in an upsurge of adultery and nontraditional relationships. But did this really add up to a *Diable au corps* (literally, a "devil in the body," a sexual itch), as the title of the novel by Raymond Radiguet, a provocative, twenty-one-year-old poet, had it? Radiguet's novel, published in 1923, was the story of one adolescent youth's sentimental education at the hands of the adulterous wife of a *poilu*. Like *La Garçonne*, it enjoyed a *succès de scandale* yet also aroused suspicion and bitterness in proportion to the fears that attached to the image of the lonely woman in wartime. What was new, and crucial, was precisely the opportunity for women to live alone, to go out alone, to assume family responsibilities alone: previously all these things had seemed impossible or dangerous. Some women even dared to write, honing patriotic metaphors to commemorate some solemn occasion or recording the hard work and misery of the war years in a journal. Compared with the few that have found publishers, how many others disappeared, and how many may remain in attics awaiting discovery and publication (as the Archives of People's Writing in Trent, Italy, has been doing for some years now)?[48]

In Italy the wartime experience of women had something of a

revolutionary aspect, because the war, which Italy joined on the Allied side in 1915, disrupted the traditional elements of the feminine identity—private life, the home, and reproduction—in a country steeped in the Mediterranean tradition of honor and Catholic ideals of morality and education and deeply influenced by Cesare Lombroso and his followers, who justified the seclusion of women on medical grounds. Paola di Cori has interpreted these changes through photographs that for the first time show women in public, at first offering assistance to the needy but later, increasingly, in the productive sphere as well. These women radiate confidence, competence, and a proud, masculine bearing. But Italian reporters still manipulated the photographic evidence to suggest that women remained confined within a sphere of their own and were hardly capable of representing the human race. Whereas the British paper *Illustrated War News* did not hesitate to show soldiers busy with housekeeping chores or ironically disguised as women, the Italian papers published only photographs of men in manly occupations. Furthermore, the commentary of Italian journalists emphasized not the possibility of future equality between the sexes but the pathological character of role reversal, at times lumping working women together with prostitutes.[49]

The Weight of Tradition and the Ambiguities of Modernity

A revolution nipped in the bud? Conditional liberty? In fact, the changes due to the war were limited, objectively and subjectively, by the preservation and even reinforcement of traditional sex roles and by a complex symbolic system that gave economic, social, and cultural priority to soldiers at the front. Other factors such as social group, age, family situation, nationality, and individual history were of course also important. Except perhaps for the first few months of the war, it is a myth that women were united in a community of suffering and service. The terms "mobilization" and "war work" cover a wide variety of individual experiences, a variety that discouraged solidarity. It was mainly younger women who savored the air of freedom. Liberated from parental surveillance, working girls enjoyed each other's company after working hours. Young middle-class women were even more "transfigured" by their social and intellectual adventure. These are of course the very women who sound a note of optimism in relatively recent, and belated, attempts to gather their oral histories. By contrast, it was working-class women with families who had the hardest time during the war, particularly in Central Europe, where shortages were quick to make themselves felt.

The United States deserves special attention because it entered the war late (April 1917) and because its population was heterogeneous. Here, women had already entered the workforce even before the war, owing to the introduction of new methods of production. The European war, which halted immigration and increased exports, led to a shortage of labor that encouraged employers to hire women long before the armed services enlisted some two million men in a gradual buildup. There was no significant increase in the number of working women in the United States during World War I (in contrast to World War II). There was, however, a shift in the pattern of employment along racial, sexual, and geographical lines. White women replaced white men in heavy industry, offices, and transportation. Black women, previously employed as farm laborers or domestics, replaced white women and black men in traditionally female sectors where the pay was low and the work was hard.[50] In the South, where racial disturbances revealed the scope of discrimination, black women organized with help from the federal government, seizing the opportunity to demonstrate their patriotism as well as to advance the cause of social reform. But the war ended too soon to accomplish any significant social change, and the subsequent rise of intolerance and conservatism put an end to many of the progressive dreams that President Wilson had symbolized.[51]

Was the Women's Committee established on April 21, 1916, in response to offers of service from women's organizations anything more than a cruel joke, an expedient for funneling middle-class women into harmless activities such as the campaign against food waste or the sale of Liberty Bonds? This is what feminist Ida Clarke argued in 1925, despite her enthusiasm during the war years, an enthusiasm that was widely shared in 1917–18 because the fighting was far away and the men remained for a long time in training.[52] Despite the authority of Anna Howard Shaw, the committee's chair, it lacked power and money and was excluded from the role of providing assistance to the troops, a task monopolized by the Red Cross and the YMCA. Some Americans organized charitable services abroad. Anne Morgan, for example, was the founder along with Mrs. Murray Dike of the American Committee for Devastated Regions, and her name still graces a medical assistance organization in the Soissonnais.[53] These philanthropists presented themselves as "modern women," who wore their hair short and took a militant attitude toward hygiene. But the mobilization of American women in general remained limited and sluggish. The suffragist movement financed the American Women's Hospitals, however, whose staff members earned many medals for meritorious service. But the hospitals had to establish themselves in Europe, not only out of solidarity with the embattled nations of the old Continent, but also because their doctors were turned away by the American army.

It was not until 1918 that pressure from feminist groups led to the creation of federal agencies charged with facilitating the employment of women in industry. Led by reformers such as Mary Van Kleeck and the trade-unionist Mary Anderson, who sought not only to train women for work but also to protect them from exploitation, the new agencies sponsored new measures of social protection but encountered resistance from employers unwilling to improve working conditions or to pay female workers as much as their male counterparts. The National War Labor Board (NWLB), which included representatives of unions, business, and government, was set up in April 1918 to arbitrate conflicts in strategic industries. It took a revolutionary step by committing itself to the principles of equal pay for equal work and a minimum wage high enough to permit women as well as men to live in "health and reasonable comfort." Yet it could not hold out against both law and tradition, which looked askance on sexual equality in the workplace: witness the board's decisions in the celebrated cases of the Cleveland and Detroit street railways just after the armistice, and likewise its refusal to accept women as members.[54]

What was striking in both Europe and the United States was the determination to limit women to a replacement role: "only for the duration," the British said. Their help was needed in wartime, but afterward their inextricable "nature" reasserted itself. The idea that only certain occupations were suitable for women enjoyed renewed vigor, along with its corollary that certain professions were exclusively male, among them those of lawyer, railway engineer, and medical scientist. "Leave the wounds to the doctors and the wounded to the nurses," one French physician put it. True, the war did add new luster to the nursing profession in France and Germany. Nurses were now awarded diplomas, and a career in nursing was considered suitable for a young woman of the middle class. But doctors topped the medical hierarchy, and devotion and discretion were considered the primary prerequisites for nurses, despite Hanna Hamilton's strenuous efforts to improve the status of nurses and to emphasize the central function of nursing care.[55] Throughout the war, charity workshops and agencies continued to be the focal point of women's activity, as volunteers prepared knitted items, bandages, and care packages for the front.

The war's effects on rural France and Italy were severe. Peasant women took the place not only of men but also of beasts requisitioned for the front. Conditions varied with region and farm size, and a great deal remains to be learned. The old division of responsibilities along sexual lines fell apart. Women plowed, sowed, swung scythes, and treated vines with copper sulphate. They helped out neighbors, quarreled with bureaucrats, and even hid young deserters (a few instances are known in the Piedmont). Soldiers returned home with newfangled ideas picked up from their comrades in the trenches, and greater access to the cash economy allowed farm women to indulge a few modest fantasies. But the work was backbreaking for all, from the youngest to the oldest, and dreams of one day escaping the hard regimen of rural labor had to be set aside. Agriculturalist ideologues assigned to women the role of preserving rural customs as well as working the land, and proper behavior was enforced by the entire community. Here more than elsewhere older women were likely to censure the young and brothers to assert their authority over sisters. If a man was drafted, his parents, in-laws, or other kin usually assumed responsibility for running the farm. Those who gained most from the situation were younger males, not females.[56]

In the factories grudgingly hired women workers met with suspicion from male co-workers and employers. The climate did little to encourage women to develop their potential. In Britain the quality of female labor was questioned throughout the war. Masculine solidarity frequently took precedence over class solidarity. In Germany, which began preparing for demobilization as early as 1915, everyone from the Reichstag to the BDF called for a return to the *status quo ante* for the sake of the soldiers and the nation. Occupational training was even rarer in Germany than in France or England, where the government joined with large firms to set up worker training programs. In order to make use of inexperienced workers, the work process was reorganized, automatic machines were introduced, and female workers were assigned to specific, limited tasks under the supervision of foremen who sometimes thought of themselves as ladies' men. These changes proved permanent, thereby creating yet another bone of contention between skilled workers and women. Industrialists everywhere "discovered" women's talents: diligence, attention to detail, and an aptitude for monotonous tasks. Some women were put to work on assembly lines manufacturing howitzers, for example, while others were assigned to machine small parts that had to be manufactured to close tolerances. These were the areas in which female workers proved most productive.

Fabulous wartime wages were not available to all, and women in the less well remunerated lines of work paid the price for the high wages offered elsewhere. Traditional female occupations were still poorly compensated, particularly for those who worked at home, where minimum wage laws (instituted in Britain in 1909 and in France in 1915) were difficult to enforce—this despite the activism of women such as Jeanne Bouvier and Sylvia Pankhurst.[57] In Germany the gap between male and female wages decreased, but real wages fell as prices soared on the black market. By contrast, real wages rose in Britain during the second half of the war and held steady in France despite rising prices. But many workers were paid by the piece, a practice that made a mockery of the principle of "equal pay for equal work." The British adopted piecework wages in the spring of 1915 in order to win the trade unions' support for "dilution." Industrialists generally paid a minimum of one pound per week, arguing that women did not do the same work as men and in any case had other sources of income. Apart from isolated instances and victories won after bitter struggle, wages remained tied to sex and were much lower for women than for men (by half on the average). Male unions in general accepted the principle of equal pay only in order to make sure that women would be readily dismissed after the war, and they refused to accept female members. Women workers did unionize, however: nearly a quarter of them belonged to the National Federation of Women Workers by the end of the war, and they learned to use the weapons of industrial combat. But their union had committed itself to the principle that the "dilutees" must be dismissed when the soldiers returned: this was the price of admission to British trade unionism.

It was in France, apparently, that women were most fully

accepted as members of the workforce and the wage gap between the sexes was lowest, a consequence of the wage schedule instituted by Albert Thomas in January 1917.[58] Nevertheless, Jean-Louis Robert notes that even in France women and the workers' movement failed to connect, despite some improvement in the climate in the spring of 1917, after strikes by *midinettes* and *munitionnettes* established an image of women as combative and committed trade unionists. But the war failed to widen breaches first opened in 1914.[59] Instead, it led to a solidifying of traditional attitudes of hostility to female labor, contempt for the alleged docility of working women, and nostalgia for the idealized working-class household. If a certain restlessness was tolerated among youth, women, along with immigrants, were marginalized by a working class that had difficulty coping with its growing diversity. Workers adopted a defensive attitude, while the official pronouncements of their leaders avoided this highly complex issue altogether. Held together by militant moralism and a powerful corporate spirit, working men failed to grasp how the presence of women on the shop floor might lead to an improvement in workplace relations and result in new social legislation beneficial to all. Labor groups called instead for specific measures of protection, at the risk, which they may or may not have calculated, that such measures would bar women from many male-dominated jobs.

The war, Deborah Thom has found, tended to reinforce the thinking of prewar social theorists, who generally viewed women as the weaker sex and held that a woman's primary role was to serve as "mother to the human race." Of course the war also led to a suspension of social laws and a deterioration in working and living conditions (crowded suburbs, inadequate transportation) and exposed women working in certain industries, particularly the arms industry, to hard, dangerous work. Any number of witnesses tell of women who arrived on the job young and robust only to sacrifice their health, and sometimes their lives, in labor that demanded eleven to twelve hours of work daily on both night and day shifts.[60] First in Britain (1915), and later in France and Germany, special committees composed of bureaucrats, industrialists, trade unionists, physicians, and feminists called for the adoption of social policies specifically intended to help female workers in war industries: more flexible working hours, meals served in factory cafeterias, and establishment of in-house dispensaries and childcare facilities.[61] The latter were rare, even in England, that supposed paragon of worker well-being, where only 108 factories offered childcare in 1917; social services and childcare were all but nonexistent in smaller plants. There was virtually total neglect, moreover, of occupational health hazards, the most serious of which was TNT poisoning.

In Germany, increasing production remained the number one priority, and social policy therefore had only a limited impact, even though the empress, Augusta Victoria, took a personal interest in the welfare of her countrywomen. Larger firms hired so-called *Fabrikpflegerinnen,* middle-class women (some of them feminists) whose job was to promote the welfare of female employees both on and off the job. They perfected techniques that would later be applied by a new category of professionals: personnel managers and social workers. The result was an effective system of social control: in sisterly solidarity women helped other women conform to middle-class standards of behavior. Perhaps this was why a comparable British measure, the so-called Lady Welfare Supervisors Program, never caught on, despite the benefits it provided. In France, the so-called *surintendantes d'usine* were a relatively late development, and their efforts met with considerable resistance. After the war they remained on the job, however, and helped to promote the government's pronatalist policies.[62] Desperate for more babies as well as more howitzers, France attempted to reconcile industrial work with motherhood. The Engerand Law of August 1917 required employers to make special nursing rooms available to breast-feeding mothers. A year later "repopulation" became the watchword of French policy, and women were reminded of their duty to procreate.

The Family Core

Prostitute or mother: for women, the sexual options remained what they had always been, a stark choice between radically opposed alternatives. More than ever, the family was considered to be the fundamental cell of society. While the dangers of sex drew unprecedented attention in the United States, the double standard—so vehemently denounced by feminists, admittedly in the name of purity more often than of sexual liberation—took on something of a patriotic coloration in Europe. While female immorality was denounced as a crime equal to treason against the state, prostitution was officially sanctioned as the soldier's necessary, not to say just, compensation. Unfaithful wives were branded unpatriotic, particularly those (more numerous in rural areas than in the cities) who had relations with prisoners of war; they were pilloried in the German press and slapped with fines and prison terms. In France the severity of the courts toward adulterous women was matched only by their leniency toward soldiers convicted of murdering culpable wives. British women were supervised like children and threatened with loss of their separation allowance in case of "impropriety." In some towns close to army bases, women were even forbidden to visit pubs or to go out at night.

Military authorities in the land of Josephine Butler even hinted at reviving the notorious Contagious Diseases Act, with its draconian controls on prostitution, but nothing came of this suggestion. Elsewhere the war put an end to the process that Alain Corbin has described in the case of France: prostitutes were forced back into licensed houses of prostitution and military bordellos (called *casini del soldato* in Italy). Advocates of regulating prostitution found their position strengthened.[63] Prostitutes were issued cards, subjected to frequent medical examination, and forcibly hospitalized. Clandestine practitioners of the trade were persecuted, and some were suspected of espionage or germ warfare. Venereal diseases, which could sap the strength of armies and debauch an entire race, were even more feared than tuberculosis. Soldiers were taught prophylactic methods and examined for signs of disease. Yet who knows how many women were infected by husbands home on leave?

Was the writer Colette right when she suggested that soldiers at the front suffered from an "orphan's complex" that caused them to marry in the hope of finding not a lover but a mother? Historians still find it difficult to write about the changing expectations of one sex toward the other. Perhaps the degrading sexual language that was so prevalent in contemporary newspapers, plays, and correspondence reflected a devaluation of women.[64]

Surely it is the history of the family that most fully reveals the dialectical and contradictory character of the conflict: military and industrial mobilization disrupted family life yet at the same time liberated political and social forces capable of restoring the traditional family structure. With the men away at the front, the state stepped into the father's role as both disciplinarian and provider. In France, for example, where married women were still legally considered minors, a law of 3 July 1915 authorized mothers to exercise parental authority and take legal action without the authorization of their husbands, provided that a court ruled that the affair was urgent and that the mobilized spouse was unable to assume his responsibilities. Furthermore, the death of large numbers of men and the decline in the birthrate focused attention on previously insignificant political movements: natalists, familialists, and hygienists. Out of this change in focus came a new demographic policy, which took a carrot-and-stick approach to the problem. Among the incentives offered to promote larger families was a new medical and social policy designed to serve the needs of mothers and children. Other countries adopted remarkably similar policies, though with minor differences in timing and justificatory rhetoric.[65]

In France, where Malthusian attitudes had long held sway and social legislation was very backward, wartime postcards with their endless variations on the theme of love, children, and family reflected the central importance of children in the culture, suggesting that natalist ideology had indeed trickled down to the lower strata of society. Bitter debate during the war eventually led to the passage (in 1920 and 1923) of laws making it illegal to advertise contraceptives or seek abortions. In Britain a decade-old campaign to protect mothers and children at last bore fruit: the number of mother and child welfare centers was doubled, the Maternal and Child Welfare Act was passed in 1918, and the ministry of health was established in 1919. The rhetoric of this campaign was increasingly hostile to female labor, however, and much of it was intended to make working mothers feel guilty, as in the National Baby Weeks Campaigns of 1917 and 1918. The disproportion of male and female populations (a consequence of the war) became an obsession: something had to be done to save the males. In Germany, where a drastic decline in the birthrate compounded the effects of the war and of recent changes in demographic behavior, the government, in response to contradictory pressures, adopted a grandiose public health program (although little was done to translate the program into practice) along with more severe penalties for contraception and abortion. This policy was adopted in the name of the *Volksgemeinschaft,* or people's community: an organicist ideology held that the family was the fundamental cell of a larger organism, the *Volk,* or people, that birth control was a symptom of a degenerative disease, and that maternity was a vital function that could not be left to individual decision. Social democrats and feminists of the BDF protested against such government interference in people's private lives, yet even they described maternity as a woman's natural duty and ultimate fulfillment as well, of course, as a service to the fatherland. The most extreme of the French natalists even described childbearing as a "blood tax" that established a sort of rough justice between the sexes here below.

Nevertheless, the pronatalist movement failed to change people's behavior. Couples managed to control births by means of coitus interruptus or abortion. Abortion was common among the lower classes, and the prohibition of contraception only increased its popularity. Women, the parties most directly concerned, often had neither the heart nor the strength to give birth under wartime conditions.

The Blood Tax

Is it out of place to speak of the suffering of women when they did not face death looming over the next ridge? In her poem *Non-Combatant* the English poet Cicely Hamilton described the dilemma of being an "idle mouth," while other women spoke of the guilt of surviving, the shame of carrying on after their men had died.[66]

Men's Deaths and Women's Pain

Even if we leave aside the casualties of civil war and intervention in Russia, the military losses incurred in World War I were staggering: nearly nine million dead. The excitement of the war's early days soon gave way to horror at the incredible slaughter. A small country like Serbia lost a quarter of its troops, while France sacrificed 1.3 million of its men, or 10 percent of the active male population and more than 3 percent of the total population. Germany lost 1.8 million men, nearly 3 percent of its population, while Italy and the United Kingdom each sacrificed around 750,000 soldiers, most of them young.

Military operations decimated the troops but spared civilians in the West, where the front stabilized quickly. Behind the lines the war scarcely made itself felt, with the exception of a few bombardments that did little more damage than accidental explosions at munitions plants, which occurred routinely. The number of civilian casualties was kept secret: they were perhaps 1,500 in England, 600 in Paris, mainly in 1918, when German raids on the city were followed up by shelling with the notorious Big Berthas. Many Parisians left the city as they had done in 1914, frightened by the advance of German troops.

Behind the numbers, one has to imagine, repeated millions of times over, tearful farewells, endless loneliness, enforced celibacy, physical hardship, and anxious waiting for the news that a husband, a son, or a lover had been wounded, taken prisoner, or "killed in the line of duty." The number of women in black dresses and long veils made public gathering places seem funereal. With images drawn from history, literature, and even religion women were exhorted to be "sowers of courage," to offer up sons and husbands bravely and accept their deaths stoically. Not all women responded appropriately, however. This we know not only from their writings but less directly from police reports and blasts from jingoists impugning their patriotism. Spirits flagged as the war dragged on and death became at once commonplace and unbearable. Women, it was alleged, often failed to exercise paternal authority and discipline their sons when necessary. Grieving mothers were immune from criticism, but widows (some 600,000 of them in France and Germany and more than 200,000 in Great Britain) were not: those suspected of insufficient sacrifice to the memory of their late husbands were vilified. The French writer Maurice Barrès proposed that dutiful widows should be honored with the right to vote in place of the fallen; this "suffrage of the dead" would also have the virtue of saving France from "rule by shirkers." In Germany, where feminists failed to persuade the government to pay wages to mothers, widows received allowances to help the "children of fallen heroes." In exchange for this installment on the nation's debt to those who sacrificed their lives, however, the government imposed strict controls on the private activities of aid recipients. Although France (in 1919) and Germany (in 1920) belatedly passed laws intended to improve the disastrous situation in which many soldiers' widows found themselves, these women remained among the war's neglected victims, as Karin Hausen has pointed out.[67]

There was no justice in the war's choice of victims. Inequality with respect to risk of death in battle cut across social lines: the wives of miners, railway engineers, and workers with essential skills enjoyed the coveted privilege of seeing their men a long way from the front, sometimes even of having them home at their sides. In France the groups most vulnerable to the war were, on the one hand, the peasantry that constituted the bulk of the infantry, and on the other hand the university students and professionals who volunteered for service in the officer corps. In England, the Eugenics Education Society, chaired by Charles Darwin's youngest son, worried about the loss of the nation's "best" reproductive stock (young men of the middle and upper classes) and sought to persuade the public that war-related disabilities were not hereditary.[68] And then there were the unfortunate young ladies whose fiancés returned without a limb, or the many others condemned to spinsterhood by the sudden shortage of eligible young men. "Virgin widows" were advised to seek surrogate motherhood by acting as devoted aunts to a sibling's children or by doing charity work on behalf of mothers and children generally.

These private ordeals, which marked so many lives, cannot be discounted as insignificant. Other ordeals still lay in store. Very little is known about the aftermath of invasion and occupation or about the cruel famine that afflicted Russia and neighboring countries.

Women's Ordeals

In the French mind the hardships of the Nazi occupation have tended to eclipse memories of life in occupied northeastern France during World War I. But the earlier German invasion also brought its share of atrocities, including the destruction of the villages of Orchies and Gerbéviller, rapes, executions of hostages, and a flood of refugees. All in all, some three million people were uprooted as the front shifted back and forth over the course of the war. And that is not counting the 500,000 repatriates, French nationals whom the Germans allowed to leave the occupied zone so as not to have to feed them, chiefly women, children, and the elderly. In Reims, a "martyr city" owing to its proximity to the front, nearly 20,000 residents lived in champagne cellars until they were forcibly evacuated on Easter of 1917, when heavy shelling resumed. Whereas the Germans placed occupied Belgium under the jurisdiction of a governor-general, the occupation army had full powers in France and used them to enforce bureaucratic terror, to confiscate supplies, and to force men and women alike to labor in the German cause.

The starving urban population survived only thanks to American aid and paid a heavy tribute in disease and death. Among the two million inhabitants of the occupied region, there were only 19,000 marriages and 93,000 births in four years compared with 190,000 deaths. In the summer of 1915 an electric fence was completed along the Dutch-Belgian border, and the Germans dismantled the escape and intelligence networks that ardent patriots had established. Edith Cavell, a British nurse who ran a hospital in Brussels, was executed on October 11. Other women of the resistance were imprisoned at the fortress of Siegburg, where Louise de Bettignies, a young woman from Lille recruited by the British Intelligence Service, died in 1918. The massive deportations of 1916 (whole towns were evacuated to remote villages) were ended in the wake of outcries in France and abroad but remained the quintessential German war crime, particularly in the eyes of French women's organizations, which mobilized sister groups in allied countries to alert the Peace Conference and demand punishment of all barbaric acts and especially indecent acts against women.

Jay Winter has called attention to a paradox of the war that emerges from a comparative study of demographic statistics: the British life expectancy actually increased. The improvement was due not so much to the government's health policy as to an increase, particularly evident in the case of the working class, in the standard of living. This success, without which victory would have been impossible, can be explained in part by the efficiency of the British administration and in part by Britain's control of the seas. The interventionist policies of Lloyd George's government, culminating in the imposition of rationing in 1918, managed to avoid serious shortages.[69] The British were even more prepared to hold out than the French, who suffered greatly from lack of coal during the long winters. Hardships were much the same on both sides of the Channel: long lines, bad bread, and no meat, alcohol, or tobacco. With the household help gone to work in the war plants, people were urged to eat less and change their dietary habits for patriotic, not health, reasons. To save energy civilians were asked to revamp household routines. Although shortages were on everyone's mind and working mothers were badly overburdened (as an increase in the infant mortality rate in France indicates), the war sometimes seemed so far away that people could almost forget it, and some returned to peacetime amusements and distractions. In

Paris the patriotic austerity of the first few months gave way to a lively round of music hall reviews and American films, which dethroned French cinema.

Meanwhile, the Central European powers, greatly hampered by the blockade, failed to manage either the food supply or the economy well enough to keep both the troops and the home front supplied. The civilian population paid dearly for this failure: Ute Daniel estimates that 700,000 people died of malnutrition in Germany alone. Most vulnerable were urban families living on fixed incomes or with large numbers of children. Children of school age were at greater risk than their younger siblings. The mortality rate for women between the ages of fifteen and thirty increased threefold between 1913 and 1918. Rationing was instituted in January 1915 and expanded in the following year to include even acorns and chestnuts. Meat consumption fell to its lowest level since 1800. The worst came in 1917, the year of the *Kohlrübenwinter,* or Rutabaga Winter, when rutabaga replaced potatoes as the staple of the civilian diet. Housewives were obliged to stand in long lines and revert to a subsistence economy, a stark contrast to the thoroughly modern economy of war. For the last time in Western Europe, the subversive tradition of the female rebel spearheading the protest of the poor manifested itself. Women of the lower classes were among the first, according to police records, to criticize the war and its profiteers and to resort to strategies of survival that ultimately undid the government's attempts to ration supplies: women trafficked in ration tickets, stole food from stores and fields, and made illegal purchases on the black market or from peasants. Sunday "hamsters" went from farm to farm in search of something to eat, as did bands of starving youths. As their numbers increased, so did their indifference to the law and its controls, as well as their violence. In 1916 women instigated food riots that turned German cities into civil-war battlegrounds; men meanwhile continued to stage disciplined demonstrations, and working-class leaders condemned what they called the "instinctive" behavior of women protesters. These women's actions destroyed the *Burgfrieden,* or civil peace, and undermined the authority and legitimacy of the imperial state, laying the groundwork for its collapse.[70]

Toward the end of the war, the weakened populations of Europe were subjected to yet another ordeal, an epidemic of Spanish influenza that no one knew how to stop. In three waves, from the spring of 1918 to the spring of 1919, the flu claimed millions of victims throughout the world, particularly younger men and women, lending a somber air to the armistice. In Paris in late October 1918 there were not enough coffins or hearses to accommodate the three hundred people who died every day.

In the West combatants harbored bitter feelings toward noncombatants, but in Germany poor women who had had to support families during the war felt even greater resentment toward so-called war profiteers. In order to appreciate the true texture of wartime experience, however, we must focus in a little more closely on individual experience, for History in the large is woven of countless individual and family histories. One of the most extraordinary documents we have is the testament of Vera Brittain (1893–1970), which shows not only how devastating the war was but also how one woman became a feminist and a pacifist as a result of her experience. Although her wartime letters and diary show us a woman apparently torn between idealized patriotism and horror of the realities of war she came to know through her work in a hospital, her later autobiography is nothing less than an antiwar manifesto and a declaration of her conversion to a Christian pacifism based on a belief in the pacific nature of women.[71]

Men's War, Women's Peace?

In the spring of 1915 Romain Rolland, the much-reviled author of *Au-dessus de la mêlée* (Above the Battle), called upon the women of Europe to be "the living embodiment of peace in the midst of war, eternal Antigones who refuse to abandon themselves to hatred and who, in suffering, can no longer distinguish between warring brothers."[72] Are women pacifists by nature? Or because they are mothers? Is there a distinctive feminine morality? Are feminism and pacifism indissociable? These questions have been on the agenda since 1914, and answers to them have often been associated with distinct conceptions of feminism.[73] It is not always easy to interpret those answers without taking account of the relevant associations. Yet there is no escaping the fact that nationalist sentiment proved stronger than pacifist sentiment among women as well as men, and that all efforts to head off war in 1914 failed. Although not enough research has been done to say what role feminists played within the pacifist movement as a whole, it is possible to understand the failure of feminist pacifism.

Feminism in 1914 was an international movement bound together by a common cause (winning women the right to vote), a growing interest in questions of motherhood, and frequent contacts among feminist activists of different nationalities. The movement had long proclaimed its attachment to peace: there were major peace marches in 1899 and 1907. And it was frequently suggested that if women got the vote, they would abolish war. But there had been no discussion of what position to take in case of actual conflict. Established at the behest of American women in 1888, the International Council of Women (ICW), headed by Lady Aberdeen of England, counted some fifteen million members in twenty-five affiliated national councils, while the more radical International Woman Suffrage Alliance (IWSA) had scheduled a congress for the fall of 1914 to be chaired by Mrs. Chapman Catt of the United States. In these international circles the BDF was criticized for its traditionalism, which had grown more pronounced after the group absorbed the Organization of Evangelical Women and Gertrud Bäumer replaced Marie Stritt as president in 1910. Meanwhile, the international movement of socialist women, which emphasized class solidarity above all and made "bourgeois women" one of its targets, was dominated by Germans (the SPD, or German Social-Democratic Party, boasted some 175,000 women members, compared with just 1,500 French women in the SFIO) and by the strong personality of Clara Zetkin.[74]

The war destroyed internationalist women's groups just as it destroyed the Worker's International. "As long as the war lasts, the enemy's women will also be the enemy," Jane Misme wrote in *La Française* for November 19, 1914. Just as feminists set aside their own demands for the sake of national union in wartime, so, too, did they renounce their international alliances in favor of a "national-feminism" which exhorted women to serve the nation. At the same time, they attempted to persuade neutral countries to join the correct side in the war and oppose any attempt to win a negotiated settlement or peace without victory. Patriotic feminists sought to inspire courage and to promote the national cause, which they identified with justice and civilization. They displayed fierce hostility toward erstwhile comrades who continued to cling to their pacifist ideals, which patriots denounced as blind, if not criminally defeatist. Nationalist feminists remained intransigent throughout the war, even as national unity began to break down and signs of impatience to end the war began to appear both among the troops and on the home front.

The Failure of Feminist Pacifism

Feminists did play a role in various pacifist initiatives, particularly in the early years of the war. These attempts to end the conflict were the work of a radical and isolated minority in the belligerent countries, joined by larger groups of women from neutral powers such as the Netherlands, the Scandinavian countries, and the United States, where Progressives believed that the progress of civilization should have made war impossible. The Women's Peace Party (WPP) was born in Washington in January 1915 at a women's peace rally organized by Jane Addams, after a visit by two dissident European suffragists. Within a year it claimed 25,000 members from all walks of life. An attempt was made to organize a federation of American pacifist groups as well as to combat the rise of pro-war sentiment in the country and to arrange for mediation of the conflict by neutral nations. Above all, the party stood for the idea that the community of women remained united against the war.

The WPP sent representatives to the International Congress for the Future Peace that was organized in the Hague by a handful of radical feminists, including Jane Addams of the United States and Dr. Aletta Jacobs of the Netherlands, after the French and British governments denied the IWSA permission to accept an invitation extended by a Dutch suffragist organization. From April 28 to May 1, 1915, 800 Dutch women, 28 Germans from Anita Augspurg's group, 47 Americans, 16 Swedes, 12 Norwegians, 2 Canadians, 1 Italian, 3 Belgians, and 3 Englishwomen protested against the war and, long before Wilson had issued his Fourteen Points, debated the conditions necessary to ensure a lasting peace: among the measures proposed were compulsory arbitration, respect for nationalities, pacifist education of children, and the vote for women. The congress established an International Women's Committee for the Permanent Peace, which in 1919 changed its name to the International Women's League for Peace and Freedom. This group sent delegates all over the world to meet with other feminist groups and to urge neutral governments to sound out belligerents about possible peace terms. Gabrielle Duchêne headed the organization's French branch, known as the Comité de la rue Fondary. She was soon expelled from the Conseil National des Femmes Françaises (CNFF) on the grounds that she was a "feminist in the service of [Kaiser] Wilhelm."[75]

Richard Evans has called attention to the fact that the Hague pacifists saw a close connection between the subjugation of women and the triumph of militarism. This gave a radical turn to the argument that granting women the vote would advance the cause of civilization, and led to attacks on the war as a male venture. But did the pacifists' concept of "nurturing maternity" indicate an inability to transcend female stereotypes, and was this inability perhaps one reason for their failure, as Barbara Steinson suggests in the case of the WPP? Or was feminist pacifism a variety of humanism, one that reflected the dream of an "androgynous" society that would not only establish gender equality but also incorporate women's moral values? Many militants saw those values—respect for life, a determination to improve living conditions, a rejection of violence as a means of resolving conflicts—as stemming more from the social experience of women than from their reproductive function.[76]

In any event, there were many reasons for the pacifists' failure. A convention of neutral countries met in Stockholm in January 1916 but soon broke up without results, and it proved impossible to hold further pacifist meetings while war raged. Feminist pacifists were suspicious of other pacifist groups, most of which denied any connection between war and masculinity. There was also government interference and repression (although the British government was relatively lenient). Pacifists were expelled from the major feminist organizations. European peace activists were therefore unable to mobilize women at the grass roots, who either passively endured their fate or enthusiastically supported their country's cause. And "patriotic" women did more than contribute to charity and attend patriotic rallies: some were veritable "rear-echelon troopers," quick to point out shirkers (with a white feather in England), to buy or persuade others to buy war bonds, and to ferret out every last vestige of the enemy's presence, even in seemingly innocuous artifacts of language: "German" shepherds, "Viennese" bread, and eau de "Cologne" all came in for criticism. Some women went to bizarre lengths: Helen Taft, the niece of former President Taft, climbed to the top of a fireman's ladder and offered to dive into a net in return for a pledge to buy $5,000 worth of Liberty Bonds.

In the United States many women joined pro-war "preparedness movements" as early as 1915. The Women's Section of the Navy League boasted more than 100,000 members in 1916. The group established training camps whose curriculum was more domestic than military. Women insisted that mothers must protect their children: they denounced pacifist sentimentalism in favor of what they felt was a more realistic outlook, one that impelled them to make common cause with men's organizations favoring American intervention in Europe. The break in diplomatic relations with Germany followed by a declaration of war on April 6, 1917 (Jeannette Rankin, the first woman elected to Congress, voted against it), dealt a fatal blow to pacifism and led to the collapse of the WPP, a majority of whose members followed Jane Addams in adopting a middle course: to support the national civil assistance while working to promote internationalism in the postwar environment. Most other feminist organizations pledged their support to President Wilson, but their patriotism remained temperate: few became chauvinists or witch-hunters. Internationally, as William O'Neill has pointed out, American feminist groups exerted a moderating influence.

Socialist women also failed to prevent or stop the war. The vast majority followed their parties in accepting policies of national union. The minority faced enormous difficulties in making its views heard, and little could be done to channel the popular discontent evident in hunger strikes and riots into an effective challenge to wartime policy. After attempting to mobilize the left wing of the SPD, Clara Zetkin issued an appeal to socialist women, calling for an international conference to be held in Bern, Switzerland, March 26–28, 1915. Seventy women from eight European countries attended. The conference adopted a resolution that was neither feminist nor defeatist in tenor. Instead, it condemned the war as a capitalist war and urged women of the proletariat— mothers, wives, and girlfriends of the dead and wounded—to save humanity by speaking for men whose tongues were no longer free. But Zetkin, who was imprisoned from July 23 to October 12, 1915, and who suffered from a heart condition, could no longer play an active role in the peace movement. Luise Zietz, the only woman in a position to take her place, vacillated for some time between loyalty to her party and opposition to the war. Forbidden to speak in public in 1916 (for having discussed shortages too frankly in the past), she was finally expelled from the SPD, whereupon she joined Clara Zetkin and the 20,000 other women of the USPD, which since April 1917 offered an alternative to women opposed to the SPD line. This split proved inauspicious for the women's movement, which lost much of its support along with the last vestiges of its autonomy.

In France the number of socialist feminists was small. Two such women played emblematic roles in the Socialist Party and the pacifist Comité pour la Reprise des Relations Internationales: Hélène Brion, a teacher and trade unionist but first and foremost a feminist, and Louise Saumoneau, a seamstress dead set against any form of cross-class alliance. Brion, who had long sought to persuade working-class organizations to recognize the cause of women, was charged with defeatism and tried by court martial. But she transformed her trial into a plea for feminism, announcing on March 29, 1918, that "I am an enemy of war because I am a feminist. War is the triumph of brutal force. Feminism can triumph only by moral force and intellectual courage." This was closer to the ideology of the Hague pacifists than to the sectarianism of Louise Saumoneau, whom Richard Evans has aptly called a "general without an army." After finding herself in the minority of the Groupe des Femmes Socialistes at the beginning of the war, she, along with two Russian students, founded the Socialist Women's Action Committee for Peace and Against Chauvinism. She also attended the Bern conference and in 1915 published several issues of *La Femme socialiste* along with several crude and interminable tracts, veritable diatribes attacking the women of the proletariat as slavish, woolly-minded, apathetic imitators of the vices of the bourgeoisie. In fact, French working women were not passive during the war. They constituted a majority of those workers, including munitions workers, who went on strike in the summer and fall of 1917. But these strikes, even in the crucial period of May-June 1917, were primarily over wages and were provoked by rising prices. Jean-Louis Robert has exposed as myth the notion that the seamstresses of Paris initiated a pacifist uprising. There were in fact two waves of strikes in May and June: one by *midinettes* in May, exclusively over higher wages and largely successful, and another by *munitionnettes* in June, a more complex affair, with strike activity paralleling the outbreak of mutiny among soldiers at the front. These later strikes expressed an ambiguous desire if not for peace, then at least for the return of the troops.[77]

Feminism, Nationalism, and the Right to Vote

There is no denying that both feminism and socialism failed to keep their commitments to resist war. Nevertheless, recent scholarship on socialist behavior has focused not on the "betrayal" of the Second International but rather on the degree of social and ideological integration of the working class in different countries.[78] Similarly, I think that historians had best abstain from characterizing the feminists of this period as "alienated" or "inauthentic" and consequently choosing the wrong battles to fight. Richard Evans is right to point to the historical connection between European feminism and nationalist ideology, as well as to the potency of class and national constraints at the turn of the century. Feminist patriotism can also be seen as expressing a desire for integration— a desire consistent with the movement's goals and quite apparent if one takes the trouble to decipher the language of the day. Take, for instance, the Pankhursts, whom historians have tended to judge harshly owing to their verbal extremism and sudden metamorphosis from "militant feminists" into "superpatriots" zealously opposed to Huns and Bolsheviks. Sandra Gilbert treats the change in the title of their newspaper from *The Suffragette* to *Britannia*, along with its new dedication, as evidence not of the Pankhursts' chauvinism but of their intuition that the war might lead to the emancipation of women in a feminized state.[79] Patriotic feminists filled their speeches with the rhetoric of gender ("heart and conscience" in France, "the mobilization of the feminine soul and male bodies" in Germany), and one can surely interpret this, too, as expressing hope that women might win the battle of the decade for the right to vote.

Prior to 1914 women campaigned for the right to vote as a way of both promoting equality and extending the maternal role, giving motherhood a social dimension by involving women in the battle against a variety of social ills. During the war the issue was initially associated with pacifism, but patriotic feminists, feeling that they had amply demonstrated their loyalty, eventually resumed agitating for the vote. In November 1915, after the sinking of the hospital ship *Anglia,* one English suffragist called in a newspaper headline for "the right to vote for heroines as well as heroes." Is Arthur Marwick right, then, when he argues that women were granted the right to vote as a reward for their wartime loyalty, thereby minimizing the importance of the long suffragist struggle? Or is Richard Evans right to emphasize both structural and war-related political factors, especially the fear of revolution that affected many countries in the war's aftermath? What importance, finally, are we to attach to the often victorious struggles waged by the English militants of the WSPU or the Americans of the National Woman's Party (NWP) as well as by more moderate groups such as the National American Woman Suffrage Association (NAWSA), the NUWSS in Britain, and the UFSF in France? Protest was contagious, moreover, eventually affecting the belligerent countries, after Denmark, Iceland, and the Netherlands followed the lead of Finland (1906).[80]

In the United States, which joined the war late, the conflict was of little importance in the suffragists' final battle, although the argument that the women's vote was necessary to the war effort and to bolstering democracy at home did play a part. While opponents of the women's vote cried blackmail and the threat of social revolution and warned of a loss of sexual identity, the NAWSA under the dynamic leadership of Carrie Chapman Catt lobbied state governments and federal agencies. The young NWP, a minority splinter group, was determined to obtain the vote through an amendment to the Constitution and adopted the English strategy of punishing the party in power. After failing to make a difference in the 1916 elections, during which it campaigned against Democrats in the twelve states where women already enjoyed the right to vote, the NWP for months stationed pickets outside the White House; some chained themselves to the fence or lay down on the sidewalk. While taking no position on the war, these activists did not hesitate, at the height of the anti-German frenzy, to refer to the President as "Kaiser Wilson." Expelled from the NAWSA, they became the first victims of wartime repression, but also martyrs to the cause. Victory, however, was delayed for three more years; at last on January 9, 1918, after years of opposition, Wilson formally announced his support for the Nineteenth Amendment, which was approved the next day by the House of Representatives. The Senate passed the amendment in June, and over the next fourteen months it was ratified by thirty-six states. To be sure, this suffragist victory coincided with Prohibition and a period of political reaction. But is it accurate to say that granting women the vote was simply a defensive reaction on the part of puritanical, white America, nothing less than an attempt by the WASP middle class to control blacks, immigrants, and the population of the cities? Such an argument implies that feminism had become essentially conservative and ignores the support that the suffragists received from immigrant communities such as the Jews of New York.[81]

By contrast, in Central Europe and in Russia reformist liberals and socialists did indeed seize on the women's suffrage issue as one way of preventing a proletarian social revolution and stabilizing democracy, following the collapse of the old imperial regimes. In Germany, for example, women were granted political rights on November 30, 1918, by a decree of the Council of People's Representatives, at a time when the gap was widening between the SPD and the Spartakists (who opposed the election of a constituent assembly). During the war German women had indeed been thanked for their work—with a day of homage (the *Frauensonntag* of June 1915) and a congratulatory telegram from Hindenburg to Gertrud Bäumer on September 17, 1917. The Kaiser promised in his Easter message of 1917 to allow his subjects a greater role in politics, but the Reichstag twice proclaimed its belief that a woman's place was in the home.

In Great Britain, despite the spectacular conversion of Prime Minister Asquith, the war affected the suffrage issue only indirectly, by way of its impact on the overall political situation. The need for sweeping electoral reform became a major issue for the British system, whose residential and property qualifications as well as its exclusion of women had made it look quite undemocratic. The crucial factor, however, was the suffragists' retreat to a defensive position: repudiating prewar promises, they accepted the inegalitarian law of February 6, 1918, which granted the vote to all men and to women over the age of thirty. This compromise might be described as either partial victory or partial defeat. It excluded some 5 out of 12 million adult women from the vote, in order to "compensate" for the large numbers of men lost in battle and even out the traditional imbalance of men and women in the population. In France the Committee on Universal Suffrage also chose a minimum voting age of thirty when, after much dithering, it finally presented the Dussaussoy voting reform bill to the Chamber of Deputies in May 1919. Other proposals, such as the family vote or the "vote of the dead," to be cast by their widows or mothers, were considered too alien to French legal tradition and were rejected. But the optimism of feminist activists concealed many problems: the fighting spirit of 1914 had subsided as the movement divided in the wake of wartime disputes, the Russian Revolution, and the personal difficulties of feminist leaders.

Although the Chamber passed the Andrieux amendment granting women political equality by a large majority, the Senate refused even to consider the bill and finally let it die in November 1922, with senators justifying their action by the most traditional sexist arguments: women had no place in the political arena, and the left (particularly the Parti Radical), was afraid that the women's vote would prove conservative.

Given the many pressing issues of the day, the woman question no longer seemed urgent to many male politicians, and the whole depopulation issue seemed to overshadow the matter of women's rights. Earlier I had alluded to the anticontraceptive law of 1920, which was passed by a very large majority and denounced by only a few feminists. This law was indeed a matter of direct concern to French women, although its purpose was not to make them citizens but to control their reproduction. France was more repressive in this area than any other country in Europe—a sign that revealed France's natalist obsession and proved to be a setback for women's rights as well as an indication of the government's determination to restore the prewar status quo in gender relations.[82]

The War and Gender Relations

Did the war really change the relations between men and women? Did it alter their actual or symbolic place in society? To be sure, the immediate postwar period witnessed a retrenchment in some areas and a series of upheavals in others, but beyond that it is not easy to arrive at an overall assessment. National differences were important, as other essays in this volume will make clear.

Postwar Retrenchment

When the armistice bells rang on November 11, 1918, the war left Europe prostrate and America triumphant. The defeated German and Austro-Hungarian empires were soon dismembered, while victorious France, Great Britain, and Italy suffered trauma in spite of triumph. The total number of civilian victims is unknown, but in Central and Eastern Europe the civilian toll was very high. Nine million soldiers had died in the conflict, and millions of survivors had to be reintegrated into civilian life. For women, despite sonorous promises of a brighter tomorrow, or at any rate of an opportunity to contribute to the postwar effort of reconstruction, the time had come to give up hard-won gains. Some were labeled war profiteers, others incompetent, but all were asked to return home and to resume their traditional female occupations for the sake of the veterans, the nation, and the race. Some refused, but others—tired by years of toil and loneliness or overjoyed at being reunited with a loved one—went willingly. The end of the conflict witnessed marriages in unprecedented numbers: there was a veritable rush to return to private life, to an existence centered on the family and child, which Marcelle Capy, at one time among the more radical French feminists, now saw as "the Messiah, the great hope."[83]

Women, the argument went, had provided a needed wartime service, but the end of the war made further sacrifice useless. Hence the demobilization of female workers was everywhere swift and merciless, particularly in the armaments industry, where women were the first to be fired. Of the warring powers France was the least generous but the most pragmatic: although there was wide agreement that a woman's place was in the home, many argued that women were needed in the workplace, even in industry. In Germany and Britain, on the other hand, demobilization policy aimed to reestablish the gender-differentiated labor market as quickly as possible and to restore the traditional family, in which the father works and the mother stays home. In Germany, women whose work had been related strictly to the war effort received no unemployment compensation. In Britain they received a decreasing allowance, but a press campaign took women to task for living on the dole and betraying their men. Protective laws were invoked against women in both countries, and unemployment compensation was denied to women who refused alternative jobs as domestics or other traditionally female work. Even clerical jobs that men ordinarily scorned were to be reserved for disabled veterans.[84] In this climate of intensifying gender warfare, 37 women were elected to Weimar's Constituent Assembly, but none of the 15 English female candidates in the December 1918 parliamentary elections was elected to the House of Commons. The only woman elected to parliament was Countess Constance Markievicz, an Irish rebel imprisoned for her role in the Easter uprising of 1916 (and spared the death penalty only because she was a woman) and a feminist whose feminism had always been intimately associated with the Irish national question.[85]

Intended to enable returning veterans to settle in to work and home life as quickly as possible, this brutal treatment of women seems to have served a psychological as well as an economic function. It not only bolstered a male identity buffeted by four years of anonymous combat but also effaced the war entirely. In a period of social ferment and political reaction, it answered a deeply felt need on the part of veterans for a restoration of the prewar world they had left behind. The English trade unionist Mary Macarthur was wrong when she suggested, in 1918, that the way men looked at women had changed. Out of a need to cling to something permanent and a desire for what they regarded as elementary justice, men wanted to find their women just as they had left them. Front-line newspapers reveal that combat troops felt not only a profound need for recognition but also a fear of being displaced on returning home; they knew little of what the home front had contributed to the war effort and longed to return as lords and masters and above all to set their women straight. More tragically, men's literature at the time and later voiced suspicions of a female conspiracy against male power and revealed a desperate quest for a new virility based on domination of women and children. "When I saw my wife again, I didn't recognize her eyes," says a decorated major in a story by Paul Géraldy.[86] It is difficult, however, to gauge what happened in private, and the evidence is contradictory. One woman interviewed remarked: "I gave them a lamb, and they gave me back a lion."[87] There are signs that domestic violence increased, and it may well be that a systematic study of police and court records would bear this out.

In the defeated nations restoration was impossible, and this led to bitterness toward the civilians held responsible for the defeat, stimulated violent sexual fantasies, and encouraged a retreat into male camaraderie, or *Männerbund:* the cult of the leader and the imposition of discipline on women would, it was hoped, lead to national regeneration. This spirit, which would eventually inform Nazi organizations and the Hitler regime, found its first embodiment in the so-called Freikorps that terrorized the young Weimar Republic.[88] In Austria, the realities of war and the dismemberment of the empire accentuated an identity crisis that had already hit intellectual Vienna before the war. Karl Kraus's *Last Days of Mankind* (1918–19) was not only a satire on war but a warning about the contemporary decadence implicit in gender mixing and the confusion of sexes.[89]

Meanwhile, the demobilization of women was accompanied

by a virulent critique of the emancipated woman and of feminism: the French novelist Colette Yver repeated in *Les Jardins du féminisme* (1920) what she had already said in her earlier novels *Les Cervelines* (1903) and *Princesses de science* (1907): that women could not be "autonomous individuals" without risk to themselves and to society. In the period of demobilization praise was also heaped on the housewife, newly crowned the queen of an eroticized and consumerist domestic unit (albeit to a lesser degree in Europe than in the United States), and above all on the mother: the United States was the first country to establish a Mother's Day in 1912, and Canada and Britain soon followed suit. France adopted the idea in 1918 for natalist reasons; the government from time to time staged public ceremonies in honor of women, as Vichy would do more systematically later on. Mothers of five or more children were awarded the Family Medal, a prize established along with birth bonuses in 1920. There were also awards for prolific fathers, "those great adventurers of the modern world." Pro-maternity discourse invoked the duties of women rather than women's rights.[90] Elsewhere, new protective legislation such as the British Maternal and Child Welfare Act of 1918 and the Sheppard-Towner Act of 1921 in the United States undoubtedly marked progress in this area, but failed to address the specific problems of working mothers.

Was the war a "time out" for women? A better image, which Margaret and Patrice Higonnet borrowed from molecular biology to apply to relations between the sexes, is that of the double helix: the changes in women's lives are at once temporary and superficial (the helix turns first one way, then the other), yet constant in that women's roles remain subordinate to men's (whether in reality or as mediated through language).[91]

War and Sexual Difference

These preliminary conclusions are valid for the short term but need to be reexamined over the long term. In regard to the evolution of the condition of women, the war in some cases impeded, in other cases accelerated changes begun in the Belle Epoque. New opportunities became available to women, and the balance of power did change somewhat. The extent of the changes varied with country, age, and social class, but changes undoubtedly occurred.

First consider labor. True, the war did little to alleviate the division of labor by sex. It made employers more reluctant than ever to hire women, and female workers came in for criticism whenever the economy weakened. In France there was a shortage of male workers and a corresponding increase in female employment in, of all things, the agricultural sector in 1921, but from then until 1968 female employment and the proportion of women in the workforce decreased every year except 1946. Thus the war marked the end of the upward trend of those two indicators that had characterized the nineteenth century.[92] Nevertheless, this overall decline conceals many changes in France and in its European neighbors. Domestic service was now seen as servile, and employment of this sort plummeted. In Great Britain persistent unemployment slowed this trend between the two world wars, however, and working conditions for domestics improved. The collapse of the sweatshop and cottage work in the textile industry increased the proportion of female workers in the light metalworking and electrical industries, where Taylor's principles of scientific management were applied. In France and Britain new mass production strategies led to increased employment of women in factory work despite opposition from the trade unions. Applying a lesson learned in the war, manufacturers assigned women to repetitive tasks requiring little skill. Women became agents of modernization: they proved better able to accept the century's innovations than older male coworkers who seemed stunned by the pace of change. Sometimes this worked to their advantage, sometimes not. The question needs to be studied in greater depth.[93]

A third change was perhaps the most important of all: job growth in the tertiary sector (commerce, banking, public services, and service professions) brought it close to being the primary employer of women. In Britain Virginia Woolf in *Three Guineas* hailed the Sex Disqualification Removals Acts of 1919 as the dawn of a new world for "the daughters of cultivated men." In France women gained equal access to secondary and higher education, fulfilling an age-old feminist demand: engineering and business schools were opened to women during the war; a women's baccalaureate was instituted in 1919, allowing women to enter universities; and in 1924 differences in the secondary curricula for boys and girls were eliminated. Combined with middle-class fears of spinsterhood and declining family fortunes, this feminization of the tertiary sector made it possible for young women of the bourgeoisie to pursue professional careers. They were therefore the principal beneficiaries of the war, and many of them were aware that their lives no longer resembled the lives of their mothers. As role models they chose active and independent women such as Suzanne Lenglen, Marie Curie, and Colette in France; at a more modest level they admired the work of professional social workers and activists, both lay and Catholic, a group that both Yvonne Knibiehler and Sylvie Fayet-Scribe see as having been more innovative and dynamic than conservative.[94]

The effects of the war on women's rights vary more widely from country to country. France, which prohibited birth control, denied women the right to vote, and waited until 1938 to lift the civil disabilities imposed on married women, seems backward when compared with Great Britain and Germany. The constitution of the Weimar Republic proclaimed equality of the sexes in principle but failed to translate that principle into concrete statutes. Some types of behavior tended to converge in different countries: couples had fewer children and, to a lesser extent, became more egalitarian. Meanwhile, suffragist groups transformed themselves into political education societies: the NAWSA became the National League of Women Voters, and the NUWSS became the National Union of Societies for Equal Citizenship. Yet the mere fact that women had the right to vote did not translate into political participation or power. Finally, such wartime policies as separation allowances and widows' pensions had established family protection as a principal aim of the welfare state: state aid was to be awarded to those whose service entitled them to it. Women thus became second-class citizens, for it was the service of the man of the family that justified their receipt of public assistance. This principle encouraged a sexist outlook in the drafting of subsequent welfare-state legislation.[95]

Progress was probably most obvious and most widely shared on another front: women in their long years of loneliness and responsibility had discovered a new freedom of behavior and movement. Unfettered by corsets, long fitted garments, and elaborate hats and hairpieces, women were at last free to move about. Compare Jacques-Henri Lartigue's photographs of women in the Roaring Twenties with those of the Belle Epoque. Read the memoirs of Clara Malraux and others. All speak of a revolution in daily life, of a new relation to body and self. Women could now participate in sports, dance to new American rhythms, go out by themselves, explore their sexuality, and in some cases decide what sort of life they wished to lead.[96] The younger generation was the principal beneficiary of these changes. Men and women joined each other in their hours of leisure long before coeducation became the norm in public schools. Like men, women knew that happiness was a fragile thing. Renouncing abstinence and modesty, they seized the day. Despite this greater permissiveness, the line was nevertheless drawn when it came to female homosexuality. Although the freewheeling sapphism of the turn of the century had proclaimed itself openly, lesbians now were condemned to hide themselves and to suffer guilt at their defiance of virile hegemony. A case in point is Radclyffe Hall's *The Well of Loneliness,* which was banned for obscenity in 1928 only to become the quintessential lesbian novel for subsequent generations.[97]

To understand the changes brought about by the war, however, one must go beyond a mere catalogue of advances, which in any case remained limited. What were the war's effects on the psychology of men and women, and, still more significantly, on the social perception of gender? The war had forcibly separated the sexes and created a barrier of misunderstanding, sometimes tinged with hatred, between the battle front and the home front. This led to a sharp cultural awareness of the contrast between two realities: in Paul Fussell's words, "the modern versus habit."[98] A firm and durable line was drawn between male and female spheres. Ancient male myths gained a new lease on life: men are made to fight and conquer, women to bear and raise children. Such a complementarity of the sexes seemed necessary if peace and security were to be restored to a world that seemed out of kilter. The Edwardian era's egalitarian aspirations and doubts about sexual identity were forgotten, and sexual dichotomy once again became the norm in social and political thought. Evidence for this can be found in the success, far beyond the borders of Italy, of Gina Lombroso's argument that women are essentially "other-centered," that is, that they cannot find happiness except by giving of themselves, and in the acceptance of family and natalist ideologies. In working-class culture (leaving aside the signal exception of 1920s Communism) women were even more identified with the home than they had been before 1914, and men with skilled labor. For example, the Austrian Social Democrats, who with the downfall of the emperor and the dismemberment of the empire had become the regime's new "father figures," established a new system of medical insurance, the so-called Viennese system, which Reinhard Sieder sees as a restoration of the patriarchal order; this went hand in hand with a marginalization of feminist activists, as other historians have pointed out.[99] The rise of Christian syndicalism with its social-Catholic ideology reinforced the pro-family attitudes of the working class.[100] Among revolutionaries, the century's conquistadors, activism took on a certain military aspect, and resolution of the "woman question" was necessarily postponed to a better day. The practice of celebrating the war's dead flattered male virility and highlighted the noncombatant role of women. Veterans' groups and associations of the disabled, which tended to be pacifist in France and more militaristic in the defeated countries, became centers of masculine social life and exerted a profound influence in the interwar period. By the late 1920s such groups claimed more than three million members in France alone. Although politically divided, they were united by common memories and a determination to exert a moral influence on government.[101]

Did women willingly accept the roles assigned to them? The question is at once crucial and delicate. Wartime experience was a permanent fixture of women's consciousness, but not all women had the same experience, and not all interpreted their experience in the same way. Depending on nationality, age, and social class, women tended to attach different relative importance to independence, suffering, and fatigue. Although class solidarity had been scarcely more evident than gender solidarity during the war, the concept of class remained paramount in societies where social barriers were still high. In Germany, where wartime hardships persisted for several years after the war's end, Christiane Eifert was bitterly critical of the alacrity with which bourgeois feminist organizations sacrificed working-class women for the sake of social acceptance.[102] Although some women discovered a new individuality and strength during the war, many wished to regain the peace and quiet of family life, especially since the postwar climate was hard on those who made other choices and tended to discourage any push toward emancipation. To be sure, many women behaved independently in the interwar years, encouraged in doing so by the permissive moral climate, the "man shortage," and a certain circulation of wealth, but the independence of individuals never coalesced in the form of a movement. Any tendency toward such a movement was soon squelched by a broad consensus that motherhood was the fulfillment of a woman's life. Even the feminists of the period seem to have marked time, or at any rate to have turned, in the majority, to a "feminism of difference."

In 1977 Richard Evans expressed his view that "1920 marked the end of the feminist era": winning the right to vote (in some countries) was at once a symptom and a cause of the movement's decline. Evans may have been too categorical, and his chronology may well need revision in light of ongoing research into the period "between two feminisms" (1920–1960). Nancy Cott has already noted that in the United States the years between 1910 and 1930 were a period not of feminist decline but rather of transition between the nineteenth-century feminist movement, a movement for the rights of *woman*—woman in general—and modern feminism, which, taking diversity into account, attempts to reconcile equality and difference, individual freedom and group solidarity.[103] More work also needs to be done on the international aspects of feminism, including both pacifist groups and groups that sought to improve the condition of women.

Prewar feminism, a movement on the march that drew strength from diversity, had issued its demands in the name of both individual equality and gender specificity. Interwar feminism seems to have accepted the commonsense view of male and female as natural constructs. This led to schisms in the movement, as radical minorities fighting for sexual freedom or workplace equality went their separate ways: these minorities include French neo-Malthusians (Madeleine Pelletier and Jeanne Humbert, for example) and their American counterparts; the group associated with the magazine *Die Frau im Staat* in Germany, which supported the positions of the Open Door Council; and the NWP in the United States, which fought for the Equal Rights Amendment.[104] The vast majority of feminists insisted on gender difference and complementarity. They exalted motherhood on moral grounds. And they invoked not the rights of women but the needs of mothers in their demands for special protection for working women. This was particularly true in Germany, where the BDF's 1919 platform defined women's duties to the national community. It was also true in Great Britain, where a minority of "equalitarians" quit the NUSEC to protest its maternalistic "new feminism" and its obsession with male violence.[105] Bear in mind, however, that the theme of maternity as a "social function" could, as in France, instill confidence in women and draw them into political action.[106]

To sum up, then, I do not think it makes sense to contrast the 1920s (allegedly a period of liberation) with the 1930s (allegedly a time of reaction). Gender did play a key role in wartime society, and the war exerted a profoundly conservative influence on gender relations in subsequent years. This is true not only of World War I and its aftermath, but of the entire century, so largely made up of war, postwar, and "between-war" periods. The conservative effects of war thus help to explain why no genuine upheaval in male-female relations occurred until the 1960s.

TRANSLATED FROM THE FRENCH BY ARTHUR GOLDHAMMER

2

The Modern Woman of the 1920s, American Style

Nancy F. Cott

THE COMPETITIVE CHALLENGE that the United States posed to world leadership in the early twentieth century came not only from American intervention in the Great War but also from the relentless march of American technology, products, and visual media overseas during succeeding decades. Similarly, the challenge that the model of the modern American woman offered to the old patriarchal or the new collectivist way of life was less attached to the flag than it was represented in goods, style, the news, and the cinema. In their diverse incarnations, modern women emerged from previous struggles for political, economic, and sexual emancipation. The decades around the turn of the century had produced the most effective feminist as well as labor and socialist movements ever seen in the United States. The 1910s saw such unprecedented gains by women in professional and white-collar occupations that the language of "emancipated womanhood" became well known. By the 1920s, agents of modernity had to take into account women's desires for the reality and the emblems of freedom and individuality.

A culturally diverse American population was

exposed to unprecedented forces of cultural uniformity in the 1920s, and the same forces operated to carry the American image abroad. Contrasts and disparities within the American population, perennially great, were more so than ever as a result of enormous immigration between 1880 and 1920. Yet in the twentieth century it became possible not only to claim a unique "American way of life," but also to advertise and broadcast it. An American mass culture became possible as mass production and marketing techniques joined with the new media (radio and the movies) and the old (newspapers and magazines) already crossing the nation. Forty percent of all homes in the U.S. acquired radios during the 1920s, and weekly attendance at movies doubled—reaching 100 to 115 million by the end of the decade. Surveys even reported that movie stars had replaced leaders in politics, business, and the arts as those most admired by the young. New forms of communication forged common information and values.

Mass Production and Consumption

In 1920, for the first time, America's population was more than half urban (living in population centers over 2,500, according to the U.S. census). An urban industrial economy of mass production, individual wage-earning, and money purchases became the designated norm. Not cities merely but large metropolitan areas accounted for almost three-quarters of the expansion of the U.S. population in the 1920s, in part thanks to the automobile, which was so popular a mode of transportation that it stimulated suburban growth. In 1910 there was one automobile for every 265 persons in the United States; in 1928, one per six. Modern habits of production, consumption, and recreation began to homogenize long-standing differences between South and North, country and city. The factory and the Ford, the new national "chain" stores, the innovation of national brand names, mail-order catalogues marketing mass-produced items—all portended a new level of standardization and uniformity of common life.[1]

Economic growth was the banner of the New Era, as Republican presidents liked to call it. Measurable in manufacturing productivity, per capita income, and the ratio of consumer outlay to net national product, economic growth and its material fruits were very unevenly distributed, without doubt. Black women tobacco workers in Durham, North Carolina, for example, washed their families' clothes in pots in the yard, used outdoor privies, and cooked on wood or oil-burning stoves in the 1920s and 1930s, when glossy magazines were displaying housewives freed from drudgery by "electric servants." (Location as well as buying power figured here: where most urban households could count on having electricity, as well as indoor plumbing and municipal gas service, rural areas were much more unevenly served by electrification.) Manufacturers who believed that industrial progress relied on high-volume purchasing went about stimulating demand with market research, advertising, and new retailing techniques. Production of consumer goods such as canned and packaged food and ready-to-wear clothes surged. With mail-order merchandising, rural as well as metropolitan households contributed to large and sustained increases in purchases of irons, stoves, vacuum cleaners, washing machines, and refrigerators.

An important specific factor in U.S. economic growth in the 1920s, and a symbol of the new emphasis on consumption, was the innovation of payment by the "installment plan": it encouraged people to swell their consumption habits beyond what they could afford, changing their focus from saving to spending. In 1925, consumers used installment credit to purchase more than two-thirds of the household furniture and gas stoves, and at least three-quarters of the passenger cars, pianos, washing machines, sewing machines, mechanical refrigerators, phonographs, vacuum cleaners, and radios sold. Manufacturers and advertisers tantalizingly translated such purchases into improvement of a family's "standard of living."[2]

Households and Families

Along with the New Era's urbanity and mass-produced material splendor, the modern American woman was sold. A portrait of the modern woman, American-style, might start with her family size. Households on the average were smaller, because marital fertility was dropping and because boarders and lodgers and live-in servants became increasingly rare. The trend toward fewer children was, of course, a long-term one. The birthrate had been declining for more than a hundred years by the time the twentieth century opened. Between 1800 and 1900 the average number of children born to a white woman was cut in half, dropping from 7 to 3.5. Abstinence, the withdrawal method *(coitus interruptus)*, abortion, spermicidal douching, and (late in the century) the condom and the rhythm method, together with sufficient motivation, were the means used—none of them (except abstinence) reliably enabling people to "plan" their families.

Limiting marital fertility became an accepted idea in the early twentieth century, although contraceptive means were still highly controversial. In the 1910s Margaret Sanger promoted the female-controlled method of the diaphragm, a significant advance in contraception. However, the birth-control clinics set up by Sanger and some of her allies operated within a narrow legal margin, only in some states, and only under medical license; they could meet only a fraction of the demand. Not until 1936 did the U.S. Supreme Court remove birth-control devices from the inclusive reach of the federal anti-obscenity law. The American Medical Association withheld its approval of doctors' dispensing birth-control devices until the following year. In the 1920s and 1930s the principal users of diaphragms were educated, prosperous married women whose physicians would privately provide prescriptions and instructions. Women's desires for contraception spread far beyond that class, however. In the space of five years in the early 1920s, Sanger received a million letters from mothers asking for methods of birth control. By whatever combination of will and traditional and new methods, the birthrate dropped especially rapidly in the 1920s and 1930s, owing most to falling fertility among foreign-born women (who were marrying later and less frequently than earlier immigrants had) and among rural women, probably because of the farm depression.[3]

Sexual Ideology and Behavior

In the context of a declining birthrate, new value was placed on marital sex apart from reproduction—indeed, new value and interest focused on sex altogether. The generation that came of age in the 1920s reaped a harvest of changes in sexual ideology and practice that had been planted before the turn of the century and had begun to ripen in the 1910s. As later revealed by sexologist Alfred Kinsey's investigations, the incidence of women's "petting," premarital and extramarital intercourse, and reaching orgasm in marital sex moved on an upward curve in the early twentieth century; the sharpest difference occurred between those born in the decade before and those born in the decade after 1900. Among women with college education the pendulum swung the widest arc. The college-educated born before 1900 were less likely than their less well-educated age-mates to have premarital sex, Kinsey showed, but those born later were *more* likely.[4]

For the young in the 1920s, acknowledging female sexuality became less a matter of rebellion than an instance of going along with the crowd. From popular, intellectual, and social-scientific writers swelled a tide of scorn for "Victorian" sexual morality, thought of as monotonously repressive and hypocritical. Movies, pulp magazines, and advertising copy made the "thrill" of sex their agenda. The moviegoer in a typical midwestern town in the mid-1920s, for instance, could choose in the course of one week from among *The Daring Years, Sinners in Silk, Women Who Give,* and *The Price She Paid;* and during the next, *Name the Man, Rouged Lips,* and *The Queen of Sin. Flaming Youth* promised "neckers, petters, white kisses, red kisses, pleasure-mad daughters, sensation-craving mothers, by an author who didn't dare sign his name." A new cultural apparatus formed around the revelation that sexual expression was a source of vitality and personality—not a drain on energy as nineteenth-century moralists had warned—and that female sexual desire was there to be exploited and satisfied.[5]

Companionate Marriage

Yet sexual expression was domesticated in a new model of marriage. A rising chorus of social scientists, social workers, journalists, and jurists championed the small family and the notion that family life was becoming a specialized arena for emotional intimacy and personal and sexual expression. Although conservatives chafed and lamented, social scientists of varying intentions converged upon a new marital ideal, called "companionate marriage" after the title of a book by Judge Ben Lindsay of Colorado, whose work with juveniles had persuaded him that young people ought to be friends and perhaps lovers before embarking on the serious matter of marrying. Professional marital advice-givers in the 1920s and 1930s looked back and saw Victorian marriage as hierarchical and emotionally barren, based on dominance and submission.

They sought to substitute an ideal of intimate sexual partnership, in which female sexuality was presumed, and marriage was valued for eliciting the partners' individuality as well as for uniting the two. Marriage advice books now made sex the centerpiece of marriage; the sexual adjustment and satisfaction of both partners became principal measures of marital harmony as well as means toward a wider social order.[6]

Just when wage-earning made it more possible than ever before for women to escape the economic necessity to marry, the emphasis on female heterosexual desires made marriage appear a sexual necessity, for "normal" satisfaction. Both professional and popular literature and fiction now portrayed the woman who didn't find a man as socially dangerous—irrational, unwholesome, mannish, or frigid. Since the companionate model portrayed marriage as indeed symmetrical, women were left little rationale for avoiding it; the objection made by feminists in prior generations that marriage was a system of domination was eliminated.

Once female sexual drives were acknowledged, too, relationships between women were inevitably reassessed. The nineteenth-century ideology of women's moral influence and glorious maternity, by veiling female eroticism, had made intimacies between women appear innocent. But the same interest among physicians, sex reformers, and ethicists that had rolled back Victorian reticence about sex placed new labels of "normality" and "abnormality" on the spectrum of human behavior from heterosexual to homosexual. Not only clinicians and social scientists but all the popular media which dabbled in psychology in the 1920s and 1930s paired attention to women's erotic nature with new recognition and incrimination of homosexuality in women.

The specter of women on their own, satisfied with and by each other, stalked through much social-scientific work. Cultural anxiety about the potential for women's escape from men's control gained credibility from newsworthy evidence of single women's exploits in the arts, entertainment, sports, and professions—as well as in civic and suffrage organizations. Since erotic drives were now admitted to be as important to women's nature as to men's—and valued apart from reproduction—women's relationships with each other seemed to compete with heterosexual pairing and thus came to be suspected as threats to existing sexual and social order. This shift of concern was so emphatic as to constitute a backlash against the idea and practice of independent women.

Whether lesbian sexual behavior was more suppressed or expressed as a result of changing sexual norms is probably impossible to measure. Kinsey's investigations did not find any increase in homosexual behavior, in contrast to the increases in all sorts of heterosexual behavior. Nonetheless it is reasonable to hypothesize that women acted in multivalent ways upon the new acceptance of the legitimacy of female sexuality. As did heterosexual women, lesbians might appropriate the greater leeway for female sexual assertiveness in the modern era. Among a small group of writers and artists, certainly, lesbianism was more overt and acknowledged in the 1920s than ever before, and the lives of some outstanding women achievers of the 1920s generation reveal sustaining sexual relationships with individuals of both sexes. Medical and social-scientific investigators confirmed that some women found sexual and emotional satisfaction with one another, even while they portrayed that choice as aberrant.[7]

How much the popularity of marriage owed to companionate marriage advocates is impossible to say, but during the interwar years the institution was more embraced than ever. Almost 10 percent of the generation born between 1865 and 1885 never married, but that proportion went down to near 6 percent among the men and women born between 1895 and 1915. The median age at first marriage declined from 26 for men and near 24 for women of the late-nineteenth-century generation, to about 25 for men and 22.5 for women among those maturing in the 1920s and 1930s.[8] The marrying trend was especially apparent among college graduates. The nineteenth-century women who attended college had remained single more often than their contemporaries who didn't, or married late in life. But as the proportion of eighteen- to twenty-two-year-old Americans in college more than quadrupled between 1890 and 1930—reaching 20 percent of the age-group—more female college graduates married and at younger ages. The less rarefied an experience college attendance became, the more did women students' marital patterns assimilate to the middle-class norm.[9]

Women's Employment: Having It All?

The generation of women who were marrying younger and making more certain to marry were also flowing into secondary and higher education and into the job market. Under pressure of compulsory schooling laws and the incentive of training for white-collar employments, high school attendance zoomed up in the 1920s and 1930s, reaching between 50 and 60 percent of teenagers—among whom girls more than held their own. Even in colleges and universities, where they had been all but shut out until the late nineteenth century, women composed almost half of the students in the 1920s. The proportion of women in the labor force held at about one-fourth from 1910 through 1940, but women workers on the average became older (as teenagers stayed in school) and were increasingly concentrated in the clerical, managerial, sales, and professional areas, more visible to social commentators than women at work had been in domestic service and agriculture and in manufacturing. Although alarmists complained that women's wage-earning would ruin the prospects of marriage, the contrary seemed to be true, since both members of an affianced couple could contribute to saving toward a household. The proportion of wives at work rose six times as fast as the proportion of single women.[10]

With the female presence in the workforce an inescapable reality, the age at marriage declining, and marriage becoming more universal than in previous generations, the issues of employment and marriage for women were inevitably joined. College women frequently named this their own, the "modern" problem. An editorial in the Smith College *Weekly* late in 1919 announced, "We cannot believe it is fixed in the nature of things that a woman must choose between a home and her work, when a man may have both. There must be a way out and it is the problem of our generation to find the way." The issue resonated in scores of articles and inquiries with titles such as "Can a Woman Run a Home and a Job, Too?" "The Wife, the Home, and the Job," "College Wives Who Work," "From Pram to Office," "Why Do Married Women Work?" "The Home-Plus-Job Woman," "Babies Plus Jobs," and "The Two-Job Wife."[11]

Wives' employment in the white-collar sector was noticeable because it was rising at a faster rate than in any other occupational area. Yet in 1930, after a decade in which the proportion doubled, still fewer than 12 percent of the married women worked for pay outside the home, according to the U.S. Census. Among employed women, however, almost half were married, divorced, widowed, or separated, and thus likely to be responsible for households and children besides their paid work. The great majority were doubly burdened menial workers in domestic or personal service, agriculture, or manufacturing. At the very most, not even 4 percent of the married women in the country could be said to be combining "marriage and career."[12]

Social Scientists' Intervention

If public concern with the balancing of women's desires for both love and work remained at the forefront, that was not only because feminists since the turn of the century had insisted on both but also because social scientists trained their attention on the "problem." Pushing aside folk wisdom and religion, having more to say about women's roles than ever before, the social sciences displayed new authoritativeness in the 1920s. Their promise to explain the nature and sources of human behavior through objective empirical observation and methodologically rigorous analysis had enormous popular as well as academic appeal. After half a century of development, by the 1920s the separate disciplines of sociology, economics, political science, psychology, and anthropology were established in institutions and had the large-scale support of corporate philanthropy. Thousands of social scientists carried on research and taught in hundreds of American colleges and universities. Their researches were popularized in print and audiovisual media. Their findings and interpretations reverberated in the practice of personnel management and in marketing strategies in business and industry, in government investigation and procedure, in journalism, and—perhaps most effectively of all with respect to public consumption—in advertising.[13]

Although social science was by no means monolithic, the field in the 1920s did present a united front on the point that its expertise was crucial to establishing a modern, realistic, effective, and democratic social order. Psychology in particular was seen as a tool to enable prediction and control of "the human element"— perhaps even to realize concepts of "social engineering" that had surfaced in the previous decade. The most influential male psychologists of the period, such as John B. Watson and Floyd Allport, believed that psychology's outstanding promise was to bring about individuals' psychological "adjustment" to salutary social norms. Although Freudian ideas had been bruited about by "advanced" thinkers since the first decade of the century, and some Freudian terms were used with superficial familiarity, it was not psycho-analysis but mental hygiene and behaviorist psychologies that dominated during the 1920s. All these shared, however, a focus on irrational sources of human behavior, the assumption that deeply buried sexual motivations underlay actions in public, and the revelation that people were motivated by mechanisms in their own psyches of which they were unaware. For instance, a female journalist displayed typical popular psychologizing as she questioned whether the college-educated woman's pursuit of a career was "a sublimation for other desires," and assumed that "the greatest cause of individual failure is psychic maladjustment, the conflicts, inhibitions, anxieties, fears and other emotional disturbances which . . . certainly are responsible for warped and distorted lives."[14]

Social science practitioners conveyed their sense that their disciplines could both explain the modern woman's problems and lead in solving them—especially the problem of reconciling women's demands for love, work, and individuality. A generation after women social scientists of the 1890s had undertaken iconoclastic empirical research to unseat Victorian beliefs about sex differences in mental functions, psychologists in the 1920s conceptualized these differences anew. They located sex differences in the realm of temperament rather than in the narrow realm of cognition. Lewis Terman and his associates led in constructing quantifiable measures of "masculinity" and "femininity," which, they claimed, were real and scientifically verifiable qualities identifiable on a range from normality to deviance. Their model of well-being matched biological sex to psychological correlates, but their so-called empirical data on the categories of masculinity and femininity were constructed from conventional assumptions.[15] Psychologists' reinvention of femininity spilled over disciplinary boundaries into sociological assessments of the pros and cons of women's careers. The arena of paid work was conventionally "masculine"; a man's ability to provide financially for his wife and children was an important component of "masculinity" as conventionally understood. Even the male sociologists seemingly most sympathetic to feminist intents warned that the woman "coarsened or hard-boiled" by business life would "repel men."[16]

Such commentary revealed how far social science—despite boasts of empiricism—had incorporated the long-standing bias that women's "adjustment" consisted in serving men's needs and pleasures. Contemporary social scientists often assumed that appropriate values would emerge from the empirical work itself, and failed to acknowledge how far the prevailing values had constructed the scientific guideposts in the first place. Their insistence on eschewing metaphysical or philosophical claims and sticking to experimental and empirical findings left room for no acknowledged critical standpoint. Insofar as it was based on the observable—and it claimed to be based entirely on the observable—social science tended to limit itself to the gender order already present, to confirm it, and to inhibit any visions of alternatives. The proportion of career women in the expanding social sciences was much larger than in medicine, natural science, or other comparable professional fields, but the feminist voice that tried to speak in the language of modern social science was by definition muted.

The New Housekeeping

The household became fair game for social science in the 1920s no less than sexual and marital relations did. Professional home economists—to a woman—took as their mandate the improvement of the status and conditions of housework. Under the influence of ideas of scientific management, they began comparative studies of time spent in housework and showed that for urban no less than rural housewives, housekeeping was full-time work. Only 10 percent of urban housewives spent less than 35 hours per week on their tasks, despite modern advantages, and the bulk of them had work weeks comparable to rural wives, over 50 hours. The English writer Vera Brittain, on a visit in 1926, jumped to the conclusion that Americans had "succeeded in abolishing the sacred immunity of the male from all forms of housework," but testimony was much less sanguine from American women themselves, especially those who were trying to pursue paying jobs outside the home and found that their husbands expected them to manage all the housework nonetheless.[17]

Home economists agreed that a principal result of technological advance applied to the home was a rising standard of household care. "Labor-saving" household appliances were more effective in raising standards of cleanliness and order—and encouraging housewives to meet them—than in shortening hours of household work. The gas stove or electric lighting and irons, which were the items in commonest use in the 1920s, improved the comfort and effectiveness of a woman's domestic labor but did not make her household responsibilities less of a full-time job. If housewives did save time by using appliances or packaged commodities, they reallocated it to childcare, shopping, or matters of household management, to improve their working environment or the result of their work. Expectations for material well-being had leapt beyond those of earlier generations. Housewives took seriously their opportunities to improve their families' health and security, as all around them home economists and advertisers proclaimed that a woman's proper care of the household could bring comfort, adjustment, and efficiency to her loved ones. Moreover, manufacturers' aggressive marketing of some household appliances in the 1920s—washing machines were the prime example—returned to the home some services that the previous generation of urban families had paid to have done outside their homes.[18]

The New Child-Rearing

Like the responsibilities of housekeeping, the duties involved in child-rearing had never been so multifariously defined. New storehouses of expertise increased the resources and advice available to parents. Emanating from public health and social work agencies, schools, women's clubs, magazines, newspapers, pulpits, and from the federal government, scientifically oriented directives swarmed to meet mothers' readiness. Half of the babies born in 1929 were touched by government-issued child-rearing advice, according to the U.S. Children's Bureau's estimate. As one study concluded, many more agencies outside the home had cropped up to assist the mother "in meeting her responsibility for child culture," but the same agencies were "increasing the work of the mother somewhat by imposing higher standards upon her."[19]

If childbearing was voluntary and could be planned—and, increasingly, at least middle-class women assumed that it was—its responsibilities appeared both more strenuous and more self-consciously accepted. Now science offered new expertise about nutrition, sanitation, and child-rearing practice, and new ways to measure parents' success or failure as well. The early-twentieth-century field of mental hygiene fed the social science consensus that the prime duty of the family in modern industrial society was no longer economic production but construction of the right environment for children's healthy and normal adjustment. Mental hygienists familiarized the public with the concept of a "normality" believed to be measurable by standardized tests. Parents were put on guard for abnormality, that is, for "infantile" or "neurotic" behavior in their growing children.[20]

Advertising in the Consumer Society

The complicated expectations for the "modern woman" provided ample terrain on which she and her friends and enemies could wage psychological battle. Advertising came into the breach to allay anxieties aroused by the new standards, grabbing the ammunition of scientific credibility from stockpiles provided by the social sciences. By means of advertising, manufacturers and retailers of household and child-related products explicated modern femininity. The homemaker was linked to the "new housekeeping" and the mother to scientific child-rearing through purchasing. In the 1920s the modern advertising industry came into its own. Twentieth-century advertising adopted science as the modern form of authority—as the standard of industry's advance and the consumer's advantage. By the turn of the century the specialized advertising agency had begun to appear, and pictorial representation entered the field. Turning the social science norms of efficiency and adjustment to sales purposes, advertisers presented themselves to consumers as educators and to their clients as especially informed manipulators of human behavior. Large companies aiming at a national market saw the advantage of superseding the local retailer by appealing directly to the consumer through nationally advertised "name brands." By the 1920s advertisers took for granted that their craft had advanced beyond supplying information, to creating "needs." (This was symbolized in the name of one of the earliest nationally advertised brands, "Uneeda" Biscuit.) Increasingly, advertising technique exploited psychological revelations of the irrational motives of behavior and employed symbolism and mental association pictorially, to set the emotions of the consumer to work to make the sale.[21]

Advertising and marketing people habitually referred to the consumer as "she." Countless publications of the 1920s cited the statistic that women made 80 percent of consumer purchases.

Home economists welcomed the link and heralded consumption as the queen of the homemaker's tasks. "Her most important work," announced one, "is that of director of family relations and family consumption." If the multifarious consequences of advertising for human perception and behavior resist exact measurement, it is nonetheless clear that most ads were beamed toward women, who presumably absorbed a larger dose of what they offered than men. In a study of almost 15,000 consumers' responses to advertising in the 1930s, housewives (over one-third of those surveyed) were the least critical of all occupational groups. Only 31 percent of housewives' comments on advertisements were complaints. In contrast, 85 percent of the comments gathered from students were complaints. Gainful employment seems to have reduced women's tolerance, especially for those who worked farthest away from the home, for 45 percent of domestic employees' responses, but 66 percent of clerical workers' assessments were complaints.[22]

Advertisers hastened to package individuality and modernity for women in commodity form. New graphic and photographic techniques enabled advertising to become a visual medium with subliminal influence as never before, intentionally selling to women not only sales pitches for products but also images of themselves. The economic power behind such images of the modern woman was many times greater than that behind any competing model. Advertisers succeeded in superimposing modern emblems on women's traditional priorities. No longer diffident, delicate, and submissive, the ideal modern woman was portrayed as vigorous and gregarious. She liked to have fun, liked men, and was attractive to them. Of course, sex appeal was big business. By 1929 the cosmetic industry was spending about as much on advertising as was the food industry, which was seventeen times bigger. But not *simply* attractive, the modern woman was also scientifically aware of the best methods for caring for her husband, children, and home and capably responsible for their welfare.[23]

Women's traditional household status and heterosexual service were now defended—even aggressively marketed—in terms of women's choice, freedom, and rationality. Advertisements worked and reworked the theme that purchasing was an arena for choice and control in which women could exert rationality and express values. This was a contention that home economists also favored, although for different purposes. Modern merchandising adopted the feminist proposal that women take control over their own lives and translated it into the consumerist notion of choice. General Electric linked "the suffrage and the [electric] switch." An ad for household products in the *Chicago Tribune* in 1930 boasted, "Today's woman gets what she wants. The vote. Slim sheaths of silk to replace voluminous petticoats. Glassware in sapphire blue or glowing amber. The right to a career. Soap to match her bathroom's color scheme."[24]

Although a few outraged individuals cried out that women were being sold a streamlined and glamorized modern image of their traditional place vis-à-vis men, popular media and advertising took the upper hand in prescribing models for fulfillment of womanhood. Feminist intentions and rhetoric were not ignored but appropriated. Advertising collapsed feminist emphasis on women's range and choice into individual consumerism; the social-psychological professions domesticated feminists' assertion of sexual freedom and entitlement to the arena of marriage; feminist defiance of the sexual division of labor was swept under the rug. Hollywood movies carried a celluloid image worth thousands of words, with the message that private intimacy equaled freedom and the plush of an expensive automobile capped the search for the good life.[25] These adaptations disarmed the challenges of feminism in the guise of enacting them.

Just as feminism, at the height of the international women's movement before World War I, was no respecter of national boundaries, neither were the forces of marketing and media. Especially through the vehicle of the American film industry, which saturated European cinemas with its products in the 1920s, the particular model of emancipation of the modern woman American-style was brought to audiences abroad, challenging European nations to counter with their own models of womanhood.[26] European consumers received the idealized picture of modern American women in more unalloyed form than Americans themselves did, not having a view of the streets to temper the silver screen or the mass-produced photograph.

The culture of modernity and urbanity absorbed the challenges of feminism and re-presented them in the form of the modern American woman. It was the particular genius of American advertising to convey several decades' worth of drastic alterations in women's opportunities as citizens and workers, and in their freedoms of social behavior and ideals and practices of marriage, as the inevitable product of technological improvement and economic expansion rather than the consequence of purposeful struggle to change gender hierarchy. Of course, the relation between a dominant cultural model of womanhood and the actual, various, and divergent experiences of women in a time and place is not direct but dynamic and interactive: what was made of the American model of modern womanhood depended on who was hearing and seeing, how and where. The economic crisis that brought the 1920s to an end also revealed that so-called modern patterns were rooted in long-lived expectations of women's subordination and domesticity. If the 1920s model had an emancipatory thrust, it was predicated on continued economic expansion through sustained consumer demand. During the Great Depression, reactionary calls for women's return to the home—especially for married women's exit from occupations—showed how thin was the aura of freedom and individuality cloaking the modern woman's prescribed role.

3

Between the Wars
in France and England

Anne-Marie Sohn

THERE HAVE BEEN FAR fewer books on the
period between the two world wars than on Victorian England or the triumphant French Third
Republic. If history in general has tended to neglect
the two decades between 1920 and 1940, women's
history, a late arrival on the scene, has neglected
the period even more. What was the character of
this ill-defined span of years, sandwiched between—if I may beg the reader's indulgence for
resorting to shorthand stereotypes—the "patriarchal" nineteenth century and the 1960s era of "the
pill" and the "sexual revolution"? What occurred
between the entry of women into the still new
industrial workforce and the advent of consumer
society with all its pleasures, supported by the
relative security of the welfare state? There were
signs of women's emancipation in the 1920s: females wore their hair short, enjoyed some of the
freedoms previously limited to unmarried males,
and in England obtained the right to vote. Yet their
daily lives changed little. The notion that the ideal
place for a woman was in the home went unchallenged, as did the concomitant division of labor.
England and France being democratic countries,
women avoided the regimentation of totalitarian
regimes. Yet for all their similarities, and despite

equivalent levels of development, the two countries were different, and the differences largely determined the place of women in each. For one thing, the Protestant and Catholic religions took different positions on contraception. For another, the farmwife all but disappeared in England, whereas in France 40 percent of the female workforce was employed in agriculture and thus subject to the unique constraints of the rural environment. In what follows, therefore, I shall be pointing out the distinctive features of each national type more often than the similarities.

From Mother to "Bachelor Girl"

Short skirts, short hair, and the portrait of the new woman as drawn in the novel *La Garçonne* (The Bachelor Girl): these have often been seen as symbols of a new type of female behavior, of the advent of the liberated woman. Despite appearances, however, traditional norms continued to hold sway.

The Bachelor Girl and the Flapper: Clichés of the Roaring Twenties

In France, nineteenth-century republicans such as Jules Ferry and Camille Sée held that marriage ought to be based on intellectual community. They hoped that education would help to narrow the "spiritual gap" *(fossé des âmes)* which they believed led to marital discord. Yet they denied that men and women could play similar roles in life: a woman's duty was to devote herself to her family. Novelists, meanwhile, had elaborated the figure of the mistress-wife: by domesticating eroticism they undermined the double standard and the usual justifications of male adultery, yet at the same time imposed on wives the duty of always meeting their husbands' sensual needs. In England, writers like George Bernard Shaw and George Wells went even further in their portraits of sexually and socially liberated women, some based on their own experience. In so doing they struck a blow as much for sexual equality as against the stultifying morality of the day. The "new woman" defied convention in search of her identity and autonomy. Meanwhile, free love and trial marriage were defended by a few marginal thinkers influenced by socialist and anarchist ideas and determined to overthrow Victorian morality, such as Léon Blum.[1]

After World War I, the "new woman" burst into the news. In England, the "flapper" was the very image of the liberated woman: she wore short skirts and loved to dance. In France Victor Margueritte crystallized the mood of the day in a vivid fictional archetype, the "bachelor girl," eponymous heroine of his novel *La Garçonne*.[2] Men back from the trenches rediscovered the joys of life, and people everywhere were transfixed by the Russian Revolution, which promised emancipation in every form human beings had ever dreamed of. It was in this climate that the bachelor girl seized the popular imagination: Margueritte's heroine hoped to achieve financial independence by pursuing a career, and she carried sexual freedom to the point of experimenting with bisexuality before settling down in a stable, egalitarian relationship with a male "companion."[3] Her creator said of her that "she thinks and acts like a man." Short hair symbolized a masculine character reflected in such "virile" qualities as talent, logic, an ability to handle money, and fierce independence ("I belong to no one but myself"). The emancipated woman, in short, was no longer a woman; she was something else, a new species, a tomboy. The novel was read by somewhere between 12 and 25 percent of the French public; a million copies were sold in twelve languages, a success equaled only by the scandal aroused by the book, which led to its author's exclusion from the Légion d'Honneur. In 1923 the British government seized copies shipped to Britain by mail, although it never publicized the fact or formally banned the book for fear of providing the author with free publicity. Debate raged not only in public—above all in the press—but also within families. Journalists, politicians, and conventional novelists condemned the "woman who lives her own life" as a "trollop" and criticized the book in the most vehement of terms. Most feminists found the novel's "pornographic" aspect shocking. The left divided on the issue: it defended freedom of expression but expressed doubts as to the book's content. The Communists, who saw the emancipation of women as an issue to be taken up after the revolution, voiced contempt for the "pseudo-demands" of a "republican bourgeois." Only revolutionary feminists, most notably schoolteachers affiliated with the CGTU, approved of the bachelor girl as an example of sexual equality. The interest of *La Garçonne*, then, is that it enables us to gauge the views of a range of official spokespersons, a majority of whom still defended a traditional image of women—that of the housewife.

The Housewife, or Woman's True Vocation

The stereotype of woman as "priestess of the hearth" and "angel of the household" became a fixture not only of literature and art but also of scientific texts in the second half of the nineteenth century. Exaltation of female "nature" and "sacred womanhood" actually served to relegate women to an inferior status. Men now pointed to women's physical weakness as a reason for protecting them and sparing them undue fatigue. Motherhood was a duty, for obvious biological reasons. Men of the elite also painted a moral portrait of woman to match this "scientific" account: sensitivity, it was argued, was a more prominent feature of woman's character than intelligence. Docility and obedience were her great virtues, whereas the pursuit of ambition or theoretical speculations could easily tax her strength or threaten her femininity. The public sphere was for men, while a woman's place was "home, sweet home." The Pre-Raphaelite woman, that decorative flower, was held out as an ideal for British upper-class women to emulate.

At the same time, a new medical literature on child-rearing increased the pressure on women to remain in the home. Starting in the nineteenth century, medical authorities began to urge women to assist the physicians in the battle against infantile mortality. The Pasteurian revolution emphasized the need for stringent measures to protect nursing children from contamination by microbes. It was the mother's duty to do whatever was necessary to protect the "race" and nation. In France especially, an early decline in the birthrate and the ensuing specter of depopulation lent added urgency to the crusade for hygiene, which joined forces with the pronatalist movement. In England it was not until 1937 that the threat of a declining birthrate and its alleged consequences for the prosperity and "maintenance of the British Empire" were mentioned for the first time in the House of Commons. The "back to the kitchen" movement of the 1930s marshaled similar arguments. Medical supervision of child-rearing practices became common only after World War I, although doctors had begun to examine nursing children as early as the 1890s. England established so-called Maternity and Infant Centers in 1918, while the number of well-baby clinics in France increased from 400 to 5,000 between the two world wars. Following the American lead, visiting nurses checked up on mothers in their homes. Physicians charged mothers with so many new responsibilities that work outside the home became difficult. Measures intended to protect children thus led first to implicit and later to explicit restrictions on women's labor, especially in France, where many married women had careers. Any mother who did not wish to be branded "an abomination of nature" was advised not to place her child in the hands of a paid wet nurse who might transmit a disease to the tender nursling. Breast-feeding meant that women had to stay home. Newspapers, novels, and politicians portrayed motherhood as the noblest of careers. In France, the Syndicat Professionnel de la Femme au Foyer, which was founded in 1935 for the purpose of demanding wages for housework, extolled motherhood as a "social function which assures harmony in families, health in children, happiness in individuals, and, consequently, prosperity in the nation."[4] The magazine *Housewife,* which began publication, significantly, in 1939, had this to say: "Happy is the man whose wife is proud of her home . . . who likes to do things well so as to make him proud of her and her children." It was around this time that the image of the French housewife changed, from that of the "household manager" carefully administering the family farm or business or, in the case of the working class, that of the "working man's minister of finance,"[5] to that of the mother who devoted herself exclusively to her children—exclusively, and at times even excessively, as in François Mauriac's *Genitrix*. So universal and incontrovertible was the propaganda in favor of the housewife that many couples internalized the new ideal. It went all but unchallenged in England after 1900. In France, however, there were regrets and questions.

Mother, Wife, and Worker

The convergence of the secular teachings of the churches, of the increased emphasis on the importance of femininity since the nineteenth century, and of the new duties imposed on women in an ever more medicalized society led to the triumph of a discourse on women in the interwar period that emphasized motherhood, wifehood, and the rejection of a "profession." The housewife, restricted to domestic chores and confined to the home, was the opposite of the bachelor girl, who by the thirties had all but disappeared from the scene. But women adapted themselves to this new, male-imposed model in ways that allowed for consider-able freedom.

The Resistance to Women's Labor

Even though women were generally portrayed as being without a profession, many did work, especially in France. Between 1906 and 1946, women accounted for between 36.6 and 37.9 percent of the workforce in France, compared with 28.5 percent in Great Britain. While it was common for young women of modest station to work prior to marriage in both countries, relatively few married women worked in England (14 to 16 percent of the workforce), whereas it was common for married women to work in France. Half of all French female workers were married in 1920, and the proportion had risen to 55 percent in 1936. Furthermore, widows with children accounted for 13.5 to 14.5 percent of women work-ers. In France in the interwar period two-thirds of working women supported families. Outside the upper and upper-middle classes French women largely ignored the pro-family propaganda, then at its height, and pursued their own goals both in the home and in the workplace.

Historians often point out that women's labor declined in both England and France after World War I, but the totals are mislead-ing. The number of women working in factories in France in-creased from one million in 1906 to 1,220,000 in 1921 and 1,470,000 in 1926. The disparity between the historians' charac-terization (and even their use of statistics) and the reality is strik-ing. The structure of the French workforce was peculiar, owing to the high percentage of women working in agriculture: 46 percent of the female workforce in 1921 and 40 percent as late as 1936, compared with only 1 or 2 percent in Great Britain. The role of women in farming actually increased in the interwar years owing to growing specialization of agricultural production and a shortage of labor due to an exodus from the countryside: "Because of the labor shortage, women usually replace male workers in agricul-ture," according to one 1929 survey.[6] In regions where livestock was raised and where the care of animals was traditionally en-trusted to women, their role expanded as farmers gambled on increased production. In Normandy, for example, two-thirds of family incomes came from dairy products. Similar changes occurred in vineyards and vegetable-growing regions. Women had long been flexible workers capable of adapting to climatic and seasonal changes. "A woman has to do a little of everything," Minot was told in Burgundy.[7] Some preferred working in the fields or vineyards to working in their kitchens. As one woman from the Aude nostalgically recalled: "I used to have a ball in the vineyard."[8] Women employed in agriculture could generally leave work for short periods to respond to family or home emergencies. Mothers of young children could quit work for a time or cut back to part-time employment. They could also rely on neighbors and grandparents for free childcare. Still, the combined burden of household chores and farm work was quite substantial.

In urban areas two out of three mothers were forced to work because their husbands earned too little to support the family.[9] Women found ready employment owing to the prevalence of small businesses in the French economy, and because the low birthrate created labor shortages despite a strong influx of immigrants. These factors had been at work since the previous century, so that it was now common to find women in the workplace: ideology may have insisted that women stay home, but reality dictated otherwise. The reports of factory supervisors collected by Annie Fourcaut show that women were attached to their jobs for more personal reasons as well. Two salaries allowed families to achieve a modest level of comfort, and the workplace was also a convivial place to meet other people: "Factory life, with its gossip, incidents, and camaraderie, amused them." It was also a source of freedom: "Work gave them a measure of independence from their husbands."[10] Women in the Nord, a region where jobs in textile mills were passed on from mother to daughter, refused to quit work when they married: "They prefer their jobs."[11]

In areas where the prevailing industries (such as mining and steel) employed relatively few female workers, women ran taverns or took in boarders or washing. Even the women who did these kinds of work scarcely counted it as labor. One garment trimmer from Saint Etienne, asked if her mother had worked after her marriage, replied, "No, never. She stayed home and did mending for anyone who asked. She never stopped for a minute."[12] Conditions being what they were, it became less and less common for women to quit work when children arrived. In Paris, one in two working women took a long leave when a child was born, but only 10 percent—generally women with large families or working in unpleasant jobs—quit work permanently.

By contrast, Great Britain afforded women more limited opportunities owing to persistent, at times explosive, unemployment. Things were so bad between 1921 and 1931, in fact, that 200,000 female blue-collar workers had to accept employment as domestics for lack of jobs in industry. In addition, the rapid growth of suburbs far from any possible place of employment made it difficult for many women to work. One final factor was the average woman's view of her social role. As early as 1913 a survey of working-class women found a growing reluctance to work outside the home. Women began to regard the need to work as a calamity. The expression "working mother" was now applied to women at home. These negative attitudes toward work hardened in the interwar period. When Margery Spring Rice surveyed working-class women in 1939, she did not ask about wage-paying jobs, and few of the women she spoke to brought the matter up.

Comparing the three factors of workforce composition, tradition of female employment, and dominant ideology, we see that French and British patterns of female labor were quite different. Yet the jobs available to women and the skills required of them were more or less similar. In both countries the branch of industry that employed more women than any other—nearly one-third of the total—was textile manufacturing. Employment in this sector declined sharply between the wars, however, as clothing manufacture was industrialized, throwing many seamstresses out of work. The trimming, lace-making, and embroidery trades all suffered, as did other "minor professions" (such as darning and dressmaking) associated with a way of life destroyed by the war. The number of textile workers in France declined from 1,471,000 in 1906 to 887,500 in 1931; women working on their own were even more severely affected (their numbers dropped from 907,500 to 429,500 over the same period). On the other hand, women began to find jobs in sectors previously considered all-male, such as the mechanical, chemical, and food industries. In England the proportion of women in the metals trades rose from 8.8 to 16.4 percent, and in the Midlands and southeastern England, home of the new mechanical industries, female employment rose steadily as more jobs became available. In these expanding sectors women did not simply fill in for men. In periods of recession they often kept their jobs while men were sacked, proof that the hiring of women reflected a certain economic logic. Indeed, the development of assembly lines and the substitution of machines for brute strength encouraged the employment of women, many of whom were assigned to unskilled jobs, less well paid than the jobs given to men. In these roles their traditional female skills, though unrecognized, proved invaluable.

Many women were hired as semiskilled workers on the new assembly lines in order to reduce labor costs. At the same time the growth of the service sector also favored the employment of women. In England the proportion of women employed in white-collar jobs increased from 2 percent in 1911 to 10 percent in 1931. In France, the ratio of female clerical to female factory workers was one to three in 1902 but had fallen to one to two by 1931. The proportion of white-collar workers among working women doubled between 1906 and 1921, and by 1931 about one million women, or 22.6 percent of the female workforce, held office jobs. Women also found employment in retail sales and in the post office as well as in new professions such as social work and nursing. Married women were the chief beneficiaries of the new opportunities. The new service-sector jobs called upon skills that women acquired through longer schooling in public classrooms and special course extensions. But male and female employees were treated differently: women were rarely promoted, for example.

In both France and Great Britain fewer people enjoyed the luxury of private incomes, and this meant a decline in the number of servants as well as a qualitative transformation in the nature of domestic service. The change was less pronounced in England, however, where one women in three continued to work as a domestic. In France, where 15 to 18 percent of working women were employed as domestics, live-in maids were replaced by cleaning women hired for the day. Many of these women were married, and because they did not reside under their employers' roofs they enjoyed much greater freedom in their private lives than the live-ins they replaced.

To sum up, if French and British women in the nineteenth century had been used chiefly as helpers and sweated labor, they now found better paid, more prestigious jobs open to them. In France, the number of employed women, and particularly employed married women, increased. Work brought women a sense of personal satisfaction and made them feel "modern," and industry began to recognize the improvement in their skills.

Working Mother or Housewife

The nature of housework changed slowly, and the American dream of a "scientifically managed" (Taylorized) household for the most part remained a myth. What the homemaker had to do, and how long it took her to do it, was largely determined by the quality of housing and the availability of running water, gas, and electricity. Improvements in these areas were slow in both countries. The English authorities pulled down a million slum apartments and built healthy, if monotonous, suburbs—progress, to be sure, but still far short of what was needed. The new "council houses" went primarily to white-collar workers. Blue-collar housing remained mediocre at best (and in a majority of cases downright unacceptable). Fifty percent of London households had no running water, and overcrowding was severe: five people lived in the average room in Bethnal Green, for example. A survey of 1,250 working-class women conducted by the Women's Health Enquiry Committee found that 6.9 percent lived in healthful, spacious apartments with hot and cold running water, but often far from downtown; 61.4 percent lived in poor, overcrowded houses, and 31 percent in dwellings "that no civilized society ought to tolerate."[13] Meanwhile, in France, a housing shortage compounded by a postwar freeze on rents led to severe overcrowding. As in Great Britain, few working-class families had more than one or two rooms. It should be noted, however, that until the 1930s the French were reluctant to spend much on housing: "We skimped on rent."[14] As recently as 1954, 42 percent of French households had no running water. Yet there had been considerable progress in rural housing since the nineteenth century: many farmers replaced dirt floors with tile or stone, added bedrooms on upper floors, and painted the main room of the house. In eastern France many farmhouses destroyed by the war were replaced with modern dwellings, some even equipped with central heating. But Brittany and the more mountainous parts of France still lagged behind the rest of the country. In regions such as the Haute-Loire, upper Champsaur, the Queyras, and the Briançonnais, peasant families still shared a room with their animals, at least during the day and quite often throughout the winter. Roads were neglected, and farmyards were thick with foul muck. In Lorraine manure was stored in open piles, and paths in the mountain village of Oisans were "blocked by piles of manure and filth."[15] With mud and animal filth everywhere, it was all but impossible to keep houses clean. Before women's attitudes toward housekeeping could be changed, something had to be done about the prevailing conditions in rural villages and farms.

In the cities overcrowding and lack of water had the same dispiriting effect. The English study mentioned above reports that "poor dwellings can be made decent only by dint of enormous effort."[16] Even expressions of remorse about the filth contain hints of insuperable squalor. The wife of one invalid sailor who lived in a one-room apartment in Croydon wrote that "there are so many beds in the room that I cannot change them, and I dry the laundry in the only space available."[17]

More than half of all women continued to perform much the same domestic chores as their mothers: very little had changed. True, those fortunate enough to have running water found themselves liberated from one chore that had consumed as much as three-quarters of an hour a day: fetching water. By 1938, moreover, 65 percent of British women and nearly as many in France had electric lighting in their homes, and this eliminated the two-and-a-half hours a week that had been devoted to cleaning and preparing oil lamps. Heating with gas or electricity could save an additional nine hours a week, but fewer than 20 percent of English women had this luxury. The majority still had to tend the fireplace or stove. And women in both countries were a long way from enjoying the benefits of household appliances; Britain, being more urbanized, led France in this respect because households had greater access to electricity.

The "domestic science movement," which originated in the United States prior to World War I, set out to improve health standards by applying Frederick Taylor's strict scientific management principles to housework. (Taylor [1856–1915] was the author of *The Principles of Scientific Management*—Trans.) Taylor's French translator, the engineer Henry Le Chatelier, brought the American's ideas to the Continent, but it was Paulette Bernège, the founder of the Institut d'Organisation Ménagère, who popularized them by organizing a series of home shows beginning in Paris in 1923. In England the Electrical Association for Women played a similar role by publicizing the use of electrical appliances in the home, a boon that promised to reduce housework by up to fifteen hours a week. Unfortunately, the new appliances appear to have been beyond the reach of the average consumer. In 1929 a washing machine cost 700 francs, or two-thirds of a Parisian worker's monthly wage, and a refrigerator cost 7,000 francs, compared with a maid's annual wages of 4,500. In 1938 only 4 percent of British households had a washing machine and only 2 percent a refrigerator. In France such innovations as electric irons caught on only in the north and east, regions with a reputation for cleanliness. Remember that it was not until the interwar period that the simple *lessiveuse,* a washpan for doing the laundry, came into widespread use. Great Britain eventually began to embrace modernity: by 1948, 86 percent of British households had an electric iron, 40 percent had a vacuum cleaner, and 75 percent had a gas or electric stove. Yet until 1939 women in both countries went on washing, cooking, and cleaning much as they had done in the previous century, although falling prices encouraged the use of new products that made home maintenance easier.

Cooking was in the main women's work, and changes affecting the kitchen had contradictory effects. Even in rural France it became extremely rare to bake bread at home. This freed up a half to a full day per week. In England widespread use of canned foods and powdered milk simplified the preparation of meals, which were kept quite simple. In modest homes supper was rarely served, and meals consisting of bread and butter, stew, pudding, a little salad, vegetables, or sometimes fish were prepared rapidly. In France two large meals were normally served, unless, as became increasingly common, the man of the house took one of his meals at the company cafeteria. In the country, particularly during harvest season, a substantial lunch and a snack were also served. The standard middle-class menu—appetizer, meat and vegetables, salad and dessert—spread to other classes, and housewives had to learn new recipes to keep up. Traditional peasant cooking did not disappear, but it called for more time and care than modern dishes. Making *milhas,* a sort of corn porridge eaten in southwestern France, required the cooperation of several neighbors. As the French standard of living rose, diet improved, and the number of dishes served with each meal increased: mothers stopped stirring their stews and began to cook more elegant meals, which required longer hours in the kitchen.

Last but not least, ready-to-wear clothing allowed women, especially working-class women, to reduce the number of hours they spent making clothes for the family. Housewives still darned socks, but the wives of English working men refused to do much sewing. Many French women continued to practice their needle work, which not only allowed families to save money on clothing but gave women something to do and continued to symbolize the feminine ideal. The decorative techniques of the nineteenth-century bourgeoisie now spread to the working class and peasantry.

In the absence of reliable data it is difficult to gauge how many hours women spent on household chores. The Electrical Association for Women gave an estimate of forty-nine hours per week, but that figure applied only to homes with the latest electrical appliances. In 1950 one French estimate put the figure at an average eighty-two hours per week, which seems quite high. Another estimate, from 1947, suggests that working women in urban France worked an average of only nine hours per week more than women who stayed home, including time devoted to household chores: working women simply spent less time doing housework. Many married women who continued to work in factory jobs claimed that "they had little to do at home."[18] In other words, working women cut back on housework; they were the principal beneficiaries of such innovations as wash tubs, canned foods, and electrical appliances. But as a result of the health crusade and culinary refinement, French homemakers probably spent more time on household tasks than did their forebears. Although pleased to have eliminated some of the more onerous tasks (apart from laundering), they still felt uneasy about having time to themselves. And much more time was now devoted to childcare.

Remember, too, that women received help from adolescent daughters and elderly mothers. English working-class women often helped out in their daughters' homes in times of sickness or childbirth; they also prepared after-school snacks for grandchildren and shared the burden of childcare. Neighbors provided invaluable assistance, but in return they insisted that community moral standards be upheld.[19] And blue-collar husbands in France were not afraid of lending a hand around the house. One Parisian woman tells of returning home while her husband was unemployed: "When I came in, I found everything ready: the house, the meal— all I had to do was slip my feet under the table."[20] Women who worked at the Panhard auto factory in Paris also had kind words for their spouses: "We got on well and shared the housework. The first one home made dinner and did the dishes."[21] Men in England and peasants in France were apparently unwilling to accept such sharing of responsibilities, however.

Mothers Triumphant?

The ideal was not just for women to stay home but to stay home as mothers. Child-rearing was increasingly portrayed as a privilege of womanhood. In the discourse on childhood fathers occupied a secondary place. The reality was more complicated, however. A distinction has to be made between nurturing and upbringing. The nurturing of infants and young children had always been a maternal function. Breast-feeding created a physical dependency, and fathers took no part in tending to their infants' physical needs. It was unthinkable for French and British fathers to coddle their youngsters.[22] Between the wars childcare experts persuaded most mothers to give up traditional methods deemed harmful to infant health. The hygienists' campaign was so successful that some historians, such as Yvonne Knibiehler and Françoise Thébaud, have gone so far as to describe it as one of maternal indoctrination. And it is certainly true that within two decades all classes had embraced modern standards. The typical mother devoted more time to physically caring for her children than ever before. Children were cleaner, or at any rate the parts that could be seen—faces and hands—were cleaner, if only to avoid criticism from the schoolteacher, who in France checked each child's appearance and could send home any pupil deemed to be dirty. Infants were not bathed daily, however, and older children bathed only weekly. Children dressed with greater variety and took better care of their clothes. Severe punishment awaited the child who soiled or destroyed an item of clothing. Children's nutrition also improved. Although French doctors failed to persuade all women of the wisdom of breast-feeding (its frequency actually declined in the interwar period), their recommendations to use fresh milk and clean bottles were heeded (this was true in England as well). Condensed and powdered milk, which became commercially available in 1925, allowed parents to prepare uncontaminated baby formula quickly and easily. Infants were weaned later and fed commercial baby foods. The harmful practice, particularly common in rural areas, of overfeeding (which could lead to fatal diarrhea) gradually disappeared. Although some of the practices that doctors recommended were time-consuming, mothers accepted them. As the birthrate declined, women were willing to invest more time caring for smaller numbers of children. In France, the use of wet nurses, still common before the war in all social classes despite the disapproval of medical authorities, declined sharply after 1918, not only because nurses were in short supply and therefore expensive but also because mothers wished to see their children every day (although they did leave them with neighbors or relatives during working hours).

In England mothers relied exclusively on the generous help of relatives to care for very young children. English mothers bore sole responsibility for early education, whereas in France *écoles maternelles* (nursery schools) served some 400,000 children in urban areas, providing competent and indispensable daycare for working mothers. The Fischer Law (1918) had provided for the creation of similar schools in England under local auspices, but the Maternity Act transferred responsibility to the ministry of health, which showed little interest in the matter: in 1932 there were still only fifty-two nursery schools in Great Britain, and by 1938 the number had increased to just 112. The absence of daycare, nursery schools, and kindergartens, combined with the shortage of home help, meant that a British woman was forced to quit work outside the home when her first child arrived.

British mothers assumed full responsibility for formal education as well. They monitored their children's progress in school and arranged for religious instruction. In France, by contrast, fathers played a more important part. The role of mothers in English working-class families was central, as Elizabeth Roberts and Richard Hoggart documented it for the 1930s and 1940s and Young and Wilmott for the 1950s. When Roberts asked women if their parents had been strict, most stressed the preeminence of their mothers: "My mother was, yes. She was the one who wore the pants in the family. She didn't just run the household; she ruled it. She was the dominant figure in the family."[23] The mother kept the family together after the children had grown. She also helped daughters with their children and offered them advice. The typical married woman in Bethnal Green saw her mother four times a week. Women often expressed a preference for daughters over sons because daughters would keep them company and ward off loneliness. In France, daughters were closer to their mothers in certain respects (they helped out more at home and were more likely to confide in their mothers about intimate matters), but they were less likely to remain as close to their mothers as English girls did, except in Armentières, where daughters attached particular importance to these relationships. Fathers were just as interested as mothers in their children's scholastic and professional careers. Many worked out strategies for social advancement. They also kept an eye on their children's friends and activities and meted out rewards and punishments. When it came to love of the children, fathers and mothers were close rivals, and people were quick to condemn those fathers who appeared to be hard-hearted and authoritarian. Of course contemporaries believed that a mother was primarily responsible for her children's moral upbringing and above all for the chastity of her daughters. Her own behavior, especially in sexual matters, must therefore be irreproachable. Remarriage after divorce was sometimes cited as grounds for denying a woman custody of her children.

Thus there were clear differences in the behavior of French and British mothers, even within similar social milieus—differences regarding work, delegation of parental authority, and the very conception of the family. Yet it is a delicate matter to interpret the implications of these differences when it comes to assessing the relative importance of the individual versus the family or the wife's role in the marriage.

Marriage and Feminine Freedom

Between the wars it became common for men and women alike to choose the person whom they wished to marry. Few parents— even in rural France, where issues of inheritance were fundamental—still dared to insist on arranged marriages. Parents were consulted, however, for children generally did not like to marry against their parents' wishes. Men began to look not just for wives but for "soul mates," and thus the problem of where to meet members of the opposite sex and how to approach them became crucial. Dance halls where "modern" steps were all the rage became popular in both France and England. No longer did the farmer's lad court the shepherd lass on the hillside, as he had done in parts of France as recently as 1900. Now he was more likely to ride his bicycle into town to meet his girl at the local dance and try to impress her with his skill on the dance floor. New courting rituals developed, and more experienced town youths had an easy time with country girls fascinated by the city and its delights, as Pierre Bourdieu showed in his study of Béarn.[24] But farm girls took advantage of the competition to explore newfound freedoms, in part the result of a weakening of paternal authority. This emancipation of young women left many young men in rural areas without marriage prospects, however. In England, meanwhile, the war made it easier for young women to go out without chaperones, and many working girls enjoyed unprecedented sexual freedom. One survey found that 7 percent of women born before 1904 had flirted and another 19 percent had had sexual relations before marriage; the corresponding figures for the generation born between 1904 and 1914 were 22 and 36 percent. Nevertheless, men clung to their traditional views of marriage. A strict division of labor persisted in working-class families: the husband was the breadwinner, the wife the "manager" of the household. The man's economic role was reflected in language: one woman referred to her husband as "the master" and said "he's the boss." Her husband frequently told her to "shut up" and did not hesitate to hit her. Although this behavior earned him criticism, his wife observed that he was "a real man."[25] French men and women shared similar views concerning the qualities that made a good partner: the ideal mate was a hard worker, good parent, and faithful spouse, neither frigid nor hysterical, physically attractive (looks played an increasing role for both sexes), and not an alcoholic or a deviant.[26] The old stereotypes had begun to fade: women were no longer expected to be gentle and gracious, and men were not asked to be domineering and virile, although the man who was "weak" or "too good" was considered poor marriage material. It was extremely rare, moreover, to find anyone in France willing to condone a husband's mistreatment of his wife. French and British attitudes toward the family thus appear to have differed markedly.

It is widely accepted that working-class women wielded a financial power that partially compensated for their inferior position in marriage. Nineteenth-century working men turned their pay over to their wives. In England this custom survived the Great War: one of every two workers turned his entire earnings over to his wife, sometimes without even opening the envelope. Others handed over part of their wages. In exchange, the wife allotted her husband a sum for pocket money, even during periods of unemployment. The wife also took care of all dealings with the authorities. French women insisted that their husbands turn over at least a sum sufficient to cover household expenses, but some men relinquished their entire pay. Many couples established a "household kitty" from which both husband and wife could draw as needed. An alcoholic husband could easily drink up the whole family budget, thereby forcing his wife to work to provide for herself and the children. It was not uncommon for the husband to manage the budget, as in the case of the Lorraine worker whose wife complained: "I was always short of money, because L. managed the finances."[27] Working wives who did not manage the household finances felt that they had claims on the joint property, and if a woman left her husband she might take the furniture and other belongings with her in proportion to her contribution to the family's wealth. Control over finances was thus a source of power, and while that power was sometimes shared in amicable fashion, it could also give rise to disputes.

Many upper-class women remained ignorant of financial matters, although husbands frequently discussed major decisions such as the purchase, sale, or rental of property with their wives. Peasant couples also conferred about important matters. In folklore the man of the house was traditionally the one who decided what to plant, who did what around the farm, where to sell the harvest and buy supplies, how to invest, and what to tell the notary. But this patriarchal style vanished between the wars, not least because the declining birthrate and rural exodus left husbands and wives alone with each other and forced them to cooperate in daily chores. To be sure, the men still sold the grain crop and the livestock, while their wives marketed the products of garden and barn (which often brought in considerable income), but investments and negotiations with the notary were matters for the couple to decide jointly. Some women enjoyed true financial independence because they kept what they earned in the marketplace and spent the profits as they chose, usually on themselves and the children. A wife's influence also depended on the amount of land she brought to the marriage, and that could be considerable: if an "heiress" in Béarn married a younger son, she became the "head of the household." One symbol of changing mores is that after World War I women in Sologne and Limousin refused to serve their husbands unless they were allowed to sit at the same table (it had been customary for the wife to stand while her family ate).

The secrets of the marital chamber are more difficult to uncover. Passivity or even frigidity on the woman's part—the fruit of an upbringing that renounced the pleasures of the flesh—emerges occasionally in response to a survey question or when a family crisis led to exposure of normally private sexual matters. The degree to which women's needs were satisfied is hard to quantify. It is also difficult to determine who decided how many children to have or what means of contraception to use. French and British demographic policies were radically different, moreover. While France, having suffered for some time from a declining birthrate, sought to eliminate anticonceptional practices, a long-prolific England completed its demographic revolution within the space of twenty years without government intervention. The birthrate, which had stood as high as 30 per thousand as late as 1896, fell to 20 in 1921 and 15 in 1933, the same level as in France. Within a generation the average number of children per mother decreased from five or six to two or three. This abrupt reversal of the trend was accompanied by intense agitation in favor of birth control, which at the very least relieved couples of guilt concerning their procreative decisions.

The Malthusian League and the British Society for the Study of Sex Psychology, founded by feminists and socialists such as Stella Browne and George Ives and supported by intellectuals such as George Bernard Shaw and Bertrand Russell, advocated birth control for economic and political reasons before 1918. The Society for Constructive Birth-Control and Racial Progress (an eye-opening appellation) was founded in 1921 by Dr. Mary Stopes with the support of neo-Malthusians such as Stella Browne. The society adopted the principles set forth by the American nurse Margaret Sanger: to stabilize the population, prevent abortion, and promote marital harmony in a traditional framework. These pioneers led a powerful movement in favor of contraception, which was promoted through lectures, books such as *Married Love* (1918) by Mary Stopes, and clinics, the first of which was opened in the town of Halloway by the same Mary Stopes. By 1939 there were throughout England more than a hundred centers providing information on birth control. The "new feminists" backed the movement, as did women of the Labour Party and the Women's Cooperative Guild. Not a few municipal councils wished to take over these clinics, and by 1939 two-thirds were operating with assistance from public funds. In 1930 the Labour-controlled health ministry lifted the ban preventing Maternity and Child

Welfare Centers from offering advice on contraception. Finally, in the same year, the British Medical Association and the Lambeth Conference of the Anglican Church both gave their sanction to birth control if the mother's health depended on it. Once birth control had acquired both legal and moral legitimacy, its use became commonplace, as a variety of studies indicate. Whereas only 18 percent of working-class families had used contraceptives in 1900, the proportion had risen to 68 percent by 1935–1939. For unskilled workers the comparable figures were 5 percent and 54 percent, and for white-collar workers, 26 percent and 73 percent. Women played a large part in this success, which reflected a deep but hidden need, as Dora Russel was astonished to discover at the Labour Women's Conference of 1923: "I and the other participants were dumbfounded by the outburst of vituperation at the idea of pregnancy. . . . These women vehemently attacked what we had been taught to regard as woman's noblest task."[28]

Within the working class, Diana Gittins has found, it was the most liberated wives (liberated in the sense of being active in the workplace or enjoying egalitarian marital relations) who had the most complete information about birth control and were the first to adopt it. But women continued to rely on methods that left their husbands in control: *coitus interruptus* and condoms were far more popular than pessaries. No sooner had the battle for birth control been won than the struggle for the decriminalization of abortion began. The 1861 Offence Against the Person Act and the 1929 Infant Preservation Act had officially banned abortion except in cases where the mother's health was in danger. In 1936 the Abortion Law Reform Association was founded with support from pro-birth control activists such as Stella Browne. And in 1938 a major legal step was taken: the courts recognized the legality of abortion in cases of "physical or mental distress." Within the space of two decades English women had all but won the freedom to bear children as they saw fit.

Meanwhile, in France, all propaganda in favor of contraception was prohibited by the law of 3 July 1920. Abortion had been a felony subject to trial by jury, but indulgent juries had been in the habit of acquitting up to 80 percent of the women brought to trial. The law of 23 March 1923 reduced abortion to a misdemeanor subject to trial by a judge only; the legislators' hope was that professional judges would prove more severe than popular juries had been. Indeed, between 1925 and 1935, the acquittal rate fell to 19 percent. But the number of prosecutions was small: between 1920 and 1930, 978 cases were brought under the 1920 antipropaganda law, and an average of 400 to 500 women were tried annually under the law prohibiting abortion. When Henriette Alquier, a schoolteacher who wrote a report on "conscious maternity" for the Groupes Féministes de l'Enseignement Laïque, was brought to trial in 1927, the public outcry in her behalf was so vociferous that she was acquitted. The number of arrests was a drop in the bucket compared to the actual number of abortions, which certainly exceeded 100,000 annually. Furthermore, the repressive, moralistic, populationist climate did nothing to halt the decline in the birthrate, which hit new lows in the 1930s, with the death rate possibly even surpassing the birthrate in some years. These statistics are hardly surprising, since the most widely used methods of birth control—withdrawal; condoms, whose use was legal for the prevention of venereal disease; and the "natural" methods advocated by Drs. Ogino and Knauss—all were permitted by law. Only diaphragms were prohibited. As for abortion, which could only be practiced in secret, the number of operations appears to have increased, along with the efficacy, the most common technique being intrauterine injection. The conservatism of the Bloc National, which was behind the *lois scélérates* (or nefarious laws, that is, the laws against contraception and abortion), and the influence of the Catholic Church in a nominally secular country may have weighed on politicians to the point that Radicals and Socialists, despite their oft-repeated hostility to the laws in question, did not dare to repeal them during the Popular Front years. But not even the virtual unanimity of government officials was able to halt the evolution of people's attitudes in favor of shared responsibility for contraception. Abortion, however, remained the business of women. Women seeking abortions relied on other women to steer them toward the *faiseuses d'anges* (angel-makers, or women who performed clandestine abortions), often without their husbands' knowledge. Angus MacLaren has suggested that such informal networks reflect a tacit feminism in everyday life. While such a conclusion goes beyond the evidence, it is clear that women resisted political, medical, and social pressures. Here the disparity between official discourse and private convictions as well as between law and practice is striking. Despite differences in French and British public policy, one can argue that there was in both countries between the wars a growing, though as yet not openly avowed, conviction that women have a right to control their own bodies.

Divorce further extended the freedom of women, but according to different timetables in France and Great Britain. In France the law of 1884 chiefly benefited women, even though it was inegalitarian in the sense that an adulterous husband could be sentenced to prison only if he kept a concubine under the same roof as his wife. In more than half of the cases brought under the new law, it was the wife who sued for divorce.[29] And the number of cases grew steadily, from 8,000 in the 1880s to 15,000 in 1914 and 25,000 in 1935. The typical divorce suit was brought by a working woman (blue- or white-collar) living in a city in a region where there had been a sharp decline in religious practice. She knew about birth control: half of those who sought divorce were childless, and the average number of children overall was 0.84. In England divorce was limited by laws defining strict grounds for separation and requiring a costly legal procedure; the only divorce court in the country was in London, moreover. At the turn of the century the number of divorces granted annually was just two hundred. In 1923, however, divorce courts were established outside London and a husband's adultery became grounds for divorce. Thus even in the absence of legal aid, which meant that only the wealthy could sue for divorce, more than 4,000 were granted annually in the period 1920–1930 and 7,500 in 1940. The Matrimonial Causes Act of 1937 further expanded the grounds for separation and nullification, but its effects were not felt until later. The public, moreover, still frowned on divorce: the marriage of King Edward VII to a divorcée was only the most notorious example. In France, divorce still had not become commonplace on the eve of World War II, but it had been accepted by emancipated women as preferable to an intolerable marriage.

Slowly but surely marriage thus evolved toward a more egalitarian partnership. Although botched abortions still took a high toll, most women found themselves liberated from the fear of unwanted pregnancy. But a small minority, the women of the "underclass" or "fourth world," as it is sometimes called, remained in thrall to biology owing to lack of education, unstable family situations, and low incomes. Other women still obeyed the biblical injunction to "be fruitful and multiply," but their numbers were dwindling.

Finally, there were women who never married: the number of single females increased after the war decimated the ranks of young men, and for a time—the reign of the "bachelor girl"—they were a newsworthy topic, but when the headlines faded they vanished once again into obscurity. For such women finding a job was essential unless they managed to live on private incomes, which inflation made it increasingly difficult to do. Many middle-class women flocked to new and relatively respectable jobs in the service sector, but little is known about their solitary lives or about the palliative to loneliness they may have sought in furtive affairs. Their history has been eclipsed by that of mothers and wives, although some authors have seen militancy in the public sphere as a distraction or an alternative form of fulfillment.

The End of Dependency?

Commentators on the French Civil Code have traditionally pointed to its sexist character: married women are treated as minors, and women generally are defined in terms of dependency on either a father or a husband. Despite attempts to clean up the law prior to 1914, France continued to lag behind England. It was not until 1907, for example, that French women obtained the legal right to control their own earnings, despite the passage of an analogous measure in England as early as 1870. Between the wars the civil status of women changed in similar ways in both countries, bestowing legal sanction on an emancipation that had already entered into people's mores.

Reducing Legal Discrimination

In France women in 1920 were granted the right to join labor unions without their husbands' authorization and after 1927 were allowed to retain their nationality in case of marriage to a foreigner. A widow's rights to inherit from her husband were strengthened vis-à-vis the husband's family, a sign of the growing importance of the couple relative to that of the male lineage. Most important of all, the law of 18 February 1938 abolished the civil disabilities of married women, in effect abrogating Article 215 of the Civil Code pertaining to the authority of the husband. Married women were henceforth entitled to testify in court, sign contracts, open bank accounts, take degrees, participate in competitive examinations, and apply for passports without permission from their husbands. Nevertheless, the husband remained the head of the family; his residence established the family's legal domicile; and he could forbid his wife to practice a profession. The wife could, however, appeal the husband's decisions to the courts. Finally, the father enjoyed sole parental authority, although he could be stripped of that authority in case of abandonment (1924) or non-payment of alimony. These legal changes affected mainly the middle and upper classes, the fine points of the Civil Code having little effect on people of more modest background.

Similar changes occurred in Great Britain. Married women gained control of their earnings and property in 1882. The Sex Disqualification Removal Act of December 23, 1919, opened previously all-male professions, and particularly the legal profession, to women. The Law of Property Act of 1922 named the wife as heir if her husband died intestate and the husband and wife as joint heirs if a child died intestate. The Matrimonial Causes Act of 1923 restored equality between husband and wife in case of adultery and divorce. The Guardianship Act of 1925 made the mother guardian of her children in case of separation; previously she risked having her children taken away. Finally, the Criminal Justice Act of 1925 abolished the legal fiction according to which a woman who committed a crime in her husband's presence was assumed to have acted under coercion, thereby ending a woman's lack of responsibility for her own actions under the law. Nevertheless, women had to remain on their guard, for attempts were made to introduce new inequalities into the law surreptitiously. In 1935, for example, special conditions were placed on married women who applied for unemployment allowances, restrictions so onerous that women could be deprived of their compensation even though they had regularly paid unemployment taxes.

Active or Passive Citizens

The most notable difference between French and English women consisted in the right to vote. The power of pre-1914 English feminism, made manifest in the large demonstrations staged by Emmeline Pankhurst's Women's Social and Political Union, played a considerable part in the adoption, on February 6, 1918, of the People Bill, which granted English women the right to vote. To be sure, the reform was incomplete, because only women above the age of thirty were allowed to vote. Full civic equality was not achieved until 1928, but it must be said that until 1918 one man in three was also denied the right to vote (indigents, domestic servants, and others were barred from the polls): universal suffrage came to Great Britain in stages. The Parliament Qualification of Powers Act of November 6, 1918, permitted women to run for seats in the House of Commons. In 1924 Margaret Bondfield, a Labour M.P., joined the MacDonald government as the first woman minister in British history.

After the end of the Great War, various bills were filed in France proposing that at least some women be granted the right to vote in reward for their contribution to the nation's victory. Then, on May 8, 1919, in an outburst of generosity, the Chamber of Deputies answered Aristide Briand's call by passing a bill granting women the right to vote without restriction. Before this bill could became law, however, it required approval of the Senate, where debate dragged on until the measure was finally rejected on November 7, 1922. Many politicians feared that the female vote would allow the Catholic Church to exercise an occult political influence through its female parishioners, who far outnumbered men among the faithful. This, coupled with the senators' profound conservatism and latent misogyny, led to a stalemate, and bills passed by the Chamber were similarly rejected by the Senate in 1925, 1932, and 1935. Feminists, though unanimously in favor of woman's suffrage, were not numerous enough to constitute an effective pressure group, even with the support of Catholic women belonging to the Union Nationale pour le Vote des Femmes (1925) and despite the spectacular efforts of Louise Weiss, founder of *La Femme Nouvelle* (1934) and a candidate for municipal office in Montrouge in 1935. Most women took only a moderate interest in this reform, much to the disappointment of Louise Weiss herself: "Peasant women stood with mouths agape when I spoke to them about the vote. Working women laughed, shop women shrugged their shoulders, and upper-class ladies turned away in horror."[30]

Even with the right to vote, it was difficult for women to participate in public life. In Great Britain only one woman held elective office in 1918, eight in 1923, and fourteen in 1929. Women played only a very small role in the Liberal and Conservative parties. In the Labour Party, which included a Woman's Section, they enjoyed somewhat more influence, but the battles the group waged were more feminine than socialist or feminist—so much so that it became known as the "married women's section." Labour Party women fought to reduce the child mortality rate by calling for cafeterias and free milk in schools. They championed not their own rights but the rights of their children by advocating compulsory schooling until age sixteen. And they called for welfare payments to needy families despite reservations elsewhere in the party, many of whose members saw welfare as a pretext for holding down wages. The number of active female party members remained small, and it was difficult to persuade the male majority to accept their views. In France, women in the reconstituted SFIO (Socialist Party) faced a similar situation. Female membership held steady at about 3 percent. The Groupe des Femmes Socialistes, revived in May 1922, claimed no more than a thousand members (about the same number as in 1914) throughout the 1930s, at a time when overall SFIO membership rose to 125,000. The Groupe des Femmes was a total failure, as none of the positions debated among its members attracted the slightest support from other elements within the party. Hence it should come as no surprise that the Popular Front government failed to grant women the right to vote; Prime Minister Léon Blum limited himself to the symbolic gesture of appointing three women as undersecretaries of state. The fate of women in the Communist Party (roughly one-tenth of the membership) was scarcely more enviable. The party championed the cause of women workers, exploited both as women and as proletarians, but it looked to the coming revolution to eliminate sexual inequalities, which it saw as the fruit of capitalism rather than of male chauvinism among workers and employers alike. Yet female Communists aligned themselves with other women by supporting the right of women to regulate births and calling for abolition of the *lois scélérates*. After 1934, however, they were obliged to abandon those positions, since the new Soviet policy on the family obliged Communists everywhere to extol motherhood and family and condemn birth control and abortion. Thus women failed to find encouragement and support in the parties theoretically most receptive to the idea of sexual equality. One reason for this lack of support, however, was that few women were party members.

The same problem hindered women in the trade unions, although the percentage of female membership in the unions was higher than in the parties. In France the number of women holding union cards rose from 39,000 in 1900 to 239,000 in 1920, or one woman for every seven men. In Great Britain, where unions were numerous and powerful, more than a million women (one-sixth of the total membership) had joined up by 1921; this figure represented about one out of five female workers. In the 1930s, however, female union membership declined to 750,000. Men gained dominance in the process of amalgamation, that is, the merger of previously separate men's and women's unions in the same branch of industry. Two seats on the board of the Trades Union Congress were reserved for women, and at one point Margaret Bondfield even chaired the group. As a result, the specific demands of women were overwhelmed by the needs of the union movement as a whole, and the maverick behavior for which women's unions had once been noted—wildcat strikes, for instance—was ended.

French women had difficulty making their views heard and getting union leaders to take their problems seriously. Women accounted for only a third of the membership of the Fédération Unitaire de l'Enseignement, a leftist teachers' union, even though female teachers had enjoyed salaries equivalent to those of men since before the war; women were also underrepresented in the union's *départemental* branch offices.[31] Women were often shunted into administrative posts such as union treasurer rather than assuming policymaking positions: only 7 to 18 percent of the union's secretaries were women. But careful research has shown that women often excluded themselves by remaining silent at union meetings. Their reserve reflected their upbringing, so much so that feminine timidity was considered not merely proper but "natural." Once women had the opportunity to acquire oratorical skills through participation in small youth and women's groups, they learned to overcome this handicap, thereby increasing their chance of being recognized as fit to assume policymaking responsibility. At this stage barriers began to crumble, and one woman, Marie Guillot, even became secretary general of the union. Bear in mind, too, that family responsibilities prevented many women from attending meetings. The leading female activists were either single or married to male union members willing to share the housework. The obstacles that prevented women from moving ahead were rooted in the family as well as in their upbringing, a situation which makes it difficult to isolate private from public life.

Between the wars, moreover, feminism was on the defensive. In England the suffragist movement, having achieved its goal, disintegrated. Some suffragists such as Pankhurst supported the

Tories, while others backed the Liberals. The most progressive former suffragists sought to broaden their critique to encompass all of social life, but they were in the minority. Some feminists turned their attention to more concrete objectives. The former Communist, now Labourite, Stella Browne, for example, worked for the legalization of birth control and abortion. In France, the success of the Russian Revolution inspired a brief proliferation of feminist groups and publications in the immediate postwar period, but the movement rapidly lost steam. *La Voix des femmes* was forced to cease publication. The feminist groups within the Fédération Unitaire de l'Enseignement dissolved when, in the hour of danger, women teachers felt that it was more important to join the struggle against fascism than to continue to fight for sexual equality. Moderate feminists, typified by the Ligue Française pour le Droit des Femmes, favored a gradualist policy that emphasized the right to vote and equal pay for equal work. Still more conservative women supported the pronatalist, moralistic views of certain politicians, thereby helping to ensure that women would remain confined within traditional roles and receive no concessions from the government.

Women thus continued to play a very small role in public life. Although women's wages still lagged behind men's in many areas, the right to work proved less controversial than the right to speak out on political issues. Women made progress toward gaining control over their bodies and property, but family roles continued to be sex-defined, especially in the bourgeoisie in both countries and in the English working class. Some husbands continued to behave as masters, and some women still appeared to be docile and devoted wives, but more often than not the reality fell somewhere between the classic stereotype and scandalous innovation. The typical woman of the interwar period was neither Ophelia nor the bachelor girl, neither a traditional housewife nor a bluestocking; she had begun to throw off the yoke of nature and to claim her rights as a married woman even while sacrificing herself, whether to motherhood or to modernity. Thus the period was one of contradictory tendencies, a complex time of transition that many contemporaries analyzed poorly.

TRANSLATED FROM THE FRENCH BY ARTHUR GOLDHAMMER

4

How Mussolini Ruled Italian Women

Victoria de Grazia

TWO QUESTIONS NEED to be addressed to explain the condition of Italian women under Mussolini's dictatorship. First, what was specifically fascist about the oppression of women in interwar Italy? Second, what did the regime's treatment of women reveal more generally about the nature of fascist rule? My argument here, in brief, is that Mussolini's dictatorship constituted a special and distinctive episode of patriarchal rule. Fascist patriarchy took as axiomatic that men and women were different by nature. It then politicized this difference to the advantage of male Italians and built it into an especially repressive, comprehensive, and unprecedented system for defining female citizenship and governing women's sexuality, wage labor, and social participation. In the end, this system was as integral to the dictatorship's strategies of state-building as were its corporatist regulation of labor, its autarchic economic policies, and its warmongering. Antifeminist outlooks were as much a part of fascist beliefs as its virulent antiliberalism, racism, and militarism.

Accordingly, I have sought to distinguish fascism's system of gender relations from that of "liberal patriarchy," as the inegalitarian order prevailing in nineteenth-century Western societies has sometimes been called. Likewise, it should be distinguished from so-called social patriarchy, a term coined to highlight women's second-class citizenship status in post–World War II capitalist welfare states, the main progenitor of which was Swedish social democracy of the 1930s.[1] By the same token, fascist practices toward women bear enough similarities to those under the Nazi dictatorship to justify analyzing them in a common light. Although it is useful to examine the condition of women within the context of a particular national history at a particular moment in time, the systemic approach I am suggesting here moves from the premise that certain changes in gender relations—both for the better, like greater educational access or companionate relations, and for the worse, like employment biases, familistic outlooks, and state regulation of sexuality—should not be ascribed solely to particular regime policies and actions; the processes at work are in reality far more complex, widespread, and enduring. If we try to explain fascist gender politics by what the dictatorship claimed to be doing, we are at a loss to grasp how fascism could at once be for and against the family, modernize female roles while claiming to restore women to "home and hearth," or promote birthrates but also inhibit them. If, however, we place the study of women under Mussolini's rule in the context of the changing strategies of state-building amidst the general crisis of European statecraft in the interwar era, we are better able to explain the paradoxes of a new gender-based system of exploitation as well as the contradictory responses it elicited among Italian women.[2]

Recasting Gender Relations

Fascist sexual politics was in many respects the peculiar Italian response to the collapse during the Great War, and its aftermath of what the British political economist John Maynard Keynes characterized in 1919 as the Victorian model of capitalist accumulation.[3] Based on a policy of minimizing consumption and restricting the exercise of citizenship rights and reinforced by an ideology of scarcity, pre–World War I European liberalism had progressed by demanding of its subjects strict social discipline and puritanical mores. The great emancipatory movement among European women (already evident in the prewar suffrage movements), with its deep well-springs in the demographic revolution and spread of liberal ideas in the mid-nineteenth century, became irreversible once millions of women were mobilized in wartime economies. Thereafter many working women moved into white-collar labor, and most urban dwellers partook in the manifestly freer sexual and social customs associated with mass culture. At the same time as governments contended with these emancipatory pressures, they were confronted with the complex concerns which policy makers addressed under the rubric of the "population problem."[4] These ran the gamut from fertility decline and what social workers now call "problem families," to male-female job competition and unpredictable consumer behaviors. Practically all of these issues bore on the multiplicity of the sometimes incompatible roles women performed in contemporary society—as mothers, wives, citizens, workers, consumers, and clients of government social services. The proposed solutions inevitably placed policy makers before a conundrum summed up in the Swedish sociologist and social reformer Alva Myrdal's incisive phrase, namely, "One sex [is] a social problem."[5]

In the interwar decades all Western governments were presented with a double challenge: democratization on the one hand, the "population question" on the other. They responded at first by sanctioning female suffrage, and then by developing new public discourses about women, legislating about their place in the labor market, and recodifying family policies. A restructuring of gender relations thus went hand in hand with what Charles Maier characterized as the "recasting" of economic and political institutions to secure conservative interests in the face of economic uncertainty and the democratization of public life.[6] The degree to which this restructuring took on an authoritarian or democratic cast, repressed labor or coopted it, allowed women to progress or was outright antifeminist, varied according to the character of the class coalitions in power and their stands on broad issues of social welfare and economic redistribution. The eventual outcome of the restructuring determined significant aspects of women's first experience of the state-interventionist capitalism emerging in the 1930s.

In fascist Italy government addressed the double issue of female emancipation and population politics by exploiting long-standing traditions of mercantilist thinking. These traditions had acquired renewed currency from the 1870s onward as European elites, reacting to heightened international competition and growing class conflicts, sought to protect domestic markets from foreign goods and build up export capacity. Like their eighteenth-century progenitors who theorized the need for a "multitude of laborious poor," neo-mercantilists worried about achieving the optimum population size to supply cheap labor, satisfy military needs, and keep up home demand.[7] By the turn of the twentieth century these concerns became complicated by declining fertility rates, ethnic minorities whose racial characteristics and nationalist strivings allegedly undermined national/state identity, and internal fertility differentials, which threatened that the so-called least-fit would multiply while the elites dwindled away. By the eve of the Great War, a new biological politics was emerging in connection with the population question. Policy makers imbued with social Darwinist notions of life as a deadly struggle for existence proposed to shape eugenicist and social welfare programs to the ends of state policy. These ends were basically twofold: to buttress declining power in the international field and to secure control over home populations. Insofar as ethnic diversity and female emancipation were identified as obstacles, biological politics was easily infused with antifeminism and anti-Semitism.

Italian fascism's positions on the population question, which might be characterized as integrally authoritarian and antifeminist, may be clarified by contrasting them with what contemporary observers saw as their opposite, namely, Swedish population policy. This was formulated in 1937, after the social democrats won the 1932 elections and established the Royal Commission on the Swedish Population Problem in 1935, consolidated their majority in both houses of parliament in 1936, and thus opened the way for the national legislature's "mothers and babies session" the following year. Swedish social democracy was at least as conscious as the fascist elite of the importance of population to maintaining state power, since Sweden counted just 6.2 million inhabitants in 1933. To overcome the "crisis" caused by declining fertility rates, the Swedish state was just as willing as Italy to overrule the distinctions between public and private power, family and governmental authority, and individual and state interests, which had guided liberal conceptions of politics and gender relations in the nineteenth century.

Beyond that, there was little similarity. The Swedish social democrats, backed by a broad-based liberal coalition that included farmers and feminists as well as labor, tied the goal of population fitness to a broad program of social and economic reform. Swedish population politics, as its chief architects Gunnar and Alva Myrdal characterized it, had as its primary goal a fit, stable population. This meant finding noncoercive ways "to get a people to abstain from not reproducing itself."[8] Policy presumed a "mild form of nationalism," as was consistent with Sweden's openness to the international economy. However, reforms were the main way to persuade Swedes that their private interests were being safeguarded even as the public welfare was being pursued. With the same spirit of redistributive justice that inspired higher wages and farm protection, the government socialized certain important aspects of consumption to equalize the burdens of bringing up children. The chief provisions were services in kind, from low-cost housing to free school luncheons. The state also affirmed its interest in replacing patriarchal family structures with more rational, efficient, and equitable means of helping women to balance weighty and sometimes incompatible burdens as wives, mothers, workers, and citizens. Social policy thus implied that women still bore the main burden for childbearing and -rearing. The point was to make the choice to have children less arbitrary and raising them less onerous. Hence women were encouraged to work as well as have children, abortion was legalized, and birth control and sex education were widely promoted on the grounds that births be neither "undesired" nor "undesirable."[9]

By contrast, fascist Italy cast the population issue in neo-mercantilist terms, and the dictatorship justified its pronatalist "battles" in terms of national salvation. This outlook bore immediate consequences for women. The state proclaimed that it was the sole arbiter of fitness. In principle, women had no say in decisions regarding childbearing. Indeed, female subjects were presumed to be antagonists of the state: whether or not they themselves took the decision to limit family size, they were regarded as the ones responsible for acting on the family's interest in doing so. Economic policy designed to limit consumption in order to cut imports and promote exports, beyond aggravating social inequalities, may actually have increased economic deterrents to childbearing as well as heightened fertility differentials between urban and rural areas. Rejecting reforms to reduce such disincentives, fascism sought to enforce childbearing by banning abortion, the sale of contraceptive devices, and sexual education. At the same time, the fascist state favored men over women in the family structure, the labor market, the political system, and society at large. This was accomplished by maneuvering the vast machinery of political and social control that made it possible in the first place to shift the burden of economic growth to the least advantaged members of society.

The Legacy of Liberal Patriarchy

Whereas Swedish social democracy's progressive positions were linked to strong traditions of liberal feminism, a well-integrated agricultural sector, and a relatively homogeneous civil culture and sexual custom, fascist patriarchalism had its roots in the weakness of newly unified Italy's liberalism and the unsettled public opinion of a belatedly and very unevenly industrializing society. The Italian women's movement emerged around the turn of the century but remained small and divided, with its middle-class and Catholic components staying clear of the public piazza, applying themselves to good works on behalf of poor women and children. Yet the "woman question" loomed large nonetheless. In part this was because the liberal elites had moved in a desultory way to integrate Italian men into a national society following Italy's patched-together unification in 1859. At the turn of the century, class, regional, and civic-cultural splits were, if anything, greater than a half-century before, aggravated not only by the lagging development of the Italian South, but also by the patent inequality of tax levies, a stunted public education system, and the postponement until 1912 of any significant suffrage reform. The "woman question" was further complicated by overlapping with the "social question"; Italian socialism, broad-based and militant, gathered a big following among working women and frustrated middle-class reformers. Moreover, Italian Catholicism was unabatingly hostile to the liberal system until 1904. Its antimodernist culture, intolerant of individualist philosophies generally, was hostile to female emancipation. Yet the Church was paternalistically protective toward women and championed itself as the chief guardian of family values.

More specifically, the liberal state's treatment of women presented certain anomalies that the fascist government would later exploit. The liberal government was laissez-faire to an unusual degree, a feature that Mussolini's propagandists later denounced to legitimate fascism's claim to be a force for reform. The 1865

Pisanelli Law was a step backward with respect to the family legislation governing Austrian Italy. Like other family codes of Napoleonic inspiration, it affirmed the state's interest in the family by reinforcing the authority of male heads of household. Women were debarred from most commercial and legal acts without their husbands' consent, prevented from acting as children's guardians, and even excluded from the "family councils" that until 1942 were legally empowered, if the father was dead or incapacitated, to dispose of collective family patrimonies, inheritance, and dowry settlement. Other family laws displayed Italian liberalism's haphazard policy. In the interest of keeping family property intact, the state disinherited the offspring of adulterous and incestuous unions, made adultery a crime for women only, and prohibited all forms of paternity suits. At the same time, liberal Italy recognized only civil marriages, though every year thousands of Italian marriages were contracted with religious rites or without any official imprimatur. The offspring of such marriages were illegitimate in the eyes of government.[10]

By 1900 governments elsewhere were likewise becoming more paternalistic, passing reforms to protect females and children if only to safeguard male wages and racial fitness. In Italy as much as 30 percent of the industrial workforce was female at the time. Yet no factory laws spoke to the issue of women's work until the Carcano Law was passed in 1902, setting a twelve-hour maximum work day for women and minors and barring women from returning to work for a month after childbirth. Predictably, it was riddled with exceptions and hard to police.

In light of this legacy of neglect, the nascent Italian women's movement—and perhaps women generally—developed an ambivalent, if not antagonistic, relationship toward liberal ideology and institutions. Some groups, the oldest ones, influenced by the egalitarianism of the radical democrat Anna Maria Mozzoni, sympathized with the burgeoning socialist movement and built ties with working-class women. In their view, female emancipation was inconceivable without thoroughgoing political and economic democratization. Other groups, which became more cohesive after 1908, were tied to the Catholic Church; they defended family and other conservative values along with women's right to organize themselves as a public presence. After 1900 increasing numbers of middle-class women were involved in so-called practical feminism.[11] Their main organizational reference point was the National

Council of Italian Women (Consiglio Nazionale delle Donne Italiane) founded in 1903. Unlike Anglo-American feminists, who emphasized equal rights, Italian bourgeois feminists little trusted market forces or the suffrage to deliver emancipation. Self-abnegating, with the familistic outlooks and patriotic fervor typical of Italy's middle classes, they regarded self-sacrifice in philanthropic endeavors as a preliminary to being granted citizenship rights. Chary of mass politics, they sought social and state recognition of women's special maternal mission in modern society. Inevitably, many proved susceptible to Mussolini's resounding claims that this had been achieved in the fascist epoch.

That this small, fragmented, and rarely militant feminist movement should have incited widespread antagonism would be inexplicable without some further remarks on liberal Italy's weak national civic culture. Emancipated female behaviors were highly conspicuous in this half-industrial, half-rural society, which, in addition to modern industrial and commercial centers like Milan or Turin, still had over 50 percent of the population living off agricultural pursuits. The liberal elites themselves abetted antifeminist attitudes, not least of all by denying women the vote. In addition, they showed little appreciation of the social services rendered by women who, guided by their belief that their "maternal sensibility" was indispensable to "temper and complete the political order," sought to cure social ills and calm working-class unrest by means of philanthropic undertakings. Failing to take action in this domain themselves, the liberal elites missed the opportunity to recognize women's volunteer work and did not have the vision to subject working-class mutualism and Catholic charity to central government authority. Conversely, this was one opportunity that the fascists did not fail to seize. In the name of their "national reconstruction," they excoriated liberal "neglect," imposed "discipline" on local associations, and mobilized tens of thousands of middle-class women volunteers in fascist associations.

Fascism was also able to tap the exasperated masculinism of Italian men. A whole study could be devoted to the social-psychological origins of the virilist posturing of Italian intellectuals after the turn of the century and to its myriad manifestations—from the erotic sensibility of the decadentist writer Gabriele D'Annunzio and the antifeminist metaphor of the influential Florentine literary review, *La Voce,* to the Futurist poet Filippo Marinetti's notorious protestations of "scorn for women" *(disprezzo per la donna)*. In Italy, mere "latin" sexism was apparently aggravated both by male frustration at being left out of the narrowly based liberal "gerontocracy" and embarrassment at Italy's modest international status at a time when male honor was staked on the outcome of imperialist exploits. Fears of demographic exhaustion added another element, though Italian fertility rates of thirty per thousand were the highest in Europe after Spain and Romania. Apparently, anxieties about sexual disorder and racial decline were aggravated by other factors: the drain on Italian manhood caused by emigration (500,000 persons departed annually on the eve of the Great War); the importance attributed to sheer numbers of hands in a capital-scarce economic environment; the startling diversity of sexual behaviors in such an unevenly developing society; and finally, the pervasive influence of positivist scientific hypotheses and Catholic doctrines in matters regarding fertility.[12]

By the eve of war, what we might call a neo-paternalistic politics was emerging in Italy. Starting around 1910, moral zealots launched campaigns against the degeneration of family life, joining forces with Catholic leagues to blame declining birthrates on urbanization, women's emancipation, and radically inspired neo-Malthusian practices. Liberal elites, although ever reluctant to intervene in social policy, were inclined to subscribe to what the prescient liberal social theorist Vilfredo Pareto denounced as the "virtuist" myths of moral reformers, hence to abandon laissez-faire and anticlerical principles in order to legislate on sexual norms.[13] With Marinetti's Futurist Manifesto of 1909, modernist culture too rallied: "We want to tear down museums and libraries, to fight against moralism, feminism, and all the opportunist and utilitarian forms of cowardice."[14]

This neo-paternalistic attitude hardly added up to a new program of ruling women, however. Nor did it lay out any clear position on the population issue, which from the mid-1920s onward would provide the intellectual and political framework within which an antifeminist program would be conceptualized and implemented. Rather, what bears emphasis here is that the fascist regime inherited a legacy of outlooks and institutions related to the "woman question." Some positions, like those of the Church, would at once support the regime and compete with it. Others, such as demographic engineering and racial attitudes, fascism freely exploited in pursuit of its own strategies of state-building. Above all, the regime was able to decry liberalism's "agnosticism" as regards the family, children, and maternity to stake its claim as a pioneering force. Not least of all, the Duce exploited the patriotic ardor, spirit of self-sacrifice, and pent-up desire for recognition on the part of many middle-class women, including numerous former feminists.

The Mainsprings of Fascist Sexual Politics

To argue that Mussolini's dictatorship developed a distinctive system for ruling women is not to say that there was any ready-made program when the Duce marched on Rome in 1922. Italian fascism was a chameleon-like movement, cuing its colors to potential allies and the shifting political terrain of the first postwar years. Thus, in 1919, the new-born movement had embraced the positions of Futurist intellectuals, ready to flout conventional morality by supporting divorce and suppressing the bourgeois family. That year too, its opportunistic populist voice spoke out in favor of giving women the vote. However, these positions were quickly abandoned in the face of the veterans' movement opposing it, fascism's own syndicalist troops' antipathy toward women working, and the rigid Catholic-rural antifeminism of landed proprietors who in 1920–21 backed the black-shirted *squadristi* assaults on the socialist leagues and cooperatives. After 1923, fascism's misogyny was reinforced by the hard-faced authoritarianism of Mussolini's allies in the Nationalist party. They were the ones to hold up the yardstick of the state interest to which all particularisms were to be subordinated; and their vision of a strong and expert state rallied criminal anthropologists, social hygienists, medical doctors, child protection advocates, and other reformers who, long frustrated by liberal inaction, hoped to breathe life into their projects for improving the Italian "stock" *(stirpe)*. After the Concordat with the Vatican in 1929, Church institutions and Catholic religious traditions and personnel lent themselves to reinforcing fascist antifeminism.

Mussolini's dictatorship was able to develop an overriding politics toward women in a society so unevenly developed thanks to fascism's doctrinal eclecticism. The Duce himself self-consciously mouthed a commonplace when he advised against discussing "whether woman was better or worse; let's just say she's different"; that reasoning could justify practically any position, in this case, either giving women the vote or denying it to them.[15] Fascist views on women thus ran the gamut: from Mussolini's rural-rooted misogyny (women were angels or devils, "born to keep house, bear children, and plant horns")[16] to the philosopher Gentile's refined neo-Hegelian doctrine of complementary essences (women, mired in petty details—"infinite nature," the "primordial principle"—were incapable of transcendence).[17] Rude positivist polemic denounced female biological inferiority, while a few pragmatists, such as fascism's leading technocrat Giuseppe Bottai, guardedly advocated female equality, reasoning that a new fascist elite needed worthy female companions and mothers to their children.[18] A huge gap thus separated, say, the Catholic zealot Amadeo Balzari, who in 1927 launched a national campaign to "moralize" shameful female dress, from the ex-Futurist Umberto Notari, a well-known Milan-based journalist and editor whose titillating tales, for example, *La donna tipo tre* (1928) (neither "courtesan" nor "mother-wife"), both parodied and promoted Italy's "new woman."[19] Likewise, self-styled "Latin feminists" such as the brilliant Teresa Labriola—who turned ideological somersaults to reconcile fascism and feminism—were far distant from the smug officials whose antifemale witticisms circulated in Roman salons. What they shared, however, was the belief that state power should be deployed to deal resolutely with private and ethical, as well as political and economic issues. In the interest of a politics of national aggrandizement, they overlooked their diverse estimates of female difference and the implications these had in the realm of policy.

Ultimately, however, the very actions which the fascist regime took to consolidate itself in power determined the overall pattern of how females were treated in interwar Italian society. In politics, fascism passed from being a movement in opposition to becoming a one-party government by the mid-1920s, and from being an authoritarian regime with shallow roots in civil society to forming a mass-based state in the 1930s. In economic policy, the dictatorship passed from laissez-faire to protectionist policies in the second half of the 1920s. In the wake of the Depression and the Ethiopian War in 1936, it pursued full-fledged autarchy. This evolution was premised on and accompanied the confirmation of the dictatorship's social alliances with conservative Italy, meaning big business and large landed proprietors, the monarchy, the military, and the

Catholic Church. In turn, the regime subjected the fascist party (PNF) to the state bureaucracy. It then used the PNF as a transmission belt to reach out to social groups—workers, peasants, and small owners—whose interests had been either ignored or systematically violated in the economic realm, integrating them into a broad if superficial political consensus.[20]

In order to secure this conservative alliance, the dictatorship put unremitting pressure on wages and consumption. As development proceeded in the 1930s, Italy's dualistic character was accentuated. At one extreme, there was its inefficient agriculture and broad stratum of small businesses, the precarious status of which was belied by official paeans to pro-rural ideologies; at the other, there was a highly concentrated industrial sector, bailed out by state aid and stimulated by rearmament after 1933. By the mid-1930s, a little over 10 percent of the national income and as much as a third of government income was spent on the armed forces. Meanwhile, labor's share of the national income continued to shrink. One indicator of fascism's "low-wage" economy was that in 1938 real incomes for industrial workers were still 3 percent short of their 1929 level, and 26 percent lower than their postwar peak in 1921. As late as 1938, over half of the average family's income was spent on food (compared to 25 percent in the United States). All told, Italy was the only industrialized country in which wages maintained a downward trend from the very start of the 1920s through the outbreak of World War II. The standard of living as measured by food budgets, purchase of consumer durables, and availability of public services put Italy well behind other industrialized nations.

These policies inevitably had far-reaching consequences for Italian women, in particular for the majority who were working-class and peasant. To pursue its population politics, fascism sought to establish more control over female bodies, especially female reproductive functions. At the same, it sought to conserve older patriarchal notions of family and paternal authority. To sustain pressure on wages and consumption, the dictatorship exploited household economic resources deliberately and to an unusual degree for a country well advanced on the path of industrialization. Consequently, it demanded that women act as careful consumers, efficient household managers, and astute clients to squeeze services out of a stinting welfare system, in addition to being part-time and often concealed wage earners to round out family incomes.

To curb the use of cheap female labor in the face of high male unemployment while maintaining Italian industry's reserve force of low-cost workers, the regime devised an elaborate system of protections and prohibitions around the exploitation of female labor. Finally, to make women responsive to the increasingly complex claims on them, as well as to exploit their pent-up desire to identify with and serve the national community, the regime walked the thin line between modernity and emancipation. By the mid-1930s it had developed mass organizations that responded to women's, especially bourgeois and young women's, desire for social participation, yet it discouraged the female solidarity, individualist values, and sense of autonomy promoted by the emancipationist networks of the liberal era.

Reproductive Politics

Fascism's attack on reproductive freedoms is perhaps the most familiar aspect of its sexual politics. In his notorious Ascension Day speech on May 26, 1927, Mussolini put policies in "defense of the race" at the very heart of fascist domestic goals; the Duce's aim by mid-century was a population of 60 million for a nation that at the time had 40. To justify this ambition, Mussolini referred to two lines of reasoning—and we can infer a third that was at least as important, namely, to reestablish or "normalize" male-female differences which had been turned topsy-turvy by the war. The first was mercantilist, in that it stressed the need for sheer quantities of people as cheap labor. The other logic more typically belonged to a nation embarked on imperialist expansion; Italy's declining population growth, a trend accelerating in the 1920s and ever more visible as the government improved population survey techniques, frustrated its leaders' expansionist ambitions. If Italy didn't become an empire, the Duce liked to repeat, it would certainly become a colony.

In its quest for "births, more births," the dictatorship vacillated between reforms and repression, exhortation to individual initiative and concrete state incentives. ONMI, the national service for infants' and mothers' welfare, best represents the reformist side. Founded on December 10, 1925, with enthusiastic support from Catholics, nationalists, and liberals, its main focus was women and children who had fallen outside the normal family structure.

Other reformist measures included tax exemptions for fathers of big families, state-provided maternity leaves and insurance, birth and marriage loans, and family allocations to salaried and wage earners. Repressive measures included the treatment of abortion as a crime of state, a ban on birth control, censorship of sex education, and a special tax levy against bachelors. In addition to these we might include career promotion for fathers of big families, a measure that, in view of high unemployment rates, was punitive toward women as well as toward the "morbidly egotistical" bachelors and childless married man.

Unlike Nazi Germany, fascist Italy swore off the negative eugenic measures. This is not to say that the ideology was not eugenicist. But fascist population engineering originated in a far different conception of race, and it advocated a different mechanism of racial selection. Unlike Germany, Italy never had a minorities problem to speak of, at least not until the Duce founded Italy's African empire with the conquest of Ethiopia in 1936 (soon thereafter it passed its first laws against racial miscegenation). Nor did Italian racial theorists fear the prolific breeding of the lower orders. Quite the contrary. They celebrated "differential fertility," and were skeptical of the pseudo-scientificity of Anglo-American and later Nazi biological selection measures. Fascism's "revolution of youth," as theorized by Italy's leading population statistician Corrado Gini, promised to tap the "sole reservoir of vital energies," namely the countryside with "its low and prolific classes, on whose changing internal composition and mixing depended the revitalization of the nation."[21] These positions were reinforced by the Catholic Church's stern admonitions against "zootechnics applied to the human species."[22] Inspired by an outlook that might be characterized one part Malthusian laissez-faire pessimism (population would outstrip resources), one part Darwinian optimism (the fittest would survive), the regime thus mostly overlooked, but at times even publicly applauded, the evident correlations its zealous demographers found between so-called numerous families and poverty, overcrowding, malnourishment, and illiteracy.

To say that fascist policy was less physically intrusive than Nazi eugenics is not to argue that it weighed less on women, especially poor women. Fascist population politics evolved a double face. On the one hand, it was strongly normative. Experts regarded women as "badly prepared" for their maternal mission, "weak and imperfect in their generative apparatuses," and thus prone to produce "abnormal" offspring.[23] The whole thrust of state policy was thus to disseminate modernized models of child-bearing and infant care. At the same time, fascist eugenics justified a hands-off policy, at least in the face of its poorest citizens. After all, reforms were not just costly but perhaps even counterproductive if the goal was more births. True, a higher standard of living might prompt the clerk's family to have a second child, a consideration that justified the dictatorship's solicitous treatment of the salaried middle class. The same improvements would only encourage excessive expectations in peasant families, causing them too to adopt the calculating outlooks that led urban families to limit births.

The consequences of this Janus-faced policy were terribly harsh. Italian women, especially urban working-class women, wanted fewer children. "One child, professor, one child is all we want," as numerous Turinese women confided to Dr. Maccone, a leading pediatrician.[24] To achieve this goal, they practiced family planning as best they could, mainly by recourse to abortion. In spite of draconian bans, this became the most widespread form of family planning by the late 1930s.[25] Since abortions were all back-street, whether performed by medical professionals or neighborhood *comare*, women ran high risks of disabling infection, permanent physical damage, and death. Moreover, the timing of the prohibition of birth control, coming at the very moment that information was once more spreading after several centuries of Counter-Reformation censorship, made fascism's anti-Malthusian campaigns especially coercive. In rural areas especially they reinforced religiously sanctioned fatalism about controlling reproductive processes. But even Northern working class girls recalled "almost with rancor" *(quasi con rancore)* that they have been left ignorant "like beasts" *(come le bestie)* about the facts of life. New state, professional, and market models set higher social standards for bearing and raising children, and they stigmatized, if not actually suppressed, traditional birthing and child-rearing practices. Yet they failed to provide the social as well as economic wherewithal to enable women to respond to the new standards without making a significant personal sacrifice. Infant mortality declined by 20 percent, from 128 per thousand in 1922 to 102 per thousand in 1940, but that was about equal to the pace of the preceding two decades, and still put infant mortality in Italy at 25 percent higher than France or Germany.[26] In general, fascist maternity was particularly labor-intensive. Not by chance, the words *sacrifice* and *stinting* run like a leitmotif through female accounts of maternity and motherhood during the 1930s.

The Family as Fortress of the State

Fascist family policies were similarly shaped by the dictatorship's unremitting claims on individual household resources. Ideologues complained about the crisis of the Italian family, its shrinking size, the alleged loss of authority by the father, the housewife's malaise, and the recalcitrance of children. However, Italian family size, though shrinking from an average of 4.7 members to 4.3 between the census of 1921 and that of 1936, was still large; a special census estimated that at least two million of Italy's 9.3 million families had seven or more living children in 1928. Nearly half of all families still lived in small towns under 10,000, and 38 percent drew a major part of their livelihoods from agriculture. Auto-consumption, meaning the total sums of goods and services generated by family enterprises and not passing through the market, was estimated at 30 percent.[27] In any case, the dictatorship seemed to be confident that Italian family ties were strong enough to withstand the pressures that resulted as it cut wages, skimmed off small savings for industrial investment and colonial undertakings, and stinted on outlays for public services, housing, and welfare. This pressure became harsher and was more publicized as the dictatorship launched its campaigns on behalf of economic self-sufficiency in the 1930s.

This programmatic exploitation of household resources was especially visible in two policies. The first was ruralization; the second, driving down the wages. The former was especially important to the regime's effort to reduce dependency on foreign food imports, especially wheat, and to deter the flood of peasants into the towns, where they boosted unemployment and welfare rolls and aggravated social unrest. The entire anticity campaign, first mentioned by Mussolini in his Ascension Day speech—when he spoke of the sterilizing influence of urbanism and the need for a return to more rural conditions of life—depended on stretching the resources of the peasant household. Steps taken starting in 1928 to deport the unemployed to their original place of residence and to tighten up on internal migration were accompanied by government support for sharecropping contracts and projects to promote homesteading by granting long-term leases in areas of land reclamation. The net effect was to thrust families into zones of low consumption where they were not covered by social legislation and often bereft of municipal and parish relief. Ruralization was thus a way to exploit the safety net of kin solidarity. It both presumed and enforced family togetherness, the beleaguered head of family drawing on unpaid female and child labor in the home, the fields, and small rural industries. There was no attempt—such as occurred in Nazi Germany—to restore *fidecommessi* or entails to keep property within the family by handing it over to the first-born son; that measure would certainly have required fascism to buck commercial agricultural interests. Instead, the regime favored the revival of a centuries-old form of tenancy, namely, sharecropping, or *mezzadria*. The so-called *vergaro* or *capoccia* was a true patriarch. To bargain with landowners at a time of declining farm prices, he wielded tight control over the labor services of his wife and offspring. Sharecropping families continued to be among the very largest, at an average of 7.35 members each, and the labor of the *massaia,* or head wife, though estimated at only two-thirds that of male kin in the most favorable farm contracts, generally exceeded that of the chief himself. On Tuscan farms in the early 1930s, according to investigaters of the National Institute of Agricultural Economy, the hardworking Giuseppe, Egisto, and Faustino each put in 2,926, 2,834, and 2,487 hours annually, while their wives, Lucia, Virginia, and Maria, respectively, 3,290, 3,001, and 3,655.[28]

The dictatorship's treatment of the "living" or "family" wage demonstrated a similarly exploitative attitude toward the working-class family unit. The notion that a man should be able to maintain wife and dependents on his earnings alone was widely regarded in Italy, as elsewhere, as crucial to building up a stable working-class family life. Before Mussolini's march on Rome, bourgeois reformers had contended as much. Catholics continued to support the notion; Pius XI's 1931 encyclical *Quadrigesimo Anno* reaffirmed Leo XIII's contention in *De Rerum novarum* (1891) that social justice demanded that "the wage paid to the working man be sufficient for the support of himself and his family."[29] By the time the Fascist Grand Council seized on the concept in March 1937 to advance the Duce's demographic policies, the census data spoke clearly enough about how radical economic reforms would have to be to achieve such a goal: as late as 1931, 45 percent or 4,280,000 of Italy's 9.3 million families depended on two or more wage earners.

As it turned out, the allocations eventually devised to supplement family incomes added little to most wages. They were originally conceived in 1934 to help workers with families who had been put on part-time to curb mass layoffs. By mid-July 1937 the allotments, funded by tri-partite contributions from state, employers, and workers, and paid out to heads of household according to the number of their dependents, covered all personnel in private as well as state concerns, agriculture, commerce, and industry. In other countries measures of this kind were vehemently opposed by unions and usually confined to depressed industries like textiles and mining. That fascist Italy was able to enact them across the board reflected the hapless position of organized labor. The fascist family allowance system, in addition to inhibiting the efforts of the fascist unions to bargain for wage increases, played the interests of workers with families against the interests of those who had none. Within families, they favored the male head of household; working wives or unmarried sons or daughters who lived at home were not entitled to benefits. Worst of all, they did not address the main problem, that family survival depended on the work of several members, often including the mother. Fascist ideology notwithstanding, the number of married women working rose, from 12 percent in 1931 to 20.7 percent in 1936. A greater percentage of married women (circa 40 percent) worked in the 1930s in Italy than in any other European country except Sweden. In that social democracy, of course, working women had the benefit of a relatively wide range of protections and services.[30]

In theory, the dictatorship's expanding social insurance and family welfare benefits calmed insecurities that resulted as Italian society became more urbanized and the economy shifted toward mass production, undercutting family solidarities based around rural and urban craft communities. Under Mussolini, propaganda alleged, when a mother bent over to dote on and care for her offspring, the whole nation bent with her. By the late 1930s, there was an alphabet soup of governmental and party agencies to which beleaguered families could turn: INFPS, IPAP, INA, CRI, INFAIL, the OND, and the GIL, to name but a handful, not to mention the already familiar ONMI. Yet the Byzantine complexity of fascist social welfare bureaucracies often aggravated uncertainty rather than allaying it. The whole system was commanded into being by political expediency, and it was grafted onto a millennial legacy of private and semi-private Catholic and municipal charities. To obtain benefits, families had to work kin-linked patronage systems. Consequently, close relatives clung together, and strategies of survival reinforced what regime propagandists sometimes denounced as the "sacro egoismo" of the "famigliuola." At the same time as the fascist dictatorship made the family a more public institution, it unwittingly reinforced the private and "familistic" behaviors commonly associated with Italian civic culture.

These same policies thrust Italian women into new roles in Italian society. In theory, fascism put women back into the home, where, as procreators and nurturers, they contributed to the good functioning of the private sphere. But as the dictatorship put more weight on the family and promoted new models for its conduct, women were compelled to become aware of public responsibilities. Not the least of them was to get children ready for fascist after-school programs and to summer at the party and municipal sun-and-seaside colonies; if the mothers were poor, they became "specialisti della assistenza" to extract state welfare benefits. Moreover, the fascist welfare state relied heavily on female volunteers to implement programs. Upper-class women thus came to play a leading role in defining new norms of family conduct as well as in assisting lower-class women to achieve them. The household operating styles they passed on to petty bourgeois and working-class women and even to rural *massaie* through the homemaker courses, child-rearing classes, and informal get-togethers sponsored by the fascist women's groups were infused with conventional bourgeois notions of respectability and "rational" home management. These could not be achieved without obsessive budgeting, fewer children, and self-absorbed calculations about how to exploit the schools, political organizations, and social services of the regime on behalf of their families. The result was a heightened consciousness of the family's dependency on the state's services. No doubt this encouraged a certain sense of gratitude toward the regime; government propaganda acclaimed the Duce as author of an inordinate number of legislative "firsts." But dependency also prompted awareness of the conflicts between family interests and patriotic duty. "You tell me, professor," a Turinese working woman said to Luigi Maccone, expostulating against the regime's demographic campaigns: "Is it just or humane that we women of the people should have many children, destined for war when they are adults? Oh never! We love our children, we raise them as best we can given our measly means, for ourselves, for an ever better future for them, but not for the Fatherland."[31]

Women at Work

Unlike Swedish social democracy, which, in the interest of its population politics, sought to reconcile women's need to work with their burdens as mothers, fascism theorized a strict division of labor: men produced and were the family providers; women reproduced and maintained the household. Yet fascist officials were also realistic enough to recognize that women worked; according to 1936 census data, 27 percent of the whole workforce was female and about 25 percent of all working-age women were employed. Moreover, sex-typing favored the feminization of white-collar work, and as a result of the Sacchi Law of 1919 women were made eligible for most state jobs, the chief exceptions being posts in the armed forces, the judiciary, and diplomatic careers. Eventually, the dictatorship evolved legislation to deter women from competing with men for work and to protect working mothers. This had an ulterior purpose as well, namely, to prevent women from conceiving paid labor as a stepping stone to emancipation. Whereas work was indispensable to the construction of a strong male identity, female employment, as Mussolini stated, "where not a direct impediment to, distracts from reproduction, foments independence and the accompanying physical-moral styles contrary to birthing."[32] Eventually, the combination of customary restraints and state intervention, operating in an economy with chronic unemployment and relying on the state as employer of last resort, created a general climate that tolerated the employment of women, whose work was carried out under worse conditions than in any other industrial nation.

By the mid-1930s discriminatory measures were manifold. The first sort, normally overlooked, was inherent in the very reorganization of labor in corporatist institutions. Fascist labor law, by barring strikes and centralizing bargaining processes, damaged workers' interests generally and women's particularly. It drove male wages down to levels competitive with women's and minors', pushed unions unable to defend wage levels or control shop-floor conditions to bargain for nonmonetary concessions, such as restrictions on female employment, and favored the best-situated workers, meaning the skilled, the senior, and employees in strategically important sectors. Most of the latter were male. Despite pleas from Regina Terruzzi, Ester Lombardo, Adele Pertici Pontecorvo, and other well-placed fascist loyalists, women were not represented in the corporate hierarchy. At most, there were a half-dozen female consultants, since fewer than two scores of Italian women possessed the prerequisite degree in law or political science to work in the Ministry of the Corporations bureaucracy.

Arguably, fascist party institutions for women offered an alternative to the corporate labor organizations. The *massaie rurali* for peasant women, founded in 1934, and the party section for factory and female home-workers (*Sezione Operaie e Lavoratrici a Domicilio* or SOLD), established in 1938, provided some of the services that the fascist unions offered men, such as courses to improve work skills and guidance on how to obtain social benefits. However, they delivered these with the clear-cut message that fascist "solidarity" meant different things for men and women. Male workers belonged to syndicalist groups and engaged in collective bargaining, whereas women were the beneficiaries of party-run groups and acceded to government benefits. Men were constituents, subject to contracts, and represented by their factory trustees *(fiduciari)*; women were clients, the objects of social work, and their main interlocutors were party-trained social workers *(visitatrici fasciste)*.

The dictatorship's significant innovations in the realm of protectionist legislation constituted a second form of discrimination. By 1938 female wage earners were entitled to a compulsory maternity leave of two months, covered by a birth bonus equal to an average two-month wage, an unpaid leave with the right to return to work of up to seven months, and two feeding periods daily until the child was a year old. The dictatorship also tightened up rules that prohibited night work for all women and dangerous and unhealthy work for minor females aged fifteen to twenty and males under age fifteen. Children under twelve were not allowed to work at all.

These measures dovetailed with the most notorious, if not the most effective kind of discriminatory measure, namely, exclusionary statutes. Since the major emigration outlet, the United States, was cut off in the early 1920s, chronic male unemployment rates worsened. These were further aggravated during the Great Depression. Instead of investing in the government works projects other nations undertook in those years, and fearful perhaps that the industrial rehiring spurred by rearmament would favor women, the government backed contractual limits on female employment in certain trades in 1934. The September 5, 1938, decree law, which set a 10 percent limit on the employment of female personnel in state and private offices, was the most draconian measure of all. It aroused anxious protests from women office workers and was just starting to be implemented in the spring of 1940, when the situation changed and most restrictions on hiring women were removed to facilitate wartime mobilization.

To sum up, fascist labor policy embodied a set of paradoxes. The regime sought to satisfy industry's appetite for cheap labor (which could just as well be appeased by women as by men). Yet it wanted to secure the market for male heads of household. Otherwise, the self-esteem of jobless men was at risk, not to mention the causes of racial fitness and population growth. Fascist legislators claimed to want women out of the workforce. But knowing this would not happen, they set out to protect those who worked in the interest of the race. Building on long-standing sexual biases in the labor market, as well as on the gender equalities which arose as Italian workers were subjected to *inquadramento* in the corporate order, the dictatorship passed protective laws, propagated discriminatory attitudes, and enacted statutes of exclusion. These interacted with labor market trends to give Italy's workforce a peculiar gender profile. The first effect was to preserve high-prestige, increasingly well-paid state bureaucratic positions for men, reversing the trend toward feminizing office work, at least in central government agencies. State policy also reassured the fascist unions that government was dealing with male unemployment, though little evidence shows that men were hired over women all else being equal, except perhaps in the politically sensitive and dreadfully unhealthful synthetic textiles industry. Moreover, state policy favored the formation of a female labor force that was part-time, intermittent, and off-the-books. The significant increase of servants testifies to this. In interwar Italy they increased from 445,631 in 1921 to 660,725 in 1936, whereas in every other place in industrialized Europe they declined. Even petty bourgeois households relied on domestic help.

Unable to defend their right to work on grounds of sexual

equality, women workers adjusted their aspirations and claims. They pleaded "family necessity" to justify their need to toil, or claimed that their work was simply a temporary expedient or that the jobs they filled were too lowly or typically female to suit men anyway. Professional women who had once allied their interests to those of working-class women, and who were now organized in altogether separate fascists institutions like ANFAL, the National Association of Women Artists and Degree-Holders, reinforced these arguments. They championed the remarkable woman's right to a career—provided it did not conflict with family duties—and they advocated training women for social work, nursing, and teaching, careers that, in addition to being especially suited to female talents, best promised to advance the nation's progress. Insofar as they spoke of career discrimination, they blamed jealous men rather than the fascist system.[33]

Political Organization

The dictatorship's rallying of women in a wide range of party organizations might at first glance appear in conflict with the regime's effort to exclude women from the public sphere. Yet fascism, unlike conservative regimes, grasped that social and gender-differentiated policies of complex societies could not be implemented without the consent of the nation's female as well as male subjects. Indeed, to the very degree that the dictatorship itself aggravated the already sharp social and sexual divisions within Italian society, it was incumbent on the PNF to promote a variety of organizations for women. By the late 1930s, the party had a full complement. These included the *fasci femminili,* mainly for the urban middle classes, the first nucleus of which had been founded in 1920; the *massaie rurali* for peasant women (1934); and the SOLD for the working class (1938), in addition to the *piccole italiane,* the girls' sections of the GUF or university student groups, and the *giovane fasciste.* On the eve of World War II, around 3,180,000 females had membership cards in one or another of the party groups.

Still, the fascist party had initially been so wary of women's emancipation movements that it long postponed sanctioning party organizations for women. The PNF had been frankly hostile to the demands for support of its early female followers, and it rudely quashed the emancipationist hopes of female fascists of the first hour by snubbing, overriding, and in a few cases expelling the founding leaders, most of whom were well-born, educated, northern women.[34] Until the early 1930s membership in Catholic women's groups exceeded those in the *fasci femminili*. The PNF made no plans to train female cadres even on a limited scale until 1931, when it founded the Academy of Orvieto, and not on any significant scale until after 1936. It was only in late 1937 that the PNF finally ordered Fiat 1100s for the fiduciaries of women's sections of the provincial federations. Before that female organizers must have traveled by public transportation. More likely, given the genteel status of many, they were chauffeured about by family drivers.

Mobilizing women on a mass scale commenced only in the early 1930s. The first call to broaden enrollments in the *fasci femminili* was issued at the start of the Depression; upper-class volunteers were to "reach out to the people" by staffing party soup kitchens and welfare offices to feed and otherwise assist the destitute. The next call, at the time of the Ethiopian War, was issued to "women of Italy" to make "every family a fortress of resistance" against the League of Nations' sanctions on Italy.[35] In 1935–1937 membership in fascist women's groups leaped upward. The third call was to convert women's *amore di patria* into a more penetrating and activist *sensibilità nazionale;* this was to prepare women for all-out war, and it collapsed all distinctions between private duty and public service, between personal self-abnegation, family interest, and social sacrifice.

Still, fascism's mobilization of women was paper-thin when compared to that of the Nazis. In Italy there was no "lady Füehrer über alles" like the Nazis' Gertrud Scholtz-Klink, who wielded influence through the NSDAP's women's bureau, was at least listed in the Nazi hierarchy, and boasted of regular colloquia with Hitler. The *fasci femminili* were run by committee under the control of the PNF secretary. Unlike the male organizations, which, by sheer force of numbers and accretions of bureaucratic authority in Rome managed to create a voice of sorts for their constituents, the women's groups were powerless to represent women's issues. Insofar as its well-born leaders had any voice, it was because they were women of wealth and social distinction or had high-placed spouses. Indeed, the regime was inclined to take back from the women's groups the very tasks it originally delegated to them, namely social work. Theorists of the totalitarian state regarded the dispensation of state aid as a mere transitory step on the path toward perfecting a comprehensive social assistance state. The presumption was that this would be guided by actuarial sciences, not sentiment, and staffed by men, not women. In the end female social work leaders, most of whom were onetime practical feminists, defended their right to staff this uniquely important public function. Women alone had the sensitivity to "penetrate the secrets of other souls and grasp their real feelings." Moreover, women had a duty toward society to be active outside of "the narrow confines of the family circle." Finally, they alone could point out the "inevitable lacunae in state action."[36]

Ultimately, the dictatorship's system for organizing Italian women was beset by a paradox. Women's duty was maternity. As *custodi del focolare,* their primary vocation was to procreate, nurture, and manage familial functions in the interest of the state. Yet they could not perform these duties without being aware of societal expectations. Unless they were engaged outside of the household, they were unable to link individual interests with those of the collectivity. In principle, under the Duce, the path out of the household led not to emancipation but to new duties toward family and state; not to autonomy, but to obedience to new masters. Managing the meaning of female political participation was inevitably a complicated task. Women leaders wanted their young charges to combine the "noblest traditions" with "modern times"; they were "creatures at once of virile daring and exquisite femininity."[37] Inevitably, political organization carried the risk of feeding women's emancipationist yearnings. At the very least, it distracted them from their primary duties as "mothers of pioneers and soldiers."

In conclusion, fascist rule of women was the product of an epoch in which population policy was closely identified with national power. Fascism confronted the problem from the perspective of a conservative social coalition and in the context of economic strategies that placed heavy burdens on labor and household resources. Through the labor market and hierarchies of authority within the family unit, the regime shifted as much of the burden as possible to women. At the same time, Mussolini's dictatorship presented a response of sorts to the laissez-faire policies of its liberal predecessors. As in politics proper, so in the realm of sexual politics, the dictatorship used emergency state power to establish a new "moral" order in repudiation of the transgressive gender politics of the liberal era. It recognized female citizenship, though denying it any emancipatory significance. Exploiting the uneasiness of many women—and men as well—with unregulated market forces, rapidly changing fertility and family patterns, and the lack of social protections afforded by the liberal state, it presented itself as protecting family interests while reconciling them with an overriding national identity.

Fascism's rule of women was thus characterized by a complex mix of paternalistic protectionism and benign neglect, positive incentives and mean constraints. Not by chance, fascist Italy's most totalitarian vision of family policy—that formulated by an arrogant but bright young Catholic social scientist, Ferdinando Loffredo—called on the regime to be more reformist *and* more repressive. In his often-cited *Politica della famiglia* (1938), Loffredo appealed for the formation of what might be called a neo-patriarchal family. Father-dominated and mother-centered, its loyalties were to the race rather than to any single regime. To promote it, Italian fascism had to forswear its "Manchesterian" charity handouts, birth bonuses, and demographic prizes, all of which pandered to individualistic logics. It also had to forswear political initiatives that undermined family solidarity, such as the party-promoted *dopolavoro* centers, the youth groups, or the collective celebrations of the fascist Epiphany for children. Real reform meant investing in the family wage, taxing in proportion to family burdens, and supplying family-oriented services in kind, much as was contemplated in contemporary Sweden. Yet these reforms not only would not solve the "social problem" caused by women, but threatened to aggravate it. The very politics that identified the centrality of women to the life of the family, and of the family to the survival of the race and nation, risked being subverted by women. Women were, by nature, most susceptible to individualist philosophies and the most prone to ally them with familistic ideologies. Hence, along with reforms, the state had to exercise total power, first to establish the "spiritual autarchy of the nation," thereby to stanch the corrupting flows of individualist ideologies from abroad, and then to rally public opinion to drive females out of the workforce and public arena. To be effective, reforms needed to go hand in hand with repression: "Women," Loffredo concluded, "must return to be under absolute subjection to man—father or husband; subjection, and therefore spiritual, cultural and economic inferiority."[38]

The very contradictoriness of fascist patriarchy inevitably

opened the door to dissent. White-collar workers petitioned Mussolini, in the wake of the September 5, 1938, Decree Law, not to let fascism turn its back on the "Italian women" who had responded with "zeal" to his demand for sacrifices in the Ethiopian War.[39] Women jurists celebrated the decennial of the Fascist Revolution, but their gloss on fascist family legislation revealed that customs had progressed far more than the new laws admitted.[40] Women novelists, shocked at the misogynist turn of Italian society after 1925, peopled their novels with submissive heroines; with masochistic fervor they avenged themselves on the world while appearing fatalistic about their lot.[41] Working-class women went on "birth strikes" in flagrant violation of the regime's command to proliferate. By the late 1930s growing numbers of female university students, like the young men of the "generation of the Fascist Littoral," seeing the aging regime as obstructing the fulfillment of legitimate career ambitions, began to espouse Marxist and social Catholic ideologies.

What linked together such widely diverse briefs was not so much any shared female sensibility as the fact that all responded to a common system of rule. Over two decades, the dictatorship articulated new notions of female citizenship, yet frustrated their achievement. From the outset, fascism resolved to treat women as a single sector, harnessing their common biological destiny as "mothers of the race" to the end of national state power. However, the fascist state, by aggravating differences of wealth and privilege, also divided women by caste and function. Laws, social services, and propaganda affirmed the paramount importance of motherhood. But poverty, a stingy welfare system, and, finally, joining the war made mothering an exceptionally arduous undertaking. Fascism spoke of the family as a pillar of the state, but strategies of family survival accentuated the antistatist tendencies within Italian society. Mass politics dictated that women participate in political life. But family demands, social customs, and the fascist leaders' own ambivalence about involving women in the public sphere prevented most women from being integrated into the ritualized enthusiasms of fascist mass politics.

All the same, the fascist system deeply conditioned the way that women—and men too—conceived of their destinies, couched their grievances, and saw the consequences of their protests. Italian women were remarkably active in the Resistance. The movement sprang up from Naples northward in the late summer of 1943, after the Grand Council, with King Victor Emmanuel II's support, ousted Mussolini in a palace coup on July 25. It then spread through the north-central regions when Marshal Badoglio's cowardly caretaker government, after signing an armistice with the Allies, fled on September 9, abandoning the country to German occupation. By early 1945, the Resistance had around 250,000 activists. Seventy thousand women were in the Women's Defense Groups and 35,000 were troops in the field. In addition, tens of thousands of other women hid and cared for resistance fighters, succored disbanded Italian and foreign soldiers, assisted Jews on the run from the Nazi-fascist police, and shielded Italian men from conscription for forced labor in Germany. Four thousand six hundred women were arrested, tortured, and tried; 2,750 were deported to German concentration camps, and 623 were executed or killed in battle.[42] Most were working-class and peasant women close to the Communist resistance, their tight-knit communities and long-time family political allegiances reinforcing oppositional networks. But there were also middle-class Catholic women and at least a score of prominent aristocrats, among them King Victor Emmanuel III's daughter-in-law, the Belgian-born, socialist-leaning Maria José.

No doubt the war itself, accompanied after 1943 by the cruel German occupation, was a major stimulus for joining the Resistance. It brought home women's inability to square the circle: namely, to fulfill their patriotic duty, which consisted of delivering up with stoicism their sons and husbands to the manifestly inept fascist war effort while putting bread on the table. After 1943 "female consciousness," to use Temma Kaplan's term, which is to say the sense of collective obligations rooted in women's acceptance of the division of social labor by sex, was joined to the "communal consciousness" that linked women and men in the struggle to liberate Italy from the Nazi-fascists.[43] To trace a specifically feminist inspiration behind women's participation is harder. As a political and social movement on behalf of freedom and social justice, headed by political parties intent on conquering positions of influence to rebuild Italy at the war's end, the Resistance did not encourage critiques of male supremacy. Nor did it try to confront the complex issues of self-identity and gender reconstruction required to challenge the insidious conditioning of two decades of national development under fascist rule. When the time came to celebrate the victories of the Resistance, the contribution of women was by and large "silenced." The new Republic, although admitting formal equality in the labor market and granting women the vote, maintained the penal codes and family laws as well as the myriad social mores and cultural behaviors carried over from the fascist era.

5

Nazi Gender Policies and Women's History

Gisela Bock

THE NATIONAL SOCIALIST movement came to power in January 1933, when the Reich president appointed Hitler as chancellor after the party had gained 33 percent of the votes in November 1932 (this was four percentage points less than it had received in the elections of July 1932). The "Hitler movement" (this was its name on the ballot) had proclaimed it would redeem the German nation from the humiliating conditions imposed on it by the 1919 Treaty of Versailles, and reverse the severe economic crisis of the late 1920s and early 1930s. To achieve these goals it was necessary to do away with Weimar republicanism and establish a true *Volksgemeinschaft* (people's, or ethnic, community). This was a twofold process, calling for the abolition of class conflict and for the renewal of national unity, self-confidence, and power. From the beginning and throughout the election campaigns both objectives were presented not just in the language of traditional nationalism and class cooperation but also in racist terms. Germany was threatened by "racial degeneration," principally caused by the Jews (denounced as capitalists as well as Marxists and Bolshevists), but also by Gypsies, Slavs, Blacks, and other undesirable and "racially inferior" minorities that endangered the

Volkskörper (people's or racial body) in its strength, health, and superiority.

In this imagery gender issues played an important part. The self-perception of the National Socialist movement and regime was explicitly male. Its propaganda described Jewish men as rapists and procurers; more generally, economic and political anti-Semitism was coupled with "sexual anti-Semitism."[1] Women's emancipation was denounced as a product of Jewish influence. (While this was not true, Jewish women had indeed played a major role in the German women's movement, advocating women's access to the professions and social recognition of the "woman's sphere," especially of physical, spiritual, and social motherhood.) The women on the "valuable" side of the racial divide were seen as "mothers of the *Volk*," and those on the other side as "degenerate" and "inferior." "Suitable" women should contribute, as mothers, to the national revival by bearing many children, since a rise in the birthrate was desirable after its long decline. "Unsuitable" women were considered unfit to bear children. In 1930, six years after Hitler had polemicized against Jewish women in *Mein Kampf* and advocated the sterilization of millions of inferior people, one of his "blood and soil" ideologues subdivided the female sex into four categories: women who were to be encouraged to have children; those whose children were not objectionable; those who ought not to have children; and those who should be prevented from having children through sterilization. Before 1933 the National Socialists had not been the only ones to propose such eugenic or race-hygienic distinctions. For instance, one influential Social Democrat had believed that one-third of the German population was "inferior" and unworthy to have children; some women, including a few feminists of the radical wing of the movement, also advocated eugenic reforms, including compulsory sterilization.[2] But National Socialism alone was to convert such ideas and attitudes into a complex, coherent, and systematic practice of race policy, which in the course of only a few years led to unheard-of massacres of "inferior" people.

Even though in the late years of the Weimar Republic and in the early years of the Nazi regime many people, including many Nazi voters, did not give it enough credence, racism—particularly anti-Jewish racism—was at the center of National Socialist policies. Consequently, racism was also at the center of National Socialist gender policies. Because most studies of women in Nazi

Germany do not deal with racism, and most studies of Nazi racism do not deal with women, it is useful to stress that neither was Nazi racism gender-neutral nor were Nazi gender policies race-neutral. And while it is understood that not all women have the same history, the differences in women's history under the Nazi regime were as stark as those between life and death. Of course, National Socialism had many other features besides racism. Nonetheless, racism was at its center, encouraged to penetrate all the dimensions of society. In many other respects the regime proved to be quite flexible and adaptive. It did not hesitate to revise many of its apparently fundamental principles when this seemed opportune, including its policy toward the "valuable" women. Yet it never revised any of its racist principles, including their gender dimensions and policies toward "inferior" women.

From Antinatalism to Genocide: Gender Dimensions of National Socialist Racism

About half of the victims of Nazi racism were women. The laws of 7 and 25 April 1933 expelled, along with political opponents, Jewish men and women from the civil service (including many female teachers; non-Jewish men could be expelled if they were married to Jewish women) and from the universities, where the proportion of women among Jewish students was much higher than among non-Jewish students. Jewish women as well as men became victims of the early anti-Jewish measures, which sought the segregation and exclusion of Jews from political, professional, economic, and cultural life. Equally, Jews of both sexes became victims of race policy when it shifted from political, economic, and cultural discrimination to attacks on body and life. In 1938 almost half of the 90 Jews who were killed in the November pogrom ("Crystal Night") were women.[3] Jews of both sexes were among the victims of the policy of state-run birth control, or antinatalism, which called for compulsory sterilization of "racially inferior" people for the purpose of "race regeneration."

In June 1933 the minister of the interior gave a programmatic speech on race and population policy. He conjured up a scenario of "cultural and ethnic decline" brought about by the influence of "alien races," particularly the Jews. The nation was threatened by "racial mixture," by over a million people with "hereditary physical and mental diseases," by "feeble-minded and inferior" people whose "progeny is no longer desired," especially not where they show "above-average procreation." He estimated that a full 20 percent of the population in Germany, that is, 12 million people, were undesirable as mothers and fathers; conversely, the birthrate of the "healthy Germans" should rise by 30 percent (about 300,000 per year). "In order to increase the number of hereditarily healthy progeny, we have first of all the duty to prevent the procreation of the hereditarily unfit."[4] Two weeks later, the antinatalist part of this program became the first National Socialist law on population policy. It mandated eugenic sterilization, to be performed by force and with police assistance if necessary. The government stressed that "biologically inferior hereditary material" was to be "eradicated," particularly among the "innumerable inferior" people who "procreate without inhibition." Sterilization "should bring about a gradual cleansing of the ethnic body," beginning with 400,000 urgent cases and ultimately covering one and a half million people. Of the 400,000 actually sterilized over the next decade (as well as an unknown number outside this law) half were women, and together with the men they constituted one percent of those of childbearing and begetting age. For this purpose, about 250 special sterilization courts were established that brought together jurists, psychiatrists, geneticists, anthropologists, and medical doctors. The newly Nazified medical establishment was mandated, by law and under state control, to search for sterilization candidates among the population. A huge propaganda campaign attempted, though with limited success, to convince the Germans of the necessity and benefits of antinatalism. Never in history had a state joined theory, propaganda, and political-institutional practice to pursue an antinatalist policy of such proportions, a "forerunner of mass murder."[5] Erroneously characterizing National Socialist policy toward women as a "cult of motherhood," feminist historiography until recently rarely considered either the dimension of racist antinatalism or the women who were its victims.

Most of the sterilizations were performed because of emotional or intellectual defects: they included real or alleged feeble-mindedness, schizophrenia, epilepsy, and manic-depressive disorders. The sterilization law did not apply exclusively to Jews, Gypsies, Blacks, and other "alien" races, but they were of course included (though Hitler thought for a while that alien races did not merit

the benefits of "racial uplift" through sterilization). The sterilization policy was an integral component of National Socialist race
policy, as the Nazi leaders often pointed out. This was because in
addition to rejecting alien races or peoples, the Nazis sought the
"regeneration" of the German Volk by means of discriminating
against the "inferior" stock among its people. Such a regeneration
was necessary to create the "master race," which did not yet exist
and had to be produced. Special provision was made for the
sterilization of Gypsies and black Germans inside and outside the
law. German Jews were thought to be particularly prone to schizophrenia, Eastern European Jews to feeble-mindedness. The case of
a German-Jewish woman in Berlin is instructive. In 1941 she was
sterilized on the grounds of schizophrenia, evidenced by "depression" and attempted suicide. Her state of mind was perhaps not
surprising: it was during that year that the Jews, already reduced
to abject misery, were forced to wear the yellow star; the number
of suicides among them was rising dramatically, and deportations
to the death camps were starting. Accordingly, in March 1942
Jews were excluded from the regular statutory sterilization procedure. But in some of the camps experiments in new methods for
mass sterilization were carried out under Himmler's command,
particularly on Jewish and Gypsy women (through injections in
the uterus). After the hoped-for Nazi victory, such uterine injections were to be used on any group of eugenically or ethnically
undesirable women across Europe.[6]

The sterilization law applied to both sexes, although initially
some experts wanted to spare women because their sterilization
involved a major operation with its attendant risks, and this might
provoke general resistance. As it turned out, sterilization policy
was indeed far from being gender-neutral. While women were only
half of the sterilization victims, they constituted about 90 percent
of the several thousand who died of it—often because they tried
to resist until the very last moment—and these deaths were sometimes compared to men's sacrifice of life for their country as
soldiers in the war. More generally, the sterilization policy was
officially proclaimed as "the primacy of the state over the sphere
of life, marriage, and the family" and as one of the areas where
the "nonpolitical" became "political"[7]—obviously an area of particular concern to women, along with all matters relating to begetting, bearing, and rearing children. Many women, especially
young women, attempted to get pregnant just before the operation,

and this type of resistance was important enough so that it was given a special name: "protest pregnancies" *(Trotzschwanger-schaften).* These were thwarted in 1935, when abortion was added to the sterilization law; abortions could now be imposed for eugenic reasons up to the sixth month of pregnancy, and they were coupled with compulsory sterilization.

Among the "undesirables" the most important group, quantitatively and strategically, was that of the "feeble-minded." They made up almost two-thirds of all those sterilized, and almost two-thirds of them were women. Two reasons accounted for this imbalance: first, women were singled out to be sterilized on the grounds that even those who were heterosexually inactive were vulnerable to involuntary pregnancy through rape; second, there were more grounds for testing female "inferiority," including irregular heterosexual behavior, their performance on the job, orderly housework, and their handling of children. Men were tested mostly on the basis of their conduct in employment. One woman, for example, was condemned to sterilization because "her knowledge is confined to mechanically acquired information; she can prepare various foodstuffs such as pudding, bread soup, or rice soup, but only in the way usual at home." A Jewish girl from Eastern Europe who worked as a cleaning woman in a Jewish hospital in Berlin was condemned to sterilization on the grounds of "feeble-mindedness" because her work was of "mechanical character."[8]

Nazi propaganda on the subjects of sterilization and racism in general was often directed specifically at women, because it was assumed that they resisted it more; this was confirmed by the evidence of secret police reports. Gender-specific propaganda confirms that the Nazi image of the female sex was diametrically opposed to the way the earlier women's movements saw it. Women were told that "regeneration" rather than childbearing had now "become the state's aim." Female "maternalism" was the object of racist polemic and condemned as "sentimental humanitarianism," along with Christian charity and Marxism. There was "danger arising precisely from women's maternalism" as well as from "the female instinct to care for all those in need of help" because maternalism, "like any egoism, acts against the race." Of the notion that "woman, because of her physical and mental characteristics," has "a particular inclination toward all living beings," it was said that there was "scarcely any worse sin against nature."

School textbooks for girls contained only three pages on the glory of German motherhood and twelve pages on the possibility of having to sterilize "one's beloved child," along with details on the prohibition to marry Jews, Gypsies, and other people of "inferior" hereditary makeup. In 1935 marriage prohibitions fortified anti-natalist policy as a further way of preventing undesirable offspring. The Nuremberg laws of September prohibited German Jews, Gypsies, and Blacks from marrying and having sexual intercourse with other Germans. Jewish women as well as Jewish men were threatened with heavy penalties in case of transgression.[9] A further law of October prohibited marriage between sterilized and nonsterilized persons.

National Socialist sterilization policy, also called "prevention of unworthy life," was a step toward the "annihilation of unworthy life" (euthanasia, or "action T4"). This step was taken in 1939, and eventually up to 200,000 ill, old, or handicapped people, women and men alike, mostly inmates of psychiatric clinics, were killed after having been selected as "incurable." The Jewish inmates were all killed without undergoing any selection, so the euthanasia program was also the first phase of the systematic destruction of the Jews. The "T4" program used a special killing gas for the first time, but this policy of massacre had its roots in National Socialist antinatalism. First, it grew from a mentality that conceived of sterilization not as a private and free choice but as a "humane" alternative to killing for the sake of the *Volkskörper*. As an "elimination without massacre,"[10] sterilization served as a political substitute for "nature" which "naturally" (that is, without the intervention of charity and medicine) would have prevented "unfit" people from surviving. Second, implementation of the sterilization policy accustomed medical and psychiatric experts to dealing with bodily intervention of this kind and consequent deaths, mostly of women. Third, the first victims of deliberate massacre (1939–40) were 5,000 handicapped children three years of age and under, whose parents the bureaucracy in charge of abortion and sterilization had failed to identify. Finally, many of those active in the "euthanasia" deaths after 1939 had earlier advocated or participated in the policy of sterilization and came to play an important role in the massacre of the Jews.

In late 1941 the T4 gas chambers and the male part of their personnel were transferred from Germany to the newly constructed death camps in the occupied Eastern territories, where they were used for the systematic and industrial-scale killing of millions of Jews and Gypsies, women as well as men. This transfer was significant in terms of technology, mentality, and strategy. It also had important gender dimensions, which have not yet been sufficiently explored. Hundreds of thousands of Jews had already been killed, however, before gas was used, mostly through mass shooting. The SS-men who did it seem to have experienced considerable "psychological difficulties," especially when shooting women and children. Even Himmler and Eichmann became sick while watching executions that included women and children. Gas technology was introduced in late 1941 not only as a means to accelerate the mass killing, but also because a "'suitable' method," a "humane" alternative to the bloodshed was required to relieve the SS-men from their largely gender-specific scruples.[11] The first mobile gas vans (in Russian and Serbia) were thus used principally for the killing of women and children, and the sources usually describe later victims as "men, women, and children." When the Jews in the newly established ghettos in Poland were deported and killed, a disproportionate number of the victims were women.[12] When the stable gas chambers in Auschwitz started to function in late 1941, it was mostly Jewish women, especially those with children, who were selected for death right upon arrival—"every Jewish child meant automatically death to its mother"—whereas Jewish men were more likely to be sent to forced labor. Almost two-thirds of the German Jews deported to the death camps and killed there were women, and 56 percent of the Gypsies who were sent into the Auschwitz gas chambers;[13] the proportion of women among the other millions of dead will forever remain unknown. A recent study of the Nazi doctors in the death camps found that these men, healers turned into killers, were able to function largely thanks to male bonding, heavy drinking, and belief in an "overall Nazi male ideal."[14]

The leading massacre experts were by no means blind to the gender dimensions of genocide, as Himmler explained in a 1943 speech: "We came to the question: what about the women and children? I have decided to find a clear solution here too. In fact I did not regard myself as justified in exterminating the men—let us say killing them or having them killed—while letting avengers in the shape of children grow up." Jewish women were thus killed as women, that is, as childbearers and mothers of the next generation. But Himmler went even further, placing the female victims at the center of his own definition of genocide: "When I was forced somewhere in some village to act against partisans and against Jewish commissars . . . then as a principle I gave the order to kill the women and children of those partisans and commissars too . . . Believe you me, that order was not so easy to give or so simple to carry out as it was logically thought out . . . But we must constantly recognize that we are engaged in a primitive, primordial, natural race struggle."[15] Here, the National Socialist *Rassenkampf* (race struggle), taking its most extreme form, was defined as a deadly struggle waged by men particularly against women and children. The significance of this woman-centered definition of race struggle has been recognized by some historians as one element of the singularity of the National Socialist genocide of the Jewish people.[16]

Female activists in Nazi race policies were a minority among the perpetrators and a minority among women generally, though a remarkably tough and efficient one. The more active among them were usually unmarried and had no children; they came from all social classes except the very highest ones; and their participation in racist policies was mostly, as in the case of many men, a function of their job or profession. While the sterilization policy was entirely directed by men, some of the female social workers and medical doctors helped select the candidates. Nurses in the six "euthanasia" centers assisted the male doctors in selecting and killing. Some women academics operated with their male superiors in Gypsy studies and laid the groundwork for the selection and extermination of Gypsies; for this purpose they used their easier access, as women, to Gypsies and Gypsy culture. Female camp guards who supervised women in the concentration camps came mostly from a lower-class background and had volunteered for the job because it offered some upward mobility. Of all Nazi women activists, they were the closest to the center of the killing operations and to the responsibility for their functioning; it is wrong to believe that they "did not affect the workings of the Nazi state."[17] In addition, many women worked alongside men in the complex genocide bureaucracy, meticulously recording in state and party offices the process of definition, segregation, expropriation, and deportation of the Jews. National Socialist racism was not only institutionalized as state policy but also professionalized.

Some historians have argued that German women's share of guilt and responsibility for the Nazi evil lay in their acquiescence to being nothing but mothers and wives; this view has been common for a long time and included the erroneous assumption that "among the persecuted and incarcerated, by far the majority were men."[18] But the image of women as mothers and wives was neither at the core of the Nazi view of the female sex nor was it specific to National Socialism. From its beginnings National Socialism had broken with this image in many ways, mostly in all aspects of its race policy; this policy, at the core of National Socialism, constituted its novelty and specificity. Those women who participated in it and were responsible for it were rarely mothers and did not act as mothers and wives; rather, they complied with the male-dominated professional and job strategies which executed the racist policies.

Women's Employment

The National Socialist regime did not exclude women from employment. Even though this has often been demonstrated since the 1930s, the myth persists that during Nazism women were fired *en masse,* by force, and for the sake of motherhood.[19] In fact the number of officially registered employed women rose from 11.5 million in 1933—36 percent of all employed persons and 48 percent of all women between the ages of fifteen and sixty—to 12.8 million in 1939 (within the German territory of 1937, but if most annexed territories are included, the figure is 14.6 million), with the corresponding figures of 37 percent and 50 percent. In 1944, 14.9 million German women were employed (including Austria), making up 53 percent of the German civilian labor force and including well over half of all German women between ages fifteen and sixty. When low employment gave way to full employment and later to labor scarcity, largely because of the expansion of war industry, the number of female workers in industry increased by 28.5 percent between 1933 (1.2 million) and 1936 (1.55 million), and by another 19.2 percent in the following two years. Not only did the number of employed single women rise, but also that of married women and mothers. Between the Weimar period and 1939, the number of married women in the labor force and their proportion among all employed women rose dramatically, and it almost doubled for married female workers in industry (21.4 percent in 1925, 28.2 percent in 1933, and 41.3 percent in 1939; all married employed women: 31 percent in 1925, 37 percent in 1933, and 46 percent in 1939). In 1939 more than 24 percent of all employed women had children, and the married ones among them made up 51 percent of all married employed women. As is usually the case, an unknown but considerable number must have been gainfully employed outside the official registration.

During World War II about 2.5 million foreign women were brought to work in German industry and agriculture, along with many more foreign men; most of them were from Eastern Europe and were forced to work. The lower their "racial value"—the lowest was that of Russians, followed by that of Poles—the higher was the percentage of women workers among their national group, particularly in the heavy munitions industry. In 1944, when almost two million foreign women were working in Germany, 51 percent of the Russian civilian workers were women (even more in the munitions industry), and 34 percent among the Poles; together they made up 85 percent of all foreign female workers. At that time, 23 percent of all women working in industry were from abroad; the rest of the foreign women worked in agriculture and in households.

The increase in women's employment since the late nineteenth century, particularly in industry, was not interrupted during the Nazi period, and the wage differential between men and women was not significantly altered, even though in some important sectors women's wages were raised to the level of men's. A considerable share of female employment was located in "nonmodern" sectors (in 1939, 35 percent of women were employed in agriculture and 10 percent in domestic service), but the overall figures demonstrate a high level of female employment in comparison to other countries. Even the policy to exclude women from the universities and many professions, which prevailed from 1933 to 1935 but which in reality influenced women's academic standing much less than it was influenced by the economic crisis and the labor market, was soon reversed; the real and lasting impact of that policy was the permanent exclusion of Jewish women and Jewish men.[20] These facts seem to require an explanation, especially in view of what has usually been seen as the official Nazi ideal of woman as mother and family-centered; it also contradicts a frequently voiced Nazi polemic against "double-earners" (men who worked illegally in addition to their regular job and women who were "supported" by a family member, usually male) during the period of high unemployment from 1930 to 1934.

One explanation is that the process of economic modernization was too strong for the regime to stop it or reverse it, so the Nazis adjusted to it and hoped for a better future without women's employment. This explanation implies, and rightly so, that the cult of motherhood was far from being a primary goal of Nazi policy in general or of Nazi gender policy in particular. Another explanation is that the process of women's "emancipation" through employment continued for German women after 1933. This assumption implies that employment was women's primary goal. But many sources show that before, and even more so during the war, most women took up employment not for the sake of emancipation or self-fulfillment but exclusively because of financial need. Indeed, during the war some female workers protested fiercely against the "ladies" who could afford to refuse work in the munitions and other war industries, disregarding the official propaganda for female war work since 1939 and labor conscription for women in 1943.[21] Actually, lower-class women attempted to quit employment whenever they could afford to do so, particularly after 1939, while no women who looked for a job were rejected in the late 1930s and throughout the war. A third explanation assumes a shift from an ideological cult of motherhood to adjustment to the need for female labor, either from the regime's beginnings (1933), or at the time of full employment (1936), or at the beginning of the war. This assumption, however, requires a full reconstruction of the Nazi view of the female sex, which has rarely been explored in depth.

During the election campaigns of 1932 the Nazis had begun to care about the women's vote. They laid great stress therefore on disproving their opponents' assertions that a Nazi regime would fire women from their jobs, speaking in the context of a propaganda strategy that promised everything to everybody, even to opposed interest groups. One of their promises was to keep up the level of women's employment, particularly that of single or nonsupported women, and to enable mothers to quit their jobs—by providing employment to their husbands—if they did not wish to work but did so out of economic necessity. It was precisely in the 1932 elections that women's support for the Nazi Party seems to have risen considerably (but figures are available only for a tiny and nonrepresentative fraction of the female electorate), to have almost closed the previous clear gender gap—fewer women than men voted for the radical right and left—and to have come close to male voting patterns (with the exception of the Catholic regions). The specific motives for this voting behavior are unknown (unlike the better-known motives which impelled 56,386 women to join the Party up to its seizure of power). These motives may or may not have been the same as those of men; they may have been gender-neutral; or they may have been prompted by a perception of a Nazi "mother cult," which was particularly stressed and denounced by anti-Nazi parties; they may also have been the result of Nazi assurances as to the continuity of female employment.[22] Actual economic developments from 1933 on largely confirmed these assurances—except that mothers, particularly working-class mothers, continued to work out of economic necessity.

Nazi pronouncements on women's employment had been far from unanimous. But the anti-"double earner" campaign was supported by Nazis and non-Nazis, by men and women alike, and it went on in all the countries that were hit by the deep economic crisis, particularly in the United States. Here, as in Germany, it subsided with decreasing unemployment, and in both countries even the much-condemned mothers' employment continued to rise. In both countries the campaign against those who were supported by another family member was spurred by a popular moral view according to which an individualistic "right to work," in a situation of limited employment opportunities, was but another expression of the same uninhibited capitalist market forces that had led to economic disaster. Jobs should be shared out not according to abstract individual "right" but according to needs which respected family bonds.[23]

National Socialism, as we have seen, was far from identifying motherhood as the exclusive task of all women. Likewise, with respect to employment, motherhood was by no means seen as a limit to it, at least no more than it had been before 1933 or in comparison to most other Western countries. The one study that has systematically explored the Nazi view of women before and during the war, comparing it to the public image of women in the United States, demonstrates that the Nazi image was not coherent but a mixture of many divergent features. It was far from an old-fashioned Victorian cult of true womanhood, it was not confined to women's "biological role," and while the Nazi ideologues no doubt welcomed the prospect of women's staying at home, they recognized right from the start that this was an impossible dream. In the real world the ideal Nazi woman owed service to the state above all else, be it on the job or in the family, in peace or at war.

The older metaphor of "spiritual motherhood," meaning "womanly" work outside the home, was now extended to any sort of hard labor, even in factories and on farms, so long as it was for the sake of "the people." In comparison, the public image of women in the United States during the 1930s was much more limited to the "occupation: housewife" stereotype. When American propaganda tried to persuade women to take up war-related work from 1941 on, it had to break a much more entrenched traditional image of women than its German counterpart had been. In Germany, the slogan "a woman's place is in the home" was not confined to the private household and family but extended to a "home" which was Germany as a whole, at peace or at war.[24]

A considerable part of the Nazi policy toward women aimed at enabling them to work for the family as well as for the market or the war. Whereas daycare was still largely rejected in the United States and elsewhere, in Germany it was advocated and established in large numbers, before and during the war, to help women combine their double workload. But not until 1942, ten years after its beginnings, did the National Socialist regime considerably improve the 1927 law for the protection of pregnant women and young mothers in extra-domestic employment, again in order to encourage them to combine employment and motherhood. For the first time, the 1942 law established the state's obligation to provide childcare facilities. Maternity leave before and after parturition remained at 12 weeks, and the maternity benefit amounted to the full wage; the woman was protected against dismissal from her job during pregnancy and four months after birth. However, maternity benefits were reserved to employed mothers only. When Robert Ley, the leader of the German Labor Front (the Nazi surrogate union), proposed in 1942 that maternity benefits be extended to nonemployed mothers too, particularly to the hardworking working-class mothers, Hitler rejected this proposal on the grounds that the state budget was needed for the "difficult tasks" of the next years, meaning the costs of war and nonmilitary massacres.[25]

The maternity protection law excluded from its benefits all Jewish women and "racially inferior" female foreign workers such as the Russian and Polish women working in Germany. Characteristically, no figures are available that show how many of them were pregnant or mothers. In the early years of the war Polish women were sent back East upon pregnancy, and it seems that many took very conscious advantage of this method to be relieved from forced labor. But from 1941 on, Polish and Russian women had to stay despite pregnancy. They were encouraged and often forced to undergo abortions, and often their children were taken away from them, in a complex interplay among Himmler's race experts, the labor offices, the employers, and the medical profession. Russian women especially were singled out for jobs which would bring about miscarriages. Work thus became a tool of antinatalist policy. The plans for the conquered Eastern territories (particularly the *Generalplan Ost*) included a large number of carefully elaborated, voluntary and nonvoluntary methods to decrease the birthrate of native children, which aimed almost exclusively at mothers and potential mothers. Whereas at the beginning of the Nazi regime the objects of large-scale antinatalism had been a minority, they were to become a majority after a Nazi victory.[26]

Family Policy, Social Reform, and National Socialist State Welfare

From the beginning, and especially in the election campaigns of the early 1930s, National Socialism had stressed the restoration and stabilization of the family along with the promise of full employment (at least for male breadwinners) and general welfare. These promises resonated against the background of economic crisis, general impoverishment, the breakup of family life, and an extremely high number of abortions largely due to epidemics and poverty. They were couched in the vocabulary of national and racial revival, including calls for a higher birthrate among the "hereditarily healthy Germans." The propaganda and the ensuing political practice combined aspects of social welfare policy, family policy, pronatalist policy, and gender policies. They were pursued with different kinds of intensity and efficiency, investments and results.

Nazi appeals for the restoration of the family were aimed at men as well as at women. Propaganda Minister Goebbels' "population policy campaign" of 1933–34 attempted to popularize both the sterilization policy and the idea that "our birthrate must rise" while "the mother will have, as in ancient Germanic times, the place due to her in public life and in the family." The minister of the interior attacked free abortion (in his 1933 speech) and underlined that "the attitude toward unborn life depends not only on the ideology of the German woman and mother, but also on that of the husband, who must be persuaded of his duty to establish a family." Indeed, a drastic anti-abortion law was planned that would reach beyond the old section 218 of the penal code and would be based on the view that abortion was an offense against the state and the race. But this was one of those plans that was superseded by more important ones. After extensive ministerial debates the authorities decided against such a law; instead, abortion on medical and eugenic grounds (to be determined by doctors) was introduced by law in 1935. About 30,000 eugenic abortions were performed during the Nazi period, many of them compulsory and all of them coupled with compulsory sterilization. The number of extralegal abortions, which very much preoccupied the authorities, was estimated to have declined only slightly in respect to the late Weimar years. In 1933–1942 the number of convictions for illegal abortions declined, in comparison to 1923–1932, by one-sixth (39,902, 70 percent of whom were women). Altogether, it seems that in practice, policies in regard to noncompulsory abortion did not change dramatically during the Nazi period in comparison to the years before and after it. Only in 1943 was the death penalty mandated for those abortionists (not for the woman herself) who "continuously injure the life of the German people"; apparently it was applied only to Eastern European doctors who performed abortions on German women.[27]

One of the repressive means aimed at restoring the family was a fierce campaign conducted against street prostitutes (Hitler had called them symbols of "the Jewification" and "mammonification of our emotional life"). Invoking the law concerning "the protection of the people and the state" of 28 February 1933 (the legal basis for the emerging dictatorship), the criminal police arrested tens of thousands of prostitutes. But from 1939 on prostitution was encouraged: not in its free version, but in bordellos for the military forces, in concentration camps for certain privileged male prisoner-workers (most of the women were from other concentration camps), and in work camps for male foreign laborers, staffed with women of the same nationalities.[28]

In addition to repressive measures, positive steps were taken to encourage stabilization of the family. New state welfare measures were passed to assist those who wished to have children, in the belief—which at the time was widely shared in other countries—that economic support would help them to make that choice. Three major social reforms were enacted to that end. In 1933 marriage loans were introduced for husbands whose wives had been employed and gave up their jobs upon marriage (but from 1936 on, with full employment, married women could keep their jobs and often were pressed to do so), to be repaid at a modest interest rate and to be forgone by one-fourth per birth, that is, up to the birth of four children. One of the main objectives of this loan was to lower the male marriage age and therefore reduce men's need for prostitution. Second, the head of household received income and inheritance tax rebates for his spouse and children. These rebates were introduced in 1934 and increased in 1939, along with a tax rise for the childless. Third, monthly child allowances were introduced in 1936, paid by the state starting with the fifth child; two years later parents received subsidies starting with the third child. Such measures were not exclusive to Germany; marriage loans were introduced in Italy, Sweden, France, and Spain during the 1930s, and similar tax reforms and state child allowances were passed by most European countries in the 1930s and 1940s.[29]

Nonetheless, the German state measures were unique in several respects. The point is not so much that the state did not cover the costs of childbearing and childraising (they should "not become a profitable business"), although in most other countries child allowances were paid starting with the first or second child. In Nazi Germany bringing children into the world was seen as a public issue, but the costs involved continued to be a private matter (in contrast to the enormous state expenses for the prevention of births). A more distinctive feature was that all family subsidies were payable not to wives and mothers, but to husbands and fathers. In the words of one Nazi minister, "Fatherhood is a concept derived from eternal natural law," and "the concept 'father' is unambiguous and must be at the center of the financial measures." The purpose of the subsidies was not to raise the status of mothers in relation to fathers but, as the ministry of finance emphasized, to raise the status of fathers in relation to bachelors. Fatherhood was perceived as "natural" and was therefore to be socially rewarded, particularly through the substantial benefits of the tax reform; unwed mothers received child allowances only if the fathers of their children were known and acceptable to the authorities. The most important and most characteristic feature was that none of these measures was meant to be universally applied: parents or children who were considered eugenically or ethnically "unfit" were excluded.[30] In fact, child allowances had to wait until the categories for desirable children had been established and the relevant legislation passed: the sterilization law of 1933, the Nuremberg laws of 1935, and the second marriage prohibition law of 1935. The marriage loan bureaucracy became a major agency for identifying sterilization candidates.[31] Viewed in the larger context of Nazi racism, the state measures for family welfare were not just a policy of family support but were part of a population policy in the strict sense: no welfare for the "undesirables," welfare for the "hereditarily healthy German family."

While the National Socialist state focused on the support of fathers, the National Socialist Party offered some benefits also to mothers; both excluded the "inferior" of both sexes. The German Labor Front, a Party affiliate, and individual employers gave some support specifically to employed mothers. The Party's welfare organization (Nationalsozialistische Volkswohlfahrt, NSV) included a "mother and child" section. Its head, Erich Hilgenfeldt, insisted that the good mother serves her children out of love and without any "wage motive"; "as soon as she claims rewards for her services, she is no longer a good mother." The NSV offered poor relief to "valuable" mothers with many children, pregnant women, and widowed, divorced, and unmarried mothers; it helped them to find employment, established kindergartens, offered vacations from home, and took over birth and food costs. It was not financed through taxes but through member fees (this was feasible because it had over 15 million members, since many Germans preferred to join the welfare-oriented NSV instead of the Party) and through collections and other fundraising activities.[32] Whereas the NSV's maternity support focused on the "valuable" poor, in 1936 Himmler created another organization to assist mothers who had children by men who were thought to belong to the racial elite, mostly SS-men, and thus to prevent the women from resorting to abortion. The Lebensborn was not an institution for forced breeding nor an SS bordello. It established well-furnished maternity hospitals (seven in Germany, later six in Norway, one in Belgium, and one in France). In Germany fewer than 2,000 women gave birth in such homes from 1936 on (plus 6,000 women in occupied Norway during the war), and two-thirds of them were unwed mothers. Before being admitted to the maternity home, they were examined as to their own and the fathers' ethnic and eugenic credentials. Starting in 1939 the maternity homes in Germany were used to house "valuable" children from the conquered territories in the East, whose parents had been killed or who had been kidnapped.[33]

The overwhelming majority of mothers received honors and propaganda rather than costly benefits. The League of Large Families, originally founded in the course of the 1918–19 revolution to lobby for welfare benefits to large and poor families, was incorporated in 1935 into the Party's Race Policy Office; here it could distribute propaganda for Nazi race policies, but it had no funds to give to poor families. It was regarded as an elite organization of the "Aryan, hereditarily healthy, and orderly families," and the leader of the Race Policy Office asserted that "we have broken with the glorification of mere numbers and distinguish strictly between those large families which are a wealth to themselves and to the people, and those others who, being large asocial families, are a burden to the life of the nation."[34] In 1937, 200 mostly male members of the League received "honor books" which gave them the right to special family benefits. In 1939 honors without benefits (a "mother cross" medal) were introduced for mothers with four children or more; the exclusionary clauses were somewhat looser than those that applied to material benefits, and so the medals were awarded to five million mothers up to 1944.

The effect of pronatalist propaganda and of welfare measures designed to promote pronatalist goals was limited. The birthrate, which was among the lowest internationally in 1933, increased by about one-third until 1936 (14.7 to 19 per thousand, the net reproduction rate rising from 0.7 to 0.9), when it reached the level of the late 1920s; it then remained almost stagnant and dropped again during World War II. Most of the increase was accounted for by couples who had not been able to marry and have the children they wanted because of the economic depression and made up for it when employment conditions had improved. Among those who married, only about a quarter applied for a marriage loan; they were usually couples who intended to have children and where the wife would quit her job anyway upon marriage. And they evidently had no reason to fear that the compulsory medical examination could uncover a defect that might lead to sterilization instead of a loan. On the average, the recipients took advantage of the debt reduction only for the first child and preferred to repay the rest of the loan in cash. Nor did child allowances lead to a further increase in births. The proportion of married women with four or more children (the number proposed by Nazi demographers as "valuable" women's "duty") among all married women declined from 25 percent in 1933 to 21 percent in 1939. Among the couples that had married in 1933, 31 percent were still childless in 1938.[35] Those who had married and had children after 1933 limited their number to one, two, or three and thus continued the demographic trend which had characterized Germany, as well as other industrialized countries, before the Nazi regime came to power.

The behavior of two particular groups illustrates both the limits and the specificity of the Nazi type of pronatalism. The Party functionaries, that is, "valuable" Germans who were the real targets of pronatalism and supporters of National Socialism, demonstrated that they believed in the pronatalist goals only for others, not for themselves. Nazi demographers deplored that among the functionaries who had married between 1933 and 1937, 18 percent were still childless in 1939, 42 percent had one child, and 29 percent had two children. Among the all-male SS members, 61 percent were unmarried in 1942, and the married ones had 1.1 children on average; the same was true for medical doctors, who were the professional group with the highest membership figures in the Party and the SS. Obviously, there was an inverse relation between adherence to National Socialism among the elite and the number of their children. Conversely, one statistical group had an above-average number of children: those whose claims for marriage loans and child allowances were rejected because of their "disorderly" conduct and their classification as "large asocial families." National Socialist demographers often pointed out that up to half of the families with above-average numbers of children were among the undesirables.[36]

During World War II, when the average figures were declining, there were two minor but conspicuous baby booms, often noted and explained by contemporaries. In 1939 employed women, particularly of the working class, were forbidden to quit their jobs because they were urgently needed for the war economy—unless they were pregnant. Pregnant women and young mothers were also exempted from the labor conscription introduced in 1943. Many German women preferred to have children instead of working for the war effort (between 1939 and 1941 the number of employed women decreased by 500,000, but by 1944 it had increased again by 800,000). Obviously, their personal strategy—babies against war-work—was the reverse of the official political strategy that had been devised for "inferior" women from Eastern Europe: war-work against babies.

Nazi propaganda for the restoration of the family and for "mothers' place in public life and in the family" had deceived many Germans of the time, including a considerable proportion of the women voting for the National Socialist Party in 1932 who may have believed—as did many women in other countries—in pronatalism as a means for raising the status of mothers and women generally. It also deceived those men and women who had not taken seriously the other equally explicit Nazi propaganda goals, such as race policy. In propaganda as well as in practical politics antinatalism had taken precedence over pronatalism, while the state welfare measures had focused on the support of fathers; assistance to selected mothers was left to Party poor relief and elite promotion. There was no profamily or prochild measure that did not exclude the usual categories of the ethnically and eugenically "inferior." Altogether, the centerpieces of Nazi population propaganda and policy were not pronatalism and a cult of motherhood but antinatalism and a cult of fatherhood and masculinity.

Although Nazi family policy did not contribute to an increase in births, it did, at least before the war, give rise to a growing belief on the part of the general public in the capacity of the Nazi regime to overcome the economic crisis. Most people perceived the child-oriented state welfare simply as a social reform that compensated for their low income and helped them survive with the children they wanted. Even though antinatalist sterilization policy was far from being popular, few people actively cared about its victims or about all those who were excluded from the benefits offered to the "hereditarily healthy and German" family. State family support as such was not specific to National Socialism nor was it a part of National Socialist racism; it was part of a larger trend toward a modern European welfare state. Yet the Nazi regime linked it to its racist policies by denying benefits to those it categorized as racially inferior. In this sense the National Socialist policy of "racial regeneration" was not one of family welfare and upgrading of motherhood, but a policy that at its core aimed at the destruction of traditional family values.

Other aspects of Nazi population policy also ran counter to

traditional family life. For instance, in 1938 a new law permitted divorce upon demand in case of one partner's "hereditary illness," sterilization, or infertility, with serious consequences for wives, especially elderly ones, and women protested accordingly. Contemporaries perceived the Nazi attempt to group the German population in same-sex and same-age organizations as a further attack on the family. One of the popular jokes of the time alluded to the overly organized family: "My father is an SA-member, my older brother is in SS, my little brother in the Hitler Youth, my mother in the National Socialist Women's League, and I am a member of the League of German girls." "But when do you see each other?" "Oh yes, we meet each year at the National Party Congress in Nürnberg."[37]

Politics, Power, and National Socialist Women's Organizations

In the early years the proportion of women among Nazi Party members was lower than that of any other party; even in 1934 it stood at 5.5 percent. In 1935 the Party considered about 40 percent of its male members and 70 percent of its female members as "inactive." More women joined and participated in the National Socialist Women's League (Nationalsozialistische Frauenschaft, NSF). It was established in 1931, in a confusing merger of local and fairly autonomous women's groups which advocated either national revival or National Socialism; in 1935 it was raised to the status of a Party affiliate and grew from 110,000 members in late 1932 to close to two million in 1935. Led by the "Reich Women's Leader" Gertrud Scholtz-Klink starting in 1934, it was intended to be a female Nazi elite, and therefore very few candidates were admitted after 1936. The aim of this elite was to organize German women and to educate them for their national and political tasks. The mass of German women (there were about 24 million over age twenty and about 30 million after the annexations of 1938) was expected to join the German Women's Organization (Deutsches Frauenwerk, DFW). This was also led by Scholtz-Klink but was not an official Party affiliate. Initially, it was formed not through individual membership but by amalgamating various groups, such as the women's organizations left over from the Weimar period; these were "coordinated" (*gleichgeschaltet*, a procedure which implied, first of all, the exclusion of Jewish women), except, of course, for the Jewish Women's League, which was dissolved in 1938. At that time the DFW had about four million corporate members, and, despite intense recruiting drives, fewer than two million individual members, almost half of them in annexed Austria and Czechoslovakia.[38]

Few NSF members (10 percent in 1935) and even fewer DFW members joined the male-dominated Party, but about one-third of the leaders of both organizations did so. In 1938 the principal leadership amounted to about 320,000 women. The major historian of National Socialist women's organizations considers these figures as an indication of the very modest commitment of women to National Socialism, particularly if compared to the commitment of men and to Scholtz-Klink's 1934 claim to have organized "all German women under one leadership." The scholar emphasizes these organizations' lack of political power, the passivity and reluctance of most women inside and outside them, and their lack of participation in Nazism's atrocities.[39] Nonetheless, the figures deserve attention in the context of women's and gender history.

Like the men in the movement, the early Nazi women's leaders had held more radical views than did the later Nazi women's elite. To begin with, many of these women had rebelled at the movement's exclusively male bonding and demanded an important role for women in the new state, including their access to employment, the professions, and politics. At the same time, they attacked the "old" women's movement for its focus on the rights of a minority of elderly middle- and upper-class women and, by taking the idea of "national socialism" seriously, demanded that the social contribution of women from all classes be recognized, including that of motherhood. Some of them argued that child allowances should be payable to mothers, deplored the fact that the male movement paid merely lip service to a "cult of motherhood," and criticized the emerging plans for family benefits because they were aimed exclusively at the fathers.[40] After 1934 such voices disappeared. Scholtz-Klink's organization, particularly its two major sections (Volkswirtschaft/Hauswirtschaft and Reichsmütterdienst, RMD), focused on women's education for housework and motherhood; from 1937 on, somewhat hesitantly, it also dealt with the promotion of women in academic professions and directed female university students to "socialist" tasks, that is, to helping working-class women on the job and with their families.

During the early phase of the movement Nazi women's groups and their leaders were often quite outspoken against male domination, but both in their earlier and in their later phases they gave top priority to national and ethnic revival, often expressed in anti-Jewish polemic. Scholtz-Klink personally insisted that the "woman question" took a second place behind the struggle against ethnic "degeneration" and the sacrifice for "our people," and that this struggle and sacrifice must be pursued in cooperation with men. In her view the old women's movement was mistaken when it "emphasized women as a special group within the people," and gender cooperation took precedence over "women's problems." Although women should leave the business of politics to men, they nonetheless should learn to "think politically," which meant that they "should not ask what National Socialism could do for them, but what they could do for National Socialism." They should be Germans first and women only second. In this view gender difference was seen as a difference not of purpose, identity, or interest—neither in general nor in respect to the Nazi movement—but only as a division of tasks toward one and the same end; referring to a current slogan of the male movement, Scholtz-Klink maintained that women, like men, should become "rectangular in body and soul." Nazi women leaders insisted fervently on a presumed difference between German and non-German, National Socialist and non-Nazi science, scholarship, and history, but they asserted that there was "no gender difference in the scientific approach," no "specifically 'female' desire for knowledge," and no "specifically 'female' method" in regard to scholarship. Most important, motherhood and marriage, the common denominator of women of all classes, had to adapt to the new race and sterilization laws which linked mothers and nonmothers to the destiny of the "people."[41]

The NSF/DFW attempted to organize and educate especially the population of full-time housewives and mothers; they had been quite reluctant to enlist in the Nazi cause, not the least because they often identified with the church.[42] The organization was able to reach far beyond the immediate membership through the RMD maternity courses. Women were instructed in health issues, housekeeping (mainly cooking German food with an eye to Germany's need for self-sufficiency), sewing, infant care, child education, and German folklore. The instructors were full- or part-time salaried or volunteer workers (the paid staff consisted of 3,500 women, subsidized in part by the government, but mostly by fund-raising).

During the war the DFW organized neighborhood assistance among women. Between 1934, when the RMD was founded, and 1944, five million women took maternity courses. In each class some 20 women participated in 24 hours of instruction distributed over 10 days. Previously, such instruction, if given at all, had reached only urban women, but the RMD also sent instructors to women in the countryside. Married and unmarried women participated in almost equal proportions. In 1937, among the gainfully employed participants in the courses, 37 percent were blue-collar and 45 percent white-collar workers; among the married participants, 34 percent were married to blue-collar and 17 percent to white-collar workers. The folklore courses were the least frequented, and more than half of the participants chose the courses on family and infant health. It seems likely that these courses were in part responsible for the significant fall in infant mortality during this period.[43]

At the same time, the health courses were used to promote the "race and population policy," being part of the larger context of National Socialist racism. Race policy, from early sterilization to later massacres, was entrusted mostly to the "health" authorities and the healing professions; to doctors, psychiatrists, and geneticists. Scholtz-Klink left no doubt as to the centrality of "race and population policy" in the "spiritual formation" of her organization's clientele. At times she deplored women's general lack of sympathy for the sterilization policy and urged that a special effort be made to get Catholic working-class women to accept sterilization (Catholic women most fervently resisted sterilization and therefore opposed the RMD; as a result, the Catholic mothers' organization was outlawed in 1935). "Hereditary hygiene" was included in the program for mothers' education from the beginning. In 1935 Scholtz-Klink became a member of the ministry of interior's Expert Committee on Population and Race Policy, the leading advisory board in this field, and in 1936 she introduced a "race policy" section into the DFW. Starting in 1935, experts (usually men) such as the head of the Nazi Party's Race Policy Office instructed NSF leaders about the subject in the Berlin University of Political Science. Jewish women, the "incurably ill," and mentally or emotionally disturbed women could not be members of the NSF/DFW.[44]

The well-organized central and regional teacher-training courses were most effective within the elite organization NSF, and the almost 380,000 women who were specially trained up to 1938 served as important propagandists for Nazi ideology among the DFW members and perhaps also among the general public. But most of the millions of women who took courses in mothering on a local level did not seem to have taken the "race and heredity care" too seriously. Even on the upper level of NSF teacher training the interest in race, heredity, and eugenics was limited. Less than a tenth of the NSF leaders were attracted by the offer of special "racial-political" courses, and the others preferred the ordinary courses on housewifery, nursing, social welfare, charity, and neighborhood aid; the same was true of the course participants on a local level. Even though references to "race and population policy" abound in the NSF/DFW propaganda and teaching materials, they rarely mentioned sterilization and anti-Semitism overtly. In this they differed, for instance, from state-mandated school textbooks for girls (of course, we do not know what was said in class). The NSF/DFW publications did not carry the sort of pornographic anti-Semitism so prevalent in leading male Nazi's publications.[45] Not that NSF and DFW leaders believed in Nazi race policy less than their male counterparts; rather, they seem to have adapted to the more pragmatic and more humane needs of their female clientele. Most tough female race hygienists preferred to publicize and to be active outside the NSF/DFW, alongside men.

The NSF/DFW had little power in the Nazi regime, not even with respect to women. Sometimes its leaders claimed to have organized separately 12 million women—sometimes "all German women"—on the basis of women's tasks and under female leadership. This was not true. Most women members of Nazi organizations found themselves under male leadership, often to the distress of the NSF/DFW leaders. The latter were prohibited from organizing girls between the ages of 10 and 20. This left only groups of girls below age 10 and women's "youth" groups between the ages of 21 and 30. The leaders thus had to confront the same generation problem they had criticized so sharply in the Weimar women's movement. The League of German Girls (Bund Deutscher Mädel) was part of the mixed, though internally segregated Hitler Youth under male leadership, and membership was compulsory from 1936 on. Most of the 12 million women that Scholtz-Klink claimed to lead were led by her only nominally and were in fact incorporated in mixed and male-led organizations. Rural housewives were claimed by the Reich Food Estate. Four million women workers were members of Robert Ley's Labor Front, and it was this organization, not the NSF/DFW, that occasionally campaigned for higher women's wages and maternity protection. Female schoolteachers, students, doctors, girls in the Labor Service, all belonged to their respective mixed organizations. Even the regional NSF activists depended less on central female leadership than on the regional male Party leaders.[46] The NSF/DFW could not even provide much-needed support for mothers; other than the large number of kindergartens it established, it offered only "spiritual formation." Its leaders did not attempt to intervene in the 1935–36 legislation on father-focused child allowances (although they were proud of the 1942 law for the protection of employed mothers). Mothers received material support neither from the state nor from the women's organization, but from the male-dominated Nazi Party welfare organization which provided, among other benefits, aid for needy mothers and kindergartens for employed mothers. Under the Nazi regime even motherhood and charity, which the earlier women's movement had claimed was "women's sphere" to be directed by women, had fallen under male leadership.

During World War II the NSF as an organization played no role in massacres and genocide. One of its major roles at that time was to help women, often very efficiently, to survive under the difficult conditions of air-raids and evacuations. But another of its objectives was to indoctrinate German women against mingling (and to refrain from sexual intercourse) with the millions of Eastern European male and female workers; sometimes it denounced the women who had contravened the strict prohibitions. This effort proved largely futile, and up to the end of the war the Nazi authorities continued to deplore women's general lack of "racial consciousness" in this respect and sought to raise it through a high number of penal convictions.[47] Nonetheless the NSF's indoctrination may have considerably contributed to the fact that most German women did not actively resist National Socialism and its race policies. Their attachment to motherhood, privacy, and family values rarely encompassed those women and men whom the regime deprived of these values. Women's resistance is still a largely unexplored field. They seem to have played an important and underestimated part in male-dominated resistance organizations. Single cases of female resistance suggest that it was often different from that of men, less structured and organized. Women's resistance included, for example, supporting the victims of persecution by hiding and protecting them. Precisely when they were most effective, these activities did not come to the attention of the secret police and other Nazi authorities, and they left fewer written sources than did male-dominated resistance organizations.[48] But unless further research demonstrates otherwise, it seems that resistance among women was no more widespread than it had been among German men.

6

The Women of Spain
from the Republic to Franco

Danièle Bussy Genevois

THE LOCAL ELECTIONS of April 12, 1931, gave
the Republican-Socialist coalition a sufficient majority to persuade King Alfonso XIII that the monarchy was finished and he had no choice but to
leave the country. On April 14 the Republic was
proclaimed to tumultuous shouts of joy—an event
that was to have profound effects on the lives of
Spanish women. For them, the Bourbon monarchy
had meant subjugation. The Constitution of 1876
had restored the alliance of throne and altar and
reinstated Catholicism as the official religion.
Spain's legal system, based on the Napoleonic
Code, was particularly harsh. Spanish women
were thus subject to the dual authority of church
and law. Political rights were nonexistent, and despite educational advances 44.4 percent of women
remained illiterate in 1930 (down from 60 percent
in 1900). The dictatorship of General Miguel
Primo de Rivera, instituted in 1923 following a
coup discreetly encouraged by the king himself,
had introduced a decree of 1924 granting women
who headed families the right to vote in local elections (a measure inspired by the example of Mussolini's Italy); the general also allowed a number
of women to sit in the Consultative Assembly. But

when the Primo de Rivera dictatorship fell in 1930, things reverted to the *status quo ante.*

The Spanish Republic came to stand in the forefront of the parliamentary democracies of Europe in granting women their rights. As early as 1931 Spanish women obtained the all-important right to vote—this despite the fact that Spain had remained neutral in the Great War—whereas the French Senate had repeatedly refused to approve legislation granting French women the right to vote, legislation that the Chamber of Deputies had passed specifically to honor the nation's women for their contribution to the war effort. Yet after such advances the generals' coup of 1936 against the legitimate republican government sought, among other things, to return women "to their only proper place, the nursery" (as the Labor Charter of 1938 put it).

Spanish women have often been portrayed in intriguing but misleading ways, from Carmen, nineteenth-century Europe's *femme fatale,* to "la Regenta" (the title character of a novel by the Spanish writer Clarín [Leopoldo Alas]), a woman torn between love and religion. And real Spanish women have become subjects of myth in service of one ideology or another, from Dolores Ibárruri, the Communist rabble-rouser popularly known as La Pasionaria, to Federica Montseny, the anarchist minister of health. Setting such images aside, let us try to trace the lives of real Spanish women as they followed the initially exciting, later terrifying path from liberation to nationalization.

Republican Progress

With the advent of the Republic power flowed to an intellectual elite composed of writers, physicians, teachers, and jurists, as well as to the Socialist Party, whose popularity had grown through long years of repression, first under the Primo de Rivera dictatorship, and then, after December 1930, under the monarchy. The San Sebastián Pact of August 18, 1930, proposed a program of fundamental structural reform and abolition of the social privileges of the "old regime" and the Church.

Women's Demands

Democratic thinkers in Spain had long proposed a variety of reforms favorable to women. Existing marital and sexual arrangements were universally denounced. Various writers complained that women were treated as inferiors culturally and legally. The extraordinarily high birthrate led to the highest infant mortality rate in Europe. Male adultery was tolerated. The proportion of illegitimate births was high. Prostitution was widespread, and venereal disease common. Antimonarchist jurists called for legal reform, and like-minded physicians called for premarital health examinations and medical assistance for women with children. Many reformers favored divorce, although a fair number of progressive men were afraid that, Spanish customs being what they were, divorce might allow men to repudiate their wives in the manner of Oriental potentates. The Socialist Party's priorities included the regulation of labor, the legalization of divorce, and the abolition of prostitution. Although anarchism was an important political force in Spain, anarchists, opposed to the state by definition, played little part in the movement that laid the groundwork for the Republic. They did, however, fight for free love and contraception and were involved in innumerable syndicalist battles.

Were women themselves active in the movement to improve their status? Many belonged to trade unions, but few were leaders. Margarita Nelken in 1919 offered a harsh assessment of women's working conditions: women gave birth to babies on the job, work at home was tantamount to slavery, and the law was widely ignored (as were the decisions of the OIT after 1920).[1] The women closest to the republican intellectuals were civil servants, mainly schoolteachers, together with a small number of journalists (a 1918 law had granted women access to certain professions).

Women's groups first emerged in Spain in the second decade of the twentieth century. As early as 1915 ties were established with the Women's League for Peace and Freedom, and in 1918 the National Association of Women (ANME) was founded. Other postwar feminist groups formed and published newspapers. Women's groups were primarily interested in the right to vote, the abolition of prostitution, new educational opportunities, and legal reform. Representatives of the workers' movement, on the other hand, expressed doubts about the right to vote, which they saw as a bourgeois demand, while feminists and some male commentators appear to have harbored doubts about the wisdom of divorce.

Proposed Reforms

No sooner did the new government take power than it began reforming the structure of the state: regional autonomy was encouraged, separation of church and state was instituted, agrarian reforms were initiated, and an overhaul of the military was begun. Measures affecting women and the family must be seen in this context. Looking back, three features stand out as surprising: the urgency of the first measures, the legalization of woman's suffrage, and the changes in family law. Within two years, the government had revamped Spanish law in the hope of changing the attitudes of the Spanish people.

The new rulers' determination to repair the injustices of the monarchy can be seen in a series of decrees issued between May 8 and May 26, 1931, in which the provisional government "examined the situation" of women and peasants.[2] Women were granted the right to run for office—a harmless enough decision, since few women possessed the necessary qualifications. Working women received maternity insurance, a measure that the Socialists had long contemplated. April and May were months for celebrating the new Republic: people wore Phrygian bonnets, the colors of the new regime were paraded about, shows were staged in music halls, and a Miss Republic was elected. The generosity of the government's early measures reflects the joyful spirit of the moment.

Women staged enthusiastic lectures and rallies in favor of the right to vote, the need for which was said to be urgent. They would have to wait, however, until Article 34 of the Constitution was approved, after arduous debate, on October 1. If granted the vote, Spanish women would constitute more than half the electorate, and as this became clear, generosity gave way to anxiety. Most Radicals believed that "women are under the thumbs of the priests," and many Socialists shared that view. Not a few Republicans harbored misogynist attitudes: women, said one, are "hysterical by nature"; no woman can vote rationally until after menopause, argued another, because the menstrual cycle interferes with a woman's reason. The outcome was determined by a historical confrontation between two women serving as deputies: the Radical-Socialist lawyer Victoria Kent and the Radical lawyer Clara Campoamor, the first women to be admitted to the bar of Madrid. Kent enjoyed the prestige of having defended Republicans implicated in the December 1930 rebellion. Campoamor was Spain's representative to the League of Nations. Both made eloquent and moving pleas, Kent arguing that implementation of the "ideal" should be delayed, while Campoamor vigorously demanded equality. Campoamor carried the day, persuading the Socialists to vote for the measure and thus bringing joy to the hearts of feminists. (The Socialist Margarita Nelken was not elected to the legislature until later; she opposed women's suffrage.)

In its desire to Europeanize and modernize Spain, the new parliament pursued a family reform policy aimed at the "redemption" of women (even the left-wing vocabulary in Spain was often tinged with religiosity). Civil marriage was recognized, and divorce was legalized after bitter debate (Article 41 of the Constitution of December 1931, law of 2 March 1932). Spanish jurists tended to look abroad for models. They rejected Soviet precedents advocated in certain quarters, however, and overlooked solutions proposed by anarchists at home (some, like young Hildegart, for example, campaigned vigorously for libertarian causes and birth control).[3] Instead they looked to the Weimar Constitution and declared that marriage is the basis of the family and that men and women are equal. They also borrowed extensively from French divorce law. In some respects, however, the new Spanish laws were original. Illegitimate children enjoyed the same rights as legitimate ones. Divorce by mutual consent was authorized. The law referred to parental rather than paternal authority. In a country where patriarchy still reigned, these changes were bold indeed.

Echoes of Change

To an objective eye, Spanish legislators seem to have been caught between conflicting tendencies. The Socialist Jiménez de Asúa, exiled by Primo de Rivera for his lectures on birth control, held that the problem of abortion "is not an issue in Spain." The president of the Republic, Alcalá Zamora, a practicing Catholic, did nothing to oppose divorce. The absence of any analysis of Spanish women's positions was a source of ambiguity: the Socialist Largo Caballero was surprised and bitterly disappointed when many working women refused to subscribe to maternity insurance policies because they did not wish to pay the premiums or because, being unmarried, they considered such insurance useless or, worse, an insult to their "honor." The minister, only too well aware of the demands of workers in other European countries, could not admit that Spain was different. His reaction reflects a lack of understanding: "What is happening is that the Spanish woman is still a slave."[4] The law was nevertheless applied, but gradually.

The statistics on divorce show that its impact was far smaller than one might have thought. The effect of the new law was felt mainly in large cities and regions that voted for the left, yet even in Madrid only eight in a thousand marriages ended in divorce.[5] Nevertheless, the new law had a galvanizing effect on the right that far transcended the actual figures: the founder of the Falange, José Antonio Primo de Rivera, the dictator's son, denounced the reign of "sensuality." In his view, the grandeur of marriage stemmed from its having "no issue other than happiness or tragedy": "The man who is incapable of burning his ships when he lands is incapable of building empires."[6]

The true impact of efforts to reform the family may have been upon the national consciousness. One gets a sense of this from contemporary newspaper accounts and autobiographies. People were seized by a passion either to promote the new laws or to oppose them. One monarchist was prepared to pay a fortune to the Church to have a bishop annul his daughter's marriage so that she would not have to divorce. A justice of the peace fled in the middle of a wedding ceremony so that he would not be obliged to marry a pair of divorcées. Civil marriage announcements congratulated "comrades who threw off the yoke of the Church." There were "lay baptisms" of children with names such as Liberty, Life, Germinal, and Floréal. Phenomena such as these—painful contradictions, exuberant and sober innovations—are probably the best evidence we have of Spaniards' feelings that they were living in unprecedented times.

Growing Tensions

Although the effort of reform continued for two years, the Republic had only a short time to live. From the moment the new regime was proclaimed, right-wing factions plotted its downfall despite internal dissensions among monarchists favorable to Alfonso XIII, Carlists, conservatives willing to tolerate the Republic, fascists, and others. The Spanish Church issued innumerable pastoral letters denouncing the reforms, while the Vatican, which officially preached prudence, secretly promoted conspiracy, as recently opened Vatican archives prove.[7] The first major coup attempt, on August 10, 1932, united all of the regime's opponents: the army, the Church, the monarchists, the conservatives, and the large landowners, who chose General Sanjurjo, former head of the Guardia Civil, as their leader.

Right-Wing Women

Although the uprising ended in failure and its instigators were exiled or imprisoned, the episode drew attention to the role that the right had in mind for women. Women were targeted by new publications launched in January and May of 1932, calling upon them to help imprisoned rightists and their families. Their mission, however, was not just to pray for them and send gifts, which flowed in from all over Spain. The new self-styled cultural publications served as substitutes for more overtly political organs banned by the government. They appeared to contain coded messages, and their distribution aroused suspicion.

In reality, women were being summoned to engage in full-fledged political activity, primarily against secularization of the state and public schools and in the electoral arena. It still is not clear whether the mobilization of women on the right is evidence of obedience to male leadership or of their own initiative. Consider the right to vote: the idea of exploiting the women's vote politically came from the leadership. The monarchists, after declaring women's suffrage to be as objectionable as universal suffrage ("a loutish ball at which everyone is obliged to dance"[8]), allowed themselves to be persuaded by the arguments of J. M. Gil Robles, the future leader of the Spanish Confederation of Autonomous Rights (CEDA) and a man who flirted for a time with Nazism. The women's vote, he insisted, was an unhoped-for "gift from the state," and the immediate task was to "organize" it. To that end, temporarily demobilized groups such as Catholic Action were to be reactivated. Such groups had acquired the necessary organizing skills under the dictatorship. Indeed, after General Primo de Rivera exhausted the patience of even his own supporters and witnessed the failure of his essentially fascistic Patriotic Union, he was delighted when women organized demonstrations in his behalf in 1929 and when newspapers such as *Mujeres españolas* were established to encourage them. But in 1932 it was no longer a matter of sending petitions of support or bouquets of flowers to an elderly general much given to tokens of female admiration. It was rather a question of enlisting women as rapidly as possible in reactivated or newly created organizations. Some 38,000 women joined Catholic Action; another 5,000 women in Madrid alone joined the group Aspiraciones, founded by the magazine of the same name; 12,000 women attended a rally in Galicia and 4,000 attended another in Salamanca. Enough of such details: the point is that within the space of a few months large numbers of women were enlisted in a movement opposed to the government. Some of these women traveled extensively: the monarchist Rosa Urraca Pastor held fifty rallies in four months. Others indoctrinated the employees of Catholic Action workshops and home workers and drew up secret lists of sympathizers. In Madrid women delivered registration cards to 230,886 voters. A society columnist promised to solicit the support of her hairdresser. Women were urged to organize "charity teas" to help the cause.

If the early initiative came from the leadership, women soon struck out on their own. They wore monarchist symbols—the cross and lily—as jewelry and refused to pay the 500-peseta fine imposed for such acts, whereupon they went to prison and became martyrs for the cause. Visitors flocked to see these heroines in their cells and called for commutation of their sentences, which were actually quite light. The bishop of Valencia went so far as to give an engraved silver-and-ebony crucifix to one young lady of the aristocracy held in prison in that city. The whole issue of religion was indeed another area in which women were especially active. Many protested against the constitution and later legislation that established a secular state, prevented the clergy from teaching, and dissolved the Company of Jesus. Protest took many forms: women marched brandishing crucifixes and sent their children to school with heavy crosses; they took members of the clergy into their homes, signed petitions, helped to collect funds with which to found private schools, and boycotted republican shopkeepers. The women's press played a role here: the magazine *Aspiraciones* (recently discovered) was at the heart of a vehemently anti-Communist, anti-Semitic religious war. And in 1932 and 1933 the Festival of the Sacred Heart became the occasion for huge rallies led by women in mourning garb.

Is it true, as many argue, that the right-wing women were responsible for the voting shift in the November 1933 elections? Careful research into the election results offers little support to this hypothesis.[9] Although it is certainly true that the right was well organized, other factors must also be taken into account. The unhappiness of moderate Republicans with the government's anti-clerical measures, the Socialists' departure from the government, the abstention of the anarchists, whose forays into revolution had been severely put down, and finally, an electoral law designed to favor the majority (the majority party won 80 percent of the seats)—all these played a part as well.

The right-wing women received little reward for their efforts, moreover. The only one to be elected to parliament in 1933 was the schoolteacher Francisca Bohigas, who had been the hope of a broad republican elite in the 1920s.

Changes among Republican Women

Women, whether conservatives or democrats, had borne the brunt of the political campaign. "Woman, take care lest the defeat of the right weigh on your conscience," said the opposition. Socialists gave speeches throughout the country: having granted the vote to women as well as men, they panicked when they saw how unprepared the country was for such momentous changes. The socialist press reflected the politicians' fears. On October 2, 1931, *El Socialista* announced that "by winning, we lost. That is the reality. . . . Let us candidly admit that we lacked political sense, even if we were acting in accord with a tenet of our party." Their campaign, too, came close to blackmail: "Mothers, may your sons, when they reach maturity, never think that they are not free because their mothers failed to liberate them."

The process that led from 1933 to the civil war is therefore particularly interesting to analyze. Growing radical tendencies in the left-wing movement issued in the so-called Asturian Revolution of 1934. Feminists and moderate republican women had refused to take a stand on the elections. The right to vote was considered a victory in itself. These women eschewed day-to-day politics in favor of long-range goals: health, education, international peace. They were the first to denounce the Nazis and their concentration camps.[10] After a shift in the majority, the ANME was taken over by more conservative feminists, some of whom attempted to create a new Independent Feminine Political Action Group in early 1934.

The group's charter made it clear that it represented a rejection of party politics as such.[11]

Certain revolutionary tendencies also declared themselves in 1933. The Spanish left was shaken by Hitler's accession to power. Meanwhile, the Komintern reorganized the previously quite weak Spanish Communist Party, with José Díaz at its head and the powerful personality of Dolores Ibárruri at his side. Communist women from Spain participated in the antifascist congress held in Paris in August 1933 and in September organized the first antifascist demonstrations in Spain.

The events of the summer and autumn of 1934 proved crucial. A strike of Socialists and anarchists caused turmoil in rural areas. Andalusian and Basque women staged demonstrations that harked back to the bread riots of old, for survival was an issue in the terrible years of the Depression. Finally, in early October, after a series of governmental crises, the president of the Republic committed the fatal error of forming a cabinet with three members of the "autonomous right," the CEDA. The left called for a general strike to protest this decision, which was compared to Hindenburg's appointment of Hitler as chancellor. Although the general strike soon failed in much of the country, it continued for several days in Catalonia and for more than three weeks in Asturias, where a revolutionary movement of sorts, led by Socialists in some areas, anarchists in others, began to form committees to take charge of administrative matters and organize resistance to the army. Ultimately, however, the Asturian "commune" was crushed by the military in a land, sea, and air assault.

Asturian women, working women shoulder to shoulder with miners' wives and daughters, participated in both the armed struggle and the revolutionary committees. The few women who took up arms soon found their memories exalted in myth: one such was the young Communist Aida Lafuente, who died machine gun in hand. Elsewhere in Spain the revolution met with a variety of reactions. Republicans split on the matter. All left-wing groups denounced the repression and the official version of events, a first instance of a deliberate attempt to poison public opinion. From exile in France Margarita Nelken organized rallies. Victoria Kent, Clara Campoamor, and Dolores Ibárruri founded Pro Infancia Obrera to save the children of Asturias. But some feminists exhibited peculiar attitudes: one feminist paper called for reinstituting the death penalty to deal with revolutionaries. Others expressed regret that "fanatics in skirts" had fought in battle and that the miners' wives had been unable to "restrain their men."[12]

Among the parties, repression worked in favor of union. All, including dissident anarchists, signed a "popular front" agreement. The Republican government that took office following the February 1936 elections would have the support of all the parties of the left. Campaign propaganda made a symbol of the woes of the women of Asturias, and La Pasionaria (Dolores Ibárruri, herself a Basque and the wife of a miner) cast her speeches in a Marxist perspective, evoking the specter of an unbroken chain of revolutionary uprisings: the Paris Commune, the Bolshevik Revolution of October 1917, the Asturian Revolution of October 1934.

A vast unity parade on May 1, 1936, included a large number of women. A new Marxist review, *Mujeres,* was launched, a tabloid edited by La Pasionaria and written by women from many countries. The paper presented a glowing image of the Soviet paradise along with praise from Margarita Nelken, who had found refuge in the USSR. A few weeks later, a group of anarchist women doctors began publishing *Mujeres libres* in order to ponder the place of women in the anarchist movement; too many men, they said, had abandoned their revolutionary ideas and returned to their homes. For the right, May 1 was a shock. José Antonio Primo de Rivera used this as a pretext for his "Letter to Soldiers" of May 4. From his prison cell he called on the army to revolt. Was there not "shame" and "dishonor," he asked, in the fact that women had been heard to shout slogans such as "Children yes! Husbands, no!"?[13]

The Spanish Civil War

The call on the military to revolt proved unnecessary. Already on February 17 General Francisco Franco had proposed a seizure of power to the interim prime minister, and from then on the plotting had continued without interruption. Despite the government's caution, rebellion broke out in July 1936. It is clear that, except in Navarre, the people opposed the rebels. Without the aid of Hitler and Mussolini and the ambiguous attitude of the Non-Intervention Committee, the affair would never have amounted to much beyond a grave military *pronunciamento*.

The civil war of course divided families and led to the first bombing of civilian populations in history. Photographs showed women dressed in black running with their children or lying dead in the streets as bombs fell on Madrid and Guernica; protests poured in from around the world, and witnesses flocked to the scene. Everyone suffered in this war, which was at once a war against fascism and a revolution (anarchist, Trotskyist, and cultural all rolled into one). But what of the fate of women in particular?

In a paradoxical way, the war furthered the cause of women. On the Republican side, there was new urgency in proceeding with cultural and legislative changes. Programs offering women occupational training and literacy courses were approved in 1936. The following year laws were passed authorizing the cohabitation of unmarried women, including widows of militiamen, and women were also allowed to work in war industries. In 1938 they obtained the right to enter pilot training courses. In addition, the anarchist Federica Montseny, minister of health, secured the legalization of abortion in October 1936, rectifying an oversight of the peacetime period. A study of hospital records now under way should be illuminating.[14]

Clearly, for many women, the civil war led to a profound change in outlook, as historical sociologists are now demonstrating with evidence formerly concealed by Franco's reconstruction of history.[15] And who can fail to be moved by the participation of women in the struggle and resistance? Historians are now trying to determine exactly what role women played. Opinions have varied: some writers have exalted the female role, while others have seen women serving the troops as cooks or prostitutes and nothing more. Soon we will have information beyond just the first names of the working-class women who died in battle. We will know more than the heroic exploits of the few—including women who commanded troops such as Mika Etchebère for the POUM (anarchists) and Lina Odena for the PCE (Communists). There were women in the front lines of the Spanish civil war, and there were also women who organized resistance behind the lines, in regions subjugated from the outset by Franco's forces, such as Navarre, where the achievements of the resistance effort are just being brought to light today.[16]

The fact is that parties and unions were divided as to the wisdom of using women at the front or behind the lines. Two factors must be taken into account: chronology and, of course, politics. In the general chaos that prevailed in the summer of 1936, militia companies were formed in great haste and all volunteers were welcome, male or female. By fall, however, a regular army was being organized, and the growing influence of Stalinists in subsequent governments led to the crushing of other factions: first the Trotskyists, later the anarchists. Eventually all female fighters were sent to the rear. Thereafter, the role of certain organizations became paramount: during the three-year siege of Madrid, the Unión de Muchachas helped defend the city and worked toward the emancipation of women; in Catalonia the Mujeres Libres, an anarchist group, organized the rear and battled prostitution. And finally, the Association of Antifascist Women (AMA), led by La Pasionaria, organized both Communist and non-Communist women in the factories and solicited international assistance: "Men to battle, women to work." Women everywhere understood that the public and private were inseparable. So long as the revolutionary movements remained viable, women overcame their political antagonisms and worked together. Women who had been members of Parliament in the Second Republic now joined the AMA, and it was not just the Communists among them who hailed the dignity and courage of Dolores Ibárruri.

The Advent of Francoism

As far as the history of women is concerned, the origins of Francoism are to be found some time before the coup of July 18, 1936. For women, the year 1934 was marked above all by the "October revolution" and the fear and hatred it unleashed. It was in December of the same year that the Woman's Falange was founded. Furthermore, leading prelates of the Catholic Church called for a restoration of moral order. The Church reasserted its authority over various publications and public spectacles: it launched a campaign against certain sports, against "nudity" on beaches, and against the "frivolity" of certain women. All this began not in 1939, but in 1934.

The Struggle over the "Crusade"

The founding of the Women's Falange and the attempt to restore the authority of the Church have one thing in common: both were intended to return the women of the right to their subordinate place. In the early days of the Republic, women had taken many initiatives on their own; now they were being asked to submit once again to the political and religious authorities. Women were urged to help the Falange "build a great imperial Spain" by assisting with propaganda and organizing efforts. Point Five of the charter of the Women's Falange states that "action is no longer your province; urge man to act." The civil war accentuated this tendency. Historians are just now pondering the paradox of the Women's Falange: it was the death of the old leaders of the Falange (José Antonio Primo de Rivera and O. Redondo) that moved Pilar Primo de Rivera, José Antonio's sister, and Mercedes Sanz Bachiller, Redondo's sister, to the head of a new movement, which the subsequent leadership (Franco and the Church) would gradually reshape. For the Falange, separation of Church and state, the struggle against "big property," and a fascist conception of society and empire were paramount. Franco began to substitute a different set of priorities while the civil war was still raging. The overtly fascist tendencies would disappear from Francoism during World War II, following the death of Mussolini and the likelihood of an Allied victory. A Falangist plot against Franco was crushed in 1937. At that point it became safe to transfer José Antonio's ashes to the Escorial and continue the indoctrination of the masses in a "national-Catholic" rather than fascist direction.[17]

The civil war allowed Franco to recruit women for service in an organization known as Auxilio Social (or Social Aid, originally named Winter Aid and based on the German Winterhilfe). Franco incorporated this "God-ordained" outpouring "of balm and grace" into the Women's Falange in 1937. Members prepared food for the troops, made uniforms, and cared for the wounded at the front and behind the lines. They also broadcast propaganda and conducted "national education" missions throughout Spain. According to the organization's own figures, 58 of its 580,000 members were killed during the war, an indication that some of the missions undertaken were dangerous. The new Falange used publications aimed at women and children to exalt Isabelle the Catholic queen and Saint Theresa of Avila, whose history was the focus of considerable research.

Legislative Rectification

Wartime Francoism had no room for any female heroines except in the service of God and no room for women in general except in the service of motherhood. In the presence of 10,000 members of the Women's Falange Pilar Primo de Rivera addressed El Caudillo in May 1939 in "celebration of victory." The "only mission assigned to women by the Fatherland," she noted, "is at home."[18] Cardinal Gomá had been saying the same thing in editorials for women's publications since the summer of 1934. His 1937 letter to the bishops of the entire world gave proof that the Church supported the rebellion. In 1939 El Caudillo and the primate recognized their mutual interests and assured each other of support in an exchange of letters.

In September 1936 "morality was restored" by a decree abolishing coeducational schools. In March 1938 the government "liberated the married woman from factories and work." Along with this "liberation" came maternity bonuses and a ban on women entering the professions. In 1938 the law on civil marriage was nullified, and the divorce law was retroactively repealed. Between 1941 and 1946 numerous laws were passed concerning abortion, adultery, and concubinage. A woman who lived as a concubine was subject to a long prison term and a heavy fine. But a man who killed his unfaithful wife and her lover was subject only to banishment; if he merely inflicted wounds without killing anyone, he was entitled to automatic acquittal. Prostitution remained legal, however.

The Church regained control of the schools. The Falange, newly reorganized, and its compulsory teachers' union aided in this enterprise. Teaching assignments were to be made by sex, and only subjects "adapted to Catholic dogma and morality" could be taught.[19] The age of majority was increased to twenty-five, and women were obliged to remain in their fathers' homes until they either married or entered a convent.

Women Reduced to Silence

Hatred of women who supported the Republic was a powerful motive. Can it help us to understand how, after 1939, even the most active women on the right—members of Parliament, engineers, teachers among them—all extolled motherhood as the "only profession worthy of a woman"? There is no denying that after January 1938 especially, when a Francoist victory became likely, the pro-Franco media began denouncing women of the left as "viragos, sluts, monsters, and bloodsuckers," to choose a few of the choicer epithets. They were responsible for the catastrophe, it was alleged, because it was they who had destroyed the Christian family and besmirched the chastity of the rest of Spanish women.

At times the coup itself was almost forgotten. The Women's Falange helped to construct an image of the ideal woman. It participated in the reeducation of "red" women and their children and established a "social service" for women, the counterpart of compulsory military service for men; any woman who did not serve could be stripped of her passport.

The history of the repression of women under Franco is similar in most respects to that of men: exile, execution, prison, reeducation of their children, denunciation, professional blacklisting, and book burning were measures that affected all Republicans. But women also endured rape, castor oil, shaved heads, and church prisons. Many paid with their lives. Exactly how many is unknown, but in Madrid in 1939 prisoners were being executed at the rate of 6,000 a month, according to figures reported by Mussolini's ambassador, Count Ciano. And of course women suffered for an offense that only they could commit, the crime of being the wife, widow, or mother of a "vanquished" Republican.

Within the space of ten years, Spanish women compressed experiences that women in other European countries had acquired over a period of several generations. They benefited from legislation more progressive than that passed by any other parliamentary democracy. Many participated in the revolution or witnessed its consequences. All suffered from the war and some from the advent of Franco's national-Catholic regime; some were exiled.

There is no denying the rapid pace of events, so rapid that it is difficult to evaluate the actual role played by women themselves or to assess the impact of early Republican efforts to change Spanish society. From scattered sources, painstakingly assembled, historians are beginning to reconstruct ever more comprehensive views—in a feminine perspective—of anarchism and socialism and of Francoism and its opposition. Divorce and maternity, education, the press, and the war have all been subjected to fresh study in recent years. Much remains to be done, however: too little is known about rural areas, labor, organizations, and connections with women in other European countries, for example.

The difficulties of research are compounded by the well-known administrative incompetence, concealment and destruction of documents, and historical distortions of the Franco era. But whatever the obstacles, political or otherwise, to uncovering the truth, nothing can diminish the proud accomplishments of Spanish women during this period.

Along with "political adulthood" (as the right to vote is often called in Spanish) Spanish women gained not only citizenship but a sense of their own worth, an awareness of themselves as individuals. These benefits accrued to women far outside the cultural and political elite. And the lesson was remembered long after 1936: during the war, Republican newspapers, letters, and observers frequently stated that women were fighting for their rights, including the right to control their own bodies.

Although it would be quite unacceptable to obscure very real political differences, it is worth pointing out that the Republic established one very important area of common ground between women of the left and right, as study of their publications makes clear: women for the first time voiced their views in public. It was no accident that right-wing women's publications vanished between 1935 and 1937, only to resume publication under strict control.

General Franco's long-lived regime was by no means monolithic. And women's lives were not all the same. After years of silence, clandestinity, "repudiation" by some of past "errors," and the enforced docility of an entire generation,[20] several factors conspired to remind large numbers of women of their social and political oppression: persistent opposition to Franco, which took a variety of forms; the strikes of the late 1950s; the economic crisis of 1960–1964, which forced many women either to emigrate or return to work; and, after 1960, foreign tourism, which made women aware of how people from other parts of the world lived and thought. The first step in the new feminist awakening was a crisis of social conscience. Many things were influential here: student associations, neighborhood groups, clandestine action by the Communist Party, and churches where social issues could be discussed, to name a few. Feminists also spoke out in 1975 and 1976 in political rallies that went beyond the limits envisaged by the political parties.[21]

Between 1975 and 1978, when a new constitution was promulgated, historians, politicians, and feminists revived memories of experiences that had been forgotten for forty years. Although the struggle for democracy and women's rights is not yet won, Spain has come a long way in recent years.

TRANSLATED FROM THE FRENCH BY ARTHUR GOLDHAMMER

7

French Women under Vichy

Hélène Eck

HISTORICAL STUDIES OF the Vichy regime over the past twenty years have demonstrated beyond a shadow of a doubt that the policy of collaboration with Nazi Germany was born early and pursued continuously. Certain aspects of the regime, moreover, have been shown to belong to a thoroughly French ideological tradition, however strange such a tradition may seem in a country that had embraced democracy in a secular, republican form and where the left played a considerable role. Clearly, the Vichy regime was not totalitarian. It certainly was, however, an authoritarian and repressive regime that defined the French people first by legally and then by physically excluding "undesirables" from its midst. The responsibility of the French government in the implementation of the Final Solution is well known. Nevertheless, the diverse ideological and political components that made up the regime, the struggles for power that pitted each of these against the others, and the internal evolution of the regime itself, which in the space of four years took it from antiliberalism to the "brink of totalitarianism," prevent us from categorizing Vichy simply as one more reactionary regime bent exclusively on preserving some image of the past. Also inherent in Vichy was a determination to improve the country's functional organization, together with a capacity for innovation manifested most strikingly in its centralized economic administration; these features of the regime were not always compatible with strict conservative ideals.[1]

A "pluralist dictatorship," Vichy, seeking to transcend its own contradictions, undertook to reorganize a society whose complexity defies easy description. If France was essentially a nation of farmers and small businessmen, it also had its share of big business and its concentrations of working-class population. Although its citizens held freedom dear, they had been plunged into disarray by the German invasion of May-June 1940 and the ensuing defeat of French forces. The relief of the armistice soon gave way to hostility toward the occupying power. In order to establish the regime's real impact on French society, to measure its "effective power," its capacity to modify social realities and political attitudes inherited from the Republic, a new synthesis is needed, along with additional research designed to delve into the material realities and discover how the French lived through these years, sometimes with the Vichy government, sometimes against it.[2] Much of the existing research on this period does take account of the role and place of women, but not sufficiently to justify any claim to extensive knowledge.[3] Such a judgment may seem paradoxical in light of the sheer number of works devoted to the Occupation years. It is less surprising when one pauses to reflect that the ability of gendered history to reveal important characteristics of a society may not have seemed especially pertinent so long as attention was focused mainly on the political complexity of Vichy and the operation of the government, which at its highest levels was of course staffed exclusively by men. Miranda Pollard's work has shown, however, that this same political history can be approached by analyzing how Vichy's discourse on women formed an integral part of the regime's intrinsic ideology.[4]

The regime's self-proclaimed goal of National Revolution held out to women a symbolic ideal of motherhood, family, and home. Meanwhile, the state, in its actual, day-to-day operations, dealt with a very different set of realities: shortages, social services, manpower for Germany. The National Revolution was by no means a failure in all its aspects. Its implementation did not automatically exclude women from the public sphere, and they were present whenever the policies of the regime interfered with their expectations or values. Of course it was not "women" in general who acted, but specific groups of women.

The Vichy government's efforts to give concrete meaning to its "Work, Family, Country" slogan pointed up the contradictions in a regime that was often obliged by circumstances to take a short-term approach to governing. But circumstances and lack of resources alone are not enough to account for the discrepancy between Vichy's dreams and the realities of the Occupation. The very structures of society resisted the new state's efforts to impose its will. Many households refused to comply with the government's orders, although their refusal was not necessarily strictly political or connected in any way with the active Resistance. Here, of course, women played an essential role: alone or with their families, in partnership with their husbands and others, they developed strategies of survival. The attitudes and values that motivated them were often a far cry from the precepts of the government. There was nothing new about this, of course, except that the disparity between the behavior of citizens and the wishes of the government was especially clear at a time when family values were being put to the test and considerable obstacles stood in the way of accomplishing even the most routine tasks. Noncooperation, subterfuge, and resistance: the behavior of women forms one important strand of French social and political history in these years.

The history of the Occupation is part of a larger history which can be periodized in a variety of ways depending on one's point of view. The history of the family, for example, obeys a different timetable from political, military, or diplomatic history. To what extent did the conditions of life under the Occupation strengthen the renewed emphasis on family life and family relationships that was already a feature of the period between the wars? Although we know that the role of women in the workforce declined in general between the 1920s and the 1960s, we still have only a poor idea of how the Occupation fits into that overall pattern. It was the disaster of World War II, moreover, that finally made citizens of French women, in the sense that they were at least granted the right to vote after the war ended. But we can also say that the Occupation hastened the politicization of women in another sense: did not the events of these years drive home the importance of politics and its consequences for everyday life? Remember that the years of collaboration and Occupation were in no way comparable to the period 1914–1918, when there had been a sharp division between front and rear, combatants and civilians, one's own country and the enemy. From 1940 to 1944 the "war" was everywhere and nowhere, with all the ambiguities that might be expected to arise from such an extraordinary situation.

Family First

The *État français* [the official designation of the Vichy regime, marking its formal distinction from *la République française*—Trans.] was born in the sudden, overwhelming defeat of May-June 1940. Beyond the immediate problem of the armistice and relations with the occupying power, the authoritarian and reactionary new regime sought to offer a comprehensive response to the military, political, and moral crisis in which France found itself. In the midst of the extreme confusion of the summer of 1940, the Vichy regime proposed solutions notable for their simplicity: the French, their government told them, had paid with defeat for the "pleasure-seeking spirit" that had reigned in the country since 1918, bringing about a moral decadence that had proved fatal. The only way to redeem this collective guilt was for each French citizen to contribute to the effort of national reconstruction, whose principles and objectives added up to Vichy's "Work, Family, Country." The National Revolution was to be carried out under the leadership of Marshal Pétain, who presented himself to the nation as a father: a true father, clear-sighted enough to scold his children for their misbehavior yet kind enough to want to alleviate their suffering. The irresponsible ones would be punished by being deprived of the right to vote. In place of the old Republic, they were offered a novel form of political contract that was fundamentally a family relationship: in return for their father's protection, they would have to promise absolute loyalty and obedience.

The organicism of Vichy condemned individualism and its corollaries, self-assertion and the pursuit of liberty. It celebrated natural groups and social institutions that guaranteed the individual a place in society while at the same time imposing discipline. It rejected abstract intellectualism as a will-o'-the-wisp with no link to vital national traditions. It advocated an ethos of service and effort, duty and solidarity, and called for the realization of concrete projects in the general interest. When the National Revolution was complete, France would find itself purged of foreign and antinational elements. The country would then be one big family, hierarchical and united.

The Vichy regime defined each person's place in society according to the group to which he or she belonged. Its ideology deprived French citizens of the free use of their rights and aptitudes, thereby condemning society to stagnation and the individual to an all but hereditary fate.

Sexual Difference and Complementarity

In defining the role of women in society Vichy pointed to sexual difference and complementarity within the family. The duties of women were implicit in the principle of sexual difference: women were destined "by nature and vocation" for motherhood. Sexual difference was also the basis for the rules of behavior to which girls were expected to conform and for the skills they were expected to acquire. It also determined what types of activity and what locales were suitable for women. Nonetheless it would be an exaggeration to say that Vichy, for reasons of misogyny, wished to confine women to the home and exclude them from all forms of participation in social life.

In a broader sense, the regime's goal was to reinforce the family, which it viewed as an organic unit of a functioning society. Family interests took precedence over the interests of its individual members. In order to function properly, the family required a strict division of physical chores, roles, and psychological attitudes: the father, as head of the family, was expected to work and to wield authority; the mother was responsible for creating a loving home. Because husband and wife were different but complementary, they could together create a stable family environment, provided that each stayed within the limits of his or her role and exhibited the virtues appropriate to his or her sex. By thus exalting and intertwining notions of duty and difference, the regime established an ideal of the family and used that ideal to glorify motherhood as the only possible destiny for women. Anything that tended to estrange women from that destiny, whether materially or psychologically, was considered unnatural, immoral, and inimical to the national interest. There was no such thing as a bad mother; there were only bad women who refused to become mothers. The decision not to have a child was not considered to be the result of a woman's free choice; it was seen, rather, as the culmination of disastrous social changes that had created a false image, causing women to forget their *raison d'être* and luring them toward one or even both of two pernicious extremes: the denial of femininity, which took the form of a quest for equality with men (and out of which came ambition, pride, and intellectualism), and the perversion of femininity through an obsession with seduction (out of which came frivolity, flirtatiousness, and infidelity).

By freely and actively embracing their destiny as mothers, women would rediscover the virtues of true femininity. This was the only way of reconciling personal happiness with social utility in a manner compatible with the regime's goals of national revolution and social regeneration. Woman as mother took her place in Vichy's Pantheon of social role models alongside the peasant and the artisan: all three were seen as preserving a tradition defined by abnegation, patience, and respect for a job well done. In return, families and society as a whole owed mothers respect and recognition: Mother's Day, which had been celebrated officially since 1926, became a private as well as communal holiday under Vichy.

Continuity and Change in the Law

"Concerned to restore the health and stability of the family" (law of July 23, 1942), the Vichy regime reinforced the institution of the family even more vigorously than the Third Republic had done in its waning years. It is important, however, to try to determine which aspects of Vichy's policies continued the policies of its predecessors and which stemmed directly from the desire of this regime of moral order to regulate individual behavior.[5] In response to the demographic decline of the interwar period, republican governments had taken steps to strengthen the family. Although the first pronatalist measures were purely repressive, the government's efforts in this area gradually expanded as demographic and social policies were belatedly and incompletely harmonized. Having inherited the Family Code voted into law under the Daladier government in July 1939, Vichy expanded its application. The corporatist inspiration of such laws as the Gounot Law of December 29, 1942 (which established links between family organizations and the government) proved to be no obstacle to keeping certain of their provisions on the books after the Liberation. Thus a new form of state intervention developed: the family became a social phenomenon of public interest.

In 1938 married women had been granted additional rights, and their capacity to act on their own initiative had been broadened. Vichy saw itself as the champion of family interests over and above the interests of individuals. Its goal was to ensure family unity and stability, and this made it imperative that a woman should be able to take her husband's place in his absence or incapacitation. Hence Vichy had no reason to limit women's newly won capacity to act in the family name, particularly since many men were still in Germany as prisoners of war or workers. There were, however, limits to this rather half-hearted evolution toward equality in marriage, and the effects of these limits continued to be felt long after 1945. Under the law of 1938 the husband remained responsible for decisions having a major impact on the life of the household. The husband enjoyed this prerogative as "head of the family" (law of September 22, 1942). In 1945, when the restored Republic was seeking ways to demonstrate its innovative spirit, jurists held that the husband's right to veto his wife's desire to work was in effect "a public-order statute" inspired by "the interest of the family in general,"[6] and as such it would remain in effect until 1965. The husband, moreover, would remain the legal "head of the family" until 1970. The authoritarian and reactionary character of the Vichy regime emerges very clearly in laws that limited the freedom of married couples and cast motherhood as a duty to the nation.

Abortion was illegal in France from 1920 to 1975, but Vichy changed the nature of the crime by characterizing abortionists as "dangerous individuals" guilty "of acts injurious to the French nation" and subject to administrative internment and judgment by state tribunals. In theory, the law of February 15, 1942, spared women who sought abortions but vigorously prosecuted those who aided them. Between 1942 and 1944 an average of nearly 4,000 people annually were found guilty under the provisions of this law. Still more striking, one female abortionist was guillotined in 1943. In order to set an example, Vichy in this instance overlooked the unwritten law that exempted women from capital punishment.

Obtaining a divorce became a long and difficult process as a result of the law of April 2, 1941, which reversed the trend of the 1930s toward simpler divorce procedures. Supporting one's family was now a "moral obligation," and "desertion" became a crime under the law of July 23, 1942. This does not mean, however, that Vichy apportioned family duties equally between husband and wife. Women still bore most of the burden, particularly when it came to marital fidelity. Because so many couples were separated, the government took steps to keep women in the fold: the law of December 23, 1942, "intended to protect the dignity of the home," specifically addressed adultery in the case of the wife of a man held as a prisoner of war. Such adultery was no longer merely a private offense but "a crime against the social order, subject to prosecution for the public good."[7] Judges proved especially vigilant in protecting the rights of POWs by interpreting in rather broad terms the provision of the law that limited prosecution to cases of "notorious concubinage."

This law raises a general and not easily answered question: did the people of France approve of the government's pro-family measures, which, being promulgated not only *for* the family but *in the name of* the family, tended to conflate private morality with the social order? French society was not entirely clear about how it stood on such matters as domestic happiness, sex roles, and women in the workplace; its values were neither uniform nor easy to ascertain. Nevertheless, it is safe to say that a new consensus had developed in the 1930s: people agreed that couples should marry for love and that children and home life were important. They also aspired to something new, something that might be called family privacy, that is, a home life free of the constraints of work and community.[8] Various Christian groups had begun thinking in the 1930s about the couple and the nature of marriage, and reflection on these themes continued during the war and flourished afterward. Readers of the new mass-market magazines for women (such as *Marie-Claire,* which first appeared in 1937, and *Confidences,* first published in 1938) also asked themselves what it took to make a successful marriage. These magazines advocated an ideal of "constructed happiness," which reconciled love with propriety and romance with everyday realities.[9] This ideal was not universally shared, much less experienced. In many rural areas the primary aim of marriage was still to preserve or enhance the family farm. And the new ideal did not necessarily coincide with the reactionary, authoritarian ideology of the National Revolution. Vichy stood for duty, obedience, and hierarchy, whereas the new thinking sought to reconcile happiness with duty and morality with freedom in a climate of love and mutual respect. Its adherents would be against undue government intervention in family matters on the grounds that couples should be allowed to make their own decisions.

Should women work? Françoise Thébaud has shown that the ideal of woman as mother, wife, and homemaker was widely shared, even on the left. The disease-prevention and social-hygiene policies of the 1930s and the new emphasis on "scientific" child-rearing increased the burden on mothers and pointed up the alleged benefits of remaining at home with the children.[10] The Depression and the very real threat of unemployment may have led many working-class women to think they would be better off at home than in the arduous, wearing, and in many cases precarious jobs available to less skilled female workers. In a report prepared in 1936 when she was working as a stockroom supervisor at the Galeries Lafayette, Berthie Albrecht noted that the women working under her "do not envy wealthy women for their clothes or luxury items. They envy them for one thing only: the tantalizing prospect of staying home." Members of the Jeunesse Agricole Catholique (Christian Farm Youth) called for rural women to be granted "the right to stay home" and exemption from the most onerous field work.[11] This renewed emphasis on family values, together with the expectation of government assistance, may explain why a substantial number of women approved of and participated in the implementation of Vichy's family policies.

Women's Civic Action

The virtuous ladies hailed by the proponents of Vichy's National Revolution were also modern women: intelligent, efficient, and delighted not to have to work, they nevertheless kept a close eye on what was going on around them for the sake of their families. Simply being an excellent housewife and mother was not enough to secure the happiness of one's family.

The Christian Role in the Education of Women

Scholars have long recognized that it was a natural extension of the role of women in the home to participate in various forms of social and charity work, especially in connection with a church-related group or organization. The interwar years saw the development of "educational enterprises run by and intended exclusively for women." These groups stressed both "their role in educating the working class and their exclusively feminine mission."[12] Their ambition was to educate women and girls and to train new youth movement leaders capable of working independently of their male counterparts.

After World War I middle- and upper-class families realized that, even if marriage was still the ideal, girls would have to prepare for the possibility that they might need to support themselves and live alone, at least for a time. In the 1930s a generation of young girls—still said to be "in the flower of life" but no longer innocent or timid—discovered the world through group activities, dances, trips to the movies, and working side-by-side with men in white-collar jobs. Later in the decade young women clad in shorts could be seen riding bicycles or hiking with backpacks from hostel to hostel in search of nature and its supposed boons. Although some priests remained convinced that "physical education is unsuitable for women," gym teachers and Girl Scout leaders no longer subscribed to such old-fashioned, prudish ideas. Indeed, physical activity was encouraged for its presumed hygienic and moral benefits. The ideal woman, most people now agreed, should have a healthy (slender yet robust) body and a frank, natural expression connoting righteousness and courage. The women's press and fashion industry publicized the new image, rejecting "the mannered, overly elaborate ideal of beauty" of a bygone era in favor of naturalness and simplicity.[13] The modern ideal emphasized the importance of the individual woman, and girls were taught to show initiative and assume greater responsibility than in the past. Of course the new woman was by no means the exclusive property of the Christian groups that taught these lessons, but the modern ideal gained ground also during the National Revolution because Catholic militants (including Jeanne Aubert, who in 1928 had founded the JOCF) played a prominent role in the Secrétariat Général à la Jeunesse (Department of Youth Affairs) between 1940 and 1943.

Vichy government's actions on behalf of young women were intended to clarify "the role of women in politics." An example of this was the establishment of the Ecole Nationale des Cadres

Féminins at Ecully in October 1940. The school's purpose was to train "responsible leaders." Most of the young women accepted by the school were "drawn from the ranks of youth groups and social workers." The theoretical and practical training they received was designed to prepare them for immediate service in running centers, first established in September 1940, for unemployed female workers between the ages of fourteen and twenty-one. These centers were intended to supplement already existing public and private training schools. In 1944 some 345 occupational training centers served approximately 20,000 young women.[14]

Women thus demonstrated their competence and efficiency in serving this youthful clientele. The educational methods were tinged with anti-intellectualism and anti-individualism, however, and there was something suspect about the whole concept of occupational training at a time when the whole republican tradition of education for women was subject to intense scrutiny. Between the wars a series of reforms had brought girls' secondary education roughly into line with boys', a change that had drawn vehement criticism from certain parents and teachers as well as from groups such as the Association des Parents de l'Ecole Libre. Critics invoked the female "personality," the vocation of women, and the supposedly distinctive "culture" of the female sex to denounce an egalitarianism that they felt failed to pay sufficient attention to gender differences. They called for research on how to teach girls "different subjects in a different manner."[15]

Nevertheless, the Vichy regime never raised a fundamental challenge to the principle of equal education for both sexes, though it did make "home economics" courses mandatory for girls at all levels (law of March 18, 1942). The law was not very widely enforced, however, in part because of material shortages but also, perhaps, because of quiet resistance to the government's orders on the part of female teachers. Was the Vichy government simply unable to revoke an established right and sweep away what was by now a venerable tradition of equal education? Or was the tightening of the selection process that followed the reform of secondary education mandated in 1941 sufficient to limit the number of girls admitted to secondary schools? (In 1938 there had been 55,000 female students in *lycées* and *collèges* throughout France and some 50,000 girls in *écoles primaires supérieures,* or middle schools.)

The Ambiguities of Social Service

Wartime shortages and other hardships justified the government's calls for mutual solidarity and support. In order to cope with the urgent needs of the moment, the government and its affiliates developed a substantial network of social services to aid families and women who suddenly found themselves without husbands. The period witnessed a sharp increase in centralized state intervention in health and social services. Workers in these fields became more professionalized, and their activities were supervised by a new government department in charge of family and health services. Certain private groups assisted the government, among them the Mouvement Populaire des Familles. The MPF, originally part of the Ligue Ouvrière Chrétienne, became a separate organization in 1941. These private groups occasionally came into conflict with state agencies and with the Secours National, the umbrella organization responsible for coordinating the activities of private relief services.

The MPF spirit, which is summed up by the slogan "see, judge, act," was ideally suited to the wartime climate. The movement urged the wives of prisoners to "deal with their own problems" and to participate in public relief efforts. In the same spirit of solving one's own problems, the wives of prisoners formed the Fédération des Associations de Femmes de Prisonniers in order to exert a direct influence on matters that interested them, circumventing cumbersome official agencies.[16]

In one sense the war marked the end of an era: never again would the social-service profession be quite so apolitical, autonomous, or exclusively female. The war years clearly pointed up the inadequacy of this social-service model. For one thing, social workers were not always politically innocent: some participated in propaganda to persuade French workers to accept work in Germany. Radio Paris in 1943 broadcast reassuring reports from any number of social workers just back from Germany. At the other extreme of the political spectrum, the Combat resistance movement in the occupied zone received help from female students at the Ecole des Surintendantes d'Usine (School of Factory Supervisors).

Looking back on their activities, several former activists in the MPF raised questions about their work: although the need for assistance was pressing and genuine, the group might have chosen a different set of goals. Some members in 1945 took "very bitter note" of their failure to contribute to the Resistance. Some social workers found themselves in a similarly delicate position at the time of the Liberation.[17]

Under Vichy, then, the public role of women fell somewhere between total emancipation and absolute subjugation to authoritarian patriarchy. The regime did not condemn the participation of women in public life and to some extent ratified it. Women were allowed to take part in municipal administration. In industry, the Labor Charter of October 1941 provided that plant committees must be set up in all firms employing more than one hundred workers. Women were not excluded, even if very few actually participated. In 1942, for example, three women sat on the plant committee of Berliet (a manufacturer of trucks). Finally, Vichy's National Council considered granting women the right to vote under a revised constitution.[18] Such recognition of the role of women could, in theory at any rate, help to enlist their support for the National Revolution. Unlike totalitarian regimes, however, Vichy never imposed mandatory service on women or placed them under direct state control. It established no official youth organization or women's organization. After 1943, though, the methods of the regime became increasingly difficult to distinguish from those of a fascist police state, and both officials and members of many Christian groups reacted defiantly to rhetoric that referred less to the family and more to helping to bring about a German victory.

What, in any case, did family and civic service mean to millions of women obliged day after day to face an endless variety of shortages and hardships? What kind of support could the government expect when the realities of the Occupation soon belied its dream of a peaceful, orderly rural society sustained by the tireless devotion of virtuous mothers?

War and Family Values

The Germans took 1,600,000 French prisoners in 1940. More than half were married men, and one-quarter were fathers. Nearly a million men remained in prisoner-of-war camps for five years. For those women fortunate enough to welcome husbands, fiancés, and sons back home soon after the defeat, respite was short-lived.

Between 1942 and 1944 some 600,000 to 700,000 French workers left for Germany under the Compulsory Labor Service (Service du Travail Obligatoire, or STO). The experience of separation this time was different from that of World War I. Soldiers in the trenches had been able to return home on leave for brief visits, but captivity meant radical separation. Although STO workers were theoretically entitled to leaves, the Germans soon suspended this privilege. The only contact with home was via mail and authorized package shipments. As in 1914–1918, women became titular heads of families and found that they could "manage fairly well on their own," yet resented being forced by circumstances to do so. Sarah Fishman has shown that the husband's absence was not by itself enough to call traditional sex-role divisions into question. Women considered themselves to be temporarily filling in for their husbands. One POW's wife recalled that "the Resistance was first of all maintaining the house, keeping hope alive, and getting things ready for his return home."[19]

Another sign of the times: adults—in an age that exalted youth—were afraid of the harmful consequences that the father's absence might have on the children's psychology and morality. Adolescents might be tempted to disobey their mothers, and smaller children might suffer from the absence of "normal" family life. Officials advised mothers to explain to the children that their father was away and that in his absence she would be assuming his responsibilities.

Women thus acted as "guardians" while their husbands were away. Men expected no less. As in World War I, many were obsessed by the thought of being abandoned or cuckolded. Several factors contributed to these fears: many prisoners of war were young and had been married for only a brief time; the prison camps were rife with rumors that divorce applications had gone way up; and, in contrast to 1914–1918, France was occupied by a foreign army. The government responded to these concerns by adopting the previously mentioned law of December 1942 "to protect the dignity of the home." It also relied on communal surveillance by neighbors, coworkers, and family members. Members of the Fédération des Femmes de Prisonniers recall having suffered a good deal from the suspiciousness of friends and neighbors, who believed that a lonely woman was bound to be weak. Some women found the heightened scrutiny unbearable and perverse. Laure, a young mother with two little girls, lived with her in-laws. In her journal she recorded her hope that she and her husband might one day share responsibilities in an independent household: "The thing is, I need you. A family is a daddy, a mommy, and children. It isn't a sovereign pair of grandparents with three children, me being the oldest." She confesses to having been jealous herself: some prisoners did have contact with foreign workers and even German women despite the German high command's repeated warnings and punishments.[20] When the war ended, some men found it difficult to resume a normal family life. The experience of captivity ended some marriages. Clearly, the above-normal number of men suing for divorce in 1945–1947 was related to the return of prisoners of war, although allowances must be made for a certain number of divorces deferred because of the war and Vichy's unusually restrictive divorce legislation.[21]

The Occupation also disrupted ordinary human bonds, loosened certain social constraints, and allowed for the expression of previously repressed emotions. It was not unusual, for example, for one member of a couple to denounce the other. The moral shock of defeat, the hardships of daily life, the temptation to reap easy profits through illicit dealings, and the need for many young people to leave home (either to join the STO or to attempt to avoid service)—all these things tended to diminish respect for parental authority and established values. After the Liberation political leaders, social critics, and psychologists worried about the future of the so-called J3's, the supply agency's code designation for a category of adolescents deemed to be fragile, demoralized, and prone to delinquency. Brigitte Friang, a woman of strict Catholic upbringing who was a student at the time, remembers that "the times were crazy enough that it was easy to make my parents believe anything." She recalls with amazement that they put up no protest when she said she would have to stay out all night because of the curfew or went out for no particular reason: "The war was their collective failure. . . . It exposed many of their cherished principles to challenge. They could no longer set themselves up as an absolute standard."[22]

At the same time, some marriages and families were strengthened by adversity and the need to survive from day to day. Some farm and merchant couples shortchanged the authorities on compulsory deliveries and sold the diverted produce on the black market, occasionally reaping windfall profits. Some families banded together to help one of their number avoid service in

Germany. Last but not least, I must also note the courage and daring of those who took risks to protect a family member wanted by the authorities. The strength of the family reasserted itself: as early as 1943 there was a surprising increase in the rate of legitimate births (from 14.7 per thousand in 1939 to 15.8 in 1943), a harbinger of the postwar baby boom. One hesitates to speculate about the reasons for this. Does it suggest that the government's family policy was a success? Or does it reflect a tendency to retreat into private life at a time when the outside world seemed threatening?

Work and Subsistence

As in World War I, women were called upon to work so that their families might survive, but this time they were not asked to contribute to the war effort. They suffered the consequences, moreover, of an economy run by a government that was not in control of its own destiny but subject to the demands of the occupying power.

Vichy and Female Labor

In October 1940 the government imposed severe restrictions on the hiring or continued employment of women by government agencies. These measures came at a time of aggravated unemployment due to the disruption of industry and the return home of many soldiers whose jobs had been taken over by women during the so-called Phony War. The new restrictions did not apply to private industry, however. Still, the law was quite unpopular, and the government was forced to explain that it was only a temporary measure designed to distribute the existing jobs in an equitable manner. In a radio broadcast a member of the staff of the secretary of state for labor, René Guerdan, insisted that "the government never intended to lay it down as a principle that married women belong at home, as some ill-informed observers may have believed." For women, however, it made little difference whether the restrictions were a matter of principle, of circumstances, or both. Prolonged captivity, the siphoning off of male workers by the STO in 1942–1943, and the low incomes of many households even after husband and wife had been reunited made female labor an economic and social reality: women had to work, both because the nation required it (male labor being scarce) and because families somehow had to make ends meet. In September 1942 the 1940 law was suspended, and even earlier the government had begun hiring women to work as teachers, postal clerks, and railway employees.

Vichy moved still further from the principles of the National Revolution by acceding to German demands that all women between the ages of fifteen and forty-five (some nine million in all) must be available for compulsory labor requisitions. Although the regime did agree to supply Germany with male workers, it never actually gave in on the matter of female workers. The laws "concerning the utilization and assignment of labor" (September 4, 1942, August 26, 1943, and February 1, 1944) applied first to single men between the ages of twenty and thirty-five and second to women between the ages of eighteen and forty-five, both single and married but not mothers; it was further specified that women requisitioned as laborers would be assigned only to jobs in France.

It appears that the Vichy government wanted to set limits to demands by the occupying power that did not exclude women *a priori*. As early as 1941, German propaganda called upon women as well as men to volunteer for work in Germany, and some women did in fact go. Early in 1943, Fritz Sauckel, the German official responsible for recruiting foreign labor, negotiated an agreement providing for 100,000 French workers, male and female, to be sent to Germany in addition to a contingent of 150,000 workers with experience in the metals industries. In April 1943 concern that single women would indeed be sent to Germany prompted various Christian groups to petition Marshal Pétain. Rev. Boegner went to Vichy for the purpose of securing a promise from the head of state that the STO would spare women.[23] In January 1944 the Germans issued new demands for workers, including women, but in a report to Hitler on the negotiations, Sauckel noted that "the Marshal did not agree to the employment of female workers in Germany but only in France."[24] Opposition mounted: the assembly of cardinals and archbishops published a protest in February 1944, while the MPF in Saint-Etienne informed the prefect of widespread fears raised by the law of February 1. The Resistance distributed tracts proclaiming "Not a single French woman for the Reich!" The restrictive clauses in the laws mentioned above did not prevent the occupying power from exerting strong local pressures, and some women were simply deported. In June 1944, 44,835 French women were at work in Germany. They made up roughly 2 percent of the total number of foreign women workers; Soviet and Polish women alone accounted for some 85 percent of the total.[25] Yet even though French women did not go to Germany in large numbers, how many worked for the Reich in French factories as the occupying authorities required?

The Employment of Women in Wartime

Between 1936 and 1946, the proportion of women with jobs increased by 3.4 percent according to contemporary data, or between 1 and 1.5 percent when the raw figures are adjusted.[26] The increase affected all age groups with the exception of the 25–34 year-olds; it was particularly significant among the 15–24 year-olds. Thus the interwar decline in the proportion of women with jobs was temporarily halted. This was especially true in the industrial sector, which employed 53 percent of women working in nonfarm jobs in 1921 but only 44 percent in 1936, and the change occurred despite a shift in the pattern of female employment that saw many women move from "textiles to publishing."[27] Yet the aggregate figures for the decade obscure the intervening fluctuations: unemployment and instability in 1936–1938, increased hiring during the Phony War, and uncertain figures for 1940–1944, a period for which the available comprehensive studies do not single out female labor as such.[28] It is therefore risky to assert that women replaced or supplemented male workers without being precise as to when, in what branch of industry, in what proportion, and in which jobs. That said, we would do well to remember the circumstances affecting the hiring of women. French industrial production overall was being strangled: "Most branches were set back more than a century," according to Alfred Sauvy's calculations.[29] Were women able to hold on to jobs they already held in these difficult times? The answer depends on the region and the type and attitude of the employer.

After 1941 French production for German consumption gradually extended "to a wide range of businesses throughout the country."[30] This production was organized in a more systematic fashion after 1943, in the wake of an accord that Albert Speer negotiated with the Bichelonne ministry. Under the terms of that agreement, firms working for the Reich were assigned a priority for the recruitment of labor and allocation of raw materials. The occupying power was in the process of assessing the available human resources. In the region of Vienne, for example, the demand for labor included 15 percent women. The Germans naturally favored sectors of the economy most useful to the war effort, such as mining; they were far less concerned with the production of intermediate or consumer goods. Synthetic textiles could not make up for the loss of wool and cotton, for example, and employment in the already declining textile sector continued to decrease, particularly in the Nord. By contrast, in Saint-Etienne, where metals firms had been severely hampered by the departure for Germany of large numbers of skilled workers, women now found themselves in demand. In the Paris area, women in the metals and electrical construction industries found that employment, which had already begun to stabilize before the war, remained stable, at least for the most skilled workers. In Marseille a recession in the foodstuffs industry and in the commercial sector substantially increased the rate of unemployment for women, which peaked in 1943; other sectors (such as the chemical and metals industries) held steady.

Under the circumstances the attitudes of businessmen proved to be crucial. Despite the shortage of raw materials, some employers held on to their female workers. The big Paris fashion houses did so, and so did smaller textile firms in western France. In Saint-Etienne the family-run Casino Company coped with adversity as it always did: the workforce was reduced as sales declined, but employees received help from the firm to protect them from total unemployment and starvation.[31] Women who could not find factory jobs were encouraged by new hiring in the public sector, where the pay was low and many men had left their jobs. Some 25,000 postal positions were held by temporary replacements, mostly women and even some very young girls. Between December 1941 and December 1943 the French national railroad hired 20,000 women.[32] What became of those jobs when committees were appointed to reduce the size and budget of public agencies in 1946–47?

For reasons discussed earlier, it would be unwise to assert categorically that more women took office jobs than factory jobs between 1940 and 1944, although that seems plausible since much of the increase in the nonindustrial, nonfarm employment of women was concentrated in this period. Just after the war it was estimated that the percentage of women in nonfarm jobs who were employed in the liberal professions and public sector had risen from 13.8 percent in 1936 to more than 21 percent.[33] It should come as no surprise that the employment of women increased despite the Vichy government's efforts to keep women home: they had to find ways to win the daily battle for survival in those difficult years.

The Daily Burden

How were women to survive with their husbands away, or even with their husbands at home, with wages frozen while prices continued to rise? And if official prices rose, black market prices soared out of sight, eating up most of the wage increases granted by the government, most notably in 1941. The average Parisian made 2,500 francs per month, but less skilled workers earned between 1,200 and 1,800, sometimes less. Disparities were even greater in other areas. In February 1944 a program broadcast on the national radio network noted that female textile workers in Normandy who were paid by the piece and often had to work with defective raw material earned less than 1,000 francs per month. That same year a kilo of butter went for 400 to 600 francs on the black market, if it could be had at all. In August 1943 the wife of a POW received a government allowance of 140 francs per week, or slightly more than the price of a blouse.

The government was not unmoved by the nation's plight. It increased various government allocations. In 1943 the special allocation for single-wage families created in 1941 was expanded to include unwed mothers. In December 1943 special indemnities and family allocations were supplemented. But such benefits could not take the place of a second income, which was indispensable to working-class families faced with food costs amounting to at least two-thirds of total family revenues. Owing to increasingly severe shortages, food rations, first established in 1940 and extended to nearly all categories of food in 1941, decreased steadily: meat rations went from 360 grams per week in 1940 to 120 in April 1943; milk fats went from 650 grams in August 1941 to 150 in August 1944. Since the regime's own ideology advocated social justice in order to put an end to class struggle, a publication like *Unité: Bulletin des Ouvriers de la Révolution Nationale* (the newsletter of "workers for the National Revolution") could in 1943 publish a vitriolic attack on "simplistic stereotypes depicting happy women surrounded by delightful children who make life a plea-sure" when the reality was more a "distressing tableau of womanly toil." The newsletter accordingly demanded "justice for working women."

By this point the National Revolution was all but forgotten. It was not governmental calls to sacrifice but everyday realities that forced women to give first priority to protecting their families and managing their households. The war obliged every woman to learn the lessons in home economics that officials wanted to teach girls in school. Newspapers, posters, and radio programs reminded women to economize and make things last and to save and recycle even the most insignificant items. The so-called feminine virtues, devotion to duty and sound common sense, were valued as never before. Women stood in endless lines, beginning with the line at city hall for the ration tickets without which it was impossible to purchase food or clothing. Then they stood in line at shops, never sure that there would be anything left to buy, for the state of supply was unpredictable. Some shipments arrived later than scheduled, and the government could at any moment decide to release stockpiled goods, so women had to be on the lookout at all times. Families organized their own private supply networks, relying on barter, "gray market" transactions, and friends and relatives in the country, where food was easier to obtain than in the cities.

There were also ways of supplementing the family diet: with gift packages from family members, through sales or distributions of food organized by businesses or organizations, through chil-dren's lunch programs and rural excursions, or by growing food in backyard gardens.[34] The health of children was a shared concern and a top priority. Social workers noticed scabies and impetigo in schoolchildren, signs of malnutrition. Young mothers were grateful for medical advice on how to minimize the effects of meager diets and cope with lack of home heating.

Shortages, scrimping, and constant vigilance continued to be part of the daily experience of most women until 1949, when rationing finally ended. Plenty did not return immediately after the Liberation, as many no doubt hoped it would. The experiences of the 1940s surely shaped the attitudes of women for many years to come. Skills learned during the Occupation served many of them well in the 1950s and early 1960s, when housing was crowded (owing to the baby boom) and labor-saving home appliances were still scarce.

The hardships of everyday life had many social and political consequences. They influenced people's attitudes toward the government. They affected the judgments people made of self-interested versus community-oriented behavior, judgments that could have political implications. There were many reasons in this period for women to beat a strategic retreat back to home and hearth and to adopt attitudes of "watchful expectation" and "self-protection."[35] The French may have decided to sit out a conflict whose military aspects unfolded elsewhere, but they could not avoid the politicization of their daily lives owing to the actions of their own government and the presence on French soil of an occupying power (extended to the entire territory of metropolitan France in November 1942). They could refrain from choosing between the Axis and Allied powers, but they could not ignore the appeals from both sides insisting that a choice was imperative. Women were not excluded from this battle. Their loyalty, like that of men, was a prize to be won, and they were therefore, with men, a target of propaganda as the opposing sides sought the support of the entire population for their ideology and strategy. Within France this world war was a war without soldiers or a front, hence women found themselves in it from the outset.

Patriotism

Cunégonde, a fictional character made familiar by Free French radio broadcasts from London, was portrayed as a woman who understood little or nothing of France's confusing political situation. Like the old comic-strip character Bécassine, Cunégonde was a bit bewildered by what went on around her, yet she was a good-hearted woman determined to act in her country's best interest. In down-to-earth terms the broadcasts explained how she could "be smart" in her daily round of activities and constantly reminded her that "the Germans are our enemy." The consistent lesson from London was that there was nothing for any individual in France to gain if the Germans won: the Occupation was a collective enslavement that turned the entire population into Germany's hostage. In this, Vichy—the "anti-France"—was not, as some

French men might think, their shield and support but Hitler's accomplice.

"Every Person in France Can Do Something"

"Do not rely on Vichy to defend you." At first London exhorted the French to resist morally by not giving in to defeat, nor submitting to Vichy, nor seeking exclusively to further their own private interests. Women were directly involved in this strategy. They became even more involved after the spring of 1942, when, at the behest of Resistance members recently arrived from France, London began placing greater emphasis on the everyday concerns of French citizens, especially in matters of diet and health. Free French radio broadcasts included angry letters from anonymous French women who proclaimed themselves to be "unyielding and undaunted" and who continued to "hold out" despite the shortages.[36] These appeals played a vital role, since the vast majority of the public saw no immediate connection between hatred of the occupying power and rejection of the Vichy regime. It was not until late in 1942 that the "connection between the two politics" became apparent. But even after Vichy, through its police and paramilitary forces *(milice),* demonstrated unambiguously that it was serving Hitler's regime, "one finds no nationwide expression of a genuine spirit of resistance and struggle."[37] In this respect, women's attitudes were no different from men's. The rights of citizenship, which men alone had enjoyed under the Third Republic, had given them no special insight and had made them no more determined to defend liberty and country than women. It would be misleading, however, to suggest that the entire population remained passive to the point of cowardice. Resignation, obsession with everyday matters, fatigue, and fear could coexist with feelings and even acts of solidarity with persecuted Jews and hunted *résistants,* yet those feelings failed to coalesce in a collective mobilization.

Women, too, faced choices, ranging from helping persons in distress to total commitment to the cause of resistance. They made up their minds as individuals, without guidance from any organized women's group or ideology. Some acted out of hostility to the Germans, others to help out a relative or a neighbor, still others out of solidarity with coworkers. A nurse might sign certificates excusing people from work. A municipal clerk might issue false ration cards or identity papers. Women working for the post office performed exemplary service, so much so that they are viewed today as having been "a linchpin of the Postal Resistance network." It is hard to quantify resistance of this kind, anonymous, diffuse, and obscure, and of course open to both sexes. Yet this "silent infrastructure" was essential to counter slander and combat isolation, and the organized Resistance relied greatly on these "accumulated individual acts."[38] Jews, first persecuted and then systematically hunted down starting in the summer of 1942, also benefited from this silent resistance.

Of course it should also be said that this reaction was a belated expression of revulsion on the part of a nation that in 1940 had stood by indifferently and allowed Vichy to promulgate discriminatory racial legislation and hand over one-quarter of the Jewish community to the Germans. Still, belated or not, revulsion did set in, and did lead French men and women to disobey a government whose methods were judged in this instance to be not just authoritarian but inhumane: a regime that celebrated the family was actually handing Jewish children over to the Germans. François Bédarida notes that "a multitude of channels, both individual and communal, spontaneous and organized, helped to ensure that the 'final solution' ordered and implemented by Nazi leaders would largely fail in France to meet its goals."[39] It was in the course of working to save Jewish children that Madeleine Barot and other leaders of the CIMADE, a Protestant rescue organization, decided to join the underground Resistance. It also became possible to use Vichy social institutions as covers: in Roanne two female officials of the Corporation Paysanne regularly placed Jewish children in rural homes.[40]

There were also protest demonstrations by women, many of them led by Communist party militants, especially Danielle Casanova, who served as secretary general of the Union des Jeunes Filles de France until 1939. In keeping with the Party's overall strategy, these actions sought to mobilize widespread popular discontent against the government. Yvonne Dumont, one of the Party officials responsible for women's actions in the northern zone, recalls that "given their numbers and concerns, [women] ultimately represented a potential for action or at least for support of the Resistance. . . . We had to make a start on getting them involved in protest and action."[41]

Women set up so-called People's Committees that called on

housewives to demonstrate in front of town halls and prefectures in order to win the release of stockpiled food supplies or to obtain coal coupons or an allotment of potatoes. Local and regional underground newspapers specifically aimed at women printed announcements of these demonstrations and explained the reasons behind them. Protests proliferated in the spring of 1942, and the Free French radio reported them as news. In Paris speakers addressed crowds of protesters at the rue de Buci and rue Daguerre markets under the protection of armed guards from the Francs-Tireurs Partisans (FTP). In addition to the usual cries of "Down with the starvation-mongers! Bread for the people!" protesters also shouted "Down with the Boches!" and, in Marseille, "Down with the Milice!" Protest leaders hoped to use purely material demands to demonstrate the collusion between the regime and the occupying forces.

It is difficult to evaluate the actual impact of the committees or their role in influencing the opinion of the female public. For women who belonged to the Communist Party, participation in the Resistance was a normal, logical continuation of their prewar commitments. The same was true of women who had started out in antifascist movements, such as Madeleine Braun. She had been a member of the steering committee of the Amsterdam-Pleyel Movement, and in 1941 she helped organize the National Front and later joined the Communist Party. Suzanne Buisson, the secretary of the National Committee of Socialist Women, was deported in the summer of 1943 and subsequently vanished. Her sacrifice, too, was a direct consequence of her prewar commitments and activities. But many other women who now joined the struggle had no previous experience of political action.

The Resistance: Fraternity and Equality Between the Sexes?

Many who joined the active Resistance rejected either the Vichy regime or the armistice or both. Networks grew by recruiting friends and acquaintances.[42] The Resistance was by nature secret, silent, and compartmentalized. Its members went about their normal daily routine, continued their regular work, and led apparently placid family lives. In many cases the Resistance was born and carried on around the family hearth. It took many forms. The early missions and assignments were not on their face either masculine or feminine. Some missions, which involved the use of private residences, clearly required the participation of both men and women: giving shelter, acting as guides, gathering intelligence, transporting supplies—such tasks were not in themselves subsidiary or reserved for women. They were also dangerous, for one of the distinctive features of the Occupation was the doctrine of collective responsibility: a suspect's entire family was liable to punishment, regardless of the actual responsibilities of each individual and in contempt for the principle of law according to which the punishment is supposed to be proportional to the crime. In November 1943, for instance, Jeanne Kahn, a mother of two, was incarcerated at Montluc in Lyon and later deported on the sole grounds that her husband had been arrested as a member of the Resistance.[43]

In ordinary warfare a woman became a heroine simply by risking her life, which in theory was something that only men were obliged to do. In the Resistance, which was underground and illegal, men and women had to master a whole range of feelings beyond the simple fear of death: anxiety in the face of constant insecurity, fear of physical torture and psychological pressure, obsessive worry about the risks to which one exposed one's family and friends. Everyone involved, regardless of rank or function, needed prudence, courage, and poise, for often the enemy had no idea whom they were dealing with and used interrogation as a way of finding out.

Yet this equality with respect to risk and reprisal does not appear to have established either an equality of responsibility or an acknowledged equality of merit. The collective memory of the Resistance honors a few major female figures, victims of repression whose names serve as reminders that women, too, paid the price of freedom: among them were Berthie Albrecht, a leader along with Henri Frenay of the Combat movement, who was arrested twice and vanished during her second imprisonment at Fresnes; Danielle Casanova, who was arrested in 1942 and died at Auschwitz; Simone Michel-Lévy, who was posthumously named a Compagnon de la Libération (only six women were honored with this title) for her work in organizing a Resistance network within the Post and Telecommunications Service and who was tortured, deported to Ravensbrück, and ultimately hanged for sabotage. But for every such woman, how many others have been forgotten by history and historiography alike? A whole generation of resisters, male and female, saw their commitment subsumed after the war by political movements, particularly the Gaullists and Communists, even though they themselves stayed out of politics. "The army of the shadows is silent."[44] And most silent of all were those who saw themselves as serving the nation rather than a political cause.

Women, having been more estranged from power and politics than men, failed to capitalize on the experience they had acquired. Did they even wish to? When the Liberation came, many who had participated in the Franc-Tireur movement did not bother to apply for certification as Resistance volunteers.[45] Their Resistance work seemed so much a part of everyday life that they forgot the risks they had run: women who, along with their husbands, had played "hostess" to members of the underground often looked upon their contribution as "routine." The role of women was probably neglected because there were fewer women than men in organized groups and very few gained command of an underground organization. Among those who did were Marie-Louise Dissart of the Françoise network, which took its orders from the British War Office; Marie-Madeleine Méric-Fourcade, who headed the Alliance intelligence network (comprising some 3,000 agents) for the British Intelligence Service; and Claude Gérard, who was responsible for organizing Combat's Secret Army in Dordogne and eventually assumed command of all partisan combat units in the seven *départements* of southwestern France.

Historians at first focused primarily on the organization of the Resistance and on armed military actions such as sabotage and guerrilla attacks. Women did not figure prominently in the organizational hierarchy of most resistance groups, and few participated in armed combat. Their contribution was elsewhere, in work as secretaries, liaison officers, and intelligence agents (one-quarter of the Alliance network's agents were women). They organized escape routes. In the fall of 1941 the British Garrow network, which had been operating in northern France, was uncovered. More than fifty people, many of them women between the ages of thirty and fifty, were arrested and deported or executed. Was there such a thing as a "women's Resistance" or at any rate a distinctive women's wing of the Resistance? There is no doubt that the Resistance used femininity as a cover, relying on the presumption, shared by the enemy, that women are innocent, fragile, and ignorant. Jeanie Rousseau, not yet twenty years old, worked as an interpreter for an economic agency that maintained liaison with the Germans. She was also the agent code-named Amniatrix in the Alliance network. "I was able to work without running major risks. There I was, tripping over the Germans' toes, with a pigtail on one side and the look of a nice, simple little girl."[46] Lucie Aubrac not only bribed a German officer but also persuaded him that she was a young girl of good background who had been seduced and abandoned by her lover (she was in fact pregnant at the time). The "seducer," with whom she thus managed to wangle an interview, was in fact her husband Raymond Aubrac, who was held by the Gestapo in Lyon and whose escape she was planning.

Women of the Resistance often tell of using feminine wiles or accoutrements in their clandestine activities: a woman might stop to adjust her garter or touch up her makeup in order to survey the area around a building. An actual or feigned pregnancy could account for loose clothing, convenient for hiding documents or other items. Handbills could be concealed in a baby carriage. The traditional shopping bag, or *cabas,* an indispensable accessory in these times of scarcity, lent itself to the transport of all sorts of items. Olga Banciv, the only woman member of the band of refugee Resistance fighters known as the Manouchian Group, used such a shopping bag to hide weapons. Does it follow from all this that the Resistance used femininity solely as a cover and looked upon women as nothing more than auxiliaries, useful and vulnerable, to be sure, but still auxiliaries? Many women say that their experience in the Resistance was one of equality and fraternity, of solidarity in the face of shared risks that made everyone involved forget the dogma of male superiority. For Brigitte Friang, the egalitarian atmosphere was the result of "a nonconventional war that made fledglings of us all. . . . For a while we forged a new society in which every person enjoyed full human dignity and was the equal of every other person. The worker was the equal of the rich man, sure, but even more striking, woman was the equal of man."[47]

Men's judgments of women very likely changed, moreover, as a result of women's attitudes. At the Ecole des Cadres in Uriage, for example, "little secretaries" at one time dismissed or ignored by the school's instructors proved to be very effective comrades when the time came for underground activities. But where military action was involved there were limits to equality, as Paula Schwartz has shown in a study of Communist partisan women involved in guerrilla warfare and sabotage (such as Madeleine Riffaud in Paris and Madeleine Baudoin in Marseille). Few women participated in this kind of activity, and most were young and unmarried. Women were involved in planning and carrying out operations and in transporting and collecting weapons, but few made use of those weapons on a regular basis. It was rare for a woman to participate in a firefight, in contrast to other countries such as Yugoslavia, where women were involved in armed resistance. Furthermore, the role of women in combat groups was increasingly restricted as the Resistance was "normalized." Despite the protests of some, women were excluded from combat units of the Forces Françaises de l'Intérieur (FFI) at the time of the Liberation. One woman whose offer of service was rejected was Jeanne Bohec, an explosives expert and instructor in sabotage connected with the Central Intelligence and Operations Office of the Free French in London.[48] Clandestinity and illegality had encouraged transgression of sex-role boundaries, but this ceased to be tolerated once the burden of the fighting shifted to an official army made up of "real" soldiers who openly engaged the enemy.

After Five Years of Torment

On December 16, 1943, Maurice Schumann spoke to his countrymen via Free French radio: "If women have contributed hundreds of heroines to the cause of freedom in this war as in the last, now, for the first time, they are also contributing hundreds of thousands of fighting troops." Free France did not merely celebrate the role of women but promised to honor it by "securing political, economic, and social equality between Yveline and her husband, between Arlette and her fiancé." To be sure, there were ambiguities in Free French discourse, which continued to confuse justice with merit and equality with difference. Women, it was argued, contributed to the renewal of France through certain specifically female virtues, virtues intimately associated with their female nature and maternal function: they "grasp the true problems," for instance, "and understand the transfiguration of love." Still, an unmistakable promise had been made, and there was real hope, confirmed by the naming of Lucie Aubrac as a delegate to the Consultative Assembly in Algiers. "The deliverance of the nation will lead to the emancipation of French women."[49] In June 1942

General de Gaulle announced that French women would be granted the right to vote, and a measure to do just that was approved by the Assembly in Algiers on March 23, 1944. This remains the most striking sign of a determination to make France anew, to end the foot-dragging and hesitation of the Third Republic. But that very determination tended to obscure both the progress toward women's suffrage in the interwar period and the battle that women had waged on their own behalf. The at-times complicated relationship between feminism and the left was erased from memory.

The "blood tax" was not enough to bring about equality, however. Despite the accession to power of a new generation of politicians that came of age in the Resistance, recognition of women's rights and aptitudes was impeded by certain values and images that not even five years of torment had been enough to destroy. In June 1945 deputy Marianne Verger found it necessary to take the podium to explain to her male colleagues that the "special requirements" proposed for women who wished to enter the Ecole Nationale d'Administration were "hopelessly outdated and unjust." Once again the lawmakers were acting out of a sense not of women's inferiority but of their difference. Verger accepted that difference yet called for passage of her amendment on the grounds that "we are claiming not our rights, but simply the right to do our duty."[50] When viewed in the context of the entire period (1930–1970), the visible and immediate consequences of the Occupation years seem limited: the women and girls who lived through the war failed to achieve major legal reforms, to win recognition of their rights, or to gain treatment as equals. Newly enfranchised citizens found their place in one or another of the major Catholic or Communist associations, but they continued to be wary of participation by women in traditional forms of political debate.[51]

In 1942 the novelist Vercors (Jean Bruller) published his underground classic, *Le Silence de la mer,* a symbolic evocation of the exemplary dignity and reserve that daily coexistence with the enemy required. The Liberation revealed the extent to which the circumstances of the Occupation had confused the boundaries of public and private life. Everyone who, for personal reasons, had attempted to profit from the German presence now had to account for his or her behavior to the courts or the *commissions d'épuration* (purge committees) even if their motivation had not been overtly political or ideological. Because the Occupation had polit-icized daily life, significant numbers of women now found them-selves in court for a variety of reasons. Women were the accused in "slightly less than 40 percent of the cases" of slander, working for the Germans, or collaboration and tried in the Orléans court in 1944–45.[52] Some had already been subjected, at the time of the Liberation, to physical humiliation in public (shaved heads, ex-posure in the nude) for having engaged in sexual relations with German soldiers. In regions where occupying troops had been concentrated, many women were tried for fraternizing with the enemy, significantly increasing the proportion of cases involving women.[53]

In the spring of 1945 the survivors of the camps returned from "an infernal world, a monstrous, utterly mad, and above all other world, *the* Other World."[54] It would be difficult if not impossible to examine in the brief space remaining how the martyrdom of women may or may not have differed from that of men. If hu-manity consists of men and women, does inhumanity maintain the distinction? The Nazi system of internment was just as arbitrary and just as harsh for women as for men. Conditions were just as wretched: forced labor, beatings, torture, and humiliations of every kind. The elderly, infirm, physically and mentally ill, were system-atically eliminated, and women received no special pity.[55] By con-trast, Nazi ideology did distinguish, in its principles and aims, between those it considered "subhumans" and others. For whole ethnic groups it was not just individuals who were exploited and mistreated to the point of death but entire families—men, women, and children—were collected for the purpose of wiping their race from the face of the earth. The extermination was intended to be complete, so that these despised races would have no offspring and never again be able to claim to be human.

The women's camp at Ravensbrück received between 110,000 and 123,000 internees from May 1939 to April 1945; of these no fewer than 90,000 died. "But someone may say, all deaths are alike. It should suffice to describe a small number, say ten typical cases, and then multiply mentally by ten thousand. But this is false. . . . We know that each agony was individual, the bitter fate of an individual woman. One hundred thousand times."[56] We know: it was this knowledge that made readaptation to the normal world so difficult after the miracle of survival. Returnees were obsessed with memories of the camp and especially of the dead: "We are alive. Too bad for us," wrote Germaine Tillion in 1947. Some women felt that deep changes had taken place in their personalities: "Officially, of course, I came back. But who was it that came back in reality?" Micheline Maurel asked herself.[57] Others, devastated to learn on returning home that their loved ones had died or that they had been left alone, spoke of "emotional death." Beyond the personal fates of individuals, all the returnees were staggered, confused, or even horrified to discover that the "normal" world did not, could not, and did not want to understand: "How can they, all of them, go on living as before, go on living period—and we most of all? Perhaps it is that which sets us apart. Or perhaps it is a totally changed scale of values."[58]

Time did not dispel these memories—far from it. In 1988 Germaine Tillion published a third book on Ravensbrück, once again asking what led ordinary people, "apparently protected by all the safeguards of our civilization," to torture, massacre, or cause to be massacred "before their eyes millions of people in cold blood day in and day out." She wrote her book with no particular hatred for any one nation: "From 1939 to 1945 I, like many others, gave in to the temptation to formulate differences, to set some apart from others: 'they' did this, 'we' would not do such a thing. Today I no longer believe a word of this, and indeed I am convinced that no nation on earth is safe from a collective moral disaster."[59]

TRANSLATED FROM THE FRENCH BY ARTHUR GOLDHAMMER

8

The Soviet Model

Françoise Navailh

"NO STATE, NO DEMOCRATICALLY enacted legislation, has done half as much for women as the Soviet government in the first few months of its existence," Lenin claimed.[1] From 1917 to 1944 the Soviet Union was a vast laboratory of social experimentation, and the case of the Soviet woman was exemplary. In exploring the condition of women we must bear this in mind to avoid repeating certain common errors and underestimating certain important phenomena.

The former Soviet Union covered a vast territory in Europe and Asia and encompassed within its boundaries more than a hundred different ethnic groups and a wide variety of cultures and religions. Here, I shall limit myself primarily to a consideration of one part of that vast territory, namely, Russia. Moscow, the center of power, attempted to impose a Russian model on the rest of the Soviet Union; the government was intent on rooting out all local ethnic, cultural, and national allegiances. A single ideal was proposed by the center and in the end accepted, at least superficially, by the republics on the periphery.

The Russian Empire that preceded the Soviet Union was an autocracy. Although serfdom was not abolished until 1861 and the first elections were not held until 1906, the opposition quickly grew radical, and the "woman question" was incorporated into a broad revolutionary program. From the beginning large numbers of women joined the revolutionary movement, accounting for between 15 and 20 percent of the active membership of the revolutionary parties.[2] In urban areas an independent feminist movement was especially active between 1905 and 1908. It concentrated its efforts chiefly on obtaining the right to vote, but in vain. On the eve of World War I Russian society consisted of a very small cultivated and westernized elite, a bourgeoisie still in embryo, and a backward peasantry that made up the remaining 80 percent of the population. People belonging to these different strata of society generally kept to themselves and knew little of other groups. This ignorance would prove a major impediment later on.

World War I broke out on August 1, 1914. Between 1914 and 1917 more than ten million men were mobilized, mostly peasants. Conditions in the countryside, already wretched, grew even worse. Many women were pressed into farm work, so many that women ultimately accounted for 72 percent of the rural workforce.[3] They also replaced men in industrial jobs: the proportion of women in the workforce rose from 33 percent in 1914 to nearly 50 percent in 1917.[4] From 1915 on, women found employment in new branches of industry and joined the government bureaucracy in large numbers. Their wages were lower than men's, however, at a time when prices were soaring. After 1916, the effort to keep food flowing to the cities and to the troops collapsed. The war, always unpopular, seemed hopeless, with no end in sight. For more than a year the country had been afflicted with bread riots and hunger strikes in which women played leading roles. Tension mounted. The regime began to crumble. The honor of initiating the revolution fell to women.

On February 23, 1917 (according to the Julian calendar, or March 8, according to our calendar), working women took their children out into the streets of Petrograd and staged a demonstration. Since the socialists had been unable to agree on a theme for the demonstration, the women improvised, calling for peace and bread. On the following day their ranks were swelled by an influx of male demonstrators, and the scope of the turmoil grew rapidly. On March 2 the czar abdicated. A provisional government was formed, and on July 20 it granted women the rights to vote and hold office (rights not granted in England until 1918 and the United States until 1920). Feminists, having achieved their goal, disappeared as an autonomous force. Liberal women lost control of events. When the Winter Palace was seized by the Bolsheviks on the night of October 25–26, it was defended by a women's contingent composed of intellectuals along with women of the bourgeoisie, aristocracy, and working class. The revolution now erupted into a bloody civil war whose outcome hung for a long time in the balance.

A Decade of Contradiction

Though surrounded by Whites, forces of the Allied powers, and nationalists, the Bolsheviks sallied forth from Moscow and Petrograd (later Leningrad) to regain control of nearly all of the territory that had constituted the old Russian Empire. They lost no time adopting a host of new laws concerning women. A decree of December 19, 1917, stipulated that in case of mutual consent divorce was to be granted automatically by the courts or the Registry offices (ZAGS); the principle according to which one party must be assigned blame was abolished, and the divorce decree no longer had to be publicized. Russia was the first country in the world to adopt such a liberal divorce policy. A decree of December 20, 1917, abolished religious marriage and standardized and simplified the civil marriage procedure. All children, legitimate or not, enjoyed the same legal rights. These two measures were extended by the Family Code of December 16, 1918—the most liberal in Europe at the time. The ZAGS became the chief agency for dealing with family matters. A man could no longer force his wife to accept his name, residence, or nationality. Husband and wife enjoyed absolute equality even with respect to the children. Maternity leave and workplace protection were guaranteed. The Family Code adopted a narrow definition of the family: direct ancestors and descendants together with brothers and sisters. A spouse enjoyed the same status as kin and collaterals, with no special privileges or prerogatives. The new family proved less stable than the old. Bonds between individuals were loosened: inheritance was outlawed in April 1918 (and only partially restored in 1923). Unrestricted abortion was legalized on November 20, 1920.

The Code of November 19, 1926, confirmed these earlier changes and took yet another step, abolishing all differences between marriages legally recorded by the ZAGS and *de facto* (com-mon-law) marriages. Divorce could henceforth be obtained on the written request of either party: "postcard divorce" was now legal. Love was freer, but mutual obligations were more onerous owing to new alimony and child support requirements.[5] The new Family Code was intended to liberate men, women, and children from the coercive regulations of another era. The past was to be completely effaced. People were urged to change their family names in March 1918 and their first names in 1924: suggestions for new names included Marlen (short for Marxism-Leninism), Engelsine, and Octobrine. Though intended to be an instrument of liberation, the code was also an instrument of coercion that could be used to strike at conservative segments of the society, particularly peasants and Muslims. In fact, the Communist Party, composed of a handful of urban intellectuals, deliberately ignored the views of those whom it sped along the road to a better tomorrow. Although lawmakers occasionally reversed themselves, their actions were always guided by two principles: to destroy czarism and build socialism.

Marxists, Women, and the Family

The essential points of the Marxist position on women and the family can be found in the *Communist Manifesto* (1848). Friedrich Engels later elaborated on this position in his *Origin of the Family, Private Property, and the State* (1884). For Marxists, the family, and therefore woman as part of the family, is determined by the economic structure and the nature of the state. The bourgeois family, based on profit, serves an exclusively (re)productive func-tion. Capitalism exploits the proletariat and destroys the proletar-ian family. The bourgeoisie shares possession of married women through adultery and working women through prostitution. On this analysis, immorality is consubstantial with capitalism and the bourgeoisie. If the economic structure of capitalism were sup-pressed, the bourgeois family would *ipso facto* disappear, as would prostitution. Women would then enjoy full civil rights. The chores of housework would be assumed by the community, and the state would take responsibility for child-rearing and education, thus enabling women to work and become economically independent. What would become of the family under these conditions? "Since monogamy exists for economic reasons, would it disappear if its causes disappeared? The answer is no, for one very good reason: not only would monogamy not disappear, it would from that very moment begin to exist in the fullest sense of the word."[6] Henceforth marriage will be based only on natural preference, undistorted by material constraints. In good logic, then, marriage should end whenever feeling so dictates, but in the eyes of Marxism's founding fathers, divorce, which they treat mainly by implication, is supposed to remain the exception rather than the rule.

August Bebel's major Marxist work, *Woman and Socialism* (1879), analyzed the economic and sexual condition of working women in the light of Marx's *Capital,* whose argument it recapitulated. Bebel concedes that men themselves and not just the bourgeois system might bear part of the blame for inequality. Yet he insists that the general problem of female alienation cannot be resolved merely by granting women rights. The only way to free women from the domination of men, he argues, is to dissolve the bonds of economic dependence. Hence women should fight shoulder-to-shoulder with the proletariat to bring about the revolution. All he says about marriage is that it must be taken seriously: couples must not neglect their marital duties and must seek to preserve their marriages.

Precise in describing the inner workings of the capitalist system, Marx, Engels, and Bebel become evasive when it comes to describing the future. The revolution, they argue, cannot fail to create new relations between the sexes—new economic relations to begin with and therefore new social and human relations as well. The crux of the matter lies in the word "therefore." After the revolution, we are told, the old family will wither away and the family structure will regenerate itself. For Marxists, as for revolutionaries generally, a purely feminist movement was a bourgeois diversion that prevented unity and delayed the revolution. Hence there was no real debate of the woman question within the left. An anecdote will help to point up the blindness of Marxists on this issue. In 1915 the Bolshevik Ines Armand set forth her views on marriage in a pamphlet that she hoped would reconcile morality, sexuality, and communism. Lenin criticized her work as a "leftist deviation" and talked her into recanting her position.[7] Alexandra Kollontai, to whose career I turn next, referred to such conflicts between woman's creative spirit and male stubbornness as the struggle between "the dragon and the dove."

Kollontai: A Reluctant Feminist

Alexandra Kollontai (1872–1952) was a pivotal figure in debates on women and the family during the first Soviet decade. She epitomizes all the contradictions of the period. Her biography is typical of her generation. Aristocratic by birth, she enjoyed a luxury-filled, dreamy childhood. After marrying at age nineteen to escape her family and milieu, she left her husband at age twenty-six and went to school in Zurich, then a Mecca for Russian intellectuals, where she became involved in politics, took increasingly radical positions, and eventually became a professional revolutionary. Her record was brilliant: as the first woman elected to the Central Committee in 1917, she voted in favor of the October insurrection. She then became the first woman to serve in the government, as people's commissar for health, and took an active part in drafting the Family Code of 1918. As an active member of the Workers' Opposition in 1920–1921, she sought to limit the vast powers of the Communist Party. In 1922 she became the first woman ambassador in the world. Her diplomatic career abroad kept her away from Moscow until 1945, yet her name is inseparable from the controversies of the 1920s, whose passions she fueled with countless articles, pamphlets, and brochures that were widely criticized, distorted, and even caricatured. She also wrote a number of theoretical tomes (*The Social Bases of the Woman Question*, 1909; *The Family and the Communist State*, 1918; *The New Morality and the Working Class*, 1918), as well as six works of fiction, all published in 1923. Although certain aspects of her work now seem dated, much of it remains remarkably up to date.

Kollontai proposed a synthesis of Marxism with a feminism she never avowed (and in fact always combated). Marxism, combined with a touch of Fourierist utopianism, would facilitate the realization of feminist goals. Like Marx and Engels, Kollontai believed that the bourgeois family had fallen apart and that revolution would lead to the regeneration of family life. She also drew extensively on the work of Bebel, particularly his idea that oppression tends to create unity among women. But she tried to go beyond these general arguments. Aware that the revolution was merely a starting point, she argued that to change the essence of marriage required changing people's attitudes and behavior. Therein lay her originality. She stressed the reifying tendency of the masculine will and noted the alienation of women who prefer any kind of marriage to solitude and are thus driven to wager everything on love.[8] So Kollontai taught that love could be a kind of sport: if tender erotic friendship were based on mutual respect, jealousy and the possessive instinct might be eliminated.[9] The "new woman," one of her recurrent subjects, was energetic and self-assertive. She let men know what she wanted; she refused to be dependent either materially or emotionally; she rebelled against socioeconomic obstacles, hypocritical morals, and "amorous captivity." Autonomous and active, she was free to explore "serial monogamy."[10] In "Make Room for Wingèd Eros," an article published in 1923, Kollontai analyzed love's many facets: friendship, passion, maternal affection, spiritual affinity, habit, and so on. "Wingless Eros," or purely physical attraction, was to make room for "wingèd Eros," wherein physical gratification was combined with a sense of collective duty, that indispensable attribute in the era of transition to socialism. Finally, once socialist society had been established, there would be room for "Eros transfigured," or marriage based on healthy, free, and natural sexual attraction.[11] To allow couples to develop, "kitchens must be separated from homes": in other words, society must build cafeterias, day-care centers, and dispensaries in order to relieve women of certain of their traditional responsibilities.[12] Last but not least, motherhood was cast in a new light: it was "no longer a private affair but a social duty."[13] Women must have children for the sake of the community. Kollontai considered abortion to be a temporary evil, to be tolerated only until the consciousness of working women had been raised to the point where it was no longer necessary. She denounced the refusal to bear children as petty-bourgeois selfishness. Nevertheless, she did not advocate the collectivization of child-rearing: parents should decide whether children were to be raised in a nursery school or at home.

As a spiritual value, however, love in general—and sex—should take precedence over the maternal instinct: "The workers' state needs a new type of relation between the sexes. A mother's narrow, exclusive love for her own child must broaden to embrace all the children of the great proletarian family. In the place of indissoluble marriage, based on the servitude of women, we look forward to the birth of free matrimony, an institution made strong by the mutual love and respect of two members of the brotherhood of Labor, equals in rights as well as obligations. In place of the individualistic, egoistic family will arise the great universal family of working people, in which everyone, men and women alike, will be first and foremost brothers and comrades."[14] Kollontai called upon women to defend, propagate, and internalize the idea that they had value as human beings in their own right.

To be sure, Kollontai's argument was framed in terms of classical Marxism, to which the economy is primary, but she also insisted on the qualitative aspect of interpersonal relations: men and women should be attentive to each other's needs and playful toward one another. Ethics mattered to her as much as politics. Well before Wilhelm Reich, she was among the first to link sexuality with class struggle: "Why is it that we are so unforgivably indifferent to one of the essential tasks of the working class? How are we to explain the hypocritical relegation of the sexual problem to the realm of 'family affairs' not requiring collective effort? As if sexual relations and the morals governing them have not been a constant factor in social struggle throughout history."[15]

Few people shared Kollontai's ideas in the Soviet Union of the 1920s. Her comrades looked upon her ideas as frivolous and ill-timed. Her views presupposed a yet-to-be-achieved social and economic infrastructure, and they came in for vehement criticism in a 1923 article by the Bolshevik P. Vinogradskaya, who had worked with Kollontai on Women's Department of the Central Committee Secretariat (*Zhenotdel*) in 1920. Vinogradskaya attacked her opponent for confusing priorities, neglecting the class struggle, and encouraging sexual anarchy in an irresponsible way, since disorder in private life could lead to counterrevolutionary agitation. The task of the moment was to protect wives and children and to champion the cause of women without attacking men. Marx and Engels had already said everything there was to be said on the question, and it was pointless to indulge in "George-Sandism."

Lenin, for his part, related everything to the economy and opted in favor of monogamous marriage, egalitarian, earnest, and devoted to the cause, like his own tranquil union with Nadezhda Krupskaya. When Ines Armand saw poetry in free love, Lenin responded that what she mistook for poetry was nothing but bourgeois immorality. He borrowed his ideal from Nikolai Chernyshevski's austere novel *What Is to Be Done?* (1863), which, as he said, "bowled him over."[16] Indeed, he thought so highly of the book that he used its title for his own theoretical work of 1902. His conversations with Clara Zetkin, which took place in 1920 but were not published until 1925, after Lenin's death, accurately reflected his rejection of lack of discipline in love and sexual matters. Lenin saw such lack of discipline as a sign of decadence and a danger to young people's health, hence to the revolution itself. He attacked the "anti-Marxist" theory according to which "in Communist society the satisfaction of sexual desires is as simple and soothing as drinking a glass of water." Lenin had nobody particular in mind. He was not attacking Kollontai, for his remarks preceded the polemic of 1923, but later Kollontai's adversaries used his wrath against her: "Of course thirst must be satisfied! But would a normal man, under normal conditions, prostrate himself in the street to drink from a filthy puddle? Or even from a glass previously soiled by dozens of other lips?" Here, purity is restored as an absolute value, and the underlying idea is that having more than one sexual partner is in itself immoral. Lenin's credo was a negative one: "No to the monk, no to the Don Juan, and no to that supposed happy medium, the German philistine."[17] To be sure, he denounced the slavery of housework: "Woman is stifled, strangled, stupefied, and humiliated by the trivial occupations of domestic life, which chain her to the kitchen and nursery and sap her strength for work that is as unproductive, difficult, and exhausting as one can imagine."[18] But he said nothing about the new family.

For orthodox Marxists, children did not figure in the conjugal scheme. They were to be taken care of either by certain designated women or by all the women of the community collectively—at the outset the choice is not clear. Fathers certainly play no role in the new system of child-rearing. The community supports, envelops, permeates, and transcends the reduced couple, in which man and woman are strict equals. The woman, like her husband, is a worker; traditional femininity is disparaged as a product of old bourgeois social relations. Equality in fact means identity of the sexes. The new industrious humanity consists of male and female twins, identical insofar as both are workers. "Economically and politically, which also means physiologically, the modern proletarian woman can and must become more and more like the modern proletarian man," wrote Marxist psychoneurologist Aaron Zalkind in 1924.[19] Sexual relations, we are told, will not be a matter of great importance for such indistinguishable twins. One can interpret this claim in two ways. If sex is merely a physiological need, then the number of partners is unimportant: this is the attitude of the youth Zhenya in Kollontai's short story, "Three

Generations of Love." The other interpretation leads to Leninist asceticism. In either case love must be restrained; it is a disruptive force. All of this was merely speculative, however. During the 1920s the private sphere remained intact, and various norms of sexual behavior coexisted.

A New Russia

In order to enforce the law, achieve economic equality, bring uniformity to a very disparate country, and accelerate the integration of women into the society, the Party in 1919 created the Zhenotdel, or Women's Department of the Central Committee Secretariat, with equivalents at every echelon of the hierarchy. Five women in succession led this Department during its existence, among them Ines Armand in 1919–20 and Alexandra Kollontai from 1920 to 1922. The Zhenotdel offered advice and assistance, settled labor and domestic conflicts, proposed laws and suggested amendments to Central Committee edicts, joined in actions such as the campaigns to eradicate illiteracy and abolish prostitution, coordinated the work of various agencies, oversaw the application of quotas that favored women in hiring and admission to soviets, dealt with problems of supply, housing, and sanitation, and inspected schools and orphanages. In addition to the Zhenotdel there was also a system of female delegates: women workers and peasants elected by their colleagues to participate in year-long training and indoctrination courses, after which they spent two months working with the soviets or the courts before returning to work. This system trained women to become "Soviet citizens." More than ten million of them signed up during the 1920s. Dasha, the heroine of Fedor Gladkov's novel Cement (1925), is a perfect example of the liberated woman. A militant delegate, she so completely threw off her old bonds that she sacrificed her marriage, her home, and even her little daughter, who died in an orphanage. There is no doubt that the Zhenotdel, together with the delegate system, had an impact on the consciousness of women. Its political influence remained negligible, however, and all too often it served only to convey the wishes of the hierarchy to the rank and file. In 1923 it was accused of "feminist deviationism," a fatal sin.

The new Russia stumbled forward. Reality—a far cry from utopian dreams—forced the government to modify its plans or to crack down on recalcitrants, provoking further reactions and further modifications, on into the mid-1930s. To begin with, there was the civil war, in which women played active roles in all areas: military, political, and medical. The war brought about massive social and economic changes, but at a heavy price: five million dead, terrible poverty, and the beginning of what was soon to become a chronic shortage of men. Traditional channels of distribution had dried up. Commerce and barter were forbidden. The government wanted goods to be distributed directly. Workers were paid in merchandise coupons, but the coupons could not be redeemed. Industrial output had fallen to 15 percent of prewar levels, and agricultural output to 60 percent. Rationing was tightened. In the cities the bread ration fell to as little as 25 grams a day. Meat, shoes, clothing, coal, and wood were all in short supply. Peasants rebelled against the endless requisitions; epidemics of typhus and cholera broke out; a terrible famine in 1920–21 saw episodes of cannibalism and claimed more than two million lives. The result, ultimately, was disaster—political, economic, and human disaster. Racked by cold and hunger, people clung desperately to life. With the total breakdown of society, *besprizorniki,* or gangs of children, roved the countryside, occupied unused buildings, begged or stole food, killed, and prostituted themselves. There were nearly seven million children in this condition in 1921. The phenomenon repeated itself with each new change of regime, and up to the beginning of the 1950s the spectacle of children in rags was a familiar one. Adoption, abolished in 1918, was reinstated in 1923 in the hope of socializing these delinquents.

In February 1921 the sailors of Kronstadt challenged the very legitimacy of the new regime. To cope with this major crisis, Lenin persuaded the March 1921 Party Congress to adopt the New Economic Policy, or NEP. In order to restore the economy as quickly as possible and save the regime, small merchants and artisans were allowed to reopen their businesses. Drastic steps were taken in 1922 and again in 1924 to restore the currency. But the fundamental sectors of the economy remained nationalized: heavy industry, transportation, foreign commerce, certain internal commerce, education, the press, medicine. The supply of food to the cities increased rapidly, although deliveries remained uncertain and there was little variety in what was available. Consumer goods, even the most necessary items, remained scarce, expensive, and of mediocre quality. Inflation was high: retail prices rose 60 percent in 1923. The standard of living rose slowly, not regaining its 1913 level until 1927. Wages were reinstituted, and compensation varied with skill and job description, undermining the egalitarian promises of 1917. To some dyed-in-the-wool Communists, unwilling to compromise, the NEP was nothing short of treason. Yet it allowed Russia to catch its breath and reorganize. At the same time, a parallel economy developed for Party members: there were special stores and restaurants, special apartments and villas, and envelopes stuffed with cash enabling those favored to secretly supplement their ostensibly modest incomes. Little by little the gap widened between rulers and ruled, and the power of material interests in human relations reasserted itself.[20]

The economy thus consisted of two unequal sectors: small, private commercial enterprises, and everything else, which was nationalized. This dichotomy accurately reflected the government's two impulses: on the one hand the wish to meet the society's needs and desires, on the other hand the desire to shape society according to a predetermined scheme regardless of the needs and desires of its people. Voluntarist legislation and art sustained the utopian ideal. Artists of every variety enthusiastically supported the revolution and enlisted in its ranks. Some penned propaganda slogans, while others, including the poet Vladimir Mayakovsky, worked as journalists. The cinema portrayed the revolution as an epic adventure. Writers sought to capture the new life, and already some architects were straining to imagine the glittering city of the future with its family communes modeled on Fourierist phalansteries and clubs for workers.

The prosaic reality of the NEP made a mockery of such grandiose dreams. The official housing allotment, for example, was 9 square meters per person. In some places it was reduced to as little as 6 square meters per person or even per family. Owing to the widespread destruction of housing and the turmoil of civil war, many people were housed in dormitories or crowded together into tiny, ill-equipped apartments. Under the so-called condensation policy, apartments were requisitioned and whole families or unmarried individuals were assigned to single rooms, with the bathroom and kitchen shared in common. Close quarters led to petty quarrels that poisoned daily life. Long lines became a familiar sight. Fine dining and elegant fashions became a thing of the past, except on movie screens or in the narrow circle of the ruling elite.

The Communist Party's control and influence varied from region to region. Despite spectacular successes in some areas, patent failures elsewhere left the country a long way from the goal of achieving socialism. Women, who had made up as much as 40 percent of the workforce in 1914, accounted for only 24 percent in 1928 owing to their lack of skills and the return home of men formerly in the army.[21] Women were slow to enter the workforce and showed little interest in politics. While 42.9 percent of urban women voted in the 1926 elections, only 28 percent of rural women availed themselves of the privilege. By 1934, however, participation in elections had risen to 89.7 and 80.3 percent, respectively.[22] Party delegates in rural villages were more often than not schoolteachers or nurses from the city rather than peasants. Peasant women had as little to do with the government as possible. In 1926 the membership of urban soviets was 18.2 percent female, compared with only 9.9 percent for rural soviets.[23]

Freedom and Disorder

Soviet society had yet to achieve stability. War and famine led to the migration of vast segments of the population. In search of food and a better life people alternately flocked to the cities and fled the cities for the countryside. "Nomads" skirted the law in order to survive. Social services such as daycare, dormitories, cafeterias, laundries, and dispensaries were curtailed as the government, faced with countless conflicting priorities, chose to put maximum effort into rebuilding the economy. Ideology was in command: since bourgeois etiquette was held in contempt, many people affected plebeian manners. Brutality became a virtue, and crudeness of language and behavior the norm. Panteleimon Romanov's novel *Without Cherry Blossoms* (1926) told the story of the permanent damage suffered by a young woman when she had a brutal first intercourse with the man she loved, in a filthy room. Prostitution and venereal disease reemerged. There was a ready supply of new prostitutes: women who lost everything they had in the revolution, together with uprooted peasant women targeted for "reeducation" by the authorities. Were these "antisocial elements" or victims? The government seemed unable to make up its mind.

In one sense, women were granted all they could have hoped for right at the outset, without a struggle. But the most difficult part of the task remained: they had to learn how to make use of their newly won rights to forge a new way of life. But given the sociohistorical context and the gaps in the codes of 1918 and 1926, new freedoms gave rise to unintended consequences.

Two signs of the times were marital instability and a widespread reluctance to have children. The number of abortions rose, the birthrate declined precipitously, and newborn babies were frequently abandoned. Orphanages, overwhelmed by new admissions, became veritable charnel houses. Infanticide and wife-murder increased. In effect, women and children were the first victims of the new order. The condition of women clearly became more dire, especially in the cities. Men abandoned their families, leaving their wives without resources. The availability of divorce merely on application by either party led to cynical abuses. The government allowed common-law marriages in order to protect women from seduction and abandonment (and also to protect any children that might result from fleeting affairs); men were required to provide for the women they left behind, and thus to assume a burden that the government itself was unable to bear. But women had to prove that an affair had taken place, and the law failed to specify what constituted proof. The courts improvised. Lengthy and often fruitless paternity suits poisoned relations between the sexes and became a recurrent theme of contemporary fiction. The laws governing alimony were just as vague, and the courts were obliged to fix amounts on a case-by-case basis. Often it was set at one-third or one-fourth of the man's monthly wage, which sometimes created insurmountable difficulties. How was a man to survive if ten rubles were deducted from his wage of forty rubles? How was he to support a child born out of wedlock when he already had four "legitimate" children to take care of? Few men earned enough to cover alimony, and many refused to pay up. Rulings of the court went unenforced in more than half the cases.

There were practical problems as well. Allocation of housing was a state monopoly, and waiting lists were extremely long. Divorced couples were therefore obliged in some cases to go on living together. Abram Room's film *Bed and Sofa* (1927) is a marvelous depiction of conditions under the NEP. It offers a new perspective on the eternal triangle, portraying a husband, wife, and lover forced to share a single room. After the seduction, moreover, the two men take a nonchalant attitude toward the situation and join in a macho alliance against the woman, the wife of one and mistress of the other.

Many women who wanted children were nevertheless forced

to seek abortions because of the scarcity of housing, low wages, short supplies, and/or lack of a man. In a survey conducted in Moscow in 1927, 71 percent of women seeking abortions cited "living conditions" as the reason and 22 percent mentioned "unstable love lives." Only 6 percent rejected motherhood on principle.[24]

Although intellectuals and quasi-intellectuals in the cities went on leading bohemian lives, some segments of the population resisted any change in traditional mores. In 1928, 77.8 percent of the population still consisted of peasants, compared with only 17.6 percent blue- and white-collar workers.[25] The Code of 1926 triggered a huge controversy that illustrates the continuing influence of the peasantry. Since accurate news was hard to come by despite innumerable published articles, brochures, and meetings, peasants were liable to be affected by unsubstantiated rumors, and many were convinced that the new code was going to make the sharing of women compulsory. The most controversial provision of the law concerned the treatment of de facto marriage as completely equivalent to lawful matrimony. The Agrarian Code of 1922 reinforced the communal organization of the village, or *mir*, and retained the undivided family property, or *dvor*. If a couple sharing in the *dvor* divorced and payment of alimony led to division of the property, the farm might cease to be viable. Wary after years of ceaseless combat (1914–1921), the peasantry, fearful of novelty, drew back and clung to its traditional values.

It was an ambiguous image of woman that emerged from all the articles, brochures, pamphlets, investigations, speeches, novels, and films of the day: sometimes she was portrayed as a member of the vanguard of the working class, wearing an earnest look, work clothes, and a red scarf; at other times she was the backward peasant with her white kerchief pulled down over her eyes; or the mannish girl of the Komsomol (Young Communists), shockingly liberated in her ways; or the pert, flirtatious typist. Woman simultaneously embodied the past and the future. Conviction vied with confusion in the minds of the masses. Novels of the late 1920s are filled with restless, confused, unhappy heroines. Urban immorality and rural conservatism were matters of concern to both rulers and ruled. Women wanted stability, men declined responsibility, and the Party wanted to keep its program on course. By 1926 it was clear that, like it or not, the family would survive. Certain sectors of light industry were sacrificed in the name of economic progress. Home and children once again became the concern of women. The woman question was held to have been resolved once and for all, and in 1929 the Zhenotdel was abolished.

"Women of the East, Lift Your Veils!"

In central Asia, however, the Zhenotdel survived until the mid-1950s. Of course the government did not have an easy time establishing its authority in this part of the Soviet Union. The region was not really pacified until 1936. Rural areas, long held by Basmachi, or rebel bandits, were not secure. Hence a policy of "liberating women" also served to break down the local economic and social structure. The de-Islamization of women was a political weapon.

Before the revolution the situation of Muslim women was by no means uniform. The Tatars of Kazan had begun reforms before socialism: as early as 1900 one in twelve Tatar women attended school, compared with only one among fifty-five Russian women. At the First Pan-Russian Muslim Congress, which opened in Moscow on May 1, 1917, the one thousand delegates, two hundred of them women, proclaimed equal rights for men and women of Islamic faith, setting an example for the entire world.[26] Despite such progress, however, the overall situation was negative. On January 19, 1918, a Central Commissariat for Muslim Affairs was created. Polygamy was abolished, along with marriage of girls under the age of puberty, levirate (a custom according to which a man was obliged under certain circumstances to marry his brother's widow), and *kalym,* or the purchase of a bride. Education was made compulsory, and all professions were opened to women. The most striking and symbolic measure was the abolition of the *paranja,* or veil, systematized after 1926. There were risks involved in tampering with such fundamental social taboos: some of the first women to remove their veils were raped or murdered by outraged husbands and brothers. More than 300 women died in 1928. In 1930 such crimes were declared counterrevolutionary, yet old customs remained stubbornly entrenched. As late as the 1950s it was still possible to find veiled women, arranged child marriages, and polygamy, even among the ruling elite. *Kalym* still survives. Progress for women slowed noticeably, as illiteracy figures prove. In 1927 more than 95 percent of central Asian women were illiterate, compared with a national average of roughly 60 percent. In 1959, for every 1,000 boys attending school in Russia there were 921 girls, whereas the comparable figure for Muslims was 613.[27] There was also resistance to women joining the workforce. Most women were employed in agriculture, while a small minority worked in industrial and office jobs. Even today, in the five republics of central Asia, 25.6 percent of the women work, compared with 43.6 percent in the Slavic republics.[28] Muslim women are also below average in political participation.

There has of course been some genuine emancipation of women in Soviet central Asia. Between 1933 and 1979 the number of women enjoying the benefits of secondary education increased thirty-three times. Women emerged from confinement to acquire education and skills. Muslim societies remain highly endogamous, however. Often the idea of a nation is embodied in tradition and religion, and women play a fundamental role in the construction of a national identity. To oppose or impede progress for women was also to resist Russification. The attempt to impose a European model on the central Asian republics met with numerous setbacks, and such success as was achieved remains superficial.

The Conservative Revolution

The NEP was unable to bring about a lasting economic recovery. The economy remained fragile and uneven. Unemployment rose from 700,000 in 1924 to 2 million in 1927. To give industry a shot in the arm the government shut down the private sector and in 1928 launched the first Five-Year Plan, which looked forward to sustained industrial growth, so it needed a series of good harvests and stable foreign trade. In March 1928 a grain-collection crisis interfered with the supply of food to the cities. Rationing was reinstated. Once again bread, sugar, milk, soap, and fabric were in short supply. The government engaged the peasantry in the test of strength that it had avoided in 1921. The contest proved to be a crucial turning point. The Party, in a hurry, decided to collectivize agriculture so as to assure a steady flow of grain for internal consumption and export. In the face of passive and overt resistance on the part of peasants, the government stepped up arrests and confiscations. Some peasant women had no compunctions about resorting to violence: they interfered with seizures, insulting and harassing government representatives. But such revolts were disorganized and of limited consequence, except in central Asia, where things again came close to the point of civil war.[29]

The "normalization" lasted until 1935. The terrible famine of 1932–33 claimed some 6 million lives, and another 2.5 million fell victim to government repression.[30] The standard of living again collapsed. Wages held steady or decreased. Inflation persisted until 1945, except for brief periods of respite.[31] Everyday merchandise vanished from the marketplace. The whole system of distribution was in chaos, and much of the population lived in poverty. From 1932 to 1976 peasants were assigned a special status of their own, which tied them to the collective farms and made them second-class citizens. The condition of the working class also deteriorated. Piecework wages were introduced in 1932, and workers were required to carry employment records as of 1938. Discipline in the factories was tightened, and worker mobility was limited, creating a kind of "barracks socialism" characterized by centralized authority, rigid hierarchy, and rapid personnel turnover through promotion and/or elimination.

Industrialization and Morality: The Return of the Family

The crisis of 1929 forced the U.S.S.R. to choose autarchy. Soviet Russia did not rejoin the international economy until 1960. Sector A (heavy industry) took priority over Sector B (light industry). Once again the present was sacrificed to the future. The nation was mobilized to build grandiose projects such as dams, giant factories, and canals, as well as prestige projects such as the Moscow subway. While the purported "hegemonic class" lived in malnourished misery in barracks, the Five-Year Plan acquired a new mystique.[32] The poet Osip Mandelstam lamented: "It may be humiliating, but mark it well: / Fornication of labor exists, and we have it in the blood."[33]

To waste one's energy on love and sex was to betray the revolution. Bohemianism and sexual liberation were condemned, while the "revolutionary sublimation" that Aaron Zalkind had heralded in his "twelve commandments" of 1924 was now exalted as dogma.[34] Society decided what was normal: homosexuality was made a criminal act in 1934, and prostitution was also declared to be a crime.

The bohemian atmosphere of the 1920s faded, and educational, social, and artistic experiments were ended. The newspapers and movie screens were filled with paeans to machines of steel, gleaming tractors, and valiant Stakhanovites. After 1934 intellectuals succumbed as though hypnotized, falling in line behind Party leaders: among them were the writers Valentin Katayev and Lydia Seifullina and the filmmaker Sergei Eisenstein. All adapted themselves to the mold of "socialist realism," which described in realist fashion the glory of achievements that lacked any reality whatsoever. But the factories favored by the Five-Year Plan were hiring everywhere.

The proportion of women in the industrial workforce rose from 28.8 percent in 1928 to 43 percent in 1940.[35] Women found jobs in new sectors such as mining, metallurgy, and the chemical industry. Some lines of work were said to be too dangerous or unhealthy for women, however. The law protected expectant mothers, but the pressures of rapid industrialization and war encouraged managers to flout the law and shorten the maternity leaves. Women were subject to forced labor along with men—yet another area in which there was no discrimination. But most held unskilled or semi-skilled jobs.

Building socialism demanded a stable society with a strong and united family unit. The population lost to war and repression had to be replaced. Economic and ideological imperatives conspired to give the family a new lease on life. Criticism of the family was now viewed as "bourgeois" or "leftist." Exit the exalted androgyne, enter the broad-hipped *materfamilias*. *Pravda* honored the champion milkmaid whose agile fingers elicited rivers of milk, symbol of fertility. In August 1935 *Izvestia* wrote that "our women, as full-fledged citizens of the freest country in the world, have received from Nature the gift of being mothers. Let them take care of this precious gift in order to bring Soviet heroes into the world!" In April 1936 Stalin, writing in the newspaper *Trud,* observed that "abortion, which destroys life, is unacceptable in our country. The Soviet woman has the same rights as the Soviet man, but equality does not exempt her from the great and noble duty that nature bestowed on her: she is mother, she gives life."

In 1935 the press launched an attack on abortion and divorce. In 1928 there were 1.5 times as many abortions as births; by 1934 in Moscow there were 3 abortions for every birth.[36] In May 1935 the urban divorce rate had reached 44.3 percent.[37] As a result, abortion (except for medical reasons) was made illegal in June 1936, despite obvious opposition from women as evidenced by many letters to the papers. In compensation, a system of family allocations was instituted and alimony payments were increased. In addition, divorce procedures became more complex: both parties had to appear in court, a record of the divorce was included in identity papers, judgments were published, and costs were increased. But common-law marriage was still recognized.

These reforms established durable connections between motherhood, permanent marriage, and a strong nuclear family. Even paternal authority was restored in 1935. The initial results were spectacular. In one year the divorce rate dropped 61.3 percent. Abortions in Moscow decreased by a factor of fifteen between October 1935 and October 1936. Births increased slightly. But the decline in the birthrate was inexorable: 44.7 per thousand in 1925, 39.2 in 1930, 31 in 1940.[38] Because the objective factors contributing to abortion had not changed, women continued to abort their pregnancies. They did so clandestinely, however, with all the attendant risks.

Stalin resorted to terror to keep society in check and the state apparatus loyal. In 1935 the death sentence could be imposed on children as young as twelve. Torture was legalized in 1937. Arbitrary, wide-scale arrests were common, and show trials staged in Moscow pointed the finger at "counterrevolutionaries." Between January 1937 and December 1938, 7 million people were arrested, and 3 million perished at the hands of firing squads or in prison camps.[39] Twelve to eighteen percent of the Communists arrested were women.[40] The charges were always the same: sabotage, Trotskyism, espionage. In August 1934 it became a crime to be the "relative of a traitor"—a law that was used mainly against the wives and sisters of accused men. A woman could be sentenced to two to five years in a prison camp for failing to denounce a husband or brother as an "enemy of the people." She could be exiled for five years simply for not knowing of the man's activities.[41] The children of imprisoned women were sent to orphanages. Denunciation, encouraged by the authorities, broke up families and friendships, while posters featuring smiling faces covered walls everywhere.

Nevertheless, some people profited from the regime. After the purges, on the eve of World War II, a veritable *petite bourgeoisie* emerged. It was a highly conformist group, attached to the rituals, emblems, and norms of the new order, which it observed, to believe the literary stereotypes of the period, from a safe distance, ensconced behind its lace curtains and geraniums. The revolution was bourgeoisified: hats and ties again became the norm. Indeed, the Stalinist reaction, for all its negative aspects, enjoyed a kind of consensus because it offered genuine opportunities for social advancement. The image of the mother, identified with nurturing Mother Russia, joined that of the robust peasant woman. There was a clear ruralization of Soviet values. Industrialization had accelerated the exodus from the countryside: between 1928 and 1940 the urban population doubled.[42] Village preferences and prejudices left a profound mark on urban attitudes, even though peasants no longer enjoyed the status of head of the family and boss of the family farm *(khozyain)*. Women on collective farms could earn more than men and gain a measure of economic independence. Deprived of status, men lost their self-respect and the respect of others. A good illustration of the new place of women, whether real or idealized, can be found in the film *Member of the Government* by Heifiz and Zarkhi (1939), which traces the career of an illiterate, battered peasant woman who, with the support of the Party, becomes the manager of a collective farm and ultimately a deputy to the Supreme Soviet. Her husband, humiliated by her success, leaves her but later returns. The message is clear: women had everything to gain—education, family, and power—by fulfilling their duty as citizens. Happiness was the reward of those who did. The film suggested that the Party was ready to intervene in the rivalry between men and women and to utilize this rivalry. The retreat from the radical libertarian positions of 1926 is clear, however: the heroine of the film is already married and has no affairs when her husband leaves her.

Nevertheless, Soviet legislation was still far in advance of other countries. The Soviet Union offered women coeducational schooling, civil marriages, legal majority at age eighteen, the right to vote and hold office, the right to pursue a political career, and a broad spectrum of occupational opportunities. In principle Soviet women were economically emancipated, enjoying equal pay for equal work. Piecework wages placed women at a disadvantage, however, because their output was less than that of men. In addition, women who worked outside the home were still expected to do the housework: the double working day was the norm. In 1937 the heroine of one novel summed up what was expected of her: "'A wife should also be a happy mother and create a serene home atmosphere without, however, abandoning her work for the common welfare. She should know how to combine these things while also watching her husband's performance on the job.' 'Right!' said Stalin."[43] The difficulty of achieving this goal was compounded by the government's failure to keep its promises. The 1936 plan to build daycare facilities and kindergartens remained a pious wish. In 1951 there were fewer such facilities than in 1934, and virtually none in rural areas.[44] Life was hard, but the hope of a better tomorrow sustained people in sacrifice.

One Step Forward, Two Steps Back

In 1940, 16 million men were employed in agriculture. When war broke out, on June 22, 1941, 13 million of those men were mobilized or drafted for work in arms factories. Within a short time more than 70 percent of the agricultural workforce consisted of women.[45] They stepped in as needed, just as they had done in 1914. By 1945 women accounted for 56 percent of all blue- and white-collar workers as well, the highest level ever in Soviet history. Women held jobs ranging all the way from laborer to executive. The war hastened the promotion of women, improved their skills, and put an end to certain archaic customs in central Asia and the Caucasus.

The end of the war brought disillusionment, as demobilized veterans returned to their old jobs. By 1950 women held only 47 percent of the jobs. The decline was particularly noticeable in certain types of job, such as directors of collective farms and state industries, where the proportion of women went from 2.6 percent in 1940 to 14.2 percent in 1943 to 2 percent in 1961 and 1.5 percent in 1975.[46] Some women found it difficult to return to the rank and file. The problems caused and encountered by the homecoming soldiers became a recurrent theme of postwar literature. Certain women were also faced with the burden of solitude, for the war had claimed millions of lives and accentuated the disequilibrium between the sexes: in 1959 there were 20 million more women than men in the Soviet Union. Nearly 30 percent of all households were headed by single women.[47] For them work was a necessity, not a choice. This situation distorted relations between men and women and between mothers and their children. Because of their "scarcity" boys were coddled and men honored.

In the meantime changes were made in the laws. In 1943 Stalin, sensing ultimate victory, began preparations for the postwar period. The *Internationale* ceased to be the national anthem; coeducational schools were eliminated. On July 8, 1944, without even a pretense of debate, an edict was issued abolishing common-law marriage, increasing family allowances, and creating the title of Heroic Mother (more than 10 children) and the Order of Maternal Glory (7 to 9 children). Unmarried individuals and childless couples were taxed. Unwed mothers were no longer allowed to file paternity suits or to receive pensions. The status of illegitimate children reverted to its pre-1917 condition. The father of an illegitimate child was exempt from any responsibility. Finally, divorce was made all but impossible: success required submitting to a lengthy court procedure, proving adequate grounds, finding witnesses, and paying exorbitant court costs. Men and women were henceforth tied to one another for life, and adultery no longer entailed negative consequences for the man.

The Cold War and the slow reconstruction of the devastated country further compounded difficulties and heightened tensions. Terror resumed; the U.S.S.R. was isolated. In February 1947 marriage to a foreigner was prohibited.

The death of Stalin in March 1953 cut short a new cycle of violence. With the "thaw" in the Cold War, the government once more began listening to the people. Abortion was again made legal without restriction on November 23, 1955. After a lengthy campaign in the press, divorce procedures were simplified in 1965, and costs were reduced. Under the Family Code of 1968, divorce can be obtained by mutual consent simply by applying to the ZAGS (if there are no children). In other cases, court action is required, but the formalities are minimal. In effect, the edicts of the Stalinist era were erased in this period as the government sought to combine some of the best features of earlier codes. The Code of 1968 repudiated both the libertarian excesses of 1926 and the austerity of 1936.

An Incontestable Failure

After so many upheavals, what assessment can one make of more than 70 years of Soviet power? For one thing, until recently, degrading images of women were not to be found in the Soviet

Union; the explosion of pornography is a recent development. Encouraged to participate in economic and social life and convinced of their total equality, women generally found it natural to work. They felt useful to society and took pride in being able to contribute.

But living conditions reveal that some of this apparent progress was illusory. Long lines, scarce or poor-quality consumer goods, ill-equipped households without labor-saving appliances, and crowded housing made daily life hard, stretched tempers to the breaking point, and claimed a heavy toll in terms of physical deterioration and fatigue. These difficulties, along with ignorance and prejudice, made sexual relations frustrating. Without access to family planning or contraception, abortion became the rule; a typical woman of 30 might have had five to seven abortions.

A Minority Majority

Thus the private sphere of Soviet life was disappointing. Did the public sphere compensate for this? If liberation means education and work, then Soviet women were liberated. In 1989 roughly 92 percent of women between the ages of 18 and 55 were either attending school or working. In 1897, 86.3 percent of Russian women were illiterate (compared with 60.9 percent of Russian men). The campaign to eradicate illiteracy *(likbez)*, launched in 1920 and systematized in the 1930s, achieved spectacular results, as the following percentages illustrate.[48]

	1926	1939	1959
Illiterate men	28.5%	4.9%	0.7%
Illiterate women	57.3%	16.6%	2.2%

The proportion of female students rose from 31 percent in 1926 to 43 percent in 1937 and 55.5 percent in 1989.[49] Women constituted 50.6 percent of the workforce in 1989, compared with 38.9 percent in 1940.[50] Women were overrepresented in certain occupations, however: in 1989 they accounted for 66 percent of physicians, 74 percent of schoolteachers, and 78 percent of sales clerks.[51] Often women had poorly paid professions or jobs that could easily be put aside for a time in order to raise children. One legacy of the war, and of a management style not especially careful of human resources, is that women were often employed in preference to machines, particularly in heavy manual labor. In 1976 women accounted for 70 to 80 percent of the two least-skilled employment categories and 5 to 10 percent of the two top categories.[52] They filled only 6 percent of the management positions.[53] Women carried out orders but did little managing and even less decision-making. Hence they had little influence over their fate. The social services that were supposed to make it easier for women to work proved inadequate. These support services were sacrificed in favor of other priorities, owing in part to the historical context (the chaos of the 1920s, the hard times of the 1930s, the war, the postwar reconstruction), in part to deliberate decision. In 1980 Soviet nursery schools charged fees and accommodated only 45 percent of young children, whereas nursery schools in France were free and served 75 percent of the relevant population.[54] Even as recently as 1988 only 60 percent of Soviet children attended nursery school.[55]

At no time were men expected to share in household chores. Liberation, though promised and attempted, was gradually curtailed. Women were sent out to work in the factories and at the same time relegated to their kitchens, while their political influence failed to grow.

To be sure, the proportion of female Party members increased, but slowly: from 7.4 percent in 1920 to 18.7 percent in 1946 and 27 percent in 1985 (when women made up 53.1 percent of the population).[56] The representation of women in the power structure was uneven. They were present mainly at the lower levels of the hierarchy, in local soviets (14 percent in 1926, 29.5 percent in 1934, 49 percent in 1987) but almost completely absent at the top.[57] Between 1924 and 1939 only four women served on the Central Committee. While the Central Committee grew (from 9 members in 1917 to 57 in 1923 to 106 in 1925), the proportion of female members decreased: 9.7 percent in 1917, 3.3 percent in 1976.[58] In any case, this bloated Central Committee was nothing more than a rubber stamp for decisions made elsewhere. Similarly, the Supreme Soviet, in which the percentage of women decreased from 33 in 1984 to 18.4 after the elections of March 1989, had no real role.[59] The real power belonged to the Politburo and the Secretariat.

In 1956 a woman joined the Politburo for the first time, for a term of three years. In 1988 another woman was admitted. The Secretariat remained an exclusive men's club. As for women in government, after Alexandra Kollontai served as the first woman minister in 1918, it was not until 1954 that the Soviet Union saw another. Since that time, women have served as ministers of culture, health, and education—that is, in areas traditionally associated with women.

A Contestable and Contested Model

By 1923 the die was cast. Although there was progress at the grass roots, there was stalemate at the top. The masses were enlisted in the struggle, but the once competent, combative, and cultivated elite was supplanted by squadrons of colorless yes-men. Strong personalities such as Alexandra Kollontai were removed or liquidated.

In the end Kollontai's fears were justified. Without a redefinition of sex roles economic emancipation proved to be a trap, for women were obliged to conform to a male model without being relieved of their burden as women. It may be that a comparable danger exists in any developing industrial society. A century of European evolution was compressed into two decades in the Soviet Union: the sexual revolution of the 1920s broke down the old family unit, while the Stalinist reaction of the 1930s reshaped the family in order to impose breakneck industrialization on a backward peasant society. The gap between the idealistic slogans and everyday reality was enormous.

The one-party state was not solely responsible for these developments, however. As in other countries, the role of women was ambiguous. Whether responding by instinct to ensure their own survival and that of their children or acting out of alienation, women accepted and internalized the rules of the Soviet game to a greater extent than men—and much to men's annoyance. Sober, long-suffering, conscientious, and disciplined, woman was one of the pillars of the regime: she did the washing, stood in line to buy food, cooked meals, took care of the children, worked in factories and offices and on collective farms, and did whatever she had to do. But to what end? Equality only added to her burden. The legacy of the roaring twenties and the austere thirties and forties was a contradictory ideal: women were expected to be energetic and industrious outside the home and tender, calm, and "feminine" inside. Women wanted strong partners: they had little use for *homo sovieticus,* who, finding himself impotent politically, took refuge in alcoholism. Whether because they wanted to or because men left them the job, women brought up their children, and in so doing reproduced certain patterns: men and women lived separate lives, as the plays of L. Petruchevskaya show.

Since 1917 Soviet law either ran ahead of Soviet society or tried to hold it back, but it never took account of what society wanted. Soviet law was an instrument of Soviet policy. It was a tool in the hands of the state rather than a reflection of evolving attitudes and behavior. If morals under the NEP were relaxed, it was because the government saw fit to encourage such relaxation, not because the society demanded it. As a result, the Soviet people suffered extreme disorientation. The ideological choices of the chosen class—the proletariat, presumed to embody all values and virtues and to be free of all blemish—were made without realizing that the problem of sexual relations transcends class.

The revolution of 1917 occurred in an underdeveloped country with a mainly agricultural economy, and many rapid changes were necessary to move from backwardness to industrialization. The Soviet model may therefore hold lessons for the Third World, where the liberation of women cannot take place without a complete reorganization of society. Its relevance to other countries is more doubtful, as the example of France proves.

In the early days the French Communist press frequently quoted Alexandra Kollontai. In 1924, however, the Fifth Congress of the Communist International stipulated that Communist parties everywhere must follow the Bolshevik line. Henceforth, "communistically speaking, there is no woman question as such," at least according to the newspaper *L'Ouvrière* (September 25, 1924). The prudishness of the East accorded well with the French Communist Party's desire to appeal to voters from the center of the political spectrum. Although Communists continued to fight for such traditional goals as women's right to vote, equal wages, and repeal of the Law of 1920 (which forbade abortion), they joined forces in 1935 with the champions of family and a higher birthrate. It was not until 1950 that the French Communist Party (PCF) welcomed the one and only woman ever to sit on its Politburo. In 1955 the Party launched an attack on "birth control," which it identified with "Malthusianism." "Since when," asked Jeannette Vermeersch (member of the Politburo and wife of the secretary of the PCF), "are working women supposed to covet the right to share the vices of the bourgeoisie? Never!"[60] In May 1956 the Party said yes to abortion and no to contraception. Was it following the example of Moscow, where abortion had been reinstated? Of course, but the polemic was also a way of avoiding the issue of de-Stalinization. "While they argue about their monthly period, they aren't giving a thought to the Khrushchev report."[61] But the Communist rank and file failed to follow the leadership, which ultimately voted in favor of the Neuwirth Law of 1967 and Veil laws of 1974 and 1979 so as not to lose touch with the base.

Ever since 1920 the PCF had offered French women a gratifying political outlet. It encouraged them to work and honored them for doing so. But the Party was fiercely Stalinist and adhered to a rigid model ill-suited to French realities. Once in the vanguard of social change, it became conservative and missed its rendezvous with history.

Inventing the Future

In the years leading up to the collapse of the Soviet Union, relations between the sexes grew tense in the midst of a grave political and economic crisis. In 1979 and 1980 a group of women intellectuals from Leningrad published two vehemently anti-male pamphlets. Since there were no more legal rights to be won, this incipient "feminist" movement denounced men as the source of all women's woes and called for a new approach to male-female relations based on mutual respect and love. The authors of the pamphlet advocated a return to stable marriages with reliable partners. For some, the movement had religious overtones. The government, fearing that the critique might be extended to the political realm, had the leaders of the movement arrested. Some were sentenced to long prison terms, while others were expelled from the Soviet Union.

What does the future hold for the women of the former Soviet Union? Soviet society began to break down during the period of stagnation under Brezhnev, a time of rampant corruption coupled with spiritual and economic malaise. Gorbachev came to power in 1985. Much was expected from his policies of *perestroika* (restructuring) and *glasnost* (openness). But the rise of nationalism coupled with economic disaster—ration tickets for sugar, soap, meat, and other commodities were reinstituted in 1989—and a deterioration of social services, especially medicine, brought the country to the brink of civil war and economic collapse. Women seemed forgotten.[62]

Now that the empire has collapsed, the situation is explosive. If the proponents of order win, women will be condemned to the status quo. If the economic and social structure of the country is drastically reshaped, the danger is that the problems of women will be deferred indefinitely or subordinated, as in 1917, to a comprehensive program for rebuilding society.

Russia, having made its revolution, is now back at square one. The woman question, which obsessed the revolutionaries of the nineteenth century, is more than ever on today's agenda.

TRANSLATED FROM THE FRENCH BY ARTHUR GOLDHAMMER

two

Women, Creation, and Representation

In the Field of Culture

It is in some ways artificial to devote a separate part of this volume to essays touching on the symbolic and on culture as the realm in which the social imagination develops. It is especially artificial in that one premise of our approach has been to deal with the social-symbolic reality on every page (which is why we may at times appear to be repeating ourselves). Yet there was no other way to raise certain crucial questions. How has the question of sexual difference, which has tormented Western culture since the Greeks, been approached by modern philosophers? What influence have cultural images or icons of women had on consumer society? What place do women occupy in the field of culture?

The essays collected here are informed by feminism, to be sure, but they also speak of controversy and change. The first of them, by Françoise Collin, takes us on a lengthy tour of twentieth-century philosophy from Georg Simmel to Simone de Beauvoir, with stops along the way to consider Freud and the disciples of Marx. Until a distinctive feminist thought emerged, philosophy was a male preserve, and sexual difference was rarely among its central concerns. As the century progressed, philosophers no longer dared adhere to a "sexist" metaphysics, an essentialist dualism that took male superiority for granted. In various ways they moved toward a revaluation of the feminine, setting aside the preoccupation with power that had been the focus of the class-based Marxist approach. As the innovative heir of much that had gone before, feminism formulated the question of sexual difference in political and paradigmatic terms. Yet no single voice dominated the discussion.

In particular, feminism pointed out that symbolic violence was as fundamental as economic violence. It denounced the age-old ostracism of women and their works, along with the claim of men, acting in the name of "universality," to control cultural production. To be sure, the situation has changed somewhat, and—to take the case of France as an example—women today enjoy greater freedom of creative expression than in the past. Still, there has been nothing like a "feminization" of literature, and female writers have yet to achieve genuine recognition. Often their work is dismissed as ephemeral because it is believed that they write of what is peculiar to one sex only. In this context, the distinction between egalitarian feminism and the feminism of difference (a distinction on which various contributors have touched) took the form of a controversy over the nature of women's writing. Nevertheless, the use of a general term like "women's writing" should not be allowed to mask the proliferating diversity of works by women and their contribution to the creation of a positive female identity.

The rise of "mass culture," another twentieth-century phenomenon associated with the development of consumer society, has led to a redrawing of the boundary between public and private that is of direct concern to women. We have come a long way since the days when mass culture was condemned as the outcome of a process of homogenization and alienation of oppressed groups. Our attitude is more ambivalent: mass culture has in some ways provided women with the means to emancipation, not only by promoting changes in behavior but also through its role in shaping the male-female representation. Seen in proper historic context, women's magazines and Hollywood films (which women attended in large numbers) turn out to be revealing; so does advertising.

Anne Higonnet introduces us to images of mass culture with the eye of an iconographer, analyzing the circumstances surrounding their production as well as their functions and visual strategies. Their purpose was to establish a visual definition of modern femininity and to create an identity, that of the woman consumer. But the principal focus of Higonnet's contribution is the place of women in the field of art: both the status of women as artists and the value of their creations. She shows how women strove to escape from old stereotypes and points out what was at stake politically in representation. She also considers the birth of contemporary feminist art, which has challenged the traditional categories of art history and proposed new images of women.

Not until the twentieth century, after all, did education finally become available to large numbers of women, who thus gained access to the instruments of theoretical, literary, and artistic expression. We have not yet seen the last of the consequences of this appropriation of the instruments of culture. But it is not too soon to inquire about the future. How will the cultural and theoretical works of women be transmitted to future generations? And how will the emergence of a genuinely mixed culture affect the way in which people view the world and represent it symbolically?

F. T.

9

Philosophical Differences

Françoise Collin

HOW DID THE QUESTION of women and sexual difference find its place in the philosophical apparatus of the twentieth century, and how has that place changed as the century progressed? In the crudest terms, a metaphysical view of sex, still influential at the turn of the century, served to prove that women are inferior to men. Little by little this view gave way to a feminine apologetics with implications for both sexes. Here I shall confine my attention to only a few of the many works that deal with sexual difference, at times in an incidental or secondary manner. In none of the works discussed was the question of women truly central. In the brief space available, it is of course impossible to consider the general structure of every work considered or even the way in which our topic relates to the work as a whole. I shall therefore concentrate on a few significant approaches which were later confronted in a new way by feminist writers of the 1970s and 1980s. For feminists, the question of sexual difference has become paradigmatic. What characterizes and unifies feminist thought is the paradigmatic nature of this question, combined with a political approach to it, rather than any uniformity in the answers it has received.

Sexual difference, insofar as it was associated

with the question of generation, played a fundamental role in the birth of philosophy in ancient Greece and continued to occupy an important place in philosophical thought ever since. Early in the twentieth century, however, the importance of this topic seemed to decline. Changes in the structure of knowledge in the late nineteenth century provide part of the explanation for this. Just as the exact sciences emerged from philosophy in the seventeenth century, the human sciences—history, sociology, and ethnology (psychoanalysis is a special case)—constituted themselves as autonomous disciplines in the late nineteenth century. Each assumed responsibility for an aspect of reality, replacing philosophical speculation with empirical analysis. Even phenomenology, a development within philosophy itself based on a renewed interest in phenomena, sought to capture the "essence" of the phenomena it studied. It may be, too, that the advancement of women, growing numbers of whom held positions in various academic disciplines, made it more difficult to subscribe to a "metaphysics of the sexes" that inevitably reflected the sexism of the ambient society. A certain vacuum developed. Meanwhile, political philosophy was wholly taken up with the Marxist question of class and the explosive issue of race; it avoided the question of sex entirely.

Surprisingly, perhaps, nearly all the works I shall consider are by men. Philosophy remained a purely male bastion longer than other disciplines, no doubt because it claimed a quasi-sacred relation to truth. The few pre-feminist women philosophers of the twentieth century did not touch the issue of sex. This is true of Jeanne Hersch, Suzanne Langer, Gisèle Brelet, Jeanne Delhomme, Simone Weil, Edith Stein, and even Hannah Arendt, whose political thought, much taken up with the question of Jewish difference, is nevertheless illuminating to consider in relation to our question. It is not my task here to elucidate the contributions of these women philosophers.

The Metaphysics of the Sexes

The metaphysics of the sexes, sometimes referred to as "essentialism," is the doctrine that there is an essential, indeed a natural, difference between women and men. It goes on to describe what the specific attributes of each sex are. Or, more precisely, it describes what the specific attributes of the female sex are, while the attributes of the male are considered to be universal. In one form or another this doctrine can be found throughout virtually the whole history of philosophy. It was still present at the turn of the twentieth century, but since then it has faded from sight, or at any rate is no longer couched in the same language.

The German sociologist and philosopher Georg Simmel developed his ideas on sexual difference in response to the significant German feminist movement of his day. The movement was controversial, and Simmel discussed the issues it raised with Marianne Weber, among others. He was keenly aware of asymmetry and hierarchy in sexual relations, which he sometimes analyzed in terms of power. "The male sex sees itself as human, as general," he observed. "The male sex judges itself to be superior to the female, not simply in a relative sense but as the representative of the universal human being that establishes the general laws which govern the manifestations of the particular male and the particular female. That it can do this depends, through a series of mediations, on the *position of power* that men occupy."[1] There was clearly injustice in this asymmetry of power, but Simmel believed that the injustice stemmed from the way in which masculine and feminine are defined, independent of their historical conditions. For him, there was something "tragic" in relations between the sexes. He was in a sense a precursor of the French psychoanalyst Jacques Lacan, who later became notorious for saying that "there is no relation between the sexes."

Woman, in Simmel's view, is wholly immersed in her femininity. Her relation to her sex is centripetal and intrinsic: it does not depend on her relation to man. By contrast, masculinity is centrifugal, in the sense that man defines himself only externally, by objectifying himself, and asserts himself as gendered only in his relation to woman. A woman is a woman in herself; a man is a man only in his sexual relations with a woman. Hence in woman individuality and femininity are confused, whereas in man masculinity and individuality are distinct. Love is thus a misunderstanding, in which the woman seeks an individual while the man seeks the femininity—the sex—that will prove his virility. The sexual relation itself is therefore problematic, and prostitution is the way that men attempt to resolve the problem, using certain women as instruments for their own benefit. Simmel analyzed possible ways out of this unfortunate situation and saw only one viable solution: to allow women sexual freedom, as some feminists of the day were already demanding. Nevertheless, he was aware that such sexual freedom was not necessarily compatible with the imperatives of femininity. The requirements of masculinity continued to define even the "liberated" woman.

Simmel's arguments are partly conventional, partly critical of the position of women. For him, there is not just a difference between the sexes; there are two distinct sexual registers, two ways of relating to the world and to gender that are difficult if not impossible to bring into harmony except through alienation of one in the other.

Simmel then asks if there are, at any rate potentially, two distinct cultures. If the dominant culture is entirely masculine, can women, by liberating themselves, develop another, or must they find their place in the existing "foreign" culture?

Simmel has no doubt that women are capable of participating in the world as it is. He even believes that their presence might have a beneficial effect, generally by accentuating subjective elements of the culture. But he denies that a specifically feminine culture can coexist with or replace the existing masculine one. True, women have a specific mode of existence, but their specificity consists precisely in immanence, in their relation to themselves, and not in externalization, or self-realization by way of objects, which is the mode of existence specific to masculinity. Thus while there may be two distinct, gendered manners of being in the world, there is only one manner of making one's mark on the world— one language. Although Simmel does not refer to his near-contemporary Freud, their positions are similar insofar as sexual duality is subordinated to a unique and exclusive masculine process of symbolization. In other words, what is particular in man is universalizable, whereas what is particular in women is merely particular. There are two sexes, but there is only one culture, the culture of one of those sexes, in which the other shares.

The Spanish philosopher José Ortega y Gasset translated Simmel's *Masculine and Feminine* into Spanish and published it in the *Revista de Occidente,* of which he was the editor. In his preface he wrote: "I do not believe that there is another analysis of the differences between the male and female psychologies as acute and penetrating as this essay by the philosopher Simmel . . . [which sheds] so much light on the eternal conflict between masculine and feminine." Nevertheless, Ortega's reading of the illuminating tensions in Simmel's thought seems simplistic and reductionist. The Spanish philosopher was inspired by the subject, however, to publish any number of articles, which reveal his position to have been far more garden-variety sexist than Simmel's.

For Ortega, woman was "constitutionally inferior" to man: "In the presence of a woman, we men immediately sense a creature who, on the plane properly ascribed to humankind, occupies a vital rank somewhat inferior to our own. No other being can claim the two attributes of being human but to a lesser degree than man." Woman is thus not so much *different* from man as *less* than man, and her aspiration to equality is not only futile but unrealistic. Woman can best fulfill her mission by accepting her condition, again defined relative to man: "Woman's destiny is to be in man's sight."[2]

Having defined woman's place, Ortega went on to point out her attributes, by their very nature ambiguous: she was a sinuous being, perpetually in confusion and doubt, "voluptuous," with an inclination for private life and a capacity for love, "that is, for disappearing into another," and beautiful. By virtue of these qualities, woman was "the complement of man," and certain types of women were best of all, in particular the "creole" of whom Ortega gave a lyrical description.

Paradoxically, however, sexual difference was not ultimately based on biology. Biology, he observed, "teaches us that the embryo is originally undifferentiated sexually and may evolve in an ambiguous or ambivalent manner," this being the explanation for the existence of masculine women and effeminate men. Sexual difference is more a cultural product, but one so deeply rooted in each individual that any attempt to subvert it, as feminists proposed, could be dangerous. Women must exercise their freedom in accordance with these facts and not against them. The status quo is not simply a product of man's will, moreover: women helped to create and perpetuate it, and they derive their identity from it. The world (and men) would lose a great deal if sexual difference were replaced by homogenizing equality.

Although Ortega's thought was supposedly inspired by that of Simmel, it clearly marked a step backward. Ortega frequently defines difference in terms of plus or minus rather than otherness, and woman is always defined in relation to man, the standard of reference whom she serves as complement. The power structure that shapes sexual relations is never mentioned, nor is the injustice to which one sex is subjected.

The position taken by Ortega (who in reality did a great deal to promote women, not least in his journal) combined denigration with celebration of woman as "man's concrete ideal, enchantment, and illusion." Women, he conceded, have much to contribute, but always in the way of sustaining and embellishing the lives and works of men.[3]

What I have called essentialism can be found in any number of works, though not always as bluntly expressed as in Ortega y Gasset. Max Scheler, for example, summed up his conception of sexual difference in a clear, if banal, passage of *On Modesty:* "Woman is the genius of life," he wrote, whereas "man is the genius of spirit."[4]

In *Nature and Forms of Sympathy* he uses the same distinction with a slightly different shade of meaning. Considering the respective roles of men and women, or, more precisely, of the masculine and feminine, in civilization, Scheler points out that women, owing to their distinctive experience, recall and defend an essential dimension of human life, which technological domination may well compromise in the future if it has not already done so. Indeed, the feminine is the repository of what Scheler is advocating, namely, "sympathy," which gives rise to relations among human beings and between humans and the world, in forms as varied as love, sexuality, and procreation, all exempt from the draconian discipline of means and ends that governs the system of production. These forms of sympathy require no purpose or explanation: they exist and they develop.

Therein lies what Scheler calls "the cosmo-vital fusion," which must be rescued from the destructive imperatives of profit inherent in the "capitalist regime, devoid of all affective unity." Here Scheler anticipates themes that would later be taken up by Herbert Marcuse. Furthermore, according to Scheler, it is precisely women and children who suffer most from capitalism and are therefore most refractory to its discipline. Women possess an emotional power that far exceeds mere maternal instinct and that spills over into the realm of what we would nowadays call ecology: "The protection of animals . . . and plants . . . the preservation of forests and landscapes . . . of the physical and psychic capabilities of peoples and races . . . all measures that ought to enjoy absolute priority over measures serving solely to increase wealth and property."

What we see in Scheler is thus the recasting of the problem of sexual difference from the psychological to the cultural realm. In the process, the feminine, sustained by women, becomes an indispensable component of the world we share, something capable of resisting the instrumentalization of modernity.

Vladimir Jankélévitch refers to Scheler in his brief consideration of the question, but such a reference is hardly necessary since all he does is repeat a commonplace. He contrasts "the virile to the feminine as the genius of the spirit to the true genius of life, the guardian angel of the biological *existant*." The former takes the initiative and the risks; it destroys in order to build. The latter preserves, maintains, and protects. The philosopher feigns astonishment: "Why should she whose whole function is to protect and preserve be so often incapable of building. . . . Yes, it was doubtless the law of alternation that divided complementary vocations between the two sexes."[5]

Twenty pages of the *Traité des vertus* are devoted to this complementarity, immediately following the chapter on fidelity. The feminine—"form without force"—needs the masculine—"force without form," and vice versa. True, the characteristic qualities of the feminine do come in for praise: woman's spirit of continuity; her respect for the law, which is always a concern with legality more than with legitimacy; her sense of fidelity. And if woman is incapable of creating beauty, at least she embodies it. But such praise is, to say the least, ambivalent, and the reader clearly senses that the author's sympathies are with the masculine qualities: "We need insecurity, lurking danger, a beating heart; the wine of springtime, which savors of war and adventure; the drums of springtime, which beat in man's breast."

In analyzing what differentiates men and women or even leads them to confront one another, Jankélévitch questions the very complementarity that is supposed to govern their relations. In the end he declares it to be something of a "misunderstanding": the polarity of the two sexes arises because the relation between them is not dialectical or complementary but one of "contradictory tension and ambivalence." Should we read this as the expression, as in Simmel, of a timid recognition of the otherness of women or of the feminine, an otherness that eludes not only men's grasp but perhaps even their capacity to comprehend? Maybe. But this otherness is still narrowly defined and entirely contained within the most traditional of dualisms; one sex is still superior to the other.

Women and Femininity: Psychoanalysis

Is psychoanalysis, which Freud founded at the turn of the century, yet another version of the "metaphysics of sex" that has been with us since human beings began to think, or is it a subversion of that metaphysics? Both interpretations have been made, and both find justification in the abundant literature produced by Freud and his successors.

Psychoanalysis, in any case, casts itself not as a new form of philosophical speculation but as a new science, the science of the unconscious, based on previously unexplored facts. Although Freud's concept of science was shaped by the positivism of his day, from which Lacan later dissociated himself, the peculiar facts that psychoanalysis proposed to explore were, like all facts, constructs; the facts themselves were implicit in a theory subject to modification and reformulation. Thus by Freud's own admission, a speculative component was not altogether lacking. The discovery of this new stratum of reality gave rise to an immense body of texts, including both interpretations of Freud's writings and papers reporting on actual practice behind the analytic couch. This vast literature is filled with controversy, moreover. Here I shall be concentrating exclusively on matters relevant to the issue at hand, and I must remind the reader that psychoanalysis does not claim to elucidate all of human experience or, for that matter, all of the issues associated with sexuality and gender.

The oedipal structure of the unconscious is the matrix of psychoanalytic theory. The theory discusses the positions of father, mother, daughter, and son and examines the long process by which the male child learns to inhabit his gendered reality and the female child learns to resign herself to hers. The law of the father forbids possession of the mother, the first object of desire. Hence desire must seek another woman in the case of a male, another sex in the case of a female. The law thereby opens the way to maturity and symbolic capability once the ordeal of castration is surmounted.

The position of each sex is correlated with its morphology. Girls differ from boys because they lack something, namely, a penis, for which they feel "envy" and for which the clitoris is an unsatisfactory substitute. The female sex is thus defined negatively in relation to the male. To become a woman is to accept that one is not a man, and the process is an arduous one.

Usually, this order is modified by the presence of bisexual proclivities. But access to the benefits of the phallus and, more precisely, to sublimation, is something for which girls must pay dearly, for they are always obliged in one way or another to choose between pleasure and work, whereas boys are able to harmonize the two. Thus, Freud noted, "a girl whose teacher hugs her every time she does good work becomes incapable of completing the most trivial assignment."

To be sure, Freud was by no means unaware of the role that culture plays in determining the place of women, but that awareness never led him to question the oedipal structure, which he saw as transcultural. It was with nostalgia, moreover, that he noted developments likely to lead "to the disappearance of the most delightful thing the world has to offer us, our ideal of femininity." He was accordingly critical of the feminism of John Stuart Mill, who called for equality between the sexes.

Freud's work was complex and constantly evolving. In schematic outline, however, he emphasized sexual dimorphism or asymmetry even though phallic monism was his first principle: all libido is masculine. Nevertheless, what the unconscious reveals appears to be astonishingly similar to what society produces. The traditional family even defines a genital, heterosexual norm. Thus many commentators (including Kofman, Schneider, and Marini) have noted that the anxiety about death that accompanies the evocation of the maternal figure leads to a profound ambivalence about femininity in the work of Freud (and his followers, including Lacan).

Of course the founder of psychoanalysis was a man with his own personal history. He tested his fundamental concepts in a self-analysis. And he was, moreover, steeped in the sexist prejudices of his day, as his correspondence with his fiancée reveals to an almost caricatural degree. Hence one can ask what bearing these circumstantial factors had on the new "science" of the unconscious. Was the science of desire undamaged by the (masculine) desire that oversaw its elaboration? Be that as it may, the further development of psychoanalytic knowledge and practice depended on sifting out the central elements of Freud's doctrine from the accidental distortions. Women as well as men contributed to this effort during Freud's own lifetime and afterward. And the simple fact that numerous women, including many feminists, have to this day turned to psychoanalysis as analysands, analysts, and theorists suggests that they find it to contain a truth that can also be their truth. The case that some women make against Freud and his heirs is a case developed within the analytic framework itself and based on its assumptions.

Toward the end of his life, Freud returned to the question of femininity, about which he had long remained silent, and in a moment of self-criticism he did not hesitate to admit that something about the nature of that "dark continent" continued to elude him. To Marie Bonaparte he put the celebrated question: "What do women want?" And he received no answer. According to Paul-Laurent Hassoun, psychoanalysis can explain female desire but not the female will, which is something else entirely.[6] Psychoanalytic understanding is not useless, but it is inadequate to account for femininity.

Is it the additional complexity of the feminine that makes it fail to fit the established structures, or is the problem that those structures were conceived and elaborated in terms of masculinity (though initially with close reference to female patients)? In Lacan's words, "one begins with man in order to appreciate the reciprocal position of the sexes."

Freud, who continually explored and made use of the notions of masculinity and femininity throughout his career, refused even at the end to define the terms: "What creates masculinity and femininity is an unknown character that eludes anatomical definition. . . . You cannot give any new content to the notions of masculine and feminine."[7] Was this a belated expression of doubt, a retreat from earlier positions, or the key to a reinterpretation of the entire oeuvre? Having opened up a new field, Freud left it for his disciples, dissident as well as orthodox, to explore.

One group of Freud's followers, generally known as the English School, corrected his work in important ways without casting doubt on the oedipal pattern.[8] The corrections had to do primarily with the status of the feminine, which for these critics was not a secondary formation but a distinctive way of life from the beginning: there is, they argued, a feminine libido which appears as early as the pregenital phase and which stems from vaginal pleasure. Thus for the critics, penis envy is not the desire to possess a male organ, accompanied by spite at not having one, but rather allo-erotic desire either of the penis or for incorporation of the penis in the form of a child. Karen Horney, who placed heavy emphasis on the sociocultural character of gender formation, remarked that, for her, "penis envy" simply reflected women's desire to share in the advantages and responsibilities that men enjoy in society and from which women are systematically excluded, leaving them with no choice but to seek refuge in sentimentality.

Thus the English School favored a primary dualism of the sexes, by means of which the richness of the feminine dimension could be treated on a par with that of the masculine. To be a woman, as the critics saw it, was not to be a man *manqué* but to be something other than a man. In the work of Melanie Klein in particular, a fundamental role in forming a girl's identity was ascribed to her relation to her mother.

This direction in psychoanalysis, which numerous women explored, was fought by Freud himself during his lifetime as well as by several of his successors. It did, in fact, undermine a key point of Freud's doctrine: the fundamental importance of the father figure, the father being not only the bearer of the penis but the symbol of the phallus (the penis/phallus distinction being one that Lacan would develop later on, as we shall see in a moment). In the critics' view, the father was reduced to a mere object of desire, analogous to the mother. The two gendered figures had symmetrical value. This rebalancing, which was associated with the debate over clitoral versus vaginal orgasm, nevertheless remained a prisoner of Freud's morphological metaphors. It did, however, inspire a way of thinking about sexual difference, which, because it was dualist, avoided hierarchy.

The French psychoanalyst Jacques Lacan proposed a return to the texts of Freud with himself as their correct interpreter. He tried to dissociate psychoanalytic concepts from their anatomical referents more than Freud had done, however. For example, the crucial referent for Lacan was not the penis, or male organ, but the Phallus, a signifier common to both sexes, each being subject in its own way to the ordeal of castration. Thus Lacan maintained the monism of the signifier and the dimorphism of the sexes while reducing the privilege that the male sex, at first sight at any rate, possessed relative to the female in the Freudian edifice.

Later, Lacan would proceed even further with this displacement. In the seminar entitled "Encore" he revised his own conceptual edifice in light of the question of the feminine and, more precisely, of the female *jouissance,* which he designated a "supplementary *jouissance* (orgasm, pleasure, ecstasy)" to phallic orgasm. This *jouissance,* though no stranger to the phallic order, exceeded its limits: "Just because it is not all in the phallic function does not mean that it is not there at all. It is not at all not there. It is completely there, but something else is there besides."[9]

Here, the feminine is portrayed as something "added to" the phallic rather than as something "taken away." The logic of the whole does not wholly account for it. Lacan is notorious for having said, "Woman does not exist," a statement that many women took to be a denial of their existence. But what he really meant was that there is no general definition of woman, no essence that accounts for what it is to be a woman. Woman is not of the order of the definable: in Lacan's algebraic shorthand, this point was made by writing *la femme* with the article *la* struck through by a slash. In the same spirit, a feminist like Luce Irigaray used the formulation *"la/une femme."*

What did it mean for psychoanalysis to treat the feminine in this way? Whereas Freud apparently felt that the feminine eluded the grasp of analytic theory and that this called for further research, Lacan believed that the feminine eluded the grasp of knowledge itself. Is the feminine "supplement" to be sought only in the realm of the orgasmic? Is it fully spent in the silent swoon, in carnal abandon? Or does it give rise to a different way of relating to the world, to a different form of language, to a strange form of "knowledge" not susceptible to "totalization," which Lacan initially associates with mysticism but later extends in certain ways to the whole practice of knowing? In any case, some men share the feminine "supplement," whatever it is: here as elsewhere Lacan breaks the seals on the categories of "femininity" and "masculinity" as they relate to the reality of men and women.

Something pivotal had thus changed in our thinking about

sexual difference. Although the change was at this stage still ambiguous, it presaged a revaluation of the feminine that men would
immediately claim for themselves: the psychoanalyst was henceforth to take the side of incompleteness, of the "not all," and the
philosopher would take the side of "difference." In a sense,
thought itself was "feminized" *(on assiste à un certain "devenir
femme" de la pensée),* yet this had no bearing on the evolution of
women *(le devenir des femmes).*

This shift can be seen in a variety of intellectual disciplines in
the second half of the twentieth century: philosophy, social and
political theory, logic, and feminism. A more or less general critique of totality, of closed systems, of logocentrism, of domination
emerged in many areas, in favor of "nontotalizing" thought, open
systems, the infinite, decenteredness, and the unlimited. In this
sense it is possible to see a certain kinship between the "whole–
not-whole" relation in Lacan and Heidegger's critique of metaphysics. The comparison is not fortuitous: Lacan, toward the
middle of his career, moved from thinking in terms of the Hegelian
dialectic toward thinking in terms of Heideggerian Difference.

Such comparisons merely indicate consonances, however, no
matter how significant. While there is no point in drawing un-
warranted parallels between distinct modes of thought, it is worth
noting the use of similar categories in distinct forms of investigation. The order of the whole—whether phallic or metaphysical—
is unavoidable, but it is "not everything." "Modernity," understood as domination of the Subject, thus loses a certain amount
of credit, and there is reason to see this as a loss of credit on the
part of "virility." Some feminist thinkers, particularly in the United
States, have rushed into the breach thus opened, taking their inspiration from French thinkers such as Jacques Derrida as well as
Luce Irigaray and Hélène Cixous.

Political Revolution and Libidinal Revolution

Marxism's contribution to the problem of sexual difference was
to pose it in historical and political terms (for Marxists, of course,
the political is rooted in the economic). The status of women,
Marxists say, is the result of a process of domination, driven by
exploitation, which can and must be overcome. In this perspective
the battle of the sexes is closely linked to the class struggle. Indeed,

it is the fundamental form of that struggle. In Engels's words, "the first class conflict to manifest itself historically coincided with the development of antagonism between man and woman in marriage, and the first class oppression coincided with sexual oppression."[10] The goal of political struggle is thus to overthrow both capitalism and the family, which are regarded as the two bastions of bourgeois power (and all power is bourgeois).

There are problems, however, with merging class and sex. One can speak of a historical formation in which capital dominated labor, but it is more problematic to conceive of a historical formation in which man dominated woman, for it would have to extend to the most remote times and places. Bachofen's hypothesis of a primitive matriarchal state thus proved useful to Marxist theorists. Although they described his theory only to refute it, it at least had the advantage of attributing a beginning and a prospective end to patriarchy. Marxists envisaged that end not as a return to matriarchy but as a dissolution of the family cell and, more generally, of any private organization resisting the collectivist ideal.

Communism was thus supposed to supplant not only capitalism but also patriarchy, giving rise to a society devoid of class or sex distinctions and therefore fully egalitarian. In Bebel's words: "Women as well as men have the right to develop and use their strengths as they see fit. Women are human beings just as men are, and they are just as free to determine their own lives. The accident of being born a woman changes nothing."[11] Thanks to liberation, women can apply their strengths to production. To that end they must be freed from household chores. Bebel does not envision men taking up those chores, however. He relies instead on technological progress and collectivization: all his hopes are invested in the "communist kitchen." If the destruction of the family allows women to invest more of themselves in social and professional life, it also has a further corollary, namely, sexual liberation for women, this having been hitherto the exclusive privilege of men. Free love, free exchange of partners, and freedom to control one's own body were values which Alexandra Kollontai stubbornly upheld, almost in defiance of the realities of her day, when contraception was much more difficult than it is now.[12] Such demands brought together various aspects of life that would prove crucial for women's liberation: family, work, libido. Later Marxist thought and above all Communist practice gave up on the goals of abolishing the family and achieving sexual liberation, to concentrate instead on reshaping the relations of production.

This subordination of liberation to the productive order, whether capitalist or not, became the focal point of criticism by thinkers who were the heirs not only of Marx but also of Freud: first Wilhelm Reich and later Herbert Marcuse, Gilles Deleuze, Felix Guattari, and François Lyotard. These writers refused to accept that revolution could be subordinated to any form of repression, whether social productivist or oedipal.

Lifting repression, which channels libidinal life into work or reproduction, is the only way to achieve a true revolution. The elimination of economic domination calls for the elimination of sexual taboos in order to permit the pure and positive deployment of the libido. Such a lifting of taboos is even more essential for women than for men, insofar as women's sexuality has been repressed to a greater degree because of their maternal role, which, according to Reich, is antagonistic to their feminine role. In one formulation or another, libidinization is for all these thinkers not only the *sine qua non* of freedom but freedom itself: Eros, in Marcuse's terms, will give rise to a new civilization.

What this analysis takes from psychoanalysis is the primacy of desire, which is what moves human beings and society. What it rejects is the reduction of the libido to its oedipal coding, which is seen as a social imperative. The liberating implications of Freud's discovery had been blunted, we are told, by psychoanalytic practice, whose goal had become to facilitate adaptation to a reality viewed not as historical but as structural and intangible. In the theory and practice there is in a sense a contradiction between the insistence on the polymorphous character of the libido and its reduction to one operative mode. This critique can be found in two works published in France in 1972 and 1974: Deleuze and Guattari's *Anti-Oedipus,* and Lyotard's *Libidinal Economy.* Both books exemplify the spirit of the 1970s, the decade that witnessed the birth of the modern feminist movement.[13]

For all three writers, the "subject" in the sense of a desiring identity does not exist. Rather, there is a "desiring machine" or "libidinal surface," a subversive, deconstructive pleasure that constantly undermines what is given or established, that disrupts hierarchies and destroys values while lurking in the most unexpected places, even in servitude and suffering. This is desire in its purest form, the ultimate subversive force that cannot be reduced to any code. It is uncontrollable, and "the political economy is first of all a libidinal economy." Revolution thus stems from the libido, over and above the objectives and strategies that the militant forces knowingly adopt. Those objectives and forces are never anything more than a rationalization of desire, an encoding, perhaps even a repression according to predetermined forms exactly like those that the revolution aims to overthrow.

But this libidinal agency cannot be reduced to "sexual freedom," though the *socius* would reduce it exclusively to genitality or even heterosexuality. In one "polymorphously perverse" movement it surges forth on all sides and circulates everywhere, over every surface, in infinite *schizes*. Hence it is fundamentally irreducible to any social order, whether reactionary or revolutionary, for it always emerges where it is least expected and is incompatible with all norms.

Such unidentifiable pleasure is neither man nor woman, neither masculine nor feminine: it crosses the sacrosanct boundary of "sexual difference." In Lyotard's words: "Freud asked, 'What do women want?' They want the human to be neither man nor woman, and they want to want for nothing more; they want for men and women, though different, to be identical in the insane plugging together of all tissue."[14] The suggestion here is that this libidinal desexualization is in essence feminine or that it somehow responds to the feminine demand for an overcoming of all dualism. Deleuze goes even further: "Women's libbers are right to say, 'We aren't castrated, and you can go to hell.' And don't think men can get out of it by the miserable little trick of answering, 'There, that's the proof that they are.' Or that you can console them by saying, 'Men are too,' while rejoicing that they wear a different mask, one that can't be covered over. Not at all. You have to admit that the women's libbers represent in a more or less ambiguous way something that is inherent in every demand for liberation: the force of the unconscious itself, desire's assault on the social field, and the withdrawal of support for repressive structures."[15]

From this point of view, then, the contribution of the feminine, and of the women's movement that supported it, was not the development of a feminine essence opposed to a phallic masculine essence but rather subversion of the phallic agency itself and of its distributive law as it pertains to father and mother, man and woman. In the words of Gilles Deleuze, "the unconscious is an orphan." As the title *Anti-Oedipus* suggests, the whole thrust of his book is to criticize psychoanalysis for restricting the libido to its oedipal mode, as if it could be reduced to a "mom-and-pop" story.

Deleuze and Guattari dissolve the question of women and their intrinsic being by not discriminating gender, without ever taking up women's actual subordinate position in social and political life. For them, of course, that position is merely the unfortunate residue of "oedipalization," hence one will end with the other. Another issue that is not dealt with is the possibility of antagonism or mismatch between two libidos, which, even if they cannot be identified with a sex, are nevertheless plural and therefore potentially incompatible. Their preestablished harmony is simply assumed: "libidinal energy" is seen as anonymous and neuter, as a polyvalent and polymorphous flux yet without internal contradictions. Thus the question of power relations is avoided: "desire" melds all desires in a positive unity from which conflict and tragedy are excluded.

Two other thinkers expressed doubts about the anti-oedipal analysis and went on to develop distinct and indeed antagonistic critiques, both of which bring the notion of power back into the sexual economy. In *De la séduction* Jean Baudrillard was harshly critical of the attempt to translate the advent of the feminine and its role in social transformation into libidinal terms. In his view, generalized eroticization was by no means incompatible with a society of production and consumption; in fact, it turned pleasure into one commodity among others available for consumption by both men and women. Now everyone could claim pleasure as a right along with the right to own a washing machine or a television set. By associating men and women indiscriminately with this consumer paradise, one only reinforced the male definition of society. Why? Because for Baudrillard, the feminine, by way of the phenomenon of seduction, was that which always refused an essentially masculine gender identification.

Femininity is the uncertainty principle that causes both sexual poles to oscillate: "It is not the pole opposed to the masculine but that which abolishes the distinctive opposition, and therefore sexuality itself, as it has been historically incarnated in masculine phallocracy and as it may be incarnated tomorrow in feminine phallocracy." Furthermore, "seduction is always more singular and more sublime than sex and is what we value most highly."[16] Thus for Baudrillard all sexuality is phallic and objectifying, and generalized eroticization is merely the annexation of women to the phallic economy of the sexes and of sex. The feminine, he argues, "is not exactly a sex but a form transversal to all sex and all power, a secret and virulent form of non-sexuality *(insexualité),*" and the masculine traditionally seeks to subdue it.

This awareness that "sexual freedom" may be merely a way of annexing women to the primacy of male sexuality leads Baudrillard to cast a suspicious eye on women's demands. Because of the real danger of confusing sexual liberation with freedom, he sees value in the traditional position of women, whose apparent lack of power actually hides the extraordinary power that he claims women maintain through seduction.

In reducing men's social power to an artificial revenge for women's "primitive" power (especially the power to bestow life, as Bruno Bettelheim shows in *Symbolic Wounds*), Baudrillard for all his new insights ends up in a fairly traditional male position: since women in fact wield immense power that men merely attempt to counter with their social power, why should they seek to exchange that power for a social power that can only be phallic? In doing so women would not only lose their identities but would lose the battle as well. Baudrillard seemingly fails to notice that if phallic social power exists, women are subject to it even in seduction, despite their supposedly exorbitant primitive superiority.

Baudrillard may well be correct that generalized eroticization (or libidinal politics) is an extension rather than a rejection of phallocentric culture and of the generalized process of consumption. But his critique is aimed more at certain theorists of the 1970s, all to some degree heirs of Wilhelm Reich, than at feminism. Although he appears to criticize phallic civilization, he fails to propose any kind of transformation. In assigning women the role of being, in Hegel's words, "the eternal irony of the community," he credits them with a long-term subversive role compared with which their "revolution" would in fact mark a retreat.

Assigning women to an "ironic" position in fact allows the phallic system to continue to function without transformation, since it is subverted by the feminine so long as that remains in its traditional position. Thus everything is for the best in the best of all possible worlds. Any potential change is seen in terms of loss rather than gain. There is no positive political perspective in Baudrillard's position, which is entirely oriented toward the past: it is a matter of playing the cards one is dealt rather than changing the way things are. Any frontal assault on the system by women would be a sign of a "phallic conversion."

In a later interview Baudrillard clarified his position and distanced himself from Michel Foucault. In contrast to Foucault, who asserted that power is everywhere, Baudrillard stated that "power does not exist . . . masculinity does not exist . . . it's a preposterous story of simulation." Real power lies with seduction, which "plays with sexual difference."[17]

The power ascribed to men is thus a sham, a façade that disappears as soon as one ceases to take it seriously. The emperor has no clothes: one has only to say so, to laugh about it. Seduction, instead of butting its head against this reality, circumvents it. It establishes new rules, which blur the boundaries between the sexes. The realm of seduction, where women have traditionally been in command, is a counter-power more apt to undermine power than any so-called political revolution.

Foucault's position, staked out in, among other places, his *Histoire de la sexualité,* is not only more "realistic" but also more analytical and descriptive. For him, "sexuality" in the pure state does not exist: it is always caught up in historical configurations *(dispositifs)* that structure it in various ways. Thus far, moreover, it has always been associated with various "patterns of alliance" in the form of the family. Foucault sets himself the task of uncovering the historical and cultural forms those patterns have taken, including that which "constituted sex itself as something desirable." In an obvious criticism of the Freudian-Marxist theorists of libidinal revolution, he remarked on the "irony of this pattern, [which is] that it wants to persuade us that our liberation is at stake."[18] Sexuality is always a *mise en discours,* a formulation in terms of theoretical and practical discourse. One discourse can replace another: in this sense feminism is not the abolition of all discourse but the substitution of one discourse for another, of a new discourse for the hitherto dominant discourse. It is not an effect of nature but one consequence among others of history and politics, whose specific modalities call for analysis.

Foucault substituted a structural approach for Marxism's causal explanations, and he uncovered multiple strata of power where Marxism had seen only one mechanism of exploitation, the economic. He thus injected new life into the study of how societies through the ages have relied in practice on various forms of exclusion. He focused his attention primarily on madmen and prisoners. When it came to male-female relations, he was suspicious of reductionism and warned against the belief in the possibility of achieving some sort of ideal situation in which the truth would be revealed. There is, he argued, no "essence" of sexuality or of intersexual relations; there are only modalities. There is no society without power; there are only displacements of power. Foucault's philosophy, for all its analytic subtlety, was by no means a "philosophy of liberation," and it should come as no surprise that it culminated in a meditation on "the ethics of the self." By introducing the notion of "bio-power," however, Foucault brought to light a process of domination that could not be reduced to the process of economic domination identified by Marx, one that shed light, in particular, on the way in which women's bodies are subjected to inspection in the course of sexuality and reproduction. Feminist critics were quick to seize hold of it.[19]

Critique of Phallogocentrism

In the mid-twentieth century the critique of modernity, of which postmodernism is the final offspring, supplanted the rationalistic, scientistic optimism that began with Descartes and was developed by the philosophers of the Enlightenment, the Positivists, and Karl Marx. Suspicion began to be cast on the idea that nature could be dominated by an all-powerful Subject capable of objectifying it for the greater good of humankind. Faith in the omnipotence of calculating reason was shaken. A transvaluation of values took place: reason, in the sense of a totalizing domination claiming to impose unity, enlightenment, and order, was challenged not by the irrational but by another form of reason, which allied itself with the obscure, the nonunified, with change itself. This shift opened up a new intellectual realm, a new way of relating to the world, reminiscent of the opposition between "feminine" and "masculine" or of the trace of the feminine within the masculine with which some feminist thinkers would later associate themselves.

Heidegger showed how the history of technology and the history of metaphysics both depended on mastery and thus progressed in tandem. This process could be traced all the way back to classical Greece, long before the modern era began. For Heidegger as for Jacques Derrida, who in this respect at least was Heidegger's heir, there is nothing "after" or "beyond" metaphysics and technology, which cannot be abolished but only deconstructed.[20]

Derrida translated this tension into sexual terms. Heidegger's critique of the "logocentrism" of Western thought became, in Derrida's hands, a critique of "phallogocentrism," that is, of logocentrism combined with phallocentrism. The phallogocentrism of knowing and doing cannot be circumvented, for its center is constantly shifting as it is shaped by "the other" which is not "its other" and which disseminates the signifier.

When Derrida takes up the question of masculine and feminine directly, when he debates the issue with feminists who have drawn on his work, he declines to frame the issue in antagonistic or even merely dualistic terms. If the struggles of women as a social group have led them to define the sexes in terms of opposition, their practice must be strategic; its goal must be its own sublation. Its dualist logic is derived, paradoxically, from the logic of the phallic. The differentiae of sexual difference are not objectifiable. Sexual difference is not of the order of the visible or definable but of the "readable." In other words, it is subject to interpretation. Between the sexes there is, to be sure, a cleavage *(coupure)*, but it is a "cleavage that creates no separation, or, to put it another way, that repairs the separation it creates" (as Derrida once put it in a discussion with Hélène Cixous). For the same reason he also says that the neuter, that which is *neither* one sex *nor* the other, cannot be translated in terms of "either/or." Adopting this as his viewpoint in an article entitled "*Geschlecht,* différence sexuelle, différence ontologique," he interprets Heidegger's *Dasein*, or being-in-the-world, with reference to two brief texts, one an excerpt from Heidegger's *Sein und Zeit (Being and Time)*, the other an excerpt from the German philosopher's Marburg Lectures.[21]

Instead of the term Man *(Mensch)*, Heidegger uses *Dasein*: "That being *(seiend)* which we ourselves are and which, among other things, possesses in its being the power to question, we call Being There." This lexical preference is interpreted by Derrida as a desire for "neutrality." Neutrality with respect to what? With respect to any anthropological characterization and with priority over any sexual characterization: "This neutrality also signifies that *Dasein* is not any one of the two sexes."

This "neutralization" is not a denial of sexualization, however, but a skepticism with respect to the usual binary formulation thereof: "Although *Dasein* as such belongs to neither one of the two sexes, this does not mean that the being it is is deprived of sex. On the contrary, one may think of it as possessing a predifferential, or, rather, predual sexuality, which does not necessarily mean unitary, homogeneous, and undifferentiated." On this interpretation, the neutrality of *Dasein* is not equivalent to the neutrality of *Mensch* (Man). The latter neutrality is a negation and dissimulation of the question of sex in "universality." The former is a reckoning with predual sexualization within a primary difference: "There is a certain neutralization that can reconstruct the phallocentric privilege. But there is another neutralization that merely neutralizes sexual opposition and not sexual difference, liberating the field of sexuality for a very *different* sexuality."[22] *Dasein* is therefore allegedly exempt from the criticism that says Man, meaning "the human," though seemingly asexual, is in fact always man, the male human, universality being nothing more than a fig leaf hiding phallocentrism. This is true insofar as *Dasein* is not a Subject in the metaphysical sense, because it includes dispersion or dissemination within its very structure. From this point of view, it is indeed true that all language, or, rather, all writing, is coextensive with sexualization yet is neither masculine nor feminine.

This affirmation of predual sexualization (unrelated to any theory of "bisexuality," which remains a prisoner of dualism) is the quintessential expression of difference, or, as Derrida likes to call it, *differance,* combining difference with deferral to indicate a temporal dimension that cannot be reduced to any substantiation in terms of specific differentiae. The critique of phallogocentrism therefore does not lead to an affirmation of *differance* or of the feminine as its other or opposite. If the feminine exists, it is by virtue of the deconstruction rather than destruction of phallogocentrism, as an instance of dissemination and undecidability irreducible to dualist logic. In this formulation, one question remains obscure and unresolved, however: how was difference deposited in the two? The problem, of course, is that the affirmation of ontological difference runs up against the sad empirical reality of a generalized dualization of social roles. What accident, what episode can justify or illuminate this passage from "neutrality" to sexualization, from perpetual *differance* to duality or, worse yet, hierarchy?

Derrida does not deal with this political aspect of the question, that is, with the relation between ontological difference and dualization and with the domination of one of two dual terms by another. But deconstruction and dissemination can be seen as the dimension through which feminine being-in-the-world escapes from the realm of mastery.

Alterity and Dialogue

By "philosophies of alterity" I mean any of the philosophies of the second half of the twentieth century which, following Husserl's phenomenology, begin with the idea that the subject is always a relation to the world of one kind or another ("all consciousness is consciousness of something") and, further, that the subject is always in relation to other subjects ("intersubjectivity"). Thus the term applies to the work of Jean-Paul Sartre, Maurice Merleau-Ponty, Emmanuel Levinas (in dialogue with Martin Buber), and, more recently, Francis Jacques, whose thought has been influenced by English philosophy of language.

It might seem logical to assume that a philosophy of alterity, or otherness, would have something to contribute to our thinking about sexual difference. But the subject has generally been avoided in two ways: forgetting about sexual difference in describing and analyzing the relations between subject and other, and assuming that the thinking subject is transcendental and therefore "asexual," an assumption that is nevertheless contradicted when the subject adopts a point of view and proceeds to describe some object. Both procedures are common in philosophy, yet they are surprising in thinkers who chose to make otherness the central theme of their reflection.

Sartre criticized Heidegger (who was seen at the time as the first "existentialist") and other existential philosophers for their failure to take account of sexuality, "so that his *Dasein* seems to have no sex." But it was sexuality itself (common to men and women) and not the difference between men and women that Sartre found interesting. If "at first sight it seems that desire and its opposite, sexual horror, are fundamental structures of being-for-others," and if it is unacceptable to hold that "the whole immense business of sexual life is just something superfluous in the human condition," it is nevertheless possible to accept "in the end" that "sexual difference belongs to the realm of 'facticity' and therefore of contingency." For real human beings masculine and feminine are contingent (as opposed to essential) attributes. Indeed, the problem of sexual differentiation has nothing to do with Existence *(Existenz)* because both man and woman "exist," "neither more nor less." The subject transcends its sexualized position, even in sexual relations.

In dealing with sexual relations Sartre (and Merleau-Ponty for that matter) thus dispenses with sexual difference altogether. Sartre justifies this "neutralized" treatment of sexual desire by minimizing its organic components: "Desire is a fundamental mode of the relation to others. In that sense it is ontological. It precedes and transcends the mere organic sexual manifestation."[23] "The desiring being is the consciousness made flesh by its own action," or, to put it another way, "consciousness chooses desire for itself."

If sexual difference is not organic, if it is not even determinative in the functioning of desire, is its foundation social and historical? Sartre does not ask this question in the course of constructing his doctrine, and when he analyzes the phenomena of oppression and exclusion he examines cases involving class and race but never sex (although Simone de Beauvoir clearly borrowed his approach for her work on sex).

This avoidance of the issue is all the more surprising in that Sartre, when pressed on the matter in the 1970s, claimed to believe that it was fundamental. Influenced perhaps by the feminist movement of the time, he even went so far as to say that "the major contradiction is the battle of the sexes and the minor contradiction is the class struggle," thus clearly stating that the former was not derivative of the latter but something with an identity all its own. Sartre did not believe in any kind of "female nature" any more than de Beauvoir did, and he was more reserved than she on the issue of whether her history as an oppressed woman gave her a certain temporary singularity. While insisting that he always considered Simone de Beauvoir "an equal," Sartre recognized, perhaps with a bit too much self-indulgence, "a certain machismo" in himself, a male chauvinism that emerges unwittingly in various images, examples, and choices of diction in his work.[24]

Maurice Merleau-Ponty, a contemporary of Sartre's who did not live long enough to encounter feminism, totally neutralized sexual difference in the many important texts he wrote on the other, the body, sexuality, and perception. He did this without prior justification of any kind, within the framework of a philosophy of incarnation less tainted by voluntarist rationalism than was Sartre's philosophy. Nor did he deal with sexual difference in his political writings, in which he engaged in an ongoing polemic with Marxism. And there is no allusion to the subject in his preface to a book by psychiatrist Jean Hesnard. Nevertheless, former students of his remember a course he gave at the Sorbonne on the "psychology of women," primarily inspired by the work of Helena Deutsch.

As in most of Sartre's works, self and other are both treated grammatically in intentionally general masculine terms even in speaking about love and sexuality (Merleau speaks of *l'aimant*, the lover, and *l'aimé*, the beloved, both masculine nouns), as in the homosexual world of the Greek *polis*. Perhaps Merleau thought of the philosophical world as homosexual as well.

This was Gilles Deleuze's point in a youthful article entitled "Description de la femme. Pour une philosophie d'autrui sexué" (Description of Woman. For a Philosophy of a Sexualized Other). Referring to Sartre's chapter on sexuality and love, Deleuze notes that "the one making love is sexualized, the lover, but not the beloved . . . as if love in the usual sense were not essentially different from pederasty." Furthermore, "Sartre's world is even more dispiriting than the other world: a world objectively composed of sexless beings about whom one thinks of nothing but making love, a quite monstrous place."

Attempts to escape from "neutrality" or silence concerning sexual difference often seem to have been based on an essentialism derived from male stereotypes. In his desire at last to formulate "a philosophy of the sexualized other" and a "description of woman," for example, Deleuze ingenuously takes this position when he states that in order to describe woman "one must stick to the naïve image: a woman wearing makeup who torments a tender, misogynist, and underhanded adolescent." This woman has no world. There is no differentiation of interior from exterior. She is a mixture of the material and the immaterial, of substance and frivolity, a futile consciousness, a deluxe object, and so on. As such, she is radically different from the "male other." Friendship with a woman is "impossible," because "friendship is the possible realization of the external world that the Male Other offers us." It is utopian, even distressing, for a woman to attempt "to express an external world."

Alterity is not merely an important theme in the work of Emmanuel Levinas, it is its central armature. Levinas replaces ontology by ethics, that is, the interrogation of the self by the other that brings "ego" out of itself. And the other is always the Other, the "completely other," that which cannot be appropriated even by understanding. The apparition of his face opens an asymmetrical space—from him to me. Now, if he is completely different, if he eludes my grasp, it is not because of his own characteristics, not because of individual or cultural differences, but by virtue of his very existence, which cannot be reduced to any "common denominator." His resistance to my attempts to get a hold of him is in effect a revelation of the Infinite. Levinas thus explicitly set himself apart from the philosophers of "intersubjectivity" (Scheler and Buber), who, by assuming reciprocity, tame the otherness of the other by enforcing a certain identity.

Central to Levinas's ethical philosophy of alterity are his reflections on what he calls "the feminine," which at times is the very matrix of alterity, at other times a somewhat bastard form thereof: the other as woman is and is not entirely Other.

The feminine in Levinas's characterization has all the traditional attributes: "youth, weakness, pure, somewhat brutish life, a warm welcome, a flirtatious look, animality." In other circumstances, however, the feminine can be an "interlocutor, collaborator, and supremely intelligent master often dominating men in the male civilization to which it has gained access."[25]

Thus there is a contradiction between a definition of the Other as "completely different" and unknowable and the series of attributes ascribed to the female other. Perhaps woman is not "entirely other," not the Other? The same position is apparent when Levinas analyzes filiation and "fecundity" exclusively from the standpoint of father and son. In the quite remarkable passages of his work where filiation is described as alterity, the role of maternity appears to be secondary.[26]

When questioned about his position, Levinas denied having a reductive concept of woman. Yet at times his work betrays, more visibly than that of some other philosophers, the gendered position of the person philosophizing despite his claim to transcend all empiricism.

Indeed, sexual difference imbues all of Levinas's thinking in a less obvious but possibly more profound sense. He continually uses the term "virility" to refer to the Subject's wish to assert its own identity by defending itself against the influence of the "totally other." Similarly, he uses feminine metaphors—typically those of "vulnerability," "passivity," even "moaning of entrails" and "hostage"—to characterize the ethical position in which the self, driven out of its hiding place behind what it claims as its "own," its "property," is summoned to answer to the demand of the other. "Virility" and "the feminine" are categories that Levinas uses to articulate his philosophy. Virility is then subjected to criticism, and the feminine is proposed as the instigator of the change that leads to the apparition of the visage of the other.

It therefore makes sense to say that ethics, and ethical philosophy, is a "*devenir femme*" (that which is in the process of becoming a woman) and that Levinas's philosophy is a philosophy of the feminine. In this respect Levinas can be placed among those philosophers who have inverted the values associated with gender division without calling the actual position of men and women into question.

Francis Jacques might well argue that it is no accident that when Levinas's philosophy is made concrete by his using it to analyze the relation of love with a woman, its effect is to objectify woman. For Jacques, "to affirm the radically heterogeneous character of the other, its absolute separateness, is philosophically courageous. Surprisingly, however, this thesis is intimately associated with the primacy of the self."[27]

There is a way of placing the other in such a position of Pride that the way in which he affects me depends ultimately on me (and my responsibility) rather than on him. For Jacques, who draws on communications theory among other things, all interpersonal relations are based on the dialogue, in which every message is ascribed to one of two enunciative agencies engaged in "immediate communication." There is reciprocity of "I" and "thou" in the construction of this relationship. The model of reciprocity is the only way of escaping the traditional view of the male-female relationship in which the female is always posited as "the other" of the male subject. Under those conditions "the female being is ultimately never anything more than that which is repressed by the male." If the other, particularly the female other, is to be taken seriously and not "condemned to subordination, hierarchization, or annexation," then it must be acknowledged that the Other is neither "another me" whom I can come to know and understand through identification or assimilation, nor an "other than me" whom I must respect in his unique solitude, pride, and transcendence. The point is to enter into a relation with the other, that is, to agree to be questioned by him as I myself question him, or, in other words, to make the other a co-subject in a relationship.

In discussing the feminist movement Jacques recognizes the validity of the protest by means of which women hope to make themselves understood, to rediscover "their sex and the fantasy of their desire and language," but he sees just two possibilities: either women can construct for themselves a Feminine Identity sufficient unto itself and closed to the outside, or they can insist that "relations between the sexes be structured henceforth as a dialogue," which he believes will lead to the liberation of men as well as women.[28] That dialogue would not only respect differences but, even more important, would capitalize on them by constantly emphasizing differentiation within, rather than prior to or outside of, the relationship itself.

Although Jean-François Lyotard does not specifically deal with the question of sexual difference, he has some illuminating things to say about dialogue and alterity in his book *Le Différend* (Disagreement). Any dialogue, any form of alterity, is a way of managing a disagreement or difference of idiom: it is always the confrontation of two idioms. Discussion requires each participant to put questions to the other and to answer questions from the other. Nonreciprocity is its matrix. There is no difference without disagreement. Dialogue, as the space of heterogeneity, is not a resolution of heterogeneity in some hypothetical common language that would reduce otherness to identity.

In this scheme, the disagreement between the sexes is no longer an obstacle to a relationship between them but rather the substrate of that relationship. Nevertheless, the enunciative positions are not isomorphic. "Progress" in communication means making room for new idioms that previously either went unheard or were heard as variants or echoes of the dominant idiom. Is some sort of "woman's idiom" one of these new modes of communication?[29]

The philosophy of dialogue takes various guises, from the original formulations of Mikhail Bakhtin, Hannah Arendt, and Jürgen Habermas to the more recent ones of Francis Jacques and François Lyotard. All make it possible to pose the question of sexual difference in terms not of substance but of performative enunciation or action. To speak, to act in plurality, is to inscribe displacement in emplacements. It is to recognize difference (between the sexes) without casting the specific differentiae in stone. In Hannah Arendt's terms, "this revelation of the *who* as opposed to the *what* . . . is implicit in everything one does and everything one says." It is a property of the *who,* moreover, to move the *what.* The "given," in this case the gendered given, is unavoidable but not identifiable.

Feminist Thought

The foregoing brief survey of twentieth-century philosophy shows that despite the persistence of certain traditional habits of thought, philosophers have indeed come up with new ways of thinking about sexual difference and women. As the century progresses, we witness a gradual decline of the various forms of a "metaphysics of the sexes" based on either nature or reason. Sexism is not absent from recent philosophical writings, but generally it emerges indirectly, in certain figures of speech and examples but more often in the form of errors of omission rather than commission: failure to consider the question or to examine the gendered position of the subject.

As we have seen, there was even a certain inversion of values, which took the form of a critique of things traditionally associated with virility (mastery, the phallic) to the benefit of things traditionally associated with the feminine (vulnerability, the undefinable). Nevertheless, this inversion of values failed to affect the actual position of men and women in the world.

The feminist thought that originated in the 1970s drew on many of the trends already discussed: Marxism, psychoanalysis, the critique of metaphysics, structuralism, postmodernism, and so on. Despite the extreme diversity of feminist thinking, it has been unified by its political approach to philosophical questions. Feminists start with the reality that male-female relations are a form of power structure in which men dominate women. From this common starting point they then diverge over how and to what end that power structure should be abolished and what becomes of sexual difference once liberated from its social and historical determinants.

Simone de Beauvoir's *Le Deuxième Sexe* (The Second Sex) is a fundamental work of feminist philosophy. Although it was published in 1949, its influence remained latent until the neo-feminist movement of the 1970s led to new readings of this classic work. The book is notable for the volume of material it drew together and for the kinds of questions it raised. It did not, however, anticipate the full range of thought that would derive from the feminist movement, which also drew on other sources of inspiration. Beauvoir's work informed the egalitarian but not the differentialist school of feminism.

"A child is not born a woman but becomes one." This famous phrase points out that the roles that women are obliged to play in society are imposed on them by "patriarchal" power by way of a complex system of educational, legislative, social, and economic constraints and not by biological necessity. Thus woman is always "the other" for the male subject. Nevertheless, an important part of Beauvoir's work is devoted to the consequences of female physiology, from menarche to motherhood to menopause. The minute description of such matters reinforces the traditional perception that the female body is a handicap.

It is thus by overcoming rather than accepting corporality that the human being, and in this instance the woman, becomes a subject. In the existentialist vocabulary of the period, the "for itself" (consciousness) frees itself from the "in itself" (the physical datum); "transcendence" is triumphantly wrested from "immanence." Freedom asserts itself within a situation from which it escapes. Thus becoming oneself is a project, not the fulfillment of some intrinsic nature.

Although Simone de Beauvoir emphasizes women's heavy burden of corporeal contingency, she nevertheless insists that they are capable of overcoming it to become fully human. At first this was an individual act which each woman must accomplish for herself. But when she encountered the feminist movement of the 1970s, Beauvoir gained a clearer idea of the collective character of liberation. She then discovered the need for a common struggle associated with other revolutionary struggles and gave it first priority. She even offered the hypothesis that women might have something unique to contribute to the world, not because of their nature but because of their historical position.[30]

The direct heirs of Simone de Beauvoir—those who explicitly invoke her influence—tend to radicalize her position by challenging not only the "social construction" of "sex" or "gender" (the latter term introduced by American feminists) but also the very reality of sex itself. Women, they argue, constitute a "class" analogous to the working class and, like it, destined to disappear once relations of domination wither away. Independent of those relations gender identification has no relevance. Not only is anatomy not destiny; it is no longer even the precondition to the exercise of freedom.

Egalitarian feminists are deeply distrustful of nature, understandably so given the fact that nature has always served as a pretext for exclusions. In French this distrust of nature has even given rise to a play on words: *Nature-elle-ment* ("of course"/ "nature-it-lies").[31] But this distrust has tempted some to proceed to the denial of natural reality in any form, on the plausible grounds that it is impossible to distinguish between the effects of nature and those of culture. History and nature are thus both dismissed in favor of a pure subject that owes nothing to either one, affirming itself instead in the sovereign neutrality of a rather disembodied self-determination.

The egalitarian variant of feminism is the heir of the Enlightenment as reinterpreted by Marxism. It identifies difference with domination because it conceives of individuals only as abstract and equivalent. But another variant developed alongside the egalitarians in the 1970s, this one derived in part from psychoanalysis.

For this second group, the inferior position of women resulted from the denial of their true nature. It was therefore essential for women to assert their specific positive—rather than relative—reality and stake out their own space in the realm of pleasure as well as of culture. It was important, moreover, to deconstruct the definition imposed on women by men in the name of an authentic feminine "essence" connected with female morphology, which gives women a unique relation to the world. The two sexes are irreducibly distinct, it was argued, and antagonism between them must give way to an "ethics of sexual difference." Furthermore, affirmation of this duality was frequently inspired, either implicitly or explicitly, by a vision of women's superiority over men, even if that superiority usually sought to formulate itself in terms of peaceful coexistence rather than domination.

If the masculine was defined by the phallic, unity, totalization, and instrumentalization, the feminine was defined by openness, non-unity, infinitude, indefiniteness, and limitlessness. These metaphors were explicitly associated with the morphology of each sex. The leading theorists of this variant of feminism nevertheless challenged the idea of a definition of "woman" as such. To Lacan's assertion that "Woman does not exist," Antoinette Fouque replied with the formulation "des femmes," and Luce Irigaray with "la/ une femme."

In effect, if, for Lacan, la "pas toute" (the "not all") was something over and above le tout (the whole), for these feminists the two were opposed. The polemical context within which feminist thought developed led to the dualization of men and women, feminine and masculine, thus radicalizing the position of the psychoanalysts of the English School. It is difficult, however, to argue that woman is purely and simply undefinable when the territory is so narrowly delimited, just as it is difficult to credit women with a non-dual logic when one begins by dualizing the sexes.

For some theorists, the feminine is inextricably associated with a morphological or physical reality, whereas for others the feminine is a category that can to one degree or another be separated from that reality. This second way of treating the feminine, or in some cases the maternal, is used mainly by feminists interested above all in the analysis of language and texts, such as Hélène Cixous, whose way of thinking has some points in common with Derrida's. Even though a man is a man in society, he can allow himself to use the feminine in his texts. Or perhaps all texts and all forms of writing are feminine. Feminine in this sense is no longer the opposite of masculine; rather, it denotes the undecidability of such categories.

The positions I have described are extremes and necessarily schematic. Feminist thought, including the work of the authors mentioned, is richer than this summary can suggest. And for the most part it is evolving thought, which avoids fixed positions or shifts rapidly from one to another.

It is difficult to accept that sexual difference is purely a product of oppression destined to wither away when oppression does, and it is just as difficult to believe that somewhere there exists an authentic women's realm innocent of any phallic influence. Assertions such as these are more programmatic than phenomenological. They reflect a project or even a desire more than they explain what actually exists.

Sexual difference is an unavoidable reality, and it cannot be dismissed as a mere "social construction." Nevertheless, to define difference by opposing, in dualistic fashion, the male "one" to the female "non-one" leads willy-nilly back to the metaphysics of sex. Furthermore, to limit one's attention to the categories of the feminine and the masculine in all their undecidability is to neglect the sociopolitical reality of men and women. The question of sexual difference thus risks becoming caught in a vicious circle, forever coming back to the same positions.

Any proposition concerning what man or woman is should of course be seen as a speech act: a performative, dialogical act which affects the positions of both those who are speaking and those who are spoken of. Every utterance contains and reactivates what men and women want to say, whether in the violence of conflict or in the harmony of understanding. Sexual difference is an act— an act that is simultaneously political, ethical, and symbolic.

The primary objective of feminism was and is to create a space that men and women can truly share, and to that end feminism has inevitably made use of theories of equality. Here, however, equality must be understood in the sense of equal rights, not equalization of identities, which in any case would favor the existing male identity. This equality must also cover individual and collective differences without attempting to predefine what they are. Democratic space is heterogeneous and creative. The twentieth century has thus modified the eighteenth century's definition of equality, which was based on a conception of citizens as abstract individuals. The question of the sexes, like that of cultures, races, and even religions, leads to a redefinition of democracy and citizenship.

Whether sexual difference ultimately disappears or changes its configuration is determined neither by the past nor by a fate inscribed in the heavens. "What do women want?" is a question that was probably never asked; its answer, in any case, is not to be found in any representation. Every action, whether individual or collective, and every speech act raises the question anew. Its answer is not a matter of intellect. What women want is to be the originators and not just the recipients of speech acts, and thus co-actors in the definition of sexual difference.[32]

Women—some women—have begun to be originators of speech acts in the intellectual sphere. Although it is not strictly speaking within the stated purpose of this chapter, it is impossible to end without mentioning work that gives an essay like this, and even an enterprise like the *History of Women,* its legitimacy. Twentieth-century feminism—the most recent episode in an already lengthy history—stands out not only for its social and political achievements but also for its achievements in the realm of knowledge, in a body of work often referred to, and even institutionalized under "feminist studies" (or women's studies or gender studies).

The age-old exclusion and inferiorization of women have not been without impact on the realm of knowledge: both the subject and object of science have been affected. The epistemological subject, by failing to consider its gendered position, can deceive itself into mistaking a unilateral position for a "neutral" or universal one. In exploring its object, the subject can mistake the reality of a single sex for the general case. These two distortions are inseparable, moreover. The only way to minimize them is to take into account the impact of sexual difference on the epistemological process itself. Although feminists agree in criticizing the omissions and falsifications inherent in mistaking the masculine for the general, they disagree as to the correctives. Limitations of space permit only a brief discussion of this issue.

Those who believe in a dualist "essentialism" of the sexes, that is, in the radical specificity of women, even in the operation of their intellect, believe that women must develop a feminine science distinct from the dominant science not only as to its content but also as to its methods and processes and modes of transmission. These theorists call for an "epistemological break." As women create a world of their own parallel to that of men, a new body of science will develop. The new women's sciences will emerge, we are told, not only in the domain of the human sciences but even (though there is not the slightest evidence for this) in the realm of the exact sciences.

Without necessarily sharing this point of view, feminist theorists have first and foremost attempted to fill in gaps in the dominant disciplines by focusing their research in sociology, history, anthropology, and literature on issues systematically "forgotten" or obscured by other researchers. "Feminist studies" in this sense is research whose object is women and can therefore be defined as the study of women.

Some women, however, have pointed out that by isolating the object "woman" in this way from the other objects of study in a particular discipline, there is a danger of making women seem even more peculiar. Hence a wiser course would be to focus attention on the relation between the sexes, the result of which would be to change the way we look not just at women but also at men. That is why some scholars prefer the term "gender studies" to "women's studies."

Broadening the definition of the field still further, some scholars hold that the feminist approach can be applied not only to relations between the sexes but to the entire realm of knowledge. The feminist approach is distinctive in that it introduces sexual difference as a parameter or interpretive grid without prejudging the significance of the results to be obtained.[33] The claim is that the results are dramatic, as far-reaching as those claimed by the dualist essentialists. But whereas the essentialists claim that new knowledge comes from introducing a female subject as the bearer and discoverer of that knowledge, here the claim is that the new knowledge stems from the use of a new interpretive grid or key (even if that key is generally constructed and used by women).

Whatever their presuppositions (and even when not clearly defined), feminist studies have already yielded important results and developed a body of texts that serve as reference works for those just entering the field. Yet it remains a fairly self-contained discipline, whose effect on other fields of knowledge is sporadic.

There are several reasons for this perhaps unfortunate state of affairs. The strategy of feminism, and of feminist studies even today, has been one of autonomous development, and only a weak effort has been made to seek exchanges with the "outside." At the same time, one should not underestimate the reluctance of the "dominant sciences" to recognize innovative contributions by outsiders. Other factors compound the effects of these two. Today, however, there is a tendency, in Europe at any rate, to regard feminist or gender studies not as a distinct specialty but as a subspecialty within other disciplines. The gender parameter is one that must be taken into account, but its importance and relevance vary with the object under study.

It is impossible to summarize here the past twenty years of work in the many different areas of research to which feminist scholars have contributed. If nothing else, this volume will at least give the reader some idea of the feminist contribution to the field of history.

Translated from the French by Arthur Goldhammer

10

The Creators of
Culture in France

Marcelle Marini

WOMEN IN TWENTIETH-CENTURY Western
societies participate in cultural production to an
unprecedented extent. Three factors have worked
to overcome resistance to their contribution. First,
feminists have clearly been successful in their battle
for equal educational opportunities, which began
in the nineteenth century. Second, since 1950,
technological advances, expanded public interest,
and increased leisure time have led to wider appreciation of art than ever before. Finally, new
agencies of cultural production, employing large
numbers of personnel, have enabled women to
achieve greater independence and social visibility.
Many women have found work in the intellectual
and artistic arenas, and the number of women so
employed has been growing at an accelerating pace
since the middle of the century.

Toward the end of the 1960s—a period of
economic growth and an expanding public role for
women—a new and powerful feminist movement
developed. Initially it might seem odd that the first
women to protest were among the most privileged:
students, artists, and intellectuals. Had they not
realized their mothers' dream of equal access to
the common culture? Were they not already practicing professions that had once seemed out of

reach for women? To rebel just as the goal was within reach—wasn't this a foolish gesture? No realm of art or thought would be closed to women from now on, or so we were told. All we had to do was demonstrate our talent. But we were in the process of discovering a bitter reality: this highly touted equality was a trap. Women, no matter how competent or talented, were still underestimated just because of their sex.

Equal access to education had finally been achieved, but equality in social and cultural life was something else. The ideal of equal educational opportunity was based on the principle that men and women share equal natural abilities. Over the course of the century educational restrictions designed to keep women in their place were gradually abolished. The success of female students demonstrated the validity of the principle. Equal education did not guarantee equal job opportunities, however, or an equal share of power, or equal recognition of artistic talent. From the 1950s on, growing numbers of women encountered the assumption that women are inferior to men, a prejudice they had thought equal education would finally lay to rest. Privileged women were indeed the first to rebel, but the paradox lay not with them but with the situation they confronted. Had discrimination merely been displaced?

It might be objected that too many women chose the wrong field of study. Too many majored in literature, for example, and too few in science. This argument would make sense if the issue were the integration of society in general, but it does not explain why, if 75 percent of literature majors are women, only 25 percent of writers are, or why only a handful of women occupy the top posts in the cultural hierarchy. And what about music, theater, film, and painting, where women's access to creative positions has been even more severely limited? There is reason to believe that an analysis of the place of women in the arts can tell us something about duplicity in the field of culture, where egalitarian rhetoric has masked discriminatory practices. An odd general law emerges: women are economically and symbolically devalued, whether they are in the minority or in the majority; whereas men are economically and symbolically overvalued. Thus any purely quantitative explanation of the famous formula "feminization=devaluation" must be rejected; the real reason for the devaluation of women is sexism, which is all the more enigmatic in that it goes unquestioned.

Literature and the arts are sometimes considered to be women's preserves, but on closer examination this belief turns out to be quite misleading. In *Le Pouvoir intellectuel en France* Régis Debray observes that "if, broadly speaking, culture is a feminine noun with affinities for the feminine, its most exalted ranks are purely masculine." He goes on to draw a distinction between the "high intelligentsia, predominantly male," and "the low intelligentsia . . . whose composition is more female."[1] Culture is thus seen to be a crucial social battleground, where the prize, of fundamental importance, is control over what society considers to be legitimate or potentially legitimate in the realm of the imagination. Debray uses feminist analyses of the "pyramid of the sexes," but he distorts the feminist argument by accepting the legitimacy of inequality, whereas feminists are critical of the fact that men arrogate to themselves the *right* to the production and control of culture. Although forced by socioeconomic and sociocultural changes to tolerate the growing presence of women in the cultural domain, men continue to look upon it as their fief. Women are fine as consumers of culture or assistants in its production, but not as creators, except in unusual circumstances, within narrowly defined limits, and without changing any of the so-called common values for which men alone are responsible by nature and/or historical heritage. The concentration of women in the lower echelons of the cultural apparatus is merely the present-day manifestation of the age-old exclusion of women and their works.

Over the course of the nineteenth century the gulf between the universal culture and the feminine subculture widened and deepened. This gulf, which reflects the social theory of the "two spheres," has constrained twentieth-century thinking about the subject. Women artists are consequently placed in a separate category with its own set of standards. Few are selected to remain in collective memory, and those few who are chosen to become representatives of (or traitors to) their sex are exalted to their proper place—in the background of the great fresco of culture.

Both men and women have internalized this dual structure. How can such a scheme, in which the masculine-universal is clearly superior, and the feminine-specific is clearly inferior, be reconciled with a system of cultural production in which the actual participation of women has been increasing? As long as only a few "exceptional women" could hope to succeed, the cultural division of the sexes remained virtually intact. But now that culture has become the common possession of an entire generation, can the chosen few truly be regarded as exceptional? Can women dream of being exceptional individuals without concerning themselves with the limits imposed on other women as a group or with the price that all must pay for the rewards meted out to a few? The crisis of the 1970s proves that the answer is no. From that time forward, women as well-versed in aesthetic theory and practice as their male counterparts have wished to assert themselves as fully active participants in the elaboration of the common culture, yet without renouncing their gender.

The period in which we are interested runs from 1970 to 1990. It is risky to write the history of such recent events, in part because we are deeply implicated in them but even more because this chapter of history is not yet closed. The role of women in cultural creation is still at issue in battles whose outcome is far from certain. Yet enough has been achieved already to justify two tentative conclusions. The period 1970–1990 witnessed a major change in the cultural history of Western women. And that change has paved the way for a new cultural practice, for a truly *mixed* culture. Hence it is not unreasonable to suggest that the past two decades have been a period of decisive progress.

1970–1990: A Decisive Period

For the first time in history the women's movement achieved a true cultural dimension, and women's demands in the cultural arena achieved a true social impact. It all began with a creative explosion intimately associated with the battle for equality and freedom. Culture became everyone's business. It was in the streets. In widely circulated pamphlets, newspapers, drawings, graffiti, songs, and videos individual and collective self-assertion reinforced each other. Every woman was by turns artist and audience. Social distinctions and boundaries crumbled. Many works were signed only with a first name, a pseudonym, or the name of a group. Women chose innovative forms to forge a positive identity for themselves, while the social movement encouraged an outpouring of new works.[2]

Take one particularly striking example. In Portugal, still under the Salazar dictatorship, the "three Marias" published the *New Portuguese Letters* in 1972.[3] The book contained poems, essays, and stories in three voices that dared to say what the dominant culture repressed in lethal silence. The authorities brought charges against the printer for obscenity and corruption of morals. Feminists mobilized, however, and the work was published in a number of countries. After Salazar was deposed in the "revolution of carnations," the printer was found innocent and treated to a public ovation. Portuguese women organized feminist groups. So great was the innovative power of the text that it transcended the social and political circumstances out of which it arose.

It is by no means rare for artistic works to reflect the aspirations of broad social groups. Such cases reflect important changes of attitude or outlook. Until recently, however, the phenomenon was discussed only in the masculine, which was identified with the universal. The social demands of the women's culture in the 1970s were therefore surprising, all the more so in that they failed to conform to two preconceived notions. They did not fit the (masculine) generational scheme by means of which art historians explained the transition from one form of symbolic legitimacy to another. And there was something else as well. Previously women had not placed themselves in a separate category of their own volition. That position had always been imposed on them, leaving them a choice of resignation or rebellion. To understand the most radical of women's demands and realize that they were neither regressive, absurd, or suicidal, one must recognize that they came from the most radical wing of the women's liberation movement: women who of their own free will chose to live apart, among other women, a choice that in some cases meant embracing lesbianism and separatism. For these women, personal life, political action, and aesthetic practice were inseparable. As women "raised their consciousness," they transformed themselves from a group that had been *condemned* to live as a minority, a fragmented group within a homogenized male culture, into a group that *chose* to live as a minority, a group that was prepared to establish its own independent values and canons and to defend them in the public arena. The *New Portuguese Letters* symbolize this change: whereas the original *Portuguese Letters* (by the seventeenth-century writer Gabriel de Guilleragues) were the passionate lament of a (fictional) lonely nun to the man who had seduced and abandoned her, the new letters were a correspondence among women.

The women's liberation movement developed at the precise moment that two series of historical events came together: the

protest movements of 1968, which constituted its immediate sociopolitical context, and the evolution of the social and cultural
role of women, which had been proceeding at a much slower pace
throughout much of the century. It was as if women simultaneously discovered both their alienation and their strength.

The youth rebellion obviously played a part in the emergence
of the women's liberation movement, but the latter was not simply
a belated echo of battles waged by young men. In fact, women's
liberation was in part retribution for the failure of many of the
protest groups, which included large numbers of young women in
their ranks, to operate in a truly democratic fashion. Their actual
functioning was so typical of the dominant masculine mode that
women found their inclusion to be not only deceptive but downright inhibiting, and they therefore seceded.

How quickly have people forgotten the disappointment of
women who—their hopes raised by such libertarian slogans as
"power to the imagination," "let everyone speak," "let everyone
create"—actually thought they might be able, without difficulty,
to participate in the building of an "alternative society" in which
not only economic and social structures would have changed but
all other aspects of life as well: the family, sexuality, the imagination, art, language, what have you. Women found that what
they had to say was discredited because of their sex. And they
were ignored not only by the enemy but by their own male comrades in the struggle against oppression in all its forms: instead of
being welcomed in a reciprocal dialogue, women found their
words dismissed.

Just to be allowed to speak in a group composed of both men
and women was an accomplishment. The same statement did not
carry the same weight if it was made by a man or by a woman.
If we so much as dared to criticize a poster, a film, or a text as
humiliating to women, the very same men who were quickest to
propose banning any work suspected of the least hint of racism
would protest that we wanted to limit freedom of speech.[4] If we
so much as ventured an unorthodox or even a novel analysis, the
reaction would at first be one of uneasiness, followed by dismissal
without debate. Sometimes the reception was one of indifference;
other times it was catcalls and jeers. Or we might hear an objection
that we had been hearing all our lives, one that Simone de Beauvoir
had already singled out for scorn: "You think that only because
you are a woman."[5]

We tried answering as Beauvoir did: "I think that because it is true," thereby "eliminating [our] subjectivity." But how were we to persuade others of the truth of what we believed? In this system it was not the individual woman who was discredited but woman as such, on the grounds that she was "subjective," whereas the male individual stood on firm ground as an objective judge simply by virtue of being a man. "It was impossible," Beauvoir pointed out, "to respond, 'You think that only because you are a man.' For it was understood that being a man was not a peculiarity. A man was within his rights in being a man; it was the woman who was wrong." Collective experience of being disqualified in this way enabled women to gauge the injustice and violence of the situation, to which they responded iconoclastically. This brought together women otherwise divided by social class, profession, political affiliation, aesthetic taste, life style, and even by their conception of femininity and sex roles. By publicly proclaiming the subjectivity of sex, the women's movement reminded men of their own sexual subjectivity and thus of the relative rather than absolute authority of their statements and works.

The two subjectivities were not equivalent, however, and the most painful discovery of those years was of our own weakness. Despite our proclamations, our assurance was artificial, because we were incapable of responding to doubts that we had in any case internalized: who were we to criticize our masters? On what grounds did we justify our claims? What female "geniuses" authorized our statements? Could we name a single woman who had made an essential contribution to civilization? With difficulty we managed to stammer out a few names, and when these were dismissed out of hand we had no idea how to defend them. The few lucky women who had enjoyed "the best education" were in the same boat as those who had taught themselves all they knew. All of us were oddly ill equipped, without a history or heritage. We had no mothers, no female ancestors of any kind. We were the bastard daughters of noble fathers and nonexistent (or unavowable) mothers. We were "women of the year zero" of Culture,[6] condemned to see ourselves as "thieves" who had stolen the words, images, and ideas of others, as in other contexts we were thieves who stole jobs, positions, and power from men.[7]

No other social movement did more than women's liberation to demonstrate that symbolic violence is as fundamental an issue as economic violence. Symbolic violence is an integral part of social violence, not a mere reflection or even a *post hoc* justification. Women are no longer fighting as they did early in the century for the right to work in certain professions or to join certain parties, trade unions, or professional groups. They have already won enough victories in those areas to begin asking about their significance. The issue now is to win the power to speak, represent, propose, and decide—the power to innovate. And that power requires freedom: the freedom not to have to whisper the correct password in order to be admitted; the freedom to criticize established models; and, more profoundly, the freedom to run the risk, as individuals, of error, bias, stupidity, foolishness, and failure without immediately being dismissed on sexual grounds or being arraigned as a representative of all women. Men have no problem allowing themselves such freedom. The question of equality therefore reemerges, but in a more radical form: by force of will the women's movement declared that women are just as *naturally cultural* as men. Men are no more masters of the true, the good, and the beautiful than women. Both sexes share the symbol-making capacity that has been held to be characteristic of the human in general, the human that invents itself by means of its cultural productions.[8] The women's liberation movement of the 1970s has been called "neo-feminism" because it shifted the focus of feminist struggles to a new issue: the sharing of sociosymbolic power in societies already judged to be liberal in their treatment of women. Criticism was thus directed at the implicit pact that turned culture, in the anthropological sense, into an exclusive preserve of men, in which women, if admitted at all, were invariably mere (maladapted) embellishments.

This collective revolution in women's identity is still the driving force behind contemporary feminism, and especially the many innovative attempts to restore the marginalized or excluded contributions of women to our common fund of images and symbolic capital. But artists have always been aware to some degree of violating a cultural taboo: their journals, notebooks, autobiographies, and letters reveal deep distress as the desire to create, the inward conviction of talent (however fragile), contends with anxiety born of misunderstanding and contempt. What the women's liberation movement has done is to relate individual destinies to sociopolitical analysis and activism on a broader scale. Conversely, artists and critics who have participated in the movement have given it a new dimension: in individual and collective statements, memoirs, and interviews they have revealed an important connection between feminism and creation. The movement, by creating a community of progressive women including many not belonging to any organized feminist group, has shaped an audience for new directions and ideas in literature and art. It has created a new zone within which women can achieve recognition, an alternative seat of judgment that can legitimize women's creations and thus sustain them in their creativity in ways other than providing material and social support. The status of women artists has changed as a result: like it or not, they have been judged by standards other than the canons of contemporary culture.[9]

What women needed was a certain number of free zones in which they could work safe from sociosymbolic violence yet still have access to the general—that is, mixed-sex—public with the power to bestow the recognition that artists require. Not only were such free zones created, but veritable networks sprang up linking all facets of the artistic process from production to reception and transmission. Women thus proved that they were collectively capable of taking full responsibility for the *socialization* of their cultural productions. Previously unknown talents were discovered in many areas, particularly in those whose function it is to link art creators to art lovers: people working in publishing, bookselling, theatrical and film production, and the organization of art shows, festivals, concerts, reviews, criticism, training, research, and so on. These networks operated at two related levels: they established autonomous structures managed exclusively by women, and they exerted influence on existing institutions (resulting in additions to publishers' series, special journal issues, TV and radio broadcasts, art retrospectives, lecture series, curriculum changes, and so on). In addition, the women's movement offered an international dimension. Official and unofficial contacts between influential individuals and feminists, militant or otherwise, helped a once marginal culture gain greater prominence in a number of countries.

In each case, bold women took the initiative. Their strategies varied, but the audience was always the crucial driving force. In the first place there was the enlightened female audience, no longer willing to settle for the standard images purveyed by fashionable as well as popular and even commercial artists. And there was also a male audience, consisting of a small but growing number of men eager to break out of the straitjacket of a unisexual culture.

The International Festival of Women's Films at Sceaux (1978), and a subsequent festival at Créteil, was surely one of the most successful achievements of the new feminist spirit in the arts, as open to innovation as it was aesthetically demanding.[10]

Though the means employed were quite fragile, they undermined the values of established art through a sort of subterranean osmosis. This could happen only after women began to exert their intrinsic strength, a strength they owed to the tenacious battles waged by their forebears, particularly in the area of education, which profoundly altered their relation to the so-called common culture. Women, because they were better trained, were now more critical and less self-conscious, and they found it easier to play with established conventions.

The well-known slogan "Woman is beautiful" crystallized various aspects of neo-feminism. Scoffers were quick to pounce on it as extreme or simplistic, but wasn't it a good idea first of all to underscore the vital necessity of the joyful challenge women were mounting to the inevitability of shame? Gone was the alienation inherent in accepting the standards and judgments of the other sex, and in its place arose at last a positive narcissism. One needs self-respect in order to have confidence and confidence in order to risk freedom and creativity, which requires the help of people similar to oneself. The revaluation of the feminine, of woman-being, which is intimately associated with the rehabilitation of women, involves the existence of an ideal community upon which individuals in search of their identity may draw as from an inexhaustible source. Judy Chicago's installation *The Dinner Party* (1979) embodies this desire for a shared spiritual femininity: it consists of a table, reminiscent of the Last Supper, with thirty-nine place settings. It bears the names of 999 historically celebrated women from a number of cultures.[11]

The proclamation of a woman's art is one version of the "woman is beautiful" theme, exemplifying a particular moment in the history of women. Another milestone of that phase in history was the debate over "women's writing" that erupted in the 1970s. Since then, a more complex appreciation of the relation between gender identity and creativity has arisen, yet the old debate flares up periodically in oddly repetitive terms. Although I shall come back to this issue later in this essay, I wanted to mention it here in its proper social, political, and cultural context in the hope that this might shed light on the issues truly at stake in the debate.

Another point that may be relevant here is that, for all the importance of Simone de Beauvoir's *Second Sex,* the basic works of feminism for many artists and critics are still Virginia Woolf's *A Room of One's Own* (1929) and *Three Guineas* (1938). In these and her various reflections on the novel she brings extraordinary lucidity to the question of why the culture appears to be incapable of allowing a dual-vision symbolization of the world.

Twenty years of feminist research have borne fruit. There is no longer an urgent need for broad surveys, thanks to such recent encyclopedic volumes as Florence Montreynaud's *Le XXe Siècle des femmes.*[12] Research has moved on to deeper levels of investigation. We have a better grasp of the significant ways in which artistic disciplines, cultures, individual careers, and historical situations may differ. Our idea of the cultural identity of women is no longer as monolithic as it once was. And since the history of art is a history of values as much as of facts, feminist criticism has questioned criteria of readability and evaluation, including its own. Different theories and methods vie for supremacy.

In view of the abundance of the literature, I must confine my attention in the remainder of this essay to literature in France. I chose literature partly because it has traditionally been the field most open (or least closed) to women and partly because it is the primary laboratory for experimenting with the imagery of sexual difference. And I chose France partly because culture there is particularly centralized and partly because it is surely no accident that the much-discussed notion of "women's writing" *(écriture féminine)* was born there.

Women in Literature

Ever since the middle of the nineteenth century there have been periodic expressions of surprise in France at the increase in the number of female writers, whether to deplore that fact or to take delight in it. At the turn of the century Paul Léautaud fulminated: "All women write . . . It's impossible nowadays to find a housekeeper." It was the "golden age" of feminism, and well-known women of letters such as Anna de Noailles, Rachilde, and Séverine protested the all-male jury for the 1903 Prix Goncourt (a prestigious literary prize) by founding the Prix Fémina (1904). Braving sarcasm, they decided to consider the entire range of literary production. Today, we women have allegedly emerged "victorious" from these literary battles, at least according to the very conservative literary magazine *Figaro littéraire,* which in 1989 ran an article entitled "The 80 Women Who Rule the World of Letters."[13] The text continued: "Not only as successful novelists, biographers, historians, and academics but also as editors, women have taken remarkable revenge in the world of letters." In contrast to "gloomy" Léautaud, the editorialist Jean-Marie Rouart offered this handsome homage to women: "They have given striking proof that literary genius has no sex any more than it has a race or nationality." What is more, "institutions have, with the usual delay, acceded to the facts," and women "have assumed their rightful place." This optimistic view of literature is widely shared, even by many women.

Nevertheless, the moment one opens a publisher's catalogue or literary magazine, glances at the list of nominees for the major literary prizes, peruses a history of twentieth-century literature, scans one of the avant-garde journals in which tomorrow's reputations are jealously fabricated, or casts an eye on a study of established or promising authors, one looks in vain for "remarkable" numbers of women. How do things really stand?

In order to find out, it is not enough to look solely at the situation of women writers. To do so would be to take gender as the fundamental criterion of judgment and to rate women writers in terms of individual talent or historical novelty—shifting criteria at best. A different interpretation emerges from a historical study of changes in the world of letters that pays due attention to the gender variable. It is immediately apparent, for instance, that the total number of authors has increased dramatically over the course of the century, as the number of readers has expanded to the point where the audience for books constitutes a true market; the increase in the number of female authors must therefore be measured against the enormous increase in the number of writers of both sexes. The *Figaro*'s arbitrary choice of "80 women" who "rule the world of letters" is therefore quite meaningless, since nothing is said about the number of men who "rule" simultaneously. Some reliable statistics would provide a clearer idea of the relation between the sexes in the literary realm. As it happens, however, while abundant information is available about the readers of books, there is very little about writers, publishers, and critics.

By piecing together rough estimates and incomplete data,

Michèle Vessilier-Ressi[14] and, working independently, Pierette Dionne and Chantal Théry[15] have calculated that approximately 70 to 75 percent of the books published in France are written by men, compared with 25 to 30 percent by women. My own research team at the University of Paris VII reviewed all books published in the "general literature" category between 1950 and 1955 (without distinction as to value) and came up with a ratio of 75 percent male authors to 25 percent female, or three to one.[16] This ratio has remained stable over a period of forty years, despite the rise of the women's liberation movement (a finding confirmed by studies carried out in Quebec). The alleged "feminization" of literature thus turns out to be a myth, if the word is supposed to mean that the balance in publishing has shifted in favor of women or at least toward equality. So does the idea that the realm of literature was occupied by women after being abandoned by men.[17] Indeed, the figures show that literature remains highly masculinized.

The gap between the sexes is even wider if we look at which writers achieve recognition for their work: only 8 percent of the writers listed in *Who's Who* are women. The figure was roughly the same in the period 1950–1955, and most of the female writers well known at that time have already been forgotten. One therefore has to wonder about the fate that lies in store for those deemed to be the "rulers of letters" today. Contrast, for example, the optimism of the *Figaro littéraire* with the pessimism of a work as weighty as *Notre siècle,* edited by the eminent historian René Rémond: only 8 women are included in connection with art, literature, and philosophy, compared with 180 men.[18] What is more, Simone Weil and Simone de Beauvoir are mentioned only for their political activity; Gyp is mentioned only because of her son; and Marcelle Auclair is mentioned in connection with the magazine *Marie-Claire.* Colette is not named at all, nor is Marguerite Yourcenar, even though she was the first woman elected to the *Académie Française.* The three women cited for their work as writers are Nathalie Sarraute, in connection with the so-called Nouveau Roman (New Novel); Marguerite Duras, for her early "traditional" novels; and Françoise Sagan, as an exemplar of "frivolity." Granted, this is an extreme example, but the work's reputation did not suffer as a result—which tells us a great deal about contemporary tolerance for contempt toward women and ignorance of their accomplishments. These findings contradict the widespread belief in cultural equality. They raise doubts about the future and force us to reflect on the way in which literature actually functions as a social and symbolic institution.

Vessilier-Ressi offers this portrait of the author most likely to succeed: he is a man of good background and with the best education, his publisher is in Paris, and he has powerful friends and associates. She assumes, however, that the male writer obliged to work at a job other than writing in order to make ends meet has just as many problems as the female writer occupied with family responsibilities, and from this rather hastily concludes that the two situations are equivalent. She forgets that most female writers also have a second job outside the home, but, even more important, she neglects social and symbolic factors: for example, it is harder for a woman to justify her choice of writing as a primary profession to professional colleagues and family members, and women, at least those just starting out as writers, are less likely to be able to avail themselves of the important but subtle networks of solidarity and influence. Dionne and Théry give a statistical overview of publishing as an institution (including publishing houses, reviews, prize juries, government cultural agencies, and so on) which shows that the system is "andocratic": in every area men control who is published and who is praised. Men also control, as we saw earlier, the mechanisms of transmission, including cultural models.

Still, these sociological findings call for a corrective historical perspective. The fact that inequality persists does not necessarily refute the notion that there are more women in the world of letters now than in the past. Indeed, at the turn of the century literature was the only profession open to poor, unmarried women who had received some education. Colette succeeded George Sand as a model of the woman writer who achieved economic and personal independence by persuading the public as well as institutional authorities of her talent. She was the second woman to sit on the Goncourt jury (after Judith Gautier, the daughter of the celebrated poet Théophile Gautier); at one point she even served as chairperson. Literature was also the most acceptable art for a bourgeois woman to practice, provided she preserved a certain "amateur" flavor in her work. Neither Colette nor the "bourgeois amateur" had much in common with the prestigious image of the man of genius who devoted his life to literature while either living on a private income or eking out a subsistence by performing menial tasks. At the time, in other words, women who knew their place might be allowed to occupy a jump-seat in the literary coach. They were, however, excluded from institutions embodying prestige and power: the universities and other top-ranked schools, academies, and even lycées where new disciplines such as the human sciences and literary and critical theory were developed.[19] But for rare exceptions, moreover, top posts in publishing and journalism were closed to females.

Today, women can be found working in nearly all professions and institutions. In this sense the Dionne-Théry article agrees with *Le Figaro*. Furthermore, substantial numbers of women are working in the human sciences and in such fields as theater and film direction. Thus there have been undeniable advances, even if inequality remains apparent everywhere. Why, then, has the percentage of female writers remained the same from 1945 to the present? Perhaps it is because women are now freer to choose among various possibilities for creative expression. Furthermore, aspiring female artists and intellectuals do not have to deal only with men. Hence despite the continuing influence of hegemonic male models, it is by no means absurd to suggest that the status and image of female writers have improved over the course of the century.

Does it follow that we are witnessing the birth of a "mixed" literature with none of the conflict or "effort" that Virginia Woolf foresaw in *A Room of One's Own*? One dark spot remains: while nearly 30 percent of all writers are women, they make up only 8 percent of honored literary figures (and the judgment of posterity may reduce this proportion still further). The usual explanation for this situation is that very few women writers manage to produce a body of work capable of withstanding the test of time or of achieving universality. Commentators differ, however, as to the reasons for this and thus as to the prognosis: those who hold that women simply lack genius find that the disease has no cure, whereas those who say that women are less experienced than men and still alienated by their condition argue that one day women may well "rival" their male counterparts. This takes us out of the realm of the quantitative into the more delicate domain of value.

Between Universal and Specific

One critic, Anne Sauvy, published an article on "Literature and Women" that stands out for the calm yet blunt manner in which its argument is set forth.[20] Sauvy offers a list of names of women writers who achieved celebrity in the period 1900–1950: Renée Vivien, Marguerite Audoux, Colette, Gyp, Rachilde, Anna de Noailles, Jeanne Galzy, Marie Noël, and others. But the exercise, she says, is pointless. None of these writers is worth rescuing from oblivion except Colette and perhaps Noailles, that is, the two generally included in the latest textbook anthologies. The bulk of women's literary production, according to Sauvy, belongs to the history of *publishing,* not of *literature.*

Sauvy is bold enough to judge the women writers of the second half of the century as well: "No great change is to be expected," she argues, because no woman has left a body of work "making as strong an impression" as that of a man. What woman will inherit the mantle of Sand and Colette? Any number of names come to mind: Sarraute, Duras, Monique Wittig, Hélène Cixous, Yourcenar, Christiane Rochefort, Susini, Beauvoir, Hyvrard, Leduc, Elsa Triolet, Cardinal, Chawaf, Sagan, the Groult sisters. And who knows what writers may emerge in the last decade of the century? It seems unthinkable that works that are an intimate part of our world are destined to disappear as though they had never existed. What can account for such devastation?

"Genius, the divine spirit that bloweth where it listeth. We can do nothing to make it happen. . . . Genius is not created in school." Conversely, nothing has ever been able to prevent true genius from making its existence known. If the divine afflatus comes to only one or two French women in every century, there is nothing to be done about it. Sauvy, thanks to the objective tone typical of academic writing, manages to pass this perfectly gratuitous observation off as truth.

If one looks at the way literary transmission actually works, one finds that men have established a three-tier system: there are geniuses, talented writers, and failures. The classification of any particular writer is open to controversy and revision, and evaluation depends on constantly changing ideas about what to expect from the written word. For women, on the other hand, there are only two tiers: genius for the lucky few and oblivion for the rest. In effect, women are excluded from the vast category of the talented; they have no place in the *art* of writing, which is a matter of apprenticeship, work, circumstances, and encounters—in short, of "schools." The art of literature thus partakes of all the historical conditions that determine what the representative literature of a society is. As everyone knows, moreover, the great women writers of history such as Sand and Colette are generally greeted with neglect and condescension. In the end, the pseudo-recognition accorded to the work of a few makes it possible to consign the work of many others to the category of the *ephemeral,* that which is presumed very quickly to become unreadable.

Opposed to this argument is the sociohistorical argument according to which the weakness of women's literature is a product (or reflection) of their alienation. Some day, when women are totally emancipated, they will become men's equals in creation. But such equality can be conceived only in terms of identity, in the name of the neutral and universal. This was Beauvoir's point of view, to which she clung rigorously throughout her life. As late as the 1970s she had this to say: "I believe that liberated women will be as creative as men. They will not, however, discover new values. To believe the contrary is to believe in the existence of a feminine nature, which I have always denied."[21] And this: "It is by no means certain that the worlds of women's ideas are different from those of men's, for it is by identifying with the latter that women will free themselves."[22] Although she envisioned, at the end of *The Second Sex,* a new relation between the sexes based on reciprocity in double alterity, she never wavered from her radical position: access to the neutral and general inevitably meant "identification" with the male model, which is the absolute human standard of reference, hence abolition of femininity, which for Beauvoir was exclusively an effect of oppression.

It was with this theory in mind that Beauvoir judged the entire range of women's literary output. No female writer escaped the damning judgment of "specificity" (as opposed to generality), which meant that women's work was classed as "inessential," whereas every male writer, however mediocre, represented the fully formed human condition. Although Beauvoir gave her sanction to the idea of "women's literature" and treated it as a literature of the oppressed, for her it was not an oppressed literature in conflict with a dominant literature. It was an inferior literature destined to disappear once women were emancipated.

Beauvoir read women writers (as her autobiography reveals), but not for the purpose of discovery. She did not read women with the expectation of changing her view of the world or her relation to language and discourse. She saw in women's literature a limited, often repetitious set of themes, a range of styles and structures more or less successfully copied from men's innovations and women's own abortive attempts. Paradoxically, the tremendous variety of techniques and styles always pointed to "woman" as such and to her alleged inability "to disclose all of reality and not merely her own personality" in the act of writing. Under the circumstances, it should come as no surprise that Beauvoir underestimated Virginia Woolf. Sartre was able to see the importance of Sarraute's *Tropismes* and subsequently wrote a long foreword to her *Portrait d'un inconnu,* whereas Beauvoir dismissed Sarraute in vehement terms that only betrayed her incomprehension. And she simply neglected many women writers of her time: Bachmann, Tsvetaeva, Anna Akhmatova, Elsa Morante, Duras, Doris Lessing, and Maraini, among others.

In fact, Beauvoir practiced a normative reading associated with her normative conception of writing: there is only one correct way to read and write, which one learns from Literature, a Pantheon of immortal masterpieces which is the same for all people in all times and all places. She never questions that Pantheon, where, transcending the vicissitudes of history and the diversity of cultures, all the best that humankind has achieved is gathered together. These masterpieces have been able to transcend the circumstances in which they were born to enter the realm of pure freedom. Accordingly, a taboo has been raised against relativizing the standards of evaluation and selection by looking at the questions of the *transmission* and *reception* of literary works within and between cultures from a sociohistorical point of view. This taboo is deeply inscribed in each one of us, from childhood on, by the authoritative discourse of the schools, inspired by official criticism. Our apprenticeship of reading and writing—our entry into the symbolic universe—is subject to a voice of authority in possession of truth and values, a voice that seems to speak from everywhere and nowhere at the same time. Beauvoir identified that voice and located it for us. No other theorist has offered so radical an analysis of the masculine appropriation of the universal and yet issued so radical a judgment against women as readers and writers. In terms of her own experience she thereby disclosed the draconian conditions imposed on the acculturation of women in France in the twentieth century: "assimilation" is the key term.

In France educational equality was achieved within the framework of a public school system designed to impart the same education to all citizens, while selecting the few destined to become members of the elite. All students used the same language and studied the same works using the same textbooks embodying the same critical discourse leading in the end to national diplomas based on a uniform set of national examinations. Like the nation's citizens, however, the nation's culture was exclusively masculine. Feminists attacked the gender segregation that seemed to be a fundamental part of this system. At the turn of the century they sought to replace the republican ideal of "liberty, equality, and fraternity" with a new ideal of *liberté, égalité, et mixité* (liberty, equality, and coeducation). Coeducation was the major goal.

The ideal of coeducation required that pupils of both sexes be given the same training. In the 1920s girls won the right to take the examination for the *baccalauréat;* their curriculum was to be the same as the boys', the exam was to be the same, and the juries were to be composed of teachers of both sexes. With the *baccalauréat* women also gained access to French universities, and to the competitive exams used to select graduates for coveted civil service jobs. The struggle for equality was long and difficult, but the unified educational system proved to be a crucial factor in the emancipation and social advancement of women. Because they received the same education as men, women were able to break out of the ghetto and into the vast field of culture and knowledge that had previously been a male preserve. Virginia Woolf's dream of a shared culture and thus an end to the separation between brothers and sisters in creation seemed at long last to have been realized. Yet culture remained under the aegis of the male universal.

The problem was that when the boys' and girls' curricula were unified in the 1920s, the new girls' curriculum was simply modeled on that of the boys; there was no merging. Girls, for example, were allowed to study classical languages and literature, which had previously been closed to them, but boys were not allowed to study modern world (that is, non-French) literature, which had been an innovation in the girls' curriculum.[23] The teaching of literature was further impoverished by the exclusion of regional cultures and the literature of francophone countries. Thus the "universal literature" offered to students under the new system embodied not only male hegemony but French hegemony as well. Works by the most celebrated women writers were no longer studied beyond the mere mention of their authors' names in a course on literary history. Their texts were not read or discussed or assigned as essay topics. These works never appeared in courses devoted to certain literary themes, nor did they figure as examples in courses on literary theory, except by some fluke. Even the rare excerpts that appeared in textbooks were generally overlooked, because it was well known that they were "of no use on the exam." So Marot was studied in preference to Marguerite de Navarre and Louise Labé. And what about Mme de La Fayette? The novel was still a minor genre in the seventeenth century, and in any case her "minor masterpiece" revealed the influence, if not the actual pen, of La Rochefoucauld. The seventeenth-century women writers known as Les Précieuses were known only from Molière's caricatures. Sand and Colette were reserved for certain select classes. The only woman whose work was discussed in regular lectures was Mme de Sévigné, who, though famous, was the author of only a collection of letters and hence remained on the fringe of literature. That about sums up the curriculum of the 1950s. There was no longer any "socialization" of works by women, and they remained cut off from the cultivated female readership. The texts were either simply ignored or else relegated to the realm of purely "private" reading, as we see so clearly in the case of Simone de Beauvoir.

Now, ever since the mythological age, readers have formed their personal identities through literary texts. Reading teaches us to understand our lives—our emotions and passions, our pleasures, our anxieties, our desire—in terms of symbols. We learn to decipher the world, society, life and death. We uncover the full depth of other selves, all that ordinarily remains beyond our ken. Literature is therefore the primary realm in which subjectivation and socialization proceed hand in hand. The interaction of reality, imagination, and language enables us to unlock social and individual models of identity, in particular models of gender identity and sexual difference. We move rapidly from one identification to another, desiring some as violently as we reject others. This is true not only at the narrative level but also at the level of points of view, metaphors, and sentences—that is, of linguistic utterance itself. Thanks to literature, we learn how to use language more freely and to experiment with the self as "speaking subject."

It is therefore a matter of the utmost importance that the subjectivation and socialization of both sexes occur under the auspices of a one-gender literature, indeed a literature neutralized (sterilized) by a monological and dogmatic critical discourse, which imposes its own stereotypes even despite the contradictions and interrogations contained within the masculine texts to which it refers. It is a matter of importance for boys as well as girls, though not in the same way: both sexes are deprived of the experiences of identification they could obtain from the imaginary and linguistic labyrinths of women's texts. Both are deprived of their feminine symbolic heritage. Both learn about sexual difference by way of the representation of a plural masculine subject always in question and transformation vis-à-vis an "eternal feminine" whose variations depend on men's history and men's representations. The asymmetry of this entry into the sociosymbolic field leads to very different modes of alienation: men lack the detour—the mediation—afforded by the imagination and voice of the other sex, but the richness of their male heritage keeps them from seeing the monolithic character of their identity. Women know what can be gained through identification with the imagination and voice of the other sex, but, cut off from all reciprocity and all identification with the imaginations and voices of recognized women writers, they find that identification turns into oppression.

The educational system exacerbates gender inequality. It confirms young males as the sole legitimate heirs and future wielders of the culture's creative powers. Girls are deprived of any legitimate way to express themselves; their role, in a system in which legitimacy is passed from male to male, is to participate in the reproduction of the system. They are destined to become readers, teachers, and press agents rather than writers, researchers, or editors. Even if they seek "assimilation" through rivalry with men on their terms, they are doomed, to borrow Marguerite Duras's term, to "plagiarism." They become used to discussing everything, even themselves, in terms of the dominant discourse, which they adopt as their own. This happens to certain female teachers and research assistants: in order to gain acceptance, they must serve as "vestal virgins" to leading authors, working within the framework of established theories. At the first sign of deviation from the official line, they run the risk of being reminded that they are not men.

Women are thus in what has been called a "schizophrenic position," subject to a double-bind: they are both students (or teachers, writers, intellectuals) and women. This double-bind points up the symbolic violence to which they are subject when they enter the sociocultural field. That violence is fiercest when women themselves support the legitimacy of the established culture. Historically, this was (and is) the price to be paid for indispensable advancement, but it should be clear that winning equality in a number of limited areas does not necessarily add up to "equality" as such. Simone de Beauvoir's terrifying formula sums up our painful self-image in the 1950s: "As long as women must fight to become human beings, they will never be creators."[24] But Beauvoir was wrong about women, just as Sartre was wrong about workers. The oppressed individual (whether woman or proletarian) is inalienably human and therefore inevitably a creator, even if his/her creativity fails to meet the norms of the dominant culture. Fortunately, neither humanity nor art belongs to the oppressors, as they would have us believe. Women writers are there to attest that women are indeed human beings who, despite the many obstacles standing in their way, create.

It would in fact be interesting to see just how women writers since Colette *(Claudine)* and Sarraute *(Enfance)* have inscribed their education in their work and their work in their education. Such a study would reveal the diversity of our apprenticeships, as well as the myriad of ways in which we have used and circumvented constraints to construct a realm of freedom. Monique Wittig's *L'Opoponax* (1964)—the novel not of an individual but of a generation—is the most recent example: the quest for identity and for the truth of desire draws deeply on that freedom, on a time of life and a body of experience that escapes gender determination in order to transcend the wrenching gap that the culture places between becoming human and becoming a woman.[25]

One could then analyze how women, not content, as Wittig puts it, merely to express themselves in writing, truly enter the realm of literature. Their strategies have been diverse. Duras is provocative on the subject: "One does not write in the same space as men," she argues, yet at the same time she refuses to see herself as participating in "feminine literature." Her goal is to change the common culture by introducing new forms of fiction and new modes of writing that transcend sexual dichotomy. At the end of *L'Ere du soupçon* Nathalie Sarraute sets herself up as a pioneer of the Nouveau Roman, in opposition to a group that marginalized her even as it welcomed her into its ranks, that stole from her without acknowledging its debt and without recognizing how radical her approach was. She, too, participated in the general literature but without "assimilating." By the strength of her writing alone she sought to show how what she had discovered by plumbing the depths of her own experience and observing others, male as well as female, could be valid for everyone. She rejected the conventional coding of gender in order to explore the relations between body and language in an indeterminate zone somewhere between the sexes; her experiment must remain incomprehensible to anyone unwilling to experiment with new ways of reading. So strange is the notion of a woman as literary innovator, however, that the standard textbook by Lagarde and Michard recounts the history of the Nouveau Roman as though the men in the group were the first to produce the major novels and theoretical texts for which it is known.[26]

Can a female artist really find a place in a group of fellow creators? Sarraute once spoke of her sense of deep solitude before an audience composed of other new novelists and critics. Duras refused to appear at the same symposium. Or, to take another example from an earlier time, think of Léonor Fini's fine letter about her unwillingness to see herself as a surrealist.[27] What woman artist has not experienced a similar solitude? This has nothing in common with the solitude afflicting male creators, for men can always hope that posterity will know how to read the message in the bottle they toss into the sea. Women have no such hope. In their case one should really speak not of solitude but of radical isolation, a prelude to the disappearance of their work. For the few who have the strength to persevere in spite of all the obstacle, how much must be given up or renounced? How many works go unfinished because the artist has lost her bearings? How many aspirations, Duras asked, go unfulfilled? Clearly the relatively small percentage of women writers in France is the result of many complex factors, and social equality by itself will not solve the problem.

Women's Writing and Literary Criticism

Today it is possible to reconsider the violent debate that erupted among French feminists in 1975–76 with (to borrow Geneviève Fraisse's phrase) greater "theoretical serenity" than in the past. At the end of *La Muse de la raison* Fraisse points out that the idea of equality belongs to the realm of politics, whereas discussion of sexual difference belongs to psychoanalysis and literature, both of which talk about love and the human passions. She proposes finding a way out of a perplexing dilemma: that one must "either assert that the future will decrease sexual difference in favor of greater similarity or else insist that female difference, though a censored resource, will ultimately issue in utopia."[28] Such are the terms of the debate.

The two camps are described in the introduction to *French Feminist Criticism,* an invaluable annotated bibliography.[29] On one side were the radical feminists who prided themselves on their Marxist materialism and adopted the position of Simone de Beauvoir. On the other side were the champions of the feminine, who were determined to launch a radical attack on the symbolic order, that is, the system of appropriation and exclusion of the maternal and the feminine that underlies the social order. This confrontation between two feminist camps coincided with a disciplinary dispute: the materialists tended to be sociologists and historians, whereas the symbolists tended to be psychoanalysts, linguists, artists, and literary critics. The whole controversy had its parallel in the debate between Marxists and structuralists in the 1960s, but since feminists in both camps were interested in transforming the prevailing theories by forcing them to take the point of view of women into account, there was hope that dialogue might provide a way out of the dilemma. But in the end it turned out to be a dialogue of the deaf. This was because the focal point of the debate soon shifted to the political arena: the group Psychanalyse et Politique attacked the struggle for equality as a symptom of total alienation in a patriarchal society and a betrayal of the feminist values that the group wished to promote as the basis of a women's revolution. It went so far as to forbid "outsiders" to claim to be part of the women's liberation movement. Hélène Cixous defended this position, whereas Julia Kristeva argued that there was no further need for feminism because women had already achieved equality.[30] More politically minded feminists responded immediately, denouncing as dangerous theories of the feminine that turned women away from concrete struggles and enmeshed them in old patriarchal patterns. For them, any investigation into the nature of sexual difference not explicitly associated with the issue of equality versus inequality became suspect. The split even had its counterpart in the world of publishing: the "Psy et Po" group published with Editions des Femmes, whereas the "feminist" group published with Tierce. Women who raised the question of difference within the context of the struggle for equality were marginalized.

Let us turn back for a moment to the time before the debate, to the libertarian phase of 1968 and the early days of the women's movement. Recall the "consciousness-raising" groups in which women searched for ways to express themselves more freely, and reread *Le Torchon brûlé,* a typical feminist newspaper of the period. What one senses immediately is an irresistible desire to "write about oneself as woman." This was the force that motivated so many newcomers to literature. Annie Leclerc's *Parole de femme* launched the movement in France, but it had its counterparts in other countries as well. A simple list of names is enough to show that this was a true literary movement with a broad diversity of works united by a common approach: Brossard, Leclerc, Cixous, Cardinal, Gagnon, Groult, Santos, Hyvrard, Lejeune, Chawaf, Huston, Sebbar, Condé, and others too numerous to mention. All these women shared a desire to discover their bodies, their imaginations, their unconscious, and their experiences, things of which they felt deprived by a censorious culture. All felt a need to forge a new language of their own in order to express themselves. And all shared a sense that their bodies, their imaginations, their unconscious, and their experience were unexplored territory, like wilderness preserves within the so-called common society and culture.

Beauvoir published Cixous's manifesto "Le Rire de la méduse" (The Laughter of the Medusa, 1975) in a special issue of the journal *L'Arc.* Cixous, Gagnon, and Leclerc together wrote *La Venue à l'écriture* (Discovering Writing), and Cardinal and Leclerc collaborated on *Les Mots pour le dire* (The Words to Say It). Women read one another, quoted one another, and searched for precursors by reprinting Woolf's works and publishing interviews with Duras (Gautier, *Les Parleuses*). New journals such as *Sorcières* came into being, while others, like *Les Cahiers du Grif,* devoted special issues to creativity and language.[31] In attempting to transform discourse so as to create for themselves a "space of subjectivation and socialization," women were truly behaving as writers. Yet Cixous's celebrated statement reveals all the ambiguities in the formula "women's writing" *(écriture féminine):* "Women must write themselves; women must write about women and bring women to writing, from which they were estranged as violently as from their own bodies."[32] The magazine *Quinzaine littéraire* made this statement the focal point of a debate under the headline "Does Literature Have a Sex?"

Writing in the radical feminist review *Questions féministes* in

321

1977, Monique Plaza launched a vehement attack on Luce Irigaray, whose *Speculum de l'autre femme* (1974) and *Ce sexe qui n'en est pas un* (1977) were the most profound and original of the new theoretical works on sexual difference. Plaza was critical of Irigaray's return to female distinctiveness, her alleged reductionist approach to women in terms of their bodies, and her reverting to an essentialist position that failed to relate the sexual to the social.[33] The criticisms were pertinent, as Irigaray's subsequent work demonstrated. Still, Irigaray had gone further than any other writer in deconstructing the discourse of psychoanalysis and philosophy, including the structuralist theories of Lévi-Strauss and Lacan, who, in the name of a symbolic order transcending all society, condemned women to the position of objects of social exchange and "subjective impasse" (Lacan). Along with Derrida, Kristeva, and Cixous, Irigaray opened the way to post-structuralism.[34] I, for one, acknowledge my debt to her, as I acknowledge my debt to Beauvoir. But what did post-structuralism leave "unthought"?

Part of the answer lies with the notion of "women's writing," which took on a peculiar meaning in post-structuralist texts. The basic idea was that there was a fundamental difference between "discourse"—which is organized and rational and entirely on the side of order, history, meaning, and power over the world ("logophallocentrism")—and "writing," which consists of the traces of instincts, emotions, elemental and labile representations at the unconscious level, sounds detached from all meaning, and so on. Writing, multifarious and ever-changing, eludes all temporal categories. Like psychoanalysis, contemporary literature moves constantly back and forth between "writing" and "discourse." But why make one the paternal-masculine and the other the maternal-feminine, as if predestined by nature? By conflating the maternal with the fantasies of early childhood and the feminine with the maternal, one deprives women of the right and the capacity to intervene in the realm of the symbolic, and one terms "feminine" everything in men that has to do with the archaic, the body, passivity, non-meaning, and so on. Why not speak instead of "instinctual writing" playing with the institutionalized discourses of literature? Then one could shift the question of sexual difference to the speaking subject. The gender variable is still important, but it is affected by (and in turn affects) other variables: historical, social, cultural, and individual.

Paradoxically, political feminists and feminists of difference share a common assumption: that of a radical alienation from the women of the past. For Beauvoir and her followers, and for Kristeva as well, they "wrote like women." For Irigaray and Cixous, they wrote "like men." The search ends in a new categorical imperative: "Write like a woman," and the debate turns on the definition and codification of what "women's writing" is. Dogmatism is the result, and this dogmatism prevents women from entering into literary discourse in order to transform it. Condemned to "write direct from the scene," they end up imitating a borrowed notion of femininity. But writing as escape either grinds to a halt or goes nowhere.

If the debate seems sterile, it is because it took place in an age of ignorance. We had been deprived of our place in history and our frame of reference. More recently, changes have begun that may lead to a way out of our dilemma. In 1981 Béatrice Slama and Béatrice Didier not only showed what was at stake in the idea of "women's writing" but also how it could impede progress; it was impossible, they argued, to define all work by women in terms of a single formula.[35] Literary critics, accustomed to spend a long time with individual texts, preferred to speak of "women and writing practices" rather than "women's writing." Christine Planté detects a trap in the whole controversy: the same dilemma has cropped up in a variety of sociocultural contexts whenever women have attempted to express themselves through literature.[36] The problem has shaped the history of female writers by forcing them to respond to it in one way or another, often by adopting the strategies of their precursors. The "women's writing" movement must therefore be seen in its historical context. It is certainly no more dogmatic than surrealism, and in any case the actual works it has produced are fortunately far richer than the theories surrounding them.

Today, the crux of the issue is: will we be able to create a culture in which identifications are possible across sex boundaries, a culture that involves an interplay between non-differentiation and differentiation, a culture of sharing, a culture that is truly a home for both sexes?

TRANSLATED FROM THE FRENCH BY ARTHUR GOLDHAMMER

11

The Ambivalent Image of Woman in Mass Culture

Luisa Passerini

OBSERVERS OF MASS CULTURE have frequently emphasized the connections they see between that culture and the concept of the feminine as it has come to be defined in the history of the West. The idea, first proposed by Edgar Morin in 1962, continued to develop, uninterrupted, until 1984. In that year participants in a conference on mass culture took a different position, rejecting the indulgent attitudes toward that culture of the past two decades.[1] Yet the linkage of the feminine with mass culture, though perplexing, should not be discarded, because of the valuable insights it yields.

According to Morin, the feminization of societies which had reached an adequate level of material progress was characterized by a certain reversal of values. While women gained access to careers previously restricted to men, moved into public life, and began taking more initiative in the private sphere (symbolized for instance by the film *To Have and Have Not,* in which Lauren Bacall started a romance by asking Humphrey Bogart for a light), men became more sentimental, tender, and weak. Mass culture played a key role in this change, at once affirming values said to be typically female, such as the personal, harmony, love, and happiness, and amplifying images of seductive women, from the "cover girl" to the Gilda played by Rita Hayworth, who represented a synthesis of two traditionally irreconcilable types: the vamp and the virgin.

Popular Culture between Male and Female

Actually, mass culture reveals, at the very moment it appropriates the female image, the ambivalence of that image in Western culture, an ambivalence that has increased rather than diminished in response to the demands of emancipation. The predominance of the female face in advertisements, on magazine covers, and on posters calls to mind the image of woman both as a subject and as a possible object. One risks, however, confusing two separate elements. On the one hand, the course of history has put women into a situation of real duplicity, especially with the advent of social and political emancipation of the last century and a half. And on the other hand, the use of historically determined values by mass culture (assigning forcefulness and aggressiveness to men, for example, and sweetness and tenderness to women) locks both sexes into rigid roles and "democratizes" these roles as they spread more widely throughout society. In addition, the predominance in everyday life of the type of eroticism promulgated by mass culture cannot but assign the role of protagonist, though very ambiguously, to the female figure, which the West has identified with sexuality itself.

Thus the limitations of the type of feminization analyzed by Morin are obvious, both on the theoretical and historical levels. Moreover, changes have taken place on the historical level: for instance, between 1962 and the present there has been an increase in representation of the male image in advertisements[2] and movies.[3] The redefinition of the special relation between the "feminine" and mass culture advanced twenty years after Morin shows greater subtlety and more precise distinctions, among them the fundamental distinction between the historical concept of the feminine and women in flesh and blood. The more recent critics also pointed out the sexist trend in political, psychological, and aesthetic discourse at the turn of the century, when mass culture and even the masses themselves were described as female (one need only mention Le Bon's equating, in 1895, the hysterical crowd and the "feminine"), while high culture remained the privileged domain of men.[4] Devaluation of the female continued, therefore, at the very same time that new images of feminine behavior were being affirmed, with the traditional denigration of "lower" forms of culture compared with the "higher" forms.

With the two phenomena growing apace—on the one hand increasing participation of women in the public sphere, and on the other the expansion of mass culture—new forms of so-called feminization allegedly developed. After the Second World War, for instance, mass culture in the United States seemed obsessed with the loss of male authority. Comic strips showed a husband, armed with a rolling pin, who was smaller and weaker than his wife. Television showed a domesticated father who looked ridiculous when he tried to be virile and resourceful.[5] This tendency was a continuation of the cult of "Mom" denounced by Philip Wylie in his novel *Generation of Vipers* (1942) and analyzed by Erik Erikson in *Childhood and Society* (1950). This phenomenon is not so interesting in itself—indeed one can easily find its countertendencies—but only insofar as it is an example of the attempt to blame women for the great historical changes which took power away from the familial and patriarchal structure. Although one cannot attribute such diabolic plots to mass culture, one must recognize its tendency to stand real problems on their heads, or at least to disguise them. One example of this, suggested by the authors cited above, is the request in the 1960s that retail clerks appear *sexy,* which could be explained as an attempt to mask with seductive femininity the appearance of many more women in the job market.

Apart from the debate on the equation of mass culture with "feminine," mass media have been accused by other critics of sexism, of favoring in various ways the masculine and males.[6] There are innumerable analyses in this vein and we will come across some in the course of this essay. This accusation of sexism is also partially correct, so long as it is adequately tied to the equation mentioned above, which in turn needs to be reworked through a critique of conventional wisdom. While it may be true that mass culture wishes to reinforce the idea of a clear division between masculine/work/social on the one hand and feminine/free time/natural on the other, as can often be seen in advertising,[7] it is also true that one cannot simply stop there. Numerous works by historians and anthropologists have shown that, in many societies in different epochs, the role of women has not been confined to the private sphere, the sphere of life called "ahistorical,"[8] but rather has existed on the border between public and private, where women have been mediators, as, for example, between their own families and the institutions of social life.

In the end, those studies are most convincing which succeed in elucidating the ambiguous relationship between women and the feminine on the one hand and mass culture on the other. Such studies allow us to recognize the real connections between the development of mass culture and the emancipation of women, together with those that exist between that culture and the persistence of old stereotypes of femininity. Thus, for example, the mass media make use of feminist-inspired arguments, such as the ads for "liberating brassieres" at the end of the 1960s, or for vacations as "freedom of choice" in the 1980s.[9] But the media also usually identify feminine images with the natural, the biological, or show them as embodiments of the "exotic" and the Other—images that easily fit ads for tourism and "the look."

But the products of mass culture must always be evaluated in relation to their interaction with the public. The most useful analyses are those which succeed in illustrating the dynamic influence of those products within the social context, be they the expansion and commercialization of free time, which women pioneered in the United States from the end of the last century until 1920[10] or a history of the cinema, which allows spectators to waver between feminine and masculine identities according to the characters presented.[11] The results of such approaches are also interesting methodologically. No longer is mass culture accused of conniving with one gender; rather, one notes ways by which it reformulates the subordination of women while keeping up with their new behavior and modes of thinking. At the same time the media are credited with a positive function for their capacity to propose a range of positions which viewers can assume toward them. In this way gender is not mechanically determined but is defined by the cultural attitudes of real people, so that women can choose, in a film for instance, to identify with a masculine position or a feminine one. What is important is that in this way social beings can reclaim some form of self-determination, while still remaining subject to conditioning and outside pressures. Hence it is important, too, not to misjudge mass culture and blame it blindly from an a priori position.

A useful question to ask is to what extent the responses and reactions of the public occur primarily on the basis of sex or on the basis of perceptions that link it to such factors as class, race, and generation. Again, the evaluation must take account of the specific circumstances. In certain times and places the sexual identity will prevail, influenced by other unconscious undercurrents. In addition, we have to take into account the topsy-turvy aspect of mass culture to which we have referred. It has been asserted, for instance, that the challenge offered by the women's movement to the male vision of feminine sexuality in the last thirty years has facilitated the production and wide dissemination of a new type of novel defined as "pornography for women."[12] And it has been observed that the "liberated" image of the one advertisement exclusively aimed at women, for sanitary napkins, conceals a return to folklore and its taboos which subtly emphasize a sense of guilt, in contrast to the overt message.[13]

Mass culture, compared by Adorno to the queen in the story of Snow White, always receives the same reassurance from the magical narcissistic mirror, which it both queries and uses as a context. Historical research corrects this illusion, revealing from time to time the culture's connivance with the dominant ideas of masculine and feminine, but it also shows how the culture can be influenced by pertinent new ideas. In the last analysis, the path of mass culture depends on the choices of women and men who are redefining the combination of feminine and masculine embodied in each individual.

Cultural Models for Mass Consumption

The processes of mass production and distribution (whose roots go back to the industrial revolution) that put out serial products for a potentially vast market, have involved women especially since the end of the nineteenth century. These processes become more pronounced and accelerated in the period between the two wars, at least as far as Europe and North America are concerned, with notable differences of level and timing not only between different countries but even between different regions and classes in the same country.

What did the transformation of "women" into "masses" mean? While women escaped the full force of the regimentation of the factory and office that applied to men, to the extent that it happened to women, it went hand in hand with the standardization that took place in the private, domestic sphere. The models advanced since the beginning of the twentieth century, in the United States for example, insist specifically on the modification and adjustment of crucial aspects of the traditional woman having to do with the care of the house and of her physical person.

The new housewife, able to rationalize domestic work in terms of time and production, is the counterpart of the man in his extra-domestic production, in which the same processes of uniformity and division of labor take place.[14] The functioning of the home must be assimilated and integrated into the organization of society. Beginning in the 1920s, with the appearance of electric appliances and new equipment, we see a real attempt to "Taylorize" domestic work. This is true not only for the United States but also, for example, for France, at least at the level of prototypes, as can be seen in the Salon des Arts Ménagers, created in 1923 and in full operation by 1926.[15] To be sure, such "modernizations" must always be measured against reality, but the important point is that they frequently influence models and ideologies even when they cannot be immediately put into practice.

The housewife must be from now on both a consumer and an administrator of the household. She becomes responsible for controlling consumption, which becomes an activity requiring careful organization and planning, installment buying, and long-term projects. In this light it is easy to see what a powerful hold the large department stores in the United States had on the imagination and in reality, especially during their golden age from 1890 to 1940. They delineate a new kind of public space for American women, a space for recreation and sociability, not merely for consumption, a space in which they are invested with authoritative roles as purchasers or heads of departments. In this sphere the culture of management, the culture of the urban bourgeoisie (customers and directors), the culture of the working classes (saleswomen), and the culture of women, bent but not destroyed by the ongoing historical process, all come together to form a new mass culture.[16] This culture can be called "mass" even when it applies as yet only to the middle and upper classes, because it has an intrinsic tendency to spread across society, owing to market pressures.

The new American woman was required to maintain a particularly well-cared-for physical appearance, in accordance with a redefinition of the feminine ideal for which the cosmetic and hygienic product industries were primarily responsible (the first absorbent Kotex came on the U.S. market in 1921).[17] Here again the mass character is proclaimed through the insistence on equal opportunity and democratization. Beauty can be achieved by all women if they devote sufficient energy to it. Uniformity of feminine appearance (and the very idea of feminine, since the suggested transformation is both exterior and interior: to know how to apply makeup, say the ads, is also to "find oneself") is extended to black women, whose personal success depends on straightened hair and lightened skin. However, differences between social levels and ages are underscored, since the same companies shrewdly target different sections of the market.

Such processes rely heavily on mass communication through magazines, advertising, and especially the movies which reinforce the "culture of beauty." Feminine images imbued with great charisma come out of Hollywood in the 1920s and 1930s, embodied in actresses who have been defined as the forerunners of the clamor for women's independence.[18] Here again it is interesting to note that some of the best-developed female characters emerged as the product of a convergence—typical of mass production—between very different phenomena: Hollywood technology, the promotional methods of the studio system, and a sexist vision of the world which was nevertheless able to include a desire for affirmation of many women.

The movie-star system was the principal medium for transmitting the American models to Europe between the two world wars. Films offered practical lessons on fashion, makeup, and manners during a period when everything that was innovative and modern was identified with the United States.[19] The promotion of the "new woman" image, bound up with the world of consumption, had a somewhat liberating effect (at least until the Second World War) because it emphasized freer behavior and greater social mobility for women.[20] Edgar Morin has argued, however, that the influence of the movie stars can encourage either narcissistic contemplation or self-affirmation.[21]

In Europe the processes of modification of domestic work and of the feminine image were already in progress independently, as a consequence of the great economic changes and changes in consumption brought on by the First World War. In France, for example, moderately developed at the time, the trend was, even for bourgeois women, to work outside the home.[22] The concomitant need to simplify domestic duties went along with the introduction of electricity and country-wide distribution of gas, promoting the evolution of a way of life which, between 1927 and 1932, moved away from the traditional mode despite the economic crisis. The succeeding decade witnessed a new way of life—especially in Paris—which included unusual attention to hygiene in the home, different eating habits (from long, complicated preparation to cheeses and "crudités"), and fewer servants. In 1939 technical progress in the home was limited to small appliances. But the images have changed, both of the home and of the wife, who in the evening must appear, smiling and attractive, in her attire and makeup. In short, certain fundamental cultural aspects had altered, at least within the ideological conception of the female role. It is no accident that the cosmetic industry became established and flourished in France in the 1930s.

The feminine press both reflected and stimulated such changes. In 1937 the new periodical *Marie Claire,* with a circulation of 800,000, made beauty care the province of French women of the Third Estate.[23] The journal's low price made it the "poor woman's *Vogue*" and here again "democratized" what before was accessible only to wealthy women. The ideal of energy, cheerfulness, cleanliness, and even a gracious coquetry—and some kind of independence—followed not only the American examples of Bette Davis and Katharine Hepburn, but gave a new dimension to the French tradition of charm and feminine freedom. It is interesting to recall that, despite the dominance of the American model, there is also in mass culture a constant reference to a vague and unattainable "other" model. In the interwar period this model, for American advertising, is that of the dream French woman, to such a degree that many American products are described as derived from French and especially Parisian prototypes.

At the end of the 1930s, the typical forms of mass media for women had become firmly established in France. In 1938 women's advice columns ("heart mail") became widespread, and the hugely popular *Confidences* dates from the same year. The journal adopted a new formula and, in recognition of women's loneliness, devoted many pages to anonymous confessions; this public display of autobiographical stories revealed women's suffering in the midst of the great changes they were experiencing. In 1939 the circulation of *Confidences* was well over a million.[24] World War II slowed down these developments, but they resumed and accelerated in the second half of the 1940s and in the following decade.

It is interesting to examine what happened in the period between the two world wars in Italy. The country differed from France and the United States not only in its level of economic development, resulting from its peculiar combination of backwardness and advanced industrialization, but also because of its then authoritarian regime and weak democratic tradition. In Italy, the idea of changing the role of women contradicted the established order and yet functioned within it, not without conflict. The program of the fascist regime fluctuated between using and uniforming women in its mass organizations (even literally, as far as clothing was concerned) and promoting the construct of the "exemplary wife and mother"[25] capable of taking on her shoulders all the weight of a demographic and imperialist policy. Women must become modern but at the same time produce many children and provide for the feeding and clothing of the whole family from the resources imposed by the autarchic economy: broom and nettle fibers instead of cotton, lanital instead of wool, lignite instead of coal. In addition to the contradictions of fascism, there was the conflicting pull of strong Catholic traditions, as the Roman Church cast a disapproving eye on the inclusion of youth and women in fascist organizations—although the ecclesiastical hierarchy supported the regime—and bitterly criticized women practicing sports, comparing it to entertainment, licentiousness, and "frivolities" which lured women away from the home.[26]

These contradictions were functional to fascism in practice, especially the tension between the process of capitalistic modernization and the requirements of the authoritarian regime. In reality the Italian woman clearly could not be the consumer and manager of the resources available to American and French women (leaving aside the differences in class and internal regions of the three countries). What occurred was a repressive modernization whose costs were borne chiefly by women, both in the working class (in restricted salaries and harsh industrial discipline) and in the middle class (with additional services required from the new housewife). These partial changes, which, during the second half of the 1930s, included more social welfare assistance and more leisure time even for the working classes (within, however, the institutional framework of a dictatorship), brought about a profound change in the relationship between public and private life.

Under fascism public power invaded the private sphere. This meant, for women, the breaking down of family ties or at least conflicting demands from the private and public sectors (the new Italian woman at political demonstrations and sporting events did not always receive the approval of her father, brother, or even of her mother if she were a devout Catholic). It also meant putting one's reproductive capacity in the service of the state. In this way motherhood was exhibited as a public function to an unparalleled extent, even if in a distorted way and against the resistance of women.[27] While the private sphere suffered interference, the public one ceased being a forum for the free exchange of ideas to become more and more a domain run by government and corporations. At the same time, the boundary between the two spheres shifted under the double pressure of political propaganda and commercial advertising, which tended to determine the choices of individuals. Such phenomena, albeit in their own specific form, resembled the processes of modernization carried out in democratic systems and announced the great changes in the relationship of public to private that occurred after the Second World War in the Western world and in Italy as well.

What happened to the individual woman in the course of such processes of standardization is the subject of a novel which represented a particular case in Italy of the time, *Nascita e morte della massaia* (Birth and Death of the Housewife) by Paola Masino. It was written in 1938–39, but the proofs were rejected by the fascist censors who judged it "defeatist and cynical." It is the story of a woman in conflict with her mother during childhood and adolescence. The daughter, "dusty and drowsy," is absorbed in a search of knowledge: "everything has a reason and I must find uncover it." The little Housewife is so hampered and vilified by her mother that she shuts herself up for years in a trunk. Finally, she gives in and agrees to "try a normal life" in order to please her mother, rather than continue searching for "her truth." The mother delights in anticipation of her child's new life: "I will make you a nice dress, I'll take you to the hairdresser's, they'll give you a wash and tint." The Housewife marries and becomes what is asked of her, occupying herself obsessively with her house and her political and social duties, to the point of obtaining the "diploma of citizen of merit" and being proclaimed a National Example. The narrator uses a grotesque and sometimes surreal tone which accents the irony toward the social reality. The uneasiness of the Housewife and her revolt, including the hyperbole with which she confronts all of this, is always apparent. Suffice it to mention a single example, the Housewife's new obsession with hygiene (she who once was "unkempt" and eschewed cleanliness). From a scene which sounds like an advertisement, where the Housewife is shown "gliding gently on floors shining like mirrors . . . with her beautiful white skirts blowing about her like sails," the reader passes to the description of her attempts to run her fingertips along the floor to see if any traces of dust remain, until, following a careful examination, she "could not restrain herself from going down on her knees and two or three times licking the floor. Her tongue slid back and forth along the flat polished marble and a pungent feeling, almost of must, rose from the joins of the tiles; an icy fermenting, a vaporization of mineral death, a teeming of stellar germs, the sign of embalmed universes. The tip of her tongue, having become ice, stuck to the floor, but she remained there, with her face to the ground, smelling and breathing the stone's breath."[28]

Among the changes which took place in the relation between the public and the private spheres we may include the manifestations of mass culture itself. In the 1930s the radio public in Italy increased enormously, from 27,000 listeners in 1926 to 800,000 in 1937. At the same time publications designed for the masses also spread, and not merely the periodicals of the fascist organizations, whose circulation reached hundreds of thousands. During the period 1930–1938, five of the most important women's magazines came into being and continued after the war (*Rakam, Annabella, Eva, Gioia,* and *Grazia*); some still exist today. These magazines display both the reactionary and progressive elements of the fascist propaganda toward women. Compared to the 1920s, there is an intensification and expansion of the advertising space, including propaganda for products of self-sufficiency. The women's magazines do not try to maintain class divisions; the publications destined for the lowest social levels use a simple and accessible vocabulary, for it must be remembered that in the period between the two world wars the majority of Italian women was semiliterate.[29] In 1921, 30.4 percent of women were illiterate compared to 24.4 percent of the men.[30] All the magazines had columns on love, domestic chores, family, religion, cooking, horoscopes, and dreams. Some, such as *Cinema Illustrazione,* included the indiscretions in Cinecittà (the Italian Hollywood). Besides the stars, some magazines—*Eva,* for instance—featured members of the Royal House and Mussolini and his family. The narratives told of heroic mothers who did not weep when their sons were killed in the war, having urged them firmly to defend their country. There were stories about dressmakers, sales clerks, and sportswomen engaged in fascist contests, sometimes in active heroic roles, as for instance in novels about the new Italian colonialism. In any case, women were depicted in more active roles, though in ambiguous ways, in comparison with the traditional silent sacrifice.

In Italy, as in France, the Second World War interrupted processes that resumed in the period after the war. The continuation of these processes was especially evident at the intersection of cultural models and consumption. It was in the 1950s that the Italian model of mass consumption came into full realization, with the growing number of users of goods such as televisions, electric appliances, and automobiles. Women exercised a leadership role in this field of new consumption, which included cosmetics, hygiene, clothing, and products for the home. The sociologist Alberoni, in a famous study of consumption, quoted young southern Italian women's preference for nightgowns in the new synthetic materials over those of the traditional trousseau, and explained it as follows:

> What meaning did the new nightgowns that she had seen in the movies have for the young woman? Accepting or even only understanding them implies rebellion. The trousseau in a stable society is fixed and immutable . . . with its white color and the austerity of its articles of intimate clothing, it is the expression of austere duties and the communal values connected with matrimony.
>
> To buy such a [new] nightgown and to prefer it to others is a rebellion; it is to abruptly rob the trousseau of its patrimonial value and thus to alter the institutional form of the dowry . . . in feminine consumption it is an expression of equality of value vis-à-vis men.
>
> More than men, women feel the need to be citizens under a new law in a new society.[31]

It is debatable to attribute to consumer goods such a disruptive power in a modern world community, a power capable of breaking local and traditional values. Today, thirty years later, one might mitigate the euphoric tone of the analysis by observing the limits of such emancipation. Nonetheless, the overall argument still holds, testifying to the importance of considering the historical and geographic context of cultural changes in order to evaluate them properly.

Apocalypse/Integration

Among scholars of mass culture there is an unspoken division between "the apocalyptics and the integrated," as Umberto Eco called them in 1964, explaining that his definition did not suggest aporia but combined two complementary terms, applicable to the critics themselves and above all to mass culture.[32] Even the apocalyptics, who consider mass culture to be a catastrophe for cultural values, foresee on its horizon a community of supermen. But that is already implicit in the object examined. It has always been characteristic of mass culture, according to Eco, to dangle in front of consumers, from whom a judicious mediocrity is requested, the dream of the superman who might someday arise within each of us, given the existing conditions and indeed thanks to them.

The most valuable aspect of this analysis is that it confirms the ambiguity of cultural products, which occasionally feed great hopes of innovation but ultimately produce responses patterned on the existing order. This duplicity is based on the historical conditions in which the lower classes have obtained access to participation in public life. They become protagonists but without the power to decide in what ways to amuse themselves, how to think, what to imagine, all of which are suggested instead by the mass media. This conclusion applies, even more acutely, to the history of women.

To illustrate the point I have chosen a specific domain as an example, that of the women's press, both because it is one of the most documented, particularly for the countries considered thus far, and because it has a long and very significant history for women. Indeed, it must be remembered that from the seventeenth century on, women in Europe were admitted to the cultural public sphere in the areas of literature (the novel) and spectacle (the theater), but not into the public sphere of politics. The feminine press thus has a historical and theoretical importance of longer duration than other areas, such as the cinema. However, before embarking on a discussion of the women's mass press, it is useful to situate it briefly in a larger context and to emphasize that this phenomenon concerns the European and North American civilizations. On the world level, the data on illiteracy for women during the period under consideration are shocking: about 40 percent in 1970, against 28 percent for men; rising to 83 percent in Africa (against 63 percent for men); 57 percent in Asia (37 percent for men); and 85 percent in the Arab states (60 percent for men). For all these women, who constitute more than a third of the women of the world, the press has very little importance. Fewer than a fourth follow television. The largest female public worldwide listens to the radio, but there is little documentation on this audience, compared to the press readership.

It is useful, when focusing on the concepts of "female masses" and "mass," to point out that these ideas have a potential value; moreover, they do not refer, in current usage, only to quantitative aspects but also to qualitative ones. The products of mass culture are not individual works of intellectuals but a stream directed toward a social mass, that is, a conglomerate without apparent distinction by class or geographical area. Next to the classical cultures rooted in a particular people, the new cultural form seems to rise from the mass media in a way that is relatively independent of local origins.[33]

Women's magazines date from the seventeenth century (the *Lady Mercury* appeared in England in 1693), but the characteristics of mass culture appear at the end of the nineteenth century. They are clearly expressed for the first time in 1886, when Laura Jean Libbey suggested for an American magazine "love stories for the young, pure and intelligent . . . stories for the masses."[34] Women's press expanded during the interwar period, but it really came into its own after the Second World War, when it became a gigantic business, counting tens of millions of readers.[35] This very diffusion soon alarmed the "apocalyptics," disturbed by the typical combination of archaic and large-scale which the critics of "massification" of the 1930s, from Ortega y Gasset to Horkheimer, had already noted.[36]

When in 1959, Gabriella Parca published *Le italiane si confessano* (Italian Women Confess),[37] an anthology of 8,000 letters to the editor of the advice column received in the three previous years by two weekly soap-opera type of comics, the Vatican daily *L'Osservatore Romano* expressed great concern that so many women seemed to have preferred writing to women's magazines over going to confession. The book reveals the Italian women's doubts, fears, obsessions, dissatisfactions, and, at the same time, their resistance to change. The letters are not a faithful mirror of social custom—if there ever were such a thing—but disclose a specific realm of the imagination, which is the world of the comics. The language of the letters was similar to that genre and served principally to express one of the national characteristics in its feminine form, namely the obsession with sex, formulated in ignorance of one's own body more often than of any contact with another body. The whole demonstrated the commingling of the old and new in which Italian women struggled, laboriously but energetically. The third edition of the book appeared in 1966, with a preface by Pier Paolo Pasolini, on whom it was not lost that every letter contained the germ of an idea "for a story or a film," that is, for the world which provided the language for the women's confessions. But he also allowed himself to be carried away by a misogynist viewpoint of apocalyptic cast, mistaking the changes made by the editors of the magazines as evidence of a linguistic leveling produced by mass culture, and interpreting it simply as a "superficial encrustation of modernity" underneath which "one finds immediately inferior levels of civilization," where the "feminine tendency toward conservatism" holds sway.

The attitudes toward women's magazines, especially those with wide circulation, reflect the uneasiness of progressive men and women scholars who approach the subject analytically, but in recent decades these attitudes have evolved. At the beginning of the 1960s contempt for these forms of mass culture gave way to regarding them with interest. There remained, nevertheless, the signs of a very critical attitude. Even Evelyne Sullerot, who is very attentive to the positive aspects of the feminine press, spoke of a "uniform inanity and mediocrity,"[38] while at the same time recognizing the responsibility of the intellectuals, their snobbishness, and fear of the extent of this medium. Sullerot admitted that the feminine public was the most conservative of all, but she noted that women read a lot and, with respect to working classes, more than men. The moral stance of the established order, which the mass press respects (with only slight deviations), seemed to be the only one that provided some security for women.

Ten years later, the "apocalyptic" Anne-Marie Dardigna criticized Sullerot's approach for its excessive "integration" and offered a harsh critique of the mystifications produced by the women's press.[39] In it, the ideal woman appears as passive, available, corrupted, and intent on manipulating men, considered only as husbands. The publications make clear class distinctions, according to Dardigna. To women of modest social status the magazines offer an uncompromising normative ideology; to the more affluent women, a continual, vicarious interaction with the real revolts of women, a position which cleverly redeems these readers. The women's press constantly suggests that the liberation of women is marching forward, indeed is almost complete. The heavy influence of the feminine press is, in this analysis, of inestimable value to the established order, since it contributes to maintaining a perspective in which the *word* is divorced from reality. A formulation of female "misery" and of the radical revolt which it could generate never seems to be a real possibility.

The apocalyptic tones which echo the voices of 1968 and the feminism of the early 1970s are not to be totally rejected. Their principal weakness is their absence of historical perspective, but some aspects of their criticism will be found in subsequent studies on women. In the mid-1970s in Italy, a historical approach was combined with a critique of the patriarchal order. As Sullerot had already begun to do, others brought economic interests to light. The feminine press was the most flourishing and solid branch of Italy's mass culture, to the extent that in many magazines advertising exceeded 50 percent of the total contents (from 1953 to 1963, the number of pages dedicated to advertising doubled, and in some cases tripled). Advertising in women's publications cost almost one and a half times more than in those for a mixed audience.[40] In reality, the readership of the feminine press is also mixed, calculated at 20 million readers, 30 percent of whom are men. This entire enormous market segment is controlled by an oligarchy: four editorial groups own more than three-quarters of the magazines.[41] The success of these publications has also given rise to an increased awareness of the role of women in cultural production and to an emphasis on the importance of the process by which more women participate in the information sector and become more openly supportive of one another.[42]

The most intriguing is one of the most popular forms of Italy's postwar mass-culture production: it is the photo-novel (or soap opera comic), a phenomenon of great importance but also an example of obstinate ideological persistence. The genre was a hybrid innovation, a combination of the techniques of the movies and of photography with that of the comics, grafted onto the tradition of the serial novel. It was widespread in the Romance-languages (including South America) feminine publications, but it appeared in Italy in 1946, first in drawings *(Grand Hôtel)* and then in 1947 with photographs *(Bolero film* and *Sogno)*. It seems that at the beginning of its history, the photo-novel was read communally (as early television was watched). In the more isolated communities, on Sundays, someone would read the lines of the characters aloud, while those who could not read or read little (for instance the old women) followed the story looking at the pictures.[43] Later, reading alone predominated and the public became feminized, though never completely so. From 1946 to the end of the 1970s at least ten thousand photo-novels were produced in Italy, and they were especially popular among the young. The titles included abridgments of great novels such as *The Betrothed* and *Tess of the d'Urbervilles*. Given the characteristics of the medium and of its use—to help the readers escape from reality—there was little advertising. The favorite themes included the secret unhappiness of famous people, the sentimental vicissitudes of maternity and childhood, and the glowing destinies of ordinary people.[44]

Following the "apocalyptic" denigration of such publications, critics began to recognize that they corresponded to "a deep need" and exercised "a function in the psychic economy," as an interlude of play.[45] Or else they were considered not merely as tools of ephemeral escapism but as means of refining sensitivity.[46] This change occurred in the context of a changed historical and political perspective in which some important women's magazines (such as *Grand Hôtel, Cosmopolitan, Amica,* and *Annabella*) came out in favor of divorce at the time of the referendum to revoke divorce, which was defeated in 1974 by 59 percent of the vote. Some commentators attributed such choices to market considerations, so that the problematic connection was acknowledged anew, between the market and consumers on the one hand and emancipation on the other.

The most interesting attempts to reconcile the apocalyptic criticism and the historical perspective of integration have occurred in the last ten years, in particular the research on the mass production of fantasies for women in the United States. A historical line has been traced linking the mass production of romantic novels (such as the Harlequin series, begun in 1958 in Toronto and reaching sales of a hundred million copies in 1977) with the sentimental novel of the eighteenth and nineteenth centuries, from Richardson's *Pamela* to the works of Jane Austen and the Brontë sisters.[47] There have been explorations of the psychological mechanisms which explain the predilection of many women for such literature. Tania Modelski has proposed a mechanism of reversal: thus, for example, the desire to be taken by force is only the overt content, masking anxiety about rape and the desire for power and vengeance, which is the latent content. She proposes interpretations which make use of the feminist experience. In this light, the "disappearing act" which women put in effect when they read escape literature suggests in reality a desire to be seen in a new way. Janice Radway has insisted on the importance, on the part of the critic, of not relegating the readers to passivity and impotence. She recognizes the duplicity of attitudes in which a temporary refusal of the social role of self-denial is also the compensation, in making a space for oneself, for not contesting that role in real life. She emphasizes, however, that in the last analysis, the texts are chosen, purchased, constructed, and used by people who put in these actions their needs, desires, and interpretative strategies. The community of women readers and authors thereby established must nevertheless undergo the mediation of the capitalistic structure, which exploits the distances between them and between their desire for change and for acceptance.[48]

The direction in which these analyses of the feminine press are heading, despite the differences between them, can also be extended to other sectors of mass culture. Modelski has applied her method to soap operas, concluding that their fantasy of a large extended family does not contradict the feminist discourse, which could indeed take up the fantasy and restate it as a desire for community which defies traditional values while seeming to reaffirm them. An unprejudiced look at mass culture can even provide some pleasant surprises, as happened to Milly Buonanno when she analyzed Italian television programs at the beginning of the 1980s. Her investigation showed that Italian information or cultural programs devalued and distorted the female figures, in contrast to their treatment of the males; these findings paralleled the conclusions of similar research on American television. But in programs of fiction, it appeared, to the amazement of the researcher, that the relationship of man/woman is not described as one of domination, and the programs present a range of female identities. Fiction favors the aspects of differentiation in women's lives, proposing different and legitimate ways of being women, giving space to the transformation of old stereotypes and roles.[49]

One observation emerges from the discussion. Never before has such a growing number of possibilities been open to women to become subjects in the fullest sense of the word, either as individuals or in partnership. The process seems long and complex, both for the full realization of the hopes for emancipation and self-discovery in the Northern Hemisphere, and for the inception and growth of processes of liberation of the majority of women of the planet. It is not necessary, but paradoxically it has happened and continues to happen, that such processes of self-affirmation work through the phenomena of mass and uniformity. The irony of history—and it abounds in such ironies—is that these phenomena can also occur in the reverse order.

TRANSLATED FROM THE ITALIAN BY JOAN BOND SAX

12

Women, Images, and Representation

Anne Higonnet

AT THE START OF the twentieth century women
faced new cultural opportunities which they
seemed at last prepared to seize. Allowed into high
art's institutions, catered to by the mass media,
women appeared free to imagine themselves in
their own terms. In the following decades many
women did take control of their visual identities
and pushed them beyond all previous limits. Many
more women participated passively in cultural
forms which at once glorified and undermined
them. But the more fully they represented themselves or were represented by men, the more problematic their images became. In the last decades of
the twentieth century women have begun to confront these contradictions and dilemmas in the
ways they are seen and the ways they see themselves.

A belief in the possibilities of change characterized the years just prior to World War I. Women
used images to make their physical presence and
their demands felt in the public sphere. Unlike the
allegorical figures of the past, the female figure in
a 1914 "Frauen Tag" poster puts her vigor in the
service of her own political cause (fig. 1). A bare-
foot woman of the people, she stands silhouetted

against the endless red banner she holds aloft, a graphic statement scandalous enough for the poster to have been banned in Berlin.

Women began to rediscover and display their bodies. Dancers like Isadora Duncan and Ruth St. Denis rejected the confinement and stylization of the ballet in favor of an unfettered lyricism. Edward Steichen evoked Duncan's choreographic philosophy in a photograph of one of her students (fig. 2). Poised on the Acropolis, she moves in harmony with the elements of rock, wind, and fire.

Paula Modersohn-Becker dared to make self-portraits in the nude. Unlike many male avant-garde artists, who used formal innovations to conceal or justify conventional treatments of female subjects, Modersohn-Becker used the radicalism of an avant-garde stance to disobey gender taboos. In images like *Self-Portrait with Amber Necklace* (fig. 3) she pictured her sensuality as a solid and natural fact, juxtaposing the dense volumes of her figure with foliage and flowers.

Then came World War I, during which military and nationalist preoccupations revived feminine archetypes, but at the same time generated some novel images of women entering the workforce. Posters like *For Every Fighter a Woman Worker* (fig. 4) not only made women's wartime effort the counterpart of men's, they also gave women's employment a dignified and collective image, while others used women's images to symbolize what men fought for. A peasant girl embodies "la douce terre de la France" for which money must be raised (fig. 5). On the other side of the battle lines, a grandly classical woman's head stands for the Austrian nation-state (fig. 6). To remind women of their potential, some posters invoked heroic women from the past: "Joan of Arc Saved France. Women of Britain, Save Your Country. Buy War Savings Certificates" (fig. 7).

Galvanized by world events, many women artists devoted their talents to political purposes in

1. *Come Out for Women's Right to Vote.* Poster for Women's Day, during Germany's "Red Week" of March 8–14, 1914. Berlin, Archiv für Kunst und Geschichte.

345

2. Edward Steichen
(American, 1879–1973),
Wind and Fire. Photograph
of Theresa (Isadora
Duncan's student) on the
Acropolis, 1921. New
York, Museum of Modern
Art.

3. Paula Modersohn-
Becker (German, 1876–
1907), *Self-Portrait with
Amber Necklace,* 1906.
Oil painting. Bremen, Lars
Lohrisch.

4. Ernest Hamlin Baker,
*For Every Fighter a
Woman Worker.* American
World War I recruiting
poster, 1918. Ekstrom
Library, University of
Louisville, Kentucky.

the century's first decades. Especially in Germany and in Russia, the way women practiced the so-called minor arts revised artistic hierarchies. Käthe Köllwitz, for instance, produced images of suffering, poverty, death, and insurrection more universal and more powerful than anyone had thought possible in the print medium (fig. 8). In the wake of the 1917 Revolution, many Russian artists both female and male overtly rejected painting's and sculpture's intellectual pretensions and turned to art forms whose significance could be at once formal, political, and functional. They designed clothes and fabric, household items, posters, magazines, and theater sets (fig. 9). Thus the arts that women had been relegated to in the past and which had marginalized their energies suddenly became vehicles for the most urgent public issues of their time.

5. *So That the Sweet Land of France May Be Fully Restored to Us.* French World War I poster to finance the war debt, 1918. Ekstrom Library, University of Louisville, Kentucky.

6. *Design 8. War Loan.*
Austrian World War I
poster. Ekstrom Library,
University of Louisville,
Kentucky.

7. *Joan of Arc Saved France. Women of Britain, Save Your Country.* British World War I poster offering war savings certificates. Ekstrom Library, University of Louisville, Kentucky.

8. Käthe Köllwitz
(German, 1867–1945),
The Survivors, 1923.
Lithograph for a poster for
the International Workers'
Guild. Washington, D.C.,
National Gallery of Art.

Like the Russian Constructivists, designers in
the West hoped to change people's lives by transforming their environments. Though the goal was
modernization, not revolution, traditionally accepted feminine competence was here too allowed
a new scope. Women continued to cluster in all
areas of clothing, furniture, and textile, graphic,
and interior design, negotiating often brilliant and
innovative careers in fields traditionally conceded
to women. Some of these were for decades almost
forgotten, victims of art-historical categories and
sexist bias. Eileen Gray's career in furniture and
house design did not fit into modernist architec-

МАСТЕРСК. МЕЙЕРХОЛЬДА

ВЕЛИКОДУШНЫЙ

КРОМЕЛИНК

РОГОНОСЕЦ

1922

САЖ

АРШ

CR

УСТАНОВКА И ПОПОВА

9. Liubov Popova
(Russian, 1889–1924),
set design for *The
Magnanimous Cuckold* by
Meyerhold. Gouache on
paper, 1922. Moscow,
Tretiakov Gallery.

tural hagiographies, for instance, while the chairs Charlotte Perriand and Le Corbusier designed together have often been attributed to Corbusier alone. Yet designers—ranging from Sonia Delaunay within the Cubist movement to Coco Chanel in haute couture—equipped women for the machine age (fig. 10). Dynamism, mobility, and efficiency became values women aspired to. Although designers seemed to deal with superficial or symbolic aspects of feminine identity, in myriad small ways they contributed to a simplification of dress and domestic tasks that dramatically altered women's daily lives.

Western designers supplied an expanding consumer economy. Advertisements used images to demonstrate the effects of the commodities they offered, effects not always clearly caused by the product itself, but which were insistently associ-

10. Sonia Delaunay
(Russian-French, 1885–
1979), clothing design
coordinated with a Citroen
5CV chassis, 1925. Paris,
Bibliothèque Nationale.

ated with new feminine ideals. Thus in an advertisement for Kotex sanitary napkins (fig. 11), the text's medical and statistical authority—"used by 85 percent of America's leading hospitals"—sanctions the image of two happy women able to play golf no matter what the circumstances, a visualization of the advertisement's promise: "Perfect freedom every day."

Advertisements urged the purchase of leisure and pleasure. They bound the cosmetic and psychological feminine traits they promoted to a consumer identity. According to advertisements, women were completely dependent on commercial products to accomplish household tasks, attract men, raise children, and win social acceptance. One advertisement for Wexbar silks even endowed its product with creative power: "Silks that transform as does the very breath of life" (fig. 12). By identifying femininity with objects, advertisements encouraged women to identify themselves as ob-

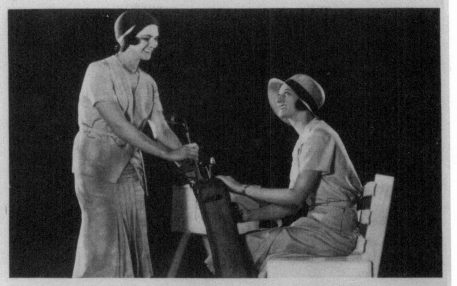

Perfect freedom every day
with this lighter, cooler sanitary protection

Costume from Kaskel & Kaskel Dunlap

Kotex stays light, cool and delicate for hours . . . it deodorizes . . . and has rounded corners for perfect fit—thus giving unique summer comfort.

MODERN living demands so much of us! Freedom and perfect poise . . . every day of every month . . for sports or business or some other interest.

This constant activity would be very difficult, particularly in summer, without the wonderful comfort provided by Kotex. Kotex . . . with its light, cool construction . . . its careful shaping . . . its safe deodorizing . . . its easy disposability . . . has ended forever so many disquieting mental and physical handicaps.

Used in hospitals

Many of the unusual comforts of Kotex are due to its unique filler of Cellucotton (not cotton) absorbent wadding. This material is used by 85% of America's leading hospitals because of its comfort, absorbency and hygienic safety.

Cellucotton absorbs *five times* as much as an equal weight of cotton, or any cotton material. This means your Kotex pad can be five times lighter than ordinary pads, yet have the same absorbency.

And Cellucotton absorbs away from the surface. It is made in sheet layers, laid lengthwise. These layers permit free circulation of air, and they carry moisture quickly away from the surface. Thus the surface is left soft and delicate . . . completely comfortable . . . and so much more hygienic.

Always inconspicuous

Kotex deodorizes . . . so doubly important in summer. And it is never conspicuous. The corners are rounded and tapered to eliminate awkward lines and bulging corners.

You dispose of Kotex just as you would a piece of tissue . . . no laundering, no embarrassment. All drug, dry goods and department stores sell Kotex. Just ask for "a package of Kotex." Kotex Company, Chicago, Ill.

IN HOSPITALS

1   85% of our leading hospitals use the very same absorbent of which Kotex is made.

2   *Kotex is soft* . . . Not a deceptive softness, that soon packs into chafing hardness. But a delicate, fleecy softness that lasts for hours.

3   *Safe, secure* . . . keeps your mind at ease.

4   *Deodorizes* . . . safely, thoroughly, by a special process.

5   *Disposable*, instantly, completely.

Regular Kotex—45c for 12
Kotex Super-Size—65c for 12
Also regular size single in vending cabinets through West Disinfecting Co.

Ask to see the KOTEX BELT and KOTEX SANITARY APRON at any drug, dry goods or department store.

KOTEX
The New Sanitary Pad which deodorizes

11. *Perfect Freedom Every Day.* Advertisement for sanitary napkins from *Ladies Home Journal*, September 1930.

12. *Silks That Transform
as Does the Very Breath of
Life.* Advertisement in
Vanity Fair, August 1920.

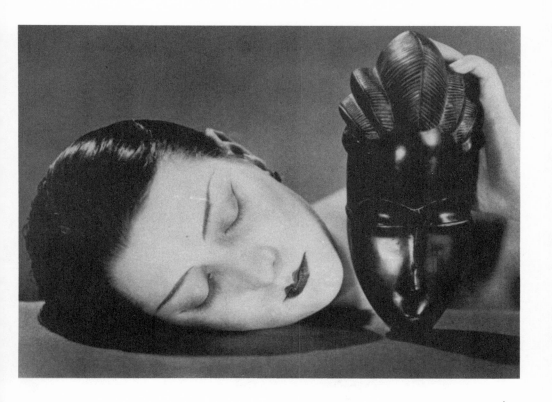

jects. The beauty of the woman adorned in Wexbar silks is the beauty of an inanimate sculpture.

Class, race, and gender factors interacted. High and mass culture worked to establish universal feminine values, but also to differentiate women. Using visual tactics similar to those of the Wexbar silks ad, Man Ray, for instance, reduced all women to equivalent objects of esthetic enjoyment, but also put white women in control over women of color (fig. 13). With her stylized make-up and hair, the white woman is almost as much of a mask as the African sculpture she holds—but not quite; she is the one who holds the African object, a "primitive" art form intended to contrast with the sophistication of European culture. Formalism glossed over white middle-class hegemony as well as masculine desire and commodity fetishism.

13. Man Ray (American, 1890–1977), *Black and White,* 1926. Photograph. Paris, Musée National d'Art Moderne, Centre Pompidou.

14. Hannah Höch
(German, 1899–1978),
*"Indian Dancer" from an
Ethnographic Museum,*
1930. Photomontage. New
York, Museum of Modern
Art.

Alternative representations were difficult to imagine. Because industrial means of reproduction rendered images of modern femininity so prevalent, because high art enjoyed enormous cultural prestige, and because visual definitions of femininity included definitions of beauty and pleasure, no one could wholly escape all gender conventions.

Some women, however, achieved critical distance from their condition by turning its assumptions against each other. Hannah Höch literally cut apart visual stereotypes and reassembled them in savagely witty photomontages. In her series *From an Ethnographic Museum* she dismantled the integrity of Western ethnocentrism and of the art-object as well, combining elements of disparate scale, origin, and status to challenge our perceptions (fig. 14). Like Höch, who turned the Dada anti-art movement to her own purposes, women like Remedios Varo, Dorothea Tanning, and Frida Kahlo found a place for themselves within the Surrealist movement. Surrealism gave women license to reject the way things were or seemed to be and picture other realities to express their own experiences or fantasies. Meret Oppenheim in her *Breakfast in Fur* confounded expectations with her fur cup, saucer, and spoon (fig. 15). Like many

15. Meret Oppenheim (American, 1913–1985), *Breakfast in Fur*, 1936. Fur-covered cup, saucer, and spoon. New York, Museum of Modern Art.

other Surrealist works by women, *Breakfast in Fur* rethinks what might have been seductive or familiar to render it perhaps repellent and certainly ambiguous.

Women artists' relationships with men artists continued to influence their self-conception and artistic production, yet career patterns were evolving. Women still sometimes needed to be valued as artists and as people by successful men, but they passed through men's orbits on the way to their own destinations. Tina Modotti provides the paradigmatic example. She made her first appearance in art as a movie actress, then became the photographer Edward Weston's model and companion. His images treat her as an abstractly sensual form (fig. 16). Once he had trained her as a photographer, she turned the camera on him and made him her model (fig. 17); she pictured him alongside his instrument, his gaze and its lens directed outward together. When she went on to create her own work, she too often depicted women, but as active subjects rather than as passive objects; her photograph of a mother and child concentrates on the mother's powerful arm grasping and supporting a child whose sturdy physical presence as well as the mother's swelling abdomen attest unsentimentally to her fertility (fig. 18). Similarly, the painters Georgia O'Keeffe, Lee Krasner, and Helen Frankenthaler all went beyond relationships with famous male artists to build entirely separate careers.

As women became the ones to make images as well as pose for them, they introduced their attitudes to traditional themes. When Frida Kahlo or Dorothea Lange, for instance, depicted suffering, they chose to represent women not as pathetic victims but as stoics enduring the deep traces pain or care had inflicted on their spirits and bodies (figs. 19, 20). While the high arts favored an exploration of women's imagination, documentary photography, whether commissioned by governments or by the new breed of photo-magazines,

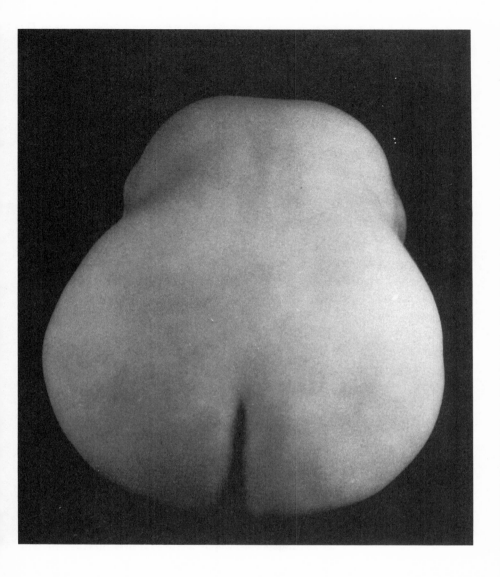

encouraged both women and men to confront and publicize hidden aspects of women's material lives. Poverty, age, infirmity, racial and ethnic diversity were very gradually being recognized and visualized.

World War II replayed many of the First World War's pictorial themes. Again traditional arche-

16. Edward Weston (American, 1886–1958), *Nude,* 1926. Photograph of Tina Modotti. Tucson, Center for Creative Photography.

17. Tina Modotti (Italian, 1886–1956), *Edward Weston with Graflex,* c. 1924–26. Photograph. Trieste, Comitato Tina Modotti.

18. Tina Modotti, *Mother and Child,* n.d. Photograph. Trieste, Comitato Tina Modotti.

types were revived for propaganda purposes. Norman Rockwell expressed "Freedom from Want" for an American government poster in the form of a family gathered around a Thanksgiving meal served by a plump and kindly grandmother (fig. 21). Once more, images of women embodying the values of home and nation for which the war was being fought coexisted with images of women newly engaged in the industrial workforce. One poster could show a bereft woman with two small children, appealing: "I Gave a Man!" (fig. 22), while another urged women to "Fight for Freedom" and included pictures of them wielding tools and repairing aeroplanes (fig. 23).

The economic and cultural pressures of the war as well as the postwar recovery reshaped femininity in several different ways. The Soviet Union advocated one extreme model, built around civic duty, productivity, collective responsibility, and public visibility. Kalashnikov and Korchunov's *Celebration of Strength and Courage* depicts this model as a photomontage of women's participation in a state-sponsored event, staging anonymous women as vigorous participants in outdoor group

362

19. Frida Kahlo (Mexican, 1910–1954), *La columna rota,* 1944. Oil painting on masonite. Mexico City, Instituto Nacional de Bellas Artes.

20. Dorothea Lange
(American, 1895–1965),
*Woman of the High Plains,
Texas Panhandle,* 1938.
Photograph made for the
U.S. Works Progress
Administration.
Washington, D.C., Library
of Congress.

21. Norman Rockwell
(American, 1894–1978),
Freedom from Want,
1943. One of "The Four
Freedoms" posters
commissioned by the U.S.
government during World
War II. Stockbridge
(Mass.), Norman Rockwell
Museum.

22. *I Gave a Man!*
American World War II
poster urging the purchase
of war bonds. Ekstrom
Library, University of
Louisville, Kentucky.

23. *Women of the Allies—
Fight for Freedom.* British
World War II recruiting
poster. Ekstrom Library,
University of Louisville,
Kentucky.

ПРАЗДНИК СИЛЫ И МУЖЕСТВА

exercises and pageants (fig. 24). At the opposite pole was the American model: domestic, maternal, individualistic, and consumerist. Advertisements promoted this feminine image skillfully. A message from General Electric, for example, sets a mother and her daughter in their home and attributes their happiness to a product for sale: "She's confident with flameless electric clothes drying" (fig. 25). The woman is pictured doing the family laundry while her invisible husband provides the family with money and goods, like the man addressed in the handwritten appeal.

The twentieth century added cinema to visual culture. Immensely popular, the cinema has played a powerful role in mass culture's definition of gender. Classic cinema represents women as visually pleasing objects of a masculine gaze. Actresses like Marilyn Monroe have become icons of sexuality,

24. M. Kalashnikov and S. Korchunov, *Celebration of Strength and Courage,* 1935. Photomontage from *Projektor* 7 (1935).

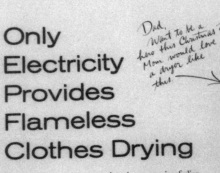

Only Electricity Provides Flameless Clothes Drying

Dad,
Want to be a
hero this Christmas?
Mom would love
a dryer like
this!

One thing most women seem to have in common is a feeling of *confidence* in the ability of flameless electric clothes dryers to handle even the most delicate fabrics safely. They know how clean and modern flameless electric clothes drying is. And may we remind you that no fumes cling to clothing dried with electricity. We truly believe that once you install a flameless electric clothes dryer in your home you'll feel both proud and practical. So see your electric appliance dealer today.

YOU LIVE BETTER ELECTRICALLY

25. *She's Confident with GE.* Advertisement for an electric clothes dryer from *Life,* November 14, 1960.

static images whose fascination resides in the fantasies projected on them (fig. 26). They function as ciphers which men use to act out the scenarios of their search for identity and satisfaction. Films like *Gone with the Wind* (fig. 27) have fixed our understanding of sexuality as an all-absorbing romantic heterosexual adventure organized according to the linear logic of the suspenseful narrative. Hollywood's "happy endings" deliver women where they belong in a patriarchal order: to the hero, to a nobly self-sacrificial death, or, if they deviate from feminine norms, to an appropriate punishment.

From the 1920s to the 1960s, but especially in the 1930s and 1940s, Hollywood produced a type of film designed for female audiences and called a "woman's film." These films, among them comedies like *Adam's Rib* (1949), medical dramas like

26. Philippe Halsman
(American, 1906–1979),
Marilyn Monroe, 1962.
Photograph. Cover picture,
Life, April 1962.

'GONE WITH THE WIND.' a David O. Selznick Technicolor Production released by Metro-Goldwyn-Mayer.   Made in U.S.A.

27. *Gone with the Wind.*
Publicity still from the
movie with Vivien Leigh as
Scarlett O'Hara and Clark
Gable as Rhett Butler,
Metro-Goldwyn-Mayer,
1939. New York, Museum
of Modern Art.

372

Dark Victory (1939), gothic stories like *Rebecca* (1940), romances like *Letter from an Unknown Woman* (1948, fig. 28) and maternal melodramas like *Stella Dallas* (1925 and 1937), all revolve around a female protagonist and deal with issues and emotions considered feminine. Yet although these films cast women as heroines and voice women's concerns, again and again they render their subjects passive or pathetic and seek to elicit the female spectator's empathetic suffering.

More than any other kind of cinema, the woman's film raises the problem of the female spectator. Did she identify with what she saw because it addressed her experience, whether imaginary or actual, or because she had to internalize the role society assigned to her? The woman's film suggests

28. *Letter from an Unknown Woman.* Publicity still from the movie directed by Max Ophuls, with Joan Fontaine as Lisa and Louis Jourdan as Stefan, 1948. New York, Museum of Modern Art.

the two possibilities cannot be separated. Women's fascination with cinematic representations of themselves oscillated between submission to disciplinary ideological frameworks and the pleasures of momentary power, fulfillment, and difference. The tension maintained between self-denial and self-affirmation in the woman's film reveals the contradictions women have had to live with and even embrace.

Television's daytime "soap operas" inherited some of the woman's film's strategies and functions. In 1976 it was estimated that 20 million people watched daytime television in the United States, four out of five of them women, and that the favorite shows among women viewers between the ages of eighteen and fifty were soap operas.[1] Shows like *As the World Turns, Days of Our Lives,* and *The Guiding Light* acquired their nickname from the household product companies that invest heavily in them and use 25 percent of their program time to advertise items like soap.[2] Endless sagas of romance, emotional upheaval, and family tribulation, soap operas at once deal with the kinds of domestic and neighborhood situations many women live with, and provide fantasy outlets by aggrandizing those situations into melodrama. Broadcast in short segments during weekdays, they integrate themselves into the housewife's daily schedules and mirror the rhythm of women's years, repetitious but punctuated by personal crises.

Cinema and television appeal to female viewers not only in their original moving forms but also in posters and especially magazines. Founded in 1917, *Photoplay* set the pattern for the "fan" magazine, which offers women the illusion of intimacy with "stars," usually entertainment celebrities but also glamorous political celebrities like England's royal princesses. Snapshot-style photography accompanied by journalistic gossip provides readers with a glimpse into the private lives of the rich and famous. Fan magazines thus allow readers to

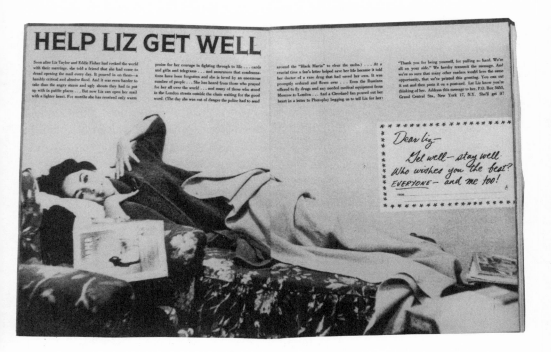

HELP LIZ GET WELL

Soon after Liz Taylor and Eddie Fisher had rocked the world with their marriage, she told a friend that she had come to dread opening the mail every day. It poured in on them—a harshly critical and abusive flood. And it was even harder to take than the angry stares and ugly shouts they had to put up with in public places . . . But now Liz can open her mail with a lighter heart. For months she has received only warm

praise for her courage in fighting through to life . . . cards and gifts and telegrams . . . and assurances that condemnations have been forgotten and she is loved by an enormous number of people . . . She has heard from those who prayed for her all over the world . . . and many of those who stood in the London streets outside the clinic waiting for the good word. (The day she was out of danger the police had to send

around the "Black Maria" to clear the mobs.) . . . At a crucial time a fan's letter helped save her life because it told her doctor of a rare drug that had saved her own. It was promptly ordered and flown over . . . Even the Russians offered to fly drugs and any needed medical equipment from Moscow to London . . . And a Cleveland fan poured out her heart in a letter to Photoplay begging us to tell Liz for her:

"Thank you for being yourself, for pulling so hard. We're all on your side." We hereby transmit the message. And we're so sure that many other readers would love the same opportunity, that we've printed this greeting. You can cut it out and then paste it on a postcard. Let Liz know you're thinking of her. Address this message to her, P.O. Box 3453, Grand Central Sta., New York 17, N.Y. She'll get it!

Dear Liz—
Get well—stay well.
Who wishes you the best?
EVERYONE— and me too!
FROM

feel involved in the extraordinary.

Magazines or shows designed for female audiences consistently address their readers as individuals and solicit their personal participation. "I" or "We" often write to "You" and suggest the possibility of reciprocity. The movie magazine piece "Help Liz Get Well" invites readers to do just that (fig. 29). In a seemingly casual picture the actress Elizabeth Taylor looks right out at the reader, engaging her in eye contact. After describing her personal troubles and dismay at her public's hostility, the piece urges readers to write to "Liz," even supplying the words: "Dear Liz—Get well—stay well." The magazine promises to mediate between reader and star: "We hereby transmit the message."

Women's magazines encourage women to help themselves. Increasingly popular since the 1830s, these publications reach a vast female audience. Five out of six women in postwar England regu-

29. *Help Liz Get Well.*
From *Photoplay* 59, 6
(June 1961).

larly read women's magazines;[3] today in America *Good Housekeeping* alone claims a readership of 24 million.[4] While some of these magazines concentrate more on fashion and others on domestic management or on leisure, they all share the boundaries of traditional femininity. With images and with words they uphold the values of cosmetic enhancement, heterosexuality, and the nuclear family. Within the security of established boundaries, however, the women's magazine preaches achievement and change. Readers are exhorted to improve their appearance, to express their individuality, to manage their households more efficiently, economically, and lovingly, and to triumph over adversity. The women's magazine reader is encouraged to take control of her situation—but not to question the situation itself.

Virtually all magazines and television shows alternate editorial or programming content with advertisements. The proportion of advertising in mass media has been rising. In 1939 the American women's magazine *Ladies Home Journal* devoted 55.6 percent of its pages to editorials and 44.4 percent to advertisements. By 1989 the percentage of advertising pages had risen to 58.2 percent of the total. Ostensibly advertisements serve media by supporting them financially. In effect, however, advertisements constitute an intrinsic component of mass media and purvey much more than information about specific products, including consistent interpretations of gender roles.

Pictures of femininity sell almost anything. By the 1980s cosmetics companies devoted up to 80 percent of their total budgets on advertisements,[5] a sum estimated by one author at $900 million for the United States in 1985 alone.[6] But a compelling association of feminine beauty with commodities is not confined to a female audience or to beauty-related products, where it seems most logical. It pervades advertising imagery of all sorts. Seagram's, for instance, pictures a man confidently holding out his whiskey to the viewer (fig. 30). A

30. *Seagram's V.O. For People Who Do Everything Just Right.* Advertisement for whiskey from *Newsweek,* September 25, 1972.

woman clings to his side. She is rendered transparent so we can see through her to another luxury item, a yacht. The caption tells us that he who drinks the whiskey is among those "people who do everything right."

To be the female model for these images is to be the most glorified item among consumer goods. At once object of adulation and object of commercial exploitation, models both enforce and serve beauty standards. Serene, self-absorbed, unmarked by any emotional or intellectual experience, the professional model sustains Fashion's rule. One trend follows another, each announcing its imperative modernity. As the baby boom generation reached adolescence, a child-like physical ideal gained a currency it has yet to lose. Its most perfect embodiment was the aptly nicknamed Twiggy (fig. 31). Twiggy produced an overnight sensation in 1967 at the age of seventeen with her frail waifish looks, managed and promoted by her boyfriend. For most adult women a body like Twiggy's could only be approximated by means of extreme dietary self-discipline. Yet weight loss has become a modern feminine goal. Glorified as a prelude to all feminine success, a slender body-image haunts women throughout the Western world. "A woman can never," the Duchess of Windsor is supposed to have said, "be too rich or too thin."

Western culture has developed very few ways to represent women positively. Like Twiggy, who appealed esthetically and sexually because she looked so vulnerable, the woman who would exert the power of attraction must deny her agency, strength, or sufficiency. Sexually available, maternal, or pathetic—what other options have been viable? Marginality cannot easily be contradicted. How can women of color, and poor, elderly, or handicapped women be pictured without slipping into negative stereotypes or, even more difficult, without playing into prejudices held by viewers?

31. *Twiggy.* From *Life* 62
(April 14, 1967).

To elicit sympathy rather than disgust or fear, Werner Bishof cast a destitute Indian woman as a mother who begs (fig. 32). His photograph, taken from below, lends her a towering presence, yet she can still be understood through a European sentimentality that neutralizes the impact of her otherness.

Stereotypes perpetuated themselves. Women artists often worked within familiarly feminine territory and received little or no encouragement to explore other subjects or attitudes. Women architects, for example, were directed during their studies to domestic projects and were more likely to receive commissions of this sort, while photo-journalists were usually assigned "human interest" stories that concentrated on portraiture, homes, the family, and emotions. The English photo-journalist Grace Robertson, for example, was assigned the subject of childbirth, and when she represented her subject as the process of a woman's labor and delivery, her employer, the *Picture Post,* censored one image of a woman's face grimacing with pain, alleging that women readers would be alarmed.

It was possible, however, for women to redefine subjects, even if only slightly. In another series, *Mother's Day Off,* Robertson managed to publish pictures of older women represented with exceptional respect. She chose to show their humor, companionship, and warmth. In one photograph (fig. 33) Robertson stages women as the ones who do the looking. Three women talk with each other, while one of them exchanges glances with us; a girl observes them through a clear pane; between these visual registers occupied by the women and the girl, we see backwards and through opaque glass the word "spirits." This evocative juxtaposition of different transparencies and gazes takes us very far from women as simple objects of sight.

The influential photographer Diane Arbus devoted herself throughout her career to both marginal and mainstream members of society. Trans-

32. Werner Bishof (German, 1916–1954), *Famine in India: Woman in Bihar Province,* 1951. Photograph. Magnum Photos.

33. Grace Robertson
(English, b. 1930),
Mother's Day Off, 1954.
From a photo-essay in
Picture Post.

vestites, dwarfs, older women, and Down's
syndrome sufferers (fig. 34) were all invested by
Arbus with a dignity that did not preclude a recognition of their condition. Her close range and
direct frontal point of view, as well as her setting
of her subjects in their own environments, invested
them with a rare confidence and pictorial importance. We may approach their images as conde-
scending voyeurs, but what we find are human
beings like ourselves.

34. Diane Arbus
(American, 1923–1971),
Untitled 5, 1970–71.
Photograph. Paris, Musée
National d'Art Moderne,
Centre Pompidou.

35. Faith Ringgold (American, b. 1930), *Who's Afraid of Aunt Jemima?* Quilt of dyed, painted, and pieced fabrics. New York, Frederick N. Collins Collection. Photo: Bernice Steinbaum Gallery.

Self-representation has eluded all but the privileged few. Now women have begun not only to make images of themselves, but to question the images that have been made of them. Women of color face a compounded problem, for they must deal not only with how they have been pictured as women, but with images that whites have used to demean, ignore, or repress all other races. Yet recent years have witnessed an increasing number of organized and assertive women artists of color, both in England and in the United States. While there have always been artists among women of color, now their work penetrates fine arts establishments and explicitly addresses racial issues. In the United States Faith Ringgold, among others, comments on racial stereotypes in her "Aunt Jemima" (fig. 35), a witty reference to the racially pejorative trademark of a popular food product (which has recently, under pressure, been changed). At the same time, she reinterprets the quilt medium, long one of slave-women's only artistic outlets. Her *Painted Story Quilts* series shows how our ideas about race and value have been shaped by images. Work like Ringgold's reveals how high the political stakes of representation have been all along.

Perhaps the most intractable problem of women's self-representation remains the body. Caught between a desire to praise the body's beauty and a fear of depicting individuals as sexual objects, women artists since the 1970s have sought new ways to treat this subject so laden with cultural connotations. One solution has been to avoid depicting the body directly and associate its energies with the elements. Ana Mendieta created imprints or signs of a female body with fire, earth, and water, orchestrated in fleeting installations she captured photographically (fig. 36).

If artists like the Cuban Mendieta located women outside of culture's definitions, others, like the American Judy Chicago, have revived women's neglected contributions to civilization. Her monumental 1974–1979 work, *The Dinner Party*, hailed the achievements of women in politics, the arts, and religion (fig. 37). *The Dinner Party* raised issues hotly debated among feminists. Should women adopt men's cult of individual heroes? Was it demeaning or courageously subversive that Virginia Woolf, among others, be represented with vaginal imagery? Why did Chicago sign the project

36. Ana Mendieta,
Untitled. Serie Volcán 2,
1979. Color photograph
by the artist. New York,
Carlo Lamagna Gallery.

when dozens of women and men participated in its execution?

Yet another tactic applies erotic imagery traditionally reserved for images of women to the representation of men. But eroticism proves to be asymmetrical; a male nude cannot carry the same art-historical or sexual meanings as the female nude; role reversal reminds us of sexual difference but cannot undo it. The British sculptor Nancy Grossman binds a male figure in leather, zippers, straps, and buckles (fig. 38). He at once repels and fascinates, causing us to recognize how our per-

ceptions of sexuality are linked to signs of power, both exerted and submitted to.

All attempts to renew the representation of the female body have to contend with deeply ingrained visual habits, and with the knowledge that eroticism can devolve into pornography. Perhaps no other pictorial issue angers women so much as the lucrative traffic in pornographic images of women (fig. 39), yet on no other issue is there less consensus about the means of redress or retaliation. The pornography industry as a whole has been estimated to generate sales of more than $7 billion a year in the early 1980s, up from $500 million in the late 1960s.[7] Visual material seems to account for the largest part of these profits. In the United States the Pacific Bell telephone company estimated that "Dial-a-Porn" services brought them $12 million between October 1984 and October 1985,[8] but a leading sexually explicit magazine sold as many as 10,617,482 copies a month in 1984,[9] while the 20 production companies that produce about 100 full-length feature pornographic films a year gross some $500 million a year in box-office receipts. *Deep Throat*, a porn "classic" made in 1972 and starring Linda Lovelace, has been called "the most profitable motion

37. Judy Chicago (American, b. 1939), *The Dinner Party*, 1974–1979. Thirty-nine sculpted ceramic plates placed on embroidered runners along three 46-foot sides of an equilateral table on a ceramic floor, recording 999 women's names. San Francisco, Museum of Modern Art.

387

38. Nancy Grossman
(English, b. 1940), *Male
Figure Sculpture*, 1971.
Leather over wood and
zippers. Jerusalem, Israel
Museum.

39. *Busty Belle.* From *Club* 15, 4 (May 1989).

picture ever made."[10] The Johnson Commission Study conducted between 1968 and 1970 found that more than 90 percent of "adult movie" attendance was male.[11]

Even committed feminists disagree about censorship. Nor do they agree about whether pornography can be attacked at the level of its specific manifestations, or whether it is so intrinsic a part of patriarchal culture that only a fundamental social critique can be effective. At the heart of the pornography debate lies the intractably complex relationship between lived experience and representations. Few people argue that images simply cause violence or women's objectification, yet few would deny that images do spring from, participate in, and perpetuate the unequal identities our culture assigns to women and to men.

Since the 1970s feminist artists, critics, and historians have shifted toward this issue of the social construction of identity. Influenced by Marxism, social history, linguistic philosophy, and psychoanalysis, they have come to question all of art history's most cherished assumptions and categories. They argue that concepts like authorship, originality, and masterpieces are not the foundations of creativity but rather the consequences of the cultural processes by which femininity and masculinity are secured.

The question of how a history of visual culture could be rethought without using traditional conceptual frameworks, as well as the question of what kinds of visual production might evade these frameworks, remain to be settled. Most critics and historians, however, have at least identified two positions they wish to avoid: at one extreme, an essentialist stance that seeks to posit a sensibility or esthetic common to all women regardless of class or race; at the other extreme, a deconstructive strategy so relativist that it forecloses political agency. For feminist critics and historians, and for artists as well, theory and practice must work together toward changes in the ways that permit both understanding history and making sense of the present.

Since the nineteenth century the arts have provided a relatively acceptable way for women to seek or assert social prominence, cultural leadership, economic independence, and civic political power. Women still constitute small minorities among tenured art history professors, registered architects, and exhibited artists; at New York's Museum of Modern Art, only 12 percent of the artists exhibited between 1981 and 1987 were women. Professional women's numbers are increasing, however, and their presence has become more vocal and visible. Women occupied 4.3 percent of American architectural positions in 1975, as against 11.3 percent in 1985.[12]

Some kind of involvement in the arts often structures women's informal sociability. In the United States all museums depend heavily on volunteer labor, a need met almost entirely by women, for whom the museum functions rather like a club. For very rich or socially ambitious women, the arts are a fashionable charity, recipients of their financial generosity but also forums for lavish parties and occasions for personal self-promotion. In 1981 Wilhelmina Holladay founded a National Museum for Women in the Arts, a controversial institution which some argue ghettoizes women's art, and others claim replicates patriarchal definitions of creativity, yet which has elicited the interest and financial commitment of more than 83,000 members across the country. As art made by women becomes more widely exhibited, published, and taught about, the art that women identify with is beginning to be in part their own.

Within an extremely varied and vigorous recent feminist artistic practice emerge a few general tendencies. One is the irreverent appropriation of canonical imagery in order to criticize its meanings or create new meanings for it. Another is the search for new or forgotten media, formats, exhibition spaces, and audiences not recognized or controlled by artistic establishments. Suzanne Lacy's *Travels with Mona* happens to do both (fig. 40). Lacy traveled to artistic pilgrimage spots around the world, painting her version of Leonardo da Vinci's iconic *Mona Lisa*. She assembled photographs of her itinerant performance project, Arlene Raven contributed a text, and this permanent but reproducible part of the project, presented as a parody of fold-out tourist postcard series, has been sold for only a few dollars a copy.

In the Louvre with the Real Thing, and the Real Thing Postcard, altered to erase and unfinish (different from Duchamp's moustache which masculinizes)—a postcard of a work of art in a postcard artwork.

40. Suzanne Lacy (American, b. 1945), *Travels with Mona.* Fold-out postcards. Text by Arlene Raven; photos by D. E. Steward and Sylvie Hencocque.

Just as Lacy simultaneously reworked a high art masterpiece and the popular postcard, many feminist artists cross artistic boundaries and address mainstream issues and markets. Barbara Kruger, for instance, juxtaposes found imagery with verbal interpellation (fig. 41), and her work therefore cannot fit into fine arts classifications; moreover, she collaborates on critical and theoretical publishing projects and also occasionally produces pieces for specific political causes such as women's reproductive rights; nonetheless her production is shown in major museums and is handled by a completely commercial art dealer.

After several centuries of division between the visual and verbal arts, and after several decades of abstract high art, feminist artists have been among the most active proponents of mixed media

and meanings. Performance artists like Lacy communicate with their viewers in various ways over time, often drawing the public into the project. Artists like Kruger who produce autonomous objects use scale and the familiarity of images, but especially words, to provoke close readings rather than detached contemplation.

Artists like Mary Kelly use their work to show how language as well as images produce meanings

41. Barbara Kruger
(American, b. 1945),
I Shop Therefore I Am.
Photograph. New York,
Mary Boone Gallery.

393

42. Mary Kelly (American, b. 1941), *Post-Partum Document. Transitional Objects, Diary and Diagram. Documentation IV*. One of 135 units organized in 6 sections; mixed media, 1973–1979. New York, Mary Kelly.

which structure our identities. In her 1976 *Post-Partum Document* Kelly explores the ancient theme of maternity from the point of view of the mother who must relinquish her physical bond to her child as he enters the adult realm of language (fig. 42). Fetish objects like bits of slate are inscribed with signs or words that chart the process

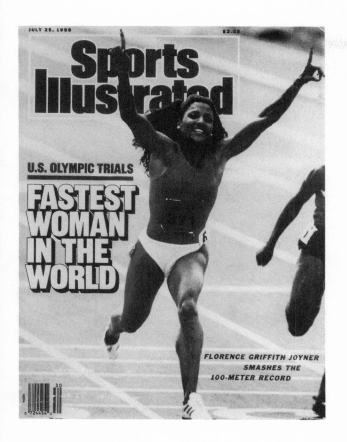

43. *Fastest Woman in the World.* Photograph of Florence Griffith Joyner on the cover of *Sports Illustrated,* July 25, 1988.

of regretful separation. In *Post-Partum Document* an interplay between sensual pleasure and intellectual rigor enables women to feel the emotional pull of a tiny fist's imprint or of the words "I love you, Mummy," and also to understand better what it is about a feminine identity that makes the pull so strong.

For women to create new images of themselves they have had to learn and cultivate new attitudes about themselves, their bodies, and their place in society. Never in history have the images both of and by women changed so radically and so quickly. Experience and representation chase each other onward. Some of the most powerful images of women in recent years move us because they

44. Raissa Page, *Greenham Common Women, January 1983.* Photograph. London, Raissa Page/ Format.

are at once about lived gestures and about the passage of those gestures into the representational realm of our visual imaginations. Florence Griffith Joyner appears on the cover of *Sports Illustrated,* breaking the women's speed record in 1988, her arms raised in exhilarated triumph (fig. 43). Above the missile site they have come to protest, the photographer Raissa Page elevates the Greenham Common women; their hands join them in a ring (fig. 44).

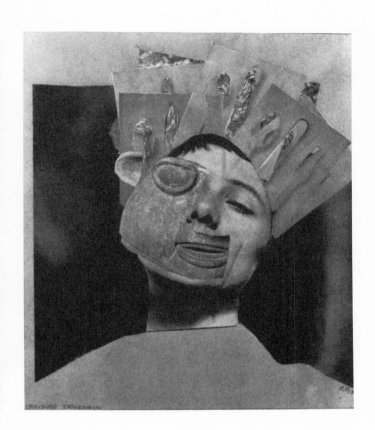

three

The Century's
Great Changes

Continuities and Ruptures

In a letter to Jean-Paul Sartre dated December 18, 1940, Simone de Beauvoir severely criticized the irresponsibility of a philosopher friend who, in "refusing the 'gymnastic exercise' which men perform who do not want to have children, left all the risk to his girlfriend . . . and therefore felt that it was her fault if anything went wrong."[1] Is it true, as Edgar Morin has argued, that the liberation of sexuality (or, to put it more precisely, sexual liberation in its various forms)—which, prior to the advent of AIDS, seemed to have ushered in an era of sex without procreation or societal standards—was the "only truly good news of modern times"?[2]

In this section we have deliberately chosen not to redo the history of motherhood, the family, or private life.[3] We also wished to avoid the well-worn genre known as "the history of everyday life," even though this was a domain in which there were notable developments that made housework easier, increased leisure time, and gave greater freedom of movement for both women and men. (At the same time, places where women once had gathered ceased to exist, while sexual taboos continued to apply to certain public places and means of transport.) Instead, we propose a historical and thematic narrative in which we question two ideas: one, widely accepted, is that access to education and jobs led to greater emancipation for women, while the other, more controversial, is that women found themselves increasingly constrained by the demands of motherhood. The three essays in this section, though very different in tone, all look for continuities and ruptures and seek to achieve an overview of such typical twentieth-century concerns as maternity and welfare, education and jobs.

The first of the three reveals a little-known aspect of early-twentieth-century feminism. This feminism, which is today characterized as "maternalist," flourished prior to World War I. It called for equality of economic and political rights and for social recognition of the value of motherhood, which was said to be equal to or outweigh that of many masculine pursuits. Early feminists were among the promoters of the welfare state, but in Europe the welfare state soon moved toward a family-assistance model that accentuated the value of paternity, whereas in the United States maternity was regarded as a purely individual issue.

The second essay is concerned with the economic, technological, and demographic changes which, over the past thirty years, have undermined the traditional family, thereby encouraging the development of a new pattern of reproduction of the population and its labor power. Characteristic features of this new pattern include the use of birth-control by women, increased medical and social assistance to mothers, and a more intellectualized, socialized approach to the labor of reproduction itself. Women have thus come to enjoy greater freedom to control their biological destinies and marital relations. Along with a concomitant evolution of civil rights (considered in the next section), women have achieved full-fledged recognition as individuals, and this has contributed—more in some countries than in others—to social equality between the sexes.

The third essay is markedly more pessimistic in tone. Despite changes in the economic structure and conjuncture, the author points to enduring inequalities in the areas of jobs and education. With each increase in the number of women in any given discipline, profession, or trade, the male-dominated society comes up with new ways to perpetuate the sexual division of knowledge and labor, which it camouflages as economic or symbolic imperatives. The most recent ploy has been the invention of a so-called need for temporary or part-time employment. Only a minority of women, those with the best educational and social backgrounds, can overcome the rules and thus claim a genuine right to work.

Because this lengthy essay deals with the combined influence of education and employment on the diversification of the labor market, it was impossible to discuss legislation or to treat the important theme of women and the trade unions. Unions themselves may be looked upon as both reflecting and contributing to the sexual division of labor through support for legislation protecting women on the job and through the unions' own gendered conception of the workplace. In France, union women such as Jeannette Laot of the CFDT and Madeleine Colin of the CGT have tried to make working-class organizations heed the pleas of women.[4] Some working women clung to the revolutionary hope that if large numbers of women entered the workplace, everyone's working conditions would improve and society would change for the better. This utopian dream of the 1970s succumbed to reality, but not before important political, material, and symbolic gains had been achieved. Although equality in the workplace has to some degree been recognized in law, it has by no means been achieved in reality and remains one of the fundamental issues in male-female relations today.

F.T.

13

Poverty and Mothers' Rights in the Emerging Welfare States

Gisela Bock

ALTHOUGH THE MODERN welfare states came into being at different times and had different histories, they came to share a considerable degree of similarity after World War II. The reforms which constituted them were manifold, but their central core presupposed state care for a specific category of the underprivileged: people who could not support themselves through paid work because of work accidents, sickness, old age, and unemployment. In the modern welfare state such people were no longer objects of poor-relief, hence subject to discriminatory means-testing or loss of citizenship. They were seen as having a social right to support that was the responsibility of the state, and this social right derived from their political rights as citizens and from their previous contribution to society as wage workers or taxpayers. (When in the 1940s the term "welfare state" was coined in Britain, "welfare" had already been disassociated from alms-giving, charity, or poor-relief.) But until World War I only men were citizens; before as well as after the war social insurance schemes discriminated against women because they were underrepresented on the labor market, and because their wages were lower than men's. Most of the national welfare reforms "focussed on the male laborer, rather than on women and children, the main beneficiaries of previous poor relief."[1] This bias is reflected in the broad scholarship dealing with the rise of the welfare states; it also focuses on reforms that concerned mainly men and male poverty. Women and female poverty appear as an appendix, at best. Likewise, the research concerning the social and political forces and pressure groups that demanded, impeded, influenced, or brought about welfare state reforms (trade unions, religious or secular groups, progressive, left, liberal, or conservative political parties) neglected the earlier ("first wave") women's movements, although they were crucial in the area of welfare reforms that concern mothers and maternity.

Since the late nineteenth century women's struggles for political and social rights, citizenship, and welfare had been closely linked, and the women's movements had focused more sharply than ever on the needs and interests of lower-class women and on female poverty. Many women fought for suffrage and full citizenship not merely for the sake of formal equality with men (in some countries not even all adult men were allowed to vote), but for the sake of shaping social policies in favor of women. Everywhere, middle-class members of the women's movements began to investigate female poverty. At the same time, poor women began to speak out for themselves and about themselves in ways unheard of before, particularly in letters and autobiographies. These documents, which one historian has analyzed as a veritable dialogue between middle- and lower-class women,[2] illustrate the multiple links of female poverty with maternity and the growing awareness and conceptualization of these issues. For example, middle-class women's claims for their right to self-earned income often included the view that employment and maternity could not and should not be combined, at least not in the early stages of motherhood. Most women of the lower classes, however, had to combine domestic work and employment outside the home—not because they wanted to, but out of economic necessity (in the late nineteenth and early twentieth centuries women's proportion of the labor force was consistently much higher in Europe—with the exception of the Netherlands and Spain—than in the United States and in Canada). Female poverty was reinforced by distinctively female life risks: motherhood, particularly in the case of mothers with many children, and the unavailability or temporary or permanent loss of a husband's income.[3] Consequently, when feminist activists focused on maternity, they targeted unmarried mothers, nonemployed and employed working-class wives, female factory workers, widows, and deserted wives. Moreover, feminists addressed motherhood *per se* regardless of women's actual poverty and occupational or marital status, arguing that the specific groups they targeted were extreme versions of a universal female condition: that of being actual or potential mothers and depending on men (with or without a family wage) for their own and their children's survival. This feminist focus on mothers' welfare, which may be described as "feminist maternalism" or "maternal feminism," was based on the assumption that motherhood was not merely a "special problem" or single issue but the unifying condition of the female sex. The approach questioned both female poverty and the male family wage, and it led from the demand for rights of poor mothers to rights for all mothers.

In this context, the women's movements fought for a kind of welfare state and a kind of citizenship that would recognize rights and needs not only of male wage earners but also of mothers, wage-earning or not. They initiated and shaped important welfare legislation, although it never fully realized their high hopes and claims. Sometimes they succeeded without having the vote, as in the case of the Italian *cassa di maternità* of 1910, which was one of the first welfare state measures in Italy; sometimes in the wake of suffrage, as in the case of the Sheppard-Towner Maternity and Infancy Act of 1921 in the United States, which was not only the first national welfare law but also the first goal and political success of newly enfranchised women. In other countries women's struggle for political equality included their demand for paid maternity leave for employed women before and after parturition, and beyond that, a universal and state-sponsored endowment of motherhood, understood as a redistribution of wealth from men to women. Under the pressure of diverse social and political pressure groups (men's as well as women's), this demand was later transformed into the proposition of "child allowances," understood as a redistribution of wealth from the childless to those with children. When such allowances were enacted in democratic countries—in France in the 1930s, in Britain, Norway, and Sweden shortly after World War II—women's pressure succeeded in making them payable directly to the mothers; when they were introduced in the interwar dictatorships, where women (as well as men) lost their political rights, these subsidies were paid to the fathers. Commenting on such reforms in democratic countries, British feminist Vera Brittain stated in 1953 that the "woman question" had been transformed under the welfare state: "In it women have become ends in themselves and not merely means to the ends of men . . . The Welfare State has been both cause and consequence of the second great change, by which women have moved within thirty years from rivalry with men to a new recognition of their unique value as women."[4] In the long struggle for the dignity of motherhood and for the rights and welfare of mothers, the continuity of certain ideas across time and space is just as striking as their transformation.

In the evolution of the welfare states and in the struggles between women's demands and those of other pressure groups, maternity-centered welfare reforms often came to be considered more as paternalist protection than as maternal rights. Claims for the overall, systemic recognition of the economic, social, and political dignity of motherhood were rarely accepted by male political leaders. Instead, they were answered by piecemeal legislation for "special problem groups" and scattered through measures for labor law, health insurance, poor relief, family law, income tax legislation, and so on. Or else the problems were dealt with by reforms that hid mothers' and women's needs behind an apparently gender-neutral legislation that focused on children or families, often also on fathers. The first of the following three sections deals with the issues raised by the women's movements in various countries concerning the relationship between female poverty, maternity, and the state—one aspect of what Katherine Anthony in 1915 called the "dollars for women" movement, alongside that of "votes for women."[5] The second section focuses on the first wave of legislation for mothers' welfare up to World War I, and the third deals with women's voices and the legislation of the interwar, wartime, and immediate post–World War II period.

Women's Movements, Maternalist Feminism, and Mothers' Rights, 1890s–1920s

A crucial issue in the feminist debate was the work related to mothering, which many feminists claimed was not in the realm of nature, but in the realm of labor. In 1904 the German feminist

Käthe Schirmacher, prominent member of the Verband Fortschrittlicher Frauenvereine, sharply attacked the science and practice of economics for its neglect of such work. At a public meeting she declared that women's domestic work was "real," "value-creating," and "productive work," though "it may look like nothing": "there is no more 'productive' work than that of the mother who, all by herself, creates the value of values called a human being." She described at length women's hard work at home and pointed out that the same type of work was remunerated in the marketplace. A woman's work for her husband was the "conditio sine qua non for [his] employment outside the home"; both he and his employer depended on it, and whereas he appears to work for two, "in fact he is merely pocketing for two." She protested against this "exploitation of the housewife and mother" and argued that women did not need, in the name of their emancipation, to accept another exploitation in the guise of a badly paid job, but that society owed them social, political, and economic recognition of their domestic work.[6]

Schirmacher's argument was not an isolated one, though the conclusion she drew from her analysis—that domestic work ought to be valued and even remunerated—was criticized by some members of the Verband as overly "individualistic." Schirmacher had lived in France, where she had encountered similar views in the 1890s and her work had been originally published in French. In that country mothers' work, their poverty, their civic and economic dependency upon the husband, and their even worse situation if there was no husband were pervasive and permanent subjects of feminist concern. At the International Congress for Women's Rights in Paris in 1878 delegates demanded that the municipalities support poor mothers for an eighteen-month period. In 1892 the first women's conference to call itself "feminist" stressed the need for "social protection of all mothers." In 1885 Hubertine Auclert, indefatigable fighter for women's suffrage and apparently the first woman who called herself a "feminist," posed her (extra-legal) candidacy for the parliamentary elections with a program that called for setting up "L'Etat mère" (which would replace the "L'Etat Minotaure," named for the monster that killed and devoured men and women alike), and secure assistance to children. In 1899 she advocated maternity allowances to be financed by a paternal tax levied on men. Some years later she proposed "payments for indispensable service to the state" for mothers and brought this up once more in 1910, when she again presented herself as a candidate for parliament. At the International Feminist Congress of 1896 in Paris, a socialist-feminist, Léonie Rouzade, declared that "motherhood is the principal social function and deserves to be subsidized by the state" and called for a petition to parliament to this avail.[7]

The subject surfaced again at the International Congress on the Conditions and the Rights of Women in 1900. There Maria Pognon intervened in a debate on the unmarried mother's right to initiate a paternity suit to name the father and make him pay for the child—the *recherche de la paternité* which had been prohibited by the Napoleonic Civil Code of 1804—arguing that a father who did not wish to support his child should not be forced to do so. Instead, a state-sponsored fund for child-support should be created, accessible to all women, married or not, which would render them independent from the fathers of their children. The conference resolved that a *caisse publique de la maternité* should be created in all civilized countries. Blanche Edwards-Pilliet reported on the double workload of female factory workers inside and outside the home; society should fully subsidize their needs because of their "enormous effort of maternity." It was resolved that women with jobs should have the right to a paid maternity leave. This issue and, more generally, the recognition of motherhood as a social service continued to be on the agenda of the Conseil National des Femmes Françaises, founded in 1901, and of the Union Française pour le Suffrage des Femmes, founded in 1909. Marguerite Durand, founder and editor of the feminist daily *La Fronde,* advocated payment for housework and maternity insurance along with equal pay for equal work. The more radical Nelly Roussel, who publicly defended contraception and in 1904 proclaimed a "strike of the womb," denounced the pain of childbirth and stressed that "of all the social functions the premier, the most magnificent, the most arduous, and the most necessary, is the only one that has never received a wage." Roussel demanded its recognition as true labor and argued for the right to maternity, compensated by "a fair wage for the noble work of motherhood." A "salaire de la maternité" would allow women who desired to do so to dedicate themselves to their children.[8]

Similar ideas and proposals emerged in all Western women's movements around the turn of the century, but the French versions seem to have come to the fore earliest and in the most pronounced and diversified ways. In all countries such proposals were advocated by radical, moderate, and socialist women alike, though not by all such women; many of them knew each other personally. In Norway one of the best-known radical advocates was Katti Anker Møller, propagandist for women's "birth-strike" and voluntary motherhood; her active involvement in politics started in 1900 when she claimed state assistance for unmarried mothers. Soon she extended this claim to include all mothers, and by 1918 she theorized that maternity should be recognized as work, be awarded a wage, and become the best-paid of all women's work. The Swedish feminist Ellen Key was less influential in her home country than on an international level; she considered motherhood as women's most noble vocation, to be supported by payment through the state.[9] In Italy the revaluation of motherhood as women's major contribution to society and to the recently unified Italian nation was a crucial topic within the women's movement, and from the 1890s many feminist groups—mostly of socialist-feminist leanings—struggled for the creation of a *cassa di maternità,* a maternity insurance for female factory workers, to be financed by contributions from men and women workers alike, or by contributions from worker parents (for their daughters), from the employers, or from the state. The first such project was launched in 1894 by Paolina Schiff on behalf of the Milan-based Lega per la Tutela degli Interessi Femminili, and subsequently the demand for a national maternity fund was taken up by the Unione Femminile Nazionale. At the latter group's first National Congress of Women's Practical Activities in 1908, Nina Sierra and Bianca Arbib proposed an insurance that would enable women, particularly working-class women, to devote themselves to their families during the years of "active motherhood" while being paid for it.[10]

In Germany too the obligatory insurance model for maternity endowment was intensely discussed. Here the issue was not so much maternity leave as such, since a law of 1878 (one year after the first such European law, enacted in Switzerland) had already introduced a mandatory leave for factory workers of three weeks after parturition. The Bismarckian health insurance act of 1883 included very modest maternity benefits for self-insured workers (a similar provision followed in Austria in 1888). Women then demanded the prolongation of this leave, its extension to other categories of workers, and most of all a mandatory benefit that amounted to the full wage or more. Some feminists argued for a separate maternity insurance instead of one that lumped pregnancy and maternity together with sickness. In 1897 and 1901 Lily Braun, a feminist and socialist, was the first publicly to advocate an independent maternity insurance; she conceived it as a means for liberating mothers from poverty and, temporarily at least, from employment. The scheme would be financed out of taxes and cover four weeks before and eight weeks after parturition. Like other German feminists, she based her claim on the notion that "Mutterschaft ist eine soziale Funktion."[11] Her proposal was a compromise between her utopian ideal—a motherhood endowment for one and a half years—and the need for job security. Subsequently, many radical, moderate, and socialist women called for maternity insurance, for example the Jewish feminists Alice Salomon and Henriette Fürth. The German Jewish feminist movement, the Jüdischer Frauenbund, placed the dignity and revaluation of motherhood at the center of its theories and activities. In 1905 the Allgemeine Deutsche Frauenverein stated in its program that "women's work" in the family "shall be valued, both economically and legally, as a fully valid cultural contribution"; but President Helene Lange explained that it was "premature" to measure its value in precise figures because such an approach was "not yet a part of the general moral consciousness." In Germany few feminists went as far as claiming state endowment for all mothers. Anita Augspurg was one of them, and in 1902 Helene Stöcker (co-founder of the Bund für Mutterschutz in 1904) was fascinated by the idea of "financial independence" for housewives and mothers. In 1909 Schirmacher protested against the gap between women's and men's earnings; the difference, rationalized by men's breadwinner role, amounted to a "sex bonus" or "family allowance" which was really due to the wives and ought to be paid to them directly. She particularly criticized the fact that the "sex bonus" was also paid to the unmarried man: "*His* pay incorporates the earnings of the legitimate wife, and *his* wages are increased in order that he can buy an *illegitimate* wife [meaning prostitution in the case of unmarried men]: the 'family allowance' is based on a twofold robbery of women."[12]

In Britain, Alys Russell demanded "payment of motherhood" as early as 1896, when she questioned August Bebel's assumption that only socialism would emancipate women. She criticized him for taking account of women more as industrial workers than as child-bearers and for relegating the "woman question" to the place of a mere appendix to the labor question; in her view higher wages, recognition of the social importance of motherhood, and equal laws for men and women were entirely possible "in an individualistic state of society."[13] At the same time, a mothers' movement developed, and some years later the issue was discussed more widely. Among the first groups to do so in Britain was the Women's Labour League (the women of the Labour Party), which in 1907 demanded monetary assistance for needy mothers "to enable them to attend to the children without having to work for wages"; in 1909 its members discussed the idea of a state-sponsored "endowment of motherhood"—this term had been coined shortly before then—whether the support should be just for childbirth or a permanent income for mothers, and whether it might lower the average wage for men since they would no longer have to support wives and children. Other women's organizations objected to "the regrettable tendency to consider the work of a wife and mother in her home of no money value."[14] State motherhood endowments or mothers' pensions (this term was mostly used for payments to widows and other needy mothers) were advocated particularly by members of the Fabian Women's Group and by the Women's Co-operative Guild, with its largely working-class membership. They were regarded as a means for promoting women's economic independence and recognizing the social value of child-rearing. In 1914 Mabel Atkinson argued that, unlike middle-class women, working-class women did not feel excluded from the realm of work, and that they did not demand "the right to work but rather the protection against the unending burden of toil." In her opinion the issue was highly political: a "state endowment" was "coming to be realized more and more clearly as the ultimate ideal of the feminist movement." Since "no act of citizenship is more fundamental" than childbearing and child-rearing, women should be remunerated for the duration of these tasks. During and shortly after World War I, Beatrice Webb and especially Eleanor Rathbone developed an economic theory of maternity allowances based on a radical feminist critique of the male family wage and the traditional income gap between men and women. "Equal pay for equal work" outside the home had to be supplemented by a maternity endowment, which ought to be entirely separate from the traditional wage system and serve as a "remuneration of women's services" as well as an antidote to the negative effects of "equal pay for equal work," which was sometimes advocated by the trade unions in order to prevent women from replacing men at a lower cost and restrict them to "unequal" work.[15]

In 1915 Katherine Anthony presented such European views to the American feminists. She considered "the economic valuation of maternity" and "the principle of state-supported motherhood" as "one of the most significant chapters in the history of the changing status of women"; even if the payment were minimal at an initial stage, it would be crucial because it would secure a "paid vacation" from employment and come "from some other source besides her husband," thereby paving the way for independence and for a fundamental change in the relationship between the sexes. She confirmed her ideas as she investigated the poverty of American working-class mothers who were forced to take jobs in addition to their family duties, and set them forth in an introduction to the American edition of the 1917 report of Rathbone's Family Endowment Committee.[16] Although few leaders of American feminism publicly shared Anthony's call for the recognition and payment of mothers' work, she was not the only one to advocate it. Even the earlier and more conservative women's club movement and organizations such as the Woman's Christian Temperance Union had placed women's domestic duties at the center of their activities, insisting on their public importance and occasionally claiming that they "should be among the compensated Industries of civilized nations." Some radical feminists, such as the advocate for birth control, Crystal Eastman, firmly believed that child-rearing ought to be "recognized by the world as work, requiring a definite economic reward and not merely entitling the performer to be dependent on some man." Alongside these conservative and radical voices other groups of feminists defended similar claims: reformers of the Progressive Era such as Jane Addams and Sophonisba Breckinridge; the feminists who founded (in 1912) and directed the Children's Bureau in the U.S. Department of Labor, Lillian Wald, Florence Kelley, Julia Lathrop, and Grace Abbott; and the mothers' movement founded in the 1890s, which was organized in the National Congress of Mothers. A broad movement developed to demand "mothers' pensions" for needy mothers. Its opponents attacked such subsidies on the grounds that they were unnatural rewards for mothers' work and would serve as an opening wedge to a universal maternity endowment. Nevertheless, both pensioned and nonpensioned women began to see such pensions as their right.[17]

It goes without saying that even though many women in many countries fought for the dignity of motherhood, for its recognition as work, and for a universal reward or partial support from the state, feminists were far from agreeing on the underlying social analysis, vision of a future society, and strategy for women's liberation; even those who did agree on these broader issues disagreed on many practical and particular aspects. Furthermore, not all the feminists who supported some or all of those views did so over the whole course of their lives; for some they were a point of departure, for others a point of arrival. In all the countries mentioned similar debates were taking place.

One major objection was that the claim for maternity endowment was exceedingly "individualistic" and egotistical. Katherin Glasier of the British Independent Labour Party condemned it for being "the sheerly individualist 'revolt' stage of our women's battle for freedom," and Charlotte Perkins Gilman maintained, against Ellen Key, that women should seek power "not for themselves, but in order to benefit the community." Payment for mothers expressed inappropriate distrust of the husbands and their use of the family wage, and it could disrupt the familial bonds.[18] British social worker Anna Martin as well as Marianne Weber (a German, married to Max Weber) formulated the most widespread objection, namely that maternity endowment and "wages for housework" would be harmful because they would relieve men of their responsibility for wife and children, thereby undermining male work incentives and bringing about men's, not women's, "emancipation." Both preferred some way of equally sharing the earnings of the husband, and Weber claimed the wife's statutory right to the household money plus some money for herself. But both were aware that this would not do much good to women whose domestic labor was the hardest because their husbands earned little.

There were other views. Many feminists feared that the state resources were insufficient for such compensatory payments. Even more problematic seemed the shift of the "labor of love" from a use-value into an exchange-value. Some women considered this as "immoral," "unnatural," and "monstrous."[19] The German Maria Lischnewska maintained that work outside the home was more productive than domestic work, that the nonemployed housewife was "only consuming," was "supported," and was of no value to the national economy, and she idealized the married factory worker, who combined unpaid domestic work and employment, as the "prototype of the New Woman." When mothers' welfare was discussed in the context of working-class women and factory legislation, the opponents of relief measures argued that no special legislation should be introduced for women workers because this would render them less competitive on the labor market and reinforce the prejudice of women's weakness. (This was the subject of the famous Italian debate between Anna Maria Mozzoni and Anna Kuliscioff.) Others expressed doubts about payment to unmarried mothers because it might encourage sexual promiscuity and undesirable progeny.[20]

Despite these objections most feminists, including those who rejected the maternity endowment, made motherhood central to their own visions of women's liberation. They did so in order to legitimate women's suffrage (as in the United States) as well as their access to nontraditional and well-paid professions (as in the German feminist concept of "spiritual" or "organized motherhood"). On the other hand, those who favored maternity endowment did not always agree on issues such as birth control, the meaning of marriage, the organization of housework, and female labor legislation. Only very few women objected to the motherhood endowment on the grounds that it would force unwilling women to perform mothers' duties; one of these was Charlotte Perkins Gilman, whose goal was to socialize and professionalize childcare. As has often been noted, during that period most women and feminists from all political and class backgrounds and from all varieties of feminism shared the assumption that domestic work and childcare, whether honored or exploited, was at any rate *women's* task—even if not *all* women's task.[21]

Feminists who insisted that motherhood is a social function, not just a physiological, private, or individual one, challenged the traditional cultural dichotomy between private/personal and public/political and struggled for a new vision of their relation not only to the larger society[22] but also to home and motherhood. Thereby they broke radically with what later came to be called a "biological" view of the sexes (the term "biology" was not yet in current use at the beginning of the period dealt with here). The words often used in describing women's rights and responsibilities were "women's nature," still echoing but also challenging the Enlightenment discourse on the "natural rights of men," which had excluded women from these rights on the basis of a "nature" that seemed to be different for women and men. Women now claimed their own citizenship rights on the basis of their own nature, understood as a unique contribution to society. By demanding rights, rewards, and protection for what used to be their private and individual duty, they did not so much question the distribution of labor between women and men as the gender division between unpaid and paid labor (both were to be paid according to their value), and therefore the gender division between powerlessness and power (including "basket power," as the Women's Co-operative Guild called it). The more radical feminists challenged the structure of society itself, which should be centered around women's activities and rewards, not around men's activities and wages. Many of them believed that maternity protection would serve not only women but society at large, and that therefore, in the words of the Italian Ersilia Majno, "feminist claims are demands for the welfare of society."[23]

Feminists who viewed state payment to mothers as a strategy for women's liberation usually stressed both the dignity and the exploitation of motherhood; in Helene Stöcker's terms: "Once the female sex will have realized that it is in maternity . . . where the deepest roots of either its slavery or its liberty lie, it will not rest until it has conquered the liberty, independence and recognition which it deserves on the ground of this contribution to society."[24] They severely criticized male-oriented societal values, the "doctrine of the supremacy, of the dominance of the masculine." But they shared the traditional Enlightenment and more recently feminist goal of "equality" in economic as well as political terms: Nelly Roussel, for example, defined feminism as "the doctrine of natural equivalence and social equality of the sexes."[25] Such feminists demanded equality with men on the grounds that mothers' activities should be recognized as work, though with the important— and proudly expressed—difference that it was a more, or the most, noble and necessary labor. State maternity benefits and endowment were thought to promote this kind of equality, insofar as they facilitated independence (from employers or from husbands) and provided "equal pay for equivalent work." Yet in order to be "equal" women should not have to accept the prevailing male-centered societal values—rather, they hoped to undermine, substitute, or at least complement them. Feminists had no illusions that equal treatment would liberate women when it led to unequal results or to equal misery, nor that economic, social, and political equality meant that women and men had to perform the same tasks, nor that women and men are essentially identical. They did not downplay the sexual difference but insisted on women's right to be different, and considered this approach not as an expression of powerlessness and resignation, but of female pride, power, and self-affirmation. French feminists summarized it as "l'égalité dans la différence." In her speech of 1904 Schirmacher put it this way: "We live in a 'male world' created by man in the first place for himself, after *his own* image, for his comfort. In this world, man has made himself the measure of all things and beings and the measure of women too. Whoever wanted to be *his equal* had to be *equal to him,* to do what he did, in order to secure his respect. For him, *equal value* lay only in *sameness; only* assimilation could count for him as equality." The speaker rejected the assumption that women's activities are inferior compared to men's; the right to equality coexisted with the right to difference. In turn-of-the-century Italy this view came to be called "femminismo sociale" or "femminismo pratico." Today this form of feminism is again a subject of analysis and debate, particularly in the approaches that distinguish between "equality" ("equity") and "social feminism," "individualist" and "relational" feminism, "liberal" and "welfare" feminism, "political" and "domestic" feminism.[26] These apparently mutually exclusive—though in fact often overlapping—categories (the second term in each set includes maternalist feminism as described above) point to the important role of maternity in the earlier women's movement's theories, demands, and hopes for liberation.

Maternity and State Benefits through World War I

The peak years of maternal feminism coincided with new legislation intended to promote the welfare of mothers and children, either through cash benefits—the subject of this section—or through services in kind. In the years before and after World War I, most governments of industrialized and industrializing countries introduced such legislation. The reform fell far short of the feminist demands, both in terms of amount of subsidies and of coverage. These usually applied either to certain categories of employed women, initially only factory workers, or to needy mothers, mostly single or widowed. Even in the case of these special groups, the welfare effect was diminished because of bureaucratic procedures, means-testing, morality controls, and the low level of benefits. But although in this respect the legislation remained within the traditions of either poor-relief or labor law, it was nonetheless a break with the past. This break was reflected in the strong resistance which the reform met in all countries. At the same time, it paved the way for farther-reaching and universal social rights in the future welfare states. While few women at this period had the right to vote and be elected (before the end of World War I female suffrage had been granted in Australia, Finland, New Zealand, Norway, Denmark, the Netherlands, and the Soviet Union; in 1918 in Sweden, Great Britain, Germany, and Austria; in 1920 in the United States and Canada), they fought to influence this legislation and succeeded to varying degrees.

In Italy it was largely the lobbying of women's organizations that led in 1910 to the establishment of the national *cassa di maternità*. The fund was based on an insurance model financed by contributions from women workers themselves, the employers, and the state. Maternity benefits were to be paid to factory workers during their obligatory maternity leave, but the allowances were too low and the contributions too high for most women to be able to take advantage of it. In the United States the first mothers' pension law was enacted in Illinois in 1911, and by 1919 thirty-nine states provided some form of mothers' aid. It was granted on two conditions, economic need and the absence of a husband's support, and thus was awarded especially to widows, but in some states also to single, deserted, or divorced women. In France the *recherche de la paternité* was admitted in 1912 and, at least in theory, fathers of out-of-wedlock children could now be obliged to support them.[27] The Engerand Act of 1909 guaranteed job security to women who stayed away from it for up to eight weeks before and after giving birth, but this maternity leave was not compulsory nor were benefits paid during this period (except for public school teachers, who were entitled to full wage replacement beginning in 1910). It took another four years of pressure and close cooperation between feminists and the few members of parliament who supported their cause before major changes were enacted. In June 1913 the Strauss Act and a financial law were passed that required certain employers to grant maternity leaves and, most important, awarded allowances to certain categories of women workers on maternity leaves. In July of the same year allowances were granted to needy families with four or more children, and in December similar benefits were extended to some categories of civil servants; in both cases they were paid to fathers, and feminists such as Nelly Roussel strongly objected to this. These three laws paved the way for the French welfare state, particularly for universal child allowances.

In Germany feminist debates preceded and influenced the 1903, 1908, and 1911 amendments of the labor and health insurance laws; these extended the period of confinement benefits to eight weeks, raised the benefits, and included obligatory insurance for domestic servants. Wives of insured wage-earners were not covered, however, though they could insure themselves voluntarily. In Britain a National Insurance Act was first introduced in 1911. The Women's Co-operative Guild succeeded in having a maternity benefit scheme included in it, not only for self-insured women but also for nonemployed dependents of insured men. When in 1911 these provisions were enacted but with payments going to the fathers, it was again the Guild that waged a battle until in 1913 the benefit (of 30 shillings) was made payable to the mothers themselves. The 1918 Maternity and Child Welfare Act provided welfare clinics and services to needy mothers, incorporating some of the features the women's groups had aimed for in the previous years. In the Netherlands a 1913 law on compulsory health insurance included maternity benefits, and in Denmark maternity benefits were included in a voluntary insurance scheme of 1915. In Norway confinement benefits for wage-earning women were provided in 1909 and 1915, and the Child Welfare Act of 1915 granted benefits, financed by taxes, to single (unmarried, widowed, divorced, and separated) mothers who were too poor to bring up their children on their own. The bill had been pushed through parliament against fierce resistance on the part of the conservatives by Johan Castberg, a former minister of justice and brother-in-law of Katti Anker Møller. But benefits were small and depended on moral supervision; "bad mothers" were excluded or had their children taken away from them; moreover, the amounts were not sufficient to cover the cost of living and the mothers were expected to find jobs in addition to tending their children. In Sweden a law of 1900 obliged employers to grant a maternity leave of four (later six) weeks after childbirth, but without providing any benefits. It took twelve more years until a maternity insurance bill was proposed; but it was withheld on the grounds that such benefits would have to be placed within the framework of an obligatory health insurance, which was not yet established. Not until the 1920s, when Swedish women sat in parliament, was the issue raised again. The results were disappointing: the Child Welfare Act of 1924 provided for intervention only in the case of child abuse and made just a few categories eligible for economic aid. Only in 1931 was health insurance established that also entitled women on maternity leave to apply for state maternity benefits.[28]

In 1917 Julia Lathrop, head of the U.S. Children's Bureau, prepared an impressive international survey of state-sponsored maternity (confinement) benefit schemes "in the hope that the information might prove useful to the people of one of the few great countries which as yet have no system of State or national assistance in maternity—the United States."[29] Her report included fifteen countries, most of them in Europe. Usually, benefits were available solely to employed mothers, and with only two exceptions—Italy and France—the benefits were part of the national health insurance scheme; the Australian law of 1912 was unique in granting maternity allowances to its "citizens" (Australian women were enfranchised in 1901) regardless of marital and occupational status. Despite the differences in the laws and, even more, in their implementation, these measures indicate an international trend toward welfare provisions for mothers or, rather, for specific groups of them. Their similarity is striking not only in view of the political, social, and economic differences between the countries, but also in view of the different specific problems that the national provisions were intended to solve. In Italy and France the new focus on mothers was in part a response to earlier, but still widespread practices of child abandonment and wet-nursing; many poor employed mothers—married as well as unmarried— would leave their children with state-sponsored institutions because they were unable to nurse them. In both countries the women who proclaimed the value of maternity hoped to abolish these institutions. In the United States mothers' pensions had finally been introduced to curb the widespread practice of placing children whose mothers worked outside the home or whose fathers were incapable of supporting the family in orphan institutions run by private charity organizations, because these were considered to be cold and inhuman surroundings; in Britain "baby-farming" was the object of similar criticism.[30] In these countries socialized, professionalized, and institutionalized childcare was to be replaced by private, though publicly supported, motherhood.

Despite its shortcomings, often noted by feminists, prewar maternity legislation certainly brought improvements for mothers. Its long-term impact was even more fundamental: the state assumed, if reluctantly and partially, the task of supporting mothers. Many feminists considered this to be a first step toward recognition of the "social function" of maternity and of women's full citizenship on their own terms. Yet the legislation was not just a response to feminist demands or to the plight of mothers, even though such rhetoric had to be mobilized in order to overcome the strong resistance of traditionalists. Among other motives that influenced legislators, the most important one was the growing public awareness of a continuous decline in the birthrate, coupled with an increasing interest in population size as a major index of national pride and power. Even though this phenomenon was an international one, common to all industrializing nations, it first came to the foreground of public debate in France because here the fertility decline had started earliest and the French defeat in the war against highly populated Germany in 1871 had charged the subject with the issue of national grandeur and European hegemony. But since the turn of the century many people in many countries felt acutely threatened by the decline in fertility; experts and would-be experts searched for measures to halt, even to reverse the trend. The two earliest but enduring approaches were the struggle against infant and child mortality, which led to movements and measures for child welfare, and the struggle against maternal mortality, which led to movements and measures for mothers' welfare. Needless to say the two were closely linked.

As soon as it was perceived that the fertility decline, which had begun among the upper classes, had reached the working classes—in Britain and Germany around 1900, in Italy much later—the public began to take interest in poor mothers, unmarried mothers, and women factory workers, particularly in countries with a considerable proportion of women in the labor force such as France, Britain, and Germany. The "birth-strike" was often attributed to feminism, infant mortality to maternal "ignorance," and both infant and maternal mortality to women's employment, particularly to factory work; given the extremely miserable female wage and work conditions at the beginning of the twentieth century, this last hypothesis came close to being the truth.[31] However, no countries ever legislated to dismiss women from factory work or from employment generally, and in any case many working-class women could not afford to dedicate themselves exclusively to home and children because the family's survival depended on their wages. Inasmuch as maternity leaves and benefits for factory workers were inspired by hopes of reversing the fertility decline, they did not intend to push mothers out of the labor force but to help them combine work and motherhood, if only for the period of pregnancy and childbirth. Yet the maternal welfare policies aimed not only at a higher survival rate of the children born, but also at a higher number of children to be born in the future. Hence they can be seen as part of a new kind of pronatalism. The rhetoric and policy that emerged in the first decade of the century, developed in the 1920s, and remained strong into the 1930s conceived of maternity welfare as a way to influence people who wanted to have children but felt they could not afford them because of overwork and poverty.

Although such maternity policies were rooted in diverse and sometimes conflicting motives, they coincided to a large extent with the feminist demands for mothers' rights. Maternalist feminists wanted motherhood recognized as part of women's citizenship; at the same time, pronatalists saw women as national assets precisely because they were mothers. Thus, in economic terms, the "birth-strike" functioned as a strike in its traditional working-class sense: not to abandon the labor of birth entirely, but to withhold it for the purpose of improving earning and working conditions. Probably nowhere else was this more visible than in France. French feminists rarely took a stand against pronatalist rhetoric; rather, they consistently used it for their own ends, sometimes genuinely believing in it, sometimes more as tactic. "If you want children, learn to honor mothers," wrote Maria Martin, editor of the *Journal des Femmes,* in 1896 in an article addressing widespread fears of "dépopulation" and "dénatalité." In 1931 Cécile Brunschvicg maintained that "both French and foreign feminists experience the same desire to save the babies, help the mothers, encourage motherhood." During World War I, when millions of men were absent or dead and the need for female labor in war-related industries was great, confinement benefits were increased in order to encourage women to be mothers as well as workers, and male "repopulators" suggested all kinds of birth incentives. Some feminists complained. In Germany in 1915 the moderate feminist Gertrud Bäumer (from 1910 to 1919 president, later vice-president of the Bund Deutscher Frauenvereine) criticized such proposals for treating "the question of the birthrate exclusively from the military viewpoint" as "an arms race by mothers," and for trying to set up "a whole bribery system of insurances, recognitions, and compensations, in order to conjure up life." Nonetheless, for feminists in Germany and elsewhere, maternity and infant care could not go far enough, and the Bund Deutscher Frauenvereine continued to demand reforms "which guarantee mothers the possibility of a fully felt experience of motherhood."[32]

French feminists had a further reason for praising maternity as a basis for women's rights and duties. In France especially, the organized male pronatalists hoped to achieve their goal by protecting fatherhood rather than motherhood, and some even considered the fertility decline as a result of a crisis not in femininity but in virility. The most vocal among them, organized in the Alliance Nationale pour l'Accroissement de la Population Française (founded in 1896, one month after the feminist congress in Paris where Léonie Rouzade had demanded state subsidies for all mothers), pleaded with men to father large families, and advocated financial incentives for fathers, especially income tax relief. Subsequently, tax rebates became the major method of those pronatalists who focused on the revaluation of fatherhood. In the Alliance's view mothers should get only decorations—a proposal which in 1903 aroused feminists such as Maria Martin and Hubertine Auclert to insist more pointedly, with some sarcasm, that state maternity allowances be paid to the mothers.[33]

World War I brought an important innovation. All belligerent countries, again with the exception of the United States, had introduced separation allowances: money paid directly to the absent soldiers' wives and widows, for themselves and for their children, the amount sometimes depending on the size of the family, sometimes on the woman's occupational status, and usually paid to wives in common law marriages as well as in legal ones. Studies of the British and German cases reveal that although officially women obtained such allowances as "dependents" of their husbands, they considered these payments as their own right and as compensation of their labor for home and children; moreover, children's welfare had demonstrably improved where their mothers had such allowances at their disposal. To Julia Lathrop and her co-workers in the Children's Bureau this novelty, based on the "most advanced and liberal ideas," seemed highly important for designing future policies in the United States.[34]

Maternity, Paternity, and Citizenship: 1920s–1950s

The maternity policies implemented during World War I remained important after its end, both for the feminist movements and the rise of the modern welfare states. In countries where women had become full voting citizens, many individual women and women's organizations used their vote and representation for improving the situation of mothers. Compared to the prewar period, the approach had changed: utopian visions had faded, more pragmatic views came to prevail, and coalitions with other policy makers had to be built. The earlier feminist tendency of denouncing the exploitation of mothers and glorifying maternity gradually subsided in most countries, to some extent among feminists themselves, even more among male policy makers and pressure groups. This was most visible in the United States, where feminists won a victory in obtaining the Sheppard-Towner Maternity and Infancy Act of 1921. It granted federal subsidies for preventive health services for mothers and children and was therefore accused by its opponents of introducing "Communism" and "collectivization" in the United States. But in the course of the 1920s a minority of the feminist movement turned away from the focus on maternity, advocating strict identity of legal provisions for women and men and stressing issues where this seemed to be desirable and feasible, notably an amendment to the Constitution providing for equality of rights. At the same time, the political victory in the field of maternity policy fell to its opponents: funding for the 1921 Act was discontinued and in 1928 the law was repealed. Its defeat reestablished the principle that maternity was a purely individual or familial, not a social responsibility. It was not until the 1935 Social Security Act, and upon the insistence of the Children's Bureau, that federal assistance was once again granted, this time to fund the gender-neutral Aid to Dependent Children program. These federal monies were administered not by the Children's Bureau women but by the Social Security Administration. No further federal law for maternity welfare was ever enacted in the United States; only decades later, in the 1960s and 1970s, did aid to dependent children emerge once again as a women's issue and play an important part in hypotheses about the "feminization of poverty."[35]

Largely as a result of women's continued lobbying, in 1919

the International Labor Office issued the Washington Convention, which recommended for all women workers a maternity leave of six weeks before and after parturition, a full maintenance grant to replace wages, and free medical services. In Germany, where equal rights of women and men as well as mothers' welfare were included in the Constitution of the Weimar Republic, female parliament members of all parties (except for the Nazi party, which had no women delegates) cooperated successfully in maintaining and even raising confinement and nursing benefits for insured women and dependents of insured men (originally a war-emergency measure). A 1919 act to this effect was considered to be the first law on which women's newly acquired civic status had left its marks, and with the 1927 Maternity Protection Act, one of the most important welfare laws of the Weimar Republic, Germany became the first major industrialized country to implement the Washington Convention. The parliamentary action in favor of working-class mothers was led by socialist as well as liberal and moderate feminists. The latter continued to focus on women's access to better-paid professions, particularly those that were considered to be expressions of "spiritual" or "social motherhood" (such as social work, teaching, medicine). Despite continuing rhetoric on motherhood and its revaluation as a "profession," German feminists no longer advocated a universal motherhood endowment regardless of occupational status; instead, they turned their attention to increasing the efficiency of housework in the hope of reducing the time women spent on it.

A different situation prevailed in Britain. Eleanor Rathbone continued her life-long struggle for universal maternity endowment, which she had earlier carried out as administrator of wartime separation allowances. After being elected president of the National Union of Women's Suffrage Societies in 1919 (later National Union of Societies for Equal Citizenship) and as an independent member of parliament since 1929, she placed her claims in the context of a theory of gender relations and feminist strategy which she called "new feminism" and "real equality for women." By this she meant "to demand what we want for women, not because it is what men have got, but because it is what women need to fulfill the potentialities of their own natures and to adjust themselves to the circumstances of their own lives," implying that "the whole structure and movement of society [should] reflect in proportionate degree [women's] experiences, their needs and their aspirations."[36] Seen against the background of prewar feminism, this view was less new than she claimed, but in the interwar years her book, *The Disinherited Family* (1924), was a major economic analysis of the need for independent cash benefits to mothers as a feminist alternative to a societal organization built around the male breadwinner's wage. She also took a definite stand against the rising tide of eugenicists (and later against anti-Semitism in Germany) and their arguments that allowances for lower-class mothers, who produced too many children anyway, would encourage them (and their husbands) to procreate even more. Rathbone countered with the claim that improving women's lives would in fact induce them to have fewer children.[37] Although her overall analysis remained the same, important details of her practical proposals were now shaped less by utopian visions and more by a search for pragmatic solutions, as well as by two decades of ongoing feminist criticism. She turned her former proposals for allowances for mothers and children into "child" or "family allowances," apparently in response to the hard feminist argument that in no case should mothers receive state allowances for anything but the children's needs. Any other assistance would risk pushing women out of the labor market.[38] As in the American case and elsewhere, the discourse began to shift from women and their difference to a gender-neutral terminology. But whatever the terminology, the feminist fighters for family allowances continued to insist that they be paid to mothers and include compensation for women's domestic labor. Opponents understood well the ongoing meaning of this emphasis.

In Britain both conservatives and the trade unions opposed these ideas. The unions continued to struggle for a male family wage, and they had some reason to believe that this struggle was jeopardized by feminist claims for benefits to mothers, even in their reduced form. Sometimes labor leaders seemed to exemplify Rathbone's male "Turk complex," though rarely as openly as the one who declared these claims to be "an insane burst of individualism" and said that "under socialism mothers' and children's right to maintenance would be honoured by the family and not by the state."[39] In the 1920s many British women's organizations (for example, the National Union and the Labour Party women) integrated the demand for family allowances into their programs, sometimes alongside the demand for free access to birth control. But another group of feminists objected to maternity-focused policies and campaigned for identical legal provisions and for women's strict equality with men, with the result—in Britain as in the United States—of a profound split in the feminist community. From the 1930s the allowances debate shifted from the "woman question" to other issues (especially the allowances' impact on wages and inflation), and the resistance of the conservatives and the trade unions stalled the enactment of family allowances until after World War II.[40] When in 1945 a bill on universal state family allowances independent of marital and occupational status was finally put before parliament, it provided for 5 shillings per week (instead of the 8 shillings recommended by the 1942 Beveridge Report on which it was based), to be paid only after the first child (the feminist proposals had included the first child) and not to the mother but to the head of the family. Rathbone and many individual women and women's organizations strongly opposed the bill on the grounds that it "will not raise the status of motherhood but will actually lower it" by treating the wife "as a mere appendage" of her husband.[41] The storm of protest succeeded in making the allowances payable to the mother. Measured against the original goals of maternalist feminism—the recognition of "maternity as a social function" and the replacement of the male breadwinner wage through redistribution of earned income from men to women—the Family Allowance Act was a defeat. But it was a victory in its recognition of mothers' right to some payment outside of the wage structure; it was remarkable especially in comparison to the contemporary European dictatorships, where family allowances actually lowered the status of motherhood.

When "child endowment" was introduced in Australia in 1941 and "family allowances" in Canada in 1944, they bore similar features and came about after similar debates within and outside the women's movement. The example of Norway shows how the ideology of motherhood and the demand for a mothers' wage, which had been so strong in the 1920s, had receded in the background when the introduction of gender-neutral "child allowances" was on the agenda for discussion in the 1930s and for legislation in 1945; the issues were no longer mother-centered but child- or family-centered. Basically, the debate was on whether child welfare should be supported through wage supplements, state benefits, or services in kind. The labor movement did not reject child allowances as such but opposed them as part of the wage system, advocating payment by the state and out of taxes. Socialist as well as nonsocialist feminists continued to plead for payment exclusively to mothers. When universal child allowances were introduced by law in 1946, they were made payable to mothers. Too small to count as a "mothers' wage," however, they were viewed as just an income supplement. Poor mothers were left to municipal support until 1957 and 1964, when widows and single mothers became entitled to payment as of right. In Sweden state maternity relief was granted in 1937, with over 90 percent of all mothers entitled to it. Needy mothers received additional special grants. The measures were largely due to women's previous proposals and pressure, but also to a new social-democratic family policy which combined pronatalism with social reform, laid down in the writings of Alva and Gunnar Myrdal. Universal child allowances were introduced by a law of 1947; as in other democratic countries, they were made payable to the mothers. In both Sweden and Norway pronatalism helped to promote this legislation—though it was less dominant there than elsewhere—and it has been convincingly argued that pronatalism served there as an instrument for women's emancipation by providing them with some independent means.[42]

The same was true for France. Pronatalism was stronger there than in any other European country among politicians and organized male pronatalists, as well as in the traditional popular culture. It remained strong throughout the interwar period, as a baby boom of the early 1920s proved short-lived and the birthrate continued to decline, reaching an all-peacetime low in the late 1930s. In 1920 the *Fête des mères* was created, and medals for mothers with five or more children were given out. Antinatalist propaganda was prohibited in 1920, and a law of 1923 provided for stricter prosecution of abortion, at the same time changing it from a crime into an offense and lowering the penalty imposed on it. The social insurance law of 1928, inspired by the German insurance system, integrated the maternity provisions of 1913 into a health insurance scheme (with feminists arguing against equating pregnancy and childbirth with sickness). The system took care of those who were insured, that is, employed women and wives of insured men; it granted free medical assistance to mothers in childbed; it extended the period of maternity leave; and it increased maternity benefits.[43]

French women's organizations and individual feminists did not reject the profamily and pronatalist consensus, and it had become difficult to distinguish pronatalist goals from maternal and child welfare as women's goals. In fact, pronatalists "convinced parents more easily of the urgency for France to have pronatalist legislation than of the necessity for them as parents to have more children."[44] In the 1930s the feminist debate on maternity as a "social" versus "family function" continued, with supporters of the (private) "family function" rejecting state payment for maternity, and supporters of the (public) "social function" favoring it. Cécile Brunschvicg spoke out for a compromise that limited the "social function" to women without husbands and to those whose husbands were unable to support them. But the Union Féminine Civique et Sociale, which was inspired by social Catholicism (unlike the largely Protestant leadership of the secular women's movement) continued to insist on maternity as a "social function." It advocated, beyond the Pope's recommendation of a male family wage in the encyclic *Quadragesimo Anno* of 1931, an *allocation de la mère au foyer*, a universal allowance to nonemployed mothers, arguing for the mother's right to dedicate herself to her children; the Union Française pour le Suffrage des Femmes supported this goal in 1933.[45] The Union Féminine's claim resembled earlier feminist propositions, but it differed from them in that it advocated a male family wage as well as a maternity wage. In this way it avoided antagonizing the Pope and the male labor organizations, which feared that money for mothers would lower men's wages.

French feminists also supported universal and state-financed family allowances. These grew out of a series of precedents similar to those of other countries: the 1913 laws on benefits for needy families and for civil servants and the business-sponsored *allocations familiales,* which were widespread in the 1920s but had remained limited to certain regions and industries. These allocations were mostly the result of employers' labor strategies and functioned through equalization funds; although the labor unions rejected them, many workers benefited from them. Given the high rate of French women's participation in the labor force, the allowances were often, though not consistently, paid directly to the mother. The Family Allowance Act of 1932 obliged all employers to join and contribute to these equalization funds within a certain period of time. Although employers were slow to implement the law, and whole categories of workers were left out for years, the law transformed an industrial wage policy into a national family policy which was inspired by a vision of family-based distributive justice. It was extended and systematized in 1938 and became the *Code de la Famille* of 1939. It provided for *allocations familiales* which consisted of a one-time bonus for the first child if born within two years after marriage, monthly allowances of 10 percent of the wage for the second and of 20 percent for each additional child, and an *allocation de la mère au foyer* of 10 percent. The amounts varied with the regional wage levels. Significantly, the Vichy regime—like all authoritarian and dictatorial regimes of the period—did not recognize a separate payment to unwaged mothers; it was integrated into the *salaire unique* of the breadwinner (male or female). In 1946 the Fourth Republic increased the child allowances (now renamed *prestations familiales*), and state-supported maternity allowances were again paid to the mothers. In the 1950s the maternity allowance was extended to the wives of the self-employed, particularly in agriculture, who previously had not been eligible. In post–World War II France, more than in any other European country, payments to mothers redistributed a substantial portion of the national income to women.[46]

While in the interwar period feminist maternalism receded internationally, it was completely driven underground in the rising dictatorships, albeit in very different ways. In Franco's Spain and fascist Italy a strong pronatalist rhetoric prevailed; in both countries it had the support of male-dominated Catholicism but little effect on the birth rate, which continued to decline. In Italy pronatalist policies started five years after Mussolini's rise to power, with a vast amount of propaganda in the daily press to bolster his 1927 proclamation that "He who is not a father is not a man."[47] Tax rebates for the head of family, based on his wife and the number of children, were introduced in the late 1920s (but brought little net gain in terms of family income, since most Italian men were too poor to pay income taxes). In 1936 state-sponsored *assegni familiari* for the wife and each dependent child were granted to employed fathers; even birth-premiums were granted to fathers in 1939, replacing the former *cassa di maternità*. All measures focused on paternity and virility, reshaping the family around the father's predominance and contrasting starkly with earlier feminist maternalism. The one exception to this rule was the state-sponsored Opera Nazionale di Maternità ed Infanzia, which provided health education and assistance to poor and mostly single mothers, even in the backward countryside, and implied some recognition of mothers' citizenship. In Spain too, where the women's movement had often focused on upgrading motherhood, novel measures rewarded fathers, upgraded paternity, and reinforced the figure of the *jefe de familia*. State family allowances *(subsidio familiar)* as of right were introduced in 1938, family bonuses *(plus de cargas familiares)* for a wider population in 1945; both supported paternity.[48]

National Socialism too pursued a cult of fatherhood and masculinity, using pronatalism and state welfare to reward and reshape paternity with such measures as marriage loans (1933), income tax rebates (1934, 1939), and child allowances (1935-36), which were payable to fathers and to unmarried mothers only if the father of the child was known to the authorities. Three partial exceptions to the paternal orientation included the organization Mother and Child, which granted assistance to "valuable" needy mothers, but this did not imply, as in Italy, state recognition of their services since it was a Nazi Party affiliate financed by fundraising; second, a medal honoring mothers of five or more children, introduced in 1939 upon the French model; and finally, the Maternity Protection Law of 1942, which improved the 1927 law and encouraged women to combine motherhood and work outside the home. But National Socialism put into practice Hubertine Auclert's "Minotaur state" by using far more incisive means than a mere cult of paternity. State welfare was circumscribed by state racism, which was at the center of National Socialism and which discriminated against "inferior" minorities on ethnic and eugenic grounds. Nazi pronatalism was never pure as in France, Italy, and Spain; an enormous antinatalist propaganda preceded and followed the Nazi rise to power, drawing upon earlier and non-Nazi antinatalist currents. The first natalist law of 1933 was not pronatalist, but antinatalist, providing for compulsory sterilization of the "biologically inferior" and "unfit."[49] Father-centered family subsidies were not, and were never meant to be, universal: people of ethnically and eugenically "inferior" stock were excluded because they were not to have children in the first place. No other country pursued an antinatalist policy of similar dimensions. National Socialism's devaluation of motherhood and human life, its antinatalism, and its cult of masculinity paved the way for the extermination of those it considered the most "inferior": about 300,000 female and male Gypsies and over five million Jewish women and men.

Eugenic and ethnic racism had not been unique to National

Socialism nor to Germany. It existed among other political groups and in other countries as well, but with profound differences in its meaning and especially in its practice. The term "race" had been employed in the populationist language of all the countries mentioned here. But the use of the term did not always imply racism, meaning discrimination on the grounds of lower ethnic or eugenic value; often it simply meant "society," "community," or "nation" with respect to their procreative potential. This was usually the case when that terminology appeared in maternity-focused feminist language. However, some of the radical feminist birth-control activists joined the rising tide of eugenics, a movement supported by many socialists and considered to be "progressive," and they advocated discrimination by recommending antinatalism specifically for the "unfit" and poor, thereby reversing the early feminist focus on maternal assistance to combat female poverty. In the United States Margaret Sanger and her collaborators, while glorifying motherhood (but not paid motherhood), came to consider antinatalism as a solution to all of women's and societal problems, and particularly to the problem of undesirable propagation of the poor and the immigrants. In Germany Helene Stöcker and Henriette Fürth went so far as to advocate compulsory sterilization for the "unfit." In part, these feminists viewed the eugenic discourse as a way to obtain public approval of abortion, sterilization, and contraception, in the same way that pronatalism had served to get mothers' services recognized by society.[50]

In France, Italy, and Spain the concept of "race" (*stirpe, raza*) included the entire national population, no group to be excluded from procreation. Norway, Sweden, and Britain had eugenic movements which aimed at excluding some undesirable sections of the population.[51] In Britain statutory eugenic sterilization was proposed but rejected in 1934, while Denmark instituted such a law in 1928, and Sweden and Norway in 1934, but they applied it to few cases. In the United States two-thirds of the states had eugenic sterilization laws by the 1930s that were closely linked to anti-immigration and other racist policies; two-thirds of these laws had clauses for compulsory intervention. But in Germany the number of legal sterilizations performed from 1934 to 1945 was ten times the number of those in the United States in 1907–1945 (with twice the population of Germany). Most important, in no country other than Germany was sterilization policy a prelude to genocide.

When German women and men were liberated from this murderous regime, they were also liberated from state antinatalism. In East Germany, which followed the model of the Soviet Union, the relevant constitutional equal rights were interpreted as women's duty to work outside the home. Domestic labor was downgraded (in accordance with Lenin's notoriously scornful views on housework) and propaganda pressed housewives to get jobs and thereby give precedence to the "We" instead of the "I," to the collectivity instead of selfishness.[52] This policy was reinforced by low wages overall, and, in 1950, by maternity provisions for employed women (maternity leave with full wage replacement). Needy mothers and widows received welfare grants only if they were incapacitated for employment, and whereas all mothers received a single grant at the birth of third and further children, a universal monthly allowance was paid only after the fourth child. In reaction to an extreme fertility decline in the 1970s, "the services of bearing and rearing children in the family were recognized and valued"[53] by the following measures: a special female labor law (a forty-hour week for mothers who tended two or more children), temporary support for single mothers who wished to quit their jobs, and a paid "baby year" at the birth of second and further children. The work of motherhood as such was not valued by the early West German state either; it also guaranteed equal rights in its constitution. Confinement benefit was improved for wage-earning women; when universal child allowances were introduced in 1954, they functioned upon the older French model of employers' equalization funds and were paid to employed fathers of third and subsequent children. Only in 1964 did the federal government take over the responsibility, gradually raising the allowance and the number of eligible children; although the law provided for payment either to the father or the mother, it was usually the father who received it. Until 1975, the major assistance tool continued to be tax deductions for wife and children.[54] In 1979 the Social-Democratic government introduced a (modestly) paid maternity leave of half a year for employed women, and in 1987 the Christian-Democrat-Liberal government replaced it with a universal "child-raising allowance" of up to 600 marks per month for a period of one-and-a-half year, regardless of occupational status. It differs from Lily Braun's ideal of over eighty years earlier in two important features: it does not fully cover needs, and it is payable either to the mother or to the father depending on who chooses childcare instead of employment.

Modern welfare states would look very different if their development had not coincided with the growth of women's movements and women's acquisition of citizenship rights. But women's impact, the shape of state welfare, and women's benefits differed substantially in different countries, most markedly as between democracies and dictatorships. Few feminists of the "second wave" took up the earlier feminist heritage. Meanwhile, employment conditions have improved considerably—even for women, and not least because of the pressure by women. In contrast, state welfare outside the traditional wage structure has brought them so little, and motherhood has become such a short-term experience (and for fewer women) that liberation, justice, and equality seem to be nearer when pursued through affirmative action in regard to work outside the home. This, together with private pressure on men to share parenthood, seems to be the approach women have chosen, rather than upholding a maternal vision of the female sex and seeking public recognition of "motherhood as a social function."

14

Maternity, Family, and the State

Nadine Lefaucheur

THE FAMILY IS NOT only the place where, traditionally, the biological reproduction of human beings has taken place, but also the focal point of social reproduction. It is where sexual difference interacts with kinship, marriage, and co-residence. Since the 1960s families in the developed nations of the world have been engulfed in turbulence on all fronts. This turmoil can be seen as the first sign of a major change stemming from the demographic, technological, and economic evolution, which has led to the emergence of a new regime in the reproduction of populations and their labor power, thereby upsetting the material and social base of gender relations and devaluing the family (in a sense that I will spell out later on).

The Family in Torment

The first warning sign was a decline in fertility. In all Western countries the birthrate, which had been declining steadily since the end of the nineteenth century, picked up in the years just prior to World War II, and the rate of increase accelerated in the postwar years. By the 1970s, however, it was clear that the baby boom was over. Some greeted the news with delight in the name of solidarity with the Third World and with the struggle against overpopulation, while others deplored it as a harbinger of the decline of the West. In any case, various indicators of fertility and natality began dropping in the mid-1960s, and before long the rate of decrease seemed precipitous, leading, within ten or fifteen years, to a situation in which the birthrate in most developed countries stood below the level needed to maintain a steady population.

A Furor over Indices

Given the death rates prevailing in today's developed countries, a fertility rate of roughly 2.1 (children per women) is required to maintain a steady population without immigration. In the United States, however, fertility fell from 3.7 in 1957 to 1.8 in 1975. In Australia it fell from 3.9 in 1960 to 1.9 in 1980, and in Canada from 3.9 to 1.7 (with Quebec going all the way from 4 in 1957 to 1.4 in 1985). In Japan fertility fell from 4.5 in 1947 to 1.7 in the 1980s.

In Northern and Western Europe the fertility rate stood above 2.5 (and in some countries 3) in 1964, but by 1975 it had fallen below 2 everywhere. By 1988 it had dropped all the way to 1.4 in West Germany, 1.5 in Austria, and 1.6 in Belgium, Luxembourg, Finland, Denmark, and Switzerland. In Southern Europe the decline began later but proceeded more rapidly. Italy and Spain, for example, still had fertility rates high enough to ensure a stable population as recently as 1975, but fifteen years later they shared with Hong Kong the distinction of having the lowest fertility rate in the world, 1.3.

To be sure, by the end of the 1980s the fertility rate had recovered somewhat in the United Kingdom, the Benelux countries, and Scandinavia, especially Sweden, where it rose from 1.6 in 1983 to 2 in 1989. But the increase reflected an increase in the average age of mothers rather than in the "final" number of children. In all countries except Japan, the decline in the fertility rate was accompanied by an increase, often quite marked, in the number of children born out of wedlock.

Those European countries in which the rate of "illegitimate" births had been quite low (around 2 percent) in the early 1960s saw that rate increase. The increase was late and moderate in the Mediterranean countries and in Belgium. By contrast, in Ireland (where divorce was prohibited), Luxembourg, and the Netherlands it was rapid and significant: a rise of 500–600 percent in twenty-five years.

The leading developed countries in the West—Canada, France, the United Kingdom, West Germany, the United States—had moderate rates of illegitimate births in the early 1960s, ranging from 6 to 8 percent of all births. With the exception of West Germany, where the rate has remained below 10 percent, all the other countries have witnessed a sharp rise to the 15–20 percent level by the mid-1980s. In France in 1990 one newborn child in four was born to unmarried parents.

As high as these figures are, they pale in comparison with those for Scandinavia, where already in 1960 one child in ten was illegitimate and by 1989 one child in two was born out of wedlock. By itself, the increase in the rate of illegitimate births, universal though uneven, suggests that marriage has taken a battering comparable to that of fertility.

While most Western countries were congratulating themselves on the "marriage boom" of the 1970s, due in large part to the arrival of the "baby-boom generation" on the matrimonial market, marital indices had already begun to fall in many countries. The marriage index is actually a measure of the probability that a person will marry before the age of 50 if present conditions do not change, and in 1960 this index stood above 90 percent for both men and women in all countries. It began to decline in the mid-1960s in Scandinavia and within a few years in most of the democracies of, first, Central Europe (West Germany, Austria, Switzerland) and, later, Western Europe (the United Kingdom and France). By the mid-1980s the marriage index in these countries ranged from 48 to 66 percent, indicating that if conditions did not change one out of every two or three people would remain celibate. In the Mediterranean countries, however, the marriage index, like the fertility rate, did not decline until the mid-1970s. Meanwhile, the percentage of unmarried couples, the divorce rate, and the proportion of single-parent families began to rise rapidly in all Western countries.

In 1980 one percent of Italian couples, 3–4 percent of English, American, and Swiss couples, 6–8 percent of French, Québecois, and West German couples, and 15 percent of Swedish couples were unmarried. In countries where the number of unwed couples increased, the phenomenon affected the old as well as the young, but it was especially marked among those under thirty: in Sweden in 1985 there were more unmarried than married couples in this age group. In the United States in 1983 more than 20 percent of unmarried women under thirty-five and not living with their parents were living with a man to whom they were not married, compared with only 10 percent of those between thirty-five and fifty-five. In France at the end of the 1980s, nearly half of all women under thirty living in couples were not married.

Even before the marriage index began to decline, divorce rates had begun to increase in most Western countries. In 1960 (excepting Denmark, where the rate was already close to 6), the annual number of divorces per 1,000 married couples stood at roughly 2 in countries where divorce was legal. Twenty years later it was above 10 in the Netherlands, the United Kingdom, and Denmark and below 5 only in Southern Europe.

Still more significant was the divorce index, which measures (as a percentage) the probability that a married couple will divorce if present conditions do not change. In the mid-1960s the index of divorce in Western Europe (leaving aside countries where divorce was illegal, such as Italy, Spain, and Ireland) ranged from 6 percent in Scotland to 18 percent in Sweden and Denmark. By 1975 it had risen to 50 percent in Sweden and 40 percent in the United Kingdom and Denmark and stood at roughly 25 percent in most other countries; over the next few years it gained another 5 to 10 points. In the United States, where the divorce index had already reached 25 by 1950, it began to rise in 1960 and by 1970 had reached 40 percent.

Divorce not only became more common but also tended to occur earlier in marriage. In Great Britain in 1959, for example, it took an average of twenty years for 14 percent of the couples married in a given year to divorce. By 1969 the figure had fallen to ten years, and by 1979 to just six years.[1]

The result of all these changes was an increase in the proportion of single-parent families in the developed countries. Sooner or later, and more or less rapidly, many countries witnessed a transition from the "old regime" to the new. Under the old regime, the majority of single parents were widows or widowers or individuals abandoned by a spouse or sexual partner. Under the new regime divorce and voluntary separation had become the chief reasons for children living primarily with one of their parents.

At the end of the 1980s a few Common Market countries still

lived under the old regime: single-parent households constituted fewer than 10 percent of all households with children, and fewer than one-quarter of single parents were divorced. This was the case in Belgium and Luxembourg but above all in countries where divorce was prohibited or recently legalized: Ireland and the Mediterranean countries. Other countries, such as Denmark, West Germany, France, the United Kingdom, and the United States, had already made the transition to the new regime: more than 10 percent of households with children were single-parent families (nearly 20 percent in Denmark and 25 percent in the United States), and of those single parents fewer than 25 percent were widowed and more than 40 percent were divorced (nearly 70 percent in Denmark). Like changes in the fertility rate and marriage index, the emergence of this new regime of single-parenting is often seen as the consequence—and symptom—of a crisis in the "nuclear family" model with its highly differentiated marital and parental roles.

Crisis in the Nuclear Family or Tempest in a Teapot?

Discussions of the family in the 1950s either celebrated or deplored the triumph of the "nuclear" family (father, mother, children) over the "extended" patriarchal family, which supposedly had once gathered several generations and clans together under one roof. In many regions, however, it had not been usual for parents, adult children, and children's offspring to share a domicile since the end of the Middle Ages. Furthermore, the baby boom coupled with the postwar housing shortage had actually increased the average number of persons per household. Households consisting of at least three persons were in the majority in all developed countries in the 1950s.

Thirty years later, things had changed: more than half of all households consisted of just one or two individuals in Scandinavia, Austria, Switzerland, Belgium, the Netherlands, France, West Germany, and the United Kingdom. Since the percentage of two-person households had changed very little, it was the number of "single-person" households that had increased dramatically. Immediately after World War II single-person households accounted for just 6 percent of the total in Canada and 19 percent in France. By 1980, one-fifth to one-third of all households in the West consisted of a man or woman living alone. The growth in the number of single-person households was due primarily to an increased life expectancy generally, and greater longevity for women than for men (elderly women accounted for the largest proportion of those living alone). But it was often seen as a sign of growing disaffection with marriage. Young people had first stopped marrying, then stopped living together. This explanation goes too far. Nevertheless, some recent studies have pointed to an increase in "non-cohabiting couples": in France, for example, one-quarter of men and one-third of women living alone in 1985 stated that they were involved in a stable amorous relationship.[2]

Since the turn of the century changes in the proportion of married women working outside the home have followed different patterns in different industrialized countries. In some countries, such as Great Britain, the rate of working women remained stable, whereas in other countries, such as Belgium and France, it declined. By contrast, it has increased steadily since World War II in North America and West Germany. The mid-1960s witnessed a sharp increase in the percentage of married working women in most countries.

Of the countries belonging to the Organization for Economic Cooperation and Development, the highest rates of married working women at the end of the 1970s were found in Scandinavia and the English-speaking countries, where more than 45 percent of women over fifteen worked (45 percent in the United Kingdom and Australia, 49 percent in the United States and Canada, 57 percent in Denmark and Sweden), many of them part-time (4 out of 10 in Scandinavia, 2 out of 10 in the United States). In 1985, the proportion of married women under fifty years of age with jobs exceeded 55 percent in five of the ten countries of the Common Market: West Germany, Belgium, Great Britain, France, and Denmark (with 87 percent). In three of these five countries—Denmark, Belgium, and France—as well as other countries, such as Italy, more than a third of women with at least one child under the age of four also held full-time jobs.

None of these phenomena is really new, except for the increase in the number of couples separating. In centuries past, high mortality rates left many parents alone with children to raise, and in many regions children left home when they married or even sooner, to find work: thus high birthrates, high death rates, and the departure of children combined to produce considerable fluctuation in household size. Illegitimate births and cohabitation without marriage increased after the Industrial Revolution. It was not the first time that the fertility rate in Europe had decreased considerably: this had happened at the end of the nineteenth century across much of the Continent and even earlier in France. And women did not wait for modern times to go to work.

Should we therefore regard the significance of changes in the demographic indices that have occurred since the mid-1960s as nothing more than a tempest in a teapot? To be sure, the changes noted above are eminently "conjunctural," as well as conjectural.[3] Many sociologists and demographers argue, moreover, that despite the alarms "the family is still doing well." They point out, for example, that West German women marry when they want children and stay home so long as the children are young; American women do not cohabit much, divorce easily, but remarry just as often; and in France in the 1980s, despite the increase in divorce, cohabitation, and out-of-wedlock births, 83 percent of people under the age of twenty were born to married parents and lived with them, while an equivalent proportion of men and women between the ages of thirty and fifty were married and had never divorced.

Many feminist writers, moreover, have sought to show that despite the high proportion of women with jobs, child-rearing remains the number one priority for most women, along with the care of physically dependent persons, family responsibilities, housework, and domestic production. These findings are supported by surveys of men's and women's schedules, which suggest little change in the division of household chores.

Focusing on the permanent features of the family institution and "sexual order" leads, however, to underestimating the magnitude of the changes that have affected the population and labor force in the West over the past century and especially since the end of World War II.

A New Regime for Motherhood

Since 1870 a series of discoveries and scientific and technological advances have decreased the mortality rate and dramatically reduced the portion of a woman's life taken up by pregnancy and nursing, thus shaking the traditional foundation of the sexual division of labor and power.

The procreation-related risks of maternal and infantile morbidity and mortality have been reduced considerably over the past century by progress in many areas of hygiene, medicine, and nutrition. In 1930 the infant mortality rate (the proportion of children dead before the age of one) was nowhere lower than 3.5 percent and stood above 10 percent in the Mediterranean countries, Central Europe, and Japan. By 1955 it had fallen below 5 percent in all Western countries, and by 1965 it was below 2.5 percent, except along the Mediterranean. In 1989 the infant mortality rate in Canada and most of Northern and Western Europe was below 0.8 percent; in Sweden and Finland it had fallen to 0.6 percent and in Japan to 0.5.

Meanwhile, life expectancy increased considerably. A woman born in France in the middle of the eighteenth century could expect, on average, to live less than thirty years. A century later her life expectancy had risen to forty. A woman born in 1930 could hope to live to sixty, whereas one born in 1987 could look forward to eighty-seven years of life.

The increase in life expectancy was greater for women than for men. In 1950 the average life expectancy of a thirty-year-old woman in the developed countries already exceeded that of a comparable man by three years. A Swedish woman of thirty could expect to live forty-six more years, a Swedish man only forty-three. Experts had expected that this disparity would diminish as male and female life-styles became more similar, but instead it increased, particularly after improvements in gynecological testing and treatment. By 1970 the life expectancy of a thirty-year-old man had marked little or no increase, whereas women of that age had gained another three years. A thirty-year-old Swedish woman could expect to live another forty-nine years, compared with forty-four for a Swedish man; in France the comparable figures were forty-eight and forty-one. Measured at birth, the disparity between the sexes was even larger: six to seven years in Sweden and most other developed countries in the mid-1980s, but more than seven years in the United States and eight in France and Finland.

The significant decline in the mortality rate was the driving force behind what has been called the "demographic transition." Since couples in the developed countries were no longer obliged to have five or six children in the hope of seeing two live to adulthood, they not only wished to limit the number of births but had the means to do so, leading to a "new demographic regime" characterized by a low mortality rate and a low fertility rate.

The move toward birth control began as early as the end of the eighteenth century in France and the end of the nineteenth century in most other Western countries, but it was not until the late 1950s that the "ultimate weapons" became available in the form of oral contraceptives and intrauterine devices.[4] Despite opposition to the use of such artificial contraception, the new techniques caught on, so that, by 1990, 48 percent of French women of childbearing age who did not wish to conceive were using oral contraceptives, 26 percent were using the coil, and fewer than 3 percent no contraception at all. In West Germany and Belgium women also preferred the pill, whereas in Northern Europe they favored the IUD. In the Netherlands, the United Kingdom, and above all the United States and Canada, surgical sterilization was common: in the mid-1980s nearly half the married women in Quebec either had had tubal ligations or were married to men who had had vasectomies.

If "modern" contraceptive methods were not quite the "ultimate weapon" they were claimed to be when first introduced, they did promise a major change in sexual relations insofar as determining who took the initiative and had control over not only contraception but perhaps the whole of sexual life. The pill and coil were much less of an impediment to sexual relations and much more reliable than earlier contraceptive methods. The failure rate of the alternatives (withdrawal, condoms, vaginal douches, diaphragms, and the "rhythm method"), as measured in various studies carried out between 1935 and 1958, ranged from a minimum of 6 all the way up to 38 percent.

Even more important, the pill and coil were methods of contraception that women could use in advance of sexual intercourse. They could decide how often they wished to become pregnant and at what point in their lives. When women chose these forms of contraception, men, for the first time in history, could no longer expose them to the risk of pregnancy against their will. The man who wanted a child could do nothing unless his partner also wanted one. What is more, progress in genetics made it more difficult for men to blame their partners for their own sterility (or for the failure to produce a son) or else to deny paternity for which they did not wish to accept responsibility.

The decline in the infant mortality rate, together with the "contraceptive revolution," dramatically decreased the amount of time that the average woman in Western society spent in pregnancy. Under the old demographic regime (which survives in many

Third World countries), pregnancy occupied four and a half years of the typical woman's life. By the time her last child was born, the average woman was roughly forty years old and could expect to live no more than twenty-three additional years. Under the new regime, a woman is pregnant for eighteen months of her life, is no more than thirty when her last child is born, and can expect to live nearly a half-century longer.[5]

Furthermore, new technologies for feeding infants, developed since the late nineteenth century and marketed widely after World War II, not only decreased the infant mortality rate but also severed the tie between childbearing and child-rearing: the average length of breast-feeding decreased, and the number of people capable of replacing the mother in caring for a young infant increased. In the old days, only another lactating mother (or, with much greater risk to the child, another mammal) could take the place of the mother who could not or would not nurse her own offspring. But with the advent of sterilized animal milk, bottles, and nipples, and the perfection of manufactured formula and baby food, anyone, regardless of sex—and thus, for the first time in history, the father—could care for a newborn. What is more, a wet nurse, if used at all, had to be used regularly, whereas bottle-feeding could be sporadic. Technically, then, an infant no longer needed its mother or any other lactating female in order to survive. It thus became possible for parents and others (family members, neighbors, friends, employees, nannies, daycare workers) to divide the work of caring for infants.

The need for mothers to stay with their very young children had given rise to the idea that it was somehow natural or rational for women to perform the labor of childcare, but the new feeding techniques undermined the legitimacy of this belief and "liberated" women—ideologically as well as physically—to enter the labor market. Further contributing to that liberation were changes in housework and, more generally, the whole range of what might be called the "labor of reproduction."

Welfare and the Labor of Reproduction

The three decades of strong economic growth that the capitalist countries experienced after World War II also witnessed widespread though uneven progress in welfare, in both senses of the word: the kind of welfare provided by the welfare state, and the welfare associated with a rising level of comfort and prosperity. Welfare is thus not only a symbol of the modern state but a driving force behind mass production and consumption, and for both reasons the traditional housekeeping and caregiving role of women changed forever.

The "Liberation" of the Housewife

The nature of the home and conditions of housework changed dramatically in the thirty years following World War II.[6] In all Western countries, even those that had suffered war damage and the ensuing crisis of housing, the housing stock expanded rapidly, and average per capita living space doubled. In France, fewer than 2 million new residences had been constructed in the interwar period and more than 1 million existing housing units had been destroyed or rendered uninhabitable by the war, but between 1945 and 1971 more than 7 million new units were constructed, more than 5 million of them with state aid. In the countries of the Common Market, seven new housing units were built for every 1,000 inhabitants every year from 1950 to 1963. In 1963 the construction rate stood at above 10 in Sweden, 9 in Switzerland, West Germany, and Finland, and 8 in Italy and the United States. Whether these were individual homes, as was generally the case in the United States, Belgium, the United Kingdom, and Denmark, or apartments, as in France and Switzerland, most of the new units contained at least four rooms and were built to modern standards of comfort including all the amenities (heat, water, sewers, electricity).

The nature of the home and the tasks necessary to maintain it changed considerably as a result both of the increase in the amount of space available and of the use of certain rooms for certain specific purposes: a standard "modern" home included a kitchen, bathroom(s), bedrooms, and living room. Running water and sewers became standard, along with gas and/or electricity for heating and cooking (and not just lighting). The "warmth of the hearth" could now be found in rooms other than the kitchen.

Some of the more onerous household chores were thus eliminated: it was no longer necessary to fetch water, coal, and wood daily, nor was there any need to light and tend the fire or carry out ashes, rinsewater, and human waste. Furthermore, many household tasks could now be at least partially mechanized by means of appliances.

Gas and electric ovens, refrigerators, electric coffee grinders, vacuum cleaners, sewing machines, washing machines, and electric irons transformed the tasks of cooking, cleaning, washing, and mending. In most Western countries, however, it was not until the 1970s that more than half of all households were equipped with the "first wave" of household appliances (including cars and television sets). Protests against "consumer society" in countries like France and Italy actually erupted before those countries had equipped 50 percent of their households with hot water, modern bathrooms, telephones, washing machines, vacuum cleaners, or TVs.

Household tasks were affected just as much by the growing use of "modern" consumer products: canned, frozen, and prepared foods, detergents and other household cleaning products, paper towels and toilet paper, synthetic fabrics, and so on. Furthermore, housewives increasingly turned to "outside suppliers" for many things formerly made at home, such as clothing and meals.

Since women no longer needed to devote full time to household chores, a vast reservoir of labor was freed up for productive work outside the home. The same transformation of housework also made such outside work necessary, because many families required two incomes in order to afford the new products, equipment, and services that partly or totally replaced traditional forms of housework.

Despite the considerable increase in industrial productivity that took place between the end of World War II and the mid-1970s, it was not enough to meet household demand stimulated by governmental policies designed to increase purchasing power. Hence industries and services supplying household needs recruited women at an accelerating pace. Between 1954 and 1980 the number of women employed in the manufacture of foodstuffs and the retail sale of food and ready-to-wear apparel grew by 80 percent, for example, while female employment in restaurants and cafés grew by 150 percent and in the manufacturing of household appliances by 250 percent.

As the comfort of homes increased, women were driven out of them to find jobs. The old "industrial" logic, whereby men took priority in jobs requiring "strength" while women worked at home, was undermined by changes in the "postindustrial" labor market owing to the rise of the service sector and the growing reliance on automation and computers.

In the early stages of industrialization, "muscle capital" had to be reconstituted every day, and the labor necessary for that reconstitution was largely delegated to others, generally at home. Now, however, "intellectual capital" counted for more than muscle power, and things changed. In essence, intellectual capital has to be acquired before an individual enters the job market, and its accumulation depends on the use of the goods and services drawn from the nation's educational, training, and cultural reserves. Necessary skills are acquired in school, but the success of schooling is strongly correlated with the cultural capital of the family, and particularly the mother of the person undergoing "socialization."

This change in the way in which the workforce is trained and maintained is largely responsible for the changes noted earlier in the various demographic indicators associated with marriage. For any given individual, the functional importance of the marital tie and the "destination family" (the family that a person creates by marrying), which was crucial in reconstituting muscle power, is marginal in the formation and "updating" of intellectual capital.

By contrast, the functional importance of the "socialization family" (the family in which a child grows up) and its cultural capital is greater than ever, and so is the influence of activities and investments associated with socialization and culture in the labor of reproduction. Thus, as Daniela del Boca writes, although "technological changes in domestic labor have increased the productivity of activities associated with *maintenance,* the same is not the case for activities of *investment.*"[7] These investment activities, particularly the chore of keeping up relations with schools and various agencies of the welfare bureaucracy, have increased as systems of social protection have grown and as the responsibility for caring for the elderly and the sick and other aspects of the labor of reproduction have been shifted either to private purveyors or to the government.[8]

The "Collectivization" of the Labor of Reproduction

In the mid-1980s, the minimum age for a child to begin compulsory schooling varied in the Common Market countries from five to seven. In France, Belgium, and Italy, full-time schooling for most children began as early as three. More than half of the children aged three to five in Germany, the Netherlands, Luxembourg, Ireland, Spain, and Greece attended a nursery school, preschool, kindergarten, or play group (generally less than six hours a day, however). Most European countries played little role in the socialization of children below the age of three, however, and little was done to free their mothers for work. The only countries in which more than 5 percent of these very young children were placed in state daycare facilities were France, Belgium, and Denmark. In France and Belgium nearly a quarter of children under three attended a communal or family daycare facility or a nursery school. In Denmark state- and community-financed daycare centers served 45 percent of children under three, and nearly 90 percent of children aged three to seven (not yet required to attend school) participated in one or another publicly funded or subsidized activity.[9]

Elderly persons may live with their adult children without being dependent on them. The elderly may give as much help as they receive, if not more. Nevertheless, the frequency of such cohabitation has diminished since World War II, and this suggests that, despite the increase in the average life expectancy, adults in the prime of life now do less to care for the elderly than in the past. Retirement pensions are now common and more generous than they once were, and many institutions have developed to serve the needs of the elderly. There are also services and subsidies available to the elderly who wish to remain in their own homes. Furthermore, the health of the population generally has improved, and more housing is available for elders who wish to live on their own. Thus in France, although the number of women over the age of seventy-five increased 71 percent between 1962 and 1982, the number of women in that group living with one of their children increased only 22 percent over the same period. And in Denmark the proportion of octogenarians without a spouse living with one of their children fell from 41 to 22 percent for men and 27 to 11 percent for women between 1962 and 1977.

Women, who once bore primary responsibility for the care of dependent generations (children and the elderly), now find their burden eased and shifted in part onto the community. In the past this burden meant that women, during at least a portion of the family life cycle, were largely confined to the home, but now they are free to remain on the job market more or less continuously, thereby opening up new career opportunities. In France, for example, the number of women working in the teaching and health professions increased fourfold from 1962 to 1982 and eighteenfold in early childcare (nursery schools, daycare).

Taken together, moreover, the social services (teaching, health, welfare, and the like) now account for one-tenth of all jobs in Austria, West Germany, and Italy, one-sixth in France, the United Kingdom, the United States, and Canada, and one-quarter in Scandinavia. This is the sector in which the growth of women's employment has been the most dramatic.

Wedded to Welfare?

The close connection between the growth in female employment and the expansion of public and private life and the "labor-power reproduction sector"—or, more familiarly, "social service sector"—has led some commentators to describe women as "wedded to the welfare state." In fact, some have argued that "women 'are' the welfare state, both as service providers and as recipients of social assistance."[10] Similarly, Helga Maria Hernes argues that the growing collectivization and professionalization of the labor of reproduction have "transformed women's erstwhile economic dependence on their fathers and husbands into economic dependence on the state, both in their roles as clients and consumers of public subsidies and services and as employees of the public sector, where they are paid essentially to do the work of reproduction."[11]

Although the argument that women are wedded to the welfare state is not entirely conclusive, the formulation is useful in that it points up the functional devaluation of marriage and the "destination family."[12] The changes in the structure of marriage (such as the increased frequency of informal cohabitation and divorce) may reflect the emergence of a postindustrial regime of reproduction characterized by the "intellectualization" and collectivization of the labor of reproduction. Under such a regime, marriage loses its functional underpinnings and is legitimated primarily by feelings of love and sexual attraction, hence it becomes a more private and less permanent matter.

The welfare state has made it possible for women to work by lightening the burdens of housekeeping, childcare, sick care, care of the elderly, and so on, and by providing a range of social protections. This has made women less dependent on marriage as an institution, allowing them to avoid marrying or to end a marriage if the benefits do not seem to outweigh the costs. Furthermore, by helping to deal with the problems of "divorced children" and providing aid to single-parent families, the welfare state has attempted to limit and collectivize the risks resulting from women's greater independence, particularly where the socialization of children is concerned. Yet not all female citizens of welfare states enjoy the same autonomy with respect to marriage, nor do they all pay the same price for the autonomy they do enjoy.

Social Service Providers and Independence

Most of those employed as social service providers, particularly in the public sector, have high school or college degrees. In recent years large numbers of women have gone into this line of work, where they were able to make use not only of the "feminine capital" acquired through a process of socialization that encouraged them to develop the qualities needed to perform the labor of social reproduction (dedication, human relations skills, educational knowhow, and so on) but also of the "educational capital" that their parents encouraged them to acquire as insurance against the vicissitudes of marriage.

By investing their feminine and educational capital simultaneously in both the job market and the matrimonial market, many social service professionals have done quite well for themselves. In France, for example, where three-fourths of social service jobs are in the public sector, women choosing this line of work have obtained the best return on their diplomas in terms of salary and access to high-level jobs.[13] Many of these positions are protected by civil service regulations, so that women who have wedded the welfare system have often found it easier than others to reconcile family life with their professional activities.

Thus, for example, many women working in retail businesses or private sector services (hotels, restaurants, housecleaning, and so on) are obliged against their will to work part-time, while many social service professionals choose to work part-time so that they have time left over for children and housework. And those who do work full-time find their jobs less consuming and less rigid when it comes to scheduling than do women in some other fields.

In France, only 12 percent of women employed as business or sales executives work less than 35 hours per week, compared with

50 percent of female graduates working in social services. And of those 12 percent of executives, 85 percent are paid for part-time work, compared with less than half of the social service workers. Given an equivalent level of education or training, French women employed in the public sector or in social services work on average several hours per week less than other women (including travel time to and from work and time spent in work or study at home), and they allocate several hours per week more to household chores; in addition, their husbands contribute more time to the household than do their counterparts. To be sure, women employed in the public sector tend to have more children than other working women, especially if they are school teachers, but they are also less likely to stop working when their children are very young. Thus it appears that they find it easier than other working women to reconcile motherhood, housework, and job. They also tend to live in couples more and to divorce less than other women with degrees. But their educational capital and job security permit them, if need be, to take the initiative in ending a marriage, and it is easier for them to cope with the financial consequences of a husband's death or departure.

The welfare state thus offers women a degree of independence and of protection from the risks of poverty associated with single-parent families, but these benefits vary from country to country, depending primarily on the size of the service sector, the level of female employment, the nature of the provider of social services (public or private), and the nature of the welfare state as determined by each country's particular social history. The situation thus depends on whether the welfare state is, to use Gosta Esping-Andersen's categories, "statist-corporatist," as in Germany, "social democratic," as in Sweden, or "liberal," as in the United States.[14]

In West Germany, where the service sector is one of the smallest in the Western world and where fewer than half of all married women work, collectivization of the labor of social reproduction, which has taken place primarily under federal auspices, has been slow and limited. The feminization of public sector jobs came to an end in the early 1960s, but in the meantime the share of the public sector in the nation's economy has increased considerably, and with it the number of women employed in the public sector (from one in fifteen working women in 1961 to one in five in 1983).

In Sweden, where the proportion of working women (and of

women working part-time) is quite high, the labor of social reproduction is highly collectivized (one out of four jobs is in social
services, almost all under state auspices). More than half of the
working women in Sweden are employed in the public sector, and
more than two-thirds of the jobs in this sector, and in social
services generally, are held by women.

In the United States, where the service sector predominates,
the collectivization of the labor of social reproduction has taken
place largely within the market; the proportion of Americans
working in the public sector has even declined since the early
1960s. But there has been a marked feminization of both public
sector jobs and service sector jobs. In 1940 the service sector
offered 3 million jobs, 59 percent of which were held by women;
forty years later, 70 percent of the 17 million jobs were held by
women, and one woman in three (but only one man in ten) was
employed in social services.[15]

In short, German women who wedded the welfare state found
in their wedding basket fewer service jobs and more limited possibilities for independence than their Swedish or American sisters.
American women enjoy less job security because of the smaller
public sector there, hence run greater risks in case a marriage ends
than do their German or above all Swedish counterparts. The
Swedes are in the best position: they enjoy both greater independence and greater security than the American and German women.

Welfare and Protection in Case of Divorce

To judge the degree of protection that various welfare states afford
in case of divorce, one can compare the respective proportions of
single-parent families and couples with children in each country
that fall below a given threshold of poverty, say, those whose
income is less than half the median.[16]

By such a measure Western countries can be divided into several groups. The first group, characterized by a high risk of poverty
associated with single parenthood and a low degree of protection
against this risk, includes such "liberal" welfare states as the
United States and Canada and, to a lesser degree, the United
Kingdom, where there is relatively little redistribution of income
among households. The proportion of "poor" households (with
incomes less than half the median) is high, and there is little in the
way of social transfer payments (social benefits less income taxes)

to reduce it: the number of "poor" households after all social transfers is not much lower (and in some instances higher!) than before. The proportion of single-parent families is high, however, ranging from 13 percent of all households with children in the United Kingdom to 23 percent in the United States. And these single-parent families are the most vulnerable to the risk of poverty: the percentage of "poor" households among them is initially (that is, before transfer payments) greater than 50 percent, and is three to four times higher than for couples with children. The risk is greater for the younger single parents: 60 to 80 percent of those under the age of thirty are "poor," and social transfers do nothing to alleviate the situation. In recent years the risk of poverty associated with single parenthood in these countries has even increased: the proportion of "poor" single-parent families (after as well as before social transfers and regardless of the age of the parent) went up in both the United States and Canada during the 1980s.

In other countries, such as West Germany and France (where the proportion of single-parent families is also fairly high, ranging from 11 to 14 percent of households with children), the risk of poverty associated with single parenthood is lower: only 25 to 40 percent of single-parent households are poor, and social transfer payments have a substantial impact, elevating roughly half of that group out of the "poor" category. In Germany, however, the social safety net works only for single mothers above the age of thirty. For younger women, the proportion left poor after social transfers is three times greater than for the older group, and it more than doubled during the 1980s. All in all, while the "statist-corporatist" welfare states accord greater benefits to single-parent households than to others, these subsidies still leave roughly two to four times as many single-parent households in the "poor" category.

The highly redistributive "social democratic" welfare states (where social transfer payments reduce the proportion of poor households by at least half) substantially limit the risks of single parenthood: the proportion of poor households is roughly the same for single-parent families as for couples with children. This is the case whether the risk of poverty is low, as in Sweden, or high, as in the Netherlands. In Sweden, the proportion of poor households prior to transfer payments is twice as great for single-parent families as for the population as a whole; in the Netherlands it is four times as great, and few single mothers, especially if they are young, have incomes high enough to escape poverty. But the protection offered by social transfers is such that in both countries it reduces the proportion of poor single-parent families by a factor of three or more. In Sweden this protection even increased during the 1980s: the proportion of poor single-parent families was decreased by a factor of almost two and was actually lower than the rate for all households.

Given these figures, it will come as no surprise that Swedish scholars have emphasized the theme of "state feminism," whereas scholars in the United States have discussed what they call the "feminization of poverty."

In summary, the benefits that women have derived from the welfare state vary widely. As with dowries, so, too, with welfare: things are not always what they seem. I have argued that, since 1950, the technological and economic basis of sexual relations has been profoundly altered by the emergence in the developed countries of a new regime for the reproduction of population and labor force. In each country, however, history—the shifting relations between social groups and the resultant welfare laws—has shaped the way in which that fundamental alteration has been reflected in the lives of men and women and of different social classes.

TRANSLATED FROM THE FRENCH BY ARTHUR GOLDHAMMER

15

A Supervised Emancipation

Rose-Marie Lagrave

THE PRINCIPAL OF a girl's school in Périgueux, speaking at the school's annual prize awards ceremony on July 23, 1908, observed that "the twentieth century will write the history of the rivalry between men and women." As we stand on the threshold of the twenty-first century, we are obliged to note that this prediction has not come true. For rivalry both sides must have some chance of winning, and the battle must be waged with equal arms. Yet despite the growing feminization of society, the contest between men and women remains too unequal for any genuine competition to take place. What characterizes the twentieth century is rather a long and slow process of legitimation of the sexual division of society, which has been achieved by perpetuating or reinventing subtle forms of segregation in both the educational system and the workplace. The social order acts as a kind of switching station, which systematically albeit imperfectly assigns men and women to separate spheres of education and labor. Its primary function is to avoid competition between the sexes and to find euphemisms for the violence of male domination.[1] Yet this has been a century in which equality of the sexes has been continually proclaimed and inscribed in gilt letters in the law, to the point where any number of observers have been inclined to characterize it as "liberating." Indeed, all analysts, no matter what the time or place, agree that women wield a growing influence over the machinery of society. There is a sort of optical illusion involved here: the impression of equality comes from observing the improvement in the condition of women without noticing that the condition of men has also improved. Thus deceived, one is tempted to pay homage to the waning century. If, however, one adopts a relational mode of thinking, the ascension of women must be measured at every moment against the progress made by men, whereupon the permanence of the gap separating men from women in education as well as the workplace becomes apparent.

It is not enough, however, to demonstrate the permanence of sexual inequality, because inequality among women is equally important. While twentieth-century women have certain common characteristics, as thinkers of all sorts constantly strive to remind them, their chances of equaling men are unevenly distributed. In France, for example, a talented female student might study the classics at an elite Catholic institution in order to compete with graduates of the all-male Ecole Normale Supérieure on the rigorous competitive examination that controls access to the country's most prestigious teaching positions, while a young woman of the working class, guided by a sort of class instinct that at times takes precedence over the gender instinct, might battle shoulder-to-shoulder with young male workers. Between the two remains all the distance that separates two social classes. Yet the existence of an inegalitarian system of differences tells us nothing about the irreversible, permanent character of the power that derives from the luck of being born on the right side of inequality, the social good fortune of being a man. In school and workplace there is no periodic reversal of majority as there is in politics: the dominant positions are always occupied by men, the devalued positions by women. A feminized occupation never becomes masculinized, and the Sorbonne, which one wag in 1919 called the "Allée des demoiselles" (Maidens' Lane), has not turned into the "Allée des messieurs." When women advance in a profession or discipline, men desert it (if they have not already done so). The situation is not one of rivalry or even honest competition but of silent defection. This avoidance behavior perpetuates the structural gap between men and women, even though the structure itself changes to adapt to changing times. This gap cannot be fully comprehended, however, without bearing in mind that any comparison between men and women, even one apparently based on solid statistical data, is in its very conception biased: all other things are never equal. The family, for instance, presents men and women with different ideological and practical burdens. Men are encouraged to work in order to meet the needs of the family, whereas women are made to feel guilty for "abandoning" the family if they take a job to make ends meet. Men "embark on careers" but women desert children and home. Way back in 1919 Pierre Hamp wrote that "with the feminization of the trades we are trampling on our children's cradles." With changes in the argument to suit the circumstances, this dictum might serve as a motto for the twentieth century: sure, educate women and give them work, but be careful to make sure that nothing adverse happens to the family. Stay within the bounds of what is thinkable for women at any given time, and see to it that the top credentials and jobs remain scarce and therefore prized and of course exclusively in the hands of men. From earliest childhood both girls and boys must be taught that their tastes and aptitudes are different and that with time those differences will embody themselves in distinct work hierarchies. Thus the twentieth century has witnessed an influx of large numbers of women into the schools and the workforce, but there remains a clear disparity in the likelihood of educational success and a clear segregation of men and women in the workplace. Some things change, but segregation remains a constant.

Work or Family?

Once the torment of World War I had come to an end and the time came to assess what women had achieved in the areas of education and jobs, many contemporaries concluded that "the war of 1914 was 1789 for women." The war did do a great deal for women: the men who had been sent to the front left their jobs behind, and women held down the home front. As long as the slaughter continued, men and women no longer competed for work. By 1917 some people had begun to think about the cessation of hostilities and the problems that would need to be solved when the men returned home. Nothing was easy. The ensuing years, the period between the two world wars, gave every indication that capitalism was suffering from an infantile disorder: depression,

455

crises, the stock-market crash, and structural unemployment revealed to an astonished world that there were no international
agencies available for regulating an economy in crisis. While the
world economy suffered from a series of structural and conjunctural disturbances, women made progress in both school and
workplace. This surprised some observers and dismayed others,
but there was general agreement that the real emergency lay elsewhere. When so many men had given their lives, if women themselves failed to perceive their duty, they needed to be reminded
of it.

From the Spirit to the Letter

Postwar rebuilding called for repopulation of depleted nations. As
the birthrate declined, the number of women workers increased.
As men returned to jobs in factories and fields, yet another ideological offensive, this one of unprecedented scope, was launched
to encourage women to return to their homes.

With strong backing from the Church, the government aimed
its family policy primarily at working women, especially the married ones. They were the root of all evil: the falling birthrate, the
rising infant mortality rate, the collapse of the family, the degeneration of morals, and the failure of parents to bring their children
up properly. Quick action was required, and the offensive was to
be two-pronged, with prohibition pure and simple constituting the
more radical, repressive side and propaganda depicting housework
in a more favorable light constituting the positive, educational
side. No government can embark on a campaign of this kind
without first protecting its rear. The French government sought
the support of Catholic women's leagues and "social Catholic"
elements of the business community. Meanwhile, international
surveys were conducted periodically to evaluate the likelihood of
success in persuading women to return to their kitchens.[2] The
answers were clear but embarrassing, in view of the difficulty of
reconciling Catholic morality with economic self-interest. Businessmen responded that while it was of course in the general
interest to ban married women from working, it might not be in
the interest of their particular firms. Was it therefore really necessary? Austrian businessmen noted that the cost of living would
rise: if women returned home, men would have to be hired to
replace them, and in Austria male workers were paid twice what

females earned. Respondents from France, Italy, and Spain reported that working mothers were more level-headed employees than younger women. A majority of those surveyed in Belgium, Italy, and Austria proposed legally prohibiting married women from working, whereas French respondents suggested that it was best to go slow, because such a move would only encourage couples to live together out of wedlock. But this argument carried no weight in Austria, where it was shown that extramarital cohabitation usually involved kept women, not "working girls." The pros and cons were carefully weighed: industry would no longer have to pay maternity allowances, but it would have to pay higher wages to men. It was far from clear that a radical approach was the best, so a coalition formed around a minimal consensus: Catholic employers should henceforth refuse to "give work to" (occuper) women with children.

This offensive lacked finesse. A more sophisticated approach was to make women themselves responsible for leaving the workplace. To do this it was necessary to whip up enthusiasm for returning to the kitchen. There was no shortage of instruments for implementing this aspect of family policy: publicists dreamed up the mother as educator and invented the rationalized, Taylorized homeworker as the keystone of the new household economy. New schools and adult-education courses were created to teach homemaking, some with accoutrements intended to appeal to the middle class, others aimed at a more popular audience. Working-class wives were taught how to avoid waste and work miracles with "the materials at hand," in other words, how to get by on a modest income. While workmen fought for decent wages, their wives were supposed to learn how to make do by stretching the budget to the limit. In 1923 the first Home Show in France awakened middle-class wives from their dogmatic slumbers: by acquiring new appliances and learning new ways to entertain, housewives could share in the surplus value of their husbands' social capital while consuming less but more wisely. In Germany housekeeping contests encouraged young women to learn new homemaking techniques, and the year 1934 was declared "the year of the housewife." Despite the grand design for the future of women, familial discourse soon began to lose favor, however: it was simply too much at odds with the interests of industry and with aspirations for social advancement that structural change made possible. The bold new propaganda did not persuade all women to stay home.

To be sure, women bore the brunt of the faltering economies' ups and downs. Although women were the first to be fired when business slowed down, female employment fared well in the storm, not advancing notably but not declining precipitously either. Statistics compiled for Europe by the League of Nations show that the proportion of working women as a percentage of the total female population was remarkably stable. Statistically speaking, the Continent can be divided into two parts: in Northern Europe, especially in Denmark, Sweden, Norway, England, and Finland—countries that had been industrialized since the middle of the nineteenth century—the number of working women increased between 1900 and 1910, held steady or declined slightly until 1930 or 1931, and then rose rapidly until 1945. Countries farther to the south tried to regain lost ground. Having begun at a very low level of female employment and having risen only slightly, Greece, Italy, and Spain "took off" between 1915 and 1920. In Greece, for example, the proportion of working women rose from 13.6 percent in 1921 to 24 percent in 1928. France led the pack, with 36 percent of women working in 1926 compared with 23 percent in Italy. Nevertheless, labor in Europe was still mainly men's business: the number of working men was two to three times as high as the number of working women. Even more revealing is the change in the number of married women working: women aged twenty-five to thirty-four, thus of an age to marry and bear children, went to work just the same. This was particularly true in France: while the proportion of working women overall decreased from 1921 to 1936, the proportion of married women with jobs increased from 35.2 to 41.4 percent. The verdict of the figures is clear: married women resisted being imprisoned in their homes.[3] The limitations of pro-family propaganda were clear, and its consequences were rather different from what was intended: the way it influenced the structure of women's employment was by encouraging women to seek bureaucratic and social variants of domestic work, that is, to search for gender-identified positions in spite of the success women had had in penetrating certain previously all-male bastions.

Men's Plans, Women's Destinies

In Europe pre-capitalist forms of labor such as home work and the family work unit gave way to wage labor. A threefold process ensued: the distribution of female labor across different industries changed, the number of women employed in the service sector increased, and women advanced in intellectual and professional careers. This structural transformation stemmed not only from changes in the economy but also from working-class strategies of social mobility and bourgeois family strategies of reproduction. Bourgeois families sought to equip their daughters with educational baggage that could take the place of a dowry or add to the dowry's value. Education was the instrument of all these plans, even though schools were still ill-adapted to the job market. Different classes made different use of the schools, which were at once more democratic and more selective, thereby broadening the horizons of some students and narrowing those of others, most notably women. Working-class women found their chances more restricted than did working-class men.

After World War I the working class changed in all European countries. It continued, however, to be characterized by occupational homogeneity, trade-union traditions, and hostility to women's work. Occupational training and general education raised the skill level of male workers but had little effect on females. Primary schooling affected everyone, however.

In France, parity between boys and girls in primary education was achieved in 1901. The weaknesses of technical education and of the obsolete apprenticeship system were compensated by on-the-job training and short-term remedial courses. Having few if any skills, women were well suited to the new industrial logic of scientific management (Taylorism), which transformed industry by widening the chasm between skilled and unskilled jobs. The goal was to derive profit from women's "natural" qualities: "Women stand out for their courage and their skill in jobs requiring a high level of motor dexterity and rapid, precise movements. What is more, women are thrifty, prudent by nature, and even avid for profit. A small increment in reward is sometimes enough to make her outdo herself on the job."[4]

Since women possess these skills "naturally," they require no training and can be assigned to low-level jobs. And women did in fact fill many unskilled positions in industry. Although the number of women working in French industry did not increase between 1918 and 1945, it did not decrease either. There was, however, a shift from traditionally female sectors such as textiles and clothing into new sectors such as chemicals, metals, and foodstuffs. The proportion of women workers in the textile sector fell from 62 percent in 1931 to 55 percent in 1954, while the number of female metal workers increased sixfold over the same period. The restructuring of industry greatly diminished the gap between men's and women's wages. In 1920 the wage differential was 31.1 percent; it remained more or less constant until 1928, fell to 19 percent in 1930, went back up to 23 percent in 1936, and fell again to 15 percent in 1945. The Matignon wage accords of 1936 had the immediate impact of encouraging employers to hire women in preference to men to reduce their wage outlay. During the postwar reconstruction period industrial employment rose sharply, and many firms were forced to turn to women working at home, peasant women ready to leave the land, and ultimately immigrant women; businesses also offered assistance to women with families.

Between 1913 and 1931 the number of women working at home shrank by half as women took jobs in factories. Foreign labor accounted for 3.95 percent of the total working population in France in 1921, 6.59 percent in 1931, and 5.34 percent in 1936. Women and immigrants constituted the reserve labor pool on which employers drew when and as needed; furthermore, the existence of this pool exerted a downward pressure on wages. Although both women and immigrants filled unskilled jobs and were the first to be laid off in a recession, they did not work in the same sectors. Italian and Polish men were employed in construction, coal mining, and public works, whereas French women were employed in textiles, metals, and food processing. The economy determined its own needs according to the laws of the segmented labor market, the sexual division of labor, and the theory of "natural" skills.

The labor marketplace strategy was one of divide and conquer: violence was directed principally toward female workers as well as toward immigrants, "men without qualities," rather than native male workers with recognized skills. Harsh working conditions drove working-class families to strive to enable their children to escape from their class of origin. Although most sons still inherited their fathers' occupation, there was ardent hope that girls might "keep their hands clean" and join other "white-collar workers" in the service sector.

It was not only the working class that hoped its daughters might find work "suitable" for women. Lower-middle and middle-class families also hoped to improve their positions by sending daughters to secondary school in order to acquire an "occupational dowry" likely to attract a better mate. So girls were sent to school all across Europe, though the figures varied from country to country. The number of girls in school in Denmark, Norway, Sweden, and Finland rose rapidly between 1900 and 1913; in Italy, Spain, Greece, and Portugal the impact was not felt until 1928. In England, the Netherlands, Belgium, and France growth in girls' education was steady.

In France the ratio of the proportion of girls in secondary school relative to the number of boys rose from 23 percent in 1911 to 28.3 percent in 1945. At the secondary level, the private-public divide almost exactly coincided with the female-male. Nearly three times as many girls attended private high schools in 1911; by 1950 this ratio had decreased to two to one. The decree of March 25, 1924, made secondary curricula for boys and girls identical in France, and as a result the instruction of girls became less sexist and more secular, although their opportunities were still more limited than those of boys. The whole educational system encouraged girls to aspire to no more than a primary school diploma or at most a high school diploma. Girls were also encouraged to seek work in the female service professions. By 1930 the number of girls attending teachers' education programs surpassed the number of boys, and there was a waiting list for girls who wished to enter the nursing school of the Salpêtrière Hospital.

The schools adjusted to the needs of the labor market by the time the service sector entered a period of rapid growth. An increasingly complex economy needed efficient administrators and bureaucrats and bankers. Many women found jobs in the fast expanding banking and insurance sectors, which were responsible for 50 percent of the jobs created between 1906 and 1936, as well as in the public service sector, where female employment doubled in the same period. Women were encouraged to quit certain kinds of jobs in view of a tacit preference for placing men in active occupations and women in sedentary ones. The notion that some jobs were reserved for women began to make headway. In a polemical work published in 1914, André Bonnefoy urged men to quit office jobs and leave things like library work to women: "Man has no place there. [Library science] is the servant of the other sciences. This subordinate role is ill suited to man's natural pride. But women don't feel humiliated to play the same role in the library that they play at home."[5]

Many women approved of such views. Citing certain intellectual and moral qualities found only in women, Suzanne Françoise Cordelier urged women to avoid fields in which they might be called upon to compete with men (*Femmes au travail*, 1935). And Gina Lombroso went even further, asking (in *La Femme dans la société actuelle*, 1929) if modern society had not gone mad, forcing women into masculine careers even though "inequality is not an injustice."[6] Women's long march toward the bureaucracy was just beginning. It would continue throughout the century. But a few women, those with the most educational capital, followed the footsteps of their elders into masculine occupations.

Higher education—"higher" though it aims—cannot escape from the logic of sexual division. In most countries, although there is now a more even distribution of women through the various departments of the university than there used to be, by far the greatest number is still found in literature departments. Few female graduates become full professors, most remaining at the associate level. In 1930 not a single woman taught in any university in Spain or Portugal, although there were quite a few female professors in Italy, carrying on a tradition that can be traced back to the eighteenth century. And some female graduates went into professions such as medicine and law.

In Germany, Austria, and Holland, the number of women doctors increased rapidly. Women were admitted to the bar—reluctantly, to be sure—in several countries. The Sex Disqualification Removal Act of December 1919 authorized English women to become solicitors and barristers; Portuguese and German women obtained the same right in 1918 and 1922, respectively. Italian feminists reacted vehemently when the appellate court of Turin ruled in November 1883 that Lydia Poët could not be admitted to the bar of that city, and ultimately, in 1919, after a long struggle, Italian women did win the right to practice law. The militant feminist Teresa Labriola was the first Italian woman to be admitted to the bar. Yet in many countries, including France, female lawyers cannot become judges, on the grounds that women lack certain powers under civil law.

Technological and industrial advances during the war led to increased demand for engineers, hence growing numbers of engineering schools and a new willingness to train women as engineers. As recently as 1930, however, Holland was the only country that had more than 150 female engineers. In France women trained as engineers held jobs not commensurate with their training. They frequently found employment as technical librarians, teachers, or analytical chemists, but few were actually allowed to design machines. Some women with advanced degrees never held jobs at all. This was by no means rare at the time, simply because the spectacle of an educated woman was in itself such an oddity. One thing is certain, however: education did lead to women marrying similarly educated men, and in many countries, most notably England and the Netherlands, educated women quit working when they married.

The sexual order thus made its effects felt in different ways. The service sector was feminized, but in the intellectual realm it was not the profession itself but the internal hierarchy within the profession that was determined by sex. The sexual order also encouraged women to limit their own professional ambitions. After overcoming all the obstacles to gain an education, many women never ventured onto the professional battleground. Pro-family ideology led them to seek a compromise between being educated professionals and housewives, and they restrained their ambitions in order to conform to the bourgeois ideal of the time. At the International Congress of Women with University Degrees, held in Geneva in 1929, the Swiss official Maurice Naef remarked that "women can now give birth in spirit as well as body." Nevertheless, a great deal of ink was spilled over even the modest advances that women made in higher education and the intellectual professions. As had happened earlier, when women took jobs in industry at the beginning of the century, critics spoke of a "tidal wave" of women about to engulf the professions. Gustave Cohen, a professor at the faculty of letters in Paris, had this to say in *Les Nouvelles littéraires* of January 4, 1930: "If someone were to ask me what was the greatest revolution we have seen since the war, I would answer that it was the invasion of the university by women. As scarce as hen's teeth in my youth thirty years ago, their numbers increased until they accounted first for one-third, then for half, then for two-thirds of the student body, to the point where one has to ask, with some anxiety, whether, having once been our mistresses, they will soon become our masters."

"Invasion, anxiety, masters": these three words capture the attitude of a time when few of either sex recognized that growing numbers of educated women could go hand in hand with increasing segregation to eliminate any danger of competition between men and women. In a time of unemployment, however, the pro-family policy would soon take on more violent overtones.

The Hour of Truth: Unemployment

Unemployment was not the same for women as for men. Throughout Europe, in 1931 and 1932 as in 1936, more men were unemployed (in absolute terms) than women, simply because of the gender imbalance in the labor market. Yet rising male unemployment was everywhere attributed to the increase in the number of female workers, and people failed to notice that women were treated as pawns to be sacrificed in time of crisis.

To be sure, more men were laid off than women. In Italy the number of unemployed males was three times the number of unemployed females in 1931. In England, however, the male unemployment rate was 23.7 percent, the female 20.4. The type of work women did naturally affected the pattern of unemployment. Each downturn of the economy affected the service sector and, even more, the industrial concerns in which the majority of women worked. Male unemployment was mostly in heavy industry. In the manufacturing sector too it was not uncommon to lay off skilled male workers and replace them with unskilled and underpaid women. In Germany the "crisis order" of September 5, 1932, was intended to stimulate the rehiring of laid-off workers. Firms were permitted to cut wages and were granted rehiring subsidies that lowered their wage bill by up to 50 percent. Industry hired large numbers of unemployed women: "A large metal-processing firm could, by rehiring 16 men and 83 women, avail itself of the authorization to cut wages for all its personnel and collect bonuses for the 99 new hires, thus obtaining 4,752 hours of work per week with a wage reduction of 94 DM."[7]

In 1936 some women began working at home while others worked two jobs and were paid under the table, at a time when many male workers were unemployed. Employers shrewdly exploited this unfair competition, leading governments in several countries to pass laws flatly prohibiting the hiring of women. In Portugal in 1935 it was made illegal to hire a woman in any sector where a single man was unemployed. In Spain at the same time the hiring of women for any work other than agriculture was prohibited. In Ireland in 1936 each branch of industry was assigned a maximum quota of women. In Belgium in 1934 and in Greece in 1936 women were banned from government jobs. If one holds women workers responsible for male unemployment, it is only logical to try to curtail the employment of women. Economic crises affected all workers, however, thus proving that female labor was not the cause of male unemployment. In Germany, for example, which beat all records for European unemployment in 1931 and 1932, male employment had increased at a far higher rate than female employment during the previous ten years.

If men were more vulnerable to unemployment than women, they were nevertheless eligible to receive greater assistance. In Austria 83.4 percent of unemployed men received unemployment benefits in 1932, compared with 72.5 percent of unemployed women, and that gap was even wider in France (81.9 versus 68.5 percent in the same year). Unemployment laws in many countries specified that women were to receive lower benefits than men, and one essentially female occupation—domestic service—was excluded from benefits altogether. In the moment of truth created by high unemployment, domestic service was declared not to be a job, hence losing it was not considered an injury. And that was not all: times of crisis tend to reawaken old demons, and targets were ready to hand, including both old victims—married women—and new—immigrants.

Like women, immigrants both served and hampered the economy. Recruited when labor was in short supply, they were dismissed when the job market shrank. In France Polish miners in the Nord and Italian miners in Lorraine were expelled from the country after hard times hit; those who were allowed to stay were more likely to lose their jobs than were French miners. Unmarried men were more likely to be sent home than married ones, but not even those with families were safe. The wife of one Polish miner in the Nord remembered the year 1929: "Hard times began with the crisis. Wages fell, and there were more and more days without work. Everywhere there were rumors that we were to be sent home. That's the way it was. A number of people had already been given tickets to return to Poland. The French claimed that we were taking their jobs. Everywhere you heard people shouting 'Go back to Poland.' What were we supposed to do?"[8]

No one had urged married women to take on jobs. According to the pro-family ideologists they shouldn't have been working in the first place. In a time of unemployment they were therefore doubly in the wrong. Hence prohibiting them from working was not so much a punishment as a recall to order. In Germany a law of January 24, 1935, granted marriage loans to young women engaged to be married and willing to quit their jobs, and in 1937 married women were excluded from the civil service. In the Netherlands married school teachers were warned to quit their posts. In France, Germany, England, and the Netherlands unemployment benefits were suspended for married women on the grounds that their husbands could support them. In Great Britain the "law of irregularities" of October 3, 1929, stripped married women of unemployment benefits unless it could be shown that the husband was also unemployed or disabled. In Germany as of 1937 young single women were required to perform compulsory service to assist mothers in rural as well as urban areas.[9] In a time of nationalism and economic crisis, it was "work, family, fatherland" for men but just plain "family" for women—the family being the only fatherland worthy of the name as far as women were concerned. Although some women said "no," the "mothers of *das Vaterland*, the Third Reich" contributed wholeheartedly to the horror as accomplices in an order that built statues to mothers the better to despise women.[10] Even in abjection and death the wretched of the earth continued to be divided by sex: when the trains arrived at the concentration camps, prisoners were sent to their deaths according to their sex, "the women to the left, the men to the right."

Consider three representative women of this period. The first is a young woman who escapes her working-class or peasant background to become a nurse, secretary, or service worker. The second is the married woman who discovers her children and rediscovers the pleasures of home. The third is the young lady of the bourgeoisie who obtains an education only to trade her diploma for a better marriage than would otherwise be available. Together these portraits define a sort of ideal type, the antithesis of the female industrial worker. But now a new figure of the ideal woman begins to emerge: the office worker.

The Disillusionment of "The Glorious Thirty" (1945–1975)

The mood in the Western world had turned to optimism. Euphoria was at its peak, and no hope seemed unreasonable. The war was over, and an economic battle that was supposed to serve the cause of women had begun. Faith in progress was immense in an age that had more than one rabbit up its sleeve. In Europe from 1960 to 1973 the gross domestic product grew at an average of 3.9 percent annually. Such growth encouraged full employment, which was most welcome after the chronic unemployment of the previous period. In England, Germany, and Sweden, tripartite commissions made up of representatives of trade unions, business, and government set the terms under which the virtually full-employment economy would operate. The state truly became a source of "welfare" for all. Many factors worked to ensure steady economic growth, among them low energy costs, increasing productivity, and worthwhile investments in education and training. And it was the beginning of the heyday of consumer society, the true driving force behind the demand for labor. Women rushed headlong into paradise, sharing at last in the wealth of nations, or so it was said. In fact, although women did participate, they hardly reaped all the expected benefits. While increasingly integrated into the educational system and workplace, they were simultaneously relegated to feminized and therefore devalued jobs or to the lowest levels of the hierarchy. What we see happening before our very eyes in this period is the naturalization of the sexual division of labor. Although this process was perceptible in the previous period, it has been intensified by changes in the economic order.

Working Women in Europe

Two phenomena stand out in this period: the incorporation of large numbers of previously independent (or self-employed) female workers into the ranks of wage earners, and the impact of wage labor on women's work patterns. The number of women working increased throughout Europe, but the proportion of wage earners was much higher in the North (85 percent in 1970) than in the South (65 percent). Italy, Greece, Spain, and especially Portugal all saw rapid increases in the number of wage-earning women between 1960 and 1970, however. Industry drew new workers from the ranks of previously independent artisans and peasants. In 1946, 41 percent of French women had worked as artisans or farmers, but that proportion had fallen to just 8.6 percent by 1975. Meanwhile, the proportion of female wage earners in the total female working population rose from 59 percent in 1954 to 84.1 percent in 1975. For the first time in France, the proportion of women employed as wage earners was higher than that of men (81.9 percent). The increase in the proportion of wage earners was due not only to the recruitment of formerly independent workers by industry but also to the decrease in the number of mothers working solely at home, which occurred everywhere in Europe except the Netherlands and Belgium. In 1975 Europe thus passed an economic and sociological milestone: independent labor in its traditional form virtually vanished, and women no longer stayed home. Women are now fully integrated into the market economy, in which the service sector, or tertiary sector as it is now called, occupies a preponderant place.

In fact, the tertiary sector played a crucial role in turning women into wage earners. The more it grew, the greater the number of women who worked for wages. This was the case in Scandinavia and the United Kingdom, where the shift of employment from the primary and secondary sectors to the tertiary began in the previous period and continued with even greater intensity in the present one. In France between 1968 and 1973 the tertiary sector alone accounted for 83 percent of the net new jobs, 60 percent of which were filled by women. The "bureaucratic phenomenon," which can be observed throughout the Continent, was thus largely feminine, except in Italy, where women are distributed more evenly among the major occupational groups. Italian women account for 48 percent of those employed in the liberal professions and affiliated services, 41 percent of other service workers, and 30 percent of office workers, whereas English women account for 74 percent of service workers and 67 percent of office workers.[11]

The European map of wage labor has its male continent and its female continent, whose contours ignore geographical boundaries and trace instead a hierarchical frontier. The male continent consists of workers and managers, whereas the female one is nothing but a vast maze of offices. Between these two extremes lies another Europe, a land of gender parity in employment, which is beginning to emerge in retail sales, the skilled trades, technical and related lines of work, teaching, law, and medicine. As the European economy expanded, it drew on an underemployed labor reserve, including one group of workers that had been sent home in an earlier period: married women.

The number of married working women increased everywhere except in the Netherlands and Belgium, and so did the period of time for which married women remained active. Between 1950 and 1960 the number of married working women doubled in Norway and rose 20 points in Sweden, 10 in Switzerland, and 5 in France, where in 1962 married women accounted for 53.2 percent of the female working population. If, however, one plots the percentage of working women versus age and number of children, the results for the period 1967–1972 vary from country to country. In Spain, Ireland, Portugal, and the Netherlands, women stopped working either when they married or when their first child was born. In Germany, France, England, and to a lesser extent in Italy, many women returned to work after raising their children. In Sweden and Finland "donkey-back" curves indicate that married women and mothers remained on the labor market. By 1975 marriage had become less of an obstacle to the practice of a profession, whereas motherhood continued to be a negative factor. The more children women have, the less they work outside the home. When women have children, not only in Southern Europe but also in Ireland and the Netherlands, they stay home. These contrasts suggest that it is idle to search for a single factor to account for the growing numbers of married women on the labor market, whether it be the desire of women to work or industry's need for more workers. Several factors worked together: "the collapse of the social base of the pro-family movement,"[12] the collective socialization of children, the availability or lack of day-care and nursery schools, the prevalence of labor-saving household appliances, the educational level of the married woman, and the husband's occupation—these are just some of the relevant factors for explaining country-to-country variations.

Furthermore, the statistics themselves are influenced by the "obvious" distribution of employment. If one wishes, as one should, to compare the behavior of fathers with that of mothers, there are no data to validate the comparison. The statisticians "instinctively" assign children to their mothers, so that we have no figures concerning the impact of the number of children on the careers of men. Yet many studies show that the presence of children has a positive effect on a man's advancement in his profession but a negative effect on a woman's advancement in hers. Furthermore, any analysis of women's careers must take account of the fact that women do housework in addition to their regular work. In 1975 working women put in three times as many hours of housework as men. Thus women do two types of work, remunerated and unremunerated, whereas most men specialize in professional labor. Yet everyone who tries to explain changes in women's work patterns, even the most quantitative of sociologists, wants to show that some kind of economic necessity is at work. There is no comparable survey data for men: for them work is a natural right, but for women it is an anomaly that has to be explained by sociologists and anthropologists. Like statistics, in other words, social science discourse can be used to reinforce preexisting sexual divisions rather than question them. Furthermore, working for wages rather than staying home or pursuing an independent occupation was perceived during the period in question (1945–1975) as a step toward women's "liberation" by both researchers and feminist activists. Paradoxically, for Marxists, who were influential at the time, wage labor is alienated labor, yet feminists and sociologists viewed the same wage labor as liberating. In any case, the integration of women into the workforce concealed the limitations that the social order placed on both their educational and workplace opportunities. That concealment was only compounded by the illusion, fostered by the schools, that a girl's chance of success was increasingly equal to that of boys.

The Educational Explosion and Social Disillusionment

Women today seek education in order to find jobs. They are encouraged to think that they will be successful, and much planning goes into making sure that the supply of graduates will fit the needs of the labor market. Although there is a clear correlation between increased education for women and the proportion of women in the workplace, the connection is far from rigid. In the Netherlands, for example, girls receive substantial schooling, but relatively few women work, so it is not possible to establish a causal connection. Conversely, a comparison of degrees earned by women with the jobs they hold can help us to measure the professional rewards of education and to gauge the likelihood of women succeeding in the workplace.

The educational system sees itself as liberating when it is in fact conservative. New curriculum options offered in the name of "broadening" the educational experience actually help to perpetuate the differences between boys and girls. Still, there was indeed an educational explosion in Europe in the sense that the number of girls attending school increased rapidly, especially between 1970 and 1975. In 1970 educational parity had been achieved in secondary education in Norway (where 58.7 percent of boys and 58.2 percent of girls attended secondary school) and France (42.1 percent of boys and 49 percent of girls). In Denmark, Spain, Sweden, and Portugal the number of female students rose more rapidly than the number of males between 1970 and 1975, whereas in France and Germany it was the other way around. By contrast, girls remained less likely than boys to obtain a higher education: many girls left school after finishing high school. Everywhere (except Luxembourg) there was a gap of at least thirty points between the percentage of male university students and the percentage of females in 1964–65, and in the Netherlands males outnumbered females two to one. In Southern Europe (excluding Portugal) the number of female students increased at a faster rate, whereas in Germany, Austria, and Belgium the rate of increase was identical.

The educational system responded to this "sexual democratization" by funneling female students into suitable, that is, "feminine," professions. The schools reproduced social divisions in the very structure of the curriculum, encouraging women to pursue certain courses of study that ultimately proved disadvantageous. In France, the *baccalauréat* degree was now awarded in different specialized areas: the F and G series "bacs" (medical, social, and administrative sciences) attracted many girls, while the C and M series "bacs" (mathematical and physical sciences, technology) attracted boys. In 1975 only 33.8 percent of the Bac C candidates and 4.2 percent of the Bac M candidates were female. Similarly, in universities throughout Europe women predominate in departments of language, literature, education, and psychology, whereas men predominate in science and math. Differences of specialization are further compounded by differences in level of education. In both technical and general courses fewer girls than boys reach the higher levels (for example, the "third cycle," equivalent to an American Ph.D.). A 1967 UNESCO study revealed that marriage was the primary reason for female students to abandon their studies in Germany, Finland, France, Italy, Norway, the Netherlands, and Sweden, but other factors combined to limit their ambitions in the first place.

Many girls end their educational careers upon finishing high school, whereas for boys the high-school diploma is often a stepping-stone to college. High-school diplomas are no longer as valuable as they once were. In France, where the number of girls receiving the bac surpassed the number of boys for the first time in 1964, the degree by itself was no longer the key to opening the doors of employment that it once was. More girls had degrees, but their degrees were not worth as much, and many found that their education ill-suited them to the present condition of the job market. For example, in France in 1956, 46 percent of the girls attending *centres d'apprentissage* were still being taught to sew, even though the textile and clothing industries were already in sharp decline. To be sure, there were more women than ever among the "fortunate few" likely to go on to college, but most girls aspired to nothing more than a high-school diploma.[13] Thus the educational system played a role in reproducing social distinctions between the sexes. Educational disparities combined with differences in family educational background to persuade many girls that their best course was to "choose" one of the "female" options. One of the most subtle and violent aspects of male domination of the educational system is precisely to force the disadvantaged to assume responsibility for their own devaluation. When girls left school and tried to cash in their diplomas on the job market, they faced even higher hurdles.

It is easy to surmise what kinds of jobs awaited female graduates. They were obviously most likely to wind up in occupations requiring the kinds of skills they had acquired in school. Education affects employment in three main ways: it encourages the student (or returnee to the workplace) to seek employment; it allows women with advanced degrees to enter male-dominated professions; and it serves as a general certificate of aptitude for work in a variety of professions. In many countries, the more education a woman has, the more likely she is to work. This is not the case for men. In 1971 in Austria, 48.3 percent of women with a primary education held jobs compared with 74.9 percent of those with a college degree; in Sweden the corresponding figures were 58.6 and 86.7 percent; in France, 28.6 and 69.3 percent. Compare these with the figures for men: in Austria, 97.3 percent of men with a primary education held jobs, compared with 94.5 percent of those with college degrees. For women, a step up the ladder of the educational hierarchy meant a step out of the kitchen and into the workplace.

If education encouraged women to seek work, it also steered them toward already feminized sectors of the economy, which consequently became even more feminized. All over Europe women are overrepresented in the tertiary sector, especially in retail sales, banking, and public and private services, whereas they are a minority in manufacturing, mining, construction, public works, and transportation. In France, medical and social services were already 80 percent female in 1968 and still attracting more women. The proportion of female office workers has been on the rise in Sweden and France. In Germany more women are employed in commerce than in any other sector. Those who escape the feminized sectors to find work in male professions find that there the sexual division is hierarchical: men give the orders and women carry them out.

Although the number of female executives, managers, and engineers has been on the rise in many places from Scandinavia to Spain, women in these positions are still far outnumbered by men. The small number of women in middle-management positions explains their virtual absence from the ranks of top executives, since they are not in positions from which they can be promoted. Those who are still do not wield the same responsibilities as their male colleagues. Two surveys—one of eight British firms conducted in 1964, another carried out in four regions of France in 1970—show the reluctance of employers to promote women to top management posts. The very idea of a woman leading a team of men is unthinkable. Similarly, in the public sector, where most skilled women are employed, few rise above the intermediate echelons. In 1974, 65 percent of the women in French civil service category C and 58 percent of those in category B were unlikely to be promoted even within their own categories, let alone moved up to category A. Throughout Europe primary and secondary teaching has become increasingly feminized since 1965, with by far the greatest number of women concentrated at the lowest levels. While it is true that 55 percent of French *lycée* teachers are women with the prestigious *agrégation* degree, this evidence of advancement for women conceals the equally salient fact that the number of male *agrégés* who move up from the *lycée* to the university teaching level is greater than the number of females. As the average level of education of the workforce in general has risen, women without diplomas are at an even greater disadvantage than in the past. The occupational groups in which employment grew between 1963 and 1973 were those that required the most education. Thus the gap between trained and untrained women only widened. Between 1954 and 1974 the percentage of French women in unskilled jobs rose in comparison to men; in 1968, 78 percent of women in industry were classed as unskilled labor, compared with 52 percent of men.

The workplace only accentuates differences already established by the educational system, so that sexual differences crystallized in the structure of the system and incorporated in people's attitudes come to seem natural, all the more so because it is difficult to perceive the incessant social construction from which such differences arise. To be sure, the pace of segregation is not always rapid enough, so that on occasion an act of overt discrimination is necessary to make sure that equal competition can never take place.

An Abortive Competition

How are women to be integrated into the workplace yet be kept professionally separate from men? One solution is to establish distinct career tracks for men and women. It is misleading, however, to think that the sexual division of labor *(la division sexuelle du travail)* is merely a division of gendered labor *(une division du travail sexué)*. The sexual division of labor fundamentally embodies a symbolic violence, and the closer one comes to equal competition between men and women, the more intense that violence must become. The logic of the thing is simple: it is essential to establish at all cost a difference where no difference exists.

Between 1945 and 1975 a spate of laws, edicts, and national and international decrees proclaimed the right to "equal pay for equal work."[14] Nevertheless, the gap between men's and women's wages held steady until 1968, when it began to shrink to the 25–35 percent range by 1975. Such a difference in pay was seen as a logical consequence of the kinds of jobs women held. Most were in feminized and therefore poorly paid trades; it was difficult for women to gain promotion to upper levels of the hierarchy; and on average women were less skilled than men. These factors seemed sufficient to explain the continued gap between men's and women's compensation. Unequal pay was purely a product, a reflection, of differences in employment.

But if that were the case, how could one account for inequalities in pay where qualifications and work load were equal? It turns out that the gap in pay increases with age and skill level. Take the example of France in 1970, and consider two graduates of the "long" technical training program, one male, the other female. At age forty-five the difference in their pay would have been 46 percent, but by age sixty it would have increased to 56 percent. Similarly, a typical female college graduate earned 43 percent less than her male counterpart at age forty-five and 53 percent less at age sixty. It appears, therefore, that the man's compensation allows for the acquisition of experience on the job, while the woman's does not. One might object that the difference is the result of some difference in the nature of the work. But the widening gap between men's and women's pay can be observed at comparable hierarchical and skill levels in banking, insurance, and retail trade. Furthermore, the lower the skill level, and the lower in the hierarchy, the smaller the disparity is. Conversely, the higher the skill level, and the higher the employee stands in the hierarchy, the greater the disparity in pay. For low-level male bank employees the pay index is 103.9 (where the average low-level female employee's pay is 100), and for men working in retail trade the index is 112.7. Top bank managers stand at 137.5, and top managers in retail sales at 142.0. The more closely a woman's career resembles a male profile, the more she is penalized in compensation.

This example might be interpreted as suggesting that equality is being achieved at the bottom of the hierarchy. An analysis of the wages of female industrial workers shows that, once again, "the imagination is in power." Women who work in all-female shops are the lowest paid of all industrial workers. Conversely, men who work in all-male shops receive the highest pay. In mixed shops, female workers earn more than women in the single-sex shop, and male workers earn less. Feminization of a job category is fatal for the paycheck, whereas masculinization brings a surplus value. In mixed shops the mode of compensation also yields pay differences. Arguing that women are more stimulated by piecework wages than men, employers will pay men a straight hourly wage and women a piece rate. In the words of one employer, "the women on the presses do the same work as the men, but we can't pay them at the same rate because in the end they would earn much more."[15] In another firm, where the tasks performed by male and female workers were absolutely identical, the shop foreman assigned men to move heavy pieces and women to jobs requiring greater rapidity so as to justify the difference in wages: "It is absolutely essential to find a way to pay men more than women."[16]

In this case physical strength is classified as a skill, but the ability to work rapidly is not. All such practices are ways of inventing distinctions where there is in fact equivalence.

Wherever the workplace is mixed, the discriminatory social logic intervenes to thwart any attempt to create parity between men and women. Part-time work is a good example. It offers several advantages: it justifies a wage differential, allows women to combine motherhood with work, lowers the firm's overall wage bill, and provides a flexible means of adjusting the supply of labor to the demand. In the period that interests us here (ending in 1975), part-time work had not yet developed to the full extent it would acquire later, but already 10 percent of European workers were employed part-time in 1975 (the number had risen sharply since 1973). Everywhere except Italy part-time employment involved mainly women. The proportion of part-time workers (and of women in part-time jobs) was highest in the United Kingdom, Germany, and Denmark. In 1973, 10.1 percent of German jobs and 16 percent of British jobs were part-time, and the proportion of part-time workers who were women was 89 percent in Germany and 90.9 percent in the United Kingdom. There is a clear correlation between growth of the tertiary sector and the development of part-time employment, especially in such service jobs as cleaning, food service, and maintenance. In France part-time employment increased for both men and women between 1971 and 1975, but the gap remained wide: 1.7 percent of men and 13.1 of women worked part-time in 1971, 2.9 percent and 16.3 percent in 1975. Thus in France much of the increase in female employment between 1968 and 1975 was in part-time work, the last bastion in which it was still legal to treat women as inferiors. Many part-time jobs held little prospect of promotion, so that while part-time employment might allow women to reconcile family and job, it prevented them from thinking in career terms. Once again, family and work were opposed, but instead of the traditional sexual division of labor one saw a sexual division of labor time: full-time for men, part-time for women. This sleight-of-hand made it possible to avoid head-to-head competition.

The segregation of women by job category, part-time work, and holding back of promotions had the effect of creating a dual labor market: one for men, highly skilled and highly productive, the other for women, underskilled, underpaid, and devalued. The economic theory of the dual labor market (primary and secondary) legitimated the sexual division of labor by portraying it as a natural part of the economy. In providing a theory to account for an empirical fact, economists forgot that duality was a social and political construct, the product of a process that is constantly inventing and reinventing distinctive new practices. What we are dealing with is in fact the same old labor market, but the deck has been reshuffled so as to create a new pattern of asymmetries. Dual-market theory prevents one from seeing and interpreting the way in which women's breakthrough into the "primary" or masculine market immediately led to more intense discrimination. It also conceals its own social function in legitimating sexual division in its modern new guise. The invention of part-time employment, which is both an economic instrument and an instrument of sexual segregation, proved effective in laying the groundwork for today's economy.

Profiting from Sexual Division (1975–1990)

It was a time of upheaval. Things went awry. The orderly economic growth of the glorious period gave way to a conjuncture marked first by slow growth (1975–1980), then (until 1986) by shrinking. The economy was sick as a result of its own expansion. Labor costs had risen faster than productivity. The service sector grew wildly and swelled to enormous proportions. National income fell. Investment slowed as investors grew wary. Inflation and unemployment grew apace. Many countries adopted austerity policies to control inflation. The goal was both to put an end to rising prices and teach a lesson to those unwilling to read the economic indicators in the "correct" manner. Labor was the first target of a long series of inflation-fighting measures. Shrinking employment, adapting supply to demand, and sharing the available work were the remedies proposed. Job mobility, flexibility, retraining, recycling—with the new interpretation came a whole new jargon. If the labor market showed signs of wage rigidity and of clinging to inveterate habits, workers would have to be taught to be more flexible; the very concept of labor would have to be changed. And as the nature of labor changed, a new word came into use to describe it: instead of labor people now spoke of "employment." Labor had already begun to fall apart, but now it literally crumbled: economists spoke of the "segmentation" or "fragmentation" of the labor market. And when it came to segmenting and fragmenting, nothing proved more effective than the sexual division of labor. The time had come to exploit its potential to the full, to derive the maximum possible profit from "rational manpower management." Sexual division became one of the levers of labor flexibility, a fundamental component of economic efficiency, the driving force behind the atomization of employment. And the first thing to do to profit from the sexual division of labor was to continue to exploit inequalities in the educational system.

The Educational Construction of Differences

After 1975 was proclaimed the International Year of Women, countless declarations, reports, laws, and position papers were drafted in favor of equal educational opportunity for both sexes, with the added proviso that there must be equal access to instruction of identical value. Yet these consensus statements and regulations left wide latitude for covert inequalities. The problem was no longer that too few girls were given the chance to obtain an education but that the schools simply reproduced existing differences and failed to prepare their graduates for the realities of the marketplace.

The increase in the number of women in secondary schools and universities and the growing number of female students majoring in supposedly "masculine" specialties created a plausible illusion of equal opportunity. Upon closer examination, however, the data speak otherwise. As more and more women availed themselves of the opportunity to obtain an education, the "feminization" of certain disciplines accelerated. Younger women followed in the footsteps of their elders, choosing already feminized disciplines. Across Europe female university students chose to major in literature, languages, pharmacy, and, to a lesser extent, medicine. In 1966, 66 percent of Norwegian women preparing for the Atrium were in the languages section, and by 1980 that proportion had risen to 84.5 percent. In Switzerland 53.9 percent of female students took up literary studies of one kind or another in 1975, and 60 percent in 1982. In France, women were already overrepresented in literature, pharmacy, and economic and social administration, and the number choosing medicine was rising sharply (43.8 percent in 1982). The attractiveness of feminized disciplines to young women, which the universities only encouraged, led to persistence of the disparity between "noble" and "devalued" specialties. Furthermore, the increase in the number of women pursuing technological and scientific studies did nothing to alter the fundamental distinctions between programs. Women in engineering remained a small minority: 7.3 percent in Belgium in 1982, 10 percent in Germany in 1981, 10.3 percent in Switzerland in 1983, and 5.5 percent in the United Kingdom. The distribution of female students in French academic institutes was typical: in 1985, 77.2 of them were pursuing careers related to informational and social services, compared with just 3.5 percent in mechanical or civil engineering. Of those studying library science, 72.3 percent were women, compared with just 1.2 percent of those in industrial arts. Thus the integration of high schools and universities and the increase in the number of women pursuing secondary and university degrees do not guarantee that women will receive an education of equal value; certain specialties remain distinctively feminine. Rather than combat sexual segregation, the educational system as a whole encourages it by maintaining specialties that are academic reflections of social stereotypes.

One must be careful, however, not to be too quick to impute the devaluation of a specialty to its feminization, because the criteria by which the "noble" disciplines are singled out do change over time. At one time, for example, the humanities were prestigious, whereas it is now mathematics and the exact sciences that separate the wheat from the chaff. The effects of gender-determined specialization are compounded by the devaluation of certain degrees. Of course this devaluation affects men as well as women, but given equal degrees, a woman is less likely to obtain a good job than a man. Among male university graduates in France, 62 percent obtained management positions in 1977 and 77 percent in 1985, whereas for women the figure was 46 percent in both years. Similarly, in 1985, 40 percent of female university graduates wound up in "intermediate professions," compared with just 20 percent of males. In other words, when men and women leave school, they seldom have the same diploma, and even if they do, the woman's is worth less on the job market than the man's. Thus the issue is not, as in the past, one of obtaining a degree but rather one of recognizing what sort of degree one has and what it is worth. All the self-satisfied rhetoric about the increase in the number of female graduates hides the fact that the diplomas they receive are worth less than in the past and that their professional opportunities are limited. This is especially true of women of modest background with no particular job skills and without a professional degree. For them, as well as for married women who wish to return to work after their children are grown, the only option is to attend an adult training program designed to help students adapt their existing knowledge and skills to the changing needs of the economy.

People have begun to question whether the educational system is capable of teaching the kinds of skills that today's workers need. Many countries have found that skilled labor is in short supply. Governments contract with employers to provide adult education, on-the-job training, and worker retraining courses intended to teach new skills and increase job mobility. Remedial courses are the latest fashion, and a whole new profession of workplace training has emerged. Workers are now faced with a plethora of training programs and self-help courses, and each individual is expected to select what he or she needs from a diverse menu of available choices. Women may choose from an array of job-market reentry programs, management training courses, and skill-upgrading seminars. In 1982 a new school, the Open Tech, began offering full-time and part-time courses to British workers in search of the latest skills. In 1985 Belgium instituted a program to train women to manage small to medium-sized companies. Although the goal of worker training in all countries was to compensate for social and sexual inequalities, it is clear that those who benefited most were those who already had some training. Given the lack of paid leave for those who signed up for training courses, few women completed their training with sufficient skills to qualify for any real promotion. Training did, however, help to broaden social and professional skills, preparing workers mentally as well as physically for a fragmentation of the labor process. The courses inculcated a new vision of work as a series of transitions from employment to training to unemployment and back again, rather than the traditional training followed by employment. As training was subdivided into smaller and smaller parcels, jobs were fragmented.

A New Mode of Employment

In a period of recession and unemployment, many European countries sought to make their industries more competitive by holding a lid on wages. The workforce was said to be maladapted to the needs of the marketplace, overpriced, and inflexible, resulting in wage rigidity that was only compounded by the stubbornness of the trade unions. What was needed, some experts contended, was greater flexibility in the labor process, in order to allow under-utilized segments of the workforce to be tapped. Women figured largely in some of these plans.

The sexual division of labor was fundamental to the way firms managed changes in the labor process. Statistics showed that women definitely wanted to work; the question was how to make that desire serve the cause of flexibility. The plan was bold, especially since the proportion of women working in Europe rose from 45.7 percent in 1975 to 48.7 percent in 1983, whereas for men it decreased by five points. In spite of recession and unemployment, women were staying in the labor market. Various factors were cited to explain this refusal on the part of woman to withdraw their offer of services: increased education, expanded public sector, new attitudes toward marriage and divorce, earlier schooling for children, a more positive image of working women. In the final analysis, however, it seems that the increase in the proportion of working women was due to the increase in the number of less-than-full-time jobs, including part-time work, off-the-books employment, home work, temporary work, and on-the-job training.

Since 1973, and even more since 1981, businesses have sought to reduce labor costs by deliberately increasing the number of part-time workers they employ. Between 1973 and 1986 the proportion of part-time employees among working women rose in all European countries except Greece, Italy, Finland, and Ireland. In 1986, 40 to 45 percent of working women in Scandinavia and the United Kingdom, 25 percent of those in Belgium and France, and 30 percent of those in Germany were employed part-time. In the same year, 90 percent of all part-time workers in Belgium, the United Kingdom, and Germany were women, as were 80 to 90 percent in Denmark, Norway, Sweden, France, and Luxembourg. In France from 1982 to 1986 women's employment increased solely because of an increase in the number of women employed part-time. The number of women at work in Europe increased because of part-time jobs, but part-time work was still insecure and disqualifying. Part-time workers were not assigned to work-related training programs; few were ever promoted; they enjoyed fewer social benefits such as pensions (not compulsory for part-time workers in certain countries); they were less well paid; they were often the first to be fired. Comparing the age of male and female part-time workers, one sees that the men tend to be elderly, the women in their prime working years. For men, part-time work is a kind of disguised pre-retirement, whereas for women it is a form of semi-employment. The employment of women on a part-time basis has further accentuated the sexual division of labor, moreover, by funneling women into an ever-narrowing range of jobs in the tertiary sector, whose growth has been made possible by part-time labor. Part-time work is women's work, expressly invented for women, yet it is frequently presented as a desirable choice when in fact it is a compulsion. Any number of surveys have shown, in fact, that only a third of women want to work part-time; the rest state that they were compelled by necessity to settle for part-time employment.[17] Part-time employment is therefore a form of underemployment. On the pretext of providing more jobs for women, part-time work reinforces workplace segregation and legitimates the practice of offering jobs without career prospects.

Of course part-time employment is not solely to blame for undermining the right of women to pursue true professional careers. Other types of temporary employment are just as effective. Working at home, for example, has taken on a whole new look. Home work in its traditional form never totally disappeared, but lately it has assumed a modern, youthful guise. Just as the sewing machine encouraged home work in the late nineteenth century, so computers and telecommunications have made it easier to work at home in the late twentieth century, which has witnessed the birth of "telecommuting." Some firms, determined to reduce wages, have identified certain types of jobs that can be done at home, such as typing, mailing, and proofreading. Increasingly, banks, insurance companies, and department stores have been installing video terminals in employees' homes in order to take advantage of slack time in computer networks and reduce office costs. What kind of work is done at home varies from country to country: in Italy, most home workers are in the manufacturing sector, where they perform such varied tasks as knitting sweaters, making shoes, and assembling automobile transmissions, whereas in Scandinavia and England most home workers do word processing or work with database programs. Female home workers tend to have low skill levels, whereas males tend to be highly skilled. According to a survey conducted by the French national economic statistics agency (INSEE) in 1986, men working at home in France earned an average of 5,285 francs per month compared with 2,952 for women.

These two forms of labor were not enough to ensure the required flexibility, however. After 1980 many workers accepted jobs as temporaries or contract workers for limited periods in order to stay off of unemployment and remain in contact with the labor market. In France 47 percent of contract workers are women (mainly office workers and junior managers), whereas men employed as contract laborers are generally blue-collar workers. Married women predominate in all jobs with reduced hours, and in Italy large numbers of married women are paid "off the books" in the illegal economy. Clearly, the existence of a parallel job market does not do away with the sexual division of labor. Full-time work, part-time work, aboveground and underground economies—women clearly have many ways of finding work, but the system devalues their contribution. Different countries emphasize different ways of introducing flexibility into the job market. In Germany, the accent is on training workers to enable them to move from job to job within the firm. England stresses external flexibility: workers laid off in one part of the country must look for work in other regions or accept part-time jobs. The Italians are prepared to try a little of this and a little of that: the family acts as a kind of safety valve, making sure that one or two members have stable jobs and thus freeing up others to accept more flexible work or even to enter the illegal economy. And there are always the less benign methods of reducing the rigidity of the labor market: lay-offs and firings. Unemployment in this period was both structural and "frictional."

During this period of shared work, there was less emphasis than in the past on propaganda urging women to stay home. Part-time work and unemployment regulated their presence on the labor market. In 1988 there were 16 million people unemployed in the Common Market countries, or 11 percent of the total working population. Except for England, female unemployment was higher than male unemployment everywhere, especially in France and Italy. In 1987 unemployment in Germany was 5.3 percent for men and 8 percent for women; in Italy 7.4 percent for men and 17.3 percent for women. Spain's 21.4 percent female unemployment rate beat all previous records, and it was followed by Belgium, Italy, and Portugal, whereas Switzerland, Sweden, and Norway had an average female unemployment rate of 3 percent. Despite temporary, part-time, and illegal work, women are more vulnerable to unemployment than men, although men tend to be out of work for longer periods. When women are out of work for long periods, it tends to be because they are employed in the tertiary sector, lack skills, and/or have worked in part-time jobs, which are particularly vulnerable to cutbacks. In France the risk of losing one's job is greater for women than for men, and that risk increased between 1968 and 1987. Women are also less likely to find new jobs. In 1981, 55 percent of laid-off male workers found a stable new job within fifteen months, compared with 43 percent of women. The primary cause of female unemployment is being laid off from temporary employment.

The best protection against unemployment for both men and women is to hold a university degree. Although women are still worse off (2.1 percent unemployment among female college graduates in 1987 compared with 0.2 percent among males), a university diploma ensures a much lower likelihood of losing one's job. Unemployment is the product of a spiral of flexibility and temporary employment. Employers adjust the supply of labor to their demand by tinkering with the range of temporary jobs and the duration of unemployment. Once women enter into the vicious circle of temporary work, unemployment is the only way out.

What has emerged since 1975 is a new social construction of employment, labor, and the sexual division of labor. The old model was education and training, leading to stable employment, leading to promotion within the firm, followed by retirement. The new model involves a sampling of specialized training courses leading in some cases to stable employment, in others to a cycle of part-time jobs followed by unemployment, contract work, retraining, or temporary work. Linear careers are a thing of the past; work now tends to be sporadic, and employment and unemployment are merely the faces of flexibility and fragmentation of the workforce. The sexual division of labor is no longer merely an effect of the division of industry by branches and sectors; it is the organizing principle of inequality with respect to employment: "real" work is for men, "supplementary" work is for women. It should therefore come as no surprise that inequality between men and women is everywhere on the rise.

A Sophisticated Segregation

Throughout this chapter we have seen how each increase in the number of women receiving an education and looking for work was followed by the invention of new ways to maintain the difference between the sexes. The time has come for an overall assessment. Experts have come up with increasingly sophisticated ways to measure sexual discrimination and segregation in the workplace.[18] They often distinguish between direct discrimination (the likelihood that a man and a woman with equal training and doing equal work will receive different pay) and indirect discrimination (procedures that give men the advantage where other factors are equal). Both types of discrimination permanently reproduce not only "different conditions but also a difference of condition."[19]

That difference is evident in all the countries we have examined. No matter what indicator is chosen (dissimilarity index, coefficient of female representation, vertical or horizontal segregation[20]), it turns out that occupational inequality is intimately associated with the structure of industry, its hiring practices, and its patterns of remuneration. Any naïve optimism that progress for women is ineluctable is categorically contradicted by the facts. Indeed, the most recent structural changes in the economy have done nothing to diminish segregation and may even have increased it. For example, "the countries with the highest proportion [of women in the workforce] also have the highest levels of segregation by occupation."[21] The Scandinavian countries are a case in point. What is more, segregation has diminished in declining sectors in all countries, particularly the manufacturing sector, whereas it has increased in expanding sectors. In Sweden, for example, a significant increase in the number of women in executive and top management positions has led to an increase in segregation. Furthermore, the arrival on the labor market of younger generations of workers has not reduced the dissimilarity index. In the United Kingdom and Germany segregation is greater among the young than among the elderly. Although many factors contribute to the persistence of segregation—concentration of women in the service sector and in a small number of professions, limited opportunities for women to acquire skills or gain promotions—part-time work is everywhere the root cause of increased

485

inequality. This new weapon against workplace equality is frighteningly effective.

Beyond the traditional sexual division of labor, there is a social construction of employment whose purpose is to attract one sex rather than another to certain jobs so as to maintain the difference between the sexes. Hence it is not surprising that a wage gap also persists. The wage gap is merely the monetary translation of the asymmetry of positions, of the value bestowed by society on women's work, or, in the case of differential pay for equally qualified individuals for the same work, of pure discrimination. In 1982 European women earned an average 20 to 40 percent less than men, although the wage gap was narrowing everywhere, most of all in Austria and least of all in France. In 1989 the average woman's wage was 31 percent less than the average man's. Italy had the smallest gap, Ireland the largest. As was the case in the previous period, the higher one looks in the hierarchy, the greater the salary gap. In France the passage of a minimum wage law (the so-called SMIG, or *salaire minimum interprofessionnel garanti*) reduced the wage gap at the bottom of the social hierarchy: unskilled female blue-collar workers earned 15 percent less than their male counterparts; for skilled workers the gap was 18 percent. Clearly, the ability of the law by itself to achieve equality of pay is limited.[22] To be sure, the limitation is inherent in the nature of law, which can only mandate equal pay for comparable jobs, and what our analysis of the sexual division of labor shows is precisely how rare it is that jobs can truly be called comparable. Hence even as governments issue orders and pass laws mandating equal pay for equal work, they create structures based on unequal work and fragmented employment. The law is legalistic: it levels its sights on the ultimate outcome of the sexual division of labor, which is the wage gap, while ignoring or pretending to ignore everything that contributes to that outcome: the existence of "female tracks" in schools and universities, the social factors influencing the choice of occupation and the formation of "taste," and industrial hiring practices. The law leaves society with a clear conscience but does nothing to halt the reproduction of inequality.

How else are we to explain why inequalities persist yet become less and less visible? I have already alluded to parts of the answer. If one looks simply at the increase in the number of women working, one fails to see that most of them are in low-level, part-time jobs. The truth is in the statistics. But there is more to it than that. There is a strange correlation between the heightening of discrimination and the proliferation of scholarly discourse about segregation. The more scholars do to reveal and denounce inequality, to analyze its causes and calculate its extent, the more it continues to bubble up from within the society, to smolder in places where it cannot be seen. Although science apparently cannot do away with inequality, at least it has not added its voice to the obscurantist campaign that has been orchestrated by the media: by selectively publicizing the testimony and portraits of a few "superwomen," the media have convinced the broad public that sexual equality has been achieved, indeed that in recent years women have achieved positions of power in unprecedented numbers. The social function of the media image of the high-powered female entrepreneur is to ensure that the forest remains hidden by the trees. The few who make it stand out against the vast number who don't. Male domination is not exercised today as it was earlier in the century, through propaganda urging women to return to their homes. Today it hides behind egalitarian laws, behind a minority of "successful" women, behind rational explanations—so many ways of anesthetizing our awareness of the unequal likelihood of success in school and at work. There has been little protest against this violence. Women and the feminist movement have delegated power to the authorities—to ministers of women's affairs, to international commissions, to the sponsors of egalitarian legislation; struggle has been played down in favor of fragile consensus. Feminists, intent on waging their struggles around the politics of the body, have all too often forgotten that many women must take their bodies to work, thus leaving the most defenseless among them to face the reality of daily discrimination in the workplace alone. Women are underrepresented in professional groups and trade unions, and this, together with the disintegration of the collective consciousness of feminism, has cleared the way for the reproduction of old inequalities and the invention of new ones. Learned treatises about the mechanisms of segregation cannot by themselves substitute for social struggle. Treatises are useful, however, for pointing out the crucial elements in the process and thus showing where the struggle for equality of opportunity should focus its efforts: the differential socialization of the sexes within the family, the "tracking" of female students into feminized and therefore devalued specialties, industrial hiring practices—in short, all the ways, old and new, in which women are made exceptions to the rule. But the moments when everything changes, when new discriminations are put in place, are increasingly insidious. Right now all the laws favor women; all schools are open to them; they are integrated everywhere. Deceived by their own triumph, they rarely protest the hidden forms of inequality and the rampant sexism they face. The status quo has the appearance of legitimacy, all the more so in that its reality is covered by a cloak of rhetoric proclaiming equality between the sexes.

What emerges from this analysis is a twofold domination, at once economic and sexual. In fact, a mutual causality is at work, in which the economy masks the sexual order of domination. The moment that men and women begin to compete professionally, the sexual order intervenes: sexual difference is an implacable force, and economic mechanisms by themselves are insufficient to overcome it. The sexual division of knowledge and labor is a sort of game in which women are earnestly risking more and more, victims of the illusion that they can be men's equals. The dice are loaded, however: women begin with handicaps, and this is a race in which only men can run the distance. The closer women come to the goal, the more they are penalized. If men took it into their heads to compete in the domestic games that women play, they, too, would be losers in their careers. But the social order has decided once and for all where the real game is being played. Only a minority of women, those with the best educational and social backgrounds, can break the rules. The game metaphor is useful in that it makes it possible to talk about advantages and handicaps, whereas most people would like to see nothing but increasingly equal opportunities. The analysis presented here is therefore disillusioning, for it shows that sexual division is basically di-vision—that is, a way of seeing double. My approach is therefore fundamentally incompatible with the view that the history of women in the twentieth century can be written exclusively in terms of social advancement. If the history of women is possible, it is because it is the history of an unequal relationship, a history of the social construction of inequality between the sexes, or, in other words, the history of male domination conceived of as one of the motors of history. Unless we bring that domination back into our story, we run the risk of writing a positive history of women, when in fact women's history should be seen above all as the history of a deposed sex, as the mirror image of the sovereign history, the history of men. One is thus forced to adopt reaction as the rhetorical figure: no sooner is an advance formulated than one immediately turns around and retracts it. In this way we can measure the "defeat of thought" that seeks to make the history of women a history in itself and for itself. History is one and indivisible, made by men and women, and within history one can make women speak from the places they occupy, places often carved out by men, places without memory, which this collective text is trying to rescue from the shadows.

<small>TRANSLATED FROM THE FRENCH BY ARTHUR GOLDHAMMER</small>

four

Current Issues

Feminism Is Plural

Can a history of contemporary feminism really be written so soon? The question is one we have often been asked, both by those who would like to see what a history of women in the twentieth century might look like and by those who are afraid that such a portrait can only turn out to be a reductive caricature. The problem is that feminism is plural: it has been marked by internal conflicts and debates and connected, despite its desire for universality, to political developments in particular countries. This volume contains no detailed accounts of individual women's experiences or of day-to-day feminist activism, important as these were for women of this generation. We have tried instead to give a theoretical and political overview of the movement centered on woman as subject—how women came to be political actors and how they acquired the power to act. How did they acquire autonomy of thought and action? How did they learn to identify the key issues for women and make those issues visible to the rest of society? How did they learn to mobilize to achieve particular political goals, such as the liberalization of laws on abortion and contraception or tougher laws on sexual violence? How did feminism change the way women (and men) live while at the same time changing the political landscape?

The case of Quebec offers an excellent example. One of the most dynamic feminist movements in the world helped to modernize the Québecois nationalist movement and to hasten the transition from a traditional Catholic way of life to a modern, secular, consumerist society.

In most Western democracies, however, the participation of female citizens in the political life of the nation remains an issue for our time, despite significant breakthroughs in this once male-dominated bastion. The participation of women, whether a matter of free choice for voters, leaders, and activists or of externally imposed quotas, requires changes in the symbolism of power and possibly in the way in which power is exercised. Are women the future of politics? Utopian dreams in this area are still permissible. Yet nowhere except in Iceland has the attempt to create a feminist party disrupted the existing political system, because political differences exist not only between the sexes but within each of them.

Feminism, in the sense of a historical movement calling for social transformation, is no longer in vogue. It fell victim to the crisis of progressive ideologies and the rise of various forms of individualism characteristic of what has been called postmodern society. Yet feminism remains in the public arena, not only in the form of organized feminist groups but even more through its role in ongoing debates: over the difference between equality and identity, for one, or the hazard of going too far in linking the personal and the political.[1] Women have also mobilized around new issues, such as sexual harassment in the workplace. Another indication of the persistence of feminism is the continuing presence of antifeminism. It can take many forms, from the proliferation of degrading images of women, to the more subtle overestimation of feminine or maternal virtues or the exaltation of a "morality of the womb," all of which fail to grapple with the truly political aspects of male-female relations.[2]

Science has developed new reproductive technologies such as in-vitro fertilization. Do these new techniques reflect an identification of women's bodies with inanimate objects, or do they represent a new right to maternity (which would replace the ancient duty to bear children)? Or again, do they constitute a new definition of the couple, with the child providing the crucial link? These new techniques, which sever reproduction from sexuality and conception from filiation and biological filiation from the affective bonds of child-rearing, call for renewed thinking about eugenics and basic human rights. The concluding essay in this section compares practices, ideologies, and policies regarding reproductive technologies in a number of countries, exposing the issues at stake and the values that underlie them. Some of those values reflect a neo-conservative attachment to blood ties and to the idea of the family and the rights of the unborn, an attachment that poses a threat to some of feminism's gains.

The last word has yet to be said about women's bodies, to be sure, and of course the discussion of the history of relations between men and women will go on forever.

F.T.

16

Law and Democracy

Mariette Sineau

BY NOW, AT THE END OF the twentieth century, the idea of legal equality between men and women is no longer new in the West. The first demands for equal rights, as well as the first legislative steps toward that end, date of course from the French Revolution. Full equality in both public and private law was demanded in the name of natural rights. Elisabeth Sledziewski has given a fine analysis of the new departure represented by the advent of "civil woman" in revolutionary law (through the definition of marriage as a civil contract and the institution of divorce, which "established the woman as her spouse's legal partner, by requiring the full participation of her reason and her will in the definition of mutual consent").[1] To be sure, the Revolution completed the exclusion of women from the political sphere for many years to come: with the advent of democracy the political disenfranchisement of women became an absolute principle, as it had not been even under the Ancien Régime. But the Revolution also associated political rights with the individual person rather than with the ownership of land, and this ultimately led to the principle of women's suffrage.

Thus the concept that individuals of different sexes should have equal rights is an old one, but it has been translated into law only relatively recently: it took almost until the dawn of the third millennium to draw the ultimate consequences of egalitarian principles. The idea of embodying equal rights for women in law met with considerable resistance, most notably in the form of the French Civil Code of 1804 (also known as the Napoleonic Code), a model widely admired and imitated in both Europe and North America (Quebec, for example). No sooner had women been liberated by the Revolution than they were once again subjugated by the Napoleonic Code. By "limiting [legal] individuality to the paterfamilias," the Code gave legitimacy to the principle that married women have no capacity to act under civil law.[2] Indirectly, the Code legitimated the denial of political rights to women: the married woman was treated as a minor child, subject to her husband's authority and deprived of all political rights. The Napoleonic model would prove durable. As recently as 1945, at the close of World War II, it was still exerting profound influence on legislation in any number of European countries. Only recently have liberal reform efforts erased from private law the last vestiges of the old subordination of women to their citizen husbands.

Even after obtaining legal equality, women still had to acquire the means to exercise the rights that went along with their new status as citizens: not just the vote but even more the right to run for office. A mere glance at the number of women holding office in Europe and North America today is enough to show that women play a very limited role in public life. Having overcome their *de jure* exclusion from the democratic process, must they now confront a *de facto* ostracism? Having fought for formal equality, feminists are now working toward a genuine sharing of power between the sexes, and they have scored some victories. Women are moving into leadership positions—but will these advances come to a dead end or do they presage an end to male domination? The political participation of women will be a major issue for decades to come.

Access to Citizenship

Contemporary history of civil and political rights for women has two major themes. First, women's rights varied widely depending on where they lived, on whether they happened to be, say, American, Canadian, French, or Portuguese. The status quo ranged from full equality to complete absence of rights. A whole range of intermediate situations could also be found: women in some places enjoyed civil rights without political rights, whereas in other places it was just the reverse.

Second, winds of reform began to blow throughout Europe in the 1960s. Major changes in the law stemmed from this reform movement—nothing short of a legal revolution, according to some scholars. The fundamental idea was that husband and wife should be equal in private law. This vast democratic movement, affecting both marriage and political society, created a sort of family resemblance among laws pertaining to the status of women throughout the West, eliminating certain "atavistic" national peculiarities.

After the defeat of totalitarianism by democracy in World War II, the postwar climate encouraged a new emphasis on individual rights. Women, who along with men had made great sacrifices in the war against fascism (including in the Resistance in France), would be among the beneficiaries. The Universal Declaration of the Rights of Man (1948) did not fail to mention equality between the sexes along with equality of the husband and wife in marriage. As various Western countries adopted new constitutions (France in 1946, Italy in 1947, West Germany in 1949) these egalitarian principles were enshrined in their fundamental laws. Nevertheless, the world's leading, if not the most, feminist democracy, the United States, refused then and still refuses today to adopt the Equal Rights Amendment, which would institute equality between the sexes in all aspects of law.

In Europe after the collapse of fascism the authorities in several countries were obliged to grant women full political rights. But the realm of private law proved more impervious to democratic pressures. In 1945 "unequal treatment was the rule, equality the exception."[3] The effect of marriage was—and for a long time would remain—to deprive women of important personal and patrimonial rights (civil competency, the right to work outside the home, the right to acquire, administer, and sell property, the right to exercise parental authority, and so on). A glance at the table on the next page reveals the disparate legal situations of women in Europe and North America. The differences are not random: they show a marked gap between countries under the influence of the Napoleonic Code, where inegalitarian conditions still prevailed after World War II, and countries subject to common law or Germanic law, where conditions were liberalized much sooner.

Table 1. Proportion of women in the lower houses of parliament (in descending order) and dates in which women acquired full political and civil rights in the major Western countries

| Country | Women in parliament | | Political rights | Civil competency (married women) |
	Year of election	% Women		
Finland	1991	38.5	1906	1919
Norway	1989	35.7	1913	1888
Sweden	1991	33.8	1921	1920
Denmark	1990	33	1915	1925
Netherlands	1989	25.3	1919	1956
Iceland	1991	23.8	1915	1923
Austria	1990	21.8	1918	1811
Germany*	1990	20.5	1919	1896
Spain	1989	14.6	1931	1975
Switzerland	1987	14	1971	1912
Luxembourg	1989	13.3	1919	1972
Canada	1988	13.2	1920	Late 19th/early 20th century
United States	1992	10.8	1920	Late 19th/early 20th century
United Kingdom	1992	10.1	1928	1882
Belgium	1991	9.4	1948	1958
Italy	1992	8.1	1945	1919
Ireland	1989	7.8	1918	1957
Portugal	1987	7.6	1976	1976
France	1993	6.0	1944	1938
Greece	1990	5.3	1952	No incompetency

Source: Union Interparlementaire, 1991.

Contrast, for example, France, where women obtained political rights in 1944 and civil rights in 1938, with English-speaking Canada, where they obtained both much earlier.

The Anglophone and Nordic Model

When the war ended, women had long been civically and politically emancipated in the anglophone and Nordic countries. By 1945 several decades had passed since women had accomplished their "revolution" and obtained the status of citizens. The religious traditions of these countries probably had something to do with their legal freedom. The Protestant ethic, so jealous of individual rights, adapted itself fairly readily to a feminist spirit which, in turn, was quick to find organizational embodiment in a mass movement that fought effectively for emancipation on two fronts. Between 1860 and 1880 the English suffragettes are said to have recruited some three million "claimants" of the right to vote. Their German counterparts, less numerous but no less militant, soon enlisted the active support of the Social Democratic Party, which made universal suffrage without regard to sex the number one plank in its Erfurt platform of 1892.

The law itself had much to do with this early rise of feminism: in countries of common-law tradition, "legal rules are envisioned as directives not for everyday life but for the resolution of conflicts."[4] More an instrument for settling disputes than for regulating order, the law generally stays out of questions of private life and personal morality. (In England, for example, adultery is a criminal matter only if carried on in a flagrantly public manner.) Thus there was never the same subordination of civil to public, of private to political, as in the Latin Catholic countries, and this probably resulted in a lesser degree of subordination of women to men.

In England another historical precondition undoubtedly hastened the legal liberation of women: industrialization came early to the British Isles. Industry, with its enormous appetite for labor, required that women be granted some measure of civil liberty. By contrast, France remained rural much longer and was able to content itself with a single, rather timid amendment to the Civil Code: the law of 1907 allowing married women to decide how to spend their own earnings.

In the Nordic and anglophone countries women obtained the

right to vote soon after the adoption of universal (male) suffrage. In some cases this universalization of suffrage came rather late: in England, for example, the "franchise" involved certain property qualifications as recently as the eve of World War I. In the United States, however, feminists were "abandoned by their abolitionist friends" after the Civil War and for the next seventy-five years were forced to fight a bitter battle for the right to vote.[5] The necessary amendment to the Constitution, to which Susan B. Anthony devoted her life, was not finally ratified until 1920.

Thus, except in the United States, the suffragist movement was carried by a powerful democratic tide, which contributed in no small measure to its early success. Scandinavian women were the first to obtain political rights, generally before or during World War I. Soon after the return of peace the Scandinavian example was imitated in nearly all the non-Latin countries of Europe. By the late 1920s women had achieved political equality in Northern Europe (except Belgium) and North America (except Quebec). By the end of World War II women in these countries had acquired considerable experience as voters and officeholders: Finnish women had enjoyed political rights for thirty-nine years, English women for seventeen. In some places women had obtained the right to vote in local elections even earlier (sometimes with, sometimes without property qualifications): women could vote in the state of Wyoming as early as 1869 and in Colorado in 1893. And women voted in municipal elections in Norway in 1901, in Denmark in 1908, and in Iceland in 1909.

When it came to civil equality, the common-law countries were the great pioneers. Civil rights were granted to married women before political rights in most states in the United States and of course in England, whose impact on the countries of the Old World was greater. By the mid-twentieth century English women had already enjoyed independence from their husbands for more than sixty years—independence with respect to both person and property. The Married Women's Property Act of 1882 not only distinguished between the property of the husband and that of the wife but allowed a married woman to dispose of her own wealth as she saw fit and to sign contracts without her husband's accord. The English law had the effect of a bombshell in countries steeped in the legal tradition of the Civil Code: even the most liberal jurists voiced shrill fears of anarchy in the marital bedchamber, while feminists hailed the new law as a beacon of liberty.

Equality of both parents vis-à-vis the children, a principle not inherent in the general rules of common law, was soon thereafter established by specific legislation (in England, the laws of 1886 and 1925). Within a few years of the end of World War II this evolution was all but complete: most of the provinces of Canada and states of the United States explicitly recognized parental equality with respect to the children.

In 1945 Scandinavian women had nothing to envy anglophone women as to the extent of their civil rights. Married women had gained legal competency in the 1920s (and even earlier in Norway) and shared parental authority in full or in part with the father. German women, whose rights were still restricted under the 1896 Bürgerliches Gesetzbuch, or BGB, would owe their equality to the promulgation of a new fundamental law in 1949. The new constitution stated forthrightly that "men and women have equal rights," and Article 117 stipulated that any law incompatible with this principle would cease to have legal force as of March 31, 1953. From that date on, German women enjoyed rights they had been denied under the BGB, especially with respect to parental authority; further legislation such as the 1957 law on equality of the sexes elaborated on these basic rights.

A comparison of Germany with France turns up some surprising differences. In France, equality between the sexes was proclaimed as a formal principle in the preamble to the Constitution of 1946 and reiterated in the Constitution of 1958, while the inequality of married women remained institutionalized in the Civil Code. More or less the same situation obtained in Italy. Different countries, different legal customs.

The Latin Model and Its "Derivatives"

In 1945 the legal situation of women in Latin countries and countries influenced by the French Civil Code was virtually the opposite of that just described: women, if not still deprived of access to political life, had enjoyed political rights for only a short time and in their private lives remained subject to the power of a husband to whom they owed obedience. Is the relative backwardness of these countries a reflection of the weakness of feminism, which presumably failed early in the century to establish a mass movement or develop a knack for political lobbying? To some extent the answer is yes, especially in Catholic countries where the law retained a strong religious underpinning: in Italy, Spain, and Portugal, the very idea of women's emancipation seemed to be in contradiction with the Catholic faith and tradition that "made" the law man's law. In France the situation was somewhat different. There, while the turn-of-the-century feminist movement was clearly vigorous, that of the interwar years was not: suffragist groups fell to internal bickering and lost support, while the political parties exhibited extremely misogynistic attitudes. In 1936 the right to vote for women was not even included in the platform of the coalition that brought Socialist Léon Blum to power.

Bear in mind, however, that two crucial events shaped the issue of women's equality in France and its neighbors over a very long period. First, the French Revolution, which excluded women from politics as a matter of principle, legitimated that principle in the eyes of generations of republicans. Second, the Civil Code of 1804, the very embodiment of legal modernity, enshrined the subordination of women in private law for a century and a half to come. Although the effect of the Code in the area of women's rights was reactionary (with respect not just to revolutionary law but even to the Ancien Régime), everyone pretended that it was a monument of legal perfection and therefore untouchable. Indeed, the principal attacks on it came from feminists (who seized on the occasion provided by the sumptuous celebration of the centenary of the Civil Code in 1904 to protest that for women it was a straitjacket).

In Latin as opposed to the anglophone countries the achievement of universal suffrage generally left women by the wayside. In 1848 France was the first European country to adopt universal male suffrage. In 1944 it was among the last to grant women the right to vote and hold office. In the period of almost a century between these two events, universal suffrage became widespread, not to say commonplace. And it was more than a century and a half since the Revolution of 1789 placed the issue of political equality on the agenda. In 1939, when the sesquicentennial of the French Revolution was celebrated at Versailles, feminists expressed outrage that "this ostracism has continued for a hundred and fifty years."[6]

France was not the only Western nation in which being male remained a prerequisite for exercising political rights until almost the middle of the twentieth century. Italy and Belgium also lagged "one war behind." Still others—Switzerland and Portugal—managed to delay granting women political rights until the 1970s, and Liechtenstein held out until the 1980s.

Following the examples of the ancient republics (Athens as well as Rome), the Mediterranean countries (except Spain) apparently clung to the belief that participation in political life ought to be reserved to those who bore arms. Of course tactical political reasons also played a part in delaying women's access to the political arena. In France, for example, it was widely assumed that women were especially vulnerable to the political influence of the clergy, hence the vote for women became a major issue dividing anticlerical republicans from the Catholics of the conservative (and perhaps royalist) right. But the whole issue of clerical influence may have been a red herring, a mask concealing deeper reservations about awarding women the right to vote. Would Radical-Socialist senators have been able to deprive women of their political rights for so long had they not felt that the great principles of the Revolution itself provided ideological justification for preserving the masculine character of politics?

"Our Civil Code, which long served as an example and model, is now quite backward with respect to women's rights."[7] This critical assessment, put forward by a French jurist in 1899, remained just as pertinent a half-century later; it applied to that whole portion of Europe that had endured the influence of Napoleon's Code. The effects of the civil incompetency of (married) women were particularly severe in countries that had simply adopted the French system (Belgium, Luxembourg, the Netherlands). Other countries, which had interpreted the Napoleonic Code more liberally, managed to lessen some of the inequalities between husband and wife (in Italy, for example, married women had enjoyed certain civil rights since 1918). Nevertheless, where religion exerted great influence on the law (as in Italy, Spain, and Portugal), women's liberties in certain areas, particularly divorce and abortion, remained limited. Last but not least, the long reign of fascist dictatorships in Spain and Portugal ensured that women would remain legally muzzled there until the mid-1970s.

Traditionally, the subordinate position of women in countries once subject to the Civil Code stemmed from both the husband's legal authority over his wife and the wife's civil incompetency. Neither had been totally eradicated from national legal codes as recently as 1945. Indeed, both would remain potent influences for years to come.

In 1945 women in many parts of Europe and even North America (Quebec), suffered a loss of legal competency when they married. Seven Western countries still denied married women competency in any civil legal matter. Legally, they did not exist; they were minors whose rights were subordinate to their husbands' will. Without her husband's authorization, a woman could not testify in court or sign a contract. A survival of the previous century, this refusal to allow women civil autonomy would endure until 1956 in the Netherlands, 1957 in Ireland, 1958 in Belgium, 1964 in Quebec, 1972 in Luxembourg, 1975 in Spain, and 1976 in Portugal. In France women received civil citizenship during the war (laws of 1938 and 1942). With men away in the army or in prison camps, there was an urgent need to grant the second sex the capacity to act (although various restrictions implicit in the laws of matrimonial property considerably limited that capacity).

For two decades after 1945, marriage in the countries of the Civil Code continued to be an association between two individuals with unequal rights and duties. French law clearly illustrates the patriarchal conception of the family then prevalent in legal systems based on the Civil Code. As the "head of the family," the husband enjoyed extensive powers over his wife's and children's persons and property. He was entitled to decide where the household would be located, to refuse to allow his wife to practice a profession, to administer community property on his own, and even to administer his wife's personal property (excepting so-called reserved property, in particular property acquired through the wife's professional activities). Although women in fact took responsibility for raising the children, the law ascribed all power concerning their upbringing to the husband (including the decision whether to enroll them in a school or summer camp). Inequality with respect to duty was no less flagrant with respect to adultery. Although both husband and wife were expected to remain faithful, failure to do so was punished much more severely in women. And divorce remained difficult, even in countries where the law had been secularized, and impossible where it remained under the influence of religion.

It has been repeated *ad nauseam* that women in the Latin countries more than compensated for their lack of political power with the extent of their domestic powers. It hardly needs emphasizing that such control over the private sphere is at best a *de facto* reality without legal implications. There is a profound harmony between law and tradition in the Latin countries, where, as Odile Dhavernas notes, tradition "situates women on the side of nature and men at the heart of culture," hence of the juridical.[8]

In 1945, and even as late as the mid-1960s, the legal systems of various countries still proposed very different concepts of woman. Some had long since accepted women's desire for independence and freedom, while others, excluding women from the dynamic of individual rights initiated by the French Revolution, left them enmeshed in that natural community, the family, under the direct authority of the family head.

As clear-cut as this contrast between legal systems and traditions is, it also points up certain similarities. No doubt the most important of these is that almost everywhere the law (or legal doctrine) continued to reflect a traditional division of responsibilities within the couple: it is the husband's role to work and earn money, while the wife is responsible for housework and childrearing. This is true not only in France and other countries with legal systems based on the Napoleonic Code but also in Germany: under the terms of the 1957 law on equality of the sexes, management of the household remained one of the natural duties of the wife, whereas a woman's right to pursue a professional career was still subject to certain limitations. Even in the United Kingdom after World War II, the Royal Commission on Marriage and Divorce criticized the Victorian system of separate property on the following grounds: "Marriage ought to be regarded as a partnership in which husband and wife work together on an equal footing and in which the woman's contribution to the common enterprise through management of the household and upbringing of the children is as precious as that of the husband, who maintains the household and provides for the needs of the family."[9] The only exceptions to the rule were the Scandinavian countries, which rejected any traditional view of sex roles.

The Winds of Reform: 1960–1980

After nearly a century of stagnation, the last thirty years have witnessed a major upheaval in family law and women's rights. Nearly all countries, no matter what their tradition, have been forced in one way or another to adapt their legal codes to changing social practices: a new, more egalitarian, more hedonistic (but less stable) conception of marriage, an increase in cohabitation without marriage, more children born out of wedlock, and a sharp rise in the number of women working and consequently desirous of greater independence. As Georges Ripert realistically observed as long ago as 1948, "The man whose wife pursues a professional career knows that he must abdicate."[10] In some countries, such as France, where the fundamental conservatism of legal doctrine was coupled with frank contempt of radical feminists for legal reforms, it may well be that the end of paternal legal autocracy was brought about primarily by millions of working women.

The general revision of the law in view of greater sexual equality has had the effect of bringing different legal systems closer together. There has been a rapprochement of both substance and form. In substance, the structure of marriage is no longer hierarchical but dyadic. The Civil Code has been stripped of some of its normative assumptions. It now envisions a range of ways in which couples may live together or choose not to live together and is thus closer to the traditionally more flexible common law. In form, there has been a blending of community and separate property regimes. Once again, it was the Scandinavian countries that led the way. As long ago as the 1920s they developed what has been called the deferred community property regime, which has the merit of not favoring any particular view of women's lives over any other: the working woman and the housewife are treated equally.

The greatest changes came in countries with legal systems based on the Napoleonic Code, where miracles were required "to adapt ancient but inadequate laws in an equitable fashion."[11] The result was nothing less than a "decolonization" of women. This decolonization not only put an end to women's legal incompetency but also did away with the ancient concept of *patria potestas,* which granted husbands powers over their wives and fathers powers over their children. The reforms embodied in law the twin ideas of sexual equality and independence of husband and wife. In France the major reform that freed women from their husbands' supervision was completed in 1965, but full realization of the principle of equality in personal as well as property law had to await the passage of additional laws in 1970 (when the notion of "head of the family" with all its connotations was replaced by that of parental authority), 1975 (when divorce by mutual consent was legalized and adultery decriminalized), and 1985 (when husband and wife gained full equality in administration of the family's wealth).

In Southern Europe, where feminism came later for religious as well as political reasons, it took even longer to replace authoritarian tradition with an egalitarian approach to the family. It was not until 1975 that reforms affecting the basic issues of women's rights began to be introduced, even as the last dictatorial regimes were crumbling. Civil marriage was introduced (and religious marriage deprived of legal sanction) in Italy in 1970 (confirmed by the referendum of 1974), in Portugal in 1975, in Spain in 1981, and in Greece in 1982. Husband and wife were also granted equal rights to administer family property and joint responsibility in childrearing (in Italy in 1975, in Portugal in 1978, in Spain in 1981, and in Greece in 1983).

This fever of reform did not spare countries that had liberalized their laws earlier. The last vestiges of male privilege in certain areas (such as divorce, parental authority, matrimonial property, choice of name) were eliminated. The German reform of marriage law (1976) may serve as an example: it reflects a desire to cleanse the law of the prevalent image of women as housewives and to renounce any predetermined notion of how responsibilities ought to be shared between husbands and wives. With the 1976 law on choice of names (allowing a woman either to take her husband's name or to keep her maiden name when she married) and the 1979 law on parental responsibility (eliminating all vestiges of parental "power" over the child), the idea of sexual equality inscribed in the West German 1949 Constitution at last found full embodiment in law.

By the beginning of the 1980s the "law of the father" was thus a relic of the past. But change never ends, and the law was still struggling to keep up. A sharp increase in the number of babies born out of wedlock (one in two in Scandinavia, one in four in France) made it necessary to insist on equality—in this case, the equal responsibility of the father in a "natural" family which, though marginal, was becoming increasingly "normal." Once again, not all European countries were in agreement as to how to proceed. Among the most egalitarian was Holland, whereas the Malhuret Law of 1987 in France gave mothers priority over fathers with respect to children born out of wedlock. In the absence of new laws, some fathers resorted to decisions of the courts to affirm their rights, if not always to assume their responsibilities.

In some countries changes in the law preceded changes in custom and jurists helped to shape women's behavior. In other places changes in attitudes and practices antedated changes in the law by a considerable margin. In countries influenced by the Napoleonic Code, where changes in the law inevitably had to reckon with doctrinal inertia, law professors rarely worked for reform. Even after reforms had been accomplished, many law professors reacted negatively to modern legislation that referred to the Code of 1804 "as the outmoded law of a vanished society."[12] In France even the most liberal legal scholars sometimes found it difficult to shed a sexist ideology that ascribed to women an essential otherness ("a different sensitivity to law, a lesser need of law, which is no doubt a great superiority"[13]) and therefore certain primary vocations (motherhood, for example, rather than autonomous creativity outside the domestic setting).

While jurists sat on the sidelines, did liberationist feminists play a key role in winning new rights for women? The answer to this simple but important question varies from country to country. In France the so-called reformist feminists of the 1950s—like their predecessors, the suffragettes—believed in the enormous transformative potential of equality before the law. According to Jean Carbonnier, the principal author of the new articles of the Civil Code, feminists "intervened effectively (in 1965) to help move the project of matrimonial law reform out of the rut in which it had become bogged down."[14] By contrast, much of the nebulous "women's liberation movement" (with the exception of a few groups such as Choisir and the Mouvement pour la Libéralisation de l'Avortement et de la Contraception) took an extralegal, extra-parliamentary position. In the name of a radicalism that opted for rejecting the entire system as it then existed, "making a revolution within the revolution," neo-feminists denounced the proposed legal reforms as "worthless." Their demands went well beyond the law, calling for "a new way of being, loving, and living."[15] As a result, the series of laws that made married women the civil equals of their husbands was drafted and passed by the National Assembly in the 1970s "without attracting the concern or even the notice of feminists."[16] It was only later that the antilegalist front collapsed, giving rise to new demands for legislation in unprecedented areas: rape, violence against women, sexual harassment, and even calls for laws against sexism modeled on existing laws against racism. Only then would an Anne Zelensky gain prominence by declaring that "for marginals like us, outlaws by definition because strangers to the prevailing law, such a law can free us from the servitude of our ancestors rather than subjugate us all the more."[17]

The evolution of American feminism is sometimes described as the exact opposite of its French counterpart. For two decades after 1970, a broad consensus of American women favored the pursuit of women's rights through legal reforms; only a few radicals objected. Spearheading the movement was the reformist National Organization for Women. For this group, total equality could be achieved only through securing full rights for women in all areas. The long struggle for the Equal Rights Amendment, which began in 1920, is not only the quintessential example of legal struggle but also clear proof of the importance ascribed to law in American neo-feminist ideology. More recently, however, doubt began to chip away at legalistic certitudes. Furthermore, theoretical challenges have been raised to the very notion of legal equality in the English-speaking countries. Disappointed by the paltry fruits of formal equality as well as by certain unintended consequences of victories in the battle for equal rights, some feminist legal scholars have moved toward protective or female-specific demands (such as granting mothers priority in parental authority or calling for wages for housework), even at the risk of perpetuating the ancient division of labor between men and women. Others have begun to deny that legal equality is a necessary (though not sufficient) stage in the destruction of sexism. It may be that the final defeat of the ERA (in 1982) and the current challenges to legal abortion have had a salutary effect on the movement. Opposition, one might argue, has reinvigorated American feminism and restored faith in a government of law by demonstrating the usefulness of the legal system for all its shortcomings.

In Southern Europe women have eagerly embraced legal reform. Having suffered from the law's oppression more severely and for a longer period than women elsewhere, they saw reform not just as liberating but as "opening the way to the future." In Italy and Spain and to a lesser degree in Portugal, family law was reformed in the face of angry pressure from feminists. In Rome and Madrid the battle for divorce and against criminal penalties for adulterous women brought thousands of women into the streets, shouting slogans such as "We are all adulterous wives."

The struggle for equal rights for women has gone on for two centuries. It took that long to establish the principle of universality in law and to bring triumph for the logic of individualism over the last vestiges of patriarchy, "vestiges which, through an alchemy peculiar to nineteenth-century law, were transformed into individual attributes of the adult male."[18]

The demand for equal rights has now been fully satisfied, with two important caveats. This legal victory has been won only in the West. The struggle for civil rights continues in Muslim countries, for example, where the religious law still prevails (as evidenced by women's demonstrations in Algeria against a family law regarded as backward). Second, even in the West, the battle is over only in the area of civil and political rights. Much remains to be done in the realm of social rights. Even with equal rights, moreover, women must still contend with inequalities of fact. In this respect, women in France, Italy, and above all Scandinavia enjoy enormous advantages over their sisters in America. European women have long benefited from legislation designed to protect them and aid them in their role as working mothers, whereas very few American women enjoy paid maternity leaves or free daycare and nursery schools.

Participation in Government

Once legal equality was obtained, the most difficult part of the struggle still remained: how to change behavior so as to enjoy in reality the freedoms and rights won in arduous combat. Did progress in the area of civil law result in true collegial decision-making by married couples? One can hardly claim that this is the case at present. Ultimately the answer will come from those who practice law in the "real world" (in the French case, the *notaires* who deal with marriage agreements and property settlements). They will tell us if married women are making full use of the new powers they have won, particularly the right to co-administer family property. One thing is certain: in some countries, France among them, divorce proceedings are initiated by women more often than by men.

Most women in Western countries have over time developed a civic sense, if not an interest in politics, as acute as that of men. In some countries, such as the United States and Sweden, more women vote than men. Equally important has been the direction in which their voting has evolved: a growing awareness of the inequalities from which they suffer has led many women to abandon the conservative parties in favor of political forces more likely to redefine sex roles. One sign of the times: in Japan, where women have traditionally been regarded as submissive, the (conservative) Liberal-Democrats have come to fear that hostility of women voters toward their party may swing the balance of power to the

Socialists, who from 1989 to 1991 were led by a woman, Mrs. Dakako Doi.

Given the political awakening of women, the failure of most institutions to respond is all the more striking. Male domination of the ruling elite has come to be seen as a sign of social obsolescence. Is politics the last refuge of virility? The apparently universal reluctance of men to share political power inevitably raises the question.

An Absolute Majority of Women Voters

Since more than half of the electorate everywhere consists of women, the female voters' potential to upset the political applecart has long been feared. The rise of women's interest in politics has alarmed men not only because it threatens their monopoly but also because the sheer number of women makes them a force to be reckoned with.

In 1945 there was a great deal of speculation (as there had been in 1918) about the presumed moderating, not to say conservative, influence of female voters. But since the political context had changed, so had the nature of the hopes and fears associated with women's suffrage: what had once been seen as a possible threat to republican institutions was now viewed as a bulwark against the possibility of a Communist upsurge. Historians of French politics generally agree that such an ulterior motive weighed on the minds of Gaullists and other rightists in the postwar period. In 1945 Georges Bidault, leader of the Mouvement Républicain Populaire (the Christian-Democrat party), allegedly told Charles d'Aragon that "with women, the bishops, and the Holy Spirit, we will have a hundred deputies."[19]

How did women vote in the first free elections after the war? Any analysis must rely on polling data (together with the actual count of separate ballot boxes for male and female voters in the few places where this practice was followed). In 1955 UNESCO sponsored a vast survey of women's political participation in Europe, with Maurice Duverger as principal investigator. Two main results emerge from this study: women were slightly more likely than men to abstain from voting and displayed less of an interest in politics; those who did vote tended to favor the moderate conservative parties (but not the extreme right). In Great Britain and Scandinavia most women voted Conservative; in Germany,

Austria, Italy, they voted for the Christian-Democratic parties that were so powerful after the war; and similarly, in France, they voted for the MRP until it collapsed, after which they turned to the Gaullists. Women accounted for between 53 and 60 percent of the vote received by these parties. Furthermore, much effort was directed toward winning the woman's vote: in Catholic countries particularly, the Church sought to influence women through affiliated women's organizations, which were quite active at the time in Italy and France. They endorsed candidates, influenced politicians, lobbied parliaments, and published countless pamphlets in the hope of swaying female voters.

Conversely, women shunned the socialist parties (the Labour Party in Britain, the Social Democrats in Scandinavia and Germany) and above all the Communist Party (where it existed). In Italy and France women never accounted for more than 40 percent of the Communist vote. Communist leaders were not unaware of their failure to appeal to women: "One of the reasons for our lack of success," observed the Italian secretary general, Palmiro Togliatti, after the 1945 general elections, "was surely our failure to campaign actively enough among women. . . . Look at the eight million votes for the Christian Democrats. . . . It is surely no mistake to say that most of them were cast by women. . . . The problem is not just to persuade the workers and peasants who voted for that party [to vote for us] but above all to persuade the masses of women."[20]

Drawing a lesson from their failure, the Communists in both Italy and France would henceforth target women voters as precisely as possible (no other parties were as energetic in this regard). They wooed women in trade unions, issued propaganda directed at housewives, and promoted women's affiliates such as the Union of Italian Women and the Union of French Women. Catholic propaganda was thus answered by Communist counter-propaganda. In the ensuing Cold War, women were not spared in the ideological battle between the Marxist left and the Catholic right, though they were treated as pawns by both sides.

In 1969 Maurice Duverger could still cling to the conclusions he had drawn in the mid-1950s: although the women's vote had not fundamentally altered the postwar political balance of power, it did on occasion suffice to determine the color of the majority: "If women had voted as men did in certain German elections, the Social Democrats would be in power instead of the Christian

Democrats. In Great Britain it was the women's vote that carried the Conservative Party into office in certain elections. In the French presidential elections of 1965, the proportion of women who voted for General de Gaulle was much greater than the proportion of men."[21] In other words, political science tended to confirm everyone's hunch: European women tended to vote conservative, or even, in Catholic countries, in favor of downright clerical reaction. North America was no exception: in Canada and the United States polling data showed that women tended to vote "conservative."

Although the reasons for this conservative predilection were intangible, some observers believed them to be durable, but they were soon proved wrong. The change came in two phases. In the early 1970s poll-takers began to report that women were more politicized, more likely to respond to complex questionnaires, and more apt to vote for the left. As time went by—a sort of apprenticeship period—the women's vote began to resemble the men's more and more closely. Many analysts believed that this evolution would end when it was no longer possible to distinguish between men's and women's political behavior: women would simply follow the lead of men.

In the 1980s, however, what has come to be called the "gender gap" began to emerge. Analysts observed a growing tendency for women to vote to the left of men: the erstwhile natural allies of conservative and Christian-Democratic parties now became the leading supporters of the noncommunist left. The phenomenon began in the United States in 1980, when women exhibited pronounced "anti-Reagan" tendencies. This unleashed a torrent of analysis by political scientists and comment by feminists. During the 1984 presidential campaign, Gloria Steinem's *Ms* magazine devoted its March issue to the phenomenon. Before long the same tendency was being observed in Canada and throughout much of Northern Europe: Denmark, Norway, Sweden, and the Netherlands. Still more surprisingly, it reached Catholic France in 1988: in the first round of the presidential election, 37 percent of women favored François Mitterrand, the Socialist candidate, compared with just 31 percent of men (according to a Bull-BVA poll).

In those European countries where both ecological Green parties and extreme right-wing parties have made electoral advances in recent years, it has been observed that women vote readily for the Greens but tend to shun the neo-fascist right. This was the case in the French presidential election of 1988 and the elections for deputies to the European Parliament in 1989. This reluctance of women to cast a protest ballot in favor of the extreme right is not new: "Wherever separate votes were counted [in Germany] before 1933, [women] cast fewer votes for the National Socialists than did men."[22]

Behind these recent divergences in political behavior it is possible to detect a divergence of political views in such crucial areas as defense, diplomacy, and foreign relations. Whether in the United States, Scandinavia, or France, women are more likely than men to support pacifist positions, to display hostility to the principle of nuclear deterrence, to hesitate to use military force, to favor reduction of the defense budget and greater spending on social programs, and to be more sensitive to the protection of the environment. They are also more feminist. What the polls in 1986 revealed was unprecedented in a country like France: for the first time "women preferred women," or at any rate they preferred the leading female politicians such as Simone Veil and Michèle Barzach over the leading men. The nomination of Edith Cresson as prime minister in 1991 only consolidated the feminism of French women: nearly 86 percent of them (compared with 77 percent of men) stated at the time that they were happy to have a woman running the government.[23] In Scandinavia women have openly displayed their feminism in casting their ballots. According to a Gallup poll conducted prior to the 1975 parliamentary elections, 40 percent of women and 7 percent of men voted for a female candidate.[24]

The emergence of this political split between men and women gives the impression that until recently politicians have failed to look upon female voters as a special target to aim at or a market to conquer. State governors in the United States have courted the women's vote by promising to appoint women to key posts in their administrations. Indeed, in 1982 six governors owed their election to the support they received from women. And the nomination of Geraldine Ferraro as Democratic candidate for vice-president in 1984 was interpreted by some commentators as an attempt to grab the "feminist vote."

How are we to interpret these changes in the political behavior of women? In the past feminists were highly critical of the work of (male) political scientists, whom they accused of being sexist or even "phallocentric." They were particularly critical of the claim that women were "politically alienated." In response to Maurice

Duverger's contention that when it comes to politics women behave like children, Andrée Michel offered this dialectical reply: "Treated as minors by parties of the left as well as the right, many adult women . . . were led to reject the paternalism of the parties" by refusing to vote for them.[25]

At present many observers have rightly reacted against the notion that there is a women's vote, a so-called gender bloc. Headlines used to scream "Women elect de Gaulle (or Giscard d'Estaing)." Now, only slightly less misleading, they report that "François Mitterrand owes his second term as president to the women's vote." In the United States the gender gap is sometimes presented as if the country were divided into two hostile camps, men and women. Some women fear that the "women's vote" is just the latest incarnation of the eternal feminine.

Thoroughgoing research has shown that there is no more a homogeneous women's vote than there is a men's vote. Furthermore, the shift in women's voting from right to left appears to be a durable phenomenon, because it is linked to structural changes that have radically modified the demographics of the female electorate.

Over the past forty years women's lives have undergone a silent revolution, and their voting reflects this. Around the world women have been centrally involved in major social changes, though to different degrees in different countries. Among those changes are the democratization of secondary and higher education, the growth of the service sector, and the expansion of wage labor. In France, for example, a sharp increase in the number of working women in the electorate has had an effect on voting patterns. There is a close correlation between the involvement of women in the economy and their willingness to vote for the left, as was seen for the first time in the 1978 French legislative elections and confirmed in the 1988 presidential election. In the first round of the 1988 election, most of the women who voted for Mitterrand worked in blue- or white-collar jobs or as middle managers.

The religious and social changes that have occurred since World War II have also led to major political changes. In Catholic countries political conservatism has always gone hand in hand with a deep involvement in religion. Most regular churchgoers were women, particularly elderly women: this explained their marked preference for right-wing parties and their hostility to Marxism. As religious practice in general declined (and as participation in the Communist Party simultaneously diminished), the battle between the Catholic right and the Marxist left—a battle that had long circumscribed the horizon of women—faded in importance.

If elderly women are nowadays less devoted to Catholicism and its associated political and cultural conservatism, young women are more rebellious than ever. Young women everywhere appear to be more disposed to vote for left-wing parties than men of the same generation. In France young Arab women, immigrants of the second generation, have shown clear signs of progressive political tendencies, as have female students. In the student demonstrations of the winter of 1986, young women led the way. These leftist tendencies among young women suggest a diffuse or delayed effect of feminism, which presumably taught the younger generation to reject a certain patriarchal order and protest against inequality in the apportionment of jobs and roles.

In France there has long been a correlation between left-wing voting and feminist beliefs, even in the absence of direct candidate endorsements by women's liberation groups. To be sure, the French feminist movement grew out of the New Left, and its most radical elements have long been opposed to electoral politics and their traditional choice between left and right: as Simone de Beauvoir put it in 1978, "I don't have a very clear idea of what the elections mean."[26] The right to vote was for a long time the most basic feminist demand, but French feminists of the second wave were contemptuous of that right. It was not until 1981 that the group known as Psychanalyse et Politique saw fit to endorse the presidential candidacy of François Mitterrand, and many other women's groups more or less tacitly approved of the Socialist government.

In Scandinavia and North America feminists adopted a more realistic, more political attitude. Instead of ignoring the influence they could wield through the ballot box, they used their lobbying strength to obtain certain desired results. Ultimately, as we shall see, this strategy led to increased political representation for women.

For a Handful of Elected Women

In many Western countries sexual equality in the concrete exercise of political rights is a goal that has yet to be attained, indeed a battle that has yet to be fought. Men still outnumber women in decision-making bodies, whether appointive or elective. The few exceptions only underscore the rule: they happened, for example, in 1985 and again in 1991 when Norwegian Labor Party leader Gro Harlem Brundtland formed governments composed half of women, half of men. The plain but eloquent truth is that there is no parliament anywhere in this last quarter of the twentieth century in which women have achieved numerical parity with men.

If women are everywhere in the minority, does it follow that they can play only a minor role in politics? The answer to this question is not simple. Participation in decision-making varies not only with time and place but with the nature of the governmental hierarchy.

Women are most advantageously placed in Northern Europe: in the five Scandinavian countries and the Netherlands they hold between 20 and 40 percent of the seats in local and national assemblies (see the table on p. 500 above). In contrast, much of Southern Europe lags behind: men hold more than 92 percent of the parliamentary seats in Portugal, Greece, Turkey, and France (Italy and Spain are exceptions). The picture is further complicated by England, where by 1992 only 6 percent of members of the House of Commons were women—the home of the suffragettes thus used to rank among the worst nations of Europe when it comes to representation of women in parliament. The 1992 elections raised the proportion of women in the House of Commons above 10 percent for the first time in history. In the United States, a powerful feminist movement has for many years coexisted with a Congress with only a handful of women senators and representatives. Recently, however, women have begun to win election to state legislatures (where their proportion tripled between 1971 and 1983) and city halls, suggesting a new upward trend. This trend is also reflected in the Congress, and in the 1992 elections the proportion of women in the House of Representatives reached the symbolic ten-percent threshold.

In 1945 the situation of women in most Western countries was the same: only a small minority could hope to gain access to the ruling elite. No country could boast of having anything more than a token woman in government or of electing a parliament with anything less than 90 percent men; the picture was just as bleak at the local level. Scandinavia was far from leading the way toward advancement for women, and one contemporary observer noted that "the Protestant countries—anglophone and Nordic—have a smaller percentage of woman deputies than does Catholic and Latin France, where women's rights were only recently introduced."[27]

Today's contrasts are therefore new, the result of other developments. In some places, including the United Kingdom, the United States, and Turkey, the number of women elected to the legislature has remained more or less stable for forty years, or even declined (as in France). In other places, including Scandinavia and the Netherlands, the representation of women began to rise sharply in the 1970s. Between 1975 and 1985 the proportion of female deputies more than doubled in the Netherlands and Norway and rose by one-fourth in Finland and one-third in Sweden. Elsewhere it is only recently that large numbers of women have begun to win elective office: in Italy, the United Kingdom, the United States, and Canada, it was only in the last elections that women won enough seats to account for more than 10 percent of the lower house.

In the past, the prize for the largest number of female deputies generally went to the left-wing parties (Communists or Socialists), followed by the Christian Democrats. In 1946, for example, 29 of 40 French female deputies were Communists, while 9 belonged to the MRP (Christian Democrats). In the German Bundestag of 1953, 46 percent of the women were Social Democrats and 42 percent Christian Democrats. Finally, in Norway, nearly all the women elected to parliament in the 1950s were Socialists.

Today, however, the left has lost its monopoly on female representation in many countries. In Scandinavia, the conservative parties, under pressure from the women's liberation movement, had to recruit more women or suffer the consequences at the ballot box. Competition between parties for votes became the most powerful force enabling women to advance in politics. In France history took a different course: the pressure for greater equality came from below. The collapse of the Communist vote forced it to renounce the lead in this area. The Socialists proved incapable of taking up the feminist torch after they became the dominant party from 1981 to 1993. In the assembly elected in June 1988, only 6.2 percent of the Socialist deputies were women compared with 7.5 percent of the RPR (the rightist Rassemblement pour la République) deputies, even though the RPR, like the Gaullist movement in general, was reputed to have little liking for feminism.

Of the major left-wing parties in Europe, the Italian Communist Party (PCI) has always been an exception, prepared to make considerable room for women on its parliamentary benches: 60 percent of the women elected to parliament in 1987 were Communists. Enrico Berlinguer, the late leader of the PCI, was especially adept at playing the feminist card and making the PCI a leading advocate of the women's cause. Meanwhile, the British Labour Party, which in the past failed to distinguish itself with a strong feminist contingent, has recently made up for lost time. In April 1992 thirty-seven women were elected to the House of Commons under the Labour banner, accounting for 13.6 percent of Labour's 271 deputies.

Political parties that were organized in recent years have generally included women in their leadership and derived electoral benefits from the decision to do so. The Greens in Germany took up many feminist issues and have taken over the title of "most feminized party" from the Social Democrats. The progress that women made in the 1987 Bundestag was due to the Greens, moreover: of 42 Green deputies, 25 were women. The reunification elections of December 1970, however, resulted in a rout of the Greens, who managed to elect only eight deputies, three of them women. Following the German example, the French Greens carefully balanced their list of candidates in the 1989 elections to the European Parliament: the result was an unprecedented success of nearly 11 percent of the vote, and 4 of the 9 Greens elected were women. This success was short-lived, however, because in the March 1993 legislative elections the coalition of the Greens and Génération Ecologie managed to attract only 17.6 percent of the votes cast, not enough to win a single seat in parliament. In Italy, the (small) Radical Party also played the feminist card: notorious above all for the "scandalous" Cicciolina, the "first X-rated deputy in the Italian parliament,"[28] the party managed to have three of its female candidates elected in the 1987 legislative elections.

None of the attempts to establish a feminist party managed to overcome the inertia of the existing party system. The only successful feminist party in the world is the Women's Party of Iceland, which in 1987 won 10 percent of the vote and elected 6 deputies, who played a key role in parliament.

Although women are often found in large numbers in peripheral party organizations, their participation tends to decrease as one moves toward the center of power. Signs of this vertical division of power between the sexes (men at the top, women at the bottom) are ubiquitous. In France, the proportion of women decreases from 17 percent at the municipal council level to 12.6 percent in regional councils and 5.4 percent in parliament (Senate and National Assembly combined). The power of women at the municipal level is interesting to analyze in detail. Although many women serve as municipal councillors, only 6 percent of mayors are female. Most women mayors head small rural communes; few hold office in large cities. When the Socialist Catherine Trautmann became mayor of Strasbourg in 1989, she set a precedent: she was the first woman to run a city with a population over 100,000. Some commentators consider the feminization of the European Parliament to be equally significant. Since 1979 (when universal suffrage was instituted), every country in Europe other than Belgium has sent a delegation to the European Parliament composed of more than 10 percent women (more than 20 percent in four instances). But this is partly because this body was considered at the time to be of relatively minor importance, with no real power at stake.

The fact that there are few women among the high-ranking civil servants who hold the most important government positions is perhaps the most serious sign of the relegation of women to the fringes of the contemporary political scene. At a time when the influence of parliaments is declining relative to that of the technocracy, it is a cause for concern that women are getting elected but are not climbing to the top of the civil service. But that is just what is happening in Scandinavia. France is to some extent a counterexample: women have done reasonably well at securing posts on ministerial staffs (holding nearly 23 percent of the available positions under Michel Rocard); better than they have succeeded at getting elected to parliament. Finding the electoral route closed, French women were forced to move ahead by obtaining degrees and skills (especially through the Ecole Nationale d'Administration, more than 20 percent of whose students are women). Of course such a choice leaves them vulnerable to the whims "of the reigning princes."

Women were not only relegated to secondary roles but also condemned to busy themselves with "good works." The growth of the welfare state facilitated, at the political level, a spontaneous recreation of the old division of labor between the masculine/

political and the feminine/social. Problems previously handled within the family were naturally assigned to the few women who sought a role in the political arena. Men handled foreign affairs, defense, interior, justice, the economy, and the treasury—all the offices embodying the sovereignty of the state. Women got the social, the familial, the cultural. This horizontal division of roles, quite visible at the governmental level, can today be found at all levels of power in all countries (except in Scandinavia). It is one way of keeping women out of the strictly political sphere—a way of hiding or erasing the error of having let them in in the first place.

Women in Politics: A Chance for Democracy?

The number of political offices occupied by women today, and the nature of those offices, give reason for pessimism about the influence that women can hope to exert in a democracy. The only way for women to make their voices heard, to influence decisions, to cease being held hostage is to make their presence felt in a major way in the political arena. Important obstacles remain to be overcome before our political institutions are truly integrated. The relatively minor role that women play in politics reflects their still subordinate status in society. Evidence of this is that a feminization of elites takes place where the ideal of equality between the sexes is being achieved, in the urban areas where women with the right qualifications to run for office live (those qualifications include a good education, professional experience, and high-level skills).

Even in a region as culturally homogeneous as Western Europe, we must bear in mind that inequality between men and women takes many forms. In Portugal centuries of oppression have resulted in a tragic situation for women today: in 1970, 38 percent of Portuguese women over twenty were illiterate, and only 7 percent had achieved a high-school reading level. In France, whatever inequalities of opportunity may remain cannot change the fact that today one out of two university students is a woman. In Portugal, men dominate the elite because women still suffer from centuries of social and cultural oppression. In France, however, a different explanation is needed for the fact that democracy has not brought power to women.

Male dominance in the corridors of power also stems from factors internal to the political world itself. In the first place, parties operate as oligarchies. It is easy to point to low levels of political participation by women to justify excluding them from key committees, just as it is a simple matter to blame a refusal to choose women candidates on the alleged misogyny of the voters. Although parties in theory are open forums for shaping platforms and choosing candidates, they actually function as narrow cliques with a particular bias against women (as well as young people). French women see their political parties for what they are: "Structures conceived by men and for men, who, when they come together, never think that they are excluding anyone but merely working for the good of all mankind—women included."[29]

Sometimes election laws encourage the reelection of the same people to office year after year. Where there is only one round of voting and the winner must gain a majority of the votes cast (as in the United Kingdom) or two rounds (as in France), it is more difficult for outsiders to win than it would be in a system of proportional representation. When the voting takes place in a relatively small district, moreover, it tends to accentuate the personal character of the election. The incumbent has the advantage, and in some countries (such as France) that advantage is multiplied by laws allowing one person to hold more than one office. Finally, in systems where members of the upper house are elected by indirect voting, the balance of power is usually held by powerful rural politicians who tend to vote for their own kind rather than for women.

"What constitutes true democracy," Léon Gambetta said, "is not to acknowledge equals but to create them." If one accepts this view, then true democracy has yet to be born. On the other hand, it is not at all implausible to anticipate that women may well wield considerable political power between now and the end of the century.

Feminism, having lost momentum as a mass movement, has belatedly turned its attention to conquering institutions. Parties, governments, and international organizations all more or less overtly proclaim feminist objectives. Some countries have established ministries to bring about equality between the sexes. Others have already promoted women to key posts. In 1989 the United Kingdom celebrated Margaret Thatcher's tenth year as prime minister, and Germany chose Rita Süssmuth to preside over the Bundestag. In 1990 Mary Robinson became president of Ireland. And in 1991 François Mitterrand chose Socialist Edith Cresson to head the government and give a "new vigor" to his policies. This appointment took on a highly symbolic value. The French press hailed it as a historic event, and a large majority of the population approved. The United Nations and the European Common Market made the participation of women in politics central issues on the international agenda. The Council of Europe chose Catherine Lalumière as its secretary general. "During my term of office," she declared, "I shall dedicate myself to advancing the cause of women." Even more important, the political parties, which dominate democratic politics, have pledged to feminize their leadership, if need be by fiat. Several major European parties have adopted quotas specifying that at least so many women must be appointed to key committees and chosen as candidates. Following the lead of the Scandinavian parties, the German Social Democrats set a quota of 40 percent women at all levels of responsibility.

Thus more and more party officials and candidates will be women. In itself this is a minor revolution, and it is also a good selling point on the campaign trail. The strategy, as we have seen, appeals not only to women but to a majority of voters. When citizens of Common Market countries were asked in 1987 if "things would go better or worse if there were more women in parliament," 28 percent answered "better" (as opposed to 49 percent "the same," 11 percent "worse," and 12 percent "no opinion").

In a time of widespread crisis—affecting the family, the economy, and the political system—women are the bearers of diffuse hopes for change. Closer to everyday human realities by virtue of their history and their lives, they may represent an alternative to the bureaucratic power of the professional male politician.

Women politicians themselves tend to emphasize this difference: they not only disparage certain obsolete ways of practicing politics but also advocate far-reaching changes in priorities and programs. Are women the future of politics? Some women think so. The feminism of former congresswoman Bella Abzug was rooted in her faith in a better world if run by women: "Would a Congress with a sufficient number of women in it have allowed this country to get to the 1970s without national health insurance? Would such a Congress have allowed this country to rank fourteenth in infant mortality among industrialized nations? Would it permit the butchery of amateur abortions? Can you imagine that a Congress full of women would have allowed the war in Vietnam to go on so long, allowing our own boys and the people of Indochina to be slaughtered?"[30]

Was Abzug right to think that women will transform government? Or is this yet another resurgence of the ancient myth of woman as redeemer? A survey I conducted of French government officials suggests the latter. In French politics the road to power is full of obstacles, which could well lead to the emergence of a distinctive female political identity, a truly feminine political culture with its own values or, rather, counter-values. Seen as different, not to say illegitimate, by their male colleagues, the few women who go into politics are well aware of being marginal, even deviant. They themselves look askance at masculine habits (of rhetoric, of speech, of dress, of ambition). But their consciousness of being different is essentially negative: it has not led to the creation of female networks of solidarity or given rise to any alternative political program. Furthermore, their conduct is largely a reaction to or overcompensation for failure (inferiority complexes, guilt feelings over neglect of their duties as wives and mothers, conformity to roles assigned by men) rather than an example for other women to follow. But France is not the United States or Scandinavia, where women politicians are said to have more of a feminist consciousness and greater hope for the future.

TRANSLATED FROM THE FRENCH BY ARTHUR GOLDHAMMER

17

Feminisms of the 1970s

Yasmine Ergas

ASKED TO COMMENT ON the last decades of the current century, attentive observers of Western societies would note the turmoil that shook the world of women. Changes that ranged from increased labor-force participation to rising incidences of divorce and single-parenting greatly altered the conditions of women's lives. But even before such changes had attracted widespread attention, "feminism" had captured public notice, becoming emblematic of women's renewed—and largely unanticipated—assertiveness.[1]

The Signs of Resurgence

The feminist renaissance showed itself in a wide array of phenomena. Most provocative at the time were the clamorous gestures which the media exalted as indicators of renewed disorder: in 1968 American women staged the "burial of traditional womanhood" with a torchlight parade at Arlington national cemetery, crowned a sheep Miss America, and threw bras, girdles, and false eyelashes into a "freedom trashcan"; two years later, French women laid a wreath dedicated to the "unknown wife of the unknown soldier" at the Arc de Triomphe in Paris and accompanied it with another wreath, inscribed with the sardonically didactic demographic observation: "one man out of every two is a woman."

If the commentators of the past decades preferred to focus on political events, they would note the massive demonstrations that helped force legislative changes on the agendas of frequently recalcitrant political systems, as in the case of the campaign for liberalization of abortion in Italy. They could also point to the flood of reformist legislation regarding "women's issues" which numerous countries approved in the 1970s and 1980s. In the United Kingdom, for instance, the Equal Pay Act of 1970 was followed by the Sex Discrimination Act (1975) and the subsequent establishment of the Equal Opportunities Commission. The Employment Protection Act (1975) mandated statutory paid maternity leave and protection from unfair dismissal during pregnancy, the Domestic Violence and Matrimonial Proceedings Act (1976) reinforced women's rights in restraining violent spouses, and the Sexual Offenses (Amendment) Act, also of 1976, improved the protection of rape victims' privacy during trial.[2] In the United States during the 1970s Congress approved 71 items of legislation, or 40 percent of all legislation regarding women's rights approved in this century.[3] Many other countries passed similar legislative innovations intended to expand women's rights.

Feminist political influence extended beyond national boundaries. International organizations inscribed the "rights of women" on their agendas: the United Nations, for instance, celebrated the Decade for Women (1975–1985) with conferences in Mexico City, Copenhagen, and Nairobi. These meetings highlighted the extensiveness of the feminist movements and their impact in "developing" as well as "developed" countries. The conferences also revealed rifts on various levels, such as between Western and non-Western militants on the definition of feminism, and between official representatives of participating governments and movement feminists, each group denying the other's legitimacy. Nonetheless, the decade itself, like the conferences, underscored the public visibility of women's issues, the emergence of strong networks of female activists, and the adoption of UN resolutions that continued to promote attention to women's concerns.

Moreover, the emergence of feminism as a political force heralded—and perhaps effected—significant redefinitions of long-standing political alignments and institutional arrangements. Analysts coined the term "gender gap" to denote women voters' migration toward more liberal or left-leaning political forces. In the United States women opposed the Reagan presidency in greater proportion than men did; in Britain, by 1983, women were less likely than men to vote for the Conservatives; in the Federal Republic of Germany in the elections of 1980 and 1983 more women than men cast their ballots in favor of the Social Democrats. Analogous patterns could be found in Canada, Sweden, and Australia.[4] And, in numerous countries, changing female electoral behavior and partisan identification were accompanied by greater political participation of women and the creation of formal institutions officially mandated to promote women's interests. In the German Federal Republic, for instance, women's representation in political parties almost doubled between 1971 and 1981 (albeit remaining significantly lower than that of men); a federal Ministry for Women was established in 1986 as part of the Ministry for Youth, Family, Women, and Health (an office of Women's Affairs had been established in 1979); and all the German *laender* had women's offices by the end of the 1980s.[5] (Significantly, as a result of German reunification, specific offices for women's issues were created together with the newly established *laender* governments in the East.) Again, analogous instances of institution-building related to women's representation were to be found in other countries.

Attentive observers would also take note of the instances in which opposition to feminism and the conflicts engendered over specific rights had served to highlight feminism's own salience. In Germany, for instance, abortion rights became a major point of contention in the negotiations regarding national unification.[6] In other European countries liberalized abortion legislation likewise generated heated, if often unsuccessful, opposition, which in turn elicited defensive feminist mobilizations. In the United Kingdom, for example, the National Abortion Campaign of 1975 defeated a bill that would have restricted the rights established by the 1967 Abortion Act. In the United States feminist mobilizations served as catalyst for the rise of "moral majorities" to national prominence, and even feminist defeats (such as the failure of the Equal Rights Amendment to win the required majority) highlighted the importance of feminism in bringing the politics of "women's issues" to the fore.[7]

Public macroevents corresponded to diffuse microprocesses of personal engagement. By the end of the 1970s feminism appeared destined to become a household term, if not a household phenomenon, in the industrialized countries of the West. *Emma,* the German feminist magazine, attained a readership of over 300,000. *Ms* magazine, in the United States, reached at least 400,000. Women's groups had formed in approximately one quarter of all Dutch towns. Feminists ran more than 200 women's shelters in the United Kingdom.[8]

Many feminist outreach initiatives—the establishment of a movement press, women's studies courses, the institution of shelters, or reproductive rights campaigns—generated diffuse support. In the Dutch town of Gouda, more than half the women interviewed by a research team in 1981–82 expressed positive attitudes towards the women's movement and felt that improvements in women's conditions could only be realized if women joined together.[9] A Canadian poll taken in 1986 found that 47 percent of the women interviewed were willing to identify themselves as feminists.[10] In the United States in the same year 56 percent of all women respondents declared to the polls that they considered themselves feminists; 71 percent felt that the women's movement had contributed to the improvement of their own lives.[11] Generally, European surveys conducted in 1983 found favorable attitudes toward women's liberation movements dominant among women in Belgium, Denmark, Germany, France, Ireland, Italy, Luxembourg, and Greece, and in a high minority among women in the Netherlands and the United Kingdom.[12] Not all feminist movements fared equally well, however. Many women preferred supporting a more neutral sounding "women's movement" rather than a "feminist movement." Others would say, "I am not a feminist, but . . ." Yet the very manner of their distancing themselves confirmed feminism's centrality as the parameter of women's politics.

By the mid-1980s, however, several once prominent feminist movements appeared to have become outmoded. The younger generation, as journalists eagerly informed their readerships in the United States and elsewhere, manifested profound indifference to its precursors' struggles and even aspirations. "Postfeminism" came to designate the new wave—a term which, paradoxically, affirmed the political primacy of a movement whose demise it was intended to signal.

The decline or eclipse of feminist mobilizations often proved less definitive than the prophets of doom had announced. In the

United States, for instance, sweeping demonstrations accompanied the Supreme Court decisions and state legislative debates of 1989 that threatened to restrict abortion rights. And if, in general, the demonstrations had become less frequent, the collectives had disbanded, and the era of grand gestures and mass gatherings that had drawn so much media attention had come to a close, they often left in their wake new forms of female political organization, a heightened visibility of women and women's issues in the public sphere, and lively debates among feminists themselves, as well as between feminists and external interlocutors. In other words, feminism's outward waning as an organized social movement implied neither the demise of feminists as political actors nor the disappearance of feminism as a developing (and contentious) set of discursive practices. Interest-group politics, mobilizations for new objectives (often defined in universalistic rather than "woman-centric" terms: peace or environmentalism in the place of abortion or sexual violence), and renewed debates took the place of the old collectives and demonstrations, expanding the range of feminism's protagonists and allowing for some—however slow—generational change. A quarter of a century after the highly visible feminist resurgence began, as the conditions in which that resurgence first took shape have altered and as feminists' concerns and resources have evolved, so, too, the loci of feminist activities and the characteristics of feminist practices have changed.

The feminist movements of the 1960s and 1970s reflected the political contexts in which they were forged. In many instances such contexts were marked by a high degree of political mobilization and by the emergence of multiple movements demanding radical social change. In particular, the ideology of the student movement, which sometimes coincided with the interests of working-class trade union and party organizations, contributed to the formation of "new lefts." Of such "new lefts" feminists became important—and critical—components. But alongside the "new lefts" and the radical social movements with which they were associated, more conventional political formations and institutions also played a role in the genesis of the new feminist movements.

The new feminist movements generally became relatively autonomous with respect to the various contexts from which they emerged, elaborating themes, developing vocabularies, identifying key issues, and demonstrating independent capacities to recruit militants and mobilize for particular ends. In fact, the feminisms which developed within the European New Left not only succeeded in asserting their legitimacy but imposed their own issues on the agendas of the New Left organizations and eventually outlived them.

Despite their autonomy, however, feminist movements inevitably remained vulnerable to the political conditions which obtained in the contexts in which they matured. Between the beginning of the feminist renaissance of the 1960s and its often proclaimed—although rarely fully achieved—quiescence two decades later, the transformation of these contexts favored changes in the forms and ends of feminist mobilization. Whereas in some countries, such as the United States, feminist movements issued in consolidated networks of independent interest group and lobbying organizations, elsewhere—as in Sweden and Norway—feminists gained positions of responsibility in political parties and state institutions. In other countries feminists developed only scanty contacts with formal political institutions, focusing either on grassroots organizations (as in the United Kingdom) or on the development of cultural projects.[13] In many instances "unobtrusive mobilizations" in seemingly unlikely places, such as the institutions of organized religion or the armed forces, advanced women's interests, sometimes in the name of feminism.[14] There has been, then, as much transformation as termination in contemporary feminism's apparent decline.

What Is Feminism?

How does one define the feminism which recently flourished in the West and in many places still maintains a lively presence, and how does one analyze its relation to particular feminist movements? The answers to these questions vary, for in the contemporary world feminism has acquired differing meanings in different settings. The dictionary views feminism discursively as "the theory of political, economic, and social equality of the sexes,"[15] and organizationally as the corresponding mobilization to "remove the restrictions that discriminate against women," but no single definition can provide an adequate guide through the complex terrain of contemporary feminist politics. Indeed, feminism is not a substantive term whose properties can be authoritatively established; but if there is a common core of phenomena to which that term refs, it is this: "feminism" indicates historically varying sets of theories and practices centered upon the constitution and empowerment of female subjects.[16]

In this perspective, what feminism is or has been is a historical rather than a definitional matter. And tracing its development requires making one's way through the untidy conflicts of the past decades during which various interpreters of feminism have disputed each other's claims, for the question of feminism's boundaries has been insistently debated by the feminist movements themselves. This process inevitably simplifies complex issues of identification and attribution.

Poignant personal tales testify to the existence of proprietary conflicts over feminism as a label. One Canadian author, for instance, recounts a moment at a movement session when feminists were asked to identify themselves. Along with other slightly older participants, those more closely linked to "traditional" women's organizations than to the recent mobilizations, she raised her hand to be counted, only to find herself facing dismissive hostility from the rest of the audience.[17] Here, in this contest over credentials, the victorious faction would win the power to define feminism.

The "sides" engaged in feminist disputes over the definition of feminism have not been frozen into particular identities by the political views they have espoused. Rather, the changing nature of feminist definitions reveals shifts in feminist identifications. In Italy, for instance, the early feminist collectives of the 1960s and 1970s specifically criticized the network of existing women's organizations. Their criticisms addressed the insufficiencies of "emancipatory culture," since Italian feminism defined itself in opposition to the idea that had been central to Western feminism, namely, that women's full access to existing rights can ensure their equality.[18] In contrast to the traditional women's organizations, Italian feminism was not ameliorative, concerned with social services, or mobilized to ensure the rights of women as mothers, wives, and workers. In the 1970s an Italian enumeration of feminism's adherents would have rejected, for instance, the National Organization of Women (NOW), clearly a principal actor in the American feminist renaissance.

Nor would the closest Italian equivalent of NOW—the Unione Donne Italiane (UDI)—have wanted to be included in a review of feminist organizations.[19] Closely related to the principal parties of the left, UDI walked a fine line between the Communist and

Socialist parties' women's divisions—which all too regularly sought to dictate the Union's positions—and its at least formally independent constituency. In the early 1970s the parties of the established left, and in particular the Communist Party, saw in feminism a form of extremism emblematic of the New Left in which the Italian feminist movement was deeply rooted.[20] And significant sectors of UDI's own constituency were leery of the feminist label.

Yet by the end of the 1970s UDI had dissolved its bureaucracy and had chosen "structurelessness," or at least a looser structure, as one way of declaring the organization's identification with the sort of feminism it had once opposed. By then the feminist movement's contours had begun to blur. Emblematically expressing the transformations of the preceding decade, in the mid-1980s a leading feminist of the 1970s assumed the general editorship of UDI's magazine. The boundaries between the old organization and the feminist movement of the previous years had broken down. And the parties of the left began to put more references to feminism in their official rhetoric. By the late 1980s, to the extent to which there was a feminist front in Italy, it included UDI along with numerous women active in the major left-wing parties.

If the position of traditional women's associations has sometimes served to demarcate one of feminism's shaky boundaries, radical perspectives have also clarified its contours. In the early 1970s Psychanalyse et Politique argued a particularly forceful melding of psychoanalytic perspectives with social critique. Its work engendered analyses stressing the essential otherness of women that have had widespread international resonance. The group, which many would consider central to French feminism, rejected the appellation of feminist. Feminism, Psychanalyse et Politique claimed, was inherently reformist, assimilationist, and ultimately bound to accept the conditions imposed by male dominance. Psychanalyse et Politique arrogated to itself the sole representation of the women's liberation movement *(mouvement de liberation des femmes),* going so far as to defend its claim to this title against other (feminist) groups in court.[21]

Analogously, in the early seventies, the term "women's liberation" also provided a label under which English activists could distance themselves from their feminist interlocutors. Juliet Mitchell and Ann Oakley, two protagonists of the period whose own analyses of women's conditions proved pivotal to the development of feminist movements of many countries, recall: "At the beginning of this phase of feminism, sometime in the sixties, there were radical feminists and women's liberationists."[22] Early radical feminists shared the views of writers such as Shulamith Firestone, whose *The Dialectic of Sex* affirmed the notion that womanhood was an essentially biological condition which provided a natural unity for women. Thus feminism entailed the alliance of women by women for women, on the basis of their belonging to a particular sex. Women's liberationists, on the other hand, as Mitchell herself had argued in two seminal works (*Women: The Longest Revolution,* and *Women's Estate*), rejected the radical feminists' biological claims. They sought, instead, to explicate women's conditions in fundamentally social terms, viewing solidarity among women as historically constructed rather than biologically grounded. Eventually, however, women's liberationists began to identify themselves as feminists and also became identified this way.

Even as feminist definitions of feminism have changed, outside observers—and many feminists as well—have sought to distinguish radical, socialist, and liberal positions, in a perspective that tends to view feminism and feminist movements as aligned with—and, in some degree, subordinate to—key political ideologies. Seen in this light, conflicts among feminists merely replicate external polemics, so that the various currents can be differentiated in terms of conventional political diction. Thus radical feminists are said to speak of female autonomy in terms reminiscent of anticolonial movements of national liberation; socialist feminists' analyses center on class conflict and contradiction; and while both radicals and socialists seem to invoke the overhauling of the social order, liberal feminists stress the importance for women of gaining equal rights within pluralist political and social frameworks.

This way of distinguishing radical, socialist, and liberal perspectives risks casting feminism as derivative, an appendix to the major political conflicts of the day. Nonetheless, it is useful as a classificatory scheme because it highlights the extent to which feminist movements have emerged in close connection with other political formations, with which they have sought to engage in dialogue. Caught in the tension between the desire to break away from external referents in favor of more internally focused concerns and the desire to maintain a capacity for action in the broader world, feminists have indeed located themselves within and without the dominant political traditions. Feminist practices and discourses have both reflected the relative importance of their outside interlocutors and contributed to the evolution of existing varieties of political discourse.[23]

The inclusion of women's rights in the rosters of demands advanced by various political organizations, the attention now at least formally paid to women's representation, and the establishment of specific forms of advocacy to promote women's interests provide tangible signs of feminism's policy effects. But it is difficult to gauge the impact of contemporary feminists' most salient—and contentious—discursive focus: the constitution and empowerment of female subject(s).

Reconstructing and Deconstructing Woman

"But first we must ask: what is a woman?" Simone de Beauvoir wrote at the outset of her classic inquiry into *The Second Sex*.[24] Contemporary feminists have differed substantially not only in their answers but in their very approaches to that question.[25] Yet it is a question to which they have insistently returned. Simultaneously affirming the primacy of womanhood as a category of political identification and questioning the nature of that category itself, feminists have sought both to construct and deconstruct the idea of womanhood. For the core of contemporary Western feminism harbors a continuous tension, one that is embodied in the "common divide [that] keeps forming in both feminist thought and action between the need to build the identity 'woman' and give it solid political meaning and the need to tear down the very category 'woman' and dismantle its all-too-solid history."[26] And so contemporary feminist movements have revolved around two antipodes: the affirmation of sexual difference as a basic existential—and therefore political—principle, and the denial of the relevance of sexual difference as a legitimate basis of social (and existential) difference.

The contemporary feminist movements of the West, it is often argued, emerged in response to the power of gender as an organizing category of social experience. Nurtured on liberal and egalitarian ideas, and confronted with the inequalities inherent in societies in which sex significantly determines life-chances, young women of the 1960s and 1970s came together in the recent feminist renaissance.[27] Challenging accepted notions relegating women to their "proper place," they attempted to free women from the constrictions of gender. The claim of today's feminism is thus the assertion of women's equal rights, and their specific objective is the attainment of a gender-neutral world.

This interpretation, however, leaves room for only one stream of contemporary feminist thought, excluding the "feminism of difference" that has explored the "otherness" of the female and insistently made women's distinction from men a central concern. Such a position is explicitly opposed to the devaluation of femininity and the assimilation of women into masculine existential modes encoded in contemporary social orders. As the members of an Italian feminist collective wrote in 1967, a woman faced two alternatives. She could opt for "masculinization" (as her newly acquired social rights seemed to portend). Or she could fall back into a role which had clearly become "exhausted and anachronistic." The "feminine" seemed increasingly bereft of social value and significance, but "masculinization" promised only alienation.[28] In this perspective, women suffer from a loss of identity to which feminism responds by revitalizing the category of womanhood. Feminism's critiques, then, are directed not at the distinctions of gender but at their incipient obsolescence.

These two perspectives have often been portrayed as polar views in the "equality versus difference" debate over the causes and characteristics of feminist movements. Not limited to the etiology of feminism, each camp in this debate has a particular understanding of the nature of feminism itself. For the "egalitarians," feminism looks beyond gender though it is linked to the oppressive pervasiveness of gender; for the "defenders of difference," feminism tends to revalidate gender and is provoked by the denial of identity from which women suffer. But the opposition between equality and difference is spurious. As Joan Scott has argued, the proper antonym of equality is inequality, not difference; that of difference, sameness, not equality.[29] Historically as well as in the recent past, feminists have claimed both equal and special rights in the name of either their identicalness with men or their difference from them.

No easy symmetry aligns difference with inequality and sameness with equality. The nineteenth- and early twentieth-century suffragists of England and the United States frequently appealed to the virtues of femininity to advance their political demands, invoking sexual difference to seek political equality. In the 1970s and 1980s, American feminists affirmed the fundamental similarity of women and men in the campaign for the Equal Rights Amendment—a campaign in which they were eventually defeated.[30] From the nineteenth century to date, those who demanded special rights for women—such as maternity leave and protective legislation—have used women's specific childbearing capacities to claim particular exemptions from the "normal" rigors of employment.[31] Finally, those who demand "affirmative action"—that is, compensatory treatment in education or in the labor market—have joined the premise of the identicalness of women and men with arguments for special consideration.

General support of women's rights does not necessarily stem from the same presuppositions. Whether sex provides a sort of physical substratum on which any gender identity can be grafted, or whether, on the contrary, gender is inexorably rooted in sex—whether, indeed, the sexed body is a given or whether physical properties can themselves result from gendering processes—are issues contemporary feminism has rendered salient.[32] Sundering sex from gender, and politicizing the space thus delineated, feminists have both posited womanhood as a foundational political identity and defined feminism as a protected political space within which the deconstruction and reconstruction of femaleness could be explicated. Especially in the first phases of the contemporary feminist movements, this fluctuation between the affirmation of a certainty (the primacy of sex as a criterion for political identification) and the iteration of doubt (the constant questioning of sexual differentiation) brought about a search for the coordinates unifying "women's condition." Later, issues relating to the distinctions and divisions among women gained salience. But in the early stages of mobilization the main issue for women in the collectives was, as one theorist and contemporary protagonist phrased it, that of women's oppression in its "endless variety and monotonous similarity."[33]

A Praxis of Separation and Distinction

But how could variety and monotony be reconciled; in what sense could women be thought to form a unified group let alone a coherent subject? Adopting vocabularies dominant on the left at the time, some used the language of class. "Women are an oppressed class. Our oppression is total, affecting every fact of our lives," wrote the American Redstockings in their Manifesto.[34] Others borrowed from anticolonial and antiracist struggles, arguing that women formed a caste, a group whose condition was inherited and immutable and thus locked into a system of domination. Others still attempted to coin specific terminologies—evoking female "otherness" or focusing on sexual difference or on the relevance of gender—to explicate the commonalities of womanhood. "Now women return from afar, from always: from 'without,' from the heath where witches are kept alive; from below, from beyond 'culture,'" wrote Hélène Cixous.[35] "Difference is an existential principle which concerns the ways of being human, the peculiarity of one's experiences, of one's goals, of one's . . . sense of existence in a given situation and in the situation which one wants to give to oneself. The difference between woman and man is the basic difference of humanity," Rivolta Femminile declared in its first major public statement.[36]

From a variety of approaches, then, feminists struggled to explicate the nature of women's commonalities, systematically and willfully transgressing the traditional distinctions demarcating the realm of the "personal" or "private" from that of the "political" or "public." The noted slogan "the personal is political" served notice that feminists were not willing to allow issues like husbands' prerogatives in marriage or sexual violence to remain confined to the niceties of individual morality, beyond the reach of political, and hence public, discussion. But "the personal is political" also denoted the importance for feminists of reconstructing female selves. The personal, in other words, represented a political project as well as a political space.

This concern with the specificity and reconstitution of the female subject was developed by feminist movements, with striking similarities, in many countries. The praxis of separation and distinction, whose elements reappeared in modified form from one movement to the next, called forth a world of women at odds with the environment, working to reconstitute female subjectivity and promote female empowerment.

Separatism and Autonomy[37]

Not all feminists endorsed separatism. On the contrary, tense confrontations focused precisely on the degree to which feminism was to be defined as women-only movement. Yet dissenting opinions notwithstanding, the exclusion of men from most activities frequently emerged as a basic organizing principle, motivated at least in part by the need to establish and defend female autonomy.[38]

In their insistence on autonomy as the goal and on separatism as the means to attain it, feminists were often said to have followed the lead of Third World and Black American nationalists.[39] The analogy illustrates the significance that today's feminists, like their predecessors, attributed to polarizing methods capable of sharply demarcating the boundaries of the collective self from the rest of the world: a crucial step in the attempt to constitute women as specific subjects.

Consciousness-Raising

Like separatism, consciousness-raising provoked dissension among feminists; nevertheless, it emerged as a fundamental technique around which contemporary feminisms were constructed.[40] Initiated in the United States around 1966–67, consciousness-raising was characterized—in the words of one activist—by the "'bitch session' cell group." This involved "ongoing consciousness expansion," including "personal recognition and testimony" and even "cross-examination," as well as "relating and generalizing individual testimony" and analyzing "classic forms of resisting consciousness" ("*or* How to avoid facing the awful truth"). The "'bitch session' cell group" also included "Starting to stop—overcoming repressions and delusions" by such means as analyzing one's fears and "developing radical feminist theory." This was to be followed by specific "consciousness-raiser (organizer) training—so that every woman in a given bitch session could herself become an organizer, in turn, of other groups."[41]

Not every feminist movement or individual collective used the vocabulary of bitch sessions for consciousness-raising. Moreover, consciousness-raising sometimes proved to be only the first of a series of methods, often heavily indebted to psychoanalytic practices and concepts, designed to promote individual self-perception as well as monitor daily behavior, and predicated on the belief that women had somehow been deprived of their "real selves." Denied positive self-images, the ability to discern their own worth, or the capacity to pursue their own interests, women could at least begin to redress their situation of fundamental "colonization" or "negation" and thus approximate if not attain an authentic form of subjectivity through collective efforts at self-understanding and self-reconstruction.

Political Symbolism and Language

Feminists developed particular codes which gathered a measure of international recognition. Throughout Western Europe and North America, for example, the conventional symbol for female was removed from the exclusive purview of biological scientists to become a sign indicating women's solidarity and power. In Europe demonstrating feminists substituted a hand-formed vulva for the clenched fist of left-wing militants as yet another way of indicating women's separateness from male politics and emphasizing their own power.[42]

Over the years a phraseology laden with political overtones emerged, to jibe with feminist analyses of women's conditions. "Sisterhood" served to indicate the strength (and quasi-genetic roots) of feminist solidarity. Other key terms, such as "patriarchy," stood for the pervasiveness of male domination and female oppression that justified women's rebellion. This language solidified the movements' bonds. But feminist codes did more than reinforce internal cohesion and external differentiation; they conveyed particular meanings which systematically underscored the commonality of women and their separateness from men.

Solidarity and Self-Help

"What stands out," wrote one Dutch feminist, "is the *social* side of feminism."[43] In establishing health clinics, rape crisis centers, and centers of advocacy, or more generally creating separate spaces for women to meet in—cafés, bookstores, seminars and study groups—and promoting a specific sociability—parties, dinners, vacations, shared living arrangements—feminists seemed to be realizing the great ambition of female solidarity.

For important sectors of the feminist movements of several countries the primacy of relations among women came to imply woman-centered sexual relations as well as preferential social ties. "The Lesbian," wrote an American feminist in 1969, "is freed of dependence on men for love, sex, and money."[44] A decade later Monique Wittig reiterated, in more articulated terms, a stance that had often been advocated: "Lesbian societies are not based on women's oppression," she stated. "Furthermore, what we aim at is not the disappearance of lesbianism, which provides the only social form we can live in, but the destruction of heterosexuality—the political system based on women's oppression."[45]

But independently of lesbianism as a political strategy, feminists emphasized female independence from male society. Self-help groups learned, for instance, to perform not only routine gynecological examinations but even abortions, and others established places for the protection of battered wives. This systematic enhancement of female support networks prefigured, or at least hinted at, the renewal of the community of women, and, with it, the reconstitution of a female social subject.

Feminist Scholarship and Women's Studies

Feminism brought with it an explosion of scholarship, one that was to touch on almost every discipline and to burgeon, with more or less support from the formal institutions of academic learning, in practically every Western country. As one critic noted: "The intrusion, advance, spread, import, insinuation . . . of feminist thought into just about every aspect of contemporary cultural life is just about general."[46] Over time, feminist scholarship has raised a myriad themes, impossible to summarize systematically. But the following three aspects stand out in the work of the new feminist movements' early years: the interest in reconstructing women's history; the attention devoted to identifying the coordinates unifying women's condition in varying contexts; and the intensity of the debate over the origins and implications of differentiation in gender roles and sexual identities.[47]

Feminists first struggled to "render visible" the female experiences that had been "cancelled from history"—as the titles of celebrated texts announced—and then attempted to move from the partial narratives of "herstory" to the rewriting of general analyses.[48] In so doing, feminist historians recovered the experiences of women's movements as well as of their daily lives: in the terms of what has been called the battle for the ownership of the past, the search for precursors bolstered the feminist creation of a feminist tradition.[49]

The "discovery" of women's history melded with analyses of women's conditions and of the significance of sexual difference to define and legitimate a female subject: establishing the commonalities on the basis of which women could identify with each other, constructing a gender-specific memory and providing—for instance, in tales of Amazons and of matriarchal societies—elements of "founding myths" which might prove serviceable as guides to the present and to the future.[50]

The Campaigns for Female Self-Possession

If what we have termed the "praxis of separation and distinction" served to highlight the centrality, especially in the early years, of the resurgence of feminist attempts to (re)constitute and empower a female social subject, nowhere was this theme more evident than in the major campaigns for reproductive rights and against sexual violence that were launched more or less concomitantly in several countries. Individual feminist movements revolved around many pressing issues: from the "dual burden" of female labor in both the home and the workplace to the question of childcare; from unfair marriage laws to women's lack of skill, training, and jobs.[51] But it was "body politics" that most frequently appeared on feminist agendas, and from these politics a plurality of issues came to be defined. The most salient were abortion and sexual violence.[52] The Boston Women's Health Book Collective titled its widely disseminated handbook *Our Bodies, Ourselves,* thus immediately declaring the existence of an inextricable connection between the realm of the corporeal and subjectivity.[53] To be expropriated of one's body was, very simply, to be expropriated of one's self. To repossess one's self necessarily entailed repossessing one's body.

Sexuality emerged, in this context, as a crucial terrain of self-reappropriation. "Sex is deep at the heart of our troubles . . . ," Kate Millet wrote in reference to Jean Genet, "and unless we eliminate the most pernicious of our systems of oppression, unless we go to the very center of the sexual politic and its sick delirium of power and violence, all our efforts at liberation will only land us again in the same primordial stews."[54] With variations, one feminist text after the other enunciated a basic position: by anchoring female sexuality to women's reproductive functions and securing male control over women's progeny, patriarchy had deprived women of the possibility of knowing their own pleasure. It had imposed, as one famous tract put it, "the myth of the vaginal orgasm."[55] In 1967 Italian feminists called on women to "free

themselves from the sexual slavery in which man has kept them."
In 1970 Germaine Greer decried *The Female Eunuch*.[56] *Our Bodies, Ourselves* included pedagogical chapters on such issues as
sexual autonomy; "we have ceased to consider frigidity an honorable alternative," one collective declared.[57] "We have been crazy.
We have been idiots," denounced a Dutch feminist of the early
1970s, recounting that a poll taken at a women's conference had
revealed that *"three-quarters* of the women have at some time
pretended to have orgasms."[58]

For many feminists, extricating female sexuality from male
domination *inter alia* entailed struggling for the liberalization of
contraception and abortion. "Boss of our own belly" proclaimed
the Dutch feminist group Dolle Mina in 1970, as they infiltrated
a gynecologists' convention and lifted their shirts to display the
slogan written on their stomachs.[59] "To speak of abortion is to
call into question our sexuality as we have experienced it until
now, the family, and the role of exploited mother and wife," one
Italian feminist declared.[60] Opposition to such views came not
only from conservatives but also from feminists who feared that
abortion (and its liberalization) would serve to reinforce masculine
privilege: "the woman asks herself: For whose pleasure did I
become pregnant? For whose pleasure am I aborting? This question contains the seeds of our liberation: formulating it women
abandon their identification with men and find the strength to
break a complicit silence which is the coronation of our colonization."[61] Nonetheless, throughout Western Europe and North
America, feminists mobilized to promote and defend liberalized
abortion legislation. France, Italy, Germany, the Netherlands, the
United States, the United Kingdom, and Spain all witnessed major
campaigns.[62] These campaigns entailed defiant admissions of culpability by both prominent women and physicians, self-incriminations, and exemplary trials, as well as the development of a "grassroots illegality" in self-help groups providing and promoting access
to abortions. The campaigns also brought a measure of international cooperation among feminists involved in the practical aspects of providing abortion services which the various national
movements developed.

In 1971, in an article published by *Stern* magazine, 375 mostly
well-known West German women declared that they had willfully
terminated pregnancies. Their statement catalyzed a widespread
mobilization culminating in a petition calling for the abolition of

the existing restrictive legislation; a declaration of support containing 86,500 signatures; and 3,000 self-indictments which were presented to the Federal Minister of Justice.[63] Eventually, this mobilization led to revised legislation, approved in 1974, which guaranteed free abortion in the first three months of pregnancy. A year later, however, the Constitutional Court declared the new legislation incompatible with the protection of life, compelling the Bundestag to pass a more restrictive law limiting the circumstances under which abortion is legal.[64]

In the same year as the German women declared their "guilt," 343 French women signed a manifesto admitting that they also had had abortions.[65] (Their statement was followed, two years later, by 345 physicians who admitted to performing abortions.) In 1972 the trial of sixteen-year-old Michèle Chevalier (she claimed to have been raped by a schoolmate who then denounced her for having obtained an illegal abortion) became a *cause célèbre.* Defended by Gisele Halimi, an attorney who had established the association Choisir to defend the 343 signatories of the abortion manifesto, Chevalier was eventually acquitted. In the meantime, the mobilization around abortion continued to expand. The Mouvement pour la Liberalization de l'Avortement et de la Contraception (MLAC) opened several illicit abortion clinics. In 1975 abortion was legalized in France, allowing a woman up to her tenth week of pregnancy to obtain an abortion, subject to medical approval.[66]

The campaigns for abortion were often accompanied, or followed by, mobilizations against sexual violence, whether with respect to battered wives, rape victims, or both.[67] In 1972 Erin Pizzey established the first British refuge for battered wives.[68] By 1980, 99 British groups had set up 200 refuges, and joined in a national organization, the Women's Aid Federation. Alongside support for battered wives, British feminists also established rape crisis centers: the first was opened in London in 1976; five years later, sixteen centers had been formed, and several rape crisis telephone lines established.[69]

The issues raised by British initiatives echoed throughout Western Europe and North America. On March 8, 1976, in celebration of International Women's Day, the International Tribunal of Crimes against Women convened in Brussels.[70] More than two thousand women from forty countries spoke out about a multiplicity of issues relating to sexual abuse—from clitoridectomies to incest. But the question of rape became especially salient. The conference organizers drew attention to its political implications: "Rape emerges clearly as a terrorist tactic used by some men, but serving to perpetuate the power of all men over women," they concluded.[71] Rape, in other words, could be understood in political terms as emblematic of women's subjugation. Organizing against rape—and against the indignities encoded in a great deal of legislation and jurisprudence regarding its victims—women mobilized to take back their bodies, that is, their selves.

The female subject that feminists were reconstructing and reappropriating in the campaigns for female self-possession quickly revealed its fragilities. "Woman" as a unitary subject was being systematically undermined by feminists' own insistence on questioning the nature of that subject itself, on divorcing "anatomy" from "destiny," on highlighting not only women's differences from men but also their similarities, indeed, identicalness, with them.[72] The indivisibility of womanhood was radically called into question when feminist attention turned from the common elements uniting women to the differences dividing them. By the mid-1970s Italian feminists were publishing a magazine entitled *Differences,* specifically dedicated to exploring the distinctions and disagreements among various collectives.[73] The issue of the multiplicity of female subjects (as well as of the plurality of feminisms) became especially sharp when Third World women accused their white, Western counterparts of imperialist and colonial tendencies.

The (implicit) imperialism of Western feminism, in its presuming to speak for Third World women (as though they were themselves a unitary category), became an issue of contention in the quinquennial conferences of the UN Decade for Women. But it had already provoked deep lacerations among American feminists, when black women found themselves profoundly alienated from white women and the feminism they espoused. In the words of one black feminist describing a common reaction to feminism among black women: "a lot of black women would say . . . feminism belongs to white women, they originated it as a form of analysis, it is a form of analysis that only takes into account their experience. Therefore, we shouldn't be involved with it."[74]

The colonialism inherent in Western feminist discourse rests, Chandra Mohanty has argued, on the presupposition that women always constitute a homogeneous group. "An analysis of 'sexual difference' in the form of a cross-culturally singular, monolithic notion of patriarchy or male dominance leads to the construction of a similarly reductive and homogeneous notion of what I call the 'third-world difference'—that stable, ahistorical something that apparently oppresses most if not all the women in these countries . . . It is in this process of discursive homogenization and systematization of the oppression of women in the third world that power is exercised in much of recent western feminist discourse, and this power needs to be defined and named."[75] But it is precisely the chimeric quality of women's commonality, of their sharing a firm collective identity, that contemporary feminism has highlighted, even as it has struggled to overcome the divisions and fragmentations of the female subject. And this legacy of ambivalence continues today, as feminists uneasily but insistently turn to the issue of the plurality of female selves.

18

From Feminine to Feminism in Quebec

Yolande Cohen

FOR FEMINISTS IN THE 1970s and 1980s, the crucial question was how to represent groups marginalized in or excluded from the political sphere. Cutting across disciplines, the political debate on this issue was aimed as much at revitalizing our thinking about democracy as at shedding light on forms of association that had previously been neglected or ignored. In the 1970s the central focus was on inverting the private welfare/public service paradigm; since then feminists have begun to explore the many new avenues opened up by the interaction of public and private, social and political, civil society and state.

Within this context of exploration, looking at the ties that bind certain nationalist women's groups to church and state can tell us a great deal about forms of behavior common in the Western world since the turn of the century. The number of voluntary associations that women have created with the aid of the political and religious authorities attests to a clear determination to enlarge the feminine private sphere so as to encompass, in part, the realm of the social and political. Some of the consequences of that determination are apparent in the emergence of certain exclusively female callings and their associated professional organizations. Women's niches developed within the broader job market: the nursing profession is the best-known example.[1] But controversy surrounds these "female callings": some commentators look upon the women's professions as employment ghettos, underpaid and undervalued precisely because they are exclusively feminine. Once again, women have been relegated to a sphere of their own. To what extent should that enclave be regarded as simply an expansion of the private role ascribed to women in earlier periods?

These questions reflect the ideological assumption that a patriarchal society has oppressed women by imposing on them a model of femininity and relegating them to a so-called women's sphere. If the theoretical stereotype of femininity underlying this role was constructed in the nineteenth century,[2] it was not implemented on a broad scale until the twentieth.[3] The process that led certain groups of women to accept this model could not have been foreseen in advance: politicians did not always behave as expected, and the resistance offered by feminists is well known. We must therefore look for historical factors capable of explaining why many twentieth-century women's groups were willing to embrace this particular representation of themselves, without prejudging what they might have deemed to be alienating or emancipating. Here, the social significance of women's professions takes on tremendous importance: it is the kernel around which women construct a social and political identity. In Quebec, as in many other places, the interaction of women's groups with nationalist movements had a significant impact on women's history. Indeed, the study of such interaction leads to a new understanding of the history of nationalism.

French-Canadian nationalism—a synonym for a change in traditional allegiances—emerged around the turn of the century with plans for integrating women into the new national entity that it was the movement's goal to create. Nationalist ideologues such as Henri Bourassa, Lionel Groulx, and the Fédération Nationale Saint-Jean-Baptiste repeatedly urged women to join their movement.[4] As guardians of the faith and of the French language, women were expected to preserve and promote a national heritage threatened by modernization. Meanwhile, women's groups saw in nationalist advances an opportunity to win wider recognition of their own role. Feeding on each other, nationalism and feminism established a new public space in which the definition of the French-Canadian identity was no longer tied solely to the Catholic

Church. The two movements thus contributed to the "deconfessionalization" of Quebec long before the Quiet Revolution completed the process in the early 1960s. Women thus played a decisive role in the constitution of the nation, not only in preserving values but also in transmitting a secular outlook that facilitated the advent of a more modern social system. This interpretation is based on a vast body of evidence, and in particular on detailed study of one of the largest (and reputedly most traditional) associations of women's groups in Quebec, the Cercles de Fermières. The history of this group reflects the major transformations of Québécois society, transformations in which it was significantly involved.

At this point it is worth citing a few statistics, which demonstrate the inexorable growth of wage labor among women and the precipitous fall in the fertility rate. At the turn of the century, fertility rates in Quebec remained at eighteenth-century levels, in sharp contrast to neighboring Ontario and nearby American states. The average rural Catholic housewife born prior to 1897 gave birth to 8.3 children. French-Canadian women were known for valuing family above all other things. Although the fertility rate declined subsequently (women born around 1915 gave birth to only 4.3 children on average), it remained quite high compared with neighboring regions. It was not until the 1970s that the fertility rate in Quebec dropped sharply, to the point where it became one of the lowest in the world: 1.45, compared with 1.81 for France, 1.75 for the United States, and 1.58 for Ontario.

This sudden decline in the birthrate cannot be explained simply as a result of the emancipation of women. Other pertinent factors include the increased number of married women who work, the availability of better paid, more highly valued jobs for women, and a major change in social values. Statistics give a rough overview of what was happening. At the turn of the century, most working women were unmarried. After World War II, however, many urban and educated women continued to work after marriage. In the early days of industrialization, most female workers were concentrated in certain sectors such as textiles, garment manufacturing, and the rubber industry, and in domestic service (some 6,000 women worked as servants in Montreal in 1881, or 7.9 percent of the city's female population). In the 1960s, however, women began to find work in other sectors of the economy. Within twenty years the proportion of working women doubled, from 26.5 percent in 1960 to 48 percent in 1983, and the range of jobs held was considerably more diverse than in the past.

These figures scarcely reflect the turmoil of a society in which the majority, Catholic and francophone, felt itself threatened if not persecuted by the minority of English-speaking Canadians. The urbanization and industrialization of Quebec were seen as part of a Quiet Revolution, a crash effort to overcome the historical "backwardness" of the province. But such a summary description sweeps a great deal of history under the rug. It is difficult, for example, to understand why nationalist ideology, which had been the hallmark of the right, was now taken up by the left. Indeed, it became the credo of the so-called progressive forces to such an extent that the nationalist Parti Québécois took on a social-democratic tinge. Nor do the statistics begin to explain how one of the most dynamic feminist movements in the West came into being in Quebec.

Among all the questions the fundamental one is: how was it that this society managed so rapid a transition from a traditional Catholic way of life to a modern, secular, consumer society? Much research has gone into the formulation of an answer. It is best not to assume at the outset that there is any one "normal" model of development.[5] One area of research that sheds a great deal of light on the changes Quebec endured is how the feminine turned into feminism.

Traditional Woman and the Survival of the Nation

Study of two magazines published by the Cercles de Fermières reveals a clear connection between the egalitarian demands of recent years and the better life for women that the group has advocated since 1915.[6] In both cases the underlying assumption is that women have a role to play in making Quebec into a nation. Together with the further assumption that men's and women's roles are complementary, this conviction paved the way for a modernist, egalitarian ideology.[7]

The inception of *La Bonne Fermière* in 1919 was followed by an outpouring of publications addressed exclusively to housewives.[8] A fountain of good works, the woman described in the magazine "pledges to concern herself exclusively with her natural domain, which is the welfare of rural women as a class."[9] Furthermore, "her primary goal is to discharge certain specific, natural, conventional duties which are incumbent on her as the mother and guardian of her children and wife and collaborator of her husband."[10]

This realm of female action occupies a special place in the economic and social organization of the community. Although single women, particularly spinsters, do not fit within this classification, they are not exempt from duties incumbent on all women. They, too, have a role to play in the broader "family" embodied in the community or parish.

Thoroughly steeped in Christian beliefs, this discourse has all the earmarks of a sermon that has been internalized and transformed into a set of norms. Though aimed specifically at rural women, *La Bonne Fermière* shared much the same view of women as other women's magazines.[11] Harmony between the sexes was promoted as an ideal, but not much space was devoted to it. The magazine's ultimate goal was to give women a sense of purpose. Its center was the family, self-discipline was the means, and the reward was participation in the Cercles de Fermières. In portraying the life of the farm wife as a calling, the magazine exalted the work done by its readers both at home and within the Cercles. A woman's bonds to her family and the land established an economic and moral connection with the future of the nation. To be sure, the magazine did not fail to avail itself of traditional ideas about the nature of women and the woman's sphere, but it added a significant new dimension with the notion that some women (perhaps an elite) could, by acquiring certain skills, endow their work with the dignity of a calling.

A veritable mysticism is evident in articles dealing with agriculture as a way of life. Rural life functioned as a kind of founding myth of the French-Canadian epic; it was viewed as having certain regenerative qualities. Working in the fields kept one far from the depravity of the cities and from the religious and ethnic intermingling to which cities gave rise. Agriculture was a vocation, which brought man closer to his Creator and woman closer to nature. For French Canadians, the future was a perpetual renewal of the founding act of colonization, and rural women were thus seen as the quintessential artisans of the patriotic project. In a period of rural exodus and agricultural transformation, they were called upon to play an active part in the modernization of farming and thus the preservation of the nation.

The lot of urban women was easier than that of rural women; indeed, the very ease of urban life was corrupting: "Shame on the proponents of women's emancipation, who seek only to undermine happy families by taking the soul out of the household, the wife away from her husband, the mother away from her children. They are undermining the foundations of the social edifice they claim to be improving."[12] There is no reason to claim equality with men, "those guardian angels—for we agree with the gentlemen."[13] In particular, feminist radicals were said to pose a threat to the family and to the equilibrium of rural society. Invoking the authority of tradition, of twenty centuries of Christianity, the magazine poured scorn on feminists "who dream of achieving happiness on this earth by amending the Constitution."[14]

In counter-attacking the position of various Montreal women's groups that favored the right to vote for women, the editors of *La Bonne Fermière* adopted an essentialist defense: "What truly emancipates women is surely not the granting of full political rights. On the contrary, the woman who votes and serves as deputy or even lieutenant-governor will have to sacrifice part of the liberty she enjoys today as queen of the household." Political freedom was thus portrayed as a limitation on the action of women, whose true vocation, according to the magazine's editors, was motherhood. Social action exalts women within their own sphere, whereas political action debases them by taking them out of that sphere: "And as illusory compensation they will receive the right to become slaves of their political passions, playthings of political contingencies, victims of political humiliations. What do you women of wisdom think of such emancipation?"[15] In plain language, the editors doubted that winning the right to vote would bring women the promised emancipation.

Because the editors of *La Bonne Fermière* took this position, the magazine has generally been categorized as traditionalist and conservative by feminist historians convinced that the battle over women's suffrage marked the dawn of a new era. These historians have been unwilling to see the magazine's position as a critique of formal democracy, a critique widespread not only in Catholic circles but within the Marxist left as well. They treat the magazine's stand reductively, as an advocacy of strict limits to the role of women in the public sphere. The editors, by assigning women at best a domestic social role and denying them the right to speak out publicly on political issues, were said to be guilty of arguing that the "natural" place for women is in the home. For these historians, the enlightened minority of women who struggled for their political rights were progressives, whereas the rural women who read the magazine were reactionaries. The real heroines of their history are the committed militants of the nationalist Fédération Nationale Saint-Jean-Baptiste such as Marie Gérin Lajoie, Caroline Beique, and Thérèse Casgrain, who fought for extending the right to vote. It was they who brought progress to traditional society.

Yet those early feminist leaders never challenged the principle of complementary sexual roles, which they shared with the Cercles de Fermières and many other women's groups.[16] Some historians have deplored the inconsistencies of this position, which they blame on the isolation of what they see as the feminist avant-garde.[17] The real problem, though, is that these historians are projecting today's preoccupations onto the past. Politics at the time was a matter of concern to a tiny elite, a small number of men and women. To be sure, more men were involved in French-Canadian politics than women, but the vast majority of both sexes preferred involvement in social and parish life to politics of any kind. This feature of life in Quebec was responsible for its alleged backwardness compared with life in English-speaking Canada and, for that matter, in the rest of North America. One could also call it "co-figurative politics," in the words of M. Mead (1977).

Seen in the proper light, the ideology of *La Bonne Fermière* was little different from the ruralist ideology prevalent in Quebec generally. Explicitly anticapitalist and antimodernist, the magazine's position had affinities with the corporatist discourse of many nationalist movements of the 1930s. In the same breath the journal advocated both closer cooperation among social classes and the development of agricultural cooperatives to promote "the social and economic advancement of the agricultural class."[18] The primary goal of its editorials was to win recognition of the value of women's work at home and to promote that work as a true profession. It never occurred to the magazine's editors to abandon the sacrosanct principles on which the fragile equilibrium of rural society was based. On no account did they wish to challenge the ideological underpinnings of the principle of complementarity. The magazine championed the achievements of French-Canadian farmers but also urged that women be given a full share in rural society.

Such a position soon proved untenable, and it required some finesse to cover up the inconsistencies. Ultimately *La Bonne Fermière* was replaced by a new monthly, *Terre et Foyer,* which, while continuing to express wariness of politics (and political passions), took yet another step toward the feminization of public space.[19]

Terre et Foyer: Cooperation and National Community

The Cercles de Fermières carried out their work in a secularizing society. While students of Québécois women's history are generally familiar with the efforts of feminists to win the right to vote, to gain access to higher education for women, and to diminish the authority of the Catholic Church, it is less well known that the Cercles also clashed with the clergy. When the bishops created a rival group, the Union Catholique des Femmes, in 1944, the Cercles de Fermières launched a secularization campaign that proved difficult to control. Although the organization continued to promote an exalted Catholic ideal of womanhood, its affirmation of women's independence put it at odds with the Church. It also intervened frequently in labor conflicts, justifying its actions on patriotic grounds.

Cooperation and solidarity were initially viewed by many women as altruistic female virtues. These virtues were needed as much in the family, "the source of social cohesion" as "in business dealings, the source of moral cohesion and Christian charity," and "in economic life, the source of progress (for example, cooperatives, credit unions, and so on)."[20] Although cooperation begins with the family, it is not limited to the family. It is, however, incompatible with the profit motive that governs capitalist business: "By contrast, a cooperative enterprise seeks to perform the service expected by the users who create it."[21] The economic and moral autarchy of the rural world in which women were encouraged to live was thus offered as a model of how society ought to function.

This vision of society as family writ large leads to identical norms for individuals and groups. Ethics and politics, the economic and the social, are inextricably intertwined. This syncretic amalgam, in which the individual is absorbed into the community, was surely inspired by Christian thought. Enriched by rural humanist traditions, Christian ideals turned into cooperative communitarian ideals. Cooperation of this type is not egalitarian; it is based, rather, on the subordination of private interests to collective interests: "Let us teach our children to forget themselves in order to serve the family community."[22]

What made this whole position coherent, presumably, was the ubiquity of a family structure that was not only patriarchal but also community-oriented. This family structure served two closely related purposes: to maintain a strict hierarchy and to ensure the survival of the nation. Such a structure assumes consensus concerning the complementarity of sex roles and of generational roles—a consensus that the structure at the same time helps to create. The whole ideology takes on a certain feminine cast. Ignoring the modern separation of public and private, the magazine cast women, especially rural women, as part of a type of civic culture that Almond and Verba characterized as both the seedbed of democracy and the ambiguous and unlikely product of a conjunction of tradition with modernity.[23] The culture combined appeals to the eternal role of women with reminders of the importance of women's work described in terms of a profession or calling. The ambiguities inherent in such a position come close to contradictions: can women really resist modernity and keep their values intact?

Redefining the Private Sphere

At one time a woman's "natural" place was said to be in the home. "Today, however, a quick look around is enough to show that 'home' is threatened on all sides by modern life: the family home is in the process of disappearing." Women are the victims of this collapse, but they are also responsible for it. "Essential pillars of the household," women must understand that "it is working outside the home, going to clubs, driving cars, going out to movies and restaurants that is slowly undermining family life."[24] They must shun these temptations because of their harmful effects on the stability of the family and nation. "Home is an affair of women, as the factory is an affair of men. And although the war and its aftermath created a dangerous confusion of roles and attributes, the truth remains the truth: with few exceptions, women can flourish only at home, as wives and mothers."[25] The argument is pure assertion, cast in the form of seemingly simple, self-evident, universal truths, yet it reflects a considerable degree of disarray. In substance, the magazine's editors are asking if working toward the common good is enough to preserve proper values in women.

We must be careful not to be misled by these appeals for good behavior. All the talk about the disappearance of traditional values is a mere litany, whose main purpose is to preserve a certain feminine ideal rather than to prescribe one. With the talk comes advice—scientific advice—from specialists on matters such as childbirth, education, economics, and politics. And there are moralistic homilies as well. A group of psychologists, for example, added their voices to the chorus deploring the "declining birthrate": "If you take away the children, you will be left with a nation headed for decadence and ultimately doomed to disappear."[26] The readers of *Terre et Foyer* continued to do their duty with the magazine's blessing, despite the peril to themselves and their offspring: "I did my divinely ordained duty. I had eleven children, eight of whom lived, while the other three died young, possibly because I was by that time just too worn out."[27] At a time when giving of oneself seemed if not old-fashioned at any rate not very attractive, the magazine resorted to psychology to justify motherhood: "The Canadian woman who continues to heed the call of motherhood with all her body and soul is neither backwards nor inferior. Physical or spiritual, motherhood is a necessity for women. Women need to 'bring something into the world.' Their psychological equilibrium largely depends on it. And so, to a certain extent, does the peace of the world."[28]

The subtle shift from traditional natalist discourse to the discourse of social motherhood reveals that a definite change has taken place. The editors would like to believe that women will continue to give birth to the children who will make the Quebec of tomorrow, but there is no longer any moral authority that can compel women to submit to continuous pregnancies. Women have become individuals, and it is up to them to decide whether it will be "physically or spiritually" that they wish to bring something into the world. Ultimately, what counts is a woman's ability to function as a parent, that is, to bring up her children and transmit healthy values to them. The change in priorities shows that what really matters is the permanence of the role.

Change within Continuity

The model of the traditional woman changed in barely perceptible ways. Broadly speaking, change came in two phases. Between 1920 and 1944, the finishing touches were put on the ideal farm wife. More prescriptive than descriptive, the ideal envisioned a radically new relation of the "professional" farm wife to her family and a new public role for her in the Cercles de Fermières. Although the Cercles avoided politics, they encouraged women to join forces to achieve common goals. In so doing, they created new networks independent of old family allegiances. The novel forms of solidarity encouraged by the Cercles allowed women to emerge in leadership roles. Well-known within their own organizations, some of these women also gained national renown. Mlle Champoux, for example, gained prominence as a teacher, known throughout Quebec for her skill at various crafts, which earned her a great many awards and prizes. Other women became known for being active in, though not necessarily leaders of, local groups. The most visible women were those elected to offices of the group at the provincial level, but they were not necessarily the best known. Remarkably enough, many leaders of the Cercles were daughters of former leaders. For example, Yolande Calvé, who served for many years as the provincial treasurer of the Cercles, was the daughter and granddaughter of women who had founded local chapters of the organization. The backgrounds of Louisette Raymond Caron, Antoinette Pelletier, and ex-provincial president Noella Huot were similar.

The second phase of modernization was marked by a change in the organization of the Cercles as well as in the content of the magazine *Terre et Foyer,* which turned toward cultural topics. The change coincided with World War II, during which many women contributed to the war effort as both volunteers and professionals. The war marked a turning point in the general public's attitudes toward women in public life. *Terre et Foyer* gave evidence of its sensitivity to these changes by accommodating itself to the diversity of its readers' interests. Although the old rhetoric persisted, it was soft-pedaled in view of such new realities as the exodus from the countryside and the employment of large numbers of women in industry and commerce. As the magazine adjusted to these changes, it advocated a broader sphere of action for women, in view of the broader responsibilities they now exercised. Although specialists were now called upon to offer their advice, that advice was almost always solicited in a manner consonant with previously established principles. The magazine was important as a mediator.

Women developed their own views about the type of nation they wanted. French-Canadian nationalists, advocates of change but with respect for tradition, welcomed women into their ranks.

Not all women were equally eager to join, but few were indifferent to the nationalist movement's appeal. Women belonging to the urban elite were the first to see the advantages of a movement that featured women as the mothers of a modern nation yet to be born. Meanwhile, rural women took charge of newly expanded social services, thereby extending into public life their traditional role within the family. All parties had to be persuaded to accept the principle of complementarity of the sexes. The magazines rejected calls for equality on the grounds that they might well lead to disorder and even revolution; instead they advocated what they called "equilibrium," although the definition of the concept was modified somewhat to accommodate the employment of women outside the home. Complementarity, the editorialists insisted, did not mean submission of women to men; rather, it meant an equitable division of responsibility and influence. Of course the two spheres were to remain strictly separate. While separation entailed professionalization of the role of mother and housewife (to the point where some commentators went so far as to hold that these functions deserved remuneration), it also meant, at least for the first half of the century, that men were reluctant to intervene in women's business and vice versa. It was because of this reluctance that *La Bonne Fermière* had opposed women's suffrage and clung to its apolitical position while insisting on the professionalism of its readers. Nevertheless, the magazines were compelled by the necessities of the day, especially the increase in the number of women working outside the home, to address themselves to working women as well as mothers.

One consequence of this change in orientation was that instead of extolling motherhood as a calling, women's magazines emphasized the role of women as consumers not just of household items but also of culture. In the case of rural women the change did not come easily. Magazines aimed at them specifically clung to the image of women as productive and reproductive agents; readers were advised to seek useful and productive lines of work, and the state was called upon to provide training and employment. Yet a great deal of space was devoted to advertising—targeting women—for household products, clothing, and other consumer goods. At first, advertisements and advice columns suggested that the most important consideration in purchasing products was saving money. But in the 1950s a new type of advertising emerged, urging women to buy ready-to-use products for pleasure, that is, in order to save not money but time and worry. The new woman was a consumer: a smart shopper, to be sure, but fully integrated into the market economy.

The two magazines I have chosen promoted an image of woman that combined modern features with a fundamentally traditional outlook. More important than the content of the magazines per se was their emphasis on the place of women in society. Women learned to recognize their own concerns and to do something about them. The associated validation of womanhood in many ways anticipated the feminist demands of the 1970s. A generation gap developed, however, and what began as a divergence of views grew into radical opposition. The resolutely "progressive" posture of Québécois nationalism after the Quiet Revolution was adopted by feminists who were determined to demonstrate that they had broken with the past. Opposing factions found common ground, however, in the ideas of equality and independence.

The End of Consensus

By the beginning of the 1960s Quebec was ready to cast aside its conservative past. The Quiet Revolution was intended to lay to rest the province's "historical backwardness" once and for all. The feminist movement of the 1970s dismissed all its predecessors (except for the suffragettes) as conservative and tinged by religion. What accounts for such rejection? What was so embarrassing about this past that it had to be covered up?

Threatened Identity

The conservatism of the women's magazines we have been examining was clearly connected with the traditional religious attitudes of rural Québécois society. Because modernization implied urbanization and rejection of traditional family values, the magazines, which opposed these developments, found themselves in the traditionalist camp. On closer examination, however, conservatism may not be the right word to convey the actual quality of the Catholic Church's concern with rural life or of the interest of agronomists in making Quebec a more prosperous place or of the effort of the women's magazines to stake out a distinctive role for women. Such simplistic views have been refuted by recent research, which shows that various farm unions opposed the government[29] and that the cooperative movement in Quebec stemmed from the pioneering efforts of certain agricultural cooperatives.[30] There is general agreement, however, that rural rhetoric was deeply tinged with moralism. In recent years, a number of scholars have defended the Church's role in defining the identity of an agricultural society under siege.[31]

In this rural community the social role of women was considered to be integral with their family role. Most observers agreed that family and language were crucial elements of the French-Canadian identity; only in relatively recent years has the idea of a specific territory been added to the mix. Rural women's magazines portrayed women as mothers and upholders of traditional values, hence as guarantors of the nation's posterity and identity. They insisted that rural women be recognized as the seedbed of French-Canadian society. Nationalists stressed the complementary roles of the sexes and thereby fostered an early form of feminism. If we set aside the clichés and stereotypes of nationalist rhetoric, what was conservative about it? Indeed, the magazines' efforts to adapt to changes soon perceived to be fundamental and their willingness to take women's concerns into account reflect a keen sensitivity to social and political changes.

To sum up, then, the magazines revised their content in important ways. They insisted that women be recognized for their intrinsic female gifts, even in the workplace. Meanwhile, the association of feminism with nationalism had various political implications. There are some similarities with the situation in Germany prior to 1933 and in Italy.[32] The nationalist-feminist nexus defined a new public space within societies in the process of reformulating their national ambitions. This new political alignment generally opposed egalitarian and socialist forces. In France a somewhat different configuration emerged: early in the history of the Third Republic, feminism deliberately sought to ally itself with socialism, but the attempt foundered on the narrowness of the egalitarian objectives espoused by its principal leaders and never attracted more than a minority of women (nor was the so-called feminism of difference any more successful). By contrast, the nationalist-feminist alliance proved advantageous to both constituencies. Perhaps the development of a feminist component of nationalist ideology, or, even more, feminist participation in the construction of the nation-state, is a necessary condition for the rise of an influential women's movement. The example of Quebec is instructive in this respect. It also shows how much influence women wielded over certain key nationalist figures.

Quebec's National Ambitions

Until 1970, "traditional" feminism grew along with the Quebec nationalist movement. Groups such as the Cercles de Fermières, the Association des Femmes pour l'Éducation et l'Action Sociale (or AFEAS, born when the Cercles d'Économie Domestique merged with the Union Catholique des Femmes in 1966), and the Fédération des Femmes du Québec (founded in the early 1970s) contributed as much to nationalist ideology as they took from it. They gave nationalism a universal dimension—that of complementarity of the sexes—as well as a base in civil society. The explosive growth of feminism in the 1970s put an end to this alliance, however, sowing confusion among the participating groups. Deep ideological and social divisions were revealed that forced political actors to revaluate their positions: nationalism no longer spoke with a single, conservative voice, and feminism was not simply a consequence of modernity.

The women's liberation movement affected all aspects of society. A whole women's world emerged from the shadows: there were consciousness-raising groups, women's health groups, and even feminist magazines ranging from *Têtes de pioches* to *La Vie en rose* with circulations approaching 100,000 in the 1980s. Women's collectives were organized to offer free legal assistance to battered women; though many of these groups were short-lived, their impact was lasting. Many women's groups organized around the fight for free access to abortion. Some women believed they were overconsumers of medication and wished to stop, while others hoped to free themselves from a medical profession that was too patriarchal for their taste. Like women in other Western countries, women in Quebec wanted to take charge of their own destinies. The women's movement was responsible for extensive social changes. Egalitarian policies were implemented to allow women greater access to credentials and positions. Trade unions and political parties raced to be the first to set up "committees on the condition of women."

A striking feature of this period of ferment is the speed with which improvised measures led to permanent institutional reforms. A case in point is the Ministère de la Condition Féminine and its various subordinate agencies: the ministry grew out of what was at first a consultative body, the Conseil du Statut de la Femme. Women's groups quickly came to rely on this council as a sponsor of various kinds of research and action, a source of both funding and information. Eventually the council was transformed into a ministry, a cog in the state apparatus, with responsibility for enforcing new laws against discrimination. All this came about within the space of ten years. During that time, Quebec experienced major political realignments—realignments explicable in part as a response to the government's rapid adaptation to women's demands. At the provincial level, the impact of the feminist movement was to further the nationalist cause, because of its primary emphasis on the issues of sovereignty and equality.

Equality for Independence

Strengthened by the women's liberation movement, a new configuration of nationalist forces took shape. This alignment first began to emerge in the early 1960s. Its central rallying cry was "modernity," now defined to mean equality of all citizens. With the support of certain feminist groups the progressive nationalists scored a victory at the polls: feminists and nationalists together joined the government formed by René Lévesque's Parti Québécois in 1976. In working toward his goal of independence from the Canadian confederation, Lévesque encountered numerous obstacles, including opposition from an unexpected quarter. In 1980 a referendum was held on independence, and the government of Quebec argued that a "yes" vote from women would lead to the equality they desired. Many women felt that they were being manipulated and patronized by Lise Payette, the minister of *la condition féminine,* who referred disparagingly to housewives as "Yvettes" and allegedly refused to acknowledge the contribution of women to the effort of building a nation. Thousands of women who prided themselves on being housewives turned Yvette against the minister herself. More than 10,000 attended a rally to demonstrate their attachment to the stereotypical Yvette and their contempt for the Parti Québécois's idea of tying women's emancipation to the independence for Quebec.

The incident burst open the underlying conflict between

women who allied themselves with traditional notions of women and nationhood and women (and men) who believed that national and sexual emancipation could be achieved only through equality and independence. There were of course partisan interpretations of what had happened. Some observers were quick to point out that the conservatives, in this instance the Parti Libéral, had used the Yvettes and possibly manipulated them. In any case, women had suddenly assumed a hitherto unimagined importance in the political arena. The Yvettes had made themselves heard by exerting public pressure through judicious use of the media. But it was above all by reminding the public of their role in Quebec's survival as a nation that they put their finger on a weak spot in the political structure of neo-nationalism. The Yvettes were the detonator that caused the Parti Québécois's program for achieving political sovereignty to explode.

In the wake of a mistake that proved so costly to the nationalist cause, political observers are today less apt to take a sectarian view of women's issues. At first the tendency was to explain the failure of the referendum in terms of an allegedly traditional fear of change on the part of women, who joined the non-French-speaking citizens in an unlikely coalition against independence for Quebec. But this explanation has not stood up well under scrutiny. Was the question on which people were asked to vote poorly framed? Did the proponents of out-and-out nationalism underestimate the importance of the changes accomplished by those they dismissed as traditionalists? Were they too quick to propose an equation between equality and independence and therefore unwilling to recognize the role that housewives (and the groups representing them) had played in establishing Quebec's national identity? In any case, since the referendum, all the political parties have been more circumspect on the question of women.

Within the space of a few years women's groups were thus able to transform the political process. Not only are the parties now obliged to pay attention to their existence; more than that, the political arena itself has been forced to accommodate new ideas about the nature of civil society. Along with other social movements, the women's movement succeeded in pressing its views on politicians and deriving influence as a result.

In contributing to a broader public role for women, a group

like the Cercles de Fermières helped to modernize certain segments of rural society, especially the rural household. By seeking recognition for the social contribution of women as farmers and housewives, the Cercles participated in a process that was as much a bid for autonomy as it was an attempt to impose a corporatist regimen on rural women. The group's efforts are difficult to categorize, even if it is tempting to see them as having first served the Church and later a state-directed nationalism.

This quiet movement of women engaged in self-consciously secular and corporatist activities anticipates modern forms of state intervention in society. Its origins were closely related to the growth of the welfare state, which, at a relatively early date, effectively supplanted the Church in Quebec, France, and other industrialized societies. While joining in group action gave women a sense of emancipation and validity, the ideological and political consequences of their efforts were not those intended. By giving of themselves women could hope to save humankind: such rhetoric, which soon defined an exclusively feminine ideal, clearly drew heavily on Christian doctrine. Meanwhile, these women's groups struck a bargain with the most traditionalist French-Canadian nationalists. Champions of the family as protector of the nation and the language, these traditionalists publicly acknowledged the role of women as the family's mainstay, hence as the "true" nationalists.

All the same, these early women's groups were ones that paved the way for contemporary feminism. Although new groups may have vied with old ones for the right to be called feminist, and despite a certain intolerance of political differences within women's groups, these organizations were responsible for a major change: it was they that made sure the cause of women was heard in Quebec. They achieved a great deal, and the visible role played by women at all levels of Québécois society is now accepted as part of the culture.

Politically, moreover, it has been shown that the conservatives did not in fact reap the benefits of the activities of the Cercles or, for that matter, of the Yvettes. The history of the women of Quebec in the twentieth century attests to another reality, one much more deeply rooted in associative and communal traditions. Tradition has contributed not only to the survival of the family but also to a remarkable intensity of social relations among women. Whether in rural or urban organizations, volunteer groups, professional societies, or political groups, women have developed a vision of society that builds on their vision of the family—at once communal and protective. In this sense they are more nationalist than conservative. In the forefront of a debate over fundamental issues, women have helped to move Québécois society toward a modernity whose effects we are just now beginning to perceive.

Feminism has played an active role in the modernization of Québécois nationalism and thus has wielded considerable political influence. Although the nationalist coalition is currently in disarray, it has drawn new strength from the support of feminists. A small society with great ideals, Quebec today is a monument to the successful efforts not only of women but of an entire society. Quebec's accomplishments are its entrée into the club of so-called advanced nations.

TRANSLATED FROM THE FRENCH BY ARTHUR GOLDHAMMER

19

Reproduction and Bioethics

Jacqueline Costa-Lascoux

WHEN SCIENCE IS BROUGHT to bear on human beings, their bodies, and the secrets of their ancestry and progeny, all of our ethical landmarks become subject to question. Choices can follow desire and will. Individuals, couples, philosophers, and theologians adopt divergent views. Increasingly, the courts are called upon to render judgment. Some denounce physicians as "producers of human beings made to order," empowered to "match individuals for reproductive purposes" and complicit in the "commercialization of the body." Others see scientific progress as a promise of victory over sterility and hereditary disease. Everyone knows that recent developments in biotechnology call for new thinking about eugenics and the fundamental rights of the individual.

Recent scientific advances have made possible a whole range of medically assisted reproductive techniques.[1] These techniques have fostered great, and sometimes illusory, hopes in sterile couples. Further research has hinted at spectacular new forms of medical and biological intervention in the transmission of life, with ample opportunity for genetic manipulation. Hope has begun to give way to anxiety.

Medically assisted reproduction is overturning

values, beliefs, and ideas once considered irrefutable. It is divorcing sexuality from reproduction, conception from filiation, and biological filiation from the bonds of emotion and nurture. The biological mother of a child need no longer be the same as the birth mother or the nurturing mother. What is our image of the mother who has received medical assistance? Of the child who is a product of science? Of the social father who cannot claim to be the biological father? What becomes of kinship, of intergenerational ties, of the notion that children have two parents, a mother and a father? Issues of biomedical ethics begin to have a bearing on our concepts of individuality and freedom.[2] Our ways of thinking about men and women depend on our answers to these crucial questions.[3]

Artificial insemination, ovocyte donation, in-vitro fertilization, embryonic transplants, surrogate motherhood, the freezing of embryos for delayed (or even post-mortem) implantation, the selection and manipulation of embryos[4]—all of these techniques have implications too broad to be left for individual conscience or medical ethics to decide. Observed abuses, a "traffic in human reproduction" involving large sums of money and considerable inequalities, and the psychological stress occasioned by the absence of ethical standards have made people aware of the consequences of artificial reproduction. Some have called for new legislation or action by the courts. Law and bioethics have interfered with the plans of couples or individuals who have expressed a desire, not to say claimed a right, to have children. What underlies that desire? In pluralistic societies with high levels of immigration from traditional societies, cultural conflicts sometimes arise: when specialists are consulted in cases of sterility, the patients sometimes explicitly express a desire for male offspring.

A comparative analysis of the state of the art as well as of ideological debate and accepted procedures in a number of different countries is beyond the scope of this essay. The literature is vast, opinions are contradictory, and laws and legal precedents vary widely. It is possible, however, to give a broad overview of the major trends with due attention to national, religious, and political differences.[5]

The issues of procreation have been widely discussed in academic colloquia, public debates, legislative committees, and the media. Opinion polls and surveys of specialists add further detail to an already variegated canvas. The most salient features of the current situation are these: first, the family as institution has been shaken by the idea of selective parenting, and, second, the various aspects of procreation have been linked to the defense of the child's interests. Some people have expressed exaggerated fears of medically assisted motherhood, elimination of the father's role, and breakdown of the traditional family. It may be, however, that the couple is in the process of rebuilding itself around the child, now regarded as an individual with full rights. If so, the significance of each participant's role and the division of labor within the family will need to be reassessed.

An Old Story

Sterility is an age-old obsession. In the ancient world it gave rise to a variety of legal fictions whose purpose was to ensure that every man could participate in the transmission of life. Scientists were encouraged to seek remedies and palliatives. Meanwhile, charlatans and others were able to turn a handsome profit by preying on the suffering and desires of childless couples.

In 1791 an English doctor by the name of Hunter was the first to conduct an artificial insemination in a married couple—a mercer and his wife. In France the first such experiment took place in 1804, the year the Napoleonic Code was adopted. The idea of artificial insemination using sperm taken from a donor outside the couple (donor artificial insemination, or DAI) at first met with resistance and was condemned by the Vatican. In the United States, in 1884, the first DAI was performed with sperm from a student chosen for his excellent scholastic record: Dr. Pancost chose a donor from the "top of the class." It was not until 1940, however, that Dr. Parker would perfect the sperm-freezing techniques that would make artificial insemination commonplace. In 1984 the Centres d'Etude et de Conservation de l'Oeuf et du Sperme (Centers for the Study and Preservation of Egg and Sperm, or CECOS) celebrated their tenth anniversary and ten-thousandth pregnancy. Since then, the number of such pregnancies has more than doubled. The problem with donor artificial insemination nowadays is no longer technical but conceptual: what is the place of the third party, the outsider in the kinship relation?

Another milestone was passed with the perfection of in-vitro fertilization and the transfer of the living embryo to the mother's womb, which ushered in the era of the so-called test-tube baby. In 1978 Louise Brown, the first test-tube baby, was born near Manchester, England, making Dr. Edwards, the physician responsible for the procedures leading to her birth, an overnight celebrity. Three years later, in France, René Frydman and Jacques Testart oversaw the birth of baby Amandine. Since then, thousands of babies have been born thanks to in-vitro techniques. Yet only 15 percent of the couples who attempt the process achieve success. Children produced in this way appear in the family photographs that festoon the offices of the doctors whom they have made famous: the gynecologist generally figures at the center of the picture, flanked by any number of mothers. The fathers usually remain off camera or on the periphery of this "family circle." An iconography of representations of medically assisted pregnancies has yet to be compiled. Such a compilation might shed a particularly harsh light on what society represses as well as on our images of women and maternity.

In 1984 Dr. Carl Wood in Melbourne supervised the birth of baby Zoe, the first frozen embryo. Other doctors in the Netherlands and England soon followed Dr. Wood's example. The pace of medical and biological advance had accelerated rapidly. Ethical controversy was inevitable. The problem was not simply that procreation had become easier. It was that the moment of procreation was now a matter of choice. "Life could now be banked as if it were capital."

In addition to choosing the time of reproduction, it was also possible to choose the number of implantations. In 1986 the simultaneous implant of a number of embryos led eventually to the birth of twins, Audrey and Loïc. Then quadruplets were born in Australia, and in Melbourne there was even a "delayed birth" of a pair of twins: Rebecca and Emma were fertilized on the same day but born sixteen months apart. The "Jesse tree" of children brought into the world through assisted reproduction sprouted new branches, which some people found terrifying. Subsequent technological developments gave rise to a new polemic on multiple pregnancies and their sometimes dramatic consequences for family life. Anything seemed possible: embryos could be manipulated, and unused embryos might become subjects for in-vitro experimentation. The bonds of kinship were stretched to the point of ascribing a "personhood" of some kind to the embryo, or "potential person" as some observers now called it. The question quickly shifted from one of kinship to the moment at which an "individual human person" could be said to emerge. In other words, what was the status of the embryo? For some, this issue became the battle cry of a renewed campaign against voluntary abortion.

Meanwhile, the number of people involved in assisted reproduction grew larger. When a child was born, a crowd gathered around its cradle: the gynecologist, the biologist, the psychologist, and even the donor (in cases where the donor was personally selected and known to the legal parents). The media made a spectacle of "miracle births." The secrets of the bedroom were now shared with specialists and experts. Medicalization thus encouraged a socialization of reproduction.

Surrogate motherhood highlights all the issues involved in medically assisted reproduction. The fantasies that have grown up around the whole subject are well illustrated here. The issues have been discussed in the press *ad nauseam*. Surrogate motherhood exemplifies, among other things, the irrepressible desire for a child, a certain proselytism in favor of reproduction, and the commercialization of the reproductive process. But one also sees remarkable displays of unselfish loyalty, as in the case of one Scottish woman who bore a child for another woman without taking a penny. Groups such as Sainte Sarah, the Cigognes, and Alma Mater have played an important role in France; despite court action against them, these groups have reconstituted and are organizing on the international level. The media have orchestrated the news and created a veritable vogue for hired wombs, yet this should not obscure the complexity of the issues or the plurality of the interests at stake. In the meantime, families have been created and destroyed on the front pages of the newspapers. Passions and fears overwhelmed reasoned argument, leaving many people in total confusion.

In the area of reproduction, every variety of argument is heard, from the loftiest of theological speculation to the basest forms of pecuniary interest. Conflicts of law, morality, and medical and scientific ethics have swirled around the unborn.[6] Bearing a child for another person has been treated as a test case for judging assisted reproduction, even though surrogate motherhood does not require elaborate medical techniques. It is reminiscent, moreover, of customs found in any number of traditional societies. It is not completely outlandish to compare the surrogate contract with the agreements that families used to make with wet nurses. Nineteenth-century parliamentary debates on wet nursing dealt with many of the same issues that one finds in the controversy over "mercenary mothers." The issue then was not science but the question of nature (kinship) versus nurture. Today, several arguments have been telescoped into one, to the detriment of careful analysis of the wide variety of situations that crop up in practice.

With each new biological or medical advance, new problems arise. Progress in prenatal diagnosis, for example, led to differentiating between the narrower issue of eugenics in individual cases and the broader one of "improving the race." It proved unfruitful to treat what was essentially a matter of individual rights as if the morality of science were at stake. The picture has been complicated by the sheer number of normative pronouncements concerning scientific progress and intervention by specialists, whose roles are no longer clearly delineated.

Which authorities are we to consult? Consider some of the texts most frequently cited: the Nuremberg Code of 1947; the Helsinki (1964) and Manila (1981) declarations on human rights; various international agreements concerning civil and political rights; theological sources ranging from papal encyclicals to episcopal letters to texts without official sanction; Advisory no. 1046 of the Council of Europe; Advisory no. 874 of the European Parliament; decisions handed down by the European Court of Justice; reports submitted by commissions of experts including the Warnock Commission of 1984, the ad hoc committee of experts of the CAHBI in Belgium, and reports prepared by the French Conseil d'Etat for the prime minister, including "Artificial Reproduction" (1986) and "The Life Sciences" (1988); Noëlle Lenoir's report on bioethics; legal statutes and administrative regulations in force in various countries; and various reports by committees on medical ethics. The theoretical literature is vast, and decisions of the courts become more numerous by the day. Meanwhile, legislatures have been slow to act. The debate has taken on an international dimension: comparing experiences may show how to transcend national institutional and cultural traditions in making ethical choices.

The storm of controversy has broken out at a time when individuals and couples are insisting on their private rights: the right *to* a child has become an issue at the same time as the rights *of* the child. Reproductive technology has sharpened the distinction between blood kinship and voluntary kinship (such as adoption). A third party—often anonymous—may be involved. The symbolism of blood contrasts with that of the will as foundation of the parental bond not only in the debate over kinship but also in the controversy surrounding nationality and political allegiance. A number of countries have revised their laws on nationality, and the passions surrounding these changes are not unlike those involved in the debate over bioethics. Whether one defines individual identity in terms of origin or membership obviously has an impact on all thinking about legal personhood.

Human beings must now confront their own creation—the new possibilities opened up by genetic manipulation of in-vitro pregnancies. Is the human body itself becoming a kind of laboratory vessel? *Le Désir de naissance* by René Frydman, *l'Oeuf transparent* by Jacques Testart, and *Produire l'Homme* by Jean-Louis Baudouin and Catherine Labrousse-Riou launched a new debate on bioethics in France. There has been much subsequent speculation. Some commentators envisage male pregnancies, uterine transplants in animals, and the use of surrogate mothers and "rented wombs" merely for convenience. Surely not all these possibilities belong on the same level. The confusion here is similar to the confusion surrounding medically assisted reproduction.

The possibility of varying the age of motherhood reflects the degree to which the body has been turned into an instrument. The unusual case of the mother who served as a surrogate for her own daughter gave rise to extensive debate, because it raised questions about the very nature and significance of human reproduction. The notion that life is transmitted from parent to child is central to all our normative discourse and legal thinking. "If man is bewildered by his own nature," then the law no longer knows which way to turn.[7]

Kinship and Science

The importance of consanguinity, of a biological link between parent and child, is evident in some of the terminology that comes up when one investigates sterility: it is not unusual to hear people draw a distinction between, on the one hand, "having a child that is all my own," a "real" child, "a child of my own flesh and blood, one I want" and, on the other hand, to use a truly terrifying phrase that came up in one interview, adopting a child "second-hand."[8]

Paradoxically, where many commentators at first saw only artificial intervention or even the "fabrication" of children by medical technology, childless couples focused primarily on the idea of the biological, on the slightest trace of a biological link, a hereditary connection, between the child and at least one of its parents. In applications for artificial insemination with donor, the parents often ask for a donor with phenotypic characteristics similar to those of the parents. Indeed, some prospective parents have gone so far as to abandon a child born by DAI because the child's ethnic appearance did not sufficiently resemble theirs, and some sperm banks (for example, the CECOS in France) were obliged to reject any application with overly specific requirements concerning the physical characteristics of the donor.

In every society couples attempt to camouflage sterility, especially male sterility, which according to psychoanalysts is the more difficult to acknowledge. Two kinds of issues are involved. First, kinship is essentially conceived in biological terms, even if many people now credit science with the ability to permit the transmission of life "untainted by hereditary disease." Second, sterility can be kept secret now that medical technology can routinely perform miracles that allow couples to keep their difficulties private while pretending to reproduce naturally.

The patient's secret and medical secrecy are intimately connected. Doctor and patient share the secret of the cause of sterility and its method of treatment. The painful secret need be revealed, if at all, only after science has triumphed over nature. When couples benefit from medical reproductive techniques, one often finds that they begin to proselytize for medical science. Doctors are only too glad to accept the credit without noting that the number of successful couples remains quite small. By contrast, silence shrouds the psychological and economic costs associated with less successful interventions, which are nevertheless justified in the name of trying to relieve suffering. Physicians like to give couples what they want, to intervene as aggressively as possible, whereas psychologists and psychiatrists try to encourage "mourning for sterility" followed in some cases, where conditions are favorable, by adoption.

Secrecy regarding sterility is most easily maintained where no outside donor is involved, regardless of whether simple insemination or embryo transfer is used. Even then, however, a new image of the body begins to develop. With the development of medical and biological techniques, the body becomes a receptacle. The consent of husband and wife takes priority over the act of procreation, or sexuality. The test tube is only an instrument, but an indispensable instrument. Where there is no outside donor, the physician gives aid and assistance to a couple in order to help them realize their wishes. He plays the role of therapist to the full; the couple's intention gives meaning to his intervention and, as a psychoanalyst might say, "cleanses it of the sins of the flesh." That is why artificial insemination with no outside donor is quite widely accepted and why religious counsel to avoid the practice is often rejected by sterile couples. From a legal standpoint, however, one fundamental question remains: does the desire to have a child take precedence even if the sperm donor dies?

Post-mortem Insemination

The so-called Paraplaix case, which was decided by the superior court of Créteil on August 1, 1984, gave rise to considerable legal debate in France over the issue of post-mortem insemination.[9] Echoing Catherine Labrousse-Riou's comments on the Créteil decision, Dean Cornu wrote: "The illegitimacy of a child born more than 300 days after the death of the husband and even the problems, admittedly enormous, connected with the laws of inheritance are of little moment compared with the principle: the structures of kinship are not a commercial matter. . . . The voluntary founding of a posthumous unilinear family is in my view illegitimate." On the other hand, two professors of law at the University of Paris II, Michelle Gobert and François Terré, were prepared to consider the possibility of posthumous insemination if accompanied by certain guarantees: by analogy with posthumous marriage, there should be a showing of "grave motives" and a stipulation as to precisely when, prior to death, the husband indicated his will to have the child and how that will was expressed. The argument emphasized the importance of an individual's will, given the ability of science to permit that will to produce an effect at a time subsequent to its original expression. Intention, in other words, has a certain temporal density. Dean Jean Carbonnier summed up the case in these terms: "It might be possible to develop a body of law around this type of filiation, or even to accept this child as an heir. In doing so, however, is there not a danger of lending credence to the fantasy that some day man will triumph over death and free himself from his mortal condition? . . . The symbolic effect of such law would itself be mortal."[10]

In fact, post-mortem insemination is an extreme, and relatively rare, test case, best left to the prudent appreciation of the judge, who is in a position to set stringent conditions and to weigh the interests of the unborn child, "born without a father by its father's will." Recently, however, the controversy erupted once again in the case of a post-mortem insemination in which one parent had died of AIDS. Since then, additional cases have gone to court in which both parents, one uninfected, the other diagnosed as HIV-positive, have clearly expressed their wish to conceive a child by means of artificial insemination.

For reasons of prudence, both the Warnock Commission in Great Britain and the Belgian CAHBI strongly advised against post-mortem insemination. The text of a proposed British law on "human fertilization and embryology" was less categorical: "Parents must indicate their wishes, should one of them die, as to the use of their embryos and gametes at the time that these are stored for preservation." What is to count from now on, therefore, is the will of the parents. By contrast, a bill filed in Italy would have expressly prohibited post-mortem insemination, and the so-called Braibant proposal prepared by a working group under the French Council of State stated that "the child must have both its parents and not just one." This principle, intended to echo the International Treaty on the Rights of the Child, mixes ambivalent arguments about biological parenthood and nurturing parenthood. In fact, post-mortem insemination strengthens both the preeminence of the biological tie and the role of the parents' will. The argument is actually based on the traditional image of the two-parent family and on the child's interest in a normal upbringing. Isn't this actually just another way of condemning the single-parent family? The readiness of some authorities to ban post-mortem insemination has unclear implications in regard to their acceptance of donor insemination. When a child is the product of donated sperm, its ancestry is complicated, and determining the child's rights becomes a more delicate matter. Nevertheless, the practice has become widespread. It is clear that the assertion of parental ties is more a symbolic act than a biological reality.

The Child Conceived with Donated Sperm

Use of donated sperm raises two sets of legal issues: one having to do with the legitimacy of such birth, the other having to do with determining the child's kin. The Warnock Commission proposed legislation to declare the child legitimate if husband and wife both consented to the procedure, in which case the child would be legally recorded as the husband's. This recommendation was adopted and embodied in the British Family Law Reform Act of 1987. In Belgium, Switzerland, the Netherlands, Portugal, and Quebec, a clause was expressly added to the Civil Code prohibiting *a posteriori* challenges to legitimacy when both husband and wife consented to the act of procreation. Meanwhile, the majority of European countries chose to presume the husband's paternity, absent proof to the contrary in the form of a legal disavowal.

In France the presumption of paternity specified in Article 312, Paragraph 1, of the Civil Code applied. Similarly, in cases where an ovule was donated, the rule was that delivery determines motherhood. Disavowal of paternity is possible if the husband can provide proof that he could not possibly be the father. A body of established case law exists in this area. In 1985 two appellate court decisions established that any interested party—that is, husband, wife, child, or heirs—was entitled to contest the paternity of the husband for a period of thirty years (forty-eight years if the action was brought by the child, owing to the suspension of the statute of limitations with respect to minor children). Disavowals of paternity by a husband or consort on grounds of absence of biological proof were held admissible by the courts, even in the case of a woman inseminated with the sperm of a donor with the prior consent of the husband or consort. Following a decision by the court of Nice on June 30, 1976, a number of judgments of this kind were handed down. The only type of parental relation not revocable on biological grounds is adoption. This position of the courts has been criticized, however, on the grounds that it threatens to undermine parental planning and family cohesion. M. Franck Serusclat and the Socialist members of the French Senate therefore filed a bill requiring that a couple record their consent to artificial insemination with the local court in order to reinforce the presumption of paternity. The Braibant proposal for its part justifies the presumption of paternity on the part of the husband by "the desire to give the child the benefit of a traditional family for the sake of its normal development." It goes on to stipulate that "the donor cannot establish any legal bond between himself and the child . . . or claim any subsidy."

Techniques of procreation involving a third-party donor, whether artificial insemination or in-vitro fertilization, raise not only the issue of disavowal of paternity but also that of the donor's anonymity. Here, again, different countries have adopted different solutions, and many points of legal controversy remain unresolved.

The vast majority of sperm banks (including those operated by the CECOS in France) maintain the anonymity of the donor. In Sweden, however, a law was passed prohibiting this practice on the grounds that every child has the right to know its progenitors. In practice, even in countries where anonymity is the rule, generally only the approved sperm banks fully protect the donor's identity. Even if the donor is not identified by name, moreover, certain information is provided in order to avoid major differences of, say, skin color and physical appearance. Strangely, these classifications by phenotype have drawn little fire from critics. The return to the "biological fiction" in reproduction has to some extent reinforced ethnicist, not to say racist, tendencies at odds with the progress that has been made in the fight against discrimination.

A certain hypocrisy is evident in the moral debate over medically assisted reproduction. Since the interests of the child can be invoked to justify either maintaining the donor's anonymity or the opposite, a further argument must have decided the issue: namely, the fear that eliminating anonymity would reduce the number of donors, since prospective donors might then have reason to worry that their offspring would sue for support. As DAI developed, considerations of profit and prestige thus proved just as important as ethical concerns about the welfare of the unborn child in determining the policies of state-approved sperm banks.

Reliable tests have facilitated the determination of biological kinship, and the courts have increasingly relied on experts in genetics as witnesses. But donor insemination involves the genetic contribution of a third party; the biological evidence gives way to fiction, and the parental bond is created by the mutual consent of the parents and the presumption of paternity. There are limits, however, to the validity of this model. What about single individuals or homosexual couples? Can they avail themselves of the services of a sperm donor?

For single individuals, particularly women, many of the associated legal issues were already thrashed out in connection with adoption. Should the right of the child to have two parents (the supposed purpose of adoption being to recreate a "normal" family) be invoked against the right of the single adopting parent? The issue in assisted reproduction is even more acute, for one begins not with a preexisting condition but with a deliberate wish to create a unilateral filiation by means of artificial insemination. In any case, the "right to have a child" was also frequently invoked in this controversy.

Likewise, the question of assisted reproduction for homosexual couples has sparked controversy. Homosexual rights organizations have made their case, but so far as I know no legislation has yet reached the floor of the French National Assembly. Because the homosexual couple is quite different from the traditional model of the family, allowing homosexuals access to medically assisted reproductive techniques has aroused fairly widespread hostility. Many homosexuals respond by arguing that homosexual couples are just as stable as heterosexual ones, if not more so, an argument that appears to have some foundation given the large number of divorces and separations occurring in heterosexual couples, particularly in the months following an artificial insemination using donated sperm. Clearly, the status of the child and a certain vision of family structure are crucial elements in the debate over medically assisted reproduction.

The Right to a Child, or the Rights of the Child?

Desire is not law. Believing in scientific progress, sterile couples go from doctor to doctor "demanding a child."[11] The desire to have a child becomes a kind of insistence, a claim that one has a right to bear children. The escalation of expectations fosters illusions that drive unhappy couples to extreme lengths, and when their efforts end in failure, the disappointment is all the more bitter. This obsession with biomedical technology has begun to worry some observers, who find that it arises out of an "objectified conception of procreation" that is beyond the control of the specialists. In *L'Oeuf transparent* Jacques Testart was critical of this growing recourse to science, which he argued led to overreliance on artificial techniques. Couples having difficulty with conception were treated as though they were sterile; in-vitro fertilization was used even when not strictly called for. In cases where time would have done its work or where sterility, properly acknowledged and worked through, followed by adoption, would have resulted in a more harmonious life, the medical profession stepped in with promises of scientific efficacy. What is the meaning of this need for a "child of one's own"?

The desire for a child is a complex need, connected with a person's ideas of his or her own identity, of the nature of parenthood, and of the structure of the family. In the twentieth century the child has become a kind of emotional focus, a social value, a proof of a person's ability to foster and transmit various qualities. We see abundant signs of this in literature and images as well as in a whole range of institutional measures for the protection of children. A semantic analysis of these indicators reveals two closely related attitudes, which may be complementary or antagonistic depending on certain normative choices: an insistence on reproductive freedom, and an emphasis on parenting in service of the child. The debates over contraception and abortion have placed the issue of reproductive freedom squarely on the agenda. Medically assisted reproduction has called attention to the implications of parental choices. Is a parental decision enough to justify any type of medical intervention?

A Child by What Right?

Reproductive freedom means much more than just bringing a child into the world. It is a projection of personal time and social space, in which the embodiment of the desire for a child functions as a proof of the totality of parental commitment. The overestimation of what science can do also heightens the quality of the parent-child relationship. Couples that seek medical assistance frequently see adoption in a different light, as a more "purposeful" task primarily involving upbringing, and less of a total, existential commitment than childbearing, because "the outcome of the struggle between the innate and the acquired presumably remains in doubt."[12] To be sure, those who adopt abandoned, unfortunate, or abused children are praised, but adoption is seen as more of a compensation for than a victory over sterility. For many sterile couples, progress in biotechnology has rekindled hopes "of having children of their own," of creating their own families. Donors are extolled for giving the gift of life, but in the meantime the parents proceed "as if" the child produced by insemination, transfer, or transplantation were really their own. Words take on a symbolic force, which critics of the commercial aspects of medically assisted reproduction tend to overlook.

Some couples have transformed the right to benefit from scientific progress in order to have a child into a kind of obligation that they would like to impose upon the government. Their desire, not to say fantasy, to have a child leads them to insist not only on the right to reproduce but on the right to have their reproduction guaranteed and subsidized by medical science and the state. This shift in emphasis has had practical consequences. There have been demands for free sperm and egg donations, for reduced costs for reproductive assistance, and for payment of all costs by the state. The government is expected to license and inspect sperm banks and other facilities and to pay all bills, as though bestowing its legitimacy on the whole process: "Money and the state legitimate the act."[13] Rather than legislate directly on the legal consequences of medically assisted reproduction, many governments have issued administrative regulations or established consultative or regulatory agencies, thereby giving hesitant, bureaucratic answers to fundamental ethical questions.

In France, two decrees dated April 8, 1988 (88-327 and 88-328) deal with regulations governing medically assisted reproduction, the preservation of human sperm, and prenatal diagnosis. A National Commission for the Medicine and Biology of Reproduction (CNMBR) was assigned the mission of informing the minister of health annually about changes in available technology. In the area of prenatal diagnosis, the intention was to establish a nationwide network of agencies subject to central control. In 1988 some 74 reproductive clinics were authorized, including 36 private clinics. A decision about the use of biological techniques was delayed, however, until February 1990, when a dozen or so laboratories were authorized to proceed (although their names were never officially published). An official nomenclature of reproductive interventions was established in order to allow for reimbursement by national health insurance.

These decisions by the French government made news. "At the end of 1988, 74 clinics were authorized to begin operation, and the media, with the connivance of the doctors, reported that this was the 'list of authorized in-vitro clinics.' This oversimplification, which may seem inconsequential, reflects the desire of the medical profession to resist any erosion of its prerogatives as a result of the new technologies."[14] When the decision of the health ministry was made public, many clinics not authorized to operate challenged the ruling either by filing suit in administrative court or submitting a petition to the minister. "It seems that roughly half the protesters won their cases before the administrative courts, which permitted them to carry on with their work. The others presumably faced immediate cessation of their activities, especially where the national health insurance plan refused to pay for medical services."[15]

Parental plans, scientific programs, and state institutions established among them a kind of self-regulating social mechanism. Bernard Edelmann has provided a comparative analysis of the German law governing "the problems raised by artificial fertilization" and "the protection of embryos" with the French proposal on "the life sciences and the rights of man" prepared at the behest of the Council of State. Edelmann stresses the philosophical assumptions underlying the provisions of the law.[16] "In the German bill, the fundamental notion was not 'parental plans' but 'the identity of the embryo,' given the risk of a discontinuous maternity." The Germans prohibited the sale or gift of sperm or eggs, on the grounds that artificial fertilization should take place only in a "durable couple." The French, on the other hand, placed the accent on "parental plans" and showed little concern about the identity of the unborn child, allowing third-party insemination:

> In the first case, the freedom of the parents was limited by the liberty of the unborn child. In the second, the liberty of the child was not even considered. The child is simply a projection of the parents' liberty, or, if you prefer, the object of their liberty. . . . What is striking in the comparison of the two bills is the difference of the relation envisioned with nature. Clearly, the German bill imitates nature in the sense that it seeks to purge the techniques of reproduction of their artificiality. The French bill is much more ambiguous. While it prohibits surrogate mothers and the formation of embryos for scientific research, it does not expressly forbid the choice of sex, and, worse yet, it allows giving embryos to third parties and scientific research institutions. The only thing about which it is

firm throughout—although an exception is made for the products of the human body—is the absence of a monetary motive.[17]

The philosophical differences seem to diminish where the agent of reproduction is not science but a surrogate human body. "Wombs for Hire," screamed the headlines, forcefully capturing some of the irrational passions surrounding the issue.

Surrogate Motherhood

The ideological, moral, and religious condemnation of surrogate mothers, particularly in continental Europe, was reminiscent in its vituperativeness of the earlier attacks on eugenics. Yet in the first case nature was deceived with little help from science beyond a routine insemination, whereas in the other science would direct the production of "demonic offspring." Human power in one case violated the rules of the identity and mystery of the human body, in the other the sacred rules governing the quality of life as given. "Gestation on behalf of another person," a practice accepted in certain traditional societies and, in its most altruistic and sublime forms, reminiscent of the biblical stories of Sarah and Mary, somehow became the object of a storm of criticism. Some charged that women were being exploited in a mercenary way. Others stressed the importance of emotional and physiological bonds formed in the womb. Still others condemned the instigation of child abandonment and perversion of the rules of adoption. Most hotly argued was the charge that while surrogate motherhood was presented as a therapy for infertility, it was in fact merely a substitution of one body for another that used the birth mother's body as nothing more than an incubator.

With the exception of a few states in the United States, most Western countries have passed laws against surrogate motherhood.[18] Yet thousands of children have already been born to surrogate mothers, and pro-surrogate groups have been formed. Although a majority of the public is apparently opposed to the practice, the reasons for the opposition vary widely. Can anyone really argue that the use of a surrogate by a woman born without a uterus is worse than engaging in the kind of traffic in children now common in international adoption circles? If money corrupts, it corrupts in other markets as well, ranging from blood transfusions to organ transplants and the long-term care required by incurable diseases. It is not a peculiar vice of surrogate motherhood. Similarly, it is nowadays common for very young children to be sent out to daycare centers and nursery schools. Is this any more or less disruptive than being nurtured in the womb of a surrogate? Mother-child relations are so complex, and the factors likely to promote healthy growth are so numerous, that one would be foolhardy to propose any simple laws or certain answers. It is easy to see why most judges, rather than rule against the principle of surrogate motherhood as such, have preferred to find technical grounds for abrogating contracts.

Nearly everyone is prepared to agree, however, that agents who specialize in selling the services of prospective surrogates are to be condemned. Many countries have imposed criminal penalties for such activities and have declared surrogacy contracts to be null and void. Yet the pressure of public opinion has brought about some changes.[19] A distinction is often made between two types of surrogate: the woman who conceives and carries her own child but decides to give it up after birth, and the woman who deliberately sets out to bear a child for someone else. And there is more fundamental disagreement over the issue of whether the reprehensible behavior consists in bearing a child for money or in the violation of the principle that "the human body is not for sale," as a French appellate court put it in a May 31, 1991, decision.[20]

Apart from problems of filiation, surrogate motherhood requires that the nature of the "bargain" be spelled out. The desire for a child, expressed in terms of individual freedom, gradually dissolves into a kind of biological conviviality, which takes advantage of a certain corporeal nondifferentiation. Whereas a profoundly individualistic philosophy was used to justify medically assisted reproduction, in which the physician allowed herself only to give concrete expression to the parents' own intentions, with surrogate motherhood we see the gradual formation of a collective constituency involving medical professionals, biologists, couples' groups, citizen pressure groups, and even intellectuals. Where, in all this, does the child's interest lie? Who will speak for the child and protect its rights?

The limits of the privatization of procreation are becoming increasingly apparent as various competing interests make their power felt. Parental roles are changing along with the family environment. What poses the greatest threat to the child is not the use of artificial techniques—family law has been based on a series of fictions for centuries—but rather the proliferation of allegiances and choices, whose complexity clouds the simple traditional image of parent-child relations. How many people have sought medical assistance for reproduction only to regret their decision later, as the fantasy of an ideal child is belied by everyday reality? How many children have been overwhelmed by their parents' enormous emotional investment in their medically assisted birth? I am thinking of one little boy, born of a frozen embryo, whose parents decided to call him Frosty.

Procreation does more than just create biological and emotional bonds between parents and child. Other family members are also involved. If there is a sperm donor, his family is involved too. Medical professionals and scientists play their part. Reproduction also has social and symbolic functions with genealogical and ethical implications. No culture can reduce filiation to engendering, mothering to pregnancy, or the child's interests to its parents' wishes. Each of us must have the courage to identify those values that we wish to affirm. Neo-conservatism, which wants to cling to one type of family structure, one vision of maternity and femaleness, has its dangers, but so has the naïve laissez-faire belief in the free market of human bodies. The debate that begins with medically assisted reproduction broadens into a consideration of eugenics in general, of the power of science over man's legacy. "Man has not yet gotten over being forced to admit that conception could be stripped of every last vestige of his dreams."[21]

After Britain adopted a new law of the family in 1990, the French legislature embarked on needed reforms by laying down general directives in the area of biomedical ethics. But the general public, along with legal scholars and politicians, remains divided over what is legitimate and what is not, and questions the wisdom of legislating in this area. Official reports are contradictory on several points. Close study of the facts of actual cases reveals enormous complexity. New questions arise every day, and choices multiply along with the power of human beings to change their destinies. We are emerging from a period haunted by fantasies and fears and approaching a time of ethical choice. It is to be hoped that we will know how to make choices that are universal without being totalitarian, that we will know how to build something for all of us without subjecting each one to a uniform general law. The multiplicity of possibilities for procreation, the many roles that women may play in the transmission of life, are proof that the patriarchal order is finished and that the time has come to reflect anew on what our values truly are.[22]

TRANSLATED FROM THE FRENCH BY ARTHUR GOLDHAMMER

five

Women's Voices

Words for Our Own Time

The twenty-first century is in part unpredictable, in part the heir of today. The future will be what the women and men of to-day and of generations to come make it, although the alchemy by which history is produced is one in which gender relations cannot be separated from other human relations.

Perhaps, with this volume and this series, we have taken a step toward fulfilling the wish that Virginia Woolf expressed at the end of *A Room of One's Own* for the rebirth of Shake-speare's sister, that "dead poetess" who never wrote a single word. To conclude this volume we have in any case chosen to open our pages to two women of this century, two among many, many others.

F.T.

Christa Wolf
"The Final Solution"

Françoise Thébaud

BORN IN 1929 IN THE eastern part of Germany, in the town
of Landsberg from which she fled with her family as Soviet troops
advanced in 1945, Christa Wolf became a citizen of the German
Democratic Republic and, in the 1960s, the speaker for a younger
generation of East German writers who expressed their views not
only in their writings but also in the questions they raised about
the Communist regime and the Iron Curtain. Through fifteen
works that drew with great originality on a variety of literary
genres, Wolf became the best known of East German writers.

Published in East Germany in 1976, *A Model Childhood* is
not a memoir but an "evocation," to use Wolf's own word, an
"invocation" of her past that attempts to go beyond ordinary
antifascist writings by laying bare the everyday reality of Nazism,
lest we forget. The book consists of questions that the author
poses and courageously asks of herself. Its complex structure involves two characters ("you," the narrator, and "she," the child
Nelly) and three narrative time frames: the period 1929–1945; a
trip taken in 1971 by the narrator along with her brother, a
companion, and her daughter Lenka to her native city, L., now in
Poland; and, finally, the time of the writing.

In this excerpt on "the final solution," Wolf asks first about
the responsibility of the Germans, of herself, and her family in a
crime that began with the indifference of ordinary citizens or with
their acceptance of Nazi rhetoric.[1] "But where were you living?"
a Communist survivor of the concentration camps asks Nelly's
mother when, in 1945, she expresses surprise at what has happened to him. Wolf also looks at how the experiences of the past
are transmitted from mother to daughter, from generation to generation, from nation to nation—especially this unique experience,

which "for all eternity an insurmountable barrier separates the sufferers from those who went free."

Defying the optimistic official view that the past has been overcome, Wolf invites her fellow citizens and readers to reexamine that past. She does this even though she writes that "it is indeed unbearable, on hearing the word 'Auschwitz,' to have to think at the same time of the little word 'I'—'I' in the past conditional, I might. I could have. I would have had to. Obey." Today, after the reunification of Germany, at a time when exclusion and hatred are taking on new faces in many different places, it is perhaps a good moment to reread and meditate on this work.

The final solution.

You've forgotten when you first heard those words. When you gave them their proper meaning; it must have been years after the war. But way after that—to this day—every tall, thickly smoking smokestack forces you to think "Auschwitz." The name cast a shadow which grew and grew. To this day, you can't bring yourself to stand in this shadow, because your otherwise lively imagination balks at the suggestion that you might take on the role of the victims.

For all eternity, an insurmountable barrier separates the sufferers from those who went free.

On July 31, 1941—a vacation day, and probably hot—Nelly may have been lying in her favorite potato furrow under the cherry trees in the garden, reading, while a lizard sunned itself on her stomach. In summertime, the radio was on the porch; perhaps Nelly jumped to her feet at the sound of the fanfares which preceded special news bulletins; perhaps she ran to the porch to hear the news of the continued German advance into Russia. Her father was no longer in the war. After the Polish campaign, his age group had been demobilized, and he, who had been deemed "fit for garrison duty at home," had been assigned a desk job as a noncommissioned officer in the orderly room of the District Command Post in L.

This was, more or less, the way Nelly spent the day on which Reichsmarshal Hermann Göring, by order of the Führer, entrusted Reinhard Heydrich, chief of security police and head of national security, with the "final solution of the Jewish problem in the zones of German influence inside Europe"—the same Heydrich who had received orders to carry out the final solution within German territory on January 24, 1939, when Nelly was not quite ten years old.

Both dates deserve to be remembered more than a number of others . . .

On page 207 of Lenka's schoolbook is a map—6″ × 4″—of "Fascist concentration camps throughout Europe during World War II." The towns aren't marked on this map. The North Sea and the Baltic Sea are indicated, as are the main rivers: sixteen larger black dots mark the major concentration camps. Five of these are underlined, to indicate that they were extermination camps. The map is studded with small dots ("secondary camps") and small crosses ("ghettos"). You can physically sense Lenka's understanding, her first, of what kind of landscape her mother spent her childhood in. From the geographical location of the extermination camps Chelmno, Treblinka, and maybe also Maidanek, one can assume that transports of human beings destined for these camps passed also through L., on the eastern railroad. Trains destined for Auschwitz and Belzec probably used the southern route. Never did Nelly hear anyone around her mention any such transport, neither during nor after the war. No one in her family worked for the German railroad in those days.

Lenka said, so far as she knew, most students in her class—including herself—hadn't examined the map very thoroughly. She said they hadn't felt (hadn't been *made* to feel, you think) that this map concerned them more than other documents in the book. Your shocked surprise, mixed with a touch of irritation, collapses as you ask yourself if it was not desirable rather than objectionable that these children no longer suffered from a guilt feeling which might have compelled them to examine the map more closely. Unto the third and fourth generation: the horrible dictum of the vengeful God. But that is not the point.

You've watched droves of people happily eating their apples and their sandwiches while tramping across the onetime drill field of Ettersberg, a sight that filled you with amazement and fear rather than with indignation. Moreover, someone tried to explain to you that the remodeling of the former SS barracks in the Buchenwald camp into a kind of tourist hotel had been an efficient way of saving material and expense. He didn't use the word "hospitality," but that was the gist of what he was saying, and he didn't understand your question: Did he really think anyone—a foreign tourist, for instance—would be able to go to sleep in that house? Frankly, he said, I don't know what you mean. Your proposition, that current visitors to the former concentration camp abstain from eating, drinking, singing, and piped-in music for the brief duration of their visit, struck him as unreasonable. Frankly, he said, that's not being realistic. You've got to take people the way they are. (Excerpts from chapter 11 of *A Model Childhood* by Christa Wolf, trans. Ursule Molinaro and Hedwig Rappolt. English translation copyright © 1980 by Farrar, Straus & Giroux, Inc. Reprinted by permission of Farrar, Straus & Giroux, Inc.)

Nelly Kaplan
"Husbands, I Salute You"

Françoise Thébaud

BORN IN 1934, a native of Argentina, the filmmaker Nelly
Kaplan is better known than Belen, her pen name as a poet. Within
the Surrealist entourage, however, she always worked in both film
and literature. As moviemaker, she collaborated with Abel Gance
and later wrote and produced a number of short subjects as well
as feature films, including *La Fiancée du pirate* (1969), which
earned her a prize at the Venice Film Festival (one of two she won)
and caused a stir in the world of film. Earlier she wrote three brief,
unusual, provocative pamphlets on the arts of loving and living:
La Géométrie dans les spasmes, La Reine des sabbats, and *Et
délivrez nous du Mâle,* which in 1966 were gathered and published
under the title *Le Réservoir des sens.*

"Husbands, I Salute You" is at once a feminist fantasy in which
the uncanny mingles with the erotic in a total reversal of sex roles
and characteristics; an insolent gibe at the men who still largely
dominated the world in the late 1950s; and a humorous brickbat
tossed into the midst of contemporary debates about Pavlovian
psychology and the existence of a primitive matriarchy. (Incidentally, the title in French, "Je vous salue, maris," is deliberately all
but identical to the opening line of the Hail Mary: "Je vous salue,
Marie . . .") This excerpt is to be savored—and the editor denies
any malice aforethought.

> For several thousand years now, the world has once again
> been living under a matriarchal regime.
>
> The women won the battle. And they won big. We're paying
> dearly now for their former servitude—we men, that is. And
> we have been paying for thousands of years.
>
> Sometimes, though, I have hope that change is possible. In
> the history of the world day follows day, but none is like any
> other. And it is to works of history that I turn in search of

reasons to hope. I am in fact one of the very few men left who still likes to read. During the long days that I spend in the cell to which I have been assigned, I read the works of our ancestors. I even understand them. It seems that, in spite of my status, my intelligence is above average. No doubt that is why they have arranged to keep me under special surveillance. But that does not prevent me from devouring works that reveal in flashes what the world was like in the distant past, long before the matriarchy. It sets me to dreaming. In vain. Because we will never escape from our situation. Hope, in truth, can only be an illusion. We cannot escape them. They have admirably arranged things so that we have what is essential: a bed, food, even comfort. A sort of anesthesia, in other words, a mental paralysis that incarcerates us more securely than any prison bars. It never even occurs to us to attempt an escape. And when on occasion I attempt to stir up a revolt, my companions look at me in panic and shun me with suspicion: they do not understand. They may even denounce me. It is the eternal masculine, with its weaknesses and its sly ways. One can scarcely trust in the weaker sex.

Of course our every whim is satisfied in this house of luxury and lasciviousness. The days pass in delightful idleness, the nights in joy. It is also true that we are well treated and never—or almost never—punished.

But I am not happy.

They know it. I think I hear them: "You will never be happy," they tell me. "You think too much. What for? It would be simpler to give in. In any case, you can never change the condition of man."

"You can't change an established fact. How do you explain that the great creators are all women?" one of them adds, her sweet voice tinged with irritation.

They are right, I know. Men never invent anything. They never create anything impressive. The women are always right, even when they seem pained by our incurable stupidity. But once again, what is to be done? Thousands of years of backwardness have destroyed us.

The days pass, and the months, in this house of which I am an inmate. From earliest childhood I have been privy to all the subtleties of the rites that the women come here to celebrate, in order to forget the fatigue of their heavy days of work and responsibility.

No sooner had I graduated from the Institute for Advanced Voluptuary Studies (IAVS) than I entered this place. Apparently I am exceptionally gifted by nature, remarkably intuitive, sometimes tender, always efficient. How could I not be, since they have thought of everything? Even when they are repulsive, we are conditioned to serve them. We are helpless to do anything else. Alas, the flesh is weak, and they have read all the books. And so it came to pass that the scientific experiments of a twentieth-century professor gave them the answer they had been looking for. They successfully put it into practice. Through long years at the IAVS, whenever they made us euphoric (and they knew just what to do!), a bell sounded in each laboratory. After many such experiences of euphoria, this produced in us a conditioned reflex, so that each time we heard the faintest sound of a bell . . . In short, whenever a woman, however unattractive, came to visit us, a clever system of carillons installed in our rooms automatically turned us into (nearly) inexhaustible, if astonished, victims.

Some day, perhaps, things will change again. My intuition tells me that the new rulers will be those strange mutants who appeared after the first Great Destruction, those worrisome androgynes with gold dust sprinkled in their eyes. For the time being they still serve us. But their strange smiles do not deceive me, any more than I am deceived as to the extent of their powers. We men and the women who rule us today will disappear in the centuries to come. And it will, I think, be no more than just.

But all that lies in the future. Right now, resigned inmate that I am, I hear footsteps on the stairs leading up to my room. The door opens. I am too tired to turn over, so I lie still, my eyes closed.

Another woman . . .

She approaches, and with a voice slurred from overindulgence in Martian liqueurs, she greets me. Then she begins to undress me. Is she beautiful or hideous? I guess it is time to open my eyes and find out. But already the sweet pealing of bells is evoking all the right responses in me. And I prefer to keep my eyes closed, to let myself go, resigned and radiant.

No revolt is possible. The matriarchy is back.   (From Belen [Nelly Kaplan], *Le Réservoir des sens*, Paris: La Jeune Parque, 1966.)

Translated from the French by Arthur Goldhammer

Notes

Explorations of Gender
FRANÇOISE THÉBAUD

1. As suggested by the title of Elizabeth Badinter's *L'Un est l'autre: des relations entre hommes et femmes* (Paris: Odile Jacob, 1986).

2. Among the principal participants in these debates are several contributors to this series, in particular Michelle Perrot, Joan Scott, and Gisela Bock. See the bibliography for suggested additional reading. An excellent source is Karen Offen, Ruth Pierson, and Jane Rendall, eds., *Writing Women's History: International Perspectives* (London: International Federation for Research in Women's History, 1991), especially Gisela Bock's chapter, "Challenging Dichotomies: Perspectives on Women's History."

3. Françoise Picq, "Le Féminisme bourgeois: une théorie élaborée par les femmes socialistes avant la guerre de 14," in *Stratégies des femmes* (Paris: Tierce, 1984); the American edition of this collective work is Judith Friedlander, ed., *Women in Culture and Politics: A Century of Change* (Bloomington: Indiana University Press, 1986); Nancy F. Cott, *The Grounding of Modern Feminism* (New Haven: Yale University Press, 1987); Bock, "Challenging Dichotomies"; Joan Scott, "Deconstructing Equality-Versus-Difference: or, The Uses of Poststructuralist Theory for Feminism," *Feminist Studies* 14, 1 (1988); Karen Offen, "Defining Feminism: A Comparative Historical Approach," *Signs* 14, 1 (1988).

4. *Savoir et différence des sexes:* spec. no. of *Cahiers du Grif* 45 (Fall 1990).

5. See the essay by Joan Scott in volume 4 of this series.

6. Margarete Buber-Neumann, *Milena* (Paris: Seuil, 1988); trans. of *Milena Kafka's Freundin* (Albert Langen-Georg Müller Verlag, 1977); idem, *Als Gefangene bei Stalin und Hitler* (Stuttgart: Seewald Verlag, 1985).

7. See Mathilde Dubesset and Michelle Zancarini-Fournel, "Parcours de femmes: réalités et représentations, Saint-Etienne 1850–1950," thesis, University of Lyon 2, 1988 (under the direction of Yves Lequin).

8. Roger-Henri Guerrand and Francis Ronsin, *Le Sexe apprivoisé: Jeanne Humbert et la lutte pour le contrôle des naissances* (Paris: La Découverte,

1990); Felicia Gordon, *The Integral Feminist: Madeleine Pelletier, 1874–1939* (London: Polity Press, 1990).

9. See, among many works, Gérard Cholvy and Yves-Marie Hilaire, *Histoire religieuse de la France contemporaine,* vol. 2 *(1880–1930)* and vol. 3 *(1930–1988)* (Toulouse: Privat, 1986 and 1988); and Sylvie Fayet-Scribe, *Associations féminines et catholicisme, XIXe–XVe siècle* (Paris: Les Editions Ouvrières, 1990). See also René Rémond, ed., *Société sécularisée et renouveau religieux, XXe siècle* (forthcoming), vol. 4 of René Rémond and Jacques Le Goff, eds., *L'Histoire de la France religieuse.*

10. Etienne-Emile Baulieu, *Génération pilule* (Paris: Odile Jacob, 1990).

11. See Yvonne Knibiehler and Régine Goutalier, *La Femme au temps des colonies* (Paris: Stock, 1985).

12. See the articles by Victoria de Grazia cited in n2 of Chapter 2 herein; see also Shari Benstock, *Femmes de la rive gauche, Paris 1900–1940* (Paris: Editions des Femmes, 1987).

13. Françoise Collin, "Ces études qui sont 'pas tout.' Fécondité et limites des études féministes," *Cahiers du Grif* 45 (Fall 1990).

14. See, for example, "Histoire et sciences sociales: un tournant critique," *Annales ESC* 6 (November-December 1989).

In the Service of the Fatherland
FRANÇOISE THÉBAUD

1. Pierre Vidal-Naquet, *Les Assassins de la mémoire* (Paris: La Découverte, 1987), translated into English by Jeffrey Mehlmann as *Assassins of Memory: Essays on the Denial of the Holocaust* (Boulder: Colorado University Press, 1993). On the controversy among historians over revisionist interpretations of fascism *(Historikerstreit),* see *Devant l'histoire: la controverse sur la singularité de l'extermination des Juifs par le régime nazi* (Paris: Cerf, 1988). [In English, see especially Charles Maier, *The Unmasterable Past* (Cambridge, Mass.: Harvard University Press, 1989)—Trans.]

2. Rita Thalmann, *La Tentation nationaliste, 1914–1945* (Paris: Deux-temps Tierce, 1990).

3. Liliane Kandel, "Féminisme et nazisme," *Les Temps Modernes,* March 1990, pp. 17–53, quotation on p. 41.

4. Rita Thalmann, *Protestantisme et nationalisme en Allemagne de 1900 à 1945* (Paris: Klincksieck, 1976); idem, *Etre femme sous le IIIe Reich* (Paris: Robert Laffont, 1982); idem, ed., *Femmes et fascismes* (Paris: Tierce, 1986); Claudia Koonz, *Mothers in the Fatherland: Women, the Family, and Nazi Politics* (New York: St. Martin's Press, 1986).

5. Djamila Amrane, *Les Femmes algériennes dans la guerre* (Paris: Plon, 1991).

6. Anne Steiner and Loïc Debray, *La Fraction Armée rouge: Guérilla urbaine en Europe occidentale* (Paris: Méridiens Klincksieck, 1988).

7. Emmanuel Reynaud, *Les Femmes, la violence et l'armée* (Paris: Fondation pour les Études de Défense Nationale, 1988).

Chapter 1. The Great War
Françoise Thébaud

I wish to thank the many colleagues and friends who sent me bibliographic references, books, and articles: Ute Daniel, Christiane Eifert, and Karin Hausen for Germany, Sîan Reynolds and Deborah Thom for Great Britain, Michela De Giorgio for Italy, and Margaret R. Higonnet, Nancy R. Jaicks, and Joan W. Scott for the United States.

1. Quoted in J. Stanley Lemons, *The Woman Citizen: Social Feminism in the 1920s* (New Haven: Yale University Press, 1973), p. 20.

2. Quoted in Françoise Thébaud, *La Femme au temps de la guerre de 14* (Paris: Stock, 1986), p. 16.

3. Antoine Prost, *Les Anciens Combattants et la société française* (Paris: Presses de la Fondation Nationale des Sciences Politiques, 1977), and "Les Monuments aux morts. Culte républicain? Culte civique? Culte patriotique?" in Pierre Nora, ed., *Les Lieux de mémoire* (Paris: Gallimard, 1990), pp. 195–225; Renato Monteleone, Pino Sarasini, "I monumenti italiani ai caduti della Grande Guerra," in Diego Leoni and Camillo Zadra, eds., *La Grande Guerra: esperienza, memoria, immagini* (Bologna: Il Mulino, 1986), pp. 631–662.

4. Anne-Marie Sohn, "La Garçonne face à l'opinion publique," *Le Mouvement Social* 80 (1972), as well as her essay in this volume.

5. In the 1920s the Carnegie Foundation for International Peace and Yale University Press began publishing an extensive series of monographs constituting an economic and social history of the First World War.

6. Georges-Henri Soutou, *L'Or et le sang: les buts de guerre économiques de la Première Guerre mondiale* (Paris: Fayard, 1989).

7. For France, see especially Jean-Jacques Becker, *1914, comment les Français sont entrés dans la guerre* (Paris: Presses de la Fondation Nationale des Sciences Politiques, 1977), and *Les Français dans la Grande Guerre* (Paris: Robert Laffont, 1980); Prost, *Les Anciens Combattants;* Jean-Louis Robert, "Ouvriers et mouvements ouvriers parisiens pendant la Grande Guerre et l'immédiat après-guerre: histoire et anthropologie," thesis, University of Paris II, 1989. On Germany and Great Britain, see Gerald D. Feldman, *Armee, Industrie und Arbeiterschaft in Deutschland 1914 bis 1918* (Berlin-Bonn, 1985); Jürgen Kocka, *Klassengesellschaft im Krieg: Deutsche Sozialgeschichte 1914–1918* (Göttingen, 1978); Arthur Marwick, *The Deluge: British Society and the First World War* (London: The Bodley Head, 1965); Jay Winter, *The Great War and the British People* (London, 1985); Richard Wall and Jay Winter, eds., *The Upheaval of War: Family, Work, and Welfare in Europe, 1914–1918* (Cambridge: Cambridge University Press, 1988).

8. David Mitchell, *Women on the Warpath: The Story of the Women of the First World War* (London: Jonathan Cape, 1966); Arthur Marwick, *Women at War, 1914–1918* (Fontana Paperbacks, 1977), and *War and Social Change in the Twentieth Century: A Comparative Study of Britain, France, Germany, Russia, and the United States* (London, 1979).

9. Gail Braybon and Penny Summerfield, *Out of the Cage: Women's Experiences in Two World Wars* (London: Pandora, 1987).

10. Interviews conducted by the author and broadcast on the program "Dossiers de l'écran," Antenne 2, May 1, 1984.

11. James F. MacMillan, *Housewife or Harlot: The Place of Women in French Society, 1870–1940* (Brighton: The Harvester Press, 1981).

12. That a generational effect was at work here is particularly clear in the case of Great Britain: see Gail Braybon, *Women Workers in the First World War* (London: Croom Helm, 1981), and Braybon and Summerfield, eds., *Out of the Cage;* and Deborah Thom, "Women and Work in Wartime Britain," in Wall and Winter, eds., *The Upheaval of War,* pp. 297–325.

13. Michelle Perrot, "The New Eve and the Old Adam: French Women's Condition at the Turn of the Century," in Margaret Higonnet et al., *Behind the Lines: Gender and the Two World Wars* (New Haven: Yale University Press, 1987), as well as her essay in Geneviève Fraisse and Michelle Perrot, eds., *A History of Women,* vol. 4 (Cambridge, Mass.: Harvard University Press, 1993); Laurence Klejman and Florence Rochefort, *L'Egalité en marche: le féminisme sous la Troisième République* (Paris: Presses de la Fondation Nationale des Sciences Politiques/Editions des Femmes, 1989); Anne-Marie Käpelli, "Feminist Scenes," in Fraisse and Perrot, eds., *A History of Women,* vol. 4.

14. Ute Daniel, *Arbeiterfrauen in der Kriegsgesellschaft* (Göttingen: Vandenhoeck & Ruprecht, 1989).

15. Colloquium organized by the Center for European Studies at Harvard University. Most of the papers are collected in Higonnet et al., eds., *Behind the Lines.* See also Michelle Perrot's review, "Sur le front des sexes: un combat douteux," *Vingtième Siècle* 3 (July 1984).

16. Joan W. Scott, "Rewriting History," in Higonnet et al., eds., *Behind the Lines,* pp. 21–30.

17. Françoise Thébaud, "Le Féminisme à l'épreuve de la guerre," in Rita Thalmann, ed., *La Tentation nationaliste, 1914–1945* (Paris: Deuxtemps Tierce, 1990); Marie-Hélène Zylberberg-Hocquard, *Féminisme et syndicalisme en France* (Paris: Anthropos, 1978).

18. Becker, *1914;* Jürgen Reulecke, "Männerbund versus the Family: Middle-class Youth Movements and the Family in the Period of the First World War," in Wall and Winter, eds., *The Upheaval of War,* pp. 439–451.

19. Eric J. Leed, *No Man's Land: Combat and Identity in World War I* (Cambridge: Cambridge University Press, 1979), chap. 2.

20. Annette Tapfert, ed., *Despatches from the Heart: An Anthology of Letters from the Front during the First and Second World Wars* (London: Hamish Hamilton, 1984), quoted in Bonnie Smith, *Changing Lives: Women in European History since 1700* (Lexington: D. C. Heath and Company, 1989); André Kahn, *Journal de guerre d'un Juif patriote, 1914–1918* (Paris: Jean-Claude Simoën, 1978).

21. Annelise Maugue, *L'Identité masculine en crise au tournant du siècle* (Marseille: Rivages, 1987); Françoise Thébaud, *La Femme au temps de la guerre de 14,* pp. 36–39.

22. Quoted in Marwick, *Women at War,* p. 27, and Thébaud, "Le Féminisme," in Thalmann, ed., *La Tentation nationaliste,* p. 21.

23. Poster reproduced in Higonnet et al., eds., *Behind the Lines,* p. 210.

24. Marianne Walle, "Contribution à l'histoire des femmes allemandes entre 1848 et 1920 à travers les itinéraires de Louise Otto, Hélène Lang, Clara Zetkin et Lily Braun," doctoral thesis, University of Paris VII, 1989; idem, "Féminisme et nationalisme dans *Die Frau,*" in Thalmann, ed., *La Tentation nationaliste.*

25. Quoted in Marwick, *Women at War,* p. 107.

26. Quoted in Thébaud, *La Femme au temps,* p. 25.

27. Patrick Fridenson, ed., *1914–1918: L'autre front, Cahier du Mouvement Social 2* (Paris: Les Editions Ouvrières, 1977).

28. Daniel, *Arbeiterfrauen;* Ute Daniel, "Fiktionen, Friktionen, und Fakten—Frauenlohnarbeit im ersten Weltkrieg," in Günter Mai, ed., *Arbeiterschaft 1914–1918 in Deutschland* (Düsseldorf, 1985), and "Women's Work in Industry and Family: German, 1914–1918," in Wall and Winter, eds., *The Upheaval of War,* pp. 267–296.

29. Richard Bessel, "Keine allzu grosse Beunruhigung des Arbeitsmarktes. Frauenarbeit und Demobilmachung in Deutschland nach dem ersten Weltkrieg," *Geschichte und Gesellschaft* 9 (1983): 211–229.

30. Alastair Reid, "The Impact of the First World War on British Workers," in Wall and Winter, eds., *The Upheaval of War,* pp. 221–233.

31. Thom, "Women and Work"; Richard Wall, "English and German Families and the First World War, 1914–1918," in Wall and Winter, eds., *The Upheaval of War,* pp. 43–105.

32. Marwick, *Women at War,* pp. 83–114; Jenny Gould, "Women's Military Service in First World War Britain," in Higonnet et al., eds., *Behind the Lines,* pp. 114–125.

33. Esther Newton and Carroll Smith-Rosenberg, "Le Mythe de la lesbienne et la femme nouvelle: pouvoir, sexualité et légitimité, 1870–1930," in *Stratégies des femmes* (Paris: Tierce, 1984), pp. 274–311; Gudrun Schwarz, "L'Invention de la lesbienne par les psychiatres allemands," idem, pp. 312–328. See also Judith Walkowitz, "Dangerous Sexualities," in Fraisse and Perrot, eds., *A History of Women,* vol. 4.

34. Quoted in Cornelie Usborne, "Pregnancy Is the Woman's Active Service. Pronatalism in Germany during the First World War," in Wall and Winter, eds., *The Upheaval of War,* pp. 389–415.

35. Quoted in Daniel, "Fiktionen," p. 308.

36. Quoted in Thébaud, *La Femme au temps,* pp. 38 and 182.

37. Thom, "Women and Work"; Diana Condell and Jean Liddiard, *Working for Victory? Images of Women in the First World War, 1914–1918* (New York: Routledge & Chapman Hall, 1988).

38. Quoted in Simonetta Ortaggi Cammarosano, "Testimonianze proletarie e socialiste sulla guerra," in Leoni and Zadra, eds., *La Grande Guerra,* pp. 577–604.

39. Photographs reproduced in Braybon and Summerfield, *Out of the Cage.*

40. Harriot Stanton Blatch, *Mobilizing Woman-Power* (New York: The Woman Press, 1918), pp. 54–55. The words "good time" are from the English feminist C. Gasquoine Hartley, *Women's Wild Oats* (New York, 1920), p. 38, quoted in William I. O'Neill, *Feminism in America: A History* (New Brunswick and Oxford: Transaction Publishers, 1989), p. 189; "fine time" is from Lorine Pruette, quoted in Lemons, *The Woman Citizen,* p. 15.

41. Sandra M. Gilbert, "Soldier's Heart: Literary Men, Literary Women, and the Great War," in Higonnet, et al., eds., *Behind the Lines,* pp. 197–226; "All the world is topsy-turvy" is a line of verse from Nina Macdonald quoted in Catherine Reilly, ed., *Scars upon My Heart: Women's Poetry and Verse of the First World War* (London: Virago, 1981). Gilbert's optimistic analysis is challenged in some respects by Helen M. Cooper et al., eds., *Arms and the Woman: War, Gender, and Literary Representation* (Chapel Hill: University of North Carolina Press, 1989), especially concerning May Sinclair.

42. Paul Fussell, *The Great War and Modern Memory* (Oxford: Oxford University Press, 1975); Leed, *No Man's Land.*

43. Elaine Showalter, *The Female Malady: Women, Madness and English Culture* (New York: Pantheon, 1985), and "Rivers and Sassoon: The Inscription of Male Gender Anxieties," in Higonnet et al., eds., *Behind the Lines,* pp. 61–69.

44. Stéphane Audoin-Rouzeau, *14–18: les combattants des tranchées* (Paris: Armand Colin, 1986).

45. Clara Malraux, *Le Bruit de nos pas: apprendre à vivre* (Paris: Grasset, 1986).

46. Quoted in Marwick, *Women at War,* p. 107; on Marie and Irène Curie, see Robert Reid, *Marie Curie, derrière la légende* (Paris: Editions du Seuil, 1979); Françoise Giroud, *Une femme honorable* (Paris: Fayard, 1981); Noëlle Loriot, *Irène Joliot-Curie* (Paris: Presses de la Renaissance, 1991).

47. Michelle Perrot, "Sur le front des sexes: un combat douteux," *Vingtième siècle* 3, 71 (July 1984); see also Philippe Ariès and Georges Duby, eds., *A History of Private Life,* vols. 4 and 5 (Cambridge, Mass.: Harvard University Press, 1989–90).

48. See, for example, in the case of France, Louise Deletang, *Journal d'une ouvrière parisienne pendant la guerre* (Paris, 1935), and Marguerite Lesage, *Journal de guerre d'une Française* (Paris, 1938).

49. Paola di Cori, "Il doppio sguardo. Visibilità dei generi sessuali nella rappresentazione fotografica (1908–1918)," in Leoni and Zadra, eds., *La Grande Guerra,* pp. 765–800; in the same work see also Michela De Giorgio, "Dalla 'Donna Nuova' alla donna della 'nuova' Italia," pp. 307–329.

50. Maurine Weiner Greenwald, *Women, War and Work: The Impact of World War I on Women Workers in the United States* (Westport: Greenwood Press, 1980).

51. William J. Breen, "Black Women and the Great War: Mobilization and Reform in the South," *The Journal of Southern History* 44 (August 1978); David M. Kennedy, *Over Here: The First World War and American Society* (New York: Oxford University Press, 1980).

52. Ida Clyde Clarke, *Uncle Sam Needs a Wife* (Chicago, 1925), p. 5, quoted in O'Neill, *Feminism in America,* p. 193.

53. Evelyne Diebolt and Jean-Pierre Laurent, *Anne Morgan: une Américaine en Soissonnais (1917–1952),* privately published by the Association Médico-sociale Anne Morgan, 1990.

54. Valerie J. Conner, "'The Mothers of the Race' in World War I. The National War Labor Board and Women in Industry," *Labor History* 21 (Winter 1980).

55. A. Mignon, chief physician of the Third Army, quoted in Thébaud, *La Femme au temps de la guerre de 14,* p. 93; on nurses see also Yvonne Knibiehler, ed., *Cornettes et blouses blanches: les infirmières dans la société française 1880–1980* (Paris: Hachette, 1984); Evelyne Diebolt, *La Maison de santé protestante de Bordeaux, 1863–1934* (Toulouse: Erès, 1990); Marie-Françoise Collière, *Promouvoir la vie* (Paris: Inter-Editions, 1982).

56. Thébaud, *La Femme au temps de la guerre de 14,* pp. 147–158; Anna Bravo, "Per una storia delle donne: donne contadine e prima guerra mondiale," *Societa e historia* 10 (1980).

57. Jeanne Bouvier, *Mes mémoires* (Paris: Découverte/Maspéro, 1983); Sylvia Pankhurst, *The Home Front* (London: Hutchinson, 1932).

58. In *1914–1918: l'autre front,* see Gerd Hardach, "La Mobilisation industrielle en 1914–1918: production, planification et idéologie"; Alain Hennebicque, "Albert Thomas et le régime des usines de guerre, 1915–1917"; Mathilde Dubesset, Françoise Thébaud, Catherine Vincent, "Les Munitionnettes de la Seine."

59. Robert, "Ouvriers et mouvement," chaps. 11 and 12.

60. See, for example, Monica Cosens, *Lloyd George's Munition Girls* (London: Hutchinson, 1916), quoted in Braybon, *Out of the Cage,* or Marcelle Capy, "La Femme à l'usine," *La Voix des Femmes* (November 17, December 17, January 18).

61. The Women's Employment Committee and The Health of Munitions Workers Committee in Great Britain, the Comité du Travail Féminin in France, and Der Nationale Ausschuss für Frauenarbeit im Kriege in Germany.

62. Besides the works of Gail Braybon and Ute Daniel cited earlier, see Laura Lee Downs, "Women in Industry, 1914–1939: The Employer's Perspective: A Comparative Study of the French and British Metals Industry," thesis, Columbia University, 1987; and Annie Fourcaut, *Femmes à l'usine en France dans l'entre-deux-guerres* (Paris: Maspéro, 1982).

63. Alain Corbin, *Filles de noce: misère sexuelle et prostitution au XIXe siècle* (Paris: Aubier-Montaigne, 1978); Emilio Franzina, "Il tempo libero dalla guerra: Case del soldato e postriboli militari," in Leoni and Zadra, eds., *La Grande Guerra,* pp. 161–230.

64. Colette, "La Chambre éclairée," *Les Heures longues* (Paris, 1917).

65. Wall and Winter, eds., *The Upheaval of War,* introduction and part 4 on "Social Policy and Family Ideology."

66. Cicely Hamilton, "Non-Combatant," in Reilly, ed., *Scars upon My Heart.*

67. Karin Hausen, "The German Nation's Obligations to the Heroes' Widows of World War I," in Higonnet et al., ed., *Behind the Lines*, pp. 126–140.

68. Richard Soloway, "Eugenics and Pronatalism in Wartime Britain," in Wall and Winter, eds., *The Upheaval of War*, pp. 369–388.

69. Jay Winter, "Some Paradoxes of the First World War," and Peter Dewey, "Nutrition and Living Standards in Wartime Britain," in Wall and Winter, eds., *The Upheaval of War*, pp. 9–42 and 197–220.

70. Ute Daniel, "The Politics of Rationing versus the Politics of Subsistence: Working-Class Women in Germany, 1914–1918," in Roger Fletcher, ed., *Bernstein to Brandt: A Short History of German Social Democracy* (London, 1987); Michelle Perrot, "La Femme populaire rebelle," in the collective volume *L'Histoire sans qualités* (Paris: Galilée, 1979), and her essay in vol. 4 of this series.

71. Lynne Layton, "Vera Brittain's Testament(s)," in Higonnet et al., eds., *Behind the Lines*, pp. 70–83.

72. Romain Rolland's appeal was published in the journal of the International Woman Suffrage Alliance and in Henri Guilbeaux's magazine *Demain*.

73. Odette Thibault, ed., *Féminisme et pacifisme: même combat* (Paris: Les Lettres Libres, 1985).

74. On feminism, see notes 13 and 24 above, and of course the three books by Richard J. Evans: *The Feminist Movement in Germany, 1894–1933* (London: Sage Publications, 1976); *The Feminists: Women's Emancipation Movements in Europe, America and Australasia, 1840–1920* (London: Croom Helm, 1977); and *Comrades and Sisters: Feminism, Socialism and Pacifism in Europe, 1870–1945* (Sussex: Wheatsheaf Books, 1987).

75. Anne Wiltsher, *Most Dangerous Women* (London, 1985); Evans, *The Feminist Movement in Germany*; O'Neill, *Feminism in America*, pp. 169–185.

76. Barbara J. Steinson, "The Mother Half of Humanity: American Women in the Peace and Preparedness Movements in World War I," in C. Berkin and C. Lovett, eds., *Women, War and Revolution* (New York: Holmes and Meier, 1980), pp. 259–285; Linda Schott, "The Woman's Peace Party and the Moral Basis for Women's Pacifism," *Frontiers* 8, 2 (1985).

77. Hélène Brion, *La Voie féministe* (Paris: Syros, 1978); Charles Sowerwine, *Les Femmes et le socialisme* (Paris: Presses de la FNSP, 1978); Robert, *Ouvriers et mouvement ouvrier*.

78. For example, "La Désunion des prolétaires 1889–1919," *Mouvement Social* 147 (April-June 1989).

79. Gilbert, "Soldiers' Heart," p. 223.

80. In addition to the previously cited works on feminism, see Steven C. Hause, *Hubertine Auclert: The French Suffragette* (New Haven: Yale University Press, 1987), and idem, "More Minerva than Mars: The French Women's Rights Campaign and the First World War," in Higonnet et al., eds., *Behind the Lines*, pp. 99–113.

81. Eleanor Lerner, "Structures familiales, typologie des emplois et soutien aux causes féministes à New York (1915–1917)," in *Stratégies des femmes,* pp. 424–442.

82. Roger-Henri Guerrand and Francis Ronsin, *Le Sexe apprivoisé: Jeanne Humbert et la lutte pour le contrôle des naissances* (Paris: La Découverte, 1990); Angus Maclaren, *Sexuality and Social Order* (New York: Holmes and Meier, 1983).

83. On the "rush to return to private life," see Albert Hirschman, *Shifting Involvements* (Princeton: Princeton University Press, 1982); and M. Capy, quoted in Thébaud, *La Femme,* p. 283.

84. Braybon, *Out of the Cage,* pp. 115–132; Bessel, "Keine allzu grosse Unberuhigung"; Susanne Rouette, "Die Erwerbslosenfürsorge für Frauen in Berlin nach 1918," *IWK* 21 (1985): 295–308, and idem, "'Gleichberechtigung' ohne 'Recht auf Arbeit': Demobilmachung der Frauenarbeit nach dem Ersten Weltkrieg," in Christiane Eifert and Susanne Rouette, eds., *Unter allen Umständen: Frauengeschichte(n) in Berlin* (Berlin: Rotation, 1986).

85. Margaret Ward, *Unmanageable Revolutionaries: Women and Irish Nationalism* (London: Pluto Press, 1983).

86. Paul Géraldy, "Femmes," in his *La Guerre, Madame* (Paris, 1936).

87. My thanks to Evelyne Diebolt, who conducted this interview.

88. Klaus Theweleit, *Männerphantasien,* 2 vols. (Frankfurt: Roter Stern, 1977–78); Reulecke, "Männerbund."

89. Jacques Le Rider, *Modernité viennoise et crises de l'identité* (Paris: Presses Universitaires de France, 1990), and idem, "Karl Kraus, satiriste de la femme en guerre," in Thalmann, ed., *La Tentation nationaliste,* pp. 63–75.

90. Françoise Thébaud, *Quand nos grands-mères donnaient la vie: la maternité en France dans l'entre-deux-guerres* (Lyon: Presses Universitaires de Lyon, 1986); the expression "adventurers of the modern world" is from the pro-family writer Henry Bordeaux, quoting Charles Péguy.

91. Higonnet and Higonnet, "The Double Helix," in Higonnet et al., eds., *Behind the Lines,* pp. 31–47.

92. Thébaud, *La Femme,* p. 291; J.-L. Robert, "Women and Work in France during the First World War," in Wall and Winter, eds., *The Upheaval of War,* pp. 251–266.

93. Sylvie Zerner, "Travail domestique et forme de travail. Ouvrières et employées entre la Première Guerre mondiale et la grande crise," doctoral thesis, University of Paris X-Nanterre, 1985; Downs, "Women in Industry."

94. Yvonne Knibiehler, *Nous les assistantes sociales* (Paris: Aubier-Montaigne, 1981); idem, *Cornettes et blouses blanches;* idem, "Le Docteur Simone Sédan et la protection de l'enfance à Marseille," in Jean Antoine Gili and Ralph Schor, eds., *Hommes. Idées. Journaux. Mélanges en l'honneur de Pierre Guiral* (Paris: Editions Ouvrières, 1990); Sylvie Fayet-Scribe, *Associations féminines et catholicisme: de la charité à l'action sociale* (Paris: Editions Ouvrières, 1990); idem, *La Résidence sociale de Levallois-Perret (1896–1936): la naissance des centres sociaux en France* (Toulouse: Erès, 1990).

95. Susan Pedersen, "Gender, Welfare and Citizenship in Britain during the Great War," *The American Historical Review* 95, 4 (October 1990).

96. Dominique Desanti, *La Femme au temps des années folles* (Paris: Stock-Laurence Pernoud, 1984).

97. Lilian Fadermann, *Surpassing the Love of Men: Romantic Friendship and Love Between Women from the Renaissance to the Present* (London: Junction Books, 1980); Newton and Smith-Rosenberg, "Le Mythe de la lesbienne."

98. Fussell, *The Great War,* p. 79.

99. Reinhard Sieder, "Behind the Lines: Working-Class Family Life in Wartime Vienna," in Wall and Winter, eds., *The Upheaval of War,* pp. 109–138; Paul Pasteur, "Femmes dans le mouvement ouvrier autrichien (1918–1934)," doctoral thesis, University of Rouen, 1986.

100. Michel Launay, *La CFTC, origines et développement, 1919–1940* (Paris: Publications de la Sorbonne, 1987); Christine Bard, "L'Apôtre sociale et l'ange du foyer: les femmes et la CFTC dans l'entre-deux-guerres," to appear in *Le Mouvement Social.*

101. Prost, *Les Anciens Combattants.*

102. Christiane Eifert, "Frauenarbeit im Krieg: Die Berliner 'Heimatfront' 1914 bis 1918," *IWK* 21 (1985).

103. Nancy F. Cott, *The Grounding of Modern Feminism* (New Haven: Yale University Press, 1987). Christine Bard is currently at work on a thesis entitled "Le Mouvement féministe en France, 1914–1939."

104. Guerrand and Ronsin, *Le Sexe apprivoisé;* Nicole Gabriel, "'Des femmes appelèrent mais on les entendit pas': Anita Augspurg et Lida Gustava Heymann," in Thalmann, ed., *La Tentation nationaliste;* Cott, *The Grounding.*

105. Susan Kingsley Kent, "The Politics of Sexual Difference: World War I and the Demise of British Feminism," *Journal of British Studies* 27 (July 1988): 232–253.

106. Anne Cova, "Cécile Brunschvicg (1877–1946) et la protection de la maternité," in Association pour l'Etude de l'Histoire de la Sécurité Sociale, *Actes du 113e congrès national des sociétés savantes* (Paris, 1989), pp. 75–104; Cova is currently at work on a thesis entitled "Droits des femmes et protection de la maternité en France. 1892–1939." See also Gisela Bock's second essay in this volume.

Chapter 2. The Modern Woman, American Style
NANCY F. COTT

1. Fuller documentation for this essay may be found in Nancy F. Cott, *The Grounding of Modern Feminism* (New Haven: Yale University Press, 1987), chap. 5.

2. Heidi I. Hartmann, "Capitalism and Women's Work in the Home, 1900–1940," Ph.D. diss., Yale University, 1974. For the Durham counter-example, see Dolores Janiewski, *Sisterhood Denied: Race, Gender and Class*

in a New South Community (Philadelphia: Temple University Press, 1985), esp. p. 32.

3. See Carl N. Degler, *At Odds: Women and the Family in America from the Revolution to the Present* (New York: Oxford University Press, 1980), pp. 178–248; Richard A. Easterlin, *The American Baby Boom in Historical Perspective* (New York: National Bureau of Economic Research, Occasional Paper #79, 1962), pp. 6–12, 15–21.

4. Alfred Kinsey et al., *Sexual Behavior in the Human Female* (Philadelphia: W. B. Saunders, 1953), pp. 242–245, 298–301, 339, 422–424, 461–462, 529, 553.

5. Robert S. Lynd and Helen Merrell Lynd, *Middletown: A Study in Modern American Culture* (New York: Harcourt, 1929), p. 266; see Linda Gordon, *Woman's Body, Woman's Right* (New York: Grossman, 1976), pp. 186–206; Estelle Freedman and John D'Emilio, *Intimate Matters* (New York: Harper and Row, 1988), pp. 222–274.

6. Christina Simmons, "Companionate Marriage and the Lesbian Threat," *Frontiers* 4 (Fall 1979): 54–59.

7. Vern Bullough and Bonnie Bullough, "Lesbianism in the 1920s and 1930s: A Newfound Study," *Signs* 2 (1977): 895–904; Leila Rupp, "'Imagine My Surprise': Women's Relationships in Historical Perspective," *Frontiers* 5 (Fall 1980): 61–71; Blanche Wiesen Cook, "'Women Alone Stir My Imagination': Lesbianism and the Cultural Tradition," *Signs* 4, 4 (Summer 1978): 718–739.

8. John Modell et al., "The Timing of Marriage in the Transition to Adulthood," in John Demos and Saranne Boocock, eds., *Turning Points: Historical and Sociological Essays on the Family* (Chicago: University of Chicago Press, 1978), p. 12.

9. Barbara Miller Solomon, *In the Company of Educated Women* (New Haven: Yale, 1985), pp. 119–122; Paula Fass, *The Damned and the Beautiful* (New York: Oxford University Press, 1977), pp. 124 and 407–408, n4.

10. Lois Scharf, *To Work and to Wed: Female Employment, Feminism, and the Great Depression* (Westport, Conn.: Greenwood, 1980), pp. 15–16, 41–42.

11. *Smith College Weekly* 10 (December 3, 1919): 2, quoted in Peter Filene, *Him/Her/Self* (New York: New American Library, 1974), p. 128.

12. Cott, *Grounding*, p. 183.

13. Edward A. Purcell, Jr., *The Crisis of Democratic Theory: Scientific Naturalism and the Problem of Value* (Lexington, Ky.: University Press of Kentucky, 1973), pp. 16–23.

14. Bessie Bunzel, "The Woman Goes to College: After Which, Must She Choose Between Marriage and a Career?" *The Century Monthly Magazine* 117 (Nov. 1928): 26–32, quotations from pp. 26 and 31; John C. Burnham, "The New Psychology: From Narcissism to Social Control," in *Change and Continuity in Twentieth-Century America: The 1920s,* John Braeman et al., eds. (Columbus: Ohio State University Press, 1968), pp. 351–398.

15. Jill Morawski, "The Measurement of Masculinity and Femininity:

Engendering Categorical Realities," *Journal of Personality* 53, 2 (June 1985): 196–223. Compare with Rosalind Rosenberg, *Beyond Separate Spheres* (New Haven: Yale University Press, 1982), on earlier generation of women social scientists.

16. Ernest Groves, "The Personality Results of the Wage Employment of Women Outside the Home and Their Social Consequences," *Annals* 143 (May 1929): 339–348.

17. Vera Brittain, "Home-Making Husbands," *Equal Rights* 13 (Jan. 29, 1927): 403.

18. See Hartmann, "Capitalism and Women's Work."

19. Gwendolyn Hughes Berry, "Mothers in Industry," *Annals* 143 (May 1929): 315.

20. See Burnham, "The New Psychology: From Narcissism to Social Control," pp. 360–366, 378–379, 381–384; Fass, *Damned*, pp. 96–101.

21. A. M. McMahon, "An American Courtship: Psychologists and Advertising Theory in the Progressive Era," *American Studies* 13 (Fall 1972): esp. 3–8, 15; Roland Marchand, *Advertising the American Dream* (Berkeley: University of California Press, 1985), pp. 5–7.

22. Chase Going Woodhouse, "The New Profession of Homemaking," *Survey* 57 (Dec. 1926): 339; see also Marchand, *Advertising*, pp. 34, 66–69, 162–163, 342–345; Neil H. Borden, *The Economic Effects of Advertising* (Chicago: Richard D. Irwin, 1942), chap. 26, esp. pp. 744–745, 763–765, 768–797.

23. On advertising volume see Robert Lynd, "The People as Consumers," in *Recent Social Trends* (New York: McGraw-Hill, 1933), vol. 2.

24. Quotation from *Chicago Tribune*, 1930, reported in Marchand, *Advertising*, p. 186; Gwendolyn Wright, *Building the Dream: A Social History of Housing in America* (New York: Pantheon Books, 1981), pp. 208–210.

25. See Lary May, *Screening Out the Past* (New York: Oxford University Press, 1980).

26. Compare with two treatments by Atina Grossman, "The New Woman and the Rationalization of Sexuality in Weimar Germany," in *Powers of Desire: The Politics of Sexuality,* Christine Stansell, ed. (New York: Monthly Review, 1983), pp. 153–171, and "*Girlkultur* or Thoroughly Rationalized Female: A New Woman in Weimar Germany?" in *Women in Culture and Politics: A Century of Change,* Judith Friedlander et al., eds. (Bloomington: Indiana University Press, 1986), pp. 62–80. For an astute and enlightening discussion of the impact of American cinema and European national responses, see Victoria de Grazia, "Mass Culture and Sovereignty: The American Challenge to European Cinemas, 1920–1960," *Journal of Modern History* 61 (March 1989): 53–87, and "'Women's Last-Best Hope'? Americanization and New Models of Modern Womanhood in Interwar Europe," paper revised for the Rockefeller Conference "Women in Dark Times," Bellagio, Italy, August 11–14, 1987. See also her *How Fascism Ruled Women: Italy, 1922–1945* (Berkeley: University of California Press, 1992), chaps. 5 and 7.

Chapter 3. Between the Wars

ANNE-MARIE SOHN

1. See Léon Blum, *Du mariage* (1908).

2. Significantly, two best-selling novels, M. Prévost's *Les Don-Juannes,* which sold 300,000 copies, and Margueritte's *La Garçonne,* both dealt with the same subject and were published around the same time (1921–22).

3. *Le Compagnon* was the title of the third novel in Victor Margueritte's trilogy *La Femme en chemin,* the first volume of which was *La Garçonne.*

4. Bulletin of the Syndicat, Bibliothèque M. Durand, Paris, dossier 396 FEM.

5. Well-described by Michelle Perrot in "L'Éloge de la ménagère dans le discours ouvrier français au XIXe siècle," *Romantisme* 13–14 (1976).

6. *Les Populations du Puy-de-Dôme. Monographies rédigées à l'occasion de l'enquête agricole de 1929* (Clermont-Ferrand, Imprimerie Gale, 1932), p. 110.

7. See F. Zonabend, *La Mémoire longue. Temps et histoire au village* (Paris: Presses Universitaires de France, 1980).

8. C. Amiel, G. Charuty, and C. Fabre-Vassas, *Jours de vigne. Les femmes des pays viticoles racontent le travail* (Atelier du Gué, Terre de l'Aude, 1981), p. 134.

9. Unemployment or illness of the husband made matters worse, according to a survey by the Union Féminine Civique et Sociale.

10. A. Fourcaut, *Femmes à l'usine dans l'entre-deux-guerres* (Paris: Maspero, 1982), pp. 103 and 119.

11. *Le Travail industriel de la mère et le foyer ouvrier* (Paris: UFCS, 1934), p. 252.

12. See J.-P. Burdy, M. Dubesset, M. Zancarini-Fournel, "Rôles, travaux et métiers féminins dans une ville industrielle: Saint-Etienne, 1900–1950," *Mouvement Social* (July-September 1987).

13. M. Spring Rice, *Working Class Wives: Their Health and Conditions* (London: Virago, 1981), pp. 135 and 141.

14. *La Vie quotidienne à Saint-Etienne entre les deux guerres* (Saint-Etienne: Centre d'Études Foréziennes, 1985), p. 7.

15. André Alix, *Un pays de haute montagne: l'Oisans. Etude géographique* (1929; repr. Marseille: J. Laffitte, 1975).

16. Rice, *Working Class Wives,* pp. 135 and 141.

17. Ibid., p. 142.

18. Fourcaut, *Femmes à l'usine,* p. 191.

19. Rosemary Crook, "'Tiddy Women': Women in the Rhondda Between the Wars," *Oral History* 10 (1982).

20. C. Germain and C. de Panafieu, *La Mémoire des femmes. Témoignages de femmes nées avec le siècle* (Paris: Sylvie Messinger, 1982), p. 191.

21. Fourcaut, *Femmes à l'usine,* p. 103.

22. Richard Hoggart, *The Uses of Literacy: Aspects of Working-Class*

Life with Special References to Publications and Entertainment (New York: Oxford University Press, 1957).

23. E. Roberts, *A Woman's Place: An Oral History of Working-Class Women, 1890–1940* (Oxford: Basil Blackwell, 1984), p. 113.

24. Pierre Bourdieu, "Célibat et condition paysanne," *Etudes Rurales* (1962).

25. Hoggart, *The Uses of Literacy,* pp. 92–93.

26. See A.-M. Sohn, "Qualità e difetti. Steretipi et realtà conjugali nelle Francia dell'Ottocento," *Memoria. Il bel matrimonio* 2 (1988).

27. Letter to the minister of justice, October 23, 1917: Archives nationales, BB^{18} 2527$^{(1)}$, dossier 2328.

28. Quoted in Jeffrey Weeks, *Sex, Politics and Society: The Regulation of Sexuality since 1800* (London: Mangman, 1981), p. 189.

29. Except in the early 1920s, when many men just back from the front sued for divorce from wives who had been unfaithful during their absence.

30. Louise Weiss, *Ce que femme veut* (Paris: Gallimard, 1946), p. 14.

31. Anne-Marie Sohn, "Féminisme et syndicalisme. Les institutrices de la Fédération unitaire de l'enseignement de 1919 à 1935," thesis, University of Paris X-Nanterre, 1973, available through Microéditions Hachette, 1974.

Chapter 4. How Mussolini Ruled Italian Women
VICTORIA DE GRAZIA

1. On the concept of "liberal patriarchy" see Linda J. Nicholson, *Gender and History: The Limits of Social Theory in the Age of the Family* (New York: Columbia University Press, 1986); see also Carole Pateman, *The Sexual Contract* (Stanford: Stanford University Press, 1988). For the concept of "social patriarchy" see Harriet Holter, ed., *Patriarchy in a Welfare Society* (Oslo: Universitetforlaget, 1984), also Carole Pateman, *The Patriarchal Welfare State* (Cambridge, Mass.: Harvard Center for European Studies Working Paper Series, 1987).

2. Victoria de Grazia, *How Fascism Ruled Women: Italy, 1922–1945* (Berkeley: University of California Press, 1992). Compare to national approaches as exemplified best by Franca Pieroni Bortolotti, *Femminismo e partiti politici in Italia, 1919–1926* (Rome: Editori Riuniti, 1978); Maria Antonietta Macciocchi, *La donna nera* (Milan: Feltrinelli, 1976); Piero Meldini, *Sposa e madre esemplare* (Rome-Florence: Guaraldi, 1975); Elisabetta Mondello, *La donna nuova* (Rome: Editori Riuniti, 1987).

3. John Maynard Keynes, *The Economic Consequences of the Peace* (1920; rpt. New York: Harper and Row, 1971), pp. 9–26.

4. Gunnar Myrdal, *Population: A Problem for Democracy* (Cambridge, Mass.: Harvard University Press, 1940); as well as Alva Myrdal and Gunnar Myrdal, *Crisis in the Population Question* (Stockholm, Albert Bonniers Forlag, 1935). D. V. Glass's work, *Population Policies and Movements in Europe* (Oxford: Clarendon Press, 1940), draws similarly broad comparisons. For a

brief overview see C. F. McCleary, "Pre-War European Population Policies," *The Milbank Memorial Fund Quarterly* 19, 2 (April 1941): 105–120.

5. Alva Myrdal, *Nation and Family, The Swedish Experiment in Democratic Family and Population Policy* (New York: Harper and Brothers, 1941), p. 398ff.

6. Charles Maier, *Recasting Bourgeois Europe* (Princeton: Princeton University Press, 1975).

7. Eli F. Heckscher, *Mercantilism*, 2 vols., trans. Mendel Shapiro (London: Allen and Unwin, 1935), vol. II, pp. 145ff. and 273ff.

8. Myrdal, *Population: A Problem for Democracy*, p. 20. The best overall account is Ann Sofie Kalvemark's *More Children of Better Quality? Aspects on Swedish Population Policy in the 1930s* (Uppsala: Acta Universitatis Upsaliensia, 1980).

9. Ibid., pp. 80, 190–191.

10. Paolo Ungari, *Storia del diritto di famiglia in Italia, 1796–1942* (Bologna: Il Mulino, 1974), p. 123ff; Maria Vittoria Ballestrero, *Dalla tutela alla parità: La legislazione italiana sul lavoro delle donne* (Bologna: Il Mulino, 1979), pp. 11–56.

11. Annarita Buttafuoco, "La filantropia come politica. Esperienze dell'emancipazionismo italiano nel Novecento," *Ragnatele di rapporti,* Lucia Ferrante, Maura Palazzi, Gianna Pomata, eds. (Turin: Rosenberg & Sellier, 1988), p. 167ff; see also her "Condizione delle donne e movimento di emancipazione femminile," *Storia della società italiana*, pt. 5, vol. XX: *L'Italia di Giolitti* (Milan: Teti, 1981), pp. 154–185. See too Franca Pieroni Bortolotti, *Alle origini del movimento femminile in Italia, 1848–1892* (Turin: Einaudi, 1963); *Socialismo e questione femminile in Italia, 1892–1922* (Milan: Mazzotta, 1974). See also Paola Gaiotti de Biase, *Le origini del movimento cattolico femminile* (Brescia: Morcelliana, 1963) and Cecilia Dau Novelli, *Società, Chiesa e associazionismo femminile* (Rome: Società A.V.E, 1988).

12. Bruno P. S. Wanrooij, *Pudore e licenza: Una storia della questione sessuale in Italia* (Venice: Marsilio Editore, 1990); George Mosse, *Nationalism and Sexuality* (New York: Howard Fertig, 1985).

13. Vilfredo Pareto, "Il mito virtuista" (1914), in *Scritti sociologici,* G. Busino, ed. (Turin: UTET, 1966), esp. pp. 425ff, 484, 602.

14. Cited in Luciano De Maria, ed., *Teoria e invenzione futurista* (Milan: Mondadori, 1983), p. 11.

15. Benito Mussolini, "La donna e il voto," *Opera Omnia*, 44 vols., E. and D. Susmel, eds. (Florence: La Fenice, 1951–1980), vol. XXI, p. 303: "Non divaghiamo a discutere se la donna sia superiore o inferiore; costatiamo che e diversa."

16. Cited in Antonio Spinosa, *I figli di Mussolini* (Milan: Rizzoli, 1983), p. 18.

17. Giovanni Gentile, "La donna e il fanciullo" (1934), cited in Simonetta Uliveri, "La donna nella scuola dall'unità d'Italia a oggi: leggi, pregiudizi, lotte e prospettive," *Nuova DWF* 2 (January-March, 1977): 116ff.

18. For example, Argo (Giuseppe Bottai), "Compiti ella donna," *Critica*

fascista 14 (1933): 267ff; also *Carta della Scuola illustrata nelle singole dichiarazioni da presidi e professori dell'Associazione fascista della Scuola* (Rome: Editore Pinciana, 1939), p. 17.

19. Umberto Notari, *La donna tipo tre* (Milan: Società anonima Notari, 1928).

20. Renzo De Felice, *Mussolini il Duce: Gli anni del consenso, 1929–1935* (Turin: Einaudi, 1974); Victoria de Grazia, *The Culture of Consent: Mass Organization of Leisure in Fascist Italy* (Cambridge and New York: Cambridge University Press, 1981); Luisa Passerini, *Torino operaia e socialista* (Rome and Bari: Laterza, 1984).

21. Claudio Pogliani, "Scienza e stirpe: eugenica in Italia, 1912–1939," *Passato e presente* 5 (1984): 79.

22. Ibid., pp. 80–81.

23. Nicola Pende, "Nuovi orientamenti per la protezione e l'assistenza della madre e del fanciullo," *Medicina Infantile* 7, 8 (August, 1936): 233.

24. Luigi Maccone, *Ricordi di un medico pediatra* (Turin: G. B. Paravia, 1936), p. 62.

25. Passerini, *Torino operaia e fascismo,* pp. 213–219; Denise Detragiache, "Un aspect de la politique demographique de l'Italie fasciste: la repression de l'avortement," *Melanges de l'Ecole Française de Rome* 92, 2 (1980): 691–735.

26. Giorgio Gattei, "Per una storia del comportamento amoroso dei bolognesi: Le nascite dall'unita al fascismo," *Società e storia,* 9 (1980): 627ff. Stefano Somogyi, *La mortalità nei primi cinque anni di età in Italia, 1863–1963* (Palermo: Ed. Ingrana, 1967), p. 42, table 7.

27. In general, Pietro Melograni, ed., *La famiglia italiana dall' Ottocento a oggi* (Rome and Bari: Laterza, 1988). Marzio Barbagli, *Sotto lo stesso tetto; Mutamenti della famiglia in Italia dal XV al XX secolo* (Bologna: Il Mulino, 1984). Vera Zamagni, "Dinamica e problemi della distribuzione commerciale e al minuto tra il 1880 e la II Guerra mondiale," in *Mercati e consumi: Organizzazione e qualificazione del commercio in Italia dal XVII al XX secolo* (Bologna: Edizioni Analisi, 1986), p. 598.

28. INEA, *Monografie di famiglie agricole.* Studi e monografie, no. 14 (Rome: 1929—), in particular, *Mezzadri di Val di Pesa e del Chianti* (1931), esp. pp. 46, 74, 94. On ruralization in general, see Domenico Preti: *La modernizzazione corporativa: 1922–1940* (Milan: Franco Angeli, 1987), pp. 53–100.

29. Cited in Igino Giordani, ed., *Le encicliche sociali dei papi,* 4th ed. (Rome: Editrice Studium, 1956), p. 200.

30. Francesca Bettio, *The Sexual Division of Labor: The Italian Case* (Oxford: Clarendon Press, 1989), p. 117. Chiara Saraceno, "La famiglia operaia sotto il fascismo," *La classe operaia durante il fascismo,* in *Annali Fondazione Giangiacomo Feltrinelli,* 20 (1979–1980); see also her "Percorsi di vita femminile nella classe operaia: tra famiglia e lavoro durante il fascismo," *Memoria* 2 (October 1981): 64–75.

31. Maccone, *Ricordi,* p. 67.

32. Mussolini, "Macchina e donna" (August 31, 1934), in *Opera Omnia,* vol. XXVI, p. 311.

33. Maria Castellani, *Donne italiane di ieri e di oggi* (Florence: Bemporad, 1937), p. 102ff.

34. Denise Detragiache, "Il fascismo femminile da San Sepolcro all'affare Matteotti, 1919–1924," *Storia Contemporanea* 2 (April, 1983): 211–251; Stefania Bartoloni, "Il fascismo femminile e la sua stampa: *La Rassegna femminile italiana* (1925–1930)," *Nuova DWF* 21 (1982): 143–169.

35. Mussolini, "Elogio alle donne d'Italia," in *Opera Omnia,* vol. XXVII, p. 266.

36. Giulia Boni, *Il lavoro sociale delle donne: le grandi organizzazioni in Italia e all'estero (Corso per visitatrici fasciste)* (Pisa: Tipografia Pellegrini, 1936), pp. 4, 9. See also Olga Modigliani, *Lavoro sociale delle donne* (Rome: 1935), p. 22.

37. Archivio Nazionale dello Stato, Segreteria particolare del Duce, Carteggio ordinario, 509.504/3 fascicolo Angiola Moretti, "Speech of May 14, 1940, to newly graduated *visitatrici fasciste* before the Queen-Empress of Italy."

38. Ferdinando Loffredo, *Politica della famiglia* (Milan: Bompiani, 1938), pp. 230–231, 376, 412, 464.

39. Archivio Centrale dello Stato, Presidenza Consiglio dei Ministri, 1937–1939, fascicolo 1/3–1, f.954.4 petition: Rome, October 6, 1938— Duce.

40. *La donna e la famiglia nella legislazione fascista* (Naples: La Toga, 1933).

41. Maria Maggi, "Rassegna letteraria: scrittrici d'Italia," *Almanacco della donna italiana, 1930,* p. 182. For examples, see: Ester Lombardo, *La donna senza cuore* (Milan: Corbaccio, 1929) and Lina Pietravalle, *Le Catene* (Milan: Mondadori, 1930).

42. Annamaria Bruzzone and Rachele Farina, *La resistenza taciuta* (Florence: La Pietra, 1976); Mirella Alloisio and Giuliana Beltrami, *Volontarie della liberta* (Milan: Mazzotta, 1981); Bianca Guidetti Serra, *Campagne: testimonianze di partecipazione politica femminile,* 2 vols. (Turin: Einaudi, 1977).

43. "Female Consciousness and Collective Action: The Case of Barcelona, 1910–1918," *Signs* 7 (Spring 1982): 545–566; Nancy F. Cott, "What's in a Name? The Limits of 'Social Feminism,' or Expanding the Vocabulary of Women's History," *Journal of American History* 76, 3 (December, 1989): 827.

Chapter 5. Nazi Gender Policies and Women's History
GISELA BOCK

1. Comité des Délégations Juives, ed., *Die Lage der Juden in Deutschland 1933* (Paris, 1934; repr. Frankfurt, 1983), p. 468; Marion Kaplan, *The Jewish Feminist Movement in Germany: The Campaigns of the Jüdischer Frauen-*

bund, 1904–1938 (Westport, Conn.: Greenwood Press, 1979), esp. ch. 3 and pp. 114–115.

2. Richard Walther Darré, *Neuadel aus Blut und Boden* (Munich, 1930), pp. 169–171; Alfred Grotjahn, *Geburten-Rückgang und Geburten-Regelung im Lichte der individuellen und sozialen Hygiene* (Berlin, 1914), pp. 144–145; Ann Taylor Allen, "German Radical Feminism and Eugenics, 1900–1918," *German Studies Review* 11 (1989): 31–56, esp. pp. 45–46.

3. Rita R. Thalmann, "Jüdische Frauen nach dem Pogrom von 1938," in Arnold Paucker, ed., *Die Juden im nationalsozialistischen Deutschland/ The Jews in Nazi Germany 1933–1943* (Tübingen: Mohr, 1986), pp. 295–302; Claudia Huerkamp, "Jüdische Akademikerinnen in der Weimarer Republik und im Nationalsozialismus," in *Geschichte und Gesellschaft* 19, 3 (1993); Raul Hilberg, *The Destruction of the European Jews,* 3 vols. (New York: Holmes and Meier, 1985).

4. Wilhelm Frick, *Bevölkerungs- und Rassenpolitik* (Berlin, 1933), pp. 3–8.

5. Robert Jay Lifton, *The Nazi Doctors: Medical Killing and the Psychology of Genocide* (New York: Basic Books, 1986), p. 22; the previous quotes are from Arthur Gütt, Ernst Rüdin, Falk Ruttke, *Gesetz zur Verhütung erbkranken Nachwuchses vom 14. Juli 1933* (Munich, 1934), p. 60.

6. Gisela Bock, *Zwangssterilisation im Nationalsozialismus. Studien zur Rassenpolitik und Frauenpolitik* (Opladen: Westdeutscher Verlag, 1986), pp. 351–362, 453–456; Theresia Seible, "Aber ich wollte vorher noch ein Kind," in *Courage* 6 (May 1981): 21–24; Hilberg, *Destruction,* vol. 3.

7. Gütt, Rüdin, and Ruttke, *Gesetz,* pp. 5, 176.

8. Quoted in Bock, *Zwangssterilisation,* pp. 357, 412.

9. Lothar Gruchmann, "'Blutschutzgesetz' und Justiz," in *Vierteljahrshefte für Zeitgeschichte* 31 (1983): 418–442; the quotes are from various contemporary women's journals, brochures, and textbooks, in Bock, *Zwangssterilisation,* pp. 129–133; cf. Barbara Greven-Aschoff, *Die bürgerliche Frauenbewegung in Deutschland 1894–1933* (Göttingen: Vandenhoeck & Ruprecht, 1981), esp. chs. 2 and 3.

10. Hans-Walter Schmuhl, *Rassenhygiene, Nationalsozialismus, Euthanasie* (Göttingen: Vandenhoeck & Ruprecht, 1987), p. 40.

11. Lifton, *Nazi Doctors,* p. 159, see also pp. 15, 147; Martin Broszat (Hg.), *Kommandant in Auschwitz. Autobiographische Aufzeichnungen des Rudolf Höss* (Munich: DTV, 1963), p. 127; Hilberg, *Destruction,* vol. 1, pp. 332–334.

12. Joan Ringelheim, "Verschleppung, Tod und Überleben: Nationalsozialistische Ghetto-Politik gegen jüdische Frauen und Männer im besetzten Polen," in Theresa Wobbe, ed., *Nach Osten: Verdeckte Spuren nationalsozialistischer Verbrechen* (Frankfurt: Neue Kritik, 1992), pp. 135–160; see also her "Women and the Holocaust," in *Signs* 10 (1985): 741–761; Eugen Kogon et al., eds., *Nationalsozialistische Massentötungen durch Giftgas* (Frankfurt: Fischer Verlag, 1986), pp. 88, 91, 93–97, 105–108, 122, 131, 134, 158, 210–215.

13. Lucie Adelsberger, *Auschwitz. Ein Tatsachenbericht* (Berlin, 1953),

pp. 126–128 (quote); Jercy Ficowski, "Die Vernichtung," in Tilman Zülch, ed., *In Auschwitz vergast, bis heute verfolgt: Zur Situation der Roma (Zigeuner) in Deutschland und Europa* (Reinbek: Rowohlt, 1979), pp. 135–136.

14. Lifton, *Nazi Doctors,* p. 462; cf. pp. 193–196, 199, 231, 312–321, 443.

15. Bradley F. Smith and Agnes F. Peterson, eds., *Heinrich Himmler: Geheimreden 1933–1945 und andere Ansprachen* (Frankfurt, 1974), pp. 201, 169.

16. Eberhard Jäckel, "Die elende Praxis der Untersteller," in *"Historikerstreit". Die Dokumentation der Kontroverse um die Einzigartigkeit der nationalsozialistischen Judenvernichtung* (Munich: Piper, 1987), p. 118. E. Nolte argued that women should not be specifically mentioned here because their role as victims of the race struggle is self-evident (ibid., pp. 229–230).

17. Claudia Koonz, *Mothers in the Fatherland: Women, the Family, and Nazi Politics* (New York: St. Martin's Press, 1987), p. 405. For various types of women's participation in race policy see Reimar Gilsenbach, "Wie Lolitschai zur Doktorwürde kam," in Wolfgang Ayass et al., *Feinderklärung und Prävention* (Berlin: Rotbuch Verlag, 1988), pp. 101–134; Henry Friedlander, in Esther Katz and Joan M. Ringelheim, eds., *Women Surviving the Holocaust* (New York: Institute for Research in History, 1983), pp. 115–116; Bock, *Zwangssterilisation,* p. 208; Gudrun Schwarz, "Verdrängte Täterinnen: Frauen im Apparat der SS (1939–1945)," in Wobbe, ed., *Nach Osten,* pp. 197–227.

18. Reinhard Kühnl, "Der deutsche Faschismus in der neueren Forschung," in *Neue Politische Literatur* 28 (1983): 71. See Koonz, *Mothers,* esp. chs. 1 and 11.

19. Koonz, *Mothers,* pp. 149–150. For the figures that follow see Rüdiger Hachtmann, "Industriearbeiterinnen in der deutschen Kriegswirtschaft, 1936–1945," in *Geschichte und Gesellschaft* 19, 3 (1993); Ulrich Herbert, *Fremdarbeiter* (Bonn: Dietz, 1985); Clifford Kirkpatrick, *Woman in Nazi Germany* (London: Jarrolds, 1939), ch. 7; Ingrid Schupetta, *Frauen- und Ausländererwerbstätigkeit in Deutschland von 1939 bis 1945* (Köln: Pahl-Rugenstein, 1983), pp. 63ff; Dörte Winkler, *Frauenarbeit im "Dritten Reich"* (Hamburg: Hoffmann and Campe, 1977), esp. chs. 2 and 3, p. 198; Stefan Bajohr, *Die Hälfte der Fabrik* (Marburg: Verlag Arbeiterpolitik, 1979), ch. 2.

20. Huerkamp, "Jüdische Akademikerinnen"; Jacques Pauwels, *Women, Nazis, and Universities: Female University Students in the Third Reich, 1933–1945* (Westport, Conn.: Greenwood Press, 1984); Jill McIntyre, "Women and the Professions in Germany, 1930–40," in Anthony Nicholls and Erich Matthias, eds., *German Democracy and the Triumph of Hitler* (London, 1971).

21. Leila J. Rupp, "'I Don't Call That Volksgemeinschaft': Women, Class and War in Nazi Germany," in Carol R. Berkin and Clara M. Lovett, eds., *Women, War, and Revolution* (New York, 1980), pp. 37–53; Winkler, *Frauenarbeit,* pp. 110–114.

22. Helen L. Boak, "'Our Last Hope': Women's Votes for Hitler—A

Reappraisal," in *German Studies Review* 12 (1989): 289–310; Jill Stephenson, *The Nazi Organisation of Women* (London: Croom Helm, 1981), p. 72; Jürgen Falter et al., *Wahlen und Abstimmungen in der Weimarer Republik* (Munich: Beck, 1986), pp. 81–85; Thomas Childers, *The Nazi Voter: The Social Foundations of Fascist Germany, 1919–1933* (Chapel Hill, 1983), pp. 239–243.

23. Alice Kessler-Harris, "Gender Ideology in Historical Reconstruction: A Case Study from the 1930s," in *Gender and History* 1 (1989): 31–49; Leila J. Rupp, *Mobilizing Women for War: German and American Propaganda, 1939–1945* (Princeton: Princeton University Press, 1978), pp. 39–40.

24. Rupp, *Mobilizing Women*, esp. pp. 14, 42–48, 51, 71, 126–127, 132–136.

25. Quoted in Bock, *Zwangssterilisation*, pp. 174–175.

26. Herbert, *Fremdarbeiter*, chs. VI–IX; see also his "Arbeiterschaft im 'Dritten Reich,'" in *Geschichte und Gesellschaft* 15 (1989): 320–360; Bock, *Zwangssterilisation*, pp. 440–451.

27. The Ministry of Propaganda and Frick quoted in Bock, ibid., pp. 120, 153; cf. Rupp, *Mobilizing Women*, pp. 32–33. The figures for abortion convictions are from *Statistisches Jahrbuch für das Deutsche Reich* 45–59 (1926–1942), see Bock, *Zwangssterilisation*, pp. 160–163, 388. According to contemporary Austrian scholars, several death penalties had been carried out in annexed Austria.

28. Gisela Bock, "'Keine Arbeitskräfte in diesem Sinne': Prostituierte im Nazi-Staat," in Pieke Biermann, ed., *Wir sind Frauen wie andere auch* (Reinbek: Rowohlt, 1980), pp. 70–106.

29. Cf. David Victor Glass, *Population Policies and Movements in Europe* (London, 1940; repr. London, 1967); Gisela Bock and Pat Thane, eds., *Maternity and Gender Policies: Women and the Rise of the European Welfare States, 1880s–1950s* (London: Routledge, 1991).

30. Cf. Bock, *Zwangssterilisation*, pp. 169–77 (quote on p. 170).

31. Gabriele Czarnowsky, *Das kontrollierte Paar* (Berlin, 1991).

32. Stephenson, *Nazi Organisation*, pp. 156–172; Hilgenfeldt quoted in Bock, *Zwangssterilisation*, p. 174.

33. Georg Lilienthal, *Der "Lebensborn e. V."* (Stuttgart: Gustav Fischer Verlag, 1985).

34. Walter Gross, "Unsere Arbeit gilt der deutschen Familie," in *Nationalsozialistische Monatshefte* 9 (1939): 103–104.

35. These and the following demographic figures are in Bock, *Zwangssterilisation*, pp. 143–144, 151–152, 156–157, 168.

36. Wolfgang Knorr, "Praktische Rassenpolitik," in *Volk und Rasse* 13 (1938): 69–73; Friedrich Burgdörfer, *Geburtenschwund* (Heidelberg, 1942), pp. 157, 184.

37. Dirk Blasius, *Ehescheidung in Deutschland 1794–1945* (Göttingen: Vandenhoeck & Ruprecht, 1987), ch. 7; Hans-Jochen Gamm, *Der Flüsterwitz im Dritten Reich* (Munich: DTV, 1979), p. 23; Rupp, *Mobilizing Women*, pp. 38–39.

38. Stephenson, *Nazi Organisation,* pp. 139–157; Michael H. Kater, "Frauen in der NS-Bewegung," in *Vierteljahrshefte für Zeitgeschichte* 31 (1983): 202–239.

39. Stephenson, *Nazi Organisation,* pp. 18, 154–155, 178–181, 206–207; Gertrud Scholtz-Klink, *Rede an die deutsche Frau* (1934), repr. in her *Die Frau im Dritten Reich. Eine Dokumentation* (Tübingen: Grabert, 1978), p. 498.

40. Irmgard Reichenau, ed., *Deutsche Frauen an Adolf Hitler* (Leipzig, 1933), pp. 7, 15, 37; Charlotte Heinrichs, "Besoldung der Mutterschaftsleistung," in *Die Frau* 41 (1934): 343–348.

41. Scholtz-Klink, *Die Frau im Dritten Reich,* pp. 131, 364, 379, 402, 486–497, 500–505, 526.

42. Stephenson, *Nazi Organisation,* pp. 17–18, 168, 170–171; Michael Phayer, *Protestant and Catholic Women in Nazi Germany* (Detroit: Wayne State University Press, 1990).

43. Stephenson, *Nazi Organisation,* esp. pp. 154, 164–165, 170–171; Scholtz-Klink, *Die Frau im Dritten Reich,* pp. 157, 173, 177, 180.

44. Ibid., pp. 69, 93, 95, 107, 156, 159, 211; Stephenson, *Nazi Organisation,* p. 152.

45. Ibid., pp. 154–161; Rupp, *Mobilizing Women,* pp. 36–37; Scholtz-Klink, *Die Frau im Dritten Reich,* pp. 500–501.

46. Stephenson, *Nazi Organisation,* pp. 83–84, 117, 132, 140–147, 157–162; Scholtz-Klink, *Die Frau,* p. 76.

47. Rupp, *Mobilizing Women,* pp. 124–125; Herbert, *Fremdarbeiter,* pp. 79–81, 122–124; Bock, *Zwangssterilisation,* pp. 438–440.

48. Gitte Schefer, "Wo Unterdrückung ist, da ist auch Widerstand," in Frauengruppe Faschismusforschung, ed., *Mutterkreuz und Arbeitsbuch. Zur Geschichte der Frauen in der Weimarer Republik und im Nationalsozialismus* (Frankfurt: Fischer, 1981), pp. 273–291.

Chapter 6. The Women of Spain
DANIÈLE BUSSY GENEVOIS

1. Margarita Nelken, *La condición social de la mujer en España* (Madrid: Minerva, 1919; repr. Madrid: CVS. Col. Ateneo, 1975).

2. *Gaceta de Madrid,* April 15, 1931.

3. On the ideas of Hildegart (Carmen Rodriguez Carballeira), see Mary Nash, *Mujer y movimiento obrero en España, 1931–1939* (Barcelona: Fontamara, 1981), pp. 165ff.

4. *El Socialista,* December 29, 1931, p. 1: "Interesantes declaraciones de nuestro camarada Largo Caballero."

5. Inés Alberdi, *Historia y sociología del divorcio en España* (Madrid: Center of Sociological Research, Col. Monografías, 9, 1979).

6. Felipe Ximénez de Sandoval, *José Antonio* (Biografía apasionada) (Madrid, 1941; repr. 1972), p. 112.

7. Manuel Tuñón de Lara, *Tres claves de la Segunda República* (Madrid: Alianza Universidad, 1985), pp. 234ff.

8. José María Pemán, "Votos e ideas," *Ellas* 1 (29 May 1932).

9. For example, Javier Tusell Gómez, *La segunda República en Madrid: elecciones y partidos políticos* (Madrid: Tecnos, Col. Ciencias políticas, 1970), pp. 107ff.

10. See *Cultura integral y femenina* (1933–1936).

11. Their newspaper was *Mundo femenino* (1921–1936): manifesto of January 1, 1934.

12. Ibid., no. 102, 1935, p. 2. Halma Angélico, "¡Mujeres en pie!"

13. José Antonio Primo de Rivera, *Textos de Doctrina política*, National Delegation of the Feminine Section of the Movement, 1971, p. 926.

14. Mary Nash, "El estudio del control de natalidad en España: ejemplos de metodologías diferentes," in *La Mujer en la Historia de España (siglos XVI–XX)* (Madrid: Autonomous University of Madrid, 1984), pp. 241–262.

15. For example, Mari-Carmen García Nieto, "Unión de Muchachas, un modelo metodológico," ibid., pp. 313–331.

16. *Las mujeres y la guerra civil española,* vol. III, Jornadas de Estudios monográficos, Salamanca, October 1989, Institute of Women, Ministry of Culture, Directorate of Governmental Archives (Madrid, 1991).

17. The expression "national-Catholic" is used by Max Gallo in *Histoire de l'Espagne franquiste* (Verviers: Marabout Université, 1969).

18. Speech by Pilar Primo de Rivera at Medina del Campo, May 30, 1939, quoted in María Teresa Gallego Méndez, *Mujer, Falange, y franquismo* (Madrid: Taurus, 1983), p. 89.

19. Law on the Spanish university, July 29, 1943.

20. *Habla la mujer,* poll conducted under the direction of M. Campo Alange (Madrid, Edicusa, 1966).

21. Amparo Moreno, *El movimiento feminista en España* (Barcelona: Anagrama, 1977).

Chapter 7. French Women under Vichy
HÉLÈNE ECK

1. Jean-Pierre Azéma, "Eléments pour une historiographie de la France de Vichy," in Institut d'Histoire du Temps Présent (hereafter, IHTP), *Le Régime de Vichy et les Français,* colloquium, Paris, June 11–13, 1990 (Paris: Fayard, 1992).

2. Henry Rousso, "L'impact du régime sur la société: ses dimensions et ses limites," in IHTP, *Le Régime de Vichy et les Français.* The IHTP is currently conducting two investigations, one on the "Time of Restrictions (1939–1949)," and the other on "Workers in France during World War II."

3. Works that I have found especially useful are cited here in the notes. I wish to thank Dominique Veillon of the IHTP for her consistent and gracious assistance.

4. Miranda Pollard, "Women and the National Revolution," in Harry

Roderick Kedward and Roger Austin, eds., *Vichy France and the Resistance: Culture and Ideology* (London: Croom Helm, 1985), pp. 36–47; idem, "Vichy et les Françaises: la politique du travail," in IHTP, *Le Régime de Vichy et les Français;* and idem, "Vichy and the Politics of Gender (1940–1944)," thesis, Department of Modern History, Trinity College, Dublin, 1990, which I was unable to consult but which is to be published shortly.

5. Aline Coutrot, "La Politique familiale," in René Rémond and Janine Bourdin, eds., *Le Gouvernement de Vichy (1940–1942)* (Paris: Presses de la Fondation Nationale des Sciences Politiques, 1972), pp. 245–265; and the works of Miranda Pollard cited in note 4 above.

6. Quoted by Guy Thuillier, *Les Femmes dans l'administration depuis 1900* (Paris: Presses Universitaires de France, 1988), pp. 77–78.

7. Michèle Bordeaux, "Femmes hors d'Etat français (1940–1944)," in Rita Thalmann, ed., *Femmes et fascismes* (Paris: Edition Tierce, 1987), p. 150.

8. See the general works in the bibliography on the history of private life and the family.

9. Marie-Geneviève Chevignard and Nicole Faure, "Système de valeurs et de références dans la presse féminine," in René Remond and Janine Bourdin, eds., *La France et les Français en 1938–1939* (Paris: Presses de la Fondation Nationale des Sciences Politiques, 1978), pp. 43–57.

10. Françoise Thébaud, *Quand nos grand-mères donnaient la vie. La maternité en France dans l'entre-deux-guerres* (Lyon: Presses Universitaires de Lyon, 1986).

11. Albrecht quote in Annie Fourcaut, *Femmes à l'usine dans l'entre-deux-guerres* (Paris: Maspero, 1982), p. 239; on the Jeunesse Agricole Catholique, see Martyne Perrot, "La Jaciste: une figure emblématique," in Rose-Marie Lagrave, ed., *Celles de la terre: Agricultrice, l'invention politique d'un métier* (Paris: Editions de l'Ecole des Hautes Etudes en Sciences Sociales, 1987), pp. 33–50.

12. Sylvie Fayet-Scribe, *Associations féminines et catholicisme; de la charité à l'action sociale, XIX–XXe siècles* (Paris: Editions Ouvrières, 1990), p. 111; Yvonne Knibiehler et al., *De la pucelle à la minette: Les jeunes filles de l'âge classique à nos jours* (Paris: Temps Actuels, 1983), pp. 224–234.

13. Dominique Veillon, *La Mode sous l'Occupation, débrouillardise et coquetterie dans la France en guerre (1939–1945)* (Paris: Payot, 1990), esp. chap. 8.

14. *Nouvelle jeunesse, bulletin de formation et d'information des cadres féminins de la jeunesse française,* no. 1, March 1941. Figures cited in Vincent Troger, *Les Centres de formation professionnelle (1940–1945), naissance des lycées professionnels* (Syndicat National des Personnels de Direction des Lycées Professionels: Imprimerie Colombes, 1987), pp. 41, 49.

15. Association des parents d'élèves de l'enseignement livre (APEL), *L'Education des filles. Quelques principes directeurs. Esquisse d'un plan général d'études* (Limoges, 1941).

16. "Les Mouvements familiaux populaires et ruraux; naissance, développement, mutations (1939–1955)," *Cahiers du GRMF* (Groupement pour

la Recherche sur les Mouvements Familiaux) 1 (1983), mimeographed; "L'Action familiale ouvrière et la politique de Vichy," *Cahiers du GRMF* 3 (1985); Sarah Fishman, "The Wives of French Prisoners of War (1940–1945)," thesis, Harvard University, Cambridge, Mass., 1987.

17. Testimony of Magdeleine Lescheira in "Les mouvements familiaux populaires et ruraux," p. 98; Yvonne Knibiehler, *Nous, les assistantes sociales. Naissance d'une profession* (Paris: Aubier-Montaigne, 1980), esp. chap. 5; Robert Vandenbussche, "Un mouvement familial: La Ligue ouvrière chrétienne sous l'Occupation," and "Eglises et chrétiens dans le Nord-Pas-de-Calais pendant la Seconde Guerre mondiale," *Revue du Nord,* 60, 238 (July-September 1978): 663–673.

18. Michèle Cointet, "Le Conseil national de Vichy. Vie politique et réforme de l'Etat en régime autoritaire (1940–1944)," doctoral thesis, University of Paris X-Nanterre, 1984, pp. 374–379.

19. Fishman, "The Wives of French Prisoners of War," part 2; testimony quoted by Yves Durand, *La Captivité. Histoire des prisonniers de guerre français 1939–1945* (Paris: Fédération Nationale des Combattants Prisonniers de Guerre, 1981), p. 228.

20. "Le Journal de Laure," in Jacqueline Deroy, ed., *Celles qui attendaient témoignent aujourd'hui* (Paris: Association Nationale pour les Rassemblements et Pèlerinages des Anciens Prisonniers de Guerre, 1985), pp. 49–61.

21. Christophe Lewin, "Le Retour des prisonniers de guerre français 1945," *Guerres mondiales et conflits contemporains* 147 (July 1987): 49–79.

22. Brigitte Friang, *Regarde-toi qui meurs (1943–1945)* (Paris: Plon, 1989), p. 24.

23. Wilfred D. Halls, *Les Jeunes et la politique de Vichy* (Paris: Syros, 1988), p. 377, states that Boegner's trip followed passage of the law of August 1943. In his deposition prior to Pétain's trial, Boegner claimed he made the trip in the spring of 1943; see *Le Procès du Maréchal Pétain, compte rendu sténographique* (Paris: Albin Michel, 1945), vol. 1, p. 369.

24. Sauckel's report to Hitler, January 25, 1944: *Procès des grands criminels de guerre devant le Tribunal militaire international de Nuremberg* (Nuremberg, 1947), vol. 26, p. 160.

25. Figure cited in *Commission consultative des dommages et des réparations. Dommages subis par la France et l'Union française du fait de la guerre et de l'Occupation ennemie (1939–1945),* vol. 9, monograph DP 1: "Exploitation de la main-d'oeuvre française par l'Allemagne," appendix II (Paris: Imprimerie Nationale, 1948).

26. Jean Fourastié, "La Population active française pendant la Seconde Guerre mondiale," *Aspects de l'économie française:* spec. no. of *Revue d'Histoire de la Deuxième Guerre Mondiale* 57 (January 1965): 5–18; corrections by Jean-Jacques Carré, Paul Dubois, Edmond Malinvaud, in *La Croissance française. Un essai d'analyse économique causale de l'après-guerre* (Paris: Editions du Seuil, 1972), pp. 69–76.

27. Sylvie Zerner, "De la couture aux presses: l'emploi féminin entre les deux guerres," *Métiers de femmes,* special issue edited by Michelle Perrot of *Le Mouvement Social* 140 (July-September 1987): 9–27; Jean-Paul Scot, "La Crise sociale des années 1930 en France. Tendances et contre-tendances dans les rapports sociaux," *Le Mouvement Social* 142 (January-March 1988): 75–101.

28. For example, the employment figures cited in *Commission consultative* (note 25), corrected by Jean-Marie d'Hoop, "La Main-d'Oeuvre française au service de l'Allemagne," *Revue d'Histoire de la Deuxième Guerre Mondiale* 1 (January 1971): 73–88, fail to note whether or not female workers were included. More detailed studies, collected in the proceedings of the colloquium on "Les Entreprises françaises pendant la Deuxième Guerre mondiale," Centre International d'Etudes Pédagogiques, Sèvres, November 25–26, 1986 (unpublished manuscript in IHTP library), reveal the diversity of regional situations but do not deal explicitly with the question of female employment.

29. Alfred Sauvy, *La Vie économique des Français de 1939 à 1945* (Paris: Flammarion, 1978), p. 156.

30. Hoop, "La Main-d'Oeuvre française au service de l'Allemagne," p. 76.

31. Examples from Monique Luirard, *La Région stéphanoise dans la guerre et dans la paix (1936–1951)* (Centre d'Etudes Foréziennes, 1980); Catherine Omnès, "Les Trajectoires professionnelles des ouvrières parisiennes au XXe siècle," unpublished research document, Délégation à la Condition Féminine (1988), kindly communicated by the author; J. P. Beauquier, "L'Activité économique dans la région marseillaise," *Revue d'Histoire de la Deuxième Guerre Mondiale* 95 (July 1974): 25–52; Veillon, *La Mode sous l'Occupation;* Michelle Zancarini-Fournel, "La Famille Casino. Saint-Etienne 1920–1960," in Yves Lequin and Sylvie Vandecasteele, eds., *L'Usine et le bureau. Itinéraires sociaux et professionnels dans l'entreprise, XIXe et XXe siècles* (Lyon: Presses Universitaires de Lyon, 1990), pp. 53–73.

32. Figures quoted in Pierre Delvincourt, "Problèmes relatifs à l'emploi dans les PTT pendant la Deuxième Guerre mondiale," *Aspects de l'économie française:* spec. no. of *Revue d'Histoire de la Deuxième Guerre Mondiale* 57 (January 1965): 41–52; Paul Durand, "La Politique de l'emploi à la SNCF pendant la Deuxième Guerre mondiale," ibid., pp. 19–40.

33. Estimates in Jean Daric, *L'Activité professionnelle des femmes en France. Etude statistique, évolution, comparaisons internationales,* Institut National d'Etudes Démographiques (INED), *Travaux et Documents,* no. 5 (Paris: Presses Universitaires de France, 1947), p. 85.

34. For example, on the work of factory committees in the Loire, see Monique Luirard, "Les Ouvriers de la Loire et la Charte du Travail," *Revue d'Histoire de la Deuxième Guerre Mondiale* 102 (April 1976): 57–82.

35. Pierre Laborie, *L'Opinion française sous Vichy* (Paris: Editions du Seuil, 1990), p. 237.

36. Texts of Radio Free France broadcasts are collected in Jean-Louis

Crémieux-Brilhac, ed., *Les Voix de la liberté (1940–1944)*, 5 vols. (Paris: La Documentation Française, 1975).

37. Laborie, *L'Opinion*, p. 333.

38. See the contributions by Rolande Trempé and Pierre Laborie to the proceedings of the colloquium held by the Comité d'Histoire de la Poste et des Télécommunications and IHTP, *L'Oeil et l'Oreille de la Résistance. Action et rôle des agents des PTT dans la clandestinité au cours de la Deuxième Guerre mondiale*, Paris, Nov. 21, 22, and 23, 1984 (Toulouse: Edition ERES, 1986), pp. 460–461.

39. François Bédarida, *Le Nazisme et le Génocide, histoire et enjeux* (Paris: Nathan, 1989), p. 33.

40. Madeleine Barot, "La Cimade et les camps d'internement de la zone sud 1940–1944," in Xavier de Montclos et al., eds., *Eglises et chrétiens dans la Deuxième Guerre mondiale (La France)*, proceedings of colloquium held in Lyon, 1978 (Lyon: Presses Universitaires de Lyon, 1982), pp. 293–303; Monique Lewi, "Le destin des Juifs et la solidarité chrétienne à Roanne entre 1940 et 1944," in *Eglises et chrétiens dans la Deuxième Guerre mondiale (La Région Rhône-Alpes)*, proceedings of colloquium held in Grenoble, 1976 (Lyon: Presses Universitaires de Lyon, 1978), p. 191.

41. Testimony quoted by Marie-Louise Coudert, with the help of Paul Hélène, *Elles, la Résistance* (Paris: Messidor-Temps Actuels, 1985), pp. 59–60.

42. Harry Roderick Kedward, *Naissance de la Résistance dans la France de Vichy. Idées et motivations 1940–1942* (Seyssel: Champ Vallon, 1989).

43. Annette Kahn, *Robert et Jeanne. A Lyon sous l'Occupation* (Paris: Payot, 1990).

44. Olivier Wiewiorka, "La Génération de la Résistance," *Vingtième siècle, Revue d'Histoire* 22 (April-June 1989): 111–116, quote p. 115.

45. Dominique Veillon, "Elles étaient dans la Résistance," *Repères, Bulletin de l'AFI* (Agence Femmes Information) 59 (May 30–June 5, 1983): 9–12.

46. Testimony quoted by Guylaine Guidez, *Femmes dans la guerre (1939–1945)* (Paris: Perrin, 1989), p. 200; on intelligence collected by "Amniatrix," see Marie-Madeleine Fourcade, *L'Arche de Noé, réseau Alliance (1940–1945)* (Paris: Plon, 1989), pp. 406–407.

47. Friang, *Regarde-toi qui meurs*, pp. 47–48.

48. Paula Schwartz, "Partisanes and Gender Politics in Vichy France," *French Historical Studies* 16, 1 (Spring 1989): 126–151; testimony of Jeanne Bohec in *Les Femmes dans la Résistance*, proceedings of colloquium organized by the Union des Femmes Françaises at the Sorbonne, Paris, Nov. 22–23, 1975 (Paris: Editions du Rocher, 1977), p. 38.

49. Maurice Schumann, broadcast "Honneur et Patrie," December 16, 1943, *Les Voix de la liberté*, vol. 4, pp. 131–132; broadcast of March 24, 1944, ibid., p. 219.

50. Quoted by Thuillier, *Les Femmes dans l'administration depuis 1900*, pp. 80–81; on the ambiguities of egalitarian discourse, see Marie-France

Brive, "L'Image des femmes à la Libération," *La Libération dans le Midi de la France,* Travaux de l'Université de Toulouse-Le Mirail, ser. A, vol. 35 (Toulouse, 1986), pp. 387–402.

51. Mattei Dogan and Jacques Narbonne, *Les Françaises face à la politique. Comportement politique et condition sociale. Cahiers de la FNSP,* no. 72 (Paris: Armand Colin, 1955).

52. Jean Goueffon, "La Cour de justice d'Orléans 1944–1945," *Revue d'Histoire de la Deuxième Guerre Mondiale et des Conflits Contemporains* 130 (April 1983): 51–64.

53. Marcel Baudot, "L'Épuration, bilan chiffré," *Bulletin de l'IHTP* 25 (September 1986): 37–52 (results covering 28 *départements*).

54. Testimony of Marinette Dambuyant in Amicale de Ravensbrück et Association des Déportées et internées de la Résistance, *Les Françaises à Ravensbrück* (Paris: Gallimard, 1987), p. 288.

55. See Anise Postel-Vinay, "Les Exterminations par gaz à Ravensbrück," in Germaine Tillion, *Ravensbrück* (Paris: Editions du Seuil, 1988), pp. 305–330.

56. *Les Françaises à Ravensbrück,* p. 293.

57. Micheline Maurel, *Un camp très ordinaire* (Paris: Editions de Minuit, 1985), p. 185.

58. *Les Françaises à Ravensbrück,* p. 305.

59. Tillion, *Ravensbrück,* p. 104.

Chapter 8. The Soviet Model

Françoise Navailh

1. André Pierre, *Les Femmes en Union soviétique* (Paris: SPES, 1960), p. 15.

2. Gail Warshofsky Lapidus, *Women in Soviet Society: Equality, Development, and Social Change* (Berkeley: University of California Press, 1978), p. 37.

3. Nicolas Werth, *La Vie quotidienne des paysans russes de la Révolution à la collectivisation (1917–1939)* (Paris: Hachette, 1984).

4. Lapidus, *Women,* p. 164.

5. Ivan Kurganov, *Semia v SSSR 1917–1967* (New York: Possev-Verlag, 1967).

6. Friedrich Engels, *The Origin of the Family, Private Property, and the State* (New York: International Publishers, 1942).

7. Richard Stites, *The Women's Liberation Movement in Russia: Feminism, Nihilism and Bolshevism. 1860–1930* (Princeton: Princeton University Press, 1978), pp. 260–261.

8. "Les Bases sociales de la question féminine," in Judith Stora-Sandor, ed., *Marxisme et révolution sexuelle* (Paris: Maspero, 1973), pp. 52–96.

9. "La Nouvelle Morale et la classe ouvrière," in ibid., pp. 156–182.

10. Ibid., pp. 100–134.

NOTES TO PAGES 223–232

627

11. "Place à Eros ailé," in Stora-Sandor, ed., *Marxisme et révolution sexuelle,* pp. 183–205.

12. "Révolution dans la vie quotidienne" (1921), in ibid., p. 216.

13. Ibid., p. 223.

14. "La Famille et l'Etat communiste," in ibid., p. 212.

15. "La Nouvelle Morale et la classe ouvrière," in ibid., pp. 171–172.

16. Nicolas Valentinov, *Mes rencontres avec Lénine* (Paris: Plon, 1964), p. 110.

17. Jean Freville, *La Femme et le Communisme. Anthologie de textes* (Paris: Editions Sociales, 1951), pp. 220–222.

18. Pierre, *Les Femmes,* p. 87.

19. Quoted by Wladimir Berelowitch, "Modèles familiaux dans la Russie des années 20," in *L'Evolution des modèles familiaux. Cultures et sociétés de l'Est,* no. 9 (Paris: IMSECO, 1988), p. 35.

20. Yves Trotignon, *Naissance et croissance de l'URSS* (Paris: Bordas, 1970), pp. 64–86.

21. Lapidus, *Women,* p. 165.

22. Ibid., p. 204.

23. Pierre, *Les Femmes,* pp. 16–17.

24. Nicolas Werth, "L'URSS: de l'amour libre à l'ordre moral," in *L'Histoire* 72 (November 1974): 76.

25. Trotignon, *Naissance et croissance de l'URSS,* p. 82.

26. Vincent Monteil, *Les Musulmans soviétiques* (Paris: Editions du Seuil, 1982), pp. 125–135.

27. Lapidus, *Women,* p. 142.

28. 1987 data from *Zhenshchiny v SSSR-1989* (Moscow: Financy i statistika, 1989), pp. 10 and 16.

29. Lynne Viola, "Babi Bunty and Peasant Women's Protest during Collectivization," *The Russian Review* 45, 1 (1986): 23–42.

30. Ivan Kourganov, "La Catastrophe démographique," *Est-Ouest* 598 (July 16, 1977): 18.

31. Basile Kerblay, *La Société soviétique contemporaine* (Paris: Armand Colin, 1977), p. 174.

32. André Gide, *Retour de l'URSS* (Paris: Gallimard, 1978), p. 51.

33. Osip Mandelstam, *Tristia et autres poèmes* (Paris: Gallimard, 1975), p. 228.

34. Werth, "L'URSS: de l'amour libre à l'ordre moral," p. 77.

35. Moshe Lewin, *La Formation du système soviétique* (Paris: Gallimard, 1987), p. 359.

36. Ivan Kurganov, *Zhenshchina i kommunizm* (Frankfurt: Possev-Verlag, 1968), p. 188.

37. Pierre, *Les Femmes,* p. 26.

38. Ibid., pp. 30–31.

39. Robert Conquest, *The Great Terror: Stalin's Purge of the Thirties* (New York: Macmillan, 1968).

40. Kurganov, *Zhenshchina,* pp. 86–87.

41. Michel Heller, *La Machine et les rouages* (Paris: Calmann-Lévy, 1985), p. 218.

42. Trotignon, *Naissance et croissance,* p. 225.

43. Fedor Panferov, "Bruski," quoted in Xenia Gasiorowska, *Women in Soviet Fiction* (Madison: University of Wisconsin Press, 1968), p. 53.

44. Louise E. Luke, "Marxian Woman: Soviet Variants," in Ernest J. Simmons, ed., *Through the Glass of Soviet Literature* (New York: Columbia University Press, 1967), pp. 27–109.

45. Basile Kerblay, "La Civilisations paysanne russe 1861–1964," course notes, University of Paris IV, 1972–1973.

46. Lapidus, *Women,* p. 179.

47. Ibid., p. 169.

48. *Malaya Sovetskaya Entsiklopediya* (Moscow, 1960), vol. 8, p. 915.

49. *Les Femmes en URSS—Chiffres et faits* (Moscow: Novosti, 1985), p. 11, and *Zhenshchiny v SSSR-1989,* p. 24.

50. *Zhenshchiny v SSSR-1989,* p. 15.

51. Ibid., p. 30.

52. Lapidus, *Women,* p. 182.

53. Kurganov, *Zhenshchina,* pp. 44–45.

54. Basile Kerblay and Marie Lavigne, *Les Soviétiques des années 80* (Paris: Armand Colin, 1985), p. 132.

55. *Zhenshchiny v SSSR-1989,* p. 7.

56. *Les Femmes en URSS—Chiffres et faits,* p. 19; Lapidus, *Women,* p. 210.

57. Lapidus, *Women,* p. 204; *Zhenshchiny v SSSR-1989,* p. 13.

58. Lapidus, *Women,* p. 219.

59. *Zhenshchiny v SSSR-1989,* p. 13; "Actualités soviétiques," *Bulletin de l'APN* 9 (7 February 1990).

60. *L'Humanité,* May 7, 1956.

61. J. Vermeersch to Dominique Desanti, quoted in Renée Rousseau, *Les Femmes rouges* (Paris: Albin Michel, 1983), p. 242.

62. In central Asia despair drove some women to self-immolation: see *Pravda,* April 21, 1988.

Chapter 9. *Philosophical Differences*
FRANÇOISE COLLIN

1. Georg Simmel, "La Femme," in *La Philosophie de la modernité* (Paris: Payot, 1989), p. 70. For an analysis of Simmel on sexual difference, see *Georg Simmel,* spec. no. of *Cahiers du Grif* 40 (Paris: Tierce, 1989).

2. José Ortega y Gasset, *El Hombre y la gente,* in *Obras Completas,* 14 vols. (Madrid: Revista de Occidente, 1962–), vol. 7, chap. 6: "Más sobre los otros y yo. Breve excursión hacia ella."

3. See Alain Guy, "La Femme selon Ortega y Gasset," in *La Femme dans la pensée espagnole* (Paris: Editions du Centre National de Recherche Scientifique, 1984).

4. Max Scheler, *Nature et formes de la sympathie* (Paris: Petite Bibliothèque Payot, 1971), pp. 152–161 and 264–267, and *De la pudeur* (Paris: Aubier, 1952), pp. 140–143. (See Bibliography for the original German titles.)

5. Vladimir Jankélévitch, *Traité des vertus* (Paris: Bordas, 1970), vol. 2, pp. 425–449.

6. Paul-Laurent Hassoun, *Freud et la femme* (Paris: Calmann-Lévy, 1983), pp. 14–19.

7. Sigmund Freud, *New Introductory Lectures on Psychoanalysis* (London: Allen and Unwin, 1971). Lacan later added his say: "As for defining what man and woman are about, what psychoanalysis shows is precisely that it is impossible." See "Le Savoir de l'analyste," Interviews at Sainte-Anne, 1971–72, session of November 4, 1971 (unpublished).

8. On this debate see Elisabeth Roudinesco, *Histoire de la psychanalyse en France* (Paris: Editions du Seuil, 1986). Roudinesco is wrong, however, to associate Simone de Beauvoir with the dualist thought of the English School. For Beauvoir, the "second sex" was more a social construction.

9. Jacques Lacan, "Encore," *Séminaire XX* (Paris: Editions du Seuil, 1972–73).

10. Friedrich Engels, *L'Origine de la famille, de la propriété privée et de l'Etat* (Paris: Editions Sociales, 1972), p. 65.

11. August Bebel, *La Femme et le Socialisme* (Paris: Editions Sociales, 1950).

12. Alexandra Kollontai, in Judith Stora-Sandor, ed., *Marxisme et révolution sexuelle* (Paris: Maspero, 1973). This is an anthology of excerpts from Kollontai's works bearing on the question.

13. Both books were published in Paris by Editions de Minuit, 1972 and 1974.

14. Jean-François Lyotard, *L'Economie libidinale* (Paris: Editions de Minuit, 1974).

15. Gilles Deleuze, *Anti-Oedipe* (Paris: Editions de Minuit, 1972), pp. 71–72.

16. Jean Baudrillard, *De la séduction* (Paris: Galilée, 1980).

17. Jean Baudrillard, interview with Diane Hunter, *Works and Days* II/12, vol. 6, nos. 1 and 2 (Spring-Summer 1988).

18. Michel Foucault, *Histoire de la sexualité* (Paris: Gallimard).

19. See, among other works, Rosi Braidotti, "Bio-éthique ou nouvelle normativité?" in spec. no. of *Cahiers du Grif 33, Hannah Arendt* (1986): 149–155, and "Les Organes sans corps," in spec. no. of *Cahiers du Grif 36, De la parenté à l'eugénisme* (1987): 7–22.

20. This is the theme of all of Jacques Derrida's work since *L'Ecriture et la Différence* (Paris: Editions du Seuil, 1967).

21. Jacques Derrida, "Geschlecht, différence sexuelle, différence ontologique," in *Psyché* (Paris: Galilée, 1967). This text appeared first in Heidegger, *Cahiers de l'Herne* (1983).

22. "Women in the Beehive: A Seminar with Jacques Derrida," in Alice Jardine and Paul Smith, eds., *Men in Feminism* (New York: Methuen, 1987).

23. Jean-Paul Sartre, *L'Etre et le Néant* (Paris: Gallimard, 1943), chap. 3, part 2.

24. "Simone de Beauvoir interroge Jean-Paul Sartre," in *L'Arc* 61 (1975): 4.

25. Emmanuel Levinas, *Totalité et Infini* (The Hague: Nijhoff, 1961), pp. 127–128.

26. Ibid., pp. 244ff.

27. Francis Jacques, *Différence et subjectivité* (Paris: Aubier, 1982), pp. 164ff.

28. Ibid., pp. 295ff.

29. Jean-François Lyotard, *Le Différend* (Paris: Editions de Minuit, 1983), p. 29.

30. "Simone de Beauvoir et la lutte des femmes," *L'Arc* 61 (1975): 11–12.

31. "Nature-elle-ment" was the title of the third issue of the journal *Questions Féministes*, 1978. Among other articles in this issue, see Colette Guillaumin, "Pratique du pouvoir et idée de nature."

32. See Françoise Collin, "L'Irreprésentable de la différence des sexes," in *Catégorisation de sexe et constructions scientifiques* (Aix: Université de Aix-en-Provence, 1989), pp. 39–40.

33. On feminist studies the literature is voluminous; see especially *Savoir et différence des sexes,* spec. no. of *Cahiers du Grif* 45 (Fall 1990); "Femmes, féminisme et recherches," *Actes du colloque du Toulouse,* 1982.

Chapter 10. The Creators of Culture in France

Marcelle Marini

1. Régis Debray, *Le Pouvoir intellectuel en France* (Paris: Ramsay, 1979), p. 247.

2. For evidence, see the newspapers, videos, and films of the period preserved in feminist libraries.

3. Maria Isabel Barreno, Maria Teresa Horta, and Maria Velho da Costa, *Les Nouvelles Lettres portugaises* (1972), French trans. (Paris: Editions du Seuil, 1974).

4. Sartre, for instance, stated that "anti-Semitism is not protected by the right of free speech" (see *Réflexions sur la question juive,* 1954). This idea was applied to racism but not to "sexism," the very term itself meeting with considerable opposition.

5. Simone de Beauvoir, *Le Deuxième Sexe* (Paris: Gallimard, 1949), vol. 1, p. 14.

6. *Libération des femmes année zéro,* special issue of *Partisans* (July–October, 1970).

7. Claudine Hermann, *Les Voleuses de langue* (Paris: Editions des Femmes, 1976).

8. On the notion of "symbolic function," see Jean-Joseph Goux, *Freud, Marx. Economie et symbolique* (Paris: Editions du Seuil, 1973). Luce Irigaray

was the first woman to offer a systematic critique, in *Speculum de l'autre femme* (Paris: Editions de Minuit, 1974).

9. Alice A. Jardine and Anne M. Menke, *Shifting Scenes. Interviews on Women, Writing and Politics in Post-68 France* (New York: Columbia University Press, 1991).

10. Created by Jackie Buet and Elisabeth Tréhard in 1979, this festival introduced a number of women directors to a worldwide audience.

11. The installation, a collective undertaking, was shown in North America, England, and Germany.

12. Florence Montreynaud, *Le XXe Siècle des femmes* (Paris: Nathan, 1989).

13. *Le Figaro littéraire,* special issue for the Salon du Livre, May 19, 1989.

14. Michèle Vessilier-Ressi, *Le Métier d'auteur* (Paris: Dunod, 1982).

15. Pierrette Dionne and Chantal Théry, "Le Monde du livre: des femmes entre parenthèses," *Recherches féministes* 2, 2 (1989).

16. Marcelle Marini and Nicole Mozet, "La Production littéraire en France depuis 1945. Analyse différentielle," 1984. Colette Julien-Bertolus designed and implemented the procedure for electronically processing the data.

17. Claude Habib, "La Femme plumée," *Cahiers de recherches de S.T.D. (Textuel),* University of Paris VII 13: *Femmes et institutions littéraires* (1984).

18. René Rémond, ed., *Notre siècle* (Paris: Fayard, 1988). The chapters on culture are the work of Jean-François Sirinelli.

19. Gérard Delfau and Anne Roche, *Histoire/Littérature* (Paris: Editions du Seuil, 1977).

20. Anne Sauvy, "La Littérature et les femmes," in Roger Chartier, ed., *Histoire de l'édition française,* vol. 4: *1900–1950* (Paris: Promodis, 1986).

21. Interview, 1972, in Claude Francis and Fernande Gontier, *Les Ecrits de Simone de Beauvoir* (Paris: Gallimard, 1979).

22. Françoise Collin, "Le Sujet et l'auteur ou lire 'l'autre femme,'" in *Cahiers du Cedref* 2: *Femmes sujets des discours* (1990).

23. Françoise Mayeur-Castellani, *L'Enseignement secondaire des jeunes filles sous la IIIe République* (Paris: Presses de la Fondation des Sciences Politiques, 1977).

24. Beauvoir, *Le Deuxième Sexe,* vol. 2.

25. Marcelle Marini, "Enfance en archipels: *l'Opoponax* de Monique Wittig," *Revue des Sciences Humaines* 222 (1991–92).

26. Marcelle Marini, "L'Élaboration de la différence sexuelle dans la pratique littéraire de la langue (Sarraute, Hyvrard)," *Cahiers du Grad* 1: *Femmes, écriture, philosophie* (University of Laval, Quebec, 1987).

27. Léonor Fini, "Lettre à Roger Borderie," *Obliques,* 14–15: *La Femme surréaliste* (Paris, 1977): 115.

28. Geneviève Fraisse, *La Muse de la raison* (Paris: Alinéa, 1989).

29. Elissa D. Gelfand and Virginia Thorndike Hules, *French Feminist Criticism: Women, Language, Literature* (New York: Garland, 1985).

30. Interviews, Françoise Van Rossum-Guyon with Hélène Cixous and Julia Kristeva, *Revue des Sciences Humaines* 168: *Ecriture, féminité, féminisme* (Lille, 1977).

31. *Cahiers du Grif* 7 (1975); also 12 and 13 (1976).

32. Hélène Cixous, "Le Rire de la méduse," *L'Arc*, 61: *Simone de Beauvoir* (Paris, 1975).

33. Monique Plaza, "'Pouvoir phallomorphique' et psychologie de 'la femme,'" *Questions Féministes* 1 (November 1977).

34. Alice Jardine, *Gynesis* (1985).

35. Béatrice Slama, "De la 'littérature féminine' à 'l'écrire femme,'" in *Littérature* 44 (December 1981); Béatrice Didier, *L'Ecriture-femme* (Paris: Presses Universitaires de France, 1981).

36. Christine Planté, *La Petite Soeur de Balzac* (Paris: Editions du Seuil, 1989).

Chapter 11. The Ambivalent Image

LUISA PASSERINI

1. See Tania Modelski, ed., *Studies in Entertainment: Critical Approaches to Mass Culture* (Bloomington: Indiana University Press, 1986). (This book contains most of the papers presented at the International Symposium on Mass Culture, held at the University of Wisconsin, Milwaukee, in April 1984.)

2. Ann Treneman, "Cashing in on the Curse: Advertising and the Menstrual Taboo," in Lorraine Gamman and Margaret Marshment, eds., *The Female Gaze: Women as Viewers of Popular Culture* (London: The Women's Press, 1988).

3. Molly Haskell, *From Reverence to Rape: The Treatment of Women in the Movies* (Chicago: University of Chicago Press, 1987).

4. Andreas Huyssen, "Mass Culture as Woman: Modernism's Other," in Modelski, ed., *Studies in Entertainment*.

5. Barbara Ehrenreich and Deirdre English, *For Her Own Good: 150 Years of the Experts' Advice to Women* (Garden City, N.Y.: Anchor Books, 1979).

6. Kath Davies, Julienne Dickey, and Teresa Stratford, eds., *Out of Focus: Writings on Women and the Media* (London: The Women's Press, 1987).

7. Judith Williamson, "Woman Is an Island: Femininity and Colonization," in Modelski, ed., *Studies in Entertainment*.

8. Gianna Pomata, "La storia delle donne: Una questione di confine," in G. De Luna, P. Ortoleva, M. Revelli, and N. Tranfaglia, eds., *Introduzione alla storia contemporanea* (Florence: La Nuova Italia, 1984).

9. Gamman and Marshment, eds., *The Female Gaze*.

10. Kathy Peiss, *Cheap Amusements: Working Women and Leisure in Turn-of-the-Century New York* (Philadelphia: Temple University Press, 1986).

11. Jackie Stacey, "Desperately Seeking Difference," in Gamman and Marshment, eds., *The Female Gaze*.

12. Avis Lewallern, "*Lace:* Pornography for Women?" in Gamman and Marshment, eds., *The Female Gaze,* an analysis of *Lace,* by Shirley Conran.

13. Treneman, "Cashing in on the Curse."

14. Gabriella Turnaturi, "La donna fra il pubblico e il privato: La nascita della casalinga e della consumatrice," *Nuova Donnawomanfemme* 12/13 (July-December 1979): 8–29.

15. Françoise Werner, "Du ménage à l'art ménager: L'évolution du travail ménager et son écho dans la presse féminine française de 1919 à 1939," *Le Mouvement Social* 129 (1984): 61–87.

16. Susan Porter Benson, *Counter Cultures: Saleswomen, Managers, and Customers in American Department Stores, 1890–1940* (Chicago: University of Illinois Press, 1986), and William R. Leach, "Transformations in a Culture of Consumption: Women and Department Stores, 1890–1925," *Journal of American History* 71, 2 (September 1984).

17. Kathy Peiss, "Mass Culture and Social Divisions: The Case of the Cosmetics Industry," lecture given at the Mass Culture and the Working Class Conference, Paris, October 14–15, 1988.

18. Haskell, *From Reverence to Rape.*

19. Victoria de Grazia, "Mass Culture and Sovereignty: The American Challenge to European Cinemas, 1920–1960," *Journal of Modern History* 61 (March 1989): 53–87.

20. Victoria de Grazia, "Puritan, Pagan Bodies: Americanism and the Formation of the 'New Woman' in Europe, 1920–1945," working paper, 1984–87.

21. Edgar Morin, *Les stars* (Paris: Seuil, 1957).

22. Werner, "Du ménage à l'art ménager."

23. Evelyne Sullerot, *La Presse féminine* (Paris: Armand Colin, 1963).

24. Ibid.

25. Piero Meldini, *Sposa e madre esemplare: Ideologia e politica della donna e della famiglia durante il fascismo* (Florence: Guaraldi, 1975).

26. Elisabetta Mondello, *La nuova italiana: La donna nella stampa e nella cultura del ventennio* (Rome: Editori Riuniti, 1987).

27. Luisa Passerini, *Torino operaia e fascismo* (Rome: Laterza, 1984).

28. Paola Masino, *Nascita e morte della massaia* (Milan: La Tartaruga, 1982; 1st ed. Milan: Bompiani, 1945), p. 183.

29. Laura Lilli, "La stampa femminile," in Valerio Castronovo and Nicola Tranfaglia, eds., *Storia della stampa italiana,* vol. 5, *La stampa italiana del neocapitalismo* (Bari: Laterza, 1976).

30. Mondello, *La nuova italiana.*

31. Francesco Alberoni, *Consumi e società* (Bologna: Il Mulino, 1964), pp. 38–43.

32. Umberto Eco, *Apocalittici e integrati: Comunicazioni di massa e teorie della cultura di massa* (Milan: Bompiani, 1964).

33. Edgar Morin, *L'esprit du temps* (Paris: Grasset, 1962).

34. Sullerot, *La presse féminine.*

35. Milly Buonanno, *Naturale come sei: Indagine sulla stampa femminile*

in Italia (Florence: Guaraldi, 1975), with an introductory note by Giovanni Bechelloni.

36. Max Horkheimer and Theodor W. Adorno, "Das Schema der Massenkultur," in T. W. Adorno, *Gesammelte Shriften* (Frankfurt am Main: Suhrkamp, 1981).

37. Gabriella Parca, *Le italiane si confessano* (Milan: Feltrinelli, 1966; 1st ed. Florence: Parenti, 1959).

38. Sullerot, *La Presse féminine*, p. 129.

39. Anne-Marie Dardigna, *Femmes-femmes sur papier glacé* (Paris: Maspero, 1974).

40. Lilli, "La stampa femminile."

41. Buonanno, *Naturale come sei.*

42. Milly Buonanno, *La donna nella stampa: Giornaliste, lettrici e modelli di femminilità* (Rome: Editori Riuniti, 1978).

43. Maria Teresa Anelli, Paola Gabbrielli, Marta Morgavi, and Roberto Piperno, *Fotoromanzo: Fascino e pregiudizio. Storia, documenti e immagini di un grande fenomeno popolare* (Milan: Savelli, 1979).

44. Buonanno, *Naturale come sei.*

45. Anelli et al., *Fotoromanzo.*

46. Buonanno, *Naturale come sei.*

47. Tania Modelski, *Loving with a Vengeance: Mass-Produced Fantasies for Women* (New York: Routledge, 1982).

48. Janice Radway, *Reading the Romance: Women, Patriarchy, and Popular Literature* (Chapel Hill: University of North Carolina Press, 1984).

49. Milly Buonanno, *Cultura di massa e identità femminile: L'immagine della donna in televisione* (Turin: ERI, 1983).

Chapter 12. Women, Images, and Representation

ANNE HIGONNET

1. Madeleine Edmondson and David Rounds, *Mary Noble to Mary Hartman: The Complete Soap Opera Book* (New York: Stein and Day, 1976), p. 187.

2. Ibid., p. 197.

3. Cynthia White, *Women's Magazines 1693–1968* (London: Joseph Michael, 1970), p. 216.

4. Cover of October 1989 *Good Housekeeping.*

5. Lois Banner, *American Beauty* (New York: Knopf, 1983), p. 273.

6. Elaine Brumberg, *Save Your Money, Save Your Face* (New York: Facts on File Publishers, 1986), p. 95.

7. Richard Randall, *Freedom and Taboo: Pornography and the Politics of a Self Divided* (Berkeley: University of California Press, 1989), p. 200.

8. Gordon Hawkins and Franklin E. Zimring, *Pornography in a Free Society* (Cambridge: Cambridge University Press, 1988), p. 42.

9. Ibid., p. 36.

10. Randall, *Freedom and Taboo,* p. 200.

11. Hawkins and Zimring, *Pornography*, p. 54.

12. Ellen Perry Berkeley, *Architecture: A Place for Women* (Washington, D.C.: Smithsonian Institution Press, 1989), p. xv.

Continuities and Ruptures
FRANÇOISE THÉBAUD

1. Simone de Beauvoir, *Lettres à Sartre, 1940–1963* (Paris: Gallimard, 1990), p. 211.

2. Edgar Morin's phrase is from "Amour et érotisme dans la 'culture de masse,'" *Arguments* (1st quarter, 1961): 52, quoted in Janine Mossuz-Lavau, "Politique des libérations sexuelles," in Pascal Ory, ed., *Nouvelle Histoire des idées politiques* (Paris: Hachette, 1987), pp. 682–694.

3. See bibliography.

4. Jeannette Laot, *Stratégie pour les femmes* (Paris: Stock, 1977); Madeleine Colin, *"Ce n'est pas aujourd'hui"* (*Femmes, syndicats, lutte de classe*) (Paris: Editions Sociales, 1975), and *Traces d'une vie: dans la mouvance du siècle* (Paris: privately published by Madeleine Vignes, 1989 and 1991).

Chapter 13. Poverty and Mothers' Rights
GISELA BOCK

This essay was inspired by a cooperative project at the European University Institute (Florence). I want to express my gratitude to the participants: Ida Blom, Annarita Buttafuoco, Anne Cova, Elisabeth Elgan, Jan Gröndahl, Hilde Ibsen, Jane Lewis, Mary Nash, Karen Offen, Ann-Sofie Ohlander, Frank Prochaska, Chiara Saraceno, Anne-Lise Seip, Bonnie G. Smith, Irene Stoehr, Angela Taeger, Pat Thane, and Elisabetta Vezzosi. Most of their contributions are published in *Maternity and Gender Policies: Women and the Rise of the European Welfare States, 1880s–1950s*, ed. Gisela Bock and Pat Thane (London: Routledge, 1991; henceforth cited as *Maternity 1991*). I am also grateful to Victoria de Grazia for helping to revise the text. The impressive work by Theda Skocpol, *Protecting Soldiers and Mothers: The Political Origins of Social Policy in the United States* (Cambridge, Mass.: Harvard University Press, 1992) appeared after this chapter was first published. I want to thank Theda Skocpol for providing important editorial advice for this version.

1. Peter Flora and Arnold J. Heidenheimer, eds., *The Development of Welfare States in Europe and America* (New Brunswick: Transaction Books, 1981), p. 27.

2. Bonnie G. Smith, "On Writing Women's Work," Working Paper HEC 91/7, European University Institute, Florence, 1991. See Margaret Llewelyn Davies, ed., *Maternity: Letters from Working Women* (1915) (London: Virago, 1978); also ed., *Life as We Have Known It, by Cooperative Working Women* (1931) (New York: Norton, 1975); Arbeiterinnensekretariat des

Deutschen Textilarbeiterverbands, ed., *Mein Arbeitstag—Mein Wochenende: 150 Berichte von Textilarbeiterinnen* (1930) (repr. ed. Frankfurt: Alf Lüdtke, 1990); Molly Ladd-Taylor, ed., *Raising a Baby the Government Way: Mothers' Letters to the Children's Bureau, 1915–1932* (New Brunswick: Rutgers University Press, 1986); Ida Blom, *Barnebegrensning—synd eller sund fornuft?* (Bergen, 1980), pp. 64–154; Annarita Buttafuoco, *Le Mariuccine* (Milan: Angeli, 1985).

3. Wolfram Fischer, *Armut in der Geschichte* (Göttingen: Vandenhoeck & Ruprecht, 1982); Hartmut Kaelble, *1880–1980, A Social History of Western Europe* (London: Gill and Macmillan, 1990).

4. Vera Brittain, *Lady into Woman* (London: Dakers, 1953), p. 224.

5. Katherine Anthony, *Feminism in Germany and Scandinavia* (New York: Holt, 1915), p. 53.

6. Käthe Schirmacher, *Die Frauenarbeit im Hause, ihre ökonomische, rechtliche und soziale Wertung* (1905) (Leipzig, 1912), pp. 3–8 (repr. in part in Gisela Brinker-Gabler, ed., *Frauenarbeit und Beruf*, Frankfurt, 1979); report in *Die Frauenbewegung* 11, 20 (15 Oct. 1905): 153–155.

7. Auclert quoted in Anne Cova, "French Feminism and Maternity: Theories and Politics, 1890–1918," in *Maternity 1991*; Rouzade quoted in Wynona H. Wilkins, "The Paris International Feminist Congress of 1896 and Its French Antecedents," *North Dakota Quarterly* (1975): 23; cf. Karen Offen, "Sur l'origine des mots 'féminisme' et 'féministe'," *Revue d'Histoire Moderne et Contemporaine* 36 (1987): 492–496; see also her "Depopulation, Nationalism, and Feminism in Fin-de-Siècle France," *American Historical Review* 89 (1984): 648–676; Claire G. Moses, *French Feminism in the 19th Century* (Albany: SUNY Press, 1984), pp. 207–208; Laurence Klejman and Florence Rochefort, *L'Egalité en marche. Le Féminisme sous la Troisième République* (Paris: Editions des Femmes, 1989), p. 260.

8. *Nelly Roussel, L'Eternelle sacrifiée* (1906), ed. Daniel Armogathe (Paris: Maité Albistur, 1979), p. 55; the other quotes are from Cova, "French Feminism" and "Féminisme et natalité: Nelly Roussel (1878–1922)," in *History of European Ideas* 5 (1992): 663–672; Offen, "Depopulation," p. 673.

9. Ida Blom, "Voluntary Motherhood 1900–1930: Theories and Politics of a Norwegian Feminist in an International Perspective," in *Maternity 1991*; Cheri Register, "Motherhood at Center: Ellen Key's Social Vision," in *Women's Studies International Forum* 5 (1982): 599–610.

10. Annarita Buttafuoco, "Motherhood as a Political Strategy: The Role of the Italian Women's Movement in the Creation of the Cassa Nazionale di Maternità," in *Maternity 1991*.

11. Lily Braun, *Die Frauenfrage* (Leipzig, 1901), p. 547; her *Die Mutterschaftsversicherung* (Berlin, 1906); Irene Stoehr, "Housework and Motherhood: Debates and Policies in the Women's Movement in Imperial Germany and the Weimar Republic," in *Maternity 1991*; Alfred G. Meyer, *The Feminism and Socialism of Lily Braun* (Bloomington: Indiana University Press, 1985), esp. pp. 125, 137.

12. Käthe Schirmacher, *Wie und in welchem Masse lässt sich die Wertung*

der Frauenarbeit steigern (Leipzig, 1909), p. 12 (repr. in Brinker-Gabler, *Frauenarbeit*); the other quotes are from Stoehr, "Housework." See Marion Kaplan, *The Jewish Feminist Movement in Germany: The Campaigns of the Jüdischer Frauenbund, 1904–1938* (Westport, Conn.: Greenwood Press, 1979), esp. ch. 3.

13. Quoted in Carol Dyhouse, *Feminism and the Family in England 1880–1939* (Oxford: Basil Blackwell, 1989), pp. 191–192.

14. Women's Industrial Council (1911), quoted in Jane Lewis, "Models of Equality for Women: The Case of State Support for Children in 20th-Century Britain," in *Maternity 1991*. The previous quotes are from Pat Thane, "Visions of Gender in the Making of the British Welfare State: The Case of Women in the British Labour Party and Social Policy, 1906–1945," in *Maternity 1991*. See Frank Prochaska, "A Mother's Country: Mothers' Meetings and Family Welfare in Britain, 1850–1950," *History* 74 (1989): 379–399.

15. Atkinson quoted in Dyhouse, *Feminism*, pp. 65–66, 93; see also pp. 96–104; Eleanor Rathbone, *The Disinherited Family* (1924), repr. with introd. by Suzy Fleming (Bristol: Falling Wall Press, 1986); Mary Stocks, *The Case for Family Endowment* (London, 1927), ch. 3; Lewis, "Models of Equality."

16. Anthony, *Feminism*, pp. 117, 127 (quotes); her *Mothers Who Must Earn* (New York: Russel Sage Foundation, 1914); her preface to *The Endowment of Motherhood* (New York, 1920).

17. Karen J. Blair, *The Clubwoman as Feminist: True Womanhood Redefined, 1868–1914* (New York: Holmes and Meier, 1980), pp. 30 (quote), 42; Crystal Eastman, *Now We Can Begin*, repr. in Blanche Wiesen Cook, ed., *Crystal Eastman: On Women and Revolution* (New York: Oxford University Press, 1978), pp. 54–57; Mary Madeleine Ladd-Taylor, "Mother-Work: Ideology, Public Policy, and the Mothers' Movement, 1890–1930," Ph.D. diss., Yale University, 1986, esp. chs. 2–4; Lela B. Costin, *Two Sisters for Social Justice. A Biography of Grace and Edith Abbott* (Urbana: University of Illinois Press, 1983).

18. Quotes from Dyhouse, *Feminism*, p. 91, and from Ladd-Taylor, *Mother-Work*, p. 148; see also the comments on Schirmacher and those by Russel (quoted above) and note 39 below.

19. Quotes from Dyhouse, *Feminism*, pp. 90, 92, and from Cova, "French Feminism"; for Anna Martin see Lewis, "Models of Equality"; Marianne Weber, "Zur Frage der Bewertung der Hausfrauenarbeit" (1912), in her *Frauenfragen und Frauengedanken* (Tübingen, 1919), pp. 80–94; Anthony, *Feminism*, pp. 118–119.

20. Lischnewska quoted in Stoehr, "Housework and Motherhood"; Franca Pieroni Bortolotti, "La Kuliscioff e la questione femminile," in *Anna Kuliscioff e l'età del riformismo. Atti del Convegno di Milano 1976* (Rome: Avanti! 1978), pp. 104–138; Rathbone, *Disinherited Family*, pp. 369–370.

21. Aileen S. Kraditor, *The Ideas of the Woman Suffrage Movement, 1890–1920* (New York: Anchor Books, 1971), esp. p. 91; Irene Stoehr, "Organisierte Mütterlichkeit': Zur Politik der deutschen Frauenbewegung um

1900," in Karin Hausen, ed., *Frauen suchen ihre Geschichte* (Munich: Beck, 1983), pp. 225–253; Ladd-Taylor, *Mother-Work*, p. 256; Ellen Ross, "'Fierce Questions and Taunts': Married Life in Working Class London 1870–1914," in *Feminist Studies* 8 (1982): 575–602.

22. Paula Baker, "The Domestication of Politics: Women and American Political Society, 1780–1920," in *American Historical Review* 89 (1984): 620–647.

23. Ersilia Majno Bronzini, "Vie pratiche del femminismo" (1902), quoted in Buttafuoco, "Motherhood as a Political Strategy"; Jean Gaffin and David Thoms, *Caring & Sharing: The Centenary History of the Co-operative Women's Guild* (Manchester: Co-operative Union, 1983), p. 43. For the Enlightenment concept of male nature and male citizen rights see Carole Pateman, *The Sexual Contract* (Cambridge: Polity Press, 1988).

24. Helene Stöcker, "Der Kampf gegen den Geburtenrückgang," *Die neue Generation* 8, 11 (1912): 602.

25. Nelly Roussel, "Qu'est-ce que le 'Féminisme'?" *La Femme Affranchie* 2 (Sept. 1904), quoted in Cova, "Féminisme et natalité."

26. Buttafuoco, "Motherhood as a Political Strategy"; Naomi Black, *Social Feminism* (Ithaca: Cornell University Press, 1989); J. Stanley Lemons, *The Woman Citizen: Social Feminism in the 1920s* (Urbana: University of Illinois Press, 1973); Karen Offen, "Defining Feminism: A Comparative Historical Approach," *Signs* 14 (1988): 119–157; Jennifer Dale and Peggy Foster, eds., *Feminists and State Welfare* (London: Routledge and Kegan Paul, 1986), pp. 5–8; Daniel Scott Smith, "Family Limitation, Sexual Control, and Domestic Feminism in Victorian America," in Lois Banner, ed., *Clio's Consciousness Raised* (New York: Harper and Row, 1974), pp. 119–136.

27. For Italy see Buttafuoco, "Motherhood as a Political Strategy." For the United States: Anthony R. Travis, "The Origins of Mothers' Pensions in Illinois," *Journal of the Illinois State Historical Society* 67 (1975): 421–428; Ada J. Davis, "The Evolution of the Institution of Mothers' Pensions in the United States," *American Journal of Sociology* 35 (1930): 573–587; Ladd-Taylor, *Mother-Work*, ch. 4. For France: Anne Cova, "French Feminism"; Mary Lynn Stewart, *Women, Work and the French State: Labour Protection and Social Patriarchy, 1879–1919* (Kingston, McGill-Queen's University Press, 1989), esp. ch. 8; Robert Talmy, *Hisotire du mouvement familial en France (1896–1939)* (Paris: Union Nationale des Caisses d'Allocations Familiales, 1962), vol. I, pp. 159–163.

28. See *Maternity 1991*, and note 29 below.

29. Julia Lathrop, introd. to Henry J. Harris, *Maternity Benefit Systems in Certain Foreign Countries* (Washington, D.C.: U.S. Department of Labor, Children's Bureau, Publication no. 57, Government Printing Office, 1917).

30. Volker Hunecke, *I trovatelli di Milano* (Bologna: Il Mulino, 1988); Rachel G. Fuchs, "Legislation, Poverty, and Child-Abandonment in 19th-Century Paris," *Journal of Interdisciplinary History* 18 (1987): 55–80; Angela Taeger, "L'Etat, les enfants trouvés et les allocations familiales en France, XIXe et XXe siècles," *Francia* 16 (1989): 15–33; Pat Thane, "Infant Welfare

in Britain, 1870s–1930s," unpubl. paper, 1990; Linda Gordon, "Single Mothers and Child Neglect, 1880–1920," *American Quarterly* 37 (1985): 173–192; Ann Vandepol, "Dependent Children, Child Custody, and the Mothers' Pensions: The Transformation of State-Family Relations in the Early 20th Century," *Social Problems* 29 (1982): 221–235.

31. Carol Dyhouse, "Working-Class Mothers and Infant Mortality in England, 1895–1914," *Journal of Social History* 12 (1978): 248–267; Rachel G. Fuchs, *Abandoned Children: Foundlings and Child Welfare in 19th-Century France* (Albany: SUNY Press, 1984).

32. Maria Martin, "Dépopulation," *Le Journal des Femmes* (June 1896); Cécile Brunschvicg, "Féminisme et natalité," *La Française*, 10 January 1931, quoted in Cova, "French Feminism"; Gertrud Bäumer, "Der seelische Hintergrund der Bevölkerungsfrage," *Die Frau* 23, 3 (1915): 129–134.

33. Offen, "Depopulation," pp. 659–660, 668–670; Françoise Thébaud, "Le Mouvement nataliste dans la France de l'entre-deux-guerres: l'Alliance Nationale pour l'Accroissement de la Population Française," *Revue d'Histoire Moderne et Contemporaine* 32 (1985): 276–301; Yvonne Knibiehler and Catherine Fouquet, *Histoire des mères du moyen-âge à nos jours* (Paris: Montalba, 1980).

34. Herbert Wolfe, *Governmental Provisions in the United States and Foreign Countries for Members of the Military Forces and Their Dependents* (Washington, D.C.: U.S. Department of Labor, Children's Bureau, Publication no. 28, Government Printing Office, 1917), p. 13; Ute Daniel, *Arbeiterfrauen im der Kriegsgesellschaft: Beruf. Familie und Politik im Ersten Weltkrieg* (Göttingen: Vandenhoeck & Ruprecht, 1989), pp. 169–183; Susan Pedersen, "Social Policy and the Reconstruction of the Family in Britain and France, 1900–1945," Ph.D. diss., Harvard University, 1989, pp. 115–130.

35. Ladd-Taylor, *Mother-Work*, esp. ch. 5; Lemons, *The Woman Citizen*, ch. 6; Joseph Benedict Chepaitis, "The First Federal Social Welfare Measure: The Sheppard-Towner Maternity and Infancy Act, 1918–1932," Ph.D. diss., Georgetown University, 1968; Hilda Scott, *Working Your Way to the Bottom: The Feminization of Poverty* (London: Pandora, 1984); Barbara Ehrenreich and Frances Fox Piven, "The Feminization of Poverty: When the 'Family-Wage System' Breaks Down," *Dissent* 31 (1984): 162–170.

36. Quoted in Jane Lewis, *The Politics of Motherhood: Child and Maternal Welfare in England, 1900–1939* (London: Croom Helm, 1980), p. 169, and in her "Models of Equality."

37. Rathbone, *Disinherited Family*, esp. pp. 316–324.

38. Dyhouse, *Feminism*, pp. 95, 102.

39. Ramsay MacDonald (leader of the Labour Party) quoted by Lewis, "Models of Equality."

40. Thane, "Visions of Gender"; John Macnicol, *The Movement for Family Allowances 1918–1945: A Study in Social Policy Development* (London: Heinemann, 1980).

41. Quoted in Suzy Fleming, intr. to Rathbone, *Disinherited Family*, p. 90.

42. Anne-Lise Seip and Hilde Ibsen, "Norway's Road to Child Allowances," in *Maternity 1991;* Ann-Sofie Ohlander, "The Struggle for a Social Democratic Family Policy in Sweden since 1900," in *Maternity 1991;* Helga Maria Hernes, "Die zweigeteilte Sozialpolitik," in Karin Hausen and Helga Nowotny, eds., *Wie männlich ist die Wissenschaft?* (Frankfurt: Suhrkamp, 1986), pp. 163–178; Bettina Cass, "Rewards for Women's Work," in Jacqueline Goodnow and Carole Pateman, eds., *Women, Social Science and Public Policy* (Sydney: Allen and Unwin, 1985), pp. 67–94; Rob Watts, "Family Allowances in Canada and Australia 1940–1945: A Comparative Critical Case Study," *Journal of Social Policy* 16 (1987): 19–48; Ann Curthoys, "Equal Pay, a Family Wage or Both: Women Workers, Feminists and Unionists in Australia since 1945," in Barbara Caine et al., eds., *Crossing Boundaries. Feminisms and the Critique of Knowledges* (Sydney: Allen and Unwin, 1988), pp. 129–140.

43. Henri Hatzfeld, *Du paupérisme à la sécurité sociale. Essai sur les origines de la sécurité sociale en France, 1850–1940* (Paris: Armand Colin, 1971); Karen Offen, "Body Politics: Women, Work, and the Politics of Motherhood in France, 1920–1950," in *Maternity 1991.*

44. Marie-Monique Huss, "Pronatalism in the Inter-War Period in France," *Journal of Contemporary History* 25 (1990): 64.

45. Cécile Brunschwicg, "La Maternité, fonction familiale ou sociale?" *La Française,* 3 May 1930; Naomi Black, "Social Feminism in France: A Case Study," in Naomi Black and Ann Baker Cottrell, eds., *Women and World Change: Equity Issues in Development* (Beverly Hills: Sage Publications, 1981), pp. 217–238; Pedersen, *Social Policy,* ch. 3.

46. Offen, "Body Politics"; Alain Barjot, *L'Allocation de salaire unique et l'allocation de la mère au foyer en France* (Bruges: Imprimerie Verbeke-Loys, 1967); Flora and Heidenheimer, *Development of Welfare States,* p. 341.

47. Benito Mussolini, preface to Richard Korherr, *Regresso delle nascite, morte dei popoli* (Rome, 1928), p. 23; see Chiara Saraceno, "Redefining Maternity and Paternity: Gender, Pronatalism and Social Policies in Fascist Italy," in *Maternity 1991;* Victoria de Grazia's article in this volume, and her *How Fascism Ruled Women: Italy, 1922–1945* (Berkeley: University of California Press, 1992).

48. Mary Nash, "Pronatalism and Motherhood in Franco's Spain," in *Maternity 1991.*

49. For the implementation of these policies, see my contributions to this volume, to *Maternity 1991,* and *Zwangssterilisation im Nationalsozialismus: Studien zur Rassenpolitik und Frauenpolitik* (Opladen: Westdeutscher Verlag, 1986).

50. Ann Taylor Allen, "German Radical Feminism and Eugenics, 1900–1918," *German Studies Review* 11 (1989): 31–56; Linda Gordon, *Woman's Body, Woman's Rights: A Social History of Birth Control in America* (Harmondsworth: Penguin, 1977), pp. 281–290, 330–331.

51. Nash, "Pronatalism"; Michele A. Cortelazzo, "Il lessico del razzismo fascista (1938)," *Movimento operaio e socialista* 7 (1984): 57–66; Claudio

Pogliano, "Scienza e stirpe: eugenica in Italia (1912–1939)," *Passato e presente* 5 (1984): 61–97.

52. "Das 'Wir' steht vor dem 'Ich,'" *Frau von heute* 39 (1959): 2, quoted in Gesine Obertreis, *Familienpolitik in der DDR 1945–1980* (Opladen: Westdeutscher Verlag, 1985), p. 146; see also pp. 51–73, 119, 136–138, 155, 292–293. For the Soviet Union see Janet Evans, "The Communist Party of the Soviet Union and the Women's Question: The Case of the 1936 Decree 'In Defence of Mother and Child,'" *Journal of Contemporary History* 16 (1981): 757–775; Bernice Q. Madison, *Social Welfare in the Soviet Union* (Stanford: Stanford University Press, 1968), ch. 3.

53. Erich Honecker, "Neue Massnahmen zur Verwirklichung des sozialpolitischen Programms des VIII. Parteitages" (1972), quoted in Obertreis, *Familienpolitik*, p. 292; see also pp. 315–318.

54. Vera Slupik, "'Kinder kosten aber auch Geld.' Die Diskriminierung von Frauen im Kindergeldrecht," in Ute Gerhard et al., eds., *Auf Kosten der Frauen. Frauenrechte im Sozialstaat* (Weinheim: Beltz Verlag, 1988), p. 195; Peter Flora, ed., *Growth to Limits: The Western European Welfare States since World War I* (Berlin: De Gruyter, 1986–87), vol. IV, pp. 278–281.

Chapter 14. Maternity, Family, and the State

NADINE LEFAUCHEUR

1. Kathleen E. Kiernan, "The British Family: Contemporary Trends and Issues," *Journal of Family Issues* 9, 3 (September 1988): 306.

2. Henri Léridon and Catherine Villeneuve-Gokalp, "Les Nouveaux Couples: nombre, caractéristiques et attitudes," *Population* 2 (1988): 331–374.

3. A country (like England in the early 1980s) can have a divorce index of 40 percent even though only 18 percent of the couples belonging to the generations most affected by divorce have already separated and even though it is likely that the final proportion of divorced couples in those generations will not exceed 30 percent. Patrick Festy, "Quelques difficultés pour apprécier les conséquences des changements familiaux," AIDELF, 1986, pp. 551–557.

4. Roger Géraud, *La Limitation des naissances* (Paris: Union Générale d'Editions, 1963), p. 104.

5. Massimo Levi-Bacci, "Le Changement démographique et le cycle de vie des femmes," in Evelyne Sullerot, ed., *Le Fait féminin* (Paris: Fayard, 1978), pp. 467–478.

6. This paragraph owes a great deal to the work of Claudette Sèze, *Evolution des activités des femmes induite par la consommation des substituts sociaux au travail domestique, 1950–1980: effets économiques et socioculturels* (Viry-Châtillon: Centre de Recherche sur l'Innovation Industrielle et Sociale, 1988).

7. Daniela del Boca, "Women in a Changing Workplace: The Case of Italy," in Jane Jenson, Elisabeth Hagen, and Ceallaigh Reddy, *Feminization of the Labour Force: Paradoxes and Promises* (Cambridge: Polity Press, 1988), p. 129.

8. "Reproduction Goes Public," in Helga Maria Hernes, *Welfare State and Woman Power: Essays in State Feminism* (Oslo and Oxford: Norwegian University Press and Oxford University Press, 1987), chap. 3, pp. 51–71.

9. Angela Phillips and Peter Moss, *Qui prend soin des enfants de l'Europe? Compte rendu du réseau des modes de garde d'enfants,* Commission des Communautés Européennes, V/1219/1/1988.

10. Harold Brackman, Steven P. Erie, and Martin Rein, "Wedded to the Welfare State," in Jenson, Hagen, and Reddy, eds., *Feminization of the Labour Force,* p. 215.

11. Hernes, *Welfare State,* p. 54.

12. Anne Gauthier, "Etat-mari, Etat-papa, les politiques sociales et le travail domestique," in Louise Vandelac et al., *Du travail et de l'amour: les dessous de la production domestique* (Montreal: Saint-Martin, 1985), pp. 257–311.

13. François de Singly and Claude Thélot, *Gens du privé, gens du public: la grande différence* (Paris: Dunod, 1988).

14. Most of the data that follow are taken from Gosta Esping Andersen, *The Three Worlds of Welfare Capitalism* (Cambridge: Polity Press, 1990), and Marie-Agnès Barrère-Maurisson and Olivier Marchand, "Structures familiales et marchés du travail dans les pays développés," *Economie et statistique* 235 (September 1990): 19–30. The data for Germany pertain to West Germany prior to reunification.

15. Brackman, Erie, and Rein, "Wedded to the Welfare State," pp. 217–218.

16. Most of the data here are taken from T. Smeeding, L. Rainwater, and S. Danziger, "Cross-National Trends in Income, Poverty, and Dependency: The Evidence for Young Adults in the Eighties," paper presented to the conference on *Poverty and Social Marginality,* Joint Center for Political Studies, Washington, Sept. 20–21, 1991.

Chapter 15. A Supervised Emancipation
ROSE-MARIE LAGRAVE

1. I make use of Max Weber's concepts of legitimacy and social order. See Weber, *Economy and Society* (Berkeley: University of California Press, 1979). Male domination is central to the social order. It is exercised primarily by means of "symbolic violence, which is one aspect of any kind of domination and the key aspect of male domination," according to Pierre Bourdieu, "La Domination masculine," *Actes de la recherche en sciences sociales* 84 (Sept. 1990): 8.

2. Surveys of 22 countries presented at the Congrès des Catholiques Sociaux in *Le Travail industriel de la mère et le foyer ouvrier. Extraits du Congrès international de juin 1933* (Paris: Union Féminine Civique et Sociale, 1933). See also the results of a questionnaire sent to various national groups affiliated with the *Union Internationale des Ligues Féminines Catholiques,* in Françoise Van Goethem, "Enquête internationale sur le travail salarié de la

femme mariée," in *Chronique sociale de France* (Lyons: Union Internationale d'Etudes Sociales, 1932).

3. See Annie Fourcaut, *Femmes à l'usine en France dans l'entre-deux-guerres* (Paris: Maspero, 1982).

4. Maurice Frois, *La Santé et le travail des femmes pendant la guerre* (Paris: Presses Universitaires de France, 1926), p. 63.

5. André Bonnefoy, *Place aux femmes. Les carrières féminines administratives et libérales* (Paris: Fayard, 1914), p. 69.

6. Gina Lombroso, *La Femme dans la société actuelle* (Paris: Payot, 1929), p. 12.

7. Marguerite Thibert, "Crise économique et travail féminin," *Revue Internationale du Travail* 27, 4 (April 1933): 31.

8. Janine Ponty, "Des Polonaises parlent," *Revue du Nord* 63, 250 (July-Sept. 1981): 730.

9. See the chapter on working conditions in Bureau International du Travail, *L'Année sociale* (Geneva).

10. Claudia Koonz, *Mothers in the Fatherland: Women, Family Life, and Nazi Ideology, 1919–1945* (New York: St. Martin's Press, 1987).

11. Françoise Lantier, *Le Travail et la formation des femmes en Europe* (Paris: La Documentation Française, 1972), vol. 4, p. 47.

12. Rémy Lenoir, "L'Effondrement des bases du familialisme," *Actes de la recherche en sciences sociales* 57–58 (June 1985): 69–88.

13. Pierre Bourdieu, *Les Héritiers: les étudiants et leurs études* (Paris: Editions de Minuit, 1964).

14. See, for example, the Equal Pay Act of 1970 in the United Kingdom, which required equal pay for jobs classified as equivalent. See also Greek Law no. 1414/84 on the principle of sexual equality in employment, and the French law on professional equality, passed in 1983.

15. Madeleine Guilbert, *Les Fonctions des femmes dans l'industrie* (The Hague: Mouton, 1966), p. 148.

16. Ibid., p. 144.

17. See, for example, Brigitte Belloc, "Le Travail à temps partiel," in *Données sociales* (Paris: INSEE, 1987), pp. 112–123.

18. See "Ségrégation professionnelle selon le sexe," in *L'Intégration des femmes dans l'économie* (Paris: Organization for Economic Cooperation and Development, 1985), pp. 40–74.

19. Pierre Bourdieu, "Classement, déclassement, reclassement," *Actes de la recherche en sciences sociales* 24 (Nov. 1978): 22.

20. The degree of segregation is measured by the ratio of the proportion of women in a given profession to the proportion of women in the working population as a whole. This ratio yields the CFR, or coefficient of feminine representation. The Dissimilarity Index (DI) is calculated as follows:

$$\frac{1}{2} \sum_{i=1}^{K} \left[\frac{Nw_i}{Nw} - \frac{Nm_i}{Nm} \right] \times 100\%,$$

where *Nw* is the total number of women in the workforce; *Nm* is the total number of men in the workforce; Nw_i is the number of women employed in category *i*; Nm_i is the number of men employed in category *i*.

See *L'Intégration des femmes dans l'économie,* pp. 44 and 73. This mathematical sophistication, which contributes to the "mythology of science," has the effect of glossing over social inequalities by expressing them in a quantitative form that is socially acceptable because it is unverifiable. See Pierre Bourdieu, "Le Nord et le Midi. Contribution à une analyse de l'effet Montesquieu," *Actes de la recherche en sciences sociales* 35 (Nov. 1980): 22–25.

21. *L'Intégration des femmes dans l'économie,* p. 46.

22. The laws and statutes concerning equal treatment and pay constitute a major legal and political victory, but they have little effect on the pay gap. *De jure* inequality and *de facto* inequality are not the same thing. See Anne Sabourin, *Le Travail des femmes dans la CEE. Conditions juridiques* (Paris: Economica, 1984). My thanks to Juliette Caniou and Tatiana Michel for their help with the documentation for this chapter.

Feminism Is Plural

FRANÇOISE THÉBAUD

1. See, for example, in France, Groupe d'Etudes Féministes de l'Université de Paris VII (GEF), *Crises de la société, féminisme et changement* (Paris: Tierce, 1991), and "Particularisme et universalisme," *Nouvelles Questions Féministes* 16–18 (1991).

2. Colloquium organized by Elisabeth de Fontenay and Roger Rotmann at the Centre Georges Pompidou on November 28 and 29, 1991, concerning the new forms of contemporary antifeminism.

Chapter 16. Law and Democracy

MARIETTE SINEAU

1. Elisabeth Guibert-Sledziewski, "Naissance de la femme civile. La Révolution, la femme, le droit," *La Pensée* 238 (March-April 1984): 45.

2. Jean Carbonnier, *Droit civil* (Paris: Presses Universitaires de France, 1983), vol. 1, p. 74.

3. United Nations, *Condition juridique de la femme mariée,* Department of Economic and Social Affairs (Geneva, 1958), p. 3.

4. Rachel Trost, "La Condition juridique de la femme mariée en France et en Angleterre," doctoral thesis, University of Nancy, 1971, p. 7.

5. Ginette Castro, *Radioscopie du féminisme américain* (Paris: Presses de la Fondation Nationale des Sciences Politiques, 1984), p. 10.

6. "Le 150e anniversaire de la Révolution," in *Le Droit des femmes* (June 1938): 12.

7. Charles Krug, *Le Féminisme et le droit civil français* (Paris: Pedone, 1899), p. 17.

8. Odile Dhavernas, "L'Inscription des femmes dans le droit: enjeux et perspectives," *Le Féminisme et ses enjeux* (Paris: Centre Fédéral FEN-Edilig, 1988), p. 321.

9. Neville I. Brown, "Angleterre," in Jean Patarin and Imre Zajtay, *Le Régime matrimonial légal dans les législations contemporaines* (Paris: Pedone, 1974), pp. 125–126.

10. Georges Ripert, *Le Régime démocratique et le droit civil moderne* (Paris: Librairie Générale de Droit et de Jurisprudence, 1948), p. 109.

11. Jacqueline Rubellin-Devichi, *L'Evolution du statut civil de la famille depuis 1945* (Paris: Editions du CNRS, 1983), p. 20.

12. Ripert, *Le Régime démocratique*, p. 23.

13. Carbonnier, *Droit civil*, vol. 2, p. 536.

14. Jean Carbonnier, *Flexible Droit* (Paris: Librairie Générale de Droit et de Jurisprudence, 1979), p. 172.

15. Odile Dhavernas, *Droits des femmes, pouvoir des hommes* (Paris: Editions du Seuil, 1978), p. 381.

16. Brigitte Jolivet, "Editorial," *Actes* 57–58 (Winter 1986–87): 5.

17. "La Ligue du droit des femmes," interview with two founders, Annie Sugier and Anne Zelensky, *Actes* 57–58 (Winter 1986–87): 59.

18. F. Rigaux, "Evolution des structures juridiques de la famille en Belgique," in Roger Nerson and Hans-Albrecht Schwarz-Liebermann von Wahlendorf, eds., *Mariage et famille en question: Allemagne* (Paris: Editions du CNRS, 1980), p. 88.

19. Quoted in Yves Lequin, *Histoire des Français* (Paris: Armand Colin, 1984), p. 311.

20. Palmiro Togliatti, "Discorsi alle Donne," pamphlet published by the women's section of the Communist Party, 1946, pp. 48–49, quoted in Dogan, 1955, p. 170.

21. Maurice Duverger, "Des conservatrices," *NEF* 26 (Oct.-Dec. 1969): 22–24.

22. Maurice Duverger, *La Participation des femmes à la vie politique* (Paris: UNESCO, 1955), p. 72.

23. Poll by the Institut Français d'Opinion Publique, *Journal du Dimanche*, May 19, 1991.

24. Torild Skard and Elina Haavio-Mannila, "Women in Parliament," in Haavio-Mannila et al., *Women in Nordic Politics* (New York: Pergamon Press, 1985), p. 58.

25. Andrée Michel, "Les Françaises et la politique," *Les Temps Modernes* 20 (July 1965): 63.

26. Interview with Pierre Viansson-Ponté, *Le Monde*, January 11, 1978.

27. Duverger, *La Participation*, p. 151.

28. *Paris-Match*, July 3, 1987.

29. Mariette Sineau, *Des femmes en politique* (Paris: Economica, 1988), p. 68.

30. Bella Abzug, *Bella! Ms. Abzug Goes to Washington* (New York: Saturday Review Press, 1972), pp. 30–31.

Chapter 17. Feminisms of the 1970s
YASMINE ERGAS

1. Throughout the 1970s and 1980s many important feminist movements developed outside Western Europe and North America. This essay, however, only attempts to address the feminisms that emerged within Western Europe and in North America. Even within this circumscribed arena, it does not attempt a systematic survey of the many movements that left profound marks on Western societies.

2. See Joyce Gelb, *Feminism and Politics: A Comparative Perspective* (Berkeley: University of California Press, 1989), pp. 12–13. For overviews of the interaction between women's movements and political systems, see inter alia Mary Fainsod Katzenstein and Carol McClurg Mueller, eds., *The Women's Movements of the United States and Western Europe: Consciousness, Political Opportunity, and Public Policy* (Philadelphia: Temple University Press, 1987), and Joni Lovenduski, *Women and European Politics: Contemporary Feminism and Public Policy* (Brighton: Wheatsheaf Books, 1986).

3. See Ethel Klein, *Gender Politics: From Consciousness to Mass Politics* (Cambridge, Mass.: Harvard University Press, 1984), p. 22.

4. There is an extensive literature on the "gender gap." For an overview, see David De Vaus and Ian McAllistair, "The Changing Politics of Women: Gender and Political Alignment in 11 Nations," *European Journal of Political Research* 17 (1989): 241–262. The data on Germany cited here are taken from Teresa Kulawik, "Identity versus Strategy: The Politics of the Women's Movement in West Germany," mimeo, n.d., pp. 28–29.

5. Christiane Lemke, "Women and Politics: The New Federal Republic of German," ms. prepared for publication in Barbara Nelson and Najma Chowdhury, eds., *Women and Politics World Wide*, 1991.

6. Ibid.

7. The 1967 Abortion Act of the United Kingdom allowed for abortion in the first 28 weeks of pregnancy when two doctors agreed that the lives of the mother or of other children were at risk or that the child was likely to be handicapped. It is worth noting more generally the many contexts in which abortion rights have emerged as a defining term of political alignments. Contests over such rights now figure prominently on the agenda of several newly reformed Eastern European political systems (such as Hungary and Poland); they have also become a key issue in, for instance, the appointments to the U.S. Supreme Court. On the American campaign for the Equal Rights Amendment and its vicissitudes, see Jane Mansbridge, *Why We Lost the ERA* (Chicago: University of Chicago Press, 1986).

8. Data cited by Mary Fainsod Katzenstein, "Comparing the Feminist Movements of the United States and Western Europe: An Overview," in Fainsod Katzenstein and McClurg Mueller, eds., *The Women's Movements of the United States and Western Europe*, p. 4.

9. Martien Briet, Bert Klandermans, Frederike Kroon, "How Women

Became Involved in the Women's Movement of the Netherlands," in ibid., p. 55.

10. See Naomi Black, *Social Feminism* (Ithaca: Cornell University Press, 1989), p. 10.

11. Mary Fainsod Katzenstein, "Comparing the Feminist Movements of the United States and Western Europe," in Fainsod Katzenstein and McClurg Mueller, eds., *The Women's Movements of the United States and Western Europe,* p. 9.

12. Ethel Klein, "The Diffusion of Consciousness in the United States and Western Europe," in ibid., p. 39.

13. For a comparison of the destinies of feminist mobilizations, see especially Joyce Gelb's discussion of the United Kingdom, the United States, and Sweden in her *Feminism and Politics.* Other comparative analyses and case studies of the parabolas of feminist mobilizations may be found in Joni Lovenduski, *Women and European Politics;* Fainsod Katzenstein and McClurg Mueller, eds., *The Women's Movements of the United States and Western Europe;* Drude Dahlerup, ed., *The New Women's Movement: Feminism and Political Power in Europe and the USA* (London: Sage, 1986); and Mary Fainsod Katzenstein and Hege Skjeie, eds., *Going Public: National Histories of Women's Enfranchisement and Women's Participation within State Institutions* (Oslo: Institute for Social Research, 1990).

14. On feminists' "unobtrusive mobilization" in the United States, see Mary Fainsod Katzenstein, "Unobtrusive Mobilization and the Feminist Movement in the U.S.," mimeo, 1988, and "Organizing on the Terrain of Mainstream Institutions: Feminism in the United States Military," in Fainsod Katzenstein and Skjeie, eds., *Going Public,* pp. 173–203.

15. Webster's *New Twentieth Century Dictionary of the English Language,* unabridged, 2nd ed. (New York: The Publisher's Guild, 1965).

16. As Teresa de Lauretis states, "feminist theory is . . . a developing theory of the female-sexed or female-embodied social subject . . . that is based on its specific, emergent, and conflictual history." Teresa de Lauretis, "Upping the Anti (sic) in Feminist Theory," in Marianne Hirsch and Evelyn Fox Keller, eds., *Conflicts in Feminism* (New York: Routledge, 1990), p. 267. For a different approach, see Karen Offen, "Defining Feminism: A Comparative Historical Approach," *Signs* 14 (1988): 118–157.

17. Black, *Social Feminism.*

18. Readers interested in contemporary Italian feminism see Biancamaria Frabotta, ed., *La politica del femminismo (1973–76)* (Rome: Savelli, 1976); Rosalba Spagnoletti, ed., *I movimenti femministi in Italia* (Rome: Savelli, 1978); Paola Bono and Sandra Kemp, eds., *Italian Feminist Thought: A Reader* (Oxford: Basil Blackwell, 1991); and Libreria delle donne di milano, *Non credece di avere dei diritti: la generazione della libertà femminile nell'idea e nelle vicende di un gruppo di donne* (Milan: Rosenberg and Sellier, 1987).

19. For a detailed discussion of the complex relationship linking UDI to the new Italian feminist movement in a variety of contexts, see Judith Adler Hellman, *Journeys among Women: Feminism in Five Italian Cities* (New

York: Oxford University Press, 1987). More generally on UDI, see Giulietta Ascoli, "L'UDI tra emancipazione e liberazione (1943–64)," in Giulietta Ascoli et al., *La questione femminile in Italia dal '900 ad oggi* (Milan: Franco Angeli, 1979); Giglia Tedesco, "Tra emancipazione e liberazione: L'UDI negli anni sessanta," in Anna Maria Crispino, ed., *Esperienza storica femminile nell'età moderna e contemporanea* (Rome: Unione Donne Italiane, 1989); and Maria Michetti, Margherita Repetto, Luciana Viviani, eds., *UDI: laboratorio di politica delle donne* (Rome: Cooperativa libera stampa, 1984).

20. See Adriana Seroni, "Ragioni e torti del femminismo," in Frabotta, ed., *La politica del femminismo (1973–76)*, pp. 218–228. Also see Carla Ravaioli, *La questione femminile: Intervista col PCI* (Milan: Bompiani, 1977).

21. For a synthetic description of the relevant events, see Jane Jenson, "Le Féminisme en France depuis mai 68," *Vingtième Siècle: Revue d'Histoire* (Oct.–Dec. 1989): 56–57.

22. Juliet Mitchell and Ann Oakley, eds., *What Is Feminism? A Re-examination* (New York: Pantheon, 1986), p. 1.

23. The significance of opening the political discourse to the articulation of women's claims has been extensively discussed by Jane Jenson, in particular, see "Liberation and New Rights for French Women," mimeo, 1984.

24. Simone de Beauvoir, *The Second Sex,* trans. and ed. H. M. Parshley (New York: Knopf, 1952), p. xv.

25. In some perspectives, this conflict within feminism practically defines feminism itself. As Denise Riley has written: "that 'women' is an unstable category, that this instability has a historical foundation, and that feminism is the site of the systematic fighting-out of that instability . . . need not worry us." Denise Riley, *Am I That Name? Feminism and the Category of "Women" in History* (Minneapolis: University of Minnesota Press, 1988), p. 5.

26. Ann Snitow, "A Gender Diary," in Hirsch and Fox Keller, eds., *Conflicts in Feminism,* p. 9. Snitow goes on to stress that the division between those who emphasize gender as a robust form of identification and those who seek to weaken its hold does not merely separate vying political perspectives. It represents, instead, a profound and diffuse existential laceration. In her words: "feminists—and indeed most women—live in a complex relationship to this central feminist divide. From moment to moment we perform subtle psychological and social negotiations about just how gendered we choose to be" (p. 9). For similar perspectives on the question of womanhood and its place in contemporary Western feminisms, see inter alia, Riley, *Am I That Name?* and Yasmine Ergas, *Nelle maglie della politica. Femminismo, istituzioni e politiche sociali nell'Italia degli anni settanta* (Milan: Franco Angeli, 1986). On this issue see also Giovanna Zincone, *Fuga dall'essenzialismo: Un bilancio degli studie su donne e politica* (Torino: Il Segnalibro Editore, 1990).

27. See, for example, Maren Carden, *The New Feminist Movement* (New York: Russell Sage, 1974).

28. Gruppo Demistificazione Autoritarismo, "Il maschile come valore dominante," in Spagnoletti, ed., *I movimenti femministi in Italia,* p. 56. This

line of reasoning has proved central to the development of contemporary Italian feminism. For a more recent explication of female difference and the bankruptcies of female emancipation, see Libreria delle donne di milano, *Non credere di avere dei diritti.*

29. Joan W. Scott, "Deconstructing Equality-Versus-Difference: Or the Uses of Poststructuralist Theory for Feminism," in *Feminist Studies* 14 (Spring 1988): 33–50, reprinted in Hirsch and Fox Keller, eds., *Conflicts in Feminism,* pp. 134–148.

30. Mansbridge, *Why We Lost the ERA.*

31. It is sometimes believed that by virtue of espousing egalitarian ideologies, feminists have relinquished the claim of special rights for women. That this is not the case is evinced by the intensity of debates among feminists in numerous countries precisely over such issues as maternity leave. As one Italian feminist wrote, arguing in favor of strengthening maternity leave as against parental leave, it would seem that in a formally egalitarian perspective maternity and paternity are the same experience, that they entail "analogous efforts and interchangeable existential dimensions." See Franca Bimbi, "differenza/paritá" in Laura Balbo, ed., *Tempi di vita. Studi e proposte per cambiarli* (Milan: Feltrinelli, 1991), p. 54. For discussions of the relevant issues in the United States, see, for example, Martha Albertson Fineman, *The Illusion of Equality: The Rhetoric and Reality of Divorce Reform* (Chicago: University of Chicago Press, 1991), and Martha Minow, "Adjudicating Differences: Conflicts Among Feminist Lawyers," in Hirsch and Fox Keller, eds., *Conflicts in Feminism,* pp. 149–163.

32. Feminist debates have concentrated most often on the relationship of "sexual difference," "gender," and sex. However, emphasis on the social nature and cultural construction of bodily experiences has recently come to the fore. See Susan Rubin Suleiman, *Subversive Intent: Gender Politics and the Avant-Garde* (Cambridge, Mass.: Harvard University Press, 1990) and Judith Butler, *Gender Trouble: Feminism and the Subversion of Identity* (New York: Routledge, 1990). On this issue, see also Catharine Gallagher and Thomas Laqueur, *The Making of the Western Body: Sexuality and Society in the Nineteenth Century* (Berkeley: University of California Press, 1987).

33. Gayle Rubin, "The Traffic in Women," in R. Reiter, ed., *Toward an Anthropology of Women* (New York: Monthly Review Press, 1975), p. 160.

34. Robin Morgan, ed., *Sisterhood Is Powerful: An Anthology of Writings from the Women's Liberation Movement* (New York: Vintage Books, 1970), p. 533.

35. Hélène Cixous, "The Laugh of the Medusa," *Signs* (1976): 877.

36. The manifesto of Rivolta Femminile was published in 1970. It is reproduced in Spagnoletti, ed., *I movimenti femministi in Italia,* pp. 102–106. On Rivolta Femminile, see Maria Luisa Boccia, "Per una teoria dell'autenticitá. Lettura di Carla Lonzi," *Memoria. Rivista di storia delle donne* 19–20 (1987): 85–108.

37. Some of the issues discussed here and in the following paragraphs concerning the praxis of separation and distinction are also examined in Ergas, *Nelle maglie della politica.*

38. Autonomy was a major theme for numerous feminist movements, especially in the early 1970s, as they struggled to define their relations with their interlocutors on the left. See the discussion of the centrality of autonomy in the German feminist movement in Kulawik, "Identity versus Strategy," mimeo, n.d.

39. This is an analogy feminists themselves often drew, and not only in the United States. "Woman is beautiful," as one of the earliest Italian feminist publications emphatically paraphrased the American Black slogan; and a coeval document of another collective, based at the University of Trent, bore the title "Women and Blacks. Sex and Color." On the close intertwining and tense conversation between American feminists and the civil rights movement, see especially Sara Evans, *Personal Politics: The Roots of Women's Liberation in the Civil Rights Movement and the New Left* (New York: Vintage Books, 1980).

40. On the centrality of consciousness-raising for contemporary feminism, see Catharine A. MacKinnon, "Feminism, Marxism, Method, and the State," *Signs* (1982): 515–544 and Dahlerup, *The New Women's Movement*.

41. This pedagogical guide to consciousness-raising was prepared by Kathie Sarachild, and then reprinted in Morgan, ed., *Sisterhood Is Powerful*, pp. xxiii–xxiv.

42. The vulva was "formed by aligning the raised fingers and lowered thumbs of both hands and turning the palms outward." Bonnie S. Anderson and Judith P. Zinsser, *A History of Their Own* (New York: Harper and Row, 1988), vol. II, p. 413.

43. Petra de Vries cited in ibid., p. 412.

44. Martha Shelly, "Notes of a Radical Lesbian," in Morgan, ed., *Sisterhood Is Powerful*, p. 307.

45. "The Second Sex—Thirty Years Later." Conference paper delivered at the New York Institute for the Humanities, 1979, pp. 74–75, cited in Anderson and Zinsser, *A History of Their Own*, p. 425. Lesbianism as a sexual preference, in other words, carried immediate political significance. On this issue, see also Adrienne Rich, "Compulsory Heterosexuality and Lesbian Experience," *Signs* 5, 4 (1980): 631–660, and Manuela Fraire, "Ordine e disordine. Ovvero dele sorti dell'amore tra donne," *Memoria. Rivista di storia delle donne* 19–20 (1987): 109–117.

46. Clifford Geertz, "A Lab of One's Own," *New York Review of Books*, November 8, 1990, p. 19.

47. Significantly, a dispute over women's history prompted the first major conference of British feminism. When a group of women attending a History Workshop at Ruskin College (Oxford) objected to the exclusion of women's history from the agenda, they decided to convene what became the Women's Liberation Conference, which was held at Ruskin in 1970 and drew 600 participants. See Joni Lovenduski, *Women and European Politics*, p. 75.

48. See, for example, Sheila Rowbotham, *Women, Resistance and Revolution: A History of Women in the Modern World* (New York: Pantheon, 1972), and *Hidden from History: Rediscovering Women in History from the Seventeenth Century to the Present* (New York: Pantheon Books, 1974);

Renate Bridenthal and Claudia Koonz, eds., *Becoming Visible: Women in European History* (Boston: Houghton Mifflin, 1977); Michelle Perrot, *Une histoire des femmes est-elle possible?* (Paris: Rivage, 1984); Joan W. Scott, *Gender and the Politics of History* (New York: Columbia University Press, 1988).

49. The importance of creating a "feminist tradition" was voiced in the early political manifestos. The Italian group, Rivolta Femminile, for instance, exhorted women to unify "the historical situations and episodes of the feminist experience." Cited in Spagnoletti, ed., *I movimenti femministi in Italia*, p. 104.

50. On the relation of memory and history with respect to women, see "Memoires des femmes," *Penelope* 12 (Spring 1985); Margaret A. Lourie and Domna C. Stanton, eds., "Women and Memory," *Michigan Quarterly Review* 26, 1 (Winter 1987).

51. To these issues the Scandinavian feminists have added a third dimension of political engagement. See Helga Maria Hernes, *Welfare State and Woman Power: Essays in State Feminism* (London: Norway University Press, 1987).

52. Elsewhere, body politics emerged in relation to a different set of issues, such as cliteridectomy in many African countries and the practice of widow-burning in India.

53. The Boston Women's Health Book Collective, *Our Bodies, Ourselves* (New York: Simon and Schuster, 1976).

54. Kate Millett, *Sexual Politics* (New York: Doubleday, 1970), p. 58.

55. Anne Koedt, "The Myth of the Vaginal Orgasm," in A. Koedt, E. Levine, and A. Rapone, eds., *Radical Feminism* (Chicago: Quadrangle, 1973).

56. Germaine Greer, *The Female Eunuch* (New York: McGraw Hill, 1971).

57. The Boston Women's Health Book Collective, *Our Bodies, Ourselves;* "Manifesto di Rivolta Femminile," in Spagnoletti, ed., *I movimenti femministi in Italia*, p. 102.

58. Cited in Anderson and Zinsser, *A History of Their Own*, p. 420.

59. Ibid., p. 413.

60. Anna, of the Movimento Femminista Romano at the ninth congress of the Unione Donne Italiane (November 1–3, 1973), cited in Silvia Tozzi, "Molecolare, creativa, materiale: la vicenda dei gruppi per la salute," *Memoria. Rivista di storia delle donne* 19–20 (1987): 161.

61. From a document by Rivolta Femminile dated July 1971, cited in Libreria delle donne di milano, *Non credere di avere dei diritti*, pp. 62, 63.

62. Cf. Lovenduski, *Women and European Politics*.

63. Kulawik, "Identity versus Strategy," p. 16.

64. Ibid.

65. For a synthesis of the relevant events, to which this reconstruction is particularly indebted, see Anderson and Zinsser, *A History of Their Own*, p. 418.

66. An analogous campaign was conducted in Italy, again meshing public defiance of existing legislation with widespread—and ultimately successful—mobilization for its repeal.

67. Similar campaigns took place in the United Kingdom, Italy, the United States, the Netherlands, and the Nordic countries. See Lovenduski, *Women and European Politics.*

68. The following reconstruction is taken from ibid., pp. 78–79. For an analysis of this aspect of the British feminist movement, see also Hilary Rose, "In Practice Supported, in Theory Denied: An Account of an Invisible Urban Movement," *Journal of Urban and Regional Research* 3 (1978): 521–537.

69. Lovenduski, *Women and European Politics,* p. 79.

70. Anderson and Zinsser, *A History of Their Own,* p. 422.

71. Cited in ibid.

72. On this issue see Zincone, *Fuga dall'essenzialismo,* and Riley, *Am I That Name?* For an emblematic analysis tending to negate the validity of sexual differences, see Cynthia Fuchs Epstein, *Deceptive Distinctions: Theory and Research on Sex, Gender, and the Social Order* (New Haven: Yale University Press, 1988).

73. A feminist journal with the same title is currently published in the United States.

74. Bell Hooks speaking in Mary Childers and Bell Hooks, "A Conversation about Race and Class," in Hirsch and Fox Keller, eds., *Conflicts in Feminism,* p. 66.

75. Chandra Talpade Mohanty, "Under Western Eyes: Feminist Scholarship and Colonial Discourses," in Chandra Talpade Mohanty, Ann Russo, Lourdes Torres, eds., *Third World Women and the Politics of Feminism* (Bloomington: Indiana University Press, 1991), pp. 53–54.

Chapter 18. From Feminine to Feminism in Quebec
Yolande Cohen

1. Barbara Melosh, *The Physician Hand Work: Culture and Conflict in American Nursing* (Philadelphia: Temple University Press, 1982); Susan Reverby, *Ordered to Care: The Dilemma of American Nursing, 1850–1945* (Cambridge: Cambridge University Press, 1987); Yolande Cohen and Michèle Degenais, "Le Métier d'infirmière: savoirs féminins et reconnaissance professionnelle," *Revue d'Histoire de l'Amérique Française* 41, 2 (Autumn 1987): 155–177.

2. Martha Vicinus, *Independent Women* (Chicago: University of Chicago Press, 1984).

3. Margaret Allen, "The Domestic Ideal and the Mobilization of Woman Power," *Women's Studies International Forum* 6 (1983): 401–412. See also the article by Michelle Perrot in Margaret Higonnet et al., *Behind the Lines: Gender and the Two World Wars* (New Haven: Yale University Press, 1987).

4. At first sight, it might appear that Quebec is a century behind New England, where the woman question was raised as early as 1820 and resolved by what has been called "the empire of motherhood." A strict separation of roles developed under U.S. democracy. In Quebec, by contrast, it was not until a secular nationalist ideology emerged that one finds a similar phenomenon.

5. Marcel Fournier, *L'Entrée dans la modernité. Science, culture et société au Québec* (Montreal: Editions Saint-Martin, 1986).

6. Here I deliberately choose to analyze two magazines reputed to be traditionalist and conservative. Both magazines not only reflected widely held views of women but helped to shape them. See Yolande Cohen, *Femmes de parole. L'histoire des Cercles de fermières du Québec, 1915–1990* (Montreal: Le Jour, 1990). There are European organizations similar to the Cercles, such as the Jeunesse Agricole Catholique in France. See Martyne Perrot, "La Jaciste, une figure emblématique," in Rose-Marie Lagrave, *Celles de la terre* (Paris: EHESS, 1987). Similar groups exist in Belgium and Italy. The Association Mondiale des Femmes Rurales organizes international meetings of groups of rural women every two years.

7. For a fuller explanation of "sexual complementarity" than I can give here, the reader may wish to see Karen Offen, "E. Legouvé and the Doctrine of 'Equality in Difference' for Women: A Case Study of Male Feminism in Nineteenth-Century French Thought," *Journal of Modern History* (June 1986): 453–484. Offen analyzes the concept of "equality in difference" first formulated by Legouvé in his *Cours d'histoire morale des femmes* (Paris: G. Sandré, 1848), and adopted late in the nineteenth century by numerous French feminist militants, including Paule Mink. Mink advocated a strict complementarity of the sexes, with men and women assigned different and exclusive zones of responsibility. To that end, she proposed to revise the division of labor, with women assuming responsibility for all services and commerce, activities at which their flair for detail and other skills made them better than men.

8. The first such magazine in Canada was *The Homemakers*, an English-language magazine for women. Belgium may also have provided examples. The French imitated only the style of the magazine, along with articles offering advice on cooking and fashions. *La Jeunesse Agricole Féminine*, which initiated the genre in France, did not appear until 1935, however. See Perrot, "La Jaciste."

9. *La Bonne Fermière*, 1, 1 (January 1920): 3 (cited hereafter as *B.F.*).

10. *B.F.* 1, 4 (October 1920): 99.

11. See M. Dumont, "La parole des femmes: les revues féminines 1938–1968," in F. Dumont et al., eds., *Idéologies au Canada-français, 1940–1976* (Montreal: Presses de l'Université de Laval), pp. 5–45, as well as the analysis of rural women's ideologies in the United States in Joan Jensen, *Loosening the Bonds: Mid-Atlantic Farm Women* (New Haven: Yale University Press, 1986), and, in France, Lagrave, *Celles de la terre.*

12. *B.F.* 2, 2 (April 1921): 38.

13. *B.F.* 5, 1 (January 1924): 10.

14. *B.F.* 9, 1 (January 1928): 30.

15. *B.F.* 11, 2 (April 1930): 56.

16. The Fédération Saint-Jean-Baptiste, which is generally considered to be the first women's nationalist organization, was founded in 1907 by women interested in social reform in Quebec. It was also considered feminist, although the feminism it espoused was Christian and social and never questioned motherhood. See M. Lavigne, Y. Pinard, and J. Stoddart, "La Fédération nationale Saint-Jean-Baptiste et les revendications féministes au début du 20e siècle," in M. Lavigne and Y. Pinard, eds., *Travailleuses et Féministes* (Montreal: Boreal Express, 1983), pp. 199–216.

17. The authors see the feminine orientation of the FNSJB and the bourgeois background of its members as the causes of its decline and cooptation (ibid., p. 215).

18. *B.F.* 3, 2 (April 1922): 46.

19. When the Union Catholique des Femmes was established in 1944, the magazine *Terre et Foyer* offered readers a women's publication with a new look. It promised to recapture some of the movement's old energy within the terms of the triad woman, family, state. As the pillar of the family, women also assured the survival of the nation through their devotion to both.

20. *Terre et Foyer* 10, 1 (January 1953): 18 (cited hereafter as *T.F.*).

21. *T.F.* 10, 7 (September 1953): 24.

22. *T.F.* 14, 5 (May-June 1957): 19.

23. Almond and Verba, *The Civic Culture* (Boston: Little, Brown, 1963).

24. *T.F.* 2, 5–6 (May-June 1946): 4.

25. *T.F.* 15, 1 (January 1958): 1.

26. *T.F.* 2, 5–6 (May-June 1946): 2.

27. *T.F.* 10, 7 (September 1953): 24.

28. *T.F.* 14, 7 (September 1957): 2.

29. Jean Bruno, *Agriculture et développement dans l'est du Québec* (Quebec: Presses de l'Université du Québéc, 1985), and M.-A. Ledoux, "L'UCC comme groupe de pression sous l'administration Duplessis," master's thesis, University of Montreal, 1971. The author analyzes the negotiating process that led the government to adopt the law of agricultural markets in 1956. He shows that the UCC was also aware of the economic needs of small farmers, whom it defended without challenging conservative ideology.

30. Beauchamp thinks that farmers saw in the dominant ideology (which included agricultural corporatism and syndicalism) only what it might be worth to them in terms of material advantages. See "Les Débuts de la coopération et du syndicalisme agricoles, 1900–1930: quelques éléments de la pratique," *Recherches Sociographiques* 20, 3 (Sept.-Dec. 1979): 380ff.

31. "Le Monde rural," *Recherches Sociographiques,* special issue edited by Yolande Cohen and Gary Caldwell (Montreal: Presses de l'Université Laval, 1989).

32. Claudia Koonz, *Mothers in Fatherland: Family Life and Nazi Ideology, 1919–1945* (New York: St. Martin's Press, 1987), and Michela De

Giorgio, "Les Demoiselles catholiques italiennes," in Yolande Cohen, ed., *Femmes et contre-pouvoirs* (Montreal: Boreal, 1987), pp. 101–126.

Chapter 19. Reproduction and Bioethics
JACQUELINE COSTA-LASCOUX

1. The principal techniques of medically assisted reproduction include intraperitoneal fertilization (IPF), in-vitro fertilization (IVF), in-vitro fertilization with transfer of the embryo (IVFTE), and intra-Fallopian gamete transfer (IFGT), which involves bringing eggs and sperm into direct contact in the Fallopian tube, where natural fertilization takes place; in addition, there is artificial insemination with sperm from the husband and artificial insemination with sperm from a third-party donor.

2. I prefer the term "biomedical ethics" to the more common "medical bioethics," because the central concept is ethics, with biomedical techniques merely instrumental objects. For an in-depth study of biomedical science in relation to ethics, see Anne Fagot-Largeault, *L'Homme bio-éthique, pour une déontologie de la recherche sur le vivant* (Paris: Maloine, 1985).

3. Two special journal issues have looked closely at the question of male-female images and roles in medically assisted reproduction: "Corps écrit," in *Naître* 21 (April 1987), and "Bioéthique et désir d'enfant," in *Dialogue, Recherches Cliniques et Sociologiques sur le Couple et la Famille* 87 (1st quarter 1985).

4. Embryo is the term for the product of fertilization up to the fetal stage, but the beginning of the fetal stage is controversial: the eighth week for the Comité National d'Éthique in France, the twelfth week for some others. Postmortem insemination is artificial insemination of a woman with the sperm of her deceased husband.

5. For further references, see the bibliography.

6. See Jean-Louis Baudouin and Catherine Labrousse-Riou, *Produire l'homme, de quel droit? Etude juridique et éthique des procréations artificielles* (Paris: Presses Universitaires de France, 1987), as well as special issues of journals cited in the bibliography. Note, also, two recent articles by Pierre-André Taguieff, which have stirred renewed controversy: "L'Eugénisme, objet de phobie idéologique," in *Esprit, la Bioéthique en panne?* 11 (November 1989), and "Sur l'eugénisme: du fantasme au débat," *Pouvoirs* 56 (1991). For a more alarmist view concerning the "biocratic temptation," see *Ethique, la Vie en question* 1 (1991).

7. Jacques Testart was one of the first biologists to draw attention to the confusion engendered by rapid progress in biotechnology. See his *L'Oeuf transparent* (Paris: Fayard, 1986).

8. Surveys conducted by the Laboratoire de Sociologie Juridique of the University of Paris II and by the Centre de Droit de la Famille of Jean Moulin University in Lyon. See the report for the Commissariat Général au Plan, François Terré and Jacqueline Rubellin-Devichi, eds., *Les Nouvelles Tech-*

niques de procréation artificielle dans les pays occidentaux, vols. 1 and 2 (1988).

9. Françoise Cahen, "La Double Illusion ou qu'est-ce qui fait courir les couples infertiles?" and Geneviève Delaisi de Parseval, "Couples stériles, médecine féconde? A propos de l'IAD," *Dialogue* 87 (1985).

10. In *Génétique, procréation et droit* (Paris: Actes Sud, 1985); see also contributions by jurists Jean Carbonnier, Michelle Gobert, Catherine Labrousse-Riou, Jean Rivero, Jacques Robert, Jacqueline Rubellin-Devichi.

11. See "Bioéthique et désir d'enfant," *Dialogue* 87, and Geneviève Delaisi de Parseval, "Le Désir d'enfant saisi par la médecine et la loi," ibid.

12. See note 8.

13. Ibid.

14. Jacques Testart, "Procréations assistées: quelle réglementation?" *Ethique. La Vie en question* 1 (1991): 88–89.

15. Ibid.

16. Bernard Edelmann, "D'un projet l'autre: France et République fédérale d'Allemagne," *Ethique* 1 (1991): 36–37; Michelle Gobert, "La maternité de substitution: réflexions à propos d'une décision rassurante," in *Les Petites Affiches* 127 (1991); Jacqueline Rubellin-Devichi, "Mères porteuses, premier et deuxième types," *Bioéthique* (1992).

17. See note 16.

18. François Giraud, *Les Mères portueses* (Paris: Publisud, 1987).

19. Rubellin-Devichi, "Mères porteuses."

20. See Dalloz, 1991, p. 417, report by Y. Chartier and D. Thouvenin.

21. Gobert, article cited in *Naître* 21 (April 1987).

22. For an overview of these issues, see especially Jean Carbonnier, *Droit civil, la famille,* vol. 2 (Paris: Presses Universitaires de France, 1991); Gérard Cornu, *La Famille* (1991); Jacqueline Rubellin-Devichi, *J.C.P.* 21 (22 May 1991), Doctrine, 3505, pp. 181–187; Catherine Labrousse-Riou, "L'homme à vif: droit et biotechnologies," *Esprit. La Bioéthique en panne?* (November 1989).

Christa Wolf

FRANÇOISE THÉBAUD

1. When did the genocide begin? and who knew what? to echo the title of a book by Stéphane Courtois and Adam Rayski, *Qui savait quoi? L'extermination des Juifs 1941–1945* (Paris: La Découverte, 1987). Christa Wolf alludes to Hitler's January 1939 speech "prophesying" the "extermination of the Jews" and to Goering's order of July 1941, which preceded the widescale massacre of Jews in occupied Soviet territory in the second half of 1941. It was at the Wannsee Conference on January 20, 1942, that "the final solution of the Jewish problem" was ordered in the greatest secrecy. Yet news of what was going on began to circulate in that same year.

Bibliography

Abel, Elizabeth. *Writing and Sexual Difference*. Chicago: University of Chicago Press, 1982.

Adams, Carolyn Teich, and Katherine Teich Winston. *Mothers at Work: Public Policies in the United States, Sweden, and China*. New York: Longman, 1980.

Addis Saba, Marina, ed. *La corporazione della donna*. Florence: Vallecchi, 1988.

Addis Saba, Marina, et al. *Storia delle donne: Una scienza possibile*. Rome: Edizione Felina Libri, 1986.

Alberoni, Francesco. *Consumi e società*. Bologna: Il Mulino, 1964.

Aleramo, Sibilla. *A Woman*, trans. R. Delmar. Berkeley: University of California Press, 1980.

Allart, Marie-Christine. "Les femmes dans trois villages de l'Artois: Travail et vécu quotidien (1919–1939)." *Revue du Nord* (July-September 1981).

Alloisio, Mirella, and Giuliana Beltrami. *Volontarie della libertà*. Milan: Mazzotta, 1981.

American Fertility Society. "Ethical Consideration of the New Reproductive Technology." *Fertile and Sterile*, 46, 3 (1986).

Amiel, Christiane, Giordana Charuty, and Claudine Fabre-Vassas. *Jours de vigne: Les femmes des pays viticoles racontent le travail*. Atelier du Gué, 1981.

Anelli, Maria Teresa, Paola Gabbrielli, Marta Morgavi, and Roberto Piperno. *Fotoromanzo: Fascino e pregiudizio—storia, documenti, e immagini di un grande fenomeno popolare*. Milan: Savelli, 1979.

Ariès, Philippe, and Georges Duby, eds. *A History of Private Life*, vol. 5: *Riddles of Identity in Modern Times*, eds. Antoine Prost and Vincent Gérard. Cambridge, Mass.: Harvard University Press, 1993.

Artom, Sandra, and Anna Rita Calabrò. *Sorelle d'Italia*. Milan: Rizzoli, 1989.

Aspesi, Natalia. *Il lusso e l'autarchia: Storia dell'eleganza italiana, 1930–1944*. Milan: Rizzoli, 1982.

Association internationale des démographes de langue française (AIDELF), 1986. *Les familles d'aujourd'hui: Démographie et évolution récente des comportements familiaux.* Colloque de Genève (September 17–20, 1984). Paris: AIDELF/Institut national d'études démographiques.

Atti del primer coloqui di historia de la dona, 1986. Barcelona, 1990.

Aubert, Nicole. *Le pouvoir usurpé: Femmes et hommes dans l'entreprise.* Paris: Laffont, 1982.

Australia, The Committee to Consider the Social, Ethical, and Legal Issues Arising from in Vitro Fertilization. "Report on the Disposition of Embryos Produced by 'in Vitro' Fertilization" (August 1984).

Ayers, Pat, and Jan Lambertz. "Marriage Relations, Money, and Domestic Violence in Working-Class Liverpool, 1919–1939," in Jane Lewis, ed., *Labour and Love: Women's Experience of House and Family, 1850–1940.* London: Basil Blackwell, 1986.

Azéma, Jean-Pierre. *De Munich à la libération (1938–1944). Nouvelle histoire de la France contemporaine.* Paris: Seuil, 1979.

Badinter, Elizabeth. *L'amour en plus: Histoire de l'amour maternel XVIIè–XXè siècle.* Paris: Flammarion, 1980.

——— *L'un est l'autre: Des relations entre hommes et femmes.* Paris: Odile Jacob, 1986.

Bailes, Kendall E. "Alexandra Kollontaï et la nouvelle morale." *Cahiers du Monde Russe et Soviétique,* 6, 4 (October-December 1965), 471–496.

Bajohr, Stefan. *Die Hälfte der Fabrik: Geschichte der Frauenarbeit in Deutschland, 1914–1945.* Marburg: Verlag Arbeiterbewegung und Gesellschaftswissenschaft, 1979.

Barrachina, Marie-Aline. "La section féminine de FET et des JONS puis du mouvement national." Thesis, University of Paris III, 1979.

Barrère-Maurisson, Marie-Agnès, and Olivier Marchand. "Structures familiales et marchés du travail dans les pays développés." *Economie et Statistique,* 235 (September 1990), 19–30.

Barrère-Maurisson, Marie-Agnès, et al. *Le sexe du travail: Structures familiales et système productif.* Grenoble: PUG, 1984.

Bashevkin, Sylvia, ed. *Women and Politics in Western Europe.* London: Cass, 1985.

Battagliola, Françoise. *La fin du mariage? Jeunes couples des années 80.* Paris: Syros, 1988.

Baudouin, J. L., and Catherine Labrousse-Riou. *Produire l'homme de quel droit? Etude juridique et éthique des procréations artificielles.* Paris: PUF, 1987.

Bawin-Legros, Bernadette. *Familles, mariage, divorce.* Liège: Pierre Mardaga, 1988.

Bebel, August. *La femme et le socialisme.* Gand: Imprimerie Coopérative, 1911.

Becker, Gary. "Human Capital, Effort, and the Sexual Division of Labor." *Journal of Labor Economics* (1985, January supplement).

Beckwith, Karen. "Women and Parliamentary Politics in Italy, 1946–1979," in Howard R. Penniman, ed., *Italy at the Polls, 1979.* Washington, D.C.: American Enterprise Institute, 1981.

Beechey, Veronica. *Unequal Work*. London: Verso, 1987.

Bell, Susan, and Karen M. Offen, eds. *Women, the Family, and Freedom*, 2 vols. Stanford: Stanford University Press, 1983.

Benetti Brunelli, Valeria. *La donna nella civiltà contemporanea*. Turin: Bocca, 1933.

Berelowitch, Vladimir. "Les débuts du droit de la famille en RSFSR." *Cahiers du Monde Russe et Soviétique*, 22, 4 (October-December 1981), 351–374.

Berges, Consuelo. *Explicación de Octubre: Historia comprimida de 4 años de república en España*. Madrid: Garcigoy, n.d.

Berkeley, Ellen Perry, ed. *Architecture: A Place for Women*. Washington, D.C.: Smithsonian Institution Press, 1989.

Berkin, Carol R., and Clara M. Lovett, eds. *Women, War, and Revolution*. New York: Holmes and Meier, 1980.

Berton-Hodge, Roberte. "La condition féminine en URSS." *Problèmes Politiques et Sociaux*, 31–32. Paris: La Documentation Française, 1970.

——— "La crise de la famille soviétique." *Problèmes Politiques et Sociaux*, 392. Paris: La Documentation Française, 1980.

Besnard-Rousseau, Pascal. "Parti communiste français, morale et sexualité." Thesis, University of Paris, 1979.

Bettio, Francesca. *The Sexual Division of Labor*. Oxford: Clarendon Press, 1989.

"La bioéthique." *Pouvoirs*, 56 (1991).

"Bioéthique et désir d'enfant: Dialogue." *Recherches Cliniques et Sociologiques sur le Couple et la Famille*, 87 (1985).

"Biologie et éthique: La maîtrise de la reproduction et l'image de l'homme." *Lumière et Vie*, 172. Lyon, 1985.

Black, Naomi. *Social Feminism*. Ithaca: Cornell University Press, 1989.

Blanc, M. *L'ère de la génétique*. Paris: Ed. La Découverte, 1986.

Blasco, Sofía. *Peuple d'Espagne: Journal de guerre de La Madrecita*. Paris: Nouvelle Revue Critique, 1938.

Blunden, Katherine. *Le travail et la vertu: Femmes au foyer—une mystification de la révolution industrielle*. Paris: Payot, 1983.

Boak, Helen L. "'Our Last Hope': Women's Votes for Hitler—A Reappraisal." *German Studies Review*, 12 (1989), 289–310.

Bock, Gisela. "'Keine Arbeitskräfte in diesem Sinne': Prostituierte im Nazi-Staat," in Pieke Biermann, ed., *Wir sind Frauen wie andere auch: Prostituierte und ihre Kämpfe*. Reinbek, 1980.

——— "Racism and Sexism in Nazi Germany: Motherhood, Compulsory Sterilization, and the State." *Signs: Journal of Women in Culture and Society*, 8, 3 (1983), 400–421.

——— "Rassenpolitik, Medizin, und Massenmord im Nationalsozialismus." *Archiv für Sozialgeschichte*, 30 (1990), 423–453.

——— *Zwangssterilisation im Nationalisozialismus: Untersuchungen zur Rassenpolitik und Frauenpolitik*. Opladen: Westdeutscher Verlag, 1986.

Bock, Gisela, and Pat Thane, eds. *Maternity and Gender Policies: Women and the Rise of the European Welfare States.* London: Routledge, 1991.

Bortolotti, Franca Pieroni. *Femminismo e partiti politici in Italia, 1919–1926.* Rome: Riuniti, 1978.

—— *Le origini del movimento femminile in Italia.* Turin: Einaudi, 1963.

—— *Socialismo e questione femminile in Italia, 1892–1922.* Milan: Mazzotta, 1974.

Bourdieu, Pierre. *La distinction, critique sociale du jugement.* Paris: Minuit, 1979.

Bourgeault, G. *La bioéthique: Son objet, sa méthode, ses questions, ses enjeux.* Montreal: Ethica, 1989.

—— *L'Ethique et le droit face aux nouvelles technologies biomédicales.* Brussels: De Boeck-Wesmael, 1990.

Braeman, J., et al. *Change and Continuity in Twentieth-Century America: The Nineteen Twenties.* Columbus: Ohio State University Press, 1968.

Braidotti, Rosi. "The Ethics of Sexual Difference: The Case of Foucault and Irigaray." *Australian Feminist Studies,* 3 (1986).

—— *Patterns of Dissonance.* Cambridge: Polity Press, 1991.

Braybon, Gail. *Women Workers in the First World War.* London: Croom Helm, 1981.

Braybon, Gail, and Penny Summerfield. *Out of the Cage: Women's Experiences in Two World Wars.* London: Pandora, 1987.

Bridenthal, Renate, and Claudia Koonz, eds. *Becoming Visible: Women in European History.* Boston: Houghton Mifflin Company, 1977; rev. ed., 1987.

Brin, Irene. *Usi e costumi.* Palermo: Sellerio, 1981.

Bruegel, Irène. "Women as a Reserve of Labour," in Mary Ewans, ed., *The Women Question.* Oxford, 1982.

Bulmer, Martin, Jane Lewis, and David Piachaud, eds. *The Goals of Social Policy.* London: Unwin Hyman, 1989.

Buonanno, Milly. *Cultura di massa e identità femminile: L'immagine della donna in televisione.* Turin: ERI, 1983.

—— *La donna nella stampa: Giornaliste, lettrice, e modelli di femminilità.* Rome: Editori Riuniti, 1978.

—— *Naturale come sei: Indagine sulla stampa femminile in Italia,* with an introduction by Giovanni Bechelloni. Rimini-Florence: Guaraldi, 1975.

Burguière, André, Christiane Klapisch-Zuber, Martine Segalen, and Françoise Zonabend, eds. *Histoire de la famille,* vol. 2: *Le choc des modernités.* Paris: Armand Colin, 1986.

Bussy-Genevois, Danièle. "Le courrier des lecteurs dans *Ellas, 1932–1935.*" *Presse et public,* ed. Carmen Salaün Sanchez. University of Rennes II, 1982.

—— "Presse féminine et républicanisme en Espagne, 1931–1936." Thesis, University of Bordeaux III, 1988.

Buttafuoco, Annarita. *Cronache femminili: Temi e momenti della stampa emancipazionista in Italia dall'Unità al Fascismo.* Siena: Università degli Studi di Siena, 1988.

————— "Condizione delle donne e movimento di emancipazione femminile," in *Storia della società italiana: L'Italia di Giolitti,* part 5, vol. 20. Milan: Teti, 1981.

————— *Le Mariuccine: Storia di un'istituzione laica—la società Mariuccia.* Milan: F. Angeli, 1985.

Byck, G., and S. Galpin-Jacquot. *Etat comparatif des règles éthiques et juridiques relatives à la procréation artificielle.* Paris: Ministère de la Justice; Ministère de la Santé et de la Famille, 1986.

Cahiers du Grif, 7, Dé/pro/re/créer, Brussels, 1975; *12, Parlez-vous française?* Brussels, 1976; *13, Elles consonnent,* Brussels, 1976; *33, Hannah Arendt,* Paris, 1985; *40, Georg Simmel,* Paris, 1989; *43, Savoir et différence des sexes,* Paris, 1990; *Femmes et philosophie,* Paris, 1991.

Campoamor, Clara. *Mi pecado mortal: El voto femenino y yo.* Barcelona: La Sal, 1981.

Canada, Ontario Law Reform Commission, 1985. "Report on Human Artificial Reproduction and Related Matters," 2 vols.

Canino, Elena. *Clotilde tra le due guerre.* Milan: Longanesi, 1957.

Capel, Rosa. *El sufragio femenino en la IIa república española.* University of Granada, 1975.

————— ed. *Mujer y sociedad en España, 1700–1975.* Madrid: Ministerio de Cultura, 1982.

Catégorisation de sexe et construction sociale. Université d'Aix-en-Provence: Collectif CEFUP, 1989.

CERM (Centre d'études et de recherches marxistes). *La condition féminine.* Paris: Editions Sociales, 1978.

Chalier, Catherine. *Figures du féminin: Lectures d'Emmanuel Lévinas.* Paris: La Nuit Surveillée, 1982.

Chalvon-Demersay, Sabine. *Concubin-concubine.* Paris: Seuil, 1983.

Chartier, Roger, ed. *Histoire de l'édition française,* vol. 4: *1900–1950.* Paris: Promodis, 1986.

Charuty, G., C. Fabre-Vassas, and Agnès Fine. *Gestes d'amont: Les femmes du pays de Sault racontent le travail.* Atelier du Gué, 1980.

Cherlin, Andrew, and Frank F. Furstenberg, Jr., eds. "The European Family." *Journal of Family Issues,* 9, 3 (September 1988), 291–424.

Childers, Thomas. *The Nazi Voter: The Social Foundation of Fascism in Germany, 1919–1933.* Chapel Hill, 1983.

Chloros, Aleck, ed. "Interspousal Relations," vol. 4 of *International Encyclopedia of Comparative Law:* "Persons and Family," 1980.

Clarke, John, Allan Cochrane, and Carol Smart. *Ideologies of Welfare: From Dreams to Disillusion.* London: Hutchinson, 1987.

Clarke, R. *Les enfants de la science.* Paris: Stock, 1984.

CLEF (Centre lyonnais d'études féministes). *Les femmes et la question du travail.* Lyon: PUL, 1984.

Cockburn, Cynthia. *Brothers, Male Dominance, and Technological Change.* London: Pluto Press, 1983.

Cohen, Yolande. *Femmes de parole: L'histoire des cercles de fermières du Québec, 1915–1990.* Montreal: Le Jour, 1990.

————, ed. *Femmes et contre-pouvoirs*. Montreal: Boréal, 1987.

Cohen, Yolande, and Gary Caldwell, eds. *Le monde rural*. Special number of *Recherches Sociographiques*, 39, 2–3 (1988).

Cointet-Labrousse, Michèle. *Vichy et le fascisme*. Brussels: Editions Complexes, 1987.

Collectif de rédaction de l'Almanach. *Femmes et Russie, 1980*. Paris: Des Femmes, 1980.

————— *Femmes et Russie, 1981*. Paris: Des Femmes, 1981.

Collin, Françoise. *Maurice Blanchot et la question de l'écriture*. Paris: Gallimard, 1971.

————— "N'etre," in *Ontologie et politique: Hannah Arendt*. Paris: Tierce, 1989.

————— "La peur," in *Emmanuel Lévinas: Cahiers de l'Herne*. Paris, 1991.

Comités d'éthique à travers le monde. Paris: Tierce, 1989.

Commaille, Jacques. *Familles sans justice? Le droit et la justice face aux transformations de la famille*. Paris: Le Centurion, 1982.

Les conceptions induites. Palermo, 1986.

Condell, Diana, and Jean Liddiard. *Working for Victory? Images of Women in the First World War, 1914–1918*. New York: Routledge & Chapman Hall, 1988.

Cooper, Helen M., Adrienne Auslander Munich, and Susan Merrill Squier, eds. *Arms and the Woman: War, Gender, and Literary Representation*. Chapel Hill: University of North Carolina Press, 1989.

Cott, Nancy E. *The Grounding of Modern Feminism*. New Haven: Yale University Press, 1987.

"Le corps aux mains du droit, dossier bioéthique." *Actes*, 49–50 (June 1985).

Coudert, Marie-Louise. *Elles, la résistance*. Paris: Messidor, 1985.

Cowan, R. "The Industrial Revolution in the Home: Household Technology and Social Change in the Twentieth Century." *Technology and Culture*, 17 (1976), 1–23.

Czarnowski, Gabriele. *Das kontrollierte Paar: Ehe—und Sexualpolitik im Nationalsozialismus*. Weinheim: Deutscher Studien-Verlag, 1991.

D'Adler, M. A., and M. Tuelade. *Les sorciers de la vie*. Paris: Gallimard, 1986.

Dale, Jennifer, and Peggy Foster, eds. *Feminists and State Welfare*. London: Routledge and Kegan Paul, 1986.

Daniel, Ute. *Arbeiterfrauen in der Kriegsgesellschaft: Beruf, Familie und Politik im Ersten Weltkrieg*. Göttingen: Vandenhoeck & Ruprecht, 1989.

Danylewicz, Marta. *Profession: Religieuse, un choix pour les québécoises, 1840–1920*. Montreal: Boréal, 1988.

Dardigna, Anne-Marie. *Femmes-femmes sur papier glacé*. Paris: Maspero, 1974.

Dau Novelli, Cecilia. *Società, Chiesa, e associazionismo femminile*. Rome: Società A. V. E., 1988.

Dauphin, Cécile, et al. "Culture et pouvoir des femmes: Essai d'historiographie." *Annales ESC*, 41 (1986).

David, D. *L'insémination artificielle humaine, un nouveau mode de filiation.* Paris: Les Editions ESF, 1984.

David, Hélène. *Femmes et emploi: Le défi de l'égalité.* Sillery: Presses de l'Université du Québec, 1986.

Davidson, Caroline. *A Woman's Work Is Never Done: A History of Housework in the British Isles, 1650–1950.* London: Chatto and Windus, 1986.

Davies, Kath, Julienne Dickey, and Teresa Stratford, eds. *Out of Focus: Writings on Women and the Media.* London: The Women's Press, 1987.

Davies, Margaret Llewelyn, ed. *Maternity Letters from Working Women.* London: Virago, 1978.

Davin, Anna. "Imperialism and Motherhood." *History Workshop,* 5 (1978).

Debray, Régis. *Le pouvoir intellectuel en France.* Paris: Ramsay, 1979.

De Céspedes, Alba. *Non si torna in dietro.* Milan: Mondadori, 1938.

Degler, Carl. *At Odds: Women and the Family in America from the Revolution to the Present.* New York: Oxford University Press, 1980.

De Grazia, Victoria. *How Fascism Ruled Women: Italy, 1920–1945.* Berkeley: University of California Press, 1991.

———— "Mass Culture and Sovereignty: The American Challenge to European Cinemas, 1920–1960." *Journal of Modern History,* 61 (March 1989), 53–87.

———— "Puritan, Pagan Bodies: Americanism and the Formation of the 'New Woman' in Europe, 1920–1945." Working paper, 1984–1987.

Delaisi de Parseval, G. *L'enfant à tout prix.* Paris: Seuil, 1983.

Delumeau, Jean, and Daniel Roche, eds. *Histoire des pères et de la paternité.* Paris: Larousse, 1990.

Didier, Béatrice. *L'écriture-femme.* Paris: PUF, 1981.

Di Febo, Giuliana. *Resistencia y movimento de mujeres en España, 1936–1976.* Madrid: Icaria, 1979.

———— *La Santa de la Raza, un culto barroco en la España franquista.* Barcelona: Icaria, 1988.

Di Giorgio, Michela, and Paola Di Cori. "Politica e sentiment: Le organizzazioni femminili fasciste cattoliche dall'eta giolittiana al fascismo." *Rivista di storia contemporanea,* 3 (1980).

Diotima. *Il pensiero delle differenza sessuale.* Milan: La Tartaruga, 1987.

Doane, Mary Ann. *The Desire to Desire.* Bloomington: Indiana University Press, 1987.

Dogan, Mattei. "Le comportement politique des femmes dans les pays de l'Europe occidentale," in *La condition sociale de la femme.* Brussels: Institut de Sociologie Solvay, 1956.

"Le droit, la médecine et la vie." *Le Débat,* 36. Paris: Gallimard, 1985.

Dufresne, J. *La reproduction humaine industrialisée.* Montreal and Quebec, 1986.

Duncan, Carol. "Virility and Domination in Early-Twentieth-Century Vanguard Painting." *Artform,* 12 (December 1973); reprinted in Norma Broude and Mary D. Garrard, eds., *Feminism and Art History: Questioning the Litany.* New York: Harper and Row, 1982.

Dunham, Vera. *In Stalin's Time: Middle-Class Values in Soviet Fiction.* New York: Cambridge University Press, 1976.

Dupaquier, Jacques, ed. *Histoire de la population française,* vol. 4: *De 1914 à nos jours.* Paris: PUF, 1988.

Duran, M. A., and Pilar Folguera, eds. *La mujer en la historia de España (siglos XVI–XX).* Actas de las II Jornadas de Investigación Interdisciplinaria, Seminario de Estudios de la Mujer, Universidad Autónoma de Madrid, 1984.

Durand, Guy. *La bioéthique.* Paris: Le Cerf, 1989.

Dyhouse, Carol. *Feminism and the Family in England, 1880–1939.* Oxford: Basil Blackwell, 1989.

Eckart, Christel, Ursula Jaerisch, and Helgard Kramer. *Frauenarbeit in Familie und Fabrik.* Frankfurt: Campus, 1979.

Eco, Umberto. *Apocalittici e integrati: Comunicazioni di massa e teorie della cultura di massa.* Milan: Bompiani, 1964.

Ehrenreich, Barbara, and Deirdre English. *For Her Own Good: One Hundred and Fifty Years of the Experts' Advice to Women.* New York: Anchor Books, 1979.

Elling, Hanna. *Frauen im deutschen Widerstand, 1933–1945.* Frankfurt: Röderberg, 1978.

Elshtain, Jean Bethke. *Public Man, Private Woman: Women in Social and Political Thought.* Princeton: Princeton University Press, 1981.

—— *Women and War.* New York: Basic Books, 1987.

"Enfants adoptés, enfants de la science, enfants de personne?" *L'Ange,* 20 (1985).

Engelhardt, H. T., Jr. *The Foundations of Bioethics.* New York: Oxford University Press, 1989.

Engels, Friedrich. *L'origine de la famille, de la propriété privée, et de l'état.* Paris: Editions Sociales, 1966.

Les enjeux éthiques et juridiques des nouvelles technologies de reproduction. Comité du Barreau du Québec, 1988.

Erenberg, L. *Steppin' Out.* Westport, Conn.: Greenwood Press, 1981.

Ergas, Yasmine. "Femminismo e crisi di sistema." *Rassegna italiana di Sociologia,* 21, 4 (October-December 1980), 543–568.

Esping-Andersen, Gosta. *The Three Worlds of Welfare Capitalism.* Cambridge and Oxford: Polity Press and Basil Blackwell, 1990.

Etchebehere, Mika. *Mi guerra de España.* Barcelona: Plaza y Janés, 1987.

"Ethique et biologie." *Cahiers STS.* CNRS, no. 11 (1986).

"Ethique et génétique." *Revue des questions scientifiques,* 1983.

"Ethique et progrès biomédicaux." *Autrement,* 1987.

Evans, Richard J. *Feminism, Socialism, and Pacifism in Europe, 1870–1945.* Sussex: Wheatsheaf Books, 1987; New York: St. Martin's Press, 1987.

Evans, Sara. *Personal Politics: The Roots of Women's Liberation in the Civil Rights Movement and the New Left.* New York: Vintage Books, 1980.

Ewen, E. "City Lights: Immigrant Women and the Rise of the Movies." *Signs,* 5 (Spring 1980 supplement), 45–66.

Ewen, S. *Captains of Consciousness.* New York: McGraw-Hill, 1976.

Fagoaga, Concha, and Paloma Saavedra. *Clara Campoamor, la sufragista española.* Madrid: Ministerio de Cultura, Instituto de la Mujer, 1986.

Fahmy-Eid, Nadia, and Micheline Dumont, eds. *Maitresses de maison, maitresses d'école: Femmes, famille, et éducation dans l'histoire du Québec.* Montreal: Boréal Express, 1983.

Falconnet, Georges, and Nadine Lefaucheur. *La fabrication des mâles.* Paris: Seuil, 1975.

Falter, Jürgen, et al. *Wahlen und Abstimmungen in der Weimarer Republik.* Munich: Beck, 1986.

Farge, Arlette, and Christiane Klapisch-Zuber, eds. *Madame ou Mademoiselle? Itinéraires de la solitude féminine, 18è–20è siècle.* Paris: Montalba, 1984.

Fass, P. *The Damned and the Beautiful: American Youth in the Nineteen Twenties.* New York: Oxford University Press, 1977.

La femme. Recueil de la Société Jean Bodin pour l'histoire comparative des institutions, 12. Brussels: Librairie Encyclopédique, 1962.

"La femme et le droit." *Revue juridique canadienne,* vol. 1, no. 2, *La femme et la reproduction.* Ottawa, 1986.

"Femmes, écriture, philosophie." *Cahiers du Grad,* 1. Quebec: Université Laval, 1987.

"Femmes et institutions littéraires." *Cahiers 34/44,* 13. Paris: University of Paris VII, 1984.

"Femmes, modes d'emploi." *Nouvelles Questions Féministes,* 14–15 (Winter 1986).

"Femmes sujets des discours." *Cahiers du Cedref,* 2. University of Paris VII, 1990.

Ferrand, Michèle, and Maryse Jaspard. *L'interruption volontaire de grossesse.* Paris: PUF, 1987.

Festy, Patrick. *La fécondité des pays occidentaux de 1870 à 1970.* Paris: PUF and Institut National d'Études Démographiques, 1979.

Filene, P. *Him/Her/Self.* New York: New American Library, 1974.

Flanz, Gisbert H., ed. *Women's Rights and Political Participation in Europe.* New York: Transnational Publishers, 1983.

Flora, Peter, ed. *Growth to Limits: The Western European Welfare States since World War II,* 4 vols. Berlin: De Gruyter, 1986–1987.

Flora, Peter, and Arnold J. Heidenheimer, eds. *The Development of Welfare States in Europe and America.* New Brunswick-London: Transaction, 1981.

"Foetus humain, à propos de son statut." *Le Supplément,* 153. Paris: Le Cerf, 1985.

Folguera, Pilar, ed. *El feminismo en España: Dos siglos de historia.* Madrid: Pablo Iglesias, 1988.

Foucault, Michel. *Histoire de la sexualité,* vol. 1: *La volonté de savoir.* Paris: Gallimard, 1976.

Fourcault, Annie. *Femmes à l'usine dans l'entre-deux-guerres.* Paris: Maspero, 1982.

Fraddosio, Maria. "La donna e la guerra. Aspetti della militanza femminile nel fascismo: Dalla mobilitazione civile alle origini del Saf nella Repubblica Sociale Italiana." *Storia contemporanea,* 20, 6 (December 1989).

Fraisse, Geneviève. *Muse de la raison: La démocratie exclusive et la différence des sexes.* Aix-en-Provence: Alinéa, 1989.

Les françaises à Ravensbrück. Paris: Gallimard, 1987, 2nd ed.

Francis, Claude, and Fernande Gontier. *Les écrits de Simone de Beauvoir.* Paris: Gallimard, 1979.

"Frauen und Politik." *Aus Politik und Zeitgeschichte,* 9, 10 (February 28, 1987), 3–37.

Frevert, Ute. *Women in German History: From Bourgeois Emancipation to Sexual Liberation,* trans. Stuart McKinnon-Evans et al. Oxford: Berg, 1989.

Frey, L., M. Frey, and J. Schneider. *Women in Western European History: A Select Chronological, Geographical, and Topical Bibliography.* Brighton: Harvester Press, 1982.

Friedlander, Judith, ed. *Women in Culture and Politics: A Century of Change.* Bloomington: Indiana University Press, 1986.

Frydman, R. *L'irrésistible désir de naissance.* Paris: PUF, 1986.

Fuente Noriega, Margarita. "Los derechos de la mujer como madre en España." *Razón y Fe,* 219 (January 1989), 56–66.

Fussell, Paul. *The Great War and Modern Memory.* New York: Oxford University Press, 1975.

Gallego Mendez, María Teresa. *Mujer, Falange y franquismo.* Madrid: Taurus, 1983.

Gamman, Lorraine, and Margaret Marshment, eds. *The Female Gaze: Women as Viewers of Popular Culture.* London: The Women's Press, 1988.

Garcia-Nieto Paris, María Carmen, ed. *Ordenamiento jurídico y realidad social de las mujeres (siglos XVI a XX).* Madrid: Seminario de Estudios de la Mujer, Universidad Autónoma de Madrid, 1986.

Gasiorowska, Zhenia. *Women in Soviet Fiction, 1917–1964.* Madison: University of Wisconsin Press, 1968.

Gelfand, Elissa D., and Virginia Thorndike Hules. *French Feminist Criticism: Women, Language, and Literature.* New York: Garland, 1985.

Génétique, procréation et droit. H. Nyssen, Actes Sud, 1985.

Gersdorff, Ursula von. *Frauen im Kriegsdienst, 1914–1945.* Stuttgart: Deutsche Verlags-Anstalt, 1969.

Gertzog, Irwin N. *Congressional Women: Their Recruitment, Treatment, and Behavior.* New York: Praeger, 1984.

"Das Geschlecht in der Philosophie." *Die Philosophin,* 2. Tübingen, 1990.

Gibson, Mary. *Prostitution and the State in Italy.* New Brunswick: Rutgers University Press, 1986.

Giddens, Anthony. *The Construction of Society.* Cambridge: Polity Press, 1984.

Giddings, Paula. *When and Where I Enter: The Impact of Black Women on Race and Sex in America.* New York: Morrow, 1984.

Gingras, Anne-Marie, Chantal Maillé, and Evelyne Tardy. *Sexe et militantisme*. Montreal: Editions du CIDIHCA, 1989.

Giraud, F. *Les mères porteuses*. Paris: Publi Sud, 1987.

Gittins, Diana. *Fair Sex: Family Size and Structure, 1900–1939*. London: Hutchinson, 1982.

Glass, David Victor. *Population Policies and Movements in Europe*. London, 1940; repr., London: Frank Cass, 1967.

Goldschmidt-Clermont, Luisella. *Unpaid Work in the Household: A Review of Economic Evaluation Methods*. Geneva: International Labor Office, 1982.

Goodnow, Jacqueline, and Carole Pateman, eds. *Women, Social Science, and Public Policy*. Sydney: Allen and Unwin, 1985.

Gordon, Linda. *Woman's Body, Woman's Right: A Social History of Birth Control in America*. New York: Crossman Publishers, 1976; Penguin Books, 1977.

Gouma-Peterson, Thalia, and Patricia Mathews. "The Feminist Critique of Art History." *Art Bulletin*, 69 (September 1987), 326–357.

Goy, Joseph, Jean-Pierre Wallot, and Rolande Bonnain, eds. *Evolution et éclatement du monde rural: Structures, fonctionnement, et évolution différentielle des sociétés rurales françaises et québécoises, 18è–20è siècles*. Montreal: Presses de l'Université de Montreal, 1986.

La Grande Guerra: Esperienza, memoria, immagini. Diego Leoni and Camillo Zadra, eds. Bologna: Il Mulino, 1986.

Greenwald, Maurine Weiner. *Women, War, and Work: The Impact of World War I on Women Workers in the United States*. Westport, Conn.: Greenwood Press, 1980.

Greven-Aschoff, Barbara. *Die bürgerliche Frauenbewegung in Deutschland, 1894–1933*. Göttingen: Vandenhoeck & Ruprecht, 1981.

Grimal, Pierre, ed. *Histoire mondiale de la femme*, vol. 4. Paris: Nouvelle Librairie de France, 1966.

Guidez, Guylaine. *Femmes dans la guerre (1939–1945)*. Paris: Perrin, 1989.

Guilbert, Madeleine. *Les fonctions des femmes dans l'industrie*. Paris: Mouton, 1966.

Haavio-Mannila, Elina, et al., eds. *Unfinished Democracy: Women in Nordic Politics*. New York: Pergamon Press, 1985.

Hachtmann, Rüdiger. *Industriearbeit im "Dritten Reich."* Göttingen: Vandenhoeck & Ruprecht, 1989.

Hamelin, France. *Femmes dans la nuit, l'internement à la Petite Roquette et au camp des Tourelles (1939–1944)*. Paris: Renaudot et Cie, 1988.

Hamilton, Roberta, and Michelle Barrett, eds. *The Politics of Diversity: Feminism, Marxism, and Nationalism*. Montreal: Book Center, 1986.

Hansson, Carola, and Karin Liden. *Moscow Women: Thirteen Interviews*. London: Allison and Busby, 1984.

Hartman, Mary, and Lois W. Banner, eds. *Clio's Consciousness Raised: New Perspectives on the History of Women*. New York: Harper and Row, 1974.

Hartmann, H. I. "Capitalism and Women's Work in the Home, 1900–1940." Ph.D. diss., Yale University, 1974.

Haskell, Molly. *From Reverence to Rape: The Treatment of Women in the Movies*. Chicago: University of Chicago Press, 1987.

Hassoun, Paul-Laurent. *Freud et la femme*. Paris: Calmann-Lévy, 1983.

Herbert, Ulrich. *Fremdarbeiter: Politik und Praxis des "Ausländer-Einsatzes" in der Kriegswirtschaft des Dritten Reiches*. Bonn-Berlin: Dietz Verlag, 1985.

Hermann, Claudine. *Les voleuses de langue*. Paris: Des Femmes, 1976.

Hernes, Helga Maria. *Welfare State and Woman Power: Essays in State Feminism*. Oxford: Oxford University Press, 1987.

Hilberg, Raul. *The Destruction of the European Jews*, 3 vols. New York: Holmes and Meier, 1986.

Hoggart, Richard. *La culture du pauvre*. Paris: Minuit, 1970.

Honneger, Claudia. *Die Ordnung der Geschlechter: Die Wissenschaft vom Menschen und das Weib*. Frankfurt, 1991.

Horkheimer, Max, and Theodor W. Adorno. *Das Schema der Massenkultur*, in Adorno, *Gesammelte Schriften*. Frankfurt: Suhrkamp, 1981.

Human Procreation: Ethical Aspects of the New Techniques. Report of a Working Party, Council for Science and Society (London). Oxford: Oxford University Press, 1984.

Huppert-Laufer, Jacqueline. *La féminité neutralisée? Les femmes cadres dans l'enterprise*. Paris: Flammarion, 1982.

Huyssen, Andreas. "Mass Culture as Woman: Modernism's Other," in T. Modleski, *Studies in Entertainment*, 1986.

Ibarruri, Dolores. *El único camino*. Paris: Editions Sociales, 1965.

Irigaray, Luce. *Speculum de l'autre femme*. Paris: Minuit, 1974.

Isidori Frasca, Rosella. . . . *e il duce le volle sportive*. Bologna: Patron, 1983.

Jardine, Alice. *Gynesis: Configurations of Woman and Modernity*. Ithaca: Cornell University Press, 1985.

Jardine, Alice, and Anne M. Menke. *Shifting Scenes: Interviews on Women, Writing, and Politics in Post-68 France*. New York: Columbia University Press, 1991.

Jenson, Jane, Elizabeth Hagen, and Ceallaigh Reddy, eds. *Feminization of the Labour Force: Paradoxes and Promises*. Cambridge and Oxford: Polity Press and Basil Blackwell, 1988.

Johnson, Barbara. *A World of Difference*. Baltimore: Johns Hopkins University Press, 1987.

Jones, Jacqueline. *Labor of Love, Labor of Sorrow: Black Women, Work, and the Family from Slavery to the Present*. New York: Basic Books, 1985.

Kälvemark, Ann-Sofie. *More Children of Better Quality? Aspects of Swedish Population Policy in the Nineteen Thirties*. Uppsala: Almquist and Wiksell, 1980.

Kamerman, Sheila B., Alfred J. Kahn, and P. Kingston. *Child Care, Family*

Benefits, and Working Parents: A Study in Comparative Policy. New York: Columbia University Press, 1981.

Kaplan, Marion. *The Jewish Feminist Movement in Germany: The Campaigns of the Jüdischer Frauenbund, 1904–1938.* Westport, Conn.: Greenwood Press, 1979.

Kater, Michael H. "Frauen in der NS-Bewegung." *Vierteljahrshefte für Zeitgeschichte,* 31 (1983), 202–239.

Kaufmann, Jean-Claude. *La chaleur du foyer: Analyse du repli domestique.* Paris: Méridiens-Klincksieck, 1988.

Kellerhals, Jean, et al. *Mariages au quotidien: Inégalités sociales, tensions culturelles et organisation familiale.* Lausanne: Favre, 1982.

Kelly, Joan. *Women, History, and Theory: The Essays of Joan Kelly.* Chicago: University of Chicago Press, 1984.

Kennedy, David M. *Over Here: The First World War and American Society.* New York: Oxford University Press, 1980.

Kent, Susan Kingsley. "The Politics of Sexual Difference: World War I and the Demise of British Feminism." *Journal of British Studies,* 27 (July 1988), 232–253.

Kergoat, Danièle. *Les ouvrières.* Paris: Le Sycamore, 1982.

Kirkpatrick, Clifford. *Women in Nazi Germany.* London: Jarrolds, 1939.

Klein, Ethel. *Gender Politics: From Consciousness to Mass Politics.* Cambridge, Mass.: Harvard University Press, 1984.

Klejman, Laurence, and Florence Rochefort. *L'égalité en marche: Le féminisme sous la Troisième République.* Paris: Des Femmes, 1989.

Klinksieck, Dorothee. *Die Frau im NS-Staat.* Stuttgart: Deutsche Verlags-Anstalt, 1982.

Knibiehler, Yvonne. *Les pères aussi ont une histoire.* Paris: Hachette, 1987.

—— *Nous les assistentes sociales: Naissance d'une profession.* Paris: Aubier, 1980.

Knibiehler, Yvonne, and Catherine Fouquet. *La femme et les médecins.* Paris: Hachette, 1983.

—— *Histoire des mères: Du moyen age à nos jours.* Paris: Montalba, 1980; Hachette, 1987.

Kocka, Jürgen. *Klassengesellschaft im Krieg: Deutsche Sozialgeschichte, 1914–1918.* Göttingen, 1978.

Kofman, Sarah. *L'énigme de la femme: La femme dans les textes de Freud.* Paris: Galilée, 1980.

—— *Lectures de Derrida.* Paris: Galilée, 1984.

Kolinsky, Eva. "The West German Greens: A Women's Party?" *Parliamentary Affairs,* 41 (January 1988), 129–148.

Koonz, Claudia. *Mothers in the Fatherland: Women, the Family, and Nazi Politics.* New York: St. Martin's Press, 1987.

Kopp, Anatole. *Ville et révolution.* Paris: Anthropos, 1967.

Koven, Seth, and Sonya Michel. "Womanly Duties: Maternalist Policies and the Origins of Welfare States in France, Germany, Great Britain, and the United States." *American Historical Review,* 95 (1990), 1076–1108.

671

Kristeva, Julia. *Recherches pour une sémanalyse*. Paris: Seuil, 1969.

Labelle, Micheline, G. Turcotte, M. Kempeneers, and D. Meintel. *Histoire d'immigrées: Itinéraires d'ouvrières colombiennes, grecques, haitiennes, et portugaises de Montréal*. Montreal: Boréal, 1987.

Laborie, Pierre. *L'opinion française sous Vichy*. Paris: Seuil, 1990.

Labourie-Racape, Annie, M. T. Letablier, and A. M. Vasseur. *L'activité féminine: Enquête sur la discontinuité de la vie professionnelle*. Paris: PUF, 1977.

Ladd-Taylor, Mary Madeleine. "Mother-Work: Ideology, Public Policy, and the Mothers' Movement, 1890–1930." Ph.D. diss., Yale University, 1986.

Lagrave, Rose-Marie, ed. *Celles de la terre: Agricultrice—l'invention politique d'un métier*. Paris: Ed. de l'EHESS, 1987.

Lamoureux, Diane. *Citoyennes? Femmes, droit de vote et démocratie*. Montreal: Ed. du Remue-Ménage, 1989.

Laqueur, Thomas. *Making Sex: Body and Gender from the Greeks to Freud*. Cambridge, Mass.: Harvard University Press, 1990.

Laurin, Nicole, Danièle Juteau, and Lorraine Duchesne. *A la recherche d'un monde oublié*. Montreal: Le Jour, 1991.

Leach, William R. "Transformations in a Culture of Consumption: Women and Department Stores, 1890–1925." *The Journal of American History*, 71, 2 (September 1984).

Le Doeuf, Michèle. *L'étude et le rouet*. Paris: Seuil, 1989.

Leed, Eric J. *No Man's Land: Combat and Identity in World War I*. Cambridge: Cambridge University Press, 1979.

Legendre, P. *L'inestimable objet de la transmission: Etude sur le principe généalogique en Occident*. Paris: Fayard, 1985.

Lemieux, Denise, with Lucie Mercier. *Les femmes au tournant du siècle, 1880–1940: Ages de la vie, maternité et quotidien*. Quebec: Institut Québécois de Recherches sur la Culture, 1989.

Lemons, J. Stanley. *The Woman Citizen: Social Feminism in the Nineteen Twenties*. Urbana: University of Illinois Press, 1973.

Lenczyk, Henryk. "Alexandra Kollontaï: Essai bibliographique." *Cahiers du Monde Russe et Soviétique*, 14, 1–2 (January-June 1973), 205–241.

Lenin, V. I. *De l'émancipation de la femme*. Paris: Bureau d'Éditions, de Diffusion, et de Publicité, 1937.

Leon, María Teresa. *Memoria de la melancolía*. Buenos Aires: Losada, 1970.

Leridon, Henri, et al. *La seconde révolution contraceptive: La régulation des naissances en France de 1950 à 1985*. Paris: PUF and Institut National d'Études Démographiques, 1987.

Levesque, Andrée. *La norme et les déviantes: Des femmes au Québec pendant l'entre-deux-guerres*. Montreal: Editions du Remue-Ménage, 1989.

Lewallern, Avis. "'Lace': Pornography for Women?" in Gammon and Marshment, *The Female Gaze*, 1988.

Lewis, Jane. *The Politics of Motherhood: Child and Maternal Welfare in England, 1900–1939*. London: Croom Helm, 1980.

—— *Women in England, 1870–1950: Sexual Divisions and Social Change*. Sussex: Wheatsheaf Books, 1984.

————, ed. *Labour and Love: Women's Experience of Home and Family, 1850–1940*. Oxford: Basil Blackwell, 1986.

Lifton, Robert Jay. *The Nazi Doctors: Medical Killing and the Psychology of Genocide*. New York: Basic Books, 1986.

Lilienthal, Georg. *Der "Lebensborn e. V.": Ein Instrument nationalsozialistischer Rassenpolitik*. Stuttgart: G. Fischer, 1985.

Lilli, Laura. *La stampa femminile*, in Valerio Castronovo and Nicola Tranfaglia, eds., *Storia della stampa italiana*, vol. V: *La stampa italiana del neocapitalismo*. Rome and Bari: Laterza, 1976.

Listhaug, Ola. "The Gender Gap in Norwegian Voting Behaviour." *Scandinavian Political Studies*, 8 (September 1985), 177–206.

Livi-Bacci, Manlio. *A History of Italian Fertility during the Last Two Centuries*. Princeton: Princeton University Press, 1972.

Lovenduski, Joni, and Jill Hills, eds. *The Politics of the Second Electorate: Women and Public Participation*. London: Routledge and Kegan Paul, 1981.

Lubove, Roy. *The Struggle for Social Security, 1900–1935*. Cambridge, Mass.: Harvard University Press, 1968.

Luker, Kristin. *Abortion and the Politics of Motherhood*. Berkeley: University of California Press, 1984.

Lynd, R. S., and H. M. Lynd. *Middletown: A Study in Modern American Culture*. New York: Harcourt Brace, 1929.

Macciocchi, Maria Antonietta. *La donna neva*. Milan: Feltrinelli, 1976.

Macnichol, John. *The Movement for Family Allowances, 1918–1945: A Study in Social Policy Development*. London: Heinemann, 1980.

Mafai, Miriam. *Pane nero*. Milan: Rizzoli, 1988.

Malherbe, J. F., and E. Bone. *Engendrés par la science*. Paris: Le Cerf, 1985.

Mansbridge, Jane. *Why We Lost the ERA*. Chicago: University of Chicago Press, 1986.

Maquieira, Virginia, and Cristina Sánchez, eds. *Violencia y sociedad patriarcal*. Madrid: Editions de la Fondation Pablo Iglesias, 1990.

Marchand, R. *Advertising the American Dream*. Berkeley: University of California Press, 1985.

Marini, Marcelle. *Lacan*. Paris: Belfond, 1986.

Maroney, Heather Jon, and Meg Luxton, eds. *Feminism and Political Economy*. Toronto: Methuen, 1987.

Martin, Martine. "Femme et société: Le travail ménager (1919–1939)." Thesis, University of Paris VII, 1984.

Martinez Sierra, María. *Una mujer por caminos de España: Recuerdos de propagandista*. Instituto de la Mujer. Madrid: Castalia, 1989.

Maruani, Margaret. *Mais qui a peur du travail des femmes?* Paris: Syros, 1985.

Maruani, Margaret, Emmanuelle Reynaud, and Claudine Romani. *La flexibilité en Italie*. Paris: Syros-Alternative, 1989.

Marwick, Arthur. *The Deluge: British Society and the First World War*. London: The Bodley Head, 1965.

———— *War and Social Change in the Twentieth Century: A Comparative*

Study of Britain, France, Germany, Russia, and the United States. London, 1979.

———— *Women at War, 1914–1918.* Fontana Paperbacks, 1977.

Masino, Paola. *Nascita e morte della massaia.* Milan: La Tartaruga, 1982.

May, L. *Screening Out the Past.* New York: Oxford University Press, 1980.

Mayeur, Françoise. *L'enseignement secondaire des jeunes filles sous la III° République.* Paris: Presses de la Fondation Nationale des Sciences Politiques, 1977.

McGovern, J. P. "The American Woman's Pre-World War I Freedom in Manners and Morals." *Journal of American History,* 55 (September 1968), 315–333.

McMahon, A. M. "An American Courtship: Psychologists and Advertising Theory in the Progressive Era." *American Studies,* 13 (Fall 1972).

McMillan, James F. *Housewife or Harlot: The Place of Women in French Society, 1870–1940.* Brighton: Harvester Press, 1981.

Meldini, Piero. *Sposa e madre esemplare: Ideologia e politica della donna e della famiglia durante il fascismo.* Rimini-Firenze, Guaraldi, 1975.

Melograni, Pietro, ed. *La famiglia nella storia d'Italia.* Bari-Rome: Laterza, 1988.

Meyer, Alfred G. *The Feminism and Socialism of Lily Braun.* Bloomington: Indiana University Press, 1985.

Michel, Andrée. *Activité professionnelle de la femme et vie conjugale.* Paris: Editions du CNRS, 1974.

———— *Sociologie de la famille et du mariage.* Paris: PUF, 2nd ed., 1978.

————, ed. *Les femmes dans la société marchande.* Paris: PUF, 1978.

Michel Foucault philosophe. Paris: Seuil, 1989.

"La militarisation et les violences à l'égard des femmes." *Nouvelles Questions Féministes,* 11–12 (Winter 1985).

Mitchell, Juliet, and Ann Oakley, eds. *The Rights and Wrongs of Women.* New York: Penguin Books, 1976.

Modleski, Tania. *Loving and Living with a Vengeance: Mass-Produced Fantasies for Women.* New York: Routledge, 1982.

————, ed. *Studies in Entertainment: Critical Approaches to Mass Culture.* Bloomington: Indiana University Press, 1986.

Mondello, Elisabetta. *La nuova italiana: La donna nella stampa e nella cultura del ventennio.* Rome: Riuniti, 1987.

Monseny, Federica. *Mis primeros cuarenta años.* Barcelona: Plaza y Janés, 1987.

Montreynaud, Florence. *Le XXè siècle des femmes.* Paris: Nathan, 1989.

Mora, Constancia de la. *Doble esplendor.* Barcelona: Crítica, 1977.

Moreno Sarda, Amparo. "La réplica de las mujeres al franquismo," in *El feminismo en España: Dos siglos de historia,* 85–110.

Moretti, J. M., and O. De Dinechin. *Le défi génétique.* Paris: Ed. Centurion, 1982.

Morin, Edgar. *L'esprit du temps.* Paris: Grasset, 1962.

———— *Les stars.* Paris: Seuil, 1957.

Mosse, George L. *Toward the Final Solution: A History of European Racism.* New York, 1978.

Mossuz-Lavau, Janine. *Les lois de l'amour: Les politiques de la sexualité en France (1950–1990).* Paris: Payot, 1991.

Mossuz-Lavau, Janine, and Mariette Sineau. *Enquête sur les femmes et la politique en France.* Paris: PUF, 1983.

——— "Le vote des femmes: L'autre événement." *Le Monde* (June 5, 1988).

Des motifs d'espérer, la procréation artificielle. Paris: Le Cerf, 1986.

Muci, Maria Rita. *La partecipazione politica femminile nei paesi del Sud d'Europa.* Milan: Università L. Bocconi, 1988.

Mueller, Carol M., ed. *The Politics of the Gender Gap.* Sage Yearbooks in Women's Policy, 1988.

Mulvey, Laura, and Peter Wollen. "Women, Art, Politics," and "The Interior and the Exterior," in *Frida Kahlo and Tina Modotti.* London: Whitechapel Gallery, 1982, pp. 9–10, 13–17.

Mutterkreuz und Arbeitsbuch: Zur Geschichte der Frauen in der Weimarer Republik und im Nationalsozialismus, ed. Frauengruppe Faschismusforschung. Frankfurt: Fischer Verlag, 1981.

Naître. Corps Écrit, 21. Paris: PUF, 1987.

Nash, Mary. *Mujer y movimento obrero en España, 1931–1939.* Barcelona: Fontamara, 1981.

——— *"Mujeres libres" España, 1936–1939.* Barcelona: Tusquets, 1976.

Navailh, Françoise. "L'image de la femme dans le cinéma soviétique," in Basile Kerblay, "L'évolution des modèles familiaux dans les pays de l'Est européen et l'URSS." *Cultures et Sociétés de l'Est,* 9. Paris: IMSECO, 1988.

Nelken, Margarita. *Por qué hicimos la revolución.* New York: International Publishers, 1936.

Nerson, Roger, ed. *Mariage et famille en question: L'évolution contemporaine du droit français.* Paris: Ed. du CNRS, 1978 and 1979, 2 vols.

——— *Mariage et famille en question: L'évolution contemporaine en Suisse, en Autriche, en Belgique, aux Pays-Bas et dans la région Scandinave.* Paris: Ed. du CNRS, 1980.

——— *Mariage et famille en question: Italie.* Paris: Ed. du CNRS, 1982.

Newland, Kathleen. *The Sisterhood of Man.* New York: W. W. Norton, 1979.

Newton, Judith L., Mary P. Ryan, and Judith R. Walkowitz, eds. *Sex and Class in Women's History: Essays from Feminist Studies.* London: Routledge and Kegan Paul, 1983; 1985.

1914–1918: L'autre front. Special number of *Mouvement Social,* Patrick Fridenson, ed. Paris: Les Editions Ouvrières, 1977.

Nolin, M. *Réflexions juridiques sur le phénomène des femmes porteuses d'enfants.* Montreal: Y. Balis, 1986.

Norris, Pippa. *Politics and Sexual Equality: The Comparative Position of Women in Western Democracies.* Brighton: Wheatsheaf, 1987.

Norton, Mary Beth. *Major Problems in American Women's History: Documents and Essays.* Lexington, Mass.: D. C. Heath, 1989.

Norvez, Alain. *De la naissance à l'école: Santé, modes de garde et préscolarité dans la France contemporaine.* Paris: PUF and Institut National d'Études Démographiques, 1990.

Nottingham, E. "Toward an Analysis of the Effects of Two World Wars on the Role and Status of Middle-Class Women." *American Sociological Review,* 12 (December 1947).

Oakley, Ann. *The Captured Womb: A History of the Medical Care of Pregnant Women.* Oxford: Basil Blackwell, 1984.

—— *Housewife.* New York: Penguin Books, 1974.

OCDE. *Les femmes et l'égalité des chances.* Paris, 1985.

—— *Les femmes et l'emploi: Politiques pour l'égalité des chances.* Paris, 1980.

—— *L'intégration des femmes dans l'économie.* Paris, 1985.

Offen, Karen M. "Defining Feminism: A Comparative Historical Analysis." *Signs,* 14 (1988), 119–157.

—— "Depopulation, Nationalism, and Feminism in Fin-de-Siècle France." *American Historical Review,* 89 (1984), 648–676.

——, ed. *Women in European Culture and Society.* Special number of *History of European Ideas,* 8, 4–5.

Offen, Karen M., Ruth R. Pierson, and Jane Rendall, eds. *Writing Women's History: International Perspectives.* The International Federation for Research in Women's History. Bloomington: Indiana University Press, 1991.

O'Leary, Véronique, and Louise Toupin, eds. *Québecoises debouttes!* Montreal: Editions du Remue-Ménage, 1982–1983, 2 vols.

O'Neill, Carlota. *Una mujer en la guerra de España.* Madrid: Turner, 1979.

"Ordre juridique et ordre technologique." *Cahiers STS,* 12. CNRS, 1986.

Ortega y Gasset, José. *El hombre y la gente,* in *Obras completas (Complete Works),* 14 vols.; vol. 7, chap. 6, "Más sobre los otros y yo: Breve excursión hacia ella." Madrid: Revista de Occidente, 1962—.

Ortner, S., and H. Whitehead, eds. *Sexual Meanings: The Cultural Construction of Gender and Sexuality.* Cambridge: Cambridge University Press, 1981.

Paillard, Rémy. *Affiches 14–18.* Copyright by Rémy Paillard, 1986.

Parca, Gabriella. *Le italiane si confessano.* Milan: Feltrinelli, 1966.

Parker, Rozsika, and Griselda Pollock. *Old Mistresses: Women, Art, and Ideology.* London: Routledge and Kegan Paul, 1981.

Passerini, Luisa. *Torino operaia e fascismo.* Rome and Bari: Laterza, 1984; English ed., New York: Cambridge University Press, 1988.

Patarin, Jean, and Imre Zajtay. *Le régime matrimonial légal dans les législations contemporaines.* Paris: Pedone, 1974.

Pateman, Carole. "The Patriarchal Welfare State," in Amy Gutman, ed., *Democracy and the Welfare State.* Princeton: Princeton University Press, 1987.

—— *The Sexual Contract.* Cambridge: Polity Press, 1988.

Pauwels, Jacques. *Women, Nazis, and Universities: Female University Students in the Third Reich, 1933–1945.* Westport, Conn.: Greenwood Press, 1984.

Paxton, Robert. *La France de Vichy (1940–1944).* Paris: Seuil, 1974.

Peiss, Kathy. *Cheap Amusements: Working Women and Leisure in Turn-of-the-Century New York.* Philadelphia: Temple University Press, 1985.

——— "Mass Culture and Social Divisions: The Case of the Cosmetics Industry." Presented at the conference "Mass Culture and the Working Class." Paris (October 14–15, 1988).

"Pères et paternités." *Revue Française des Affaires Sociales,* 42 (November 1988).

Perreux, Gabriel. *La vie quotidienne des civils en France pendant la Grande Guerre.* Paris: Hachette, 1966.

Perrot, Michelle, ed. *Une histoire des femmes est-elle possible?* Marseilles-Paris: Rivages, 1984.

Perrot, Michelle, et al. "Métiers de femmes." *Le Mouvement Social,* 140 (July-September 1987).

Phayer, Michael. *Protestant and Catholic Women in Nazi Germany.* Detroit: Wayne State University Press, 1990.

Pierre, André. *Les femmes en Union Soviétique.* Paris: SPES, 1960.

Planté, Christine. *Le petite soeur de Balzac.* Paris: Seuil, 1989.

Plessix Gray, Francine du. *Soviet Women Walking the Tightrope.* London: Doubleday, 1990.

Pogliani, Claudio. "L'utopia igienista, 1870–1920." *Storia d'Italia, Annali,* 7, pp. 587–631.

"The Politics of Tradition: Placing Women in French Literature." *Yale French Studies,* 75 (1988).

Pomata, Gianna. *La storia della donne: Una questione di confine,* in *Introduzione alla storia contemporanea,* ed. Giovanni De Luna, Peppino Ortoleva, Marco Revelli, and Nicola Tranfaglia. Florence: La Nuova Italia, 1984.

Porter Benson, Susan. *Counter Cultures: Saleswomen, Managers, and Customers in American Department Stores, 1890–1940.* Chicago: University of Illinois Press, 1986.

Pozner, Vladimir. *Descente aux enfers, récits de déportés et de SS d'Auschwitz.* Paris: Juilliard, 1980.

Prentice, Alison, et al. *Canadian Women: A History.* Toronto: Harcourt Brace Jovanovich, 1988.

President's Commission on Social Trends. *Recent Social Trends.* New York: McGraw-Hill, 1933.

Prioux, France, ed. *La famille dans les pays développés: Permanences et changements. Actes* of conference at Vaucresson, October 1987. Paris: INED-UIESP-CNAF-CNRS, 1990.

Procréation artificielle génétique et droit. Colloque de Lausanne des 29 et 30 novembre 1985, Institut Suisse de Droit Comparé. Zurich: Schulthers Polygraphischer Verlag, 1986.

La propagande sous Vichy (1940–1944). Paris: BDIC, 1990.

Quand la technologie transforme la maternité. Conseil du statut de la femme du Québec, 1987.

Questions Féministes, 1. Paris: Tierce, 1977.

Radway, Janice. *Reading the Romance: Women, Patriarchy, and Popular Literature*. Chapel Hill: University of North Carolina Press, 1984.

Randall, Vicky. *Women and Politics*. London: Macmillan, 1987.

Randolph-Higonnet, Margaret, Jane Jenson, Sonya Michel, and Margaret Collins Weitz, eds. *Behind the Lines: Gender and the Two World Wars*. New Haven: Yale University Press, 1987.

Rapp, R., and E. Ross. "The Twenties' Backlash: Compulsory Heterosexuality, the Consumer Family, and the Waning of Feminism," in A. Swerdlow and H. Lessinger, eds., *Class, Race, and Sex: The Dynamics of Control*. Boston: G. K. Hall, 1983.

Rapport 1984, 1985, 1986. Paris: Documentation Française (1985, 1986, 1987).

Rathbone, Eleanor. *The Disinherited Family*. Repr. with an introduction by Suzy Fleming. Bristol: Falling Wall Press, 1986.

Recherches Féministes, 2, 2, "Convergences." Quebec: Université Laval, 1989.

Reese, Dagmar. *"Straff, aber nicht stramm—herb, aber nicht derb": Zur Vergesellschaftung von Mädchen durch den Bund Deutscher Mädel im sozialkulturellen Vergleich zweier Milieus*. Weinheim: Beltz Verlag, 1989.

Le régime de Vichy et les français. IHTP (Paris, June 11–13, 1990). Paris: Fayard, 1992.

Reilly, Catherine, ed. *Scars upon My Heart: Women's Poetry and Verse of the First World War*. London: Virago, 1981.

Rémond, René, and Janine Bourdin, eds. *Le gouvernement de Vichy (1940–1942)*. Paris: FNSP, 1972.

Revelli, Nuto. *L'anello forte*. Turin: Einaudi, 1985.

Revue des Sciences Humaines, 168, "Ecriture, féminité, féminisme" (Lille, 1977); 222, "Le récit d'enfance" (Lille, 1991).

Rhein, Catherine. "Jeunes femmes au travail dans le Paris de l'entre-deux-guerres." Thesis, University of Paris VII, 1977.

Riley, Denise. *Am I That Name? Feminism and the Category of "Women" in History*. London: Macmillan, 1988.

——— *War in the Nursery: Theories of the Child and Mother*. London: Virago, 1983.

Ringelheim, Joan, and Esther Katz, eds. Proceedings of the conference "Women Surviving the Holocaust." New York: Institute for Research in History, 1983.

Rioux, J. *L'insémination artificielle thérapeutique*. Quebec: Laval, 1983.

Roberts, Elizabeth. *A Woman's Place: An Oral History of Working-Class Women, 1890–1940*. London: Basil Blackwell, 1984.

Rodrigo, Antonina. *Mujeres de España (las silenciadas)*. Barcelona: Plaza y Janés, 1980.

Rosenberg, Rosalind. *Beyond Separate Spheres: Intellectual Roots of Modern Feminism*. New Haven: Yale University Press, 1982.

Rossi, Alice S., ed. *Gender and the Life Course*. New York: Aldine, 1985.

Rossiter, Margaret L. *Women in the Resistance*. New York: Praeger, 1986.

Rousseau, Renée. *Les femmes rouges*. Paris: Albin Michel, 1983.

Roussel, Louis. *La famille incertaine*. Paris: Odile Jacob, 1989.

Rowbotham, Sheila. *Hidden from History*. London: Pluto Press, 1973.

——— *A New World for Women: Stella Brown—Socialist, Feminist*. London: Pluto Press, 1977.

——— *Women, Resistance, and Revolution*. London: Allen Lane, 1972; New York, 1972.

Roy, D., and M. De Wachter. *The Life Technology and Public Policy*. Montreal: Institut de Recherches Politiques, 1987.

Rupp, Leila J. "'I Don't Call That *Volksgemeinschaft*': Women, Class, and War in Nazi Germany," in Berkin and Lovett, eds., *Women, War, and Revolution*. New York: Holmes and Meier, 1980, pp. 37–53.

——— "'Imagine My Surprise': Women's Relationships in Historical Perspective." *Frontiers*, 5 (Fall 1980), 61–71.

——— *Mobilizing Women for War: German and American Propaganda, 1939–1945*. Princeton: Princeton University Press, 1978.

Ryan, M. P. "The Projection of a New Womanhood: The Movie Moderns in the Nineteen Twenties," in L. Scharf and J. M. Jensen, eds., *Decades of Discontent: The Women's Movement, 1920–1940*. Westport, Conn.: Greenwood Press, 1983.

Sabourin, Annie. *Le travail des femmes dans la CEE*. Paris: Economica, 1984.

Sachse, Carola. *Betriebliche Sozialpolitik als Familienpolitik in der Weimarer Republik und im Nationalsozialismus*. Hamburg: Hamburger Institut für Sozialforschung, 1987.

——— *Siemens: Der Nationalsozialismus und die moderne Familie*. Hamburg: Rasch and Röhring, 1990.

Saraceno, Chiara. "La famiglia operaia sotto il fascismo." *Annali della Fondazione Giangiacomo Feltrinelli*, 20 (1979–80), 189–230.

Scanlon, Geraldine. *La polémica feminista en la España contemporánea, 1868–1974*. Madrid, Siglo XXI, 1976.

Scharf, L. *To Work and to Wed: Female Employment, Feminism, and the Great Depression*. Westport, Conn.: Greenwood Press, 1980.

Scheler, Max. *Uber Scham und Schamgefühl in Schriften aus dem Nachlass*, vol. 10, *Gesammelte Werke*.

——— *Wesen und Formen der Sympathie*, vol. 7, *Gesammelte Werke*. Bern: Francke.

Schupetta, Ingrid. *Frauen und Ausländererwerbstätigkeit in Deutschland von 1939 bis 1945*. Cologne: Pahl-Rugenstein, 1983.

Schwartz, Gudrun. *Nationalsozialistische Lager*. Frankfurt: Campus, 1990.

Schwartz-Liebermann von Wahlendorf, Hans-Albrecht, ed. *Mariage et famille en question: Allemagne*. Paris: Ed. du CNRS, 1979.

——— *Mariage et famille en question: Angleterre*. Paris: Ed. du CNRS, 1979.

"Sciences de la vie de l'éthique au droit: Etude du Conseil d'Etat." Paris, Documentation Française (1988).

Scott, Joan W. *Gender and the Politics of History*. New York: Columbia University Press, 1988.

Shannon, Thomas E. *Revisited Bioethics: Basic Writings on Key Ethical Questions That Surround the Major Modern Biological Possibilities and Problems*. Mahwah, N.J.: Paulist Press, 1981.

Shideler, J. "Flappers and Philosophers and Farmers: Rural-Urban Tensions of the Twenties." *Agricultural History*, 47, 4 (October 1973), 283–299.

Showstack Sassoon, Anne, ed. *Women and the State: The Shifting Boundaries of Public and Private*. London: Hutchinson, 1987.

Simard, Carolle. *L'administration contre les femmes: La reproduction des différences sexuelles dans la fonction publique canadienne*. Montreal: Boréal Express, 1983.

Simmel, Georg. *On Women, Sexuality, and Love*, trans. with an introduction by Guy Oakes. New Haven: Yale University Press, 1984.

Simmons, C. "Companionate Marriage and the Lesbian Threat." *Frontiers*, 4 (Fall 1979), 54–59.

Simone de Beauvoir et la lutte des femmes. *L'Arc*, 61. Aix-en-Provence, 1975.

"Simone de Beauvoir, Witness to a Century." *Yale French Studies*, 72 (1986).

Sineau, Mariette. *Des femmes en politique*. Paris: Economica, 1988.

Singly, François de. *Fortune et infortune de la femme mariée: Sociologie de la vie conjugale*. Paris: PUF, 1987.

———, ed. *La famille: L'état des savoirs*. Paris: La Découverte, 1991.

Sklar, R. *The Plastic Age, 1917–1930*. New York: Braziller, 1970.

Smith, Bonnie G. *Changing Lives: Women in European History since 1700*. Lexington, Mass.: D. C. Heath, 1989.

Smith, Harold L., ed. *British Feminism in the Twentieth Century*. London: Edward Elgar, 1990.

Smith-Rosenberg, C. *Disorderly Conduct*. New York: Knopf, 1985.

Snowden, R., and G. D. Mitchell. *La famille artificielle, réflexions sur l'insémination artificielle par donneur*. Paris: Anthropos, 1984.

Sociologies et Sociétés, 19, 1 (1987).

Sofer, Catherine. *La division du travail entre hommes et femmes*. Paris: Economica, 1985.

Sohn, Anne-Marie. "Exemplarité et limites de la participation féminine à la vie syndicale: Les institutrices de la C. G. T. U." *Revue d'Histoire Moderne et Contemporaine* (July-September 1977).

——— "La Garçonne face à l'opinion publique: Type littéraire ou type social des années 20." *Le Mouvement Social* (July-September 1972).

——— "Qualità e difetti: Stereotipi e realtà conjugali nelle Francia dell'ottocento." *Memoria: Il bel matrimonio*. 1988.

——— "Les rôles féminins dans la vie privée: Approche méthodologiques et bilan de recherches." *Revue d'Histoire Moderne et Contemporaine* (October-December 1981).

Solaris, Claudia. Le futuriste. Milan: Edizione delle donne, 1982.

Soldon, Norbert S. *Women in British Trade Unions: 1874–1976.* Dublin: Rowen and Littlefield, 1978.

Solomon, B. M. *In the Company of Educated Women.* New Haven: Yale University Press, 1985.

Sortir la maternité du laboratoire. Actes du forum international sur les nouvelles technologies de la reproduction. Conseil du Statut de la Femme du Québec, 1988.

Spring Rice, Margery. *Working-Class Wives: Their Health and Conditions.* London: Virago, 1981.

Stacey, Jackie. "Desperately Seeking Differences," in Gamman and Marshment, *The Female Gaze,* 1988.

Stein, Sally. "The Graphic Ordering of Desire." *Heresies,* 18, pp. 7–16.

Steinert, Marlies G. *Hitlers Krieg und die Deutschen.* Düsseldorf, 1970.

Stephenson, Jill. "Middle-Class Women and National Socialist 'Service.'" *History,* 67 (1982), 32–44.

———— *The Nazi Organization of Women.* London: Croom Helm, 1981.

———— "Reichsbund der Kinderreichen: The League of Large Families in the Population Policy of Nazi Germany." *European Studies,* 9, 3 (1979), 351–375.

———— *Women in Nazi Society.* London: Croom Helm, 1975.

Stern, Mikhaïl. *La vie sexuelle en URSS.* Paris: Albin Michel, 1979.

Stetson, Dorothy. *Women's Rights in the U.S.A.: Policy Debates and Gender Roles.* Pacific Grove: Brooks/Cole Publishing, 1990.

Stites, Richard. *The Women's Liberation Movement in Russia: Feminism, Nihilism, and Bolshevism, 1860–1930.* Princeton: Princeton University Press, 1978.

Stora-Sandor, Judith. *Alexandra Kollontaï: Marxisme et révolution sexuelle.* Paris: Maspero, 1975.

Stuart, Mary Lynn. *Women, Work, and the French State: Labour Protection and Social Patriarchy, 1879–1919.* Kingston: McGill-Queen's University Press, 1989.

Suleiman, Susan Rubin, ed. *The Female Body in Western Culture: Contemporary Perspectives.* Cambridge, Mass.: Harvard University Press, 1986.

Sullerot, Evelyne. *Les françaises au travail.* Paris: Hachette, 1973.

———— *Histoire et sociologie du travail féminin.* Paris: Gauthier, 1968.

———— *La presse féminine.* Paris: Armand Colin, 1963.

Tabet, Paola. "Fécondité naturelle, reproduction forcée," in Nicole-Claude Mathieu, ed., *L'arraisonnement des femmes: Essais en anthropologie des sexes.* Paris: *Cahiers de l'Homme,* éditions de l'Ecole des Hautes Études en Sciences Sociales, 1985.

"La tentation biocratique." *Ethique,* 1: *La vie en question* (1991).

Testart, J. *L'oeuf transparent.* Paris: Fayard, 1986.

————, ed. *Le magasin des enfants.* Paris: F. Bourin, 1990.

Thalmann, Rita. *Etre femme sous le IIIe Reich.* Paris: Editions Laffont, 1982.

————, ed. *Femmes et fascismes*. Paris: Tierce, 1986.

————, ed. *La tentation nationaliste, 1914–1945*. Paris: Tierce, 1990.

Thane, Pat. *The Foundations of the Welfare State*. London: Longman, 1982.

Thébaud, Françoise. *La femme au temps de la guerre de 14*. Paris: Stock, 1986.

———— *Quand nos grand-mères donnaient la vie: La maternité en France dans l'entre-deux-guerres*. Lyon: Presses Universitaires de Lyon, 1986.

Théry, Irène, and Christian Biet, eds. *La famille, la loi, l'état, de la Revolution au code civil*. Paris: Imprimerie Nationale et Centre Georges-Pompidou, 1989.

Thibaud, O. *Les enfants comment? Les techniques artificielles de procréation*. Ed. Chronique Sociale, 1984.

Tickner, Lisa. "The Body Politic: Female Sexuality and Women Artists since 1970." *Art History*, 1, 2 (June 1978); reprinted in Parker and Pollock, *Framing Feminism*, 1987.

Tillion, Germaine. *Ravensbrück*. Paris: Seuil, 1988.

Tilly, Louise A., and Joan W. Scott. *Les femmes, le travail, et la famille*. Marseille: Rivages/Histoire, 1987; American ed., 1978.

Treneman, Ann. "Cashing in on the Curse: Advertising and the Menstrual Taboo," in Gammon and Marshment, *The Female Gaze*, 1988.

Trofimenkoff, Susan Mann. *Visions nationales: Une histoire du Québec*. Quebec: Editions du Trécarré, 1986.

Turnaturi, Gabriella. "La donna fra il pubblico e il privato: La nascita della casalinga e della sonsumatrice." *Nuova donnawomanfemme*, 12–13 (July-December 1979), 8–29.

Ungerson, Clare, ed. *Gender and Caring: Work and Welfare in Britain and Scandinavia*. Hemel Hempstead: Harvester Wheatsheaf, 1990.

United States Department of Health Education and Welfare, May 4, 1979, "Support of Research Involving Human in Vitro Fertilization and Embryo Transfer."

Vacquin, M. *Frankenstein ou les délires de la raison*. Paris: Ed. F. Bourin, 1989.

Vandelac, Louis, et al. *Du travail et de l'amour: Les dessous de la production domestique*. Montreal: St. Martin, 1985.

Vanek, J. "Household Technology and Social Status: Rising Living Standards and the Status and Residence Difference in Housework." *Technology and Culture*, 19 (June 1978), 361–375.

Veillon, Dominique. *La mode sous l'Occupation, débrouillardise et coquetterie dans la France en guerre (1939–1945)*. Paris: Payot, 1990.

Verdier, Yvonne. *Façons de dire, façons de faire*. Paris: Gallimard, 1979.

"Vers la procréatique, une société où les enfants viennent par la science." *Projet*, 195. Paris, 1985.

Vessilier-Ressi, Michèle. *Le métier d'auteur*. Paris: Dunod, 1982.

Vianello, Mino, Renata Siemienska et al. *Gender Inequality: An International Study of Discrimination and Participation*. London: Sage, 1989.

Von Gersdorff, Ursula. *Frauen im Kriegsdienst, 1914–1945*. Stuttgart: Verlags-Anstalt, 1969.

Walker, Alice. *In Search of Our Mothers' Gardens: Womanist Prose.* San Diego: Harcourt Brace Jovanovich, 1984.

Wall, Richard, and Jay Winter, eds. *The Upheaval of War: Family, Work, and Welfare in Europe, 1914–1918.* Cambridge: Cambridge University Press, 1988.

Wandersee, W. *Women's Work and Family Values, 1920–1940.* Cambridge, Mass.: Harvard University Press, 1981.

Wanrooij, Bruno. *Castità e licenza.* Padua: Marsilio, 1991.

Warshofsky Lapidus, Gail. *Women in Soviet Society: Equality, Development, and Social Change.* Berkeley: University of California Press, 1978.

Weeks, Jeffrey. *Sex, Politics, and Society: The Regulation of Sexuality since 1800.* London: Longman, 1981.

Weindling, Paul. *Health, Race, and German Politics between National Unification and Nazism, 1870–1945.* Cambridge: Cambridge University Press, 1989.

Weiner, L. *From Working Girl to Working Mother.* Chapel Hill: University of North Carolina Press, 1985.

Werner, Françoise. "Du ménage à l'art ménager: L'évolution du travail ménager et son écho dans la presse féminine française de 1919 à 1939." *Mouvement Social,* 129 (1984), 61–87.

Werth, Nicolas. *La vie quotidienne des paysans russes de la Révolution à la collectivisation, 1917–1930.* Paris: Hachette, 1984.

White, Cynthia. *Women's Magazines, 1693–1968.* London: Michael Joseph, 1970.

Whitelegg, Elizabeth, ed. *The Changing Experience of Women.* Oxford: Basil Blackwell, 1982.

Williamson, Judith. *Consuming Passions: The Dynamics of Popular Culture.* New York: Marion Boyars, 1986.

——— "Woman Is an Island: Femininity and Colonization," in Modleski, *Studies in Entertainment,* 1986.

Wiltsher, Anne. *Most Dangerous Women: Feminist Peace Campaigners of the Great War.* London: Pandora, 1985.

Winkler, Dörte. *Frauenarbeit im "Dritten Reich."* Hamburg: Hoffmann und Campe, 1977.

Wobbe, Theresa, ed. *Nach Osten: Verdeckte Spuren nationalsozialistischer Verbrechen.* Frankfurt: Neue Kritik, 1992.

Wright, G. *Building the Dream: A Social History of Housing in America.* New York: Pantheon Books, 1981.

Young, Richard, and Peter Wilmott. *Family and Kinship in East London.* New York: Penguin Books, 1957; 1962.

Yver, Colette. *Femmes d'aujourd'hui, enquête sur les nouvelles carrières féminines.* Paris: Calmann-Lévy, 1929.

Zavalloni, Marysa, ed. *L'émergence d'une culture au féminin.* Montreal: St. Martin, 1987.

Zetkin, Clara. *Souvenirs sur Lénine.* Paris: Bureau d'Éditions, de Diffusion, et de Publicité, 1926.

683

Contributors

GISELA BOCK Professor of history at the University of Bielefeld, formerly professor at the European University in Florence. She has published books and articles in a number of languages on the political thought of modern Italy, the American labor movement, the history of domestic labor, Nazism racism and sexism, and the theory and methodology of gender in history.

DANIÈLE BUSSY GENEVOIS Professor at the University of Paris VIII. Specializing in the history of Spain, she has worked primarily on the press and women in contemporary Spain, on which she has published widely. Her thesis is entitled "Presse féminine et républicanisme en Espagne 1931–1936." Her current work is concerned more with the history of ideas and *mentalités,* including a collective project on violence in Spain at the turn of the twentieth century.

YOLANDE COHEN Professor of history at the University of Quebec in Montreal. Her research has been concerned primarily with the history of social movements in France and Quebec in the first half of the twentieth century. She is the author of *Femmes de parole. L'Histoire des Cercles de fermières du Québec* and of a monograph entitled *Les Jeunes, le socialisme et la guerre. Histoire des mouvements de jeunesse en France.* She is also the co-author of a study of *Juifs marocains à Montréal* and the editor of two collective works, *Femmes et contrepouvoirs* and *Femmes et politique.* She is currently writing a book on the professionalization of nursing.

FRANÇOISE COLLIN A philosopher and writer, Collin has published novels, stories, and philosophical essays, including *Maurice Blanchot et la question de l'écriture,* as well as numerous essays on women and sexual difference. In 1973 she founded the journal *Les Cahiers du Grif* and edits a collection called *Littérales* for Editions Tierce. After many years as a professor in Brussels, she now teaches feminist theory at the Centre Parisien d'Etudes Critiques. She is currently working on a study of Hannah Arendt.

JACQUELINE COSTA-LASCOUX   Director of research at the Centre National de Recherche Scientifique and member of the Haut Conseil de la Population et de la Famille, Costa-Lascoux's work is in the field of legal sociology and focuses on how cultural conflicts pose challenges to legal categories. Following the publication of her *Evolution de la délinquance des jeunes de 1825 à 1968* and of studies on African law, she became interested in immigration (*De l'immigré au citoyen*), discrimination, and bioethics (co-author of the report to the Commissariat Général au Plan on *Les Nouvelles Techniques de procréation* and of *Bioéthique et Droit*).

NANCY COTT   She is Stanley Woodward Professor of History and American Studies at Yale University. Her principal works include *The Bonds of Womanhood: "Woman's Sphere" in New England, 1780–1835; The Grounding of Modern Feminism;* and *A Woman Making History: Mary Ritter Beard through Her Letters.*

HÉLÈNE ECK   *Agrégée d'histoire,* lecturer at the University of Paris X-Nanterre. Her research focuses on the history of propaganda during World War II. She is the editor of *La Guerre des ondes: histoire des radios de langue française pendant la Deuxième Guerre mondiale.*

YASMINE ERGAS   A sociologist currently interested in the law, she has done research in Italy and the United States and has published widely on contemporary feminism, in particular *Nelle maglie della politica. Femminismo, istituzioni e politiche sociali nell'Italia degli anni 70.*

VICTORIA DE GRAZIA   Teaches at Rutgers University, where she is currently director of the Center for Historical Studies. She is the author of *The Culture of Consent: Mass Organization of Leisure in Fascist Italy* and of *How Fascism Ruled Women: Italy (1922–1945).* She has also published numerous essays on the Americanization of Europe and is a founder of the *Radical History Review.*

ANNE HIGONNET   Assistant Professor of Art at Wellesley College, where she teaches the history of the visual culture of the nineteenth and twentieth centuries. She has published a biography of the impressionist painter Berthe Morisot as well as a study of Morisot's works (published by Harvard).

ROSE-MARIE LAGRAVE   A sociologist and lecturer at the Ecole des Hautes Etudes en Sciences Sociales. Lagrave's research concerns peasants in Europe. She is the author of *Le Village romanesque* and of *Celles de la terre. Agricultrices: l'invention politique d'un métier,* as well as of numerous articles on feminist scholarship.

NADINE LEFAUCHEUR A sociologist and researcher at the Centre National de Recherche Scientifique. Her work is concerned mainly with the sociopolitical treatment of maternity outside wedlock and single-parent families. She is currently working on a history of medical eugenics in France. She is the author of *La Fabrication des mâles* (with Georges Falconnet) and of many essays and articles, some of them published in *Lectures sociologiques du travail social; La Famille, la loi, l'Etat de la Révolution au Code civil,* and *La Famille: l'état des savoirs.*

MARCELLE MARINI Lecturer at the University of Paris VII. She is the author of *Territoires du féminin avec Marguerite Duras* and of *Lacan.* She contributed to *Stratégies des femmes* and to the special issue "Savoir et différence des sexes" of *Cahiers du Grif.* She has also published articles in feminist and literary reviews and, with Nicole Mozet, directs a research team on "Literary Production in France since 1945."

FRANÇOISE NAVAILH Teaches Russian (in Paris). A specialist in the Soviet cinema, she is working on a thesis (under Marc Ferro) on images of women in Soviet film. Among her many articles: "L'Image de la femme dans le cinéma soviétique contemporain," in *Film et Histoire;* "Le Renouveau religieux dans le cinéma russe," in *Slovo—Cinéma et culture nationale en URSS;* and "La Commissaire de Berditchev—une nouvelle de V. Grossman, un film de A. Askoldov," in *Pardes.*

LUISA PASSERINI Teaches research methodology at the University of Turin. Her research focuses on the historical use of oral testimony and memory, in particular for the history of fascism and of the social movements of 1960–1970. She has edited a number of anthologies, including a special issue of *Mouvement Social* devoted to "Mémoires et histoires de 1968." Among her publications are *Torino operaia e fascismo; Storia e soggettività. Le fonti orali, la memoria; Autoritratto di gruppo; Mussolini immaginario. Storia di una biografia 1915–1939;* and *Storie di donne e femministe.*

MARIETTE SINEAU Political scientist, research associate at the Centre National de Recherche Scientifique, she works at the Centre d'Etude de la Vie Politique Française of the Fondation Nationale des Sciences Politiques in Paris. Her specialty is the study of women's political attitudes and behavior, on which she has published widely, including *Enquête sur les femmes et la politique en France* (with Janine Mossuz-Lavau). Her most recent book, *Des femmes en politique,* deals with women politicians and their images, expectations, and roles.

ANNE-MARIE SOHN *Agrégée d'histoire,* lecturer at the University of Paris I. A specialist in the history of women, she is the author of "La Garçonne: type littéraire ou type social des années 20?" Her thesis is entitled "Féminisme et syndicalisme. Les institutrices de la Fédération Unitaire de l'Enseignement de 1919 à 1935." She is the author of various articles, including "Les Attentats à la pudeur sur les fillettes et la sexualité quotidienne en France (1870–1939)," in *Violences sexuelles, Mentalités.* She is completing a second thesis on "Les Rôles féminins dans la vie privée à l'époque de la IIIe République."

FRANÇOISE THÉBAUD Lecturer at the Université Lumière Lyon 2, specialist in the history of women in the twentieth century. She has written extensively on this subject in collective volumes such as *1914–1918: l'Autre front; Femmes et fascismes;* and *La Tentation nationaliste.* She has also published *La Femme au temps de la guerre de 14* and *Quand nos grand-mères donnaient la vie: la maternité en France dans l'entredeux-guerres.*

Illustration Credits

Index

701